P9-DBM-925

CONFLICT

Second Edition

& COOPERATION

Documents on Modern Global History

EDITED BY **TRACEY J. KINNEY**

OXFORD
UNIVERSITY PRESS

OXFORD
UNIVERSITY PRESS

8 Sampson Mews, Suite 204, Don Mills, Ontario M3C 0H5
www.oupcanada.com

Oxford University Press is a department of the University of Oxford.
It furthers the University's objective of excellence in research, scholarship,
and education by publishing worldwide in

Oxford   New York

Auckland   Cape Town   Dar es Salaam   Hong Kong   Karachi   Kuala Lumpur   Madrid   Melbourne
Mexico City   Nairobi   New Delhi   Shanghai   Taipei   Toronto

With offices in

Argentina   Austria   Brazil   Chile   Czech Republic   France   Greece   Guatemala   Hungary   Italy
Japan   Poland   Portugal   Singapore   South Korea   Switzerland   Thailand   Turkey   Ukraine   Vietnam

Oxford is a trade mark of Oxford University Press in the UK and in certain other countries

Published in Canada by Oxford University Press

Copyright © 2010 Oxford University Press Canada

The moral rights of the author have been asserted

Database right Oxford University Press (maker)

First Published 2010

All rights reserved. No part of this publication may be reproduced, stored in a retrieval system, or transmitted,
in any form or by any means, without the prior permission in writing of Oxford University Press, or as expressly
permitted by law, or under terms agreed with the appropriate reprographics rights organization. Enquiries
concerning reproduction outside the scope of the above should be sent to the Rights Department, Oxford
University Press, at the address above.

You must not circulate this book in any other binding or cover
and you must impose this same condition on any acquirer.

Previous edition copyright © 2005 Oxford University Press Canada

Library and Archives Canada Cataloguing in Publication

Conflict and cooperation : documents on modern global history / [edited
by] Tracey J. Kinney. — 2nd ed.

Includes bibliographical references and index.
ISBN 978-0-19-543129-2

1. History, Modern—20th century—Sources. I. Kinney, Tracey Jane, 1966–

D411.C63 2010   909.82   C2009-906156-2

Cover image: (top) © Peeterv/istockphoto.com
(bottom) UN Photo/Eskinder Debebe United Nations peacekeeping soldiers from the Canadian Battalion,
part of the United Nations Support Mission in Haiti (UNSMIH), talking with an upset Port-au-Prince woman.
Port-au-Prince, Haiti.

This book is printed on permanent acid-free paper ♾.
Printed and bound in Canada.

4 5 — 14 13 12

CONTENTS

From the Publisher   xv
Preface   xvi

Chapter One: The World and the West

DADABHAI NAOROJI, The Blessings of British Rule   3
KIDO KOIN, Observations on Returning from the West, 1873   5
ITO HIROBUMI, On the Constitution of 1889   7
SAYYID JAMAL AL-DIN AL-AFGHANI, Lecture on Teaching and Learning   9
KANG YOUWEI, Comprehensive Consideration of the Whole Situation   11
WU TINGFANG, The Awakening of China   12
RABINDRANATH TAGORE, East and West   16
Tips for Analysis   17
Web Resources   17
Recommended Reading   18
Recommended Viewing   18

Chapter Two: Global Capitalism and Imperialism

ADAM HOCHSCHILD, King Leopold's Ghost   21
JULES FERRY, Speech Before the French Chamber of Deputies, 1884   23
EVELYN BARING, EARL OF CROMER British Rule in Egypt   25
BAL GANGADHAR TILAK, The Tenets of the New Party   28
Accounts of the Amritsar (Jallianwala Bagh) Massacre, 1919   30
WINSTON CHURCHILL, On India   35
CAIO PRADO JUNIOR, The Coffee Cycle in Brazil   37
W.E.B. DU BOIS, The Negro   40
V.I. LENIN, Imperialism, the Highest Stage of Capitalism   42
Tips for Analysis   44
Web Resources   45
Recommended Reading   45
Recommended Viewing   45

Chapter Three: War and Peace

ERICH MARIA REMARQUE, All Quiet on the Western Front   49
NOVOE VREMYA, Russian Women in Combat   52
A. HENRY MCMAHON / ARTHUR JAMES BALFOUR, The McMahon Letter /
     The Balfour Declaration   55

THE ARMENIAN NATIONAL INSTITUTE, Press Reports on the
    Armenian Genocide   57
WOODROW WILSON, Fourteen Points Speech   61
MARCUS GARVEY, Advice of the Negro to the Peace Conference   64
J.M. KEYNES, The Economic Consequences of the Peace   66
H.G. WELLS, ET AL., The Idea of the League of Nations   68
HENRY CABOT LODGE, On the League of Nations, 1919   70
Tips for Analysis   72
Web Resources   72
Recommended Reading   73
Recommended Viewing   73

Chapter Four: The Appeal of Revolutionary Change

ROSA LUXEMBURG, The Junius Pamphlet   77
VLADIMIR LENIN, The Beginning of the Revolution in Russia   80
NIKITA KHRUSHCHEV, Khrushchev Remembers   83
SUN YAT-SEN, Fundamentals of National Reconstruction   85
SOONG CHING-LING, The Struggle for New China   88
LI DAZHAO, The Victory of Bolshevism   91
JAWAHARLAL NEHRU, The Socialist Creed   93
MUSTAPHA KEMAL ATATÜRK, October 1927 Speech   94
Tips for Analysis   97
Web Resources   97
Recommended Reading   97
Recommended Viewing   98

Chapter Five: The Authoritarian Alternative

ANTONIO CIPPICO, Italy: The Central Problem of the Mediterranean   101
BENITO MUSSOLINI, Fascist Doctrines   104
FRANCESCO NITTI, Probabilities of War in Europe   108
THE AMUR SOCIETY, Anniversary Statement   110
JOSEPH STALIN, On Opposition and The Socialist Fatherland   112
EVGENIIA GINZBURG, Journey Into the Whirlwind   115
JOSEPH GOEBBELS, The Reich Ministry of Popular Enlightenment and
    Propaganda   118
ADOLF HITLER, To the National Socialist Frauenbund   120
DAVID BUFFUM, On Kristallnacht   122
FORTUNE MAGAZINE, Getúlio Vargas and the 'Estado Novo'   125
Tips for Analysis   127
Web Resources   127
Recommended Reading   128
Recommended Viewing   128

Chapter Six: Global Depression

HEINRICH HAUSER, With Germany's Unemployed   132

GEORGE ORWELL, The Road to Wigan Pier   135

FRANKLIN D. ROOSEVELT, Inaugural Address of the President,
4 March 1933   139

PAUL COMLY FRENCH, Children on Strike   143

LÁZARO CÁRDENAS, Speech to the Nation   146

W.E.B. DU BOIS, Liberia, the League, and the United States, 1933   149

NEVILLE CHAMBERLAIN, Speech to the House of Commons, 3 October 1938 /
W.L. MACKENZIE KING, Telegram from Prime Minister William L.
Mackenzie King to British Prime Minister Neville Chamberlain   152

Tips for Analysis   155

Web Resources   155

Recommended Reading   156

Recommended Viewing   156

Chapter Seven: Global War and Genocide

MARGARET FREYER, Eyewitness Account of the Firestorm in Dresden   159

TOTAL WAR RESEARCH INSTITUTE, The Greater East Asia
Co-Prosperity Sphere   161

HAROLD TIMPERLEY, An Eyewitness Account at Nanjing   164

GAO XINGZU, WU SHIMIN, HU YUNGONG, and CHA RUIZHEN, The Nanjing
Massacre   166

MURIEL KITAGAWA, Letters to Wes   169

VICTOR KLEMPERER, I Will Bear Witness   175

STELLA WIESELTIER, Rejoining the Human Race   179

SINISA DJURIC (translator), Police Report on the Cleansing of Serbs   181

US WAR DEPARTMENT, Release on the New Mexico Test   185

Tips for Analysis   188

Web Resources   188

Recommended Reading   189

Recommended Viewing   189

Chapter Eight: A New World Order?

FRANKLIN D. ROOSEVELT and WINSTON CHURCHILL, The Atlantic Charter   192

HARRY S. TRUMAN, WINSTON CHURCHILL, AND CHIANG KAI-SHEK, The Potsdam
Proclamation   194

UNITED NATIONS, The Universal Declaration of Human Rights   196

MOHANDAS K. GANDHI, 'Quit India' Resolution   201

HO CHI MINH, Declaration of Independence of the Democratic Republic
of Viet Nam   203

ANGLO-AMERICAN COMMITTEE OF INQUIRY, Testimony on the
  Creation of the State of Israel   205
LESTER B. PEARSON, On Peacekeeping   210
Tips for Analysis   213
Web Resources   213
Recommended Reading   214
Recommended Viewing   214

Chapter Nine: Origins and Implications of the Cold War

WINSTON CHURCHILL, Iron Curtain Speech   217
JOSEPH STALIN Response to Churchill, 14 March 1946   221
JOSEPH MCCARTHY, On Communists in Government   225
MILOVAN DJILAS, The New Class   228
NIKITA KHRUSHCHEV, Secret Speech   231
G.H. BLAKESLEE, Draft Memorandum by G.H. Blakeslee, April 1945   235
ROBERT MCNAMARA, Memorandum for the President by McNamara,
  8 November 1961   237
Tips for Analysis   239
Web Resources   240
Recommended Reading   240
Recommended Viewing   240

Chapter Ten: The Re-emergence of Asian Power

MAO ZEDONG, The Foolish Old Man Who Removed the Mountains   244
FOX BUTTERFIELD, Lihua   247
CHAI LING, June Four: A Chronicle of the Chinese Democratic Uprising 249
HU JINTAO, China's Development is an Opportunity for Asia   252
KAMEI KATSUICHIRO, Return to the East   254
CHITOSHI YANAGA, Big Business in Japanese Politics   259
SUVENDRINI KAKUCHI, Amid Recession the New Poor Demand Safety Nets   262
Tips for Analysis   265
Web Resources   265
Recommended Reading   265
Recommended Viewing   266

Chapter Eleven: Anti-Colonial Movements and Independence

UNITED NATIONS, UN Declaration on Colonial Independence   269
PAUL RAMADIER, Speech to the National Assembly, 18 March 1947   270
FRONT DE LIBÉRATION NATIONALE, Proclamation of 1 November 1954   273
SEKOU TOURÉ, The Republic of Guinea   275
CLEMENT ATTLEE, Debates of the House of Commons, 15 March 1946   278

JAWAHARLAL NEHRU, Speech on the Eve of Independence   280

KWAME NKRUMAH, I Speak of Freedom   283

A.L. GEYER, The Case for Apartheid   285

DESMOND TUTU, My Vision for South Africa   287

Tips for Analysis   289

Web Resources   290

Recommended Reading   290

Recommended Viewing   290

Chapter Twelve: Technology and the Environment

JOHN F. KENNEDY, On the Space Race   294

VALENTINA TERESHKOVA, On the Soviet Space Programme   296

MARSHALL MCLUHAN, The Playboy Interview   299

RACHEL CARSON, A Fable for Tomorrow   302

REX WEYLER, Waves of Compassion   304

ALBERT GORE, Nobel Lecture   307

STEPHEN HAWKING, Why We Should Go into Space   310

Tips for Analysis   312

Web Resources   313

Recommended Reading   313

Recommended Viewing   313

Chapter Thirteen: The Challenge of Neo-Colonialism

KWAME NKRUMAH, Neo-Colonialism: The Last Stage of Imperialism   317

FRANTZ FANON, The Collaborating Class in Neo-Colonialism   320

D. ZIZWE POE, Afrocentric Summary of Nkrumah's Major
   Contributions   322

FIDEL CASTRO, On the Exploitation of the Cuban Nation   324

RICHARD F. BEHRENDT, The Uprooted: A Guatemala Sketch   329

ERNESTO 'CHÉ' GUEVARA, A New Old Interview   332

Tips for Analysis   336

Web Resources   336

Recommended Reading   336

Recommended Viewing   337

Chapter Fourteen: Paths to Modernization

LEOPOLD SENGHOR, Some Thoughts on Africa   339

PATRICE LUMUMBA and GRAHAM HEATH, Congo: My Country   341

JULIUS NYERERE, The Arusha Declaration   345

P.J. O'ROURKE, Inside Tanzania   347

THE ATLANTIC MONTHLY, Rwanda 1964   352

HUEY P. NEWTON, Uniting against a Common Enemy: 23 October 1971   357
Tips for Analysis   358
Web Resources   359
Recommended Reading   359
Recommended Viewing   359

Chapter Fifteen: The Middle East in the Postwar Era

GOVERNMENT OF GREAT BRITAIN, The White Paper of 1939   361
UNITED NATIONS SECURITY COUNCIL, Resolution 242, 22 November 1967 /
   PALESTINE NATIONAL COUNCIL, The Palestinian National Charter   366
GOLDA MEIR, Remarks to President Sadat   370
Joint US/Soviet Statement on Peace in the Middle East, September 1977   373
HAMAS, The Covenant of the Islamic Resistance Movement, 1988   374
EDWARD SAID, Truth and Reconciliation   378
Tips for Analysis   383
Web Resources   383
Recommended Reading   383
Recommended Viewing   384

Chapter Sixteen: Ideological Change

ELEANOR ROOSEVELT, Women Must Learn to Play the Game
   as Men Do   387
ALEXANDRA KOLLONTAI, The Soviet Woman—A Full and Equal Citizen
   of Her Country   392
REDSTOCKINGS, A Feminist Manifesto   394
JEAN-PAUL SARTRE, Existentialism   396
The Chicago Seven Trial Transcript: Abbie Hoffman   398
MARTIN LUTHER KING JR, I Have a Dream   403
KWAME ANTHONY APPIAH, Identity, Authenticity, Survival   407
Tips for Analysis   409
Web Resources   409
Recommended Reading   410
Recommended Viewing   410

Chapter Seventeen: The End of the Cold War and Its Aftermath

LUDVIK VACULÍK, Two Thousand Words to Workers, Farmers,
   Scientists, Artists, and Everyone   414
VÁCLAV HAVEL, Disturbing the Peace   416
MIKHAIL GORBACHEV, On the Closing of the 27th Congress of the CPSU   418
ALEKSANDR SOLZHENITSYN, Rebuilding Russia   422
BENJAMIN BARBER, Jihad versus McWorld   425

ROBERT KAPLAN, Old Serbia and Albania: Balkan 'West Bank';
  Moldova: 'Conditioned to Hate'   430
Tips for Analysis   436
Web Resources   436
Recommended Reading   436
Recommended Viewing   437

Chapter Eighteen: State-Building and Its Discontents

RAMI CHHABRA, An Interview with Indira Gandhi   439
SYED ABUL A'ALA MAUDUDI, Replacing Western Forms with Islamic Law 442
MU'AMMAR AL-QADHAFI, The Green Book   444
NELSON MANDELA, State of the Nation Address, 1994   446
PHILIP GOUREVITCH, We Wish To Inform You That Tomorrow We Will
  Be Killed With Our Families   452
STEPHEN LEWIS, UN Briefing on HIV/AIDS in Africa   457
ROBERT KAPLAN, The Coming Anarchy   462
Tips for Analysis   463
Web Resources   464
Recommended Reading   464
Recommended Viewing   464

Chapter Nineteen: History in the Making: Into the Twenty-First Century

S.P. UDAYAKUMAR and JOHN A. POWELL, Race, Poverty, and Globalization   467
NAOMI KLEIN, No Logo   472
ROBERT KAPLAN, World Government   476
MANGOSUTHU BUTHELEZI, Democracy at Work in Africa   478
MOHAMED ELHACHMI HAMDI, Islam and Liberal Democracy   481
THE GUARDIAN, Blast from the Past   483
NOAM CHOMSKY, On the Antiwar Movement   489
OSAMA BIN LADEN Speech on American Policy, October 2004   494
HUGO CHÁVEZ, Speech on the Opening of G-15 Summit, 2004   497
VLADIMIR PUTIN, Speech at the 43rd Munich Conference on Security
  Policy, 2007   501
Tips for Analysis   504
Web Resources   504
Recommended Reading   504
Recommended Viewing   505

Suggestions for Further Reading   506
Acknowledgements   512
Index   515

Geographical Table of Contents

Canada

W.L. MACKENZIE KING, Telegram from Prime Minister William L. Mackenzie
    King to British Prime Minister Neville Chamberlain   152
MURIEL KITAGAWA, Letters to Wes   169
LESTER B. PEARSON, On Peacekeeping   210
MARSHALL MCLUHAN, The *Playboy* Interview   299
REX WEYLER, Waves of Compassion   304

Central and South America

LÁZARO CÁRDENAS, Speech to the Nation   146
RICHARD F. BEHRENDT, The Uprooted: A Guatemala Sketch   329
FIDEL CASTRO, On the Exploitation of the Cuban Nation   324
ERNESTO 'CHÉ' GUEVARA, A New Old Interview   332
CAIO PRADO JÚNIOR, The Coffee Cycle in Brazil   37
FORTUNE MAGAZINE, Getúlio Vargas and the '*Estado Novo*'   125
HUGO CHÁVEZ, Speech on the Opening of G-15 Summit, 2004   497

Central and South Asia

DADABHAI NAOROJI, The Blessings of British Rule   3
RABINDRANATH TAGORE, East and West   16
BAL GANGADHAR TILAK, The Tenets of the New Party   28
Accounts of the Amritsar (Jallianwala Bagh) Massacre, 1919   30
WINSTON CHURCHILL, On India   35
JAWAHARLAL NEHRU, The Socialist Creed   93
MOHANDAS K. GANDHI 'Quit India' Resolution   201
CLEMENT ATTLEE, Debates of the House of Commons, 15 March 1946 278
JAWAHARLAL NEHRU, Speech on the Eve of Independence   280
RAMI CHHABRA An Interview with Indira Gandhi   439
SYED ABUL A'ALA MAUDUDI, Replacing Western Forms with Islamic Law 442
SAYYID JAMAL AL-DIN AL-AFGHANI, Lecture on Teaching and Learning 9

East Asia

KIDO KŌIN, Observations on Returning from the West, 1873   5
ITO HIROBUMI, On the Constitution of 1889   7
THE AMUR SOCIETY, Anniversary Statement   110
TOTAL WAR RESEARCH INSTITUTE, The Greater East Asia
    Co-Prosperity Sphere   161
HAROLD TIMPERLEY, An Eyewitness Account at Nanjing   164
GAO XINGZU, WU SHIMIN, HU YUNGONG, and CHA RUIZHEN,
    The Nanjing Massacre   166
KAMEI KATSUICHIRŌ, Return to the East   254

CHITOSHI YANAGA, Big Business in Japanese Politics   259
SUVENDRINI KAKUCHI, Amid Recession the New Poor Demand Safety Nets   262
KANG YOUWEI, Comprehensive Consideration of the Whole Situation   11
WU TINGFANG, The Awakening of China   12
SUN YAT-SEN, Fundamentals of National Reconstruction   85
SOONG CHING-LING, The Struggle for New China   88
LI DAZHAO, The Victory of Bolshevism   91
MAO ZEDONG, The Foolish Old Man Who Removed the Mountains   244
FOX BUTTERFIELD, Lihua   247
CHAI LING, June Four: A Chronicle of the Chinese Democratic Uprising   249
HU JINTAO, China's Development is an Opportunity for Asia   252

Europe

ERICH MARIA REMARQUE, All Quiet on the Western Front   49
NOVOE VREMYA, Russian Women in Combat   52
ROSA LUXEMBURG, The Junius Pamphlet   77
J.M. KEYNES, The Economic Consequences of the Peace   66
ANTONIO CIPPICO, Italy: The Central Problem of the Mediterranean   101
BENITO MUSSOLINI, Fascist Doctrines   104
FRANCESCO NITTI, Probabilities of War in Europe   108
JOSEPH GOEBBELS, The Reich Ministry of Popular Enlightenment
    and Propaganda   118
ADOLF HITLER To the National Socialist Frauenbund   120
DAVID BUFFUM, On Kristallnacht   122
HEINRICH HAUSER, With Germany's Unemployed   132
GEORGE ORWELL, The Road to Wigan Pier   135
NEVILLE CHAMBERLAIN, Speech to the House of Commons,
    3 October 1938   152
MARGARET FREYER, Eyewitness Account of the Firestorm in Dresden   159
VICTOR KLEMPERER, I Will Bear Witness   175
STELLA WIESELTIER, Rejoining the Human Race   179
SINISA DJURIC (translator), Police Report on the Cleansing of Serbs   181
WINSTON CHURCHILL, Iron Curtain Speech   217
MILOVAN DJILAS, The New Class   228
PAUL RAMADIER, Speech to the National Assembly, 18 March 1947   271
CLEMENT ATTLEE, Debates of the House of Commons, 15 March 1946   278
JEAN-PAUL SARTRE, Existentialism   396
LUDVÍK VACULÍK, Two Thousand Words to Workers, Farmers, Scientists,
    Artists, and Everyone   414
VÁCLAV HAVEL, Disturbing the Peace   416
ROBERT KAPLAN, Old Serbia and Albania: Balkan 'West Bank'; Moldova:
    'Conditioned to Hate'   430

North Africa

FRONT DE LIBÉRATION NATIONALE, Proclamation of 1 November 1954   273

MU`AMMAR AL-QADHAFI, The Green Book   444

MOHAMED ELHACHMI HAMDI, Islam and Liberal Democracy   481

Russia (The Soviet Union)

V.I. LENIN Imperialism, the Highest Stage of Capitalism   42

V.I. LENIN, The Beginning of the Revolution in Russia   80

NOVOE VREMYA, Russian Women in Combat   52

NIKITA KHRUSHCHEV, Khrushchev Remembers   83

JOSEPH STALIN, On Opposition and The Socialist Fatherland   112

EVGENIIA GINZBURG, Journey Into the Whirlwind   115

JOSEPH STALIN Response to Churchill, 14 March 1946   221

NIKITA KHRUSHCHEV, Secret Speech   231

ALEXANDRA KOLLONTAI, The Soviet Woman—A Full and Equal Citizen
of Her Country   392

MIKHAIL GORBACHEV, On the Closing of the 27th Congress of the CPSU   418

ALEKSANDR SOLZHENITSYN, Rebuilding Russia   422

VLADIMIR PUTIN, Speech at the 43rd Munich Conference
on Security Policy, 2007   501

Southeast Asia

HO CHI MINH, Declaration of Independence of the Democratic Republic
of Viet Nam   203

G.H. BLAKESLEE, Draft Memorandum by G.H. Blakeslee, April 1945   235

ROBERT MCNAMARA, Memorandum for the President by McNamara,
8 November 1961   237

Southwestern Asia and the Middle East

A. HENRY MCMAHON / ARTHUR JAMES BALFOUR, The McMahon Letter /
The Balfour Declaration   55

THE ARMENIAN NATIONAL INSTITUTE, Press Reports on the
Armenian Genocide   57

MUSTAPHA KEMAL ATATÜRK, October 1927 Speech   94

GOVERNMENT OF GREAT BRITAIN, The White Paper of 1939   361

ANGLO-AMERICAN COMMITTEE OF INQUIRY, Testimony on the Creation
of the State of Israel   205

UNITED NATIONS SECURITY COUNCIL, Resolution 242, 22 November 1967 /
PALESTINE NATIONAL COUNCIL, The Palestinian National Charter   366

GOLDA MEIR, Remarks to President Sadat   370

Joint US/Soviet Statement on Peace in the Middle East, September 1977   373

HAMAS, The Covenant of the Islamic Resistance Movement, 1988   374

EDWARD SAID, Truth and Reconciliation   378

THE GUARDIAN, Blast from the Past   483

NOAM CHOMSKY, On the Antiwar Movement   489

OSAMA BIN LADEN, Speech on American Policy, October 2004   494

Sub-Saharan Africa

ADAM HOCHSCHILD, King Leopold's Ghost   21

SEKOU TOURÉ, The Republic of Guinea   275

KWAME NKRUMAH, I Speak of Freedom   283

KWAME NKRUMAH, Neo-Colonialism: The Last Stage of Imperialism   317

FRANTZ FANON, The Collaborating Class in Neo-Colonialism   320

D. ZIZWE POE, Afrocentric Summary of Nkrumah's Major Contributions   322

LEOPOLD SENGHOR, Some Thoughts on Africa   339

PATRICE LUMUMBA and GRAHAM HEATH, Congo: My Country   341

JULIUS NYERERE, The Arusha Declaration   345

P.J. O'ROURKE, Inside Tanzania   347

HUEY P. NEWTON, Uniting against a Common Enemy: 23 October 1971   357

A.L. GEYER, The Case for Apartheid   285

DESMOND TUTU, My Vision for South Africa   287

NELSON MANDELA, State of the Nation Address, 1994   446

MANGOSUTHU BUTHELEZI, Democracy at Work in Africa   478

THE ATLANTIC MONTHLY, Rwanda 1964   352

PHILIP GOUREVITCH, We Wish To Inform You That Tomorrow We Will
    Be Killed With Our Families   452

ROBERT KAPLAN, The Coming Anarchy   462

The United States

WOODROW WILSON, Fourteen Points Speech   61

MARCUS GARVEY, Advice of the Negro to the Peace Conference   64

HENRY CABOT LODGE, On the League of Nations, 1919   70

W.E.B. DU BOIS, Liberia, the League, and the United States, 1933   149

ELEANOR ROOSEVELT, Women Must Learn to Play the Game as Men Do   387

FRANKLIN D. ROOSEVELT, Inaugural Address of the President,
    4 March 1933   139

PAUL COMLY FRENCH, Children on Strike   143

US WAR DEPARTMENT, Release on the New Mexico Test   185

FRANKLIN D. ROOSEVELT and WINSTON CHURCHILL, The Atlantic Charter   192

HARRY S. TRUMAN, WINSTON CHURCHILL, and CHIANG KAI-SHEK, The Potsdam
    Proclamation   194

JOSEPH MCCARTHY, On Communists in Government   225

ROBERT MCNAMARA, Memorandum for the President by McNamara,
    8 November 1961   237

G.H. BLAKESLEE, Draft Memorandum by G.H. Blakeslee, April 1945   237

JOHN F. KENNEDY, On the Space Race   294

RACHEL CARSON, A Fable for Tomorrow   302

MARTIN LUTHER KING JR, I Have a Dream   403

HUEY P. NEWTON, Uniting against a Common Enemy: 23 October 1971   357

REDSTOCKINGS, A Feminist Manifesto   394

The Chicago Seven Trial Transcript: Abbie Hoffman   398

KWAME ANTHONY APPIAH, Identity, Authenticity, Survival   407

ALBERT GORE, Nobel Lecture   307

World Organizations/International Movements

W.E.B. DU BOIS, The Negro   40

H.G. WELLS, ET AL., The Idea of the League of Nations   68

HENRY CABOT LODGE, On the League of Nations, 1919   70

W.E.B. DU BOIS, Liberia, the League, and the United States, 1933   149

UNITED NATIONS, The Universal Declaration of Human Rights   196

UNITED NATIONS, UN Declaration on Colonial Independence   269

LESTER B. PEARSON, On Peacekeeping   210

RACHEL CARSON, A Fable for Tomorrow   302

REX WEYLER, Waves of Compassion   304

ALBERT GORE, Nobel Lecture   307

STEPHEN HAWKING, Why We Should Go into Space   310

BENJAMIN BARBER, Jihad versus McWorld   425

S.P. UDAYAKUMAR and john a. powell, Race, Poverty, and Globalization   467

NAOMI KLEIN, No Logo   472

ROBERT KAPLAN, World Government   476

MOHAMED ELHACHMI HAMDI, Islam and Liberal Democracy   481

FROM THE PUBLISHER

Ten reasons you need this new edition of

Conflict and Cooperation:
Documents on Modern Global History

1. Expanded to include 144 readings, including 48 new selections with extended geographic and historical breadth, providing a more comprehensive introduction to modern global history.

2. A new chapter, 'History in the Making: Into the Twenty-First Century', connects the history of the twentieth century with current events, making the text more relevant to students.

3. With new readings on Latin America, the Middle East, and a further developed treatment of African history, the text has a more balanced coverage of Western and non-Western modern global history that ensures students receive a complete introduction to 20th century world history.

4. New **Tips for Analysis** boxes added in each chapter help students consider primary sources more critically.

5. A new **Web Resources** section added to the existing recommended reading and viewing sections in each chapter offers a more useful guide to further research.

6. New **Study Questions** included in each chapter help students better understand the material and provide directions for further research and classroom discussion.

7. Informative introductions situate the readings in their historical context and encourage students to draw links to other materials in the text.

8. A new geographical table of contents provides alternate methods of structuring material and new ways of interpreting readings.

9. Enhanced visuals—including a new design, new maps, and updated images throughout—complement readings and make history come alive for students.

10. Now accompanied by a new suite of ancillaries, featuring an **Instructor's Manual** containing sample syllabi for incorporating readings with a core text or using *Conflict and Cooperation* as a stand-alone text, and a **Student Study Guide** that offers chapter summaries and goals, essay questions, objective questions, and additional weblinks and suggested readings.

Preface

The twentieth century was profoundly shaped both by the threat and the reality of war. As a result, conflict must be seen as one of the defining issues of the twentieth century. However, this was also the century that witnessed genuine attempts to build co-operative global institutions. These institutions and organizations were designed to prevent war, to facilitate communication among all peoples, and to improve the human condition in a meaningful way. These two seemingly contradictory impulses—conflict and co-operation—are thus the defining themes that weave together this collection of primary documents. For example, conflict among the nations of Europe, evident in Jules Ferry's speech to the French National Assembly, fueled the drive for colonies; however, co-operative efforts among the colonized peoples, as advocated in Kwame Nkrumah's discussion of decolonization, accelerated the breakdown of colonialism.

In creating this collection, I was motivated by the realization that, increasingly, students find themselves generations removed from many of the critical developments that shaped the twentieth century. Even the end of the Cold War occurred before many first year undergraduates were born. I have found it essential, therefore, to provide a means by which students can meaningfully connect to the past. Primary documents can serve this function by allowing students to 'witness' essential moments in history through the words of the men and women who experienced these events. The section on war and genocide, for example, includes the testimony of Holocaust survivors who recall the terror, the deprivation, and the utter hopelessness of their situation in a way that enables contemporary readers to make a personal connection to what might otherwise have been simply an event in the increasingly distant past. Above all, this compilation seeks to show students that history can be studied as a collection of living documents, all of which represent human experience at moments of profound importance.

In the process of creating the second edition of *Conflict and Co-operation* I have been able to address a number of significant omissions from the first edition. Most importantly, key documents related to technology and the environment are now featured in the collection. As well, the absence of important documents on Latin America and on the Islamic world has been corrected. Though the process of choosing which documents to remove was difficult, in the final analysis, the present collection is hopefully more relevant and more accessible.

Historians often debate whether undergraduates—particularly first-year students—have the necessary analytical tools to interpret primary documents in a meaningful way. I have found that any reader can work successfully with primary sources if guided by several simple analytical questions. Therefore the second edition of *Conflict and Cooperation* includes a section entitled 'Tips for Analysis'. Here students will find all of the key questions necessary for a critical reading of a primary document. As in the first edition, each of the documents in this collection is accompanied by the information necessary to read the document in a critical and informed way: the author's background and the document's context are reviewed in each introduction; informational notes clarify unfamiliar references in the text of the document; and study questions reinforce key issues and alternate interpretations. Students will finish this book better informed about modern global history and better able to work critically with a wide variety of historical sources.

This collection focuses not only on the politicians and diplomats who shaped the twentieth century, but also, wherever possible, on the testimony of ordinary men and women who witnessed crucial moments in history. The documents are arranged in thematic chapters, each corresponding to a major issue or development in the twentieth century. The chapters progress in a broadly chronological narrative, though thematic consistency at times has necessitated breaks within a strict chronological progression. The chapter intro-ductions are intended to provide a brief history of the events under consideration and to summarize the documents that follow. In each chapter, an attempt has been made to include a number of different viewpoints so that readers might begin to understand the many sides of any given issue. The study question at the end of each document also encourages the reader to challenge commonly held assumptions and to consider alternative viewpoints. Finally, each chapter concludes with a list of key Internet resources along with suggested reading and viewing material that, though by no means definitive, is intended to provide additional insights into the themes under discussion. In selecting websites I have been mindful of the fact that web addresses change frequently and links can often become outdated. I have therefore tried as far as possible to include only long-standing sites with stable URLs. The photographs and illustrations in the collection have been substantially updated in order to provide an additional means by which the reader can connect with past events.

This collection of documents has been a number of years in the making. Earlier versions included different documents, alternate study questions, and different formatting. In producing the second edition I have once again taken into account the candid responses of my students, past and present, to the earlier collections. In most cases, I have chosen the documents and questions that evoked the strongest student reactions—both positive and negative—and those that produced the greatest debate. As a result, this collection is strongly informed by my interactions with students, and I thank all who provided input. Many of my colleagues at Kwantlen Polytechnic University have also contributed helpful advice and feedback on different parts of the manuscript. Any errors that remain are, of course, my own.

I would also like to thank Julia Jevmenova, formerly at Oxford University Press, who brought the manuscript of the first edition to the Higher Education Division. Thanks also to Peter Chambers who has served as developmental editor on the current edition and Jessie Coffey for her editorial assistance. The digital photograph archives at the US National Archives and Records Office and the Library of Congress provided an invaluable source for many of the photographs and illustrations that accompany the documents. Finally, thanks to my husband, Jonathan, whose support and guidance were essential to the completion of both the first and second editions.

CHAPTER ONE

THE WORLD
AND THE WEST

◇

THE RHODES COLOSSUS
STRIDING FROM CAPE TOWN TO CAIRO.

A Punch Cartoon entitled 'The Rhodes Colossus' reflects the British desire for an African Empire stretching from the Cape in the south to Cairo in the north. Reproduced with permission of Punch Ltd., www.punch.co.uk.

The western world has come to view the turn of the twentieth century as a pivotal transitional point in human history. Western power had reached a high point, the result of early industrialization and its resulting technological and military advantages. Western optimism seemed boundless. At the 1893 Chicago World's Fair Nikola Tesla's alternating current had illuminated the buildings and grounds and introduced the public to the idea of inexpensive, widespread electrical power. In 1895 Guglielmo Marconi sent the first wireless signal over a distance of one and a half miles. The age of radio had been born, and with it a revolution in global communications. In 1896 Thomas Edison presented the first publicly projected motion picture in New York City, thereby transforming popular entertainment. In 1903 at Kitty Hawk, North Carolina, Orville Wright flew a man-made craft for twelve seconds—thirty-seven metres—and revolutionized international transportation in the process. Finally, in 1905 Albert Einstein, then a patent clerk in Switzerland, published his special theory of relativity, and altered the very foundations of the modern scientific worldview.

Yet the turn of the century holds little importance for non-western nations. The most profound changes for the nations of Asia, Africa, and South America had been initiated much earlier in the nineteenth century. In China, the Opium Wars (1839–42 and 1856–60) had triggered a decisive confrontation with western power and western ideas. The consequences of China's increasing loss of sovereignty would preoccupy the Qing emperors for the remainder of the nineteenth century, finally culminating in the Xinhai Revolution in 1911. In Japan, the closed society of the late Tokugawa era was forced open by the steady pressure of foreign efforts to negotiate new trade treaties beginning in the 1850s. The resulting era of reform— the Meiji period—stretched well into the twentieth century. In Africa, the arrival of the industrialized powers of the west, beginning in the 1870s, brought profound change to some nations and the consequences of colonial conquest would be felt for nearly 100 years. The Ottoman Empire had begun its decline long before the turn of the new century. The clash between those who looked to an Islamic revival to secure change and those who looked to the west as a source of modernization would continue even as the Ottoman Empire itself disintegrated in the wake of the First World War. Finally, in South and Central America the challenge of building new national identities and functional political systems, which had begun in the 1820s and 1830s, continued well into the twentieth century.

Nonetheless, intellectuals and political leaders around the world were confronted by the challenge of western power during the nineteenth and early twentieth centuries. Many modernizers in Asia and the Middle East looked favourably upon western education and western political systems as a means to achieve comprehensive reforms in their own countries. However, political leaders often struggled to find ways to meet the challenge of the West while retaining their distinctive cultures and traditions. Chinese reformers phrased this struggle in terms of preserving 'ti' (the essence of Chinese culture) while focusing on 'yong' (that which was useful from the 'barbarians'). Intellectuals who embraced the need to reform also differed over the best way to achieve this goal. In Meiji Japan (1868–1912) political, economic, and military systems were imported wholesale from the West, though the resulting Japanese equivalents managed to retain many uniquely Japanese elements, such as the divinity of the emperor. In China, demands for reform often met strong resistance from those who sought to preserve the traditional imperial system, even in the face of ongoing foreign intervention. Other reformers sought strength through co-operation as in the case of the pan-Islamist and pan-Africanist movements. Yet those who advocated unity and co-operation often found that national and ethnic divisions worked against the core goals of their movements.

This chapter examines a variety of responses to the challenge of the West. Dadabhai Naoroji reflects on the advantages which British rule brought to India; Rabindranath Tagore, in contrast, laments the lack of true understanding between India and Britain (and more generally between the East and the West). Kido Kōin and Ito Hirobumi, Japanese reformers, comment on the form and necessity of constitutional government. Jamal al-Din al-Afghani calls on Islamic leaders to recognize the importance of western science. Both Kang Youwei and Wu Tingfang recognize the need for substantive reforms in late-Qing China. Kang argues that the institutions of the West are too remote to be of use in China; however, the methods of the Meiji reformers could be beneficial. Writing some ten years later Wu sees many positive strides towards 'the awakening of China'.

DADABHAI NAOROJI

Dadabhai Naoroji (1825–1917) was educated in British schools in India and spent time in England in the 1850s and 1860s. He played an important role in the founding of the Indian National Congress and consistently advocated a moderate position with respect to British rule in India. In the 1890s, after returning again to England, he was elected to parliament, representing both his local constituency and the broader issues facing the people of India.

Naoroji was particularly concerned with the impact of British economic policies in India. In 1906 he began to argue for Swaraj or home rule for India, but remained determined that this would be achieved through moderate means. The speech which follows was the presidential address at the opening of the second session of the Indian National Congress in 1886. The response of the audience is noted in parentheses.

THE BLESSINGS OF BRITISH RULE

The assemblage of such a Congress is an event of the utmost importance in Indian history. I ask whether in the most glorious days of Hindu rule, in the days of Rajahs like the great Vikram,[1] you could imagine the possibility of a meeting of this kind, where even Hindus of all different provinces of the kingdom could have collected and spoken as one nation. Coming down to the later empire of our friends, the Mahomedans,[2] who probably ruled over a larger territory at one time than any Hindu monarch, would it have been, even in the days of the great Akbar himself, possible for a meeting like this to assemble composed of all classes and communities, all speaking one language, and all having uniform and high aspirations of their own?

Well, then, what is it for which we are now met on this occasion? We have assembled to consider questions upon which depend our future, whether glorious or inglorious. It is our good fortune that we are under a rule which makes it possible for us to meet in this manner. [Cheers] It is under the civilizing rule of the Queen and people of England that we meet here together, hindered by none, and are freely allowed to speak our minds without the least fear and without the least hesitation. Such a thing is possible under British rule and British rule only. [Loud cheers] Then I put the *question* plainly: Is this Congress a nursery for sedition and rebellion against the British Government [cries of 'no, no']; or is it another stone in the foundation of the stability of that Government [cries of 'yes, yes']? There could be but one answer, and that you have already given, because we are thoroughly sensible of the numberless blessings conferred upon us, of which the very existence of this Congress is a proof in a nutshell. [Cheers] Were it not for the blessings of British rule I could not have come here, as I have done, without the least hesitation and without the least fear that my children might be robbed and killed in my absence; nor could you have come from every corner of the land, having performed, within a few days, journeys which in former days would have occupied as many months. [Cheers] These simple facts bring home to all of us at once some of those great and numberless blessings which British rule has conferred upon us. But there remain even greater blessings for which we have to be grateful. It is to British rule that we owe the education we possess; the people of England

were sincere in the declarations made more than half a century ago that India was a sacred charge entrusted to their care by Providence, and that they were bound to administer it for the good of India, to the glory of their own name, and the satisfaction of God. [Prolonged cheering] When we have to acknowledge so many blessings as flowing from British rule—and I could descant on them for hours, because it would simply be recounting to you the history of the British empire in India—is it possible that an assembly like this, every one of whose members is fully impressed with the knowledge of these blessings, could meet for any purpose inimical to that rule to which we owe so much? [Cheers]

The thing is absurd. Let us speak out like men and proclaim that we are loyal to the backbone [cheers]; that we understand the benefits English rule has conferred upon us; that we thoroughly appreciate the education that has been given to us, the new light which has been poured upon us, turning us from darkness into light and teaching us the new lesson that kings are made for the people, not people for their kings; and this new lesson we have learned amidst the darkness of Asiatic despotism only by the light of free English civilization. [Loud cheers]

Notes

1. [de Bary] Vikramāditya, a great and good king in Indian legend.
2. Muslims

Study Question

1. Do you believe that Naoroji's flattery of the British was more or less effective than the tactics of the extremists in challenging British rule in India?

KIDO KŌIN

Kido Kōin[1] (1833–77) was a Choshu[2] Samurai who opposed the Tokugawa refusal to open Japan to western influences. During the Meiji period Kido was an active participant in the creation of a modern Japanese state. In 1871 he travelled to Europe as part of an official fact-finding mission to study the functioning of government in the West. He returned more convinced than ever of Japan's *relative lack of development and the need for constitutional reform. Believing it would take many years to bring Japan up to the level of the western powers, Kido advocated avoiding foreign conflicts in order to concentrate on internal development. In the following excerpt Kido reflects on the roles of the Emperor and of the citizen in Japan and in the nations that he had visited.*

OBSERVATIONS ON RETURNING FROM THE WEST, 1873

It was thought advisable, as early as the spring of 1868 when the northern provinces were still subdued, to summon together at the palace all the officials and nobles of the empire. The Emperor then prayed to the gods of heaven and earth and pronounced an Oath containing five clauses, which was thereupon published throughout the empire, indicating to what end the Constitution should tend, and guiding the ideas of the people in one fixed direction. The heading of this Oath states: 'By this Oath We set up as Our aim the establishment of the national weal[3] on a broad basis and the framing of a constitution and laws.' This led at last to granting the petitions for leave to restore the fiefs to the Emperor, which occasioned the abolition of feudal titles and the unification of the divided national authority. Is not all this consonant with the prevailing view in the powerful countries of the five great continents? And if this be so, then surely we must consider those five clauses as the foundation of our Constitution. Now the Constitution is a thing which sets on a firm basis the weal of the entire nation, which prevents officials from taking unauthorized steps on their own judgment, and which by placing under one control all the business of administration, renders it necessary that all measures conform to it. Is there at the present time any subject of the empire

who does not gratefully acknowledge its profound and farsighted policy and admire the loftiness of the Emperor's views?

However, in enlightened countries, though there may be a sovereign, still he does not hold sway in an arbitrary fashion. The people of the whole country give expression to their united and harmonious wishes, and the business of the State is arranged accordingly, a department (styled the government) being charged with the execution of their judgments, and officials appointed to transact business. For this reason all who hold office respect the wishes of the whole nation and serve their country under a deep sense of responsibility, so that even in extraordinary crises, they take no arbitrary step contrary to the people's will. The strictness [of the constitution] of these governments is such as I have just described, but as an additional check upon illegal acts, the people have parliamentary representatives whose duty it is to inspect everything that is done and to check arbitrary proceedings on the part of officials. Herein lies the best quality of these governments. But if the people are not yet sufficiently enlightened, it becomes necessary, at least for a time, that the Sovereign should by his superior discernment anticipate their unanimous wishes and act for them in arranging the affairs of State and in entrusting to officials the execution of their wishes. By this means he will gradually lead them forward in the path of enlightenment. Such a course is consonant with natural principles, and I am inclined to believe that the thought of the Emperor when he inaugurated by an oath his energetic policy was based on this idea. My belief is that although Japan is not yet ready for parliamentary inspection of the affairs of state, in the importance of its laws and the magnitude of its affairs it is no different from those countries of Europe and America the conduct of whose governments embodies the will of the people. It is important that our officials should not be forgetful of their responsibility and should take as their model our five-clause Constitution. . . .

Every citizen's object in life is to preserve his natural liberty by exercising his rights, and to assist in carrying on the government by sharing its obligations. Therefore, [these rights and obligations] are specified in writing and men bind themselves by a solemn promise to permit no infringement of them, but to act as mutual checks on each other in maintaining them. These writings are what we call laws. The laws grow out of the Constitution, for the Constitution is the root of every part of the government, and there is nothing which does not branch out from it. For this reason, every country, when the time comes for changing its constitution, bestows on it the greatest care and the ripest consideration and ascertains to the full the general wishes. No new measures are put in force unless they are imperatively called for by the circumstances, [nor are any adopted] lightly or hastily. In a country whose sovereign generously decides to meet the wishes of the people, the greatest care must be taken to ascertain them with accuracy, the internal conditions of the country must be profoundly studied, what the people produce must be taken into account, and, most important of all, policies must be suited to the degree of civilization of the people.

Again, in ordering the affairs of a nation, its strength must be taken into account. If not, one good will be converted into a hundred evils. The poor man's son who tries to rival the son of the rich man ruins his property and his house, and in the end does not make a show equal to his rival. Those who order the affairs of a nation should remember, before taking action, to consider the due sequence of measures, and should proceed by gradual steps in nourishing its strength, for no nation ever attained to a perfect state of civilization in a single morning. . . .

When I consider the results of the measures of the past few years with reference to the present condition of our country it appears to me that the trend of the times still lacks direction. The people's minds are perversely turned in one direction, and instead of exercising their rights, many of them mimic idly the arts of civilization; instead of discharging their responsibilities to the state, they are much given to ill-judged pretensions to enlightenment. The consequence is that although they are gradually acquiring the outward appearance of refinement, and the old rustic coarseness is gradually changing, they have not suddenly become enlightened in their hearts.

Notes

1. Also known as Kido Takayoshi and Katsura Kogoro.
2. Choshu Samurai were strongly anti-foreign when western ships made their first appearance in Japan. However, they soon realized that Japan as it existed in the 1850s and 1860s would be unable to resist the advancing foreign forces. Thus, many of the Choshu Samurai abandoned their isolationist sentiments and began to study Western technology. They would play a prominent role in the Meiji era.
3. Literally the 'national welfare'.

Study Question

1. How accurate is Kido's reading of the way government functions in the western world?

◇

ITO HIROBUMI

Like Kido Kōin, Ito Hirobumi (1841–1909) was also a Choshu Samurai. Despite the self-enforced isolation of the Tokugawa period, Ito had travelled to Europe in the early 1860s, working as a deckhand on an English ship. After the Meiji Restoration, Ito became one of the leading advocates of Westernization. He served the Meiji Emperor in the ministries of foreign affairs, *finance, and industry. Entrusted with the task of preparing a new constitution, Ito established a constitutional commission that again travelled to the West in search of suitable models. There he came to admire greatly Bismarck's newly unified Germany. In the following comments on the new constitution Ito reflects on the origins and value of representative government.*

◇

ON THE CONSTITUTION OF 1889

If we reflect upon the history of civilization in this country it will be perceived, I think, that while several influences have been at work, still the introduction of such alien religious systems as Confucianism and Buddhism, which were largely instrumental in elevating our people, and the development of such works as have conduced to their welfare, have been due to the benevolent guidance and encouragement of the sovereign. We may therefore say with truth that the civilization which we now possess is a gift from the Throne. . . .

I shall now proceed to discuss the subject of the participation of the people in the government of the state. It is only by the protection of the law that the happiness of the nation can be promoted and the safety of person and property secured, and to attain these ends the people may elect their representatives and empower the latter to deliberate on laws with a view to the promotion of their own happiness and the safeguarding of their rights. This, gentlemen, is enacted by the Constitution, and I think you will agree that it

constitutes a concession to the people of a most valuable right. Under an absolute system of government the sovereign's will is his command, and the sovereign's command at once becomes law. In a constitutional country, however, the consent of that assembly which represents the people must be obtained. It will be evident, however, that as the supreme right is one and indivisible, the legislative power remains in the hands of the sovereign and is not bestowed on the people. While the supreme right extends to everything, and its exercise is wide and comprehensive, its legislative and executive functions are undoubtedly the most important. These are in the hands of the sovereign; the rights pertaining thereto cannot be held in common by the sovereign and his subjects; but the latter are permitted to take part in legislation according to the provisions of the Constitution. In a country which is under absolute rule the view of the sovereign is at once law; in a constitutional country, on the other hand, nothing being law without a concurrence of views between the sovereign and the people, the latter elect representatives to meet at an appointed place and carry out the view of the sovereign. In other words, law in a constitutional state is the result of a concord of ideas between the sovereign and subject; but there can be no law when these two are in opposition to each other. . . .

If we trace back to its origin the principle of a representative body, we find that it first manifested itself among an ancient German people. It has been, and still is indeed, affirmed that it is a growth of the English people, but it is not so in fact, for in an old German law, that in the levying of a tax the taxpayer should be consulted, we find the germ of the popular representative principle. The system prevailing in England must be an offshoot from the seedling that appeared in Germany, and from which the principle developed largely in later times in the west of Europe, though it never gained a hold in the central and eastern parts. Till about a century ago it was held that representative bodies should have a monopoly of the legislative right, and the theory of thus dividing the supreme right found much favor. But this conclusion has been held to be illogical by modern scholars. They say the state is like a human body. Just as one brain controls the diverse actions of the limbs and other parts, so should one supreme power superintend and control all the other members of a nation, though such members may play various parts in the whole. This view is perhaps in its turn a little antiquated, but it is sufficient to show the absurdity of the tripartite theory that maintains that the representative body should monopolize the right of legislation. If we remember that the legislative right is a part of the supreme prerogative and that the latter is the sole possession of the emperor, it will be apparent that no such monopoly is possible. But the sovereign may permit the representative body to take part in the process of practically applying the legislative right. Since the tripartite theory lost favor it has come to be recognized that the supreme right must be vested in one person and indivisible. . . .

If we look back into the history of the world to the origin of the representative body, we shall find that the principle has undergone an extraordinary degree of development. At the Restoration the institution [representative government], then well grown in Europe, was by an enlargement and extension of the scope of our national policy adopted in Japan. Now, by carefully adapting the principle to our national characteristics, manners, and customs, and by retaining what is excellent and discarding what is faulty, we are about to put into practice a system of constitutional politics that is without rival in the East. And this leads us not unnaturally to discuss briefly the English constitution, which in many quarters has been thought worthy of imitation. I shall, however, speak solely of the difference in the history and evolution of the two constitutions, and shall not attempt to define their relative merits. In England there is no codified constitution, and you must bear in mind how the English people obtained the so-called Great Charter. The nobles of England, as you no doubt are aware, not only form a large section of the population, but they were, and still are, powerful. The sovereign of that day, having engaged in unnecessary warfare with a foreign country, levied heavy burdens on the people, which policy led to much discontent. But the complaints were not confined to the mass of the people; the nobles were also angered by the monarch's actions and refused to obey his commands. Eventually they combined and required him to sign the Magna Carta; he at first refused but was at length compelled by force to comply. You will see then that while it is quite true that the king had oppressed the people, as a matter of fact this Magna Carta pledge was extorted from him by the nobles at the point of the sword. The case of Japan is totally different. The most cordial relations prevail between the Throne and the people while our Constitution is granted. The position of our court cannot be at all compared with that of England when the Magna Carta was granted, for we know that our Imperial House has a single aim—the welfare and happiness of the nation. Not only were there no such discontented barons in this country, but our feudal lords, great and small, joined in requesting the Crown to take back the military and political rights which for centuries they had enjoyed. Could any two things be more radically different than the origins of the English and Japanese Constitutions? If the English people felicitate themselves on the influence exercised in promoting and developing the national welfare and interest, by a Charter given under such ominous circumstances as was theirs, how much more should we congratulate ourselves on having received from our benevolent sovereign, under the most happy and peaceful auspices, the Constitution of the Japanese empire!. . .

The course which lies now before the Japanese empire is plain. Both ruler and ruled should apply their efforts smoothly and harmoniously to preserve tranquility; to elevate the status of the people; to secure the rights and promote the welfare of each individual; and finally, by manifesting abroad the dignity and power of Japan, to secure and maintain her integrity and independence.

Study Question

1. What does Ito mean when he says that the legislative power must remain in the hands of the Sovereign?

Sayyid Jamal al-Din al-Afghani

Jamal al-Din al-Afghani (1838/1839–97)[1] was an Islamic reformer and proponent of Islamic nationalism (or pan-Islamism). He travelled widely and visited many of the major western capitals including London, Paris, and St Petersburg. His travels led him to conclude that advances in scientific knowledge were essential to a thriving civilization. Thus, successful resistance to the colonial rulers who dominated nations such as India and Egypt would depend upon a new attitude towards scientific education. The lecture which follows was delivered in November 1882 at the Albert Hall in Calcutta.

Lecture on Teaching and Learning

The Ottoman Government and the Khedivate of Egypt have been opening schools for the teaching of the new sciences for a period of sixty years, and until now they have not received any benefit from those sciences. . . .

The first Muslims had no science, but, thanks to the Islamic religion, a philosophic spirit arose among them, and owing to that philosophic spirit they began to discuss the general affairs of the world and human necessities. This was why they acquired in a short time all the sciences with particular subjects that they translated from the Syriac, Persian, and Greek into the Arabic language at the time of Manṣūr Davānaqī.[2]

It is philosophy that makes man understandable to man, explains human nobility, and shows man the proper road. The first defect appearing in any nation that is headed toward decline is in the philosophic spirit. After that, deficiencies spread into the other sciences, arts, and associations.

. . . Muslims these days do not see any benefit from their education. For example, they study grammar, and the purpose of grammar is that someone who has acquired the Arabic language be capable of speaking and writing. The Muslims now make grammar a goal in itself. For long years they expend philosophic thought on grammar to no avail, and after finishing they are unable to speak, write, or understand Arabic.

Rhetoric, which they call *literature*, is the science that enables man to become a writer, a speaker, and poet. However, we see these days that after studying that science they are incapable of correcting their everyday speech.

Logic, which is the balance for ideas, should make everyone who acquires it capable of distinguishing every truth from falsehood and every right from wrong. However, we see that the minds of our Muslim logicians are full of every superstition and vanity, and no difference exists between their ideas and the ideas of the masses of the bazaar.

Philosophy is the science that deals with the state of external beings, and their causes, reasons, needs, and requisites. It is strange that our ulama[3] . . . call themselves sages, and despite this they cannot distinguish their left hand from their right hand, and they do not ask: Who are we and what is right and proper for us? They never ask the causes of electricity, the steamboat, and railroads. . . .

The strangest thing of all is that our ulama these days have divided science into two parts. One they call Muslim science, and one European science. Because of this they forbid others to teach some of the useful sciences. They have not understood that science is that noble thing that has no connection with any nation, and is not distinguished by anything but itself. Rather, everything that is known is known by science, and every nation that becomes renowned becomes renowned through science. Men must be related to science, not science to men.

How very strange it is that the Muslims study those sciences that are ascribed to Aristotle with the greatest delight, as if Aristotle were one of the pillars of the Muslims. However, if the discussion relates to Galileo, Newton, and Kepler, they consider them infidels. The father and mother of science is proof, and proof is neither Aristotle nor Galileo. The truth is where there is proof, and those who forbid science and knowledge in the belief that they are safeguarding the Islamic religion are really the enemies of that religion. The Islamic religion is the closest of religions to science and knowledge, and there is no incompatibility between science and knowledge and the foundation of the Islamic faith. . . .

The first education obtained by man was religious education, since philosophical education can only be obtained by a society that has studied some science and is able to understand proofs and demonstrations. Hence we can say that reform will never be achieved by the Muslims except if the leaders of our religion first reform themselves and gather the fruits of their science and knowledge.

If one considers, he will understand this truth, that the ruin and corruption we have experienced first reached our ulama and religious leaders, and then penetrated the rest of the community.

Notes

1. There is substantial debate regarding al-Afghani's birth. Scholars differ as to whether he was born in 1838 or 1839; there is even less consensus as to his place of birth—Afghanistan or Iran. For more information on this debate see Roderic H. Davison, 'Jamal al-Din Afghani: A Note on his Nationality and on his Burial', *Middle Eastern Studies* 24, 1 (Jan. 1988): 110–12.

2. [Keddie] A nickname for the first important Abbasid caliph, who ruled AD 754–75. In fact the main translations were done later under al_ Ma'mūn (813–33).

3. The Ulama [ulema] are Muslim scholars, though the term is often used to describe Islamic clerics.

Study Question

1. al-Afghani argues that there is no incompatibility between science and faith. Do you think that his contemporaries would have agreed with this claim?

KANG YOUWEI

Kang Youwei (1858–1927) was one of the best known reformers in late-Qing China. He played a major role in the Hundred Days Reform movement, which was launched shortly after this document was produced in January 1898. Kang's works called for a thorough reform of traditional institutions, using the ideas of Confucius as the basis of his reform program. Like many other reformers of this era Kang was troubled by China's defeat in the Sino-Japanese War (1894–95) but he looked favourably on the Meiji reforms which had so strengthened Japanese power. The document which follows was addressed to the reform-minded Guangxu emperor.

COMPREHENSIVE CONSIDERATION OF THE WHOLE SITUATION

A survey of all states in the world will show that those states that undertook reforms became strong while those states that clung to the past perished. The consequences of clinging to the past and the effects of opening up new ways are thus obvious. If Your Majesty, with your discerning brilliance, observes that trends in other countries you will see that if we can change, we can preserve ourselves; but if we cannot change, we shall perish. Indeed, if we can make a complete change, we shall become strong, but if we only make limited changes, we shall still perish. If Your Majesty and his ministers investigate the source of the disease, you will know that this is the right prescription.

Our present trouble lies in our clinging to old institutions without knowing how to change. In an age of competition between states, to put into effect methods appropriate to an era of universal unification and laissez-faire is like wearing heavy furs in summer or riding a high carriage across a river. This can only result in having a fever or getting oneself drowned. . . .

It is a principle of things that the new is strong but the old weak; that new things are fresh but old things rotten; that new things are active but old things static. If the institutions are old, defects will develop. Therefore there are no institutions that should remain unchanged for a hundred years. Moreover, our present institutions are but unworthy vestiges of the Han, Tang, Yuan, and Ming dynasties; they are not even the institutions of the [Manchu] ancestors. In fact, they are the products of the fancy writing and corrupt dealing of petty officials rather than the original ideas of the ancestors. Furthermore, institutions are for the purpose of preserving one's territories. Now that the ancestral territory cannot be preserved, what good is it to maintain the ancestral institutions? . . .

Although there is a desire to reform, yet if the national policy is not fixed and public opinion not united, it will be impossible for us to give up the old and adopt the new. The national policy is to the state just as the rudder is to the boat or the pointer is to the compass. It determines the direction of the state and shapes the public opinion of the country.

Nowadays the court has been undertaking some reforms, but the action of the emperor is obstructed by the ministers, and the recommendations of the able scholars are attacked by old-fashioned bureaucrats. If the charge is not 'using barbarian ways to change China', then it is 'upsetting the ancestral institutions'. Rumours and scandals are rampant, and people fight each other like fire and water. To reform in this way is as ineffective as attempting a forward march by walking backward. It will inevitably result in failure. Your Majesty knows that under the present circumstances reforms are imperative and old institutions must be abolished. I beg Your Majesty to make up your mind and to decide on the national policy. . . .

After studying ancient and modern institutions, Chinese and foreign, I have found that the institutions of the sage kings and three dynasties [Xia, Shang, and Zhou] were excellent, but that the ancient times were different from today. I hope Your Majesty will daily read Mencius[1] and follow his example of loving the people. The development of the Han, Tang, Song, and Ming dynasties may be learned, but it should be remembered that the age of universal unification is different from that of sovereign nations. I with Your Majesty would study Guanzi[2] and follow his idea of managing the country. As to the republican

governments of the United States and France and the constitutional governments of Britain and Germany, these countries are far away and their customs are different from ours. Their changes occurred a long time ago and can no longer be traced. Consequently I beg Your Majesty to adopt the purpose of Peter the Great of Russia as our purpose and to take the Meiji Reform of Japan as the model for our reform. The time and place of Japan's reform are not remote and her religion and customs are somewhat similar to ours. Her success is manifest; her example can be easily followed.

Notes

1. Mencius lived during the fourth century BCE. His interpretations of the writings of Confucius are considered, by many, to be definitive.

2. Guanzi [Guan Zhong] (~725–645 BCE) was a minister in the State of Qi who successfully carried out a number of reforms to the administrative and economic structure of the state. Guanzi advocated rigid control over the population (legalism).

Study Question

1. Why would Kang reject the governments of the West as a suitable model for China, yet commend the western-inspired Meiji model?

WU TINGFANG

Wu Tingfang (1842–1922) served in the diplomatic corps of the late Qing dynasty. He held posts in the United States, Spain, Mexico, Peru, and Cuba. In 1914 Wu wrote America through the Spectacles of an Oriental Diplomat. *Prior to his diplomatic work*

he had been a lawyer and journalist. After the 1911 Revolution Wu became Minister of Foreign Affairs and Minister of Justice in the provisional republican government. The following speech was given in New York City on 5 May 1908.

THE AWAKENING OF CHINA

The mere mentioning of this subject—'The Awakening of China'—is sufficient to make my countrymen thrill with pleasure and flush with pride. China, the country which made the dying Missionary, the famous Xavier,[1] exclaim in 1552, 'O Rock, Rock, when wilt thou open?' is at last, indeed, opened, and changes are taking place in that hoary Empire, which bid fair to constitute the miracle of the Twentieth Century.

China has been dubbed 'The Sick Man of the Far East', 'The Sleeping Lion', 'The Tottering Empire'; and other names more or less picturesque and complimentary have been bestowed upon her. With some people it is the conviction that China has only a historical interest, that her glory is of the past, that the leopard may change its spots, but China remains forever in her ruts, the same yesterday, to-day, and to-morrow.

But while this gloomy picture of the state of affairs might have been partly true of China of a few decades ago, it is no longer true now. The 'Sick Man' is rapidly convalescing, the 'Sleeping Lion' is awake, and the hoary and tottering Empire has had new blood injected into her system. China is moving, and she is moving with a rapidity difficult for one who has not personally witnessed the wonderful changes to understand and realize. . . .

First and foremost, is the spread of education—and by this I mean the diffusion of general knowledge, knowledge of men, and of affairs of the world. It is a far cry from the time when high officials in Peking, to whom the wonderful performance of the Morse telegraph apparatus was shown and explained, expressed simply their opinion that China got along without it for four thousand years; to the present day when every official residence and department in Peking is connected by the telephone and every provincial yamen, or administrative office, is supplied with the telegraph service.

Wu Tingfang during his tenure as a Qing diplomat, photographed in New York City. New York World-Telegram and the Sun Newspaper Photograph Collection. Courtesy of the Library of Congress, Prints and Photographs Division (LC-DIGggbain-00605).

Repeated defeats at the hand of the foreign powers soon convinced our people of the futility of matching bows and arrows against modern guns and explosives, while our wooden junks went down before the onslaught of armored cruisers and battleships like wheat before the scythe. The inability of our former so-called modern army and navy to encounter those of other nations demonstrated to us clearly that modern weapons of war without the properly trained men to handle them and without scientific leaders to direct and control are of no more value than bows and arrows and wooden junks. . . .

Students poured into foreign countries by the hundreds, and particularly those that went to Japan devoted a large part of their time to the editing of magazines and the translation of books, a veritable flood of literature thus pouring back to their fatherland, and reaching every nook and corner of the Empire. Some of this literature, flowing from the pens of young men flushed with the new learning and burning with patriotism, was naturally somewhat violent in tone and made sensational reading, but it produced its effect on our people who needed something unusual to wake them out of their lethargy.

Nor must I omit to mention the services of the missionary body, particularly the American branch of it, whose indefatigable efforts in the establishment of educational institutions and in the diffusion of literature of general knowledge, formed a part of the leaven which has leavened the whole Empire of China. The onward movement derived great impetus and received much encouragement from the successes of our island neighbor, Japan. The cry was that what Japan could do, China by adopting similar reforms and taking similar steps can and will do. . . .

The anxiety of young men and women to acquire a modern education in schools at home and abroad, and the joyful sacrifice on the part of parents and elders of luxuries and comforts, to which they have been accustomed for years, in order that the younger generation may receive a liberal education, costing ten or twenty times more than the old method, affords a sight unparalleled in our history. Female education, very much neglected in the past, is recognized as work of the first importance, and the position of women is approaching, though at present slowly, the ideal of that in the west.

A movement of striking significance, on account of the remarkable success it has met, is that started by the Anti-Foot-Binding Society. Foot-binding, originally only intended to check the feet of young women from attaining abnormal and disfiguring size, grew into a most horrible custom, through the perverted ideas of beauty, until it became the exception rather than the rule for women to possess a pair of natural feet. I could never bring myself to see the beauty of human feet, compressed

and arbitrarily shaped by artificial means, and from my boyhood I always expressed my strong condemnation of the absurd fashion. I remember I agitated in my early days the question by exposing the absurdity and cruelty of the practice, and with a view of its gradual discontinuance I endeavored to persuade my friends and relatives to join with me in forming a league pledging ourselves to prohibit the compression of our daughters' feet. But to my dismay I could not induce anyone to become a member of my proposed association. It was, therefore, with genuine pleasure and agreeable surprise that some years ago I learned that an anti-foot-binding society was organized by a few foreign ladies, whose object was to accomplish the same thing that I had previously aimed to do. Through the instrumentality of public meetings, pamphlets and leaflets, which were supported by official proclamations and Imperial decrees, the people in a short time have been awakened to the folly and injuriousness of the custom and the appeal has met with a response that must be gratifying to all the people who would hold their bodies as sacred. Today, one walks the streets of the larger cities and hardly ever sees a girl of ten or under with bound feet, and ladies of middle age, whose extremities have been cramped for a score of years, deem it their patriotic duty to liberate themselves from their bondage. Recently the work of the committee of that society has been handed over to a group of prominent Chinese gentlemen, who, it was believed, could better advance the interests of the society now that it has passed its period of infancy.

Another popular movement, which has given great joy to all friends and well-wishers of China, has been the efforts for the suppression of opium. No event in China has given more and better evidence of the hopeful vitality and the solid moral character of our people than the enthusiastic and energetic manner in which the vice of opium smoking is being attacked. On the part of the

Government, the highest officials in Peking have been suspended from office for not curing themselves of the habit, creating a sensation in mandarindom.[2] Decrees and proclamations have been issued commanding an annual decrease in the cultivation of the poppy, the closing of public opium dens, the registration of smokers, and other measures which will result in the wiping out of the national curse in eight or ten years. Only a few days ago, I received by cable two Imperial Decrees issued on the 7th and 10th of last month which strengthen the growing conviction that my Government is thoroughly in earnest in its efforts to suppress the opium habit. By the first decree Prince Kung and three other high officials in Peking have been appointed members of an Imperial Commission whose duty is to find out and to see that all officials addicted to the use of the drug in Peking and in all the provinces are cured of the habit, and that in case any opium-smoking official should be discovered, he and his superior for failing to report the same should be both punished. The second commands that all the members of the diplomatic and consular corps abroad must give up their noxious people at once, while those too old in age or too inveterate in the use of the drug to do so must retire from the service. Our people in foreign countries are also urged to exert themselves in putting an end to the use of opium. But the more encouraging feature is the attitude of the people towards the opium question. A few years ago, opium smoking was no more condemned than cigars or cigarettes, and it was the fashion for giddy youths to sleep and eat with the deadly drug. Today an opium smoker confesses his habit with shame, and all society regards him as more or less an outcast.

And it is this healthful change in public opinion that will liberate my country from the chain of the opium devil. At the recent closing of the opium dens in the important cities, the students turned out *en masse*, with their flags and banners and musical instruments, celebrating the occasion as if it were a victory in war, and so earnest were the people in their efforts to suppress the evil that the very keepers of the dens themselves gathered together their vile instruments of smoking and made a huge bonfire of them. . . .

What does this awakening of China mean to the world? To my mind, it means, in the first place, true and lasting peace in the Far East. The moment China becomes strong enough after her awakening to maintain her sovereign rights and protect herself from aggression, the Far Eastern question will have been solved. Again, the awakening of China means the development of commerce, and the day is not distant when the Pacific Ocean will rival the Atlantic with the number of ships that sail on its surface. The world will then witness an expansion of trade never before known in its history, and this trade will also be a safeguard in the interests of universal peace.

Notes

1. St Francis Xavier (1506–52).
2. The traditionally powerful scholarly elite, schooled in the teachings of Confucius.

Study Question

1. Wu claims that a stronger China is the key to peace in East Asia. Is this an accurate assessment?

RABINDRANATH TAGORE

Rabindranath Tagore (1861–1941) was a Bengali writer who was particularly renowned for his poetry. Tagore spent some time in England in his late teenage years and travelled widely after his literary works became well-known. In 1913 he received the Nobel Prize in Literature. In addition to his poetry, Tagore wrote numerous essays and *was, at times, involved in the Indian nationalist movement. The document that follows was written later in Tagore's life, after he had renounced the knighthood conferred upon him by King George V, in protest over the massacre at Amritsar in 1919. (See also the documents on the Amritsar Massacre in Chapter Two.)*

EAST AND WEST

Rabindranath Tagore, photographed three years after he received the Nobel Prize for Literature.

Lately I went to visit some battlefields of France which had been devastated by war. The awful calm of desolation, which still bore wrinkles of pain—death-struggles stiffened into ugly ridges—brought before my mind the vision of a huge demon, which had no shape, no meaning, yet had two arms that could strike and break and tear, a gaping mouth that could devour, and bulging brains that could conspire and plan. It was a purpose, which had a living body, but no complete humanity to temper it. Because it was passion—belonging to life, and yet not having the wholeness of life—it was the most terrible of life's enemies.

Something of the same sense of oppression in a different degree, the same desolation in a different aspect, is produced in my mind when I realize the effect of the West upon Eastern life—the West which, in its relation to us, is all plan and purpose incarnate, without any superfluous humanity.

I feel the contrast very strongly in Japan. In that country the old world presents itself with some ideal of perfection, in which man has his varied opportunities of self-revelation in art, in ceremonial, in religious faith, and in customs expressing the poetry of social relationship. There one feels that deep delight of hospitality which life offers to life. And side by side, in the same soil, stands the modern world, which is stupendously big and powerful, but inhospitable. It has no simple-hearted welcome for man. It is living; yet the incompleteness of life's ideal within it cannot but hurt humanity.

The wriggling tentacles of a cold-blooded utilitarianism, with which the West has grasped all the easily yielding succulent portions of the East, are causing pain and indignation throughout the Eastern countries. The West comes to us, not with the imagination and sympathy that create and unite, but with a shock of passion—passion for power and wealth. This passion is a mere force, which has in it the principle of separation, of conflict.

I have been fortunate in coming into close touch with individual men and women of the Western countries, and have felt with them their sorrows and shared their aspirations. I have known that they seek the same God, who is my God—even those who deny Him. I feel certain that, if the great light of culture be extinct in Europe, our horizon in the East will mourn in darkness. It does not hurt my pride to acknowledge that, in the present age, Western humanity has received its mission to be the teacher of the world; that her science, through the mastery of laws of nature, is to liberate human souls from the dark dungeon of matter. For this very reason I have realised all the more strongly, on the other hand, that the dominant collective idea in the Western countries is not creative. It is ready to enslave or kill individuals, to drug a great people with soul-killing poison, darkening their whole future with the black mist of stupefaction, and emasculating entire races of men to the utmost

degree of helplessness. It is wholly wanting in spiritual power to blend and harmonize; it lacks the sense of the great personality of man.

The most significant fact of modern days is this, that the West has met the East. Such a momentous meeting of humanity, in order to be fruitful, must have in its heart some great emotional idea, generous and creative. There can be no doubt that God's choice has fallen upon the knights-errant of the West for the service of the present age; arms and armour have been given to them; but have they yet realised in their hearts the single-minded loyalty to their cause which can resist all temptations of bribery from the devil? The world to-day is offered to the West. She will destroy it, if she does not use it for a great creation of man. The materials for such a creation are in the hands of science; but the creative genius is in Man's spiritual ideal.

> ### Study Question
>
> 1. Contrast Tagore's view of British rule with that of Naoroji earlier in this chapter. Whose assessment of the intentions of the West seems more accurate?

TIPS FOR ANALYSIS

Assessing the Author

Ask yourself three key questions: who is the author, what is his or her background, and when did the author live? This will allow you to consider the events which the author experienced in his or her life. These events will influence the author's perception of the world. No writer can be entirely objective; therefore, the author will be influenced by his or her upbringing, education, and experiences.

WEB RESOURCES

Internet Modern History Sourcebook: The Long Nineteenth Century
http://www.fordham.edu/halsall/mod/modsbook3.html

Perry-Castañeda Library Map Collection
http://www.lib.utexas.edu/maps
Internet East Asia Sourcebook
http://www.fordham.edu/halsall/eastasia/eastasiasbook.html
The Middle East Network Information Center
http://library.csusm.edu/subject_guides/history/online_primary.asp

RECOMMENDED READING

Lafcadio Hearn (Koizumi Yakumo), *Kokoro: Hints & Echoes of Japanese Inner Life* (New York: Routledge, 2002). This collection of essays from Hearn, a European-born naturalized citizen of Japan, reflects on the inner workings of Japanese society during the pivotal encounter between traditional Japan and the rapid modernization of the Meiji Era. Hearn attempts to capture the essential elements of Japanese culture that seemed to be disappearing.

Junichiro Tanizaki, *Some Prefer Nettles* (New York: Vintage, 1995). Tanizaki's *Some Prefer Nettles*, written in 1928, examines the conflict between traditional and modern Japanese culture during the Meiji era. The cities of Tokyo and Osaka appear as contrasting symbols of modern and traditional Japan. As Tanizaki himself had done, the novel's main character eventually abandons the modern world.

Eric Liu, *The Travels of Lao Can* (Honolulu, HI: University Press of the Pacific, 2001). Set in the latter years of the Qing dynasty, Liu's novel considers the possibility of political reform through a radical revision of Confucian values. Condemning the decadence of the late-Qing era, the author examines the conflict between traditional China and its Confucian values, and the forces of modernization.

Arthur Conan Doyle, *The Lost World* (New York: Tor Classics, 1997). Though contemporary audiences may be more familiar with the Michael Crichton novel rather than Conan Doyle's 1912 depiction, *The Lost World* remains a classic adventure story. Many of the attitudes that drove British imperialism are captured: the excitement of discovery, love of adventure, and scientific curiosity, as well as the less noble attitudes towards indigenous populations.

RECOMMENDED VIEWING

Age of Hope (UK/USA, 1999). Director: Jonathan Lewis/WGBH Boston/BBC (Documentary). *Age of Hope* opens with the 1900 Paris Exposition and examines the sources of both turn-of-the-century optimism and disillusionment. Interviews and contemporary film footage create a fascinating narrative.

The Last Samurai (USA, 2003). Director: Edward Zwick. Set in late-nineteenth-century Japan, the film portrays the struggle between Meiji reformers, who wanted to create a modern conscript army, and the Samurai, who attempted to preserve the old order. The film is not historically accurate, but it does capture some of the conflict within Japanese society regarding the turn towards western models.

The Opium War (China, 1997). Director: Xie Jin. Xie Jin's film begins in 1838 with the first large-scale importation of opium into China. The film provides a balanced look at the events that resulted in the humiliating Treaty of Nanjing, including the reaction of Commissioner Lin and the attitudes of British officials.

Empress Dowager (Hong Kong, 1975). Director: Li Han-hsiang. Against the backdrop of late Qing China and the instabilities caused by foreign intervention, Westernization, and internal unrest, Li Han-hsiang dramatizes the life of the Empress Dowager Cixi, and the machinations that installed and maintained her position of power.

CHAPTER TWO

GLOBAL CAPITALISM
AND IMPERIALISM

◇

In the early part of the twentieth century the British Empire ruled over some 400 million people. This was by far the greatest proportion of the almost 80 per cent of the world that found itself under direct or indirect colonial control. However, France, Germany, Portugal, Belgium, the Ottoman Turks, and Japan also dominated substantial territories. Additionally, the United States had asserted, through the Monroe Doctrine and the Roosevelt Corollary, its right to influence political and economic developments throughout the Americas. This 'informal' influence would lay the foundations for American neo-colonialism in Central and South America throughout the twentieth century.

While colonial policies and the degree of control varied widely among imperial nations, the effects on the colonized peoples tended to be similar. Throughout the colonial world the local populations became second- and even third-class citizens in their own countries; western educational, legal, and judicial systems were often imposed; and, in many of the European-controlled areas, land was reserved for white settlement. Repression and violence occurred in differing degrees in regions under imperial control, though the Belgian Congo, where the citizens lived under a draconian system of terror, experienced the most sustained abuses. Under neo-colonialism the overt mechanisms of control were absent but the restrictions inherent in the production of cash crops grown for export, left the indigenous populations impoverished and politically powerless.

Around the world resistance to the attitudes and consequences of colonial control was quick to form. In India, members of the Indian National Congress condemned the economic and social consequences of colonial control. Writers such as W.E.B. Du Bois drew attention to the fate of the black population around the world, calling for a co-operative effort to achieve liberation, and Vladimir Lenin denounced imperialism as the last gasp of global capitalism.

This chapter considers the causes and consequences of global imperialism. Adam Hochschild offers a perspective on colonialism in the Belgian Congo. Jules

Ferry and the Earl of Cromer defend the need for colonial control over foreign territory. B.G. Tilak offers a persuasive argument against British rule in India and proposes the boycott as an effective weapon in the fight to regain indigenous control. The documents on the Amritsar Massacre and Winston Churchill's wartime speech show just how determined the British were to maintain their hold on 'the jewel in the crown'. Turning to neo-colonialism, Brazilian historian Caio Prado Júnior explains the vulnerability of the cash-crop economies of South America. Lenin's assessment of imperialism as 'the highest stage of capitalism' offers an important explanation for the rapid rise of the colonial empires of the late nineteenth century. W.E.B. Du Bois points to the emerging Pan-African movement as the key to freedom for the black peoples of the world.

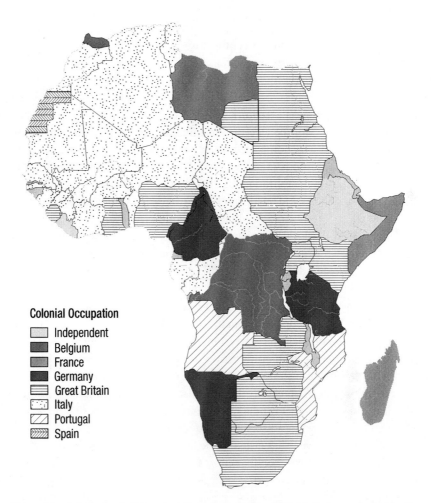

Colonial Occupation

- Independent
- Belgium
- France
- Germany
- Great Britain
- Italy
- Portugal
- Spain

Africa at the height of colonial control. Note the vast size of the territories controlled by France and Great Britian.

ADAM HOCHSCHILD

Adam Hochschild has written on a wide variety of topics, including Stalin's legacy in the Soviet Union and the apartheid era in South Africa, as well as contributing pieces to The New Yorker, The New York Review of Books, *and* The Nation. *Born in 1942, Hochschild—a New York native—teaches writing at the Graduate School of Journalism at the*

University of California, Berkeley. The following excerpt from King Leopold's Ghost *discusses the terror system established in Leopold's Belgian Congo in order to maintain control at little cost to the Europeans. It also touches upon the rationale invoked by many of the European administrators in the Congo around the turn of the twentieth century.*

KING LEOPOLD'S GHOST

Stanislas Lefranc, a devout Catholic and monarchist, was a Belgian prosecutor who had come to the Congo to work as a magistrate. Early one Sunday morning in Leopoldville,[1] he heard the sound of many children screaming desperately.

On tracing the howls to their source, Lefranc found 'some thirty urchins, of whom several were seven or eight years old, lined up and waiting their turn, watching, terrified, their companions being flogged. Most of the urchins, in a paroxysm of grief . . . kicked so frightfully that the soldiers ordered to hold them by the hands and feet had to lift them off the ground. . . . 25 times the whip slashed down on each of the children.' The evening before, Lefranc learned, several children had laughed in the presence of a white man, who then ordered that all the servant boys in town be given fifty lashes. The second installment of twenty-five lashes was due at six o'clock the next morning. Lefranc managed to get these stopped, but was told not to make any more protests that interfered with discipline.

Lefranc was seeing in use a central tool of Leopold's Congo, which in the minds of the territory's people, soon became as closely identified with white rule as the steamboat or the rifle. It was the *chicotte*—a whip of raw, sun-dried hippopotamus hide, cut into a long sharp-edged corkscrew strip.

Usually the *chicotte* was applied to the victim's bare buttocks. Its blows would leave permanent scars; more than twenty-five strokes could mean unconsciousness; and a hundred or more—not an uncommon punishment—were often fatal.

Lefranc was to see many more *chicotte* beatings, although his descriptions of them, in pamphlets and newspaper articles he published in Belgium, provoked little reaction.

> The station chief selects the victims. . . . Trembling, haggard, they lie face down on the ground. . . . two of their companions, sometimes four, seize them by the feet and hands, and remove their cotton drawers. . . . Each time that the torturer lifts up the chicotte, a reddish stripe appears on the skin of the pitiful victims, who, however firmly held, gasp in frightful contortions. . . . At the first blows the unhappy victims let out horrible cries which soon become faint groans. . . . In a refinement of evil, some officers, and I've witnessed this, demand that, when the sufferer gets up, panting, he must graciously give the military salute.

The open horror Lefranc expressed succeeded only in earning him a reputation as an oddball or troublemaker. He 'shows an astonishing ignorance of things which he ought to know because of his work. A mediocre agent,' the acting governor general wrote in a personnel evaluation. In an attempt to quiet his complaints, Lefranc wrote, officials ordered that executions at his post be carried out in a new location instead of next to his house.

Except for Lefranc, few Europeans working for the regime left records of their shock at the sight of officially sanctioned terror. The white men who passed through the territory as military officers, steamboat captains, or state or concession company officials generally accepted the use of the *chicotte* as unthinkingly as hundreds of thousands of other men in uniform would accept their assignments, a half-century later, to staff the Nazi and Soviet concentration camps. 'Monsters exist,' wrote Primo Levi of his experience at Auschwitz. 'But they are too few in number to be truly dangerous. More dangerous are . . . the functionaries ready to believe and to act without asking questions.' . . .

Although some whites in the Congo enjoyed wielding the *chicotte*, most put a . . . symbolic distance between themselves and the dreaded instrument. 'At first I . . . took upon myself the responsibility of meting out punishment to those whose conduct during the previous day seemed to warrant such treatment,' recalled Raoul de Premorel, who worked for a company operating in the Kasai River basin. 'Soon . . . I found it desirable to assign the execution of sentences to others under my direction. The best plan seemed to be to have each *capita* [African foreman] administer the punishment for his own gang.'

And so the bulk of *chicotte* blows were inflicted by Africans on the bodies of other Africans. This,

for the conquerors, served a further purpose. It created a class of foremen from among the conquered. . . . Just as terrorizing people is part of conquest, so is forcing someone else to administer the terror.

Finally, when terror is the unquestioned order of the day, wielding it efficiently is regarded as a manly virtue, the way soldiers value calmness in battle. This is the ultimate in 'becoming used to it'. Here, for instance, a station chief named Georges Bricusse describes in his diary a hanging he ordered in 1895 of a man who had stolen a rifle:

The gallows is set up. The rope is attached, too high. They lift up the nigger and put the noose around him. The rope twists for a few moments, then *crack*, the man is wiggling on the ground. A shot in the back of the neck and the game is up. It didn't make the least impression on me this time!! And to think that the first time I saw the *chicotte* administered, I was pale with fright. Africa has some use after all. I could now walk into fire as if to a wedding.

Note

1. Leopoldville was the capital of the Belgian Congo, named in a tribute to the Belgian King.

Study Question

1. Why was popular opposition to the atrocities committed in the Congo so ineffective in bringing about any change in the conditions?

JULES FERRY

Jules Ferry (1832–93) was a leading member of the Provisional Government of National Defence, established in 1870 after Napoleon III was deposed. He was also Minister of Instruction, Minister of Foreign Affairs, and was the Premier of France twice (1880–81, 1883–85). During his tenure he introduced free, secular, and mandatory primary education, and barred members of Catholic orders from serving as

public school teachers. Believing that France required a powerful colonial empire, Ferry oversaw the occupation of Tunis, Tonkin, and Madagascar, and ordered the French expansion into both the Niger region and the Congo. A religious zealot assassinated Ferry in 1893. In the following address before the French Chamber of Deputies Ferry defends colonialism on political, economic, and moral grounds.

Contract labourers in Saigon. Ferry's outspoken advocacy of colonialism led the French to consolidate their hold on Indochina and its resources. Frank and Frances Carpenter Collection. Courtesy of the Library of Congress, Prints and Photographs Division (LC-USZ62-120614).

SPEECH BEFORE THE FRENCH CHAMBER OF DEPUTIES

The policy of colonial expansion is a political and economic system . . . that can be connected to three sets of ideas: economic ideas; the most far-reaching ideas of civilization; and ideas of a political and patriotic sort.

In the area of economics, I am placing before you, with the support of some statistics, the considerations that justify the policy of colonial expansion, as seen from the perspective of a need, felt more and more urgently by the industrialized population of Europe and especially the people of our rich and hardworking country of France: the need for outlets [for exports]. Is this a fantasy? Is this a concern [that can wait] for the future? Or is this not a pressing need, one may say a crying need, of our industrial population? I merely express in a general way what each one of you can see for himself in the various parts of France. Yes, what our major industries, irrevocably steered by the treaties of 1860 into exports, lack more and more are outlets. Why? Because next door Germany is setting up trade barriers; because across the ocean the United States of America have become protectionists, and extreme protectionists at that; because not only are these great markets . . . shrinking, becoming more and more difficult to access, but these great states are beginning to pour into our own markets products not seen there before. This is true not only for our agriculture, which has been so sorely tried . . . and for which competition is no longer limited to the circle of large European states. . . . Today, as you know, competition, the law of supply and demand, freedom of trade, the effects of speculation, all radiate in a circle that reaches to the ends of the earth. . . . That is a great complication, a great economic difficulty; . . . an extremely serious problem. It is so serious, gentlemen, so acute, that the least informed persons must already glimpse, foresee, and take precautions against the time when the great South American market that has, in a manner of speaking, belonged to us forever will be disputed and perhaps taken away from us by North American products. Nothing is more serious; there can be no graver social problem; and these matters are linked intimately to colonial policy.

Gentlemen, we must speak more loudly and more honestly! We must say openly that indeed the higher races have a right over the lower races. . . .

I repeat, that the superior races have a right because they have a duty. They have the duty to civilize the inferior races. . . . In the history of earlier centuries these duties, gentlemen, have often been misunderstood; and certainly when the Spanish soldiers and explorers introduced slavery into Central America, they did not fulfill their duty as men of a higher race. . . . But, in our time, I maintain that European nations acquit themselves with generosity, with grandeur, and with sincerity of this superior civilizing duty.

I say that French colonial policy, the policy of colonial expansion, the policy that has taken us under the Empire [the Second Empire, of Napoleon III], to Saigon, to Indochina [Vietnam], that has led us to Tunisia, to Madagascar—I say that this policy of colonial expansion was inspired by . . . the fact that a navy such as ours cannot do without safe harbours, defences, supply centres on the high seas. . . . Are you unaware of this? Look at a map of the world.

Gentlemen, these are considerations that merit the full attention of patriots. The conditions of naval warfare have greatly changed. . . . At present, as you know, a warship, however perfect its design, cannot carry more than two weeks' supply of coal; and a vessel without coal is a wreck on the high seas, abandoned to the first occupier. Hence the need to have places of supply, shelters, ports for defence and provisioning. . . . And that is why we needed Tunisia; that is why we needed Saigon and Indochina; that is why we need Madagascar . . . and why we shall never leave them! . . . Gentlemen, in

Europe such as it is today, in this competition of the many rivals we see rising up around us, some by military or naval improvements, others by the prodigious development of a constantly growing population; in a Europe, or rather in a universe thus constituted, a policy of withdrawal or abstention is simply the high road to decadence! In our time nations are great only through the activity they deploy; it is not by spreading the peaceable light of their institutions . . . that they are great, in the present day.

Spreading light without acting, without taking part in the affairs of the world, keeping out of all European alliances and seeing as a trap, an adventure, all expansion into Africa or the Orient—for a great nation to live this way, believe me, is to abdicate and, in less time than you may think, to sink from the first rank to the third and fourth.

Study Question

1. To what extent was Ferry correct when he claimed that every nation needed to take part in the scramble for colonies or risk falling irrevocably behind?

EVELYN BARING, EARL OF CROMER

Evelyn Baring, 1st Earl of Cromer (1841–1917), was a diplomat who served as Controller-General in Egypt during the period in which the British established control over the weak Egyptian monarchy. Baring believed that British rule would bring Egypt into a new era of modernization and progress, whereas a victory by Arab forces would have plunged the country into an 'age of ignorance'. The following excerpt was taken from Baring's 1908 history of modern Egypt, which was written after he was dismissed from the Egyptian administration.

The Suez Canal in 1898. Within a few years of the canal's opening in 1869 it became a vital shipping link for European and American interests. Courtesy of the Library of Congress, Prints and Photographs Division (LC-USZ62-103002).

British Rule in Egypt

It is always a somewhat unprofitable proceeding to speculate on what might have been in politics, but I cannot close this portion of the narrative without hazarding conjecture as to whether any foreign occupation of Egypt could have been avoided. Mistakes were, without doubt, committed. The true nature of the Arábi revolt was misunderstood. It was more than a mere military mutiny. It partook in some degree of the nature of a bona fide national movement. . . . It was, in a great degree, a movement of the Egyptians against Turkish rule. . . . I ask myself, where were the elements for the formation of any stable government to have been found when, in pursuance of the policy of 'Egypt for the Egyptians', there had been eliminated, as would probably have been the case, first, the Europeans, with all their intelligence, wealth, and governing power; secondly, the Khedive in whose place some illiterate Egyptian, of the type of Arábi[1] or Mahmoud Sami, would have been appointed; thirdly, the Syrians and Armenians, with all their industry and capacity for sedentary employment; fourthly, the native aristocracy, largely composed of Turks, who were at that time the principal large landowners in the country, and amongst whom, in spite of many defects, the habits and traditions of a governing class still lingered; when, in fact, the nationalists and mutineers had got rid of all the classes, who then governed, and who for several centuries had governed the country? The residue would have consisted, first, of the mass of the fellaheen population who were sunk in the deepest ignorance. . .; secondly, of a certain number of small proprietors, village Sheikhs, Omdehs, etc., who constituted the squirearchy of the country, and who, in point of knowledge and governing capacity, were but little removed from the fellaheen; thirdly, of the Copts, whose religion would certainly, sooner or later, have prevented them from acting in complete harmony

with the Arábists, and who, even if tolerated by the Mohammedan population, could neither have obtained any influence over the Mohammedans, nor, even if that influence had been obtained could have used it to the general advantage of the country; fourthly, of the hierarchy, consisting principally of the Ulema of the El-Azhar Mosque. . . . They would have been the Jacobins of the movement, which, whether nationalist or military, would certainly have been reactionary in so far as it would have tended to destroy whatever germs of civilisation had been implanted into Egypt. . . . An attempt would have been made to regulate, not only the government, but also the social life of the country upon those principles of the Mohammedan faith which are most antiquated, obsolete, and opposed to the commonplace ideas of modern civilisation.

Egypt may now almost be said to form part of Europe. It is on the high road to the Far East. It can never cease to be an object of interest to all the powers of Europe, and especially to England. A numerous and intelligent body of Europeans and of non-Egyptian Orientals have made Egypt their home. European capital to a large extent has been sunk in the country. The rights and privileges of Europeans are jealously guarded, and, moreover, give rise to complicated questions, which it requires no small amount of ingenuity and technical knowledge to solve. Exotic institutions have sprung up and have taken root in the country. . . . The population is heterogeneous and cosmopolitan to a degree almost unknown elsewhere. Although the prevailing faith is that of Islam, in no country in the world is a greater variety of religious creeds to be found amongst important sections of the community. . . .

Is it probable that a government composed of the rude elements described above, and led by men of such poor ability as Arábi and his coadjutors, would have been able to control a complicated machine of this nature? Were the Sheikhs of the El-Azhar Mosque likely to succeed where Tewfik Pasha and his Ministers, who were men of comparative education and enlightenment, acting under the guidance and inspiration of a first-class European power, only met with a modified success after years of patient labour? There can be but one answer to these questions. . . . Neither is it in the nature of things that any similar movement should, under the present conditions of Egyptian society, meet with any better success. The full and immediate execution of a policy of 'Egypt for the Egyptians', as it was conceived by the Arábists in 1882, was, and still is, impossible.

History, indeed, records some very radical changes in the forms of government to which a State has been subjected without its interests being absolutely and permanently shipwrecked. But it may be doubted whether any instance can be quoted of a sudden transfer of power in any civilised or semi-civilised community to a class so ignorant as the pure Egyptians, such as they were in the year 1882. These latter have, for centuries past, been a subject race. Persians, Greeks, Romans, Arabs from Arabia and Baghdad, Circassians, and finally, Ottoman Turks, have successively ruled over Egypt, but we have to go back to the doubtful and obscure precedents of Pharaonic times to find an epoch when, possibly, Egypt was ruled by Egyptians. Neither, for the present, do they appear to possess the qualities which would render it desirable, either in their own interests, or in those of the civilised world in general, to raise them at a bound to the category of autonomous rulers with full rights of internal sovereignty.

If, however, a foreign occupation was inevitable or nearly inevitable, it remains to be considered whether a British occupation was preferable to any other. From the purely Egyptian point of view, the answer to this question cannot be doubtful. The intervention of any European power was preferable to that of Turkey. The intervention of one European power was preferable to

international intervention. The special aptitude shown by Englishmen in the government of Oriental races pointed to England as the most effective and beneficent instrument for the gradual introduction of European civilization into Egypt. . . .

By the process of exhausting all other expedients, we arrive at the conclusion that armed British intervention was, under the special circumstances of the case, the only possible solution of the difficulties which existed in 1882. Probably also it was the best solution. The arguments against British intervention, indeed, were sufficiently obvious. It was easy to foresee that, with a British garrison in Egypt, it would be difficult that the relations of England either with France or Turkey should be cordial. With France, especially, there would be a danger that our relations might become seriously strained. Moreover, we lost the advantages of our insular position. The occupation of Egypt necessarily dragged England to a certain extent within the arena of Continental politics. . . .

There can be no doubt of the force of these arguments. The answer to them is that it was impossible for Great Britain to allow the troops of any other European Power to occupy Egypt. When it became apparent that some foreign occupation was necessary, that the Sultan would not act save under conditions which were impossible of acceptance, and that neither French nor Italian cooperation could be secured, the British government acted with promptitude and vigour. A great nation cannot throw off the responsibilities which its past history and its position in the world have imposed upon it. English history affords other examples of the government and people of England drifting by accident into doing what was not only right, but was also most in accordance with British interests.

Note

1. Modern transliteration: Ahmed Orabi (Egyptian)/Ahmed Urabi

<table>
<tr><td>

Study Question

1. Baring claims that 'Egypt for the Egyptians' was an impossible goal.

</td><td>

Based on this document, what were the main obstacles to this aim (apart from the British presence)?

</td></tr>
</table>

◇

BAL GANGADHAR (B.G.) TILAK

Bal Gangadhar Tilak (1856–1920) was a prominent Indian nationalist and a key member of the Indian National Congress. Tilak argued that British rule depended on the active cooperation of the Indian population; therefore, boycotts would cripple the ability of the British to maintain their hold. Branded an extremist by the British, Tilak was arrested in 1908 and imprisoned in Burma until 1914. He remained a lifelong advocate of Swaraj (home rule). The speech which follows was delivered in Calcutta in January 1907. Tilak contrasts his views with those of Dadabhai Naoroji and the so-called 'moderates' in Congress.[1]

◇

THE TENETS OF THE NEW PARTY

Two new words have recently come into existence with regard to our politics, and they are *Moderates* and *Extremists*. These words have a specific relation to time, and they, therefore, will change with time. The Extremists of today will be Moderates tomorrow, just as the Moderates of today were Extremists yesterday. When the National Congress was first started and Mr Dadabhai's views, which now go for Moderates, were given to the public, he was styled an Extremist, so that you will see that the term Extremist is an expression of progress. We are Extremists today and our sons will call themselves Extremists and us Moderates. Every new party begins as Extremists and ends as Moderates. The sphere of practical politics is not unlimited. We cannot say what will or will not happen 1,000 years hence—perhaps during that long period, the whole of the white race will be swept away in another glacial period. We must, therefore, study the present and work out a program to meet the present condition.

It is impossible to go into details within the time at my disposal. One thing is granted, namely, that this government does not suit us. As has been said by an eminent statesman—the government of one country by another can never be a successful, and therefore, a permanent government. There is no difference of opinion about this fundamental proposition between the old and new schools. One fact is that this alien government has ruined the country. In the beginning, all of us were taken by surprise. We were almost dazed. We thought that everything that the rulers did was for our good and that this English government has descended from the clouds to save us from the invasions of Tamerlane and Chingis Khan, and, as they say, not only from foreign invasions but from internecine warfare, or the internal or external invasions, as they call it. We felt happy for a time, but it soon came to light that the peace which was established in this country did this, as Mr Dadabhai has said in one place—that we were prevented from going at each other's throats, so that a foreigner might go at the throat of us all. *Pax Britannica* is being gradually realized in these days. . . . We believed in the benevolent intentions of the government, but in politics there is no benevolence. Benevolence is used to sugar-coat the declarations of self-interest and we were in those days deceived by the apparent benevolent intentions under which rampant self-interest was concealed. That was our state then. But soon a change came over us. English education, growing poverty, and better familiarity with our rulers, opened our eyes and our leaders; especially, the venerable leader who presided over the recent Congress was the first to tell us that the drain from the country was ruining it, and if the drain was to continue, there was some great disaster awaiting us. . . .

We have come forward with a scheme which if you accept [it], shall better enable you to remedy this state of things than the scheme of the old school. Your industries are ruined utterly, ruined by foreign rule; your wealth is going out of the country and you are reduced to the lowest level which no human being can occupy. In this state of things, is there any other remedy by which you can help yourself? The remedy is not petitioning but boycott. We say prepare your forces, organize your power, and then go to work so that they cannot refuse you what you demand. . . . We are not armed, and there is no necessity for arms either. We have a stronger weapon, a political weapon, in boycott. We have perceived one fact, that the whole of this administration, which is carried on by a handful of Englishmen, is carried on with our assistance. We are all in subordinate service. This whole government is carried on with our assistance and they try to keep us in ignorance of our power of cooperation between ourselves by which that which is in our own hands at present can be claimed by us and administered by us. The point is to have the entire control in our hands. I want to have the key of my house, and not merely one stranger turned out of it. Self-government is our goal; we want a control over our administrative machinery. We don't want to become clerks

and remain [clerks]. At present, we are clerks and willing instruments of our own oppression in the hands of an alien government, and that government is ruling over us not by its innate strength but by keeping us in ignorance and blindness to the perception of this fact. Professor Seeley shares this view. Every Englishman knows that they are a mere handful in this country and it is the business of every one of them to befool you in believing that you are weak and they are strong. This is politics. We have been deceived by such policy so long. What the new party wants you to do is to realize the fact that your future rests entirely in your own hands. If you mean to be free, you can be free; if you do not mean to be free, you will fall and be for ever fallen. So many of you need not like arms; but if you have not the power of active resistance, have you not the power of self-denial and self-abstinence in such a way as not to assist this foreign government to rule over you? This is boycott and this is what is meant when we say, boycott is a political weapon. We shall not give them assistance to collect revenue and keep peace. We shall not assist them in fighting beyond the frontiers or outside India with Indian blood and money. We shall not assist them in carrying on the administration of justice. We shall have our own courts, and when time comes we shall not pay taxes. Can you do that by your united efforts? If you can, you are free from tomorrow. Some gentlemen who spoke this evening referred to half bread as against the whole bread. I say I want the whole bread and that immediately. But if I can not get the whole, don't think that I have no patience.

I will take the half they give me and then try for the remainder. This is the line of thought and action in which you must train yourself. We have not raised this cry from a mere impulse. It is a reasoned impulse. Try to understand that reason and try to strengthen that impulse by your logical convictions. I do not ask you to blindly follow us. Think over the whole problem for yourselves.

If you accept our advice, we feel sure we can achieve our salvation thereby. This is the advice of the new party. Perhaps we have not obtained a full recognition of our principles.

Old prejudices die very hard. Neither of us wanted to wreck the Congress, so we compromised, and were satisfied that our principles were recognized, and only to a certain extent. That does not mean that we have accepted the whole situation. We may have a step in advance next year, so that within a few years our principles will be recognized, and recognized to such an extent that the generations who come after us may consider us Moderates. This is the way in which a nation progresses, and this is the lesson you have to learn from the struggle now going on.

This is a lesson of progress, a lesson of helping yourself as much as possible, and if you really perceive the force of it, if you are convinced by these arguments, then and then only is it possible for you to effect your salvation from the alien rule under which you labour at this moment.

Note

1.   See the document by Naoroji in Chapter One.

Study Question

1.   Under what circumstances can boycott be an effective weapon against colonial rule?

ACCOUNTS OF THE AMRITSAR (JALLIANWALA) BAGH[1] MASSACRE, 1919

In March 1919 the British Government in India passed the Rowlatt Acts, which gave the authorities a wide range of emergency powers to deal with anti-colonial protests. The net result for the Indian population was the loss of a number of hard-won civil rights, including the right to public assembly. In protest Mohandas Gandhi called for a general strike, a call that resonated most strongly in the Punjab, where *nationalist leaders had already organized a powerful resistance movement to British rule. In Amritsar a protest meeting was organized for 13 April, a meeting which would ultimately be attended by some 10,000 men, women, and children. Determined to put an end to such protests British General R.E.H. Dyer decided to fire on the crowd. Most estimates put the final death toll at 379, with another 1,200 wounded.*

AMRITSAR DEPUTY COMMISSIONER'S LETTER TO THE COMMISSIONER OF LAHORE DIVISION

The following letter was sent by Miles Irving, Deputy Commissioner of Amritsar, to Kitchin, Commissioner of the Lahore Division, on 8 April 1919, five days before the massacre, with an advance copy to Michael O'Dwyer, the Lt Governor of Punjab.

This account of the events of last Sunday (6th April) is for your information and that of Government.

It was in the evening about 5 PM at a cricket match, that it was suddenly announced by Dr Kitchlew, Dr

Satyapal[2] and others that the hartal[3] should take place. It is said that this was a consequence of the belief that the meeting of Honorary Magistrates at my house had promised to stop the hartal, and was intended to show that they could do nothing. But it is much more likely to have been simply due to Dr Kitchlew not wishing to give us too long a notice. Anyhow a secret meeting was called at Dr Satyapal's house, and by 9.10 a small party, swelled to 200 by sightseers, was going round the town proclaiming the hartal by beat of drum. After 2 AM notices were pasted to the same effect.

In the morning all shops were closed. I hear of no violence being offered, but there was the dumb threat of numbers, and the fear of being boycotted. . . .

As for the future in Amritsar, the first point I want to press urgently is the necessity for an increase in the military forces. It is absurd to attempt to hold Amritsar city with a company of British infantry and half a company of Garrison Artillery. Any resolute action in the city would leave Civil Lines almost undefended. I know what the situation as regards British troops in India is, but another company

would be of enormous value. And whether this can be supplied or not, I would earnestly press for a motor machine gun unit, *and some Lewis or Maxim or Vickers Maxim guns* [emphasis added]. We have at present only two machine guns one of which has a parapet mounting only. The problem of holding the railway as the line of defence would be greatly simplified by a machine gun on each bridge while armored motor cars are an ideal arm for so small a force covering an area so great. As it is, we must abandon nine-tenths of the city to a riot, holding only the kotwali [district] communications, and, even so, will be hard pressed to defend the station and Civil Lines.

Secondly, we cannot go indefinitely with the policy of keeping out of the way, and congratulating ourselves that the mob has not forced us to interfere. . . . I think that we shall by prohibiting some strike or procession that endangers the public peace. But for this a really strong force will have to be brought in and we shall have to be ready to try conclusions to the end to see who governs Amritsar. For this I should want a movable column from Lahore available at 6 hours' notice. . . .

GENERAL DYER'S REPORT ON THE MASSACRE

I fired and continued to fire till the crowd dispersed, and I considered that this is the least amount of firing which would produce the necessary moral and widespread effect, it was my duty to produce if I was to justify my action. If more troops had been at hand the casualties would have been

greater in proportion. It was no longer a question of merely dispersing the crowd, but one of producing a sufficient moral effect from a military point of view, not only on those who were present, but more specially throughout the Punjab. There could be no question of undue severity. . . .

GENERAL DYER'S STATEMENTS BEFORE THE HUNTER COMMITTEE[4]

The following questions and answers are from the enquiry conducted by the Hunter Committee appointed by the British Government.

Q: I think you had an opportunity to make up your mind while you were marching to decide what was the right course. You came to the conclusion that if there really was a meeting, the right thing for you would be to fire upon them straightaway?

A: I had made up my mind. . . .

Q: No question of having your forces attacked entered into your consideration at all?

A: No. The situation was very, very serious. I had made up my mind that I will do all men to death if they were going to continue the meeting.

Q: Does it or does it not come to this: you thought that some striking act would be desirable to make people not only in Amritsar but elsewhere to consider their position more correctly?

A: Yes, I had to do something very strong.

Q: When you got into the Bagh, what did you do?

A: I opened fire.

Q: At once?

A: Immediately. I had thought about the matter, and I don't imagine it took me more than 30 seconds to make up my mind as to what my duty was.

Q: Did the crowd at once start to disperse as soon as you fired?

A: Immediately.

Q: Did you continue firing?

A: Yes.

Q: The crowds were making an effort to go away by some of the entrances at the farther end of the Bagh?

A: Yes.

Q: I take it that towards these exits the crowd was rather thick than at other places?

A: Yes.

Q: From time to time you changed your firing and directed it to places where the crowds were thickest?

A: That is so.

Q: Is that so?

A: Yes.

Q: And for the reasons you have explained to us you had made up your mind to open fire at the crowd.

A: Quite right.

Q: When you heard of the contemplated meeting at 12.40 you made up your mind that if the meeting was going to be held you would go and fire?

A: I had made up my mind that I would fire immediately in order to save the military situation. The time had come now when we should delay no longer. If I had delayed any longer, I was liable for court-martial.

Q: Supposing the passage was sufficient to allow the armored cars to go in, would you have opened fire with machine guns?

A: I think, probably, yes.

Q: In that case the casualties would have been very much higher?

A: Yes.

Q: I take it that your idea in taking the action (shooting in the Bagh) was to strike terror?

A: Call it what you like. I was going to punish them. My idea from the military point of view was to make a wide impression.

Q: To strike terror not only in the city of Amritsar but throughout the Punjab?

A: Yes, throughout the Punjab. I wanted to reduce their morale, the morale of the rebels.

Eye-Witness Accounts of the Massacre

The following excerpt is from Lala Nathu Ram's statement before the Congress Enquiry Committee.

I went to the top storey of my house to find out what it was. I then came down. A few moments later, a boy came running to me, with the news that many had been killed and wounded in the Jallianwala Bagh. As I knew that my son and brother had gone to the Bagh to attend the meeting I became very anxious and at once proceeded to the Bagh. I found my son safe, and he was fortunately not in the meeting when the troops opened fire. I took my son with me, and entered the Bagh by climbing over the wall. We went into the Bagh, five minutes after the firing was over. We saw a very large heap of the dead and the wounded near the exits. . . All the exits were blocked by a very large number of the dead and the wounded I searched for my brother, and had to turn over every dead person till at last I found him lying dead under three or four dead bodies near the foot of the raised ground. He was 25 years of age. There were about 200 dead bodies at this spot alone. I believe that about 1,500 were killed in the Jallianwala Bagh. Lots of kites were hovering very low over the dead and the wounded, so much so that it was with great difficulty that one could keep his turban on his head. . . .

RATTAN DEVI STATED THE FOLLOWING BEFORE THE CONGRESS ENQUIRY COMMITTEE

I was in my house near the Jallianwala Bagh when I heard the shots fired. I was then lying down. I went as I was anxious because my husband had gone to the Bagh. I began to cry and went to the place accompanied by two women to help me. There I saw heaps of dead bodies and I began to search for my husband. After passing through that heap, I found the dead body of my husband. The way towards it was full of blood and of dead bodies. After a short time, both the sons of Lala Sundar Das came there and I asked them to bring a charpai (cot) to carry the dead body of my husband to home. The boys accordingly went home and sent away the two women also. By this time it was 8 o'clock and no one could stir out of his house because of the curfew order. I stood on, waiting and crying. At about 8:30 a Sikh gentleman came. There were others also who were looking for something amongst the dead. I did not know them. I entreated the Sikh gentleman to help me in removing my husband's body to a dry place, for that place was overflowing with blood. He caught the body by the head and I by the legs, and we carried it to a dry place and laid it down on a wooden block. I waited up to 10 PM but no one arrived there. I got up and started towards Ablowa Patra. I thought of asking some students from the Thakurdwara to help me in carrying my husband home. I had not gone far when some men sitting in a window in an adjacent house asked me where I was going at that late hour. I said I wanted some men to carry my husband's body and as it was past 8 PM nobody could help me then. . . . So, I went back and seated myself by the side of my dead husband. Accidentally I found a bamboo stick which I kept in my hand to keep off dogs. I saw three men writhing in agony, a buffalo struggling in great pain, and a boy about twelve years old in agony entreated me not to leave the place. I told him that I could not go anywhere leaving the dead body of my husband. I asked him if he wanted any wrap, and if he was feeling cold, I could spread it over him. He asked for water, but water could not be procured at that place.

I heard the clock striking at regular intervals (of one hour) At 2 o'clock, a Jat belonging to Sultan village, who was lying entangled in a wall, asked me to go near him and to raise his leg. I got up and taking hold of his clothes drenched in blood raised his leg up. After that no one else came till half past five. At about six, L. Sundar Das, his sons, and some people from my street came there with a charpai and I brought my husband home. I saw other people at the Bagh, in search of their relatives. I passed my whole night there. It is impossible for me to describe what I felt. Heaps of dead bodies lay there, some on their backs, and some with their faces turned. A number of them were poor, innocent children. I shall never forget the sight. . . .

British Newspaper on Jallianwala Bagh Massacre

The following excerpts are from the comments made by the British newspaper Daily Herald *on the Jallianwala Bagh massacre, which were reproduced in the Amrita Bazar Patrika of 12 January 1920.*

The first detailed account of the April shootings at Amritsar, in the Punjab, shows it to have been one of the most bloody massacres of modern history.

Of the various stories of imperial oppression and the revolt against it by the subject races of the British Empire which we print today, the most amazing and stupefying in its naked horror is that of the massacre of Amritsar. The report of the evidence given by the General Dyer before the Committee of Investigation presided by Lord Hunter is not yet official, but it is so full and so well authenticated that no doubts have been cast upon its authenticity, so far as we know by anyone over here. According to the report of General Dyer's evidence, over 400 Indians were killed and 1,500 wounded by the deliberate firing on a crowd of 5,000 who were listening to a speech.

No blacker or fouler story has ever been told. General Dyer is reported as admitting that the crowd might have gone away peacefully and without bloodshed, and that his motive for the slaughter was merely that the crowd would in that case have come back again and laughed, and he would have made a fool of himself!

According to his reported evidence, he admits that, with incredible indifference to human suffering, the British authorities left the wounded unattended in the streets. This, we presume, was done in order to teach men and women, of a different civilization and a different religion, what a beautiful and merciful thing Christianity is, and how sacred we British hold the law of Him who said that we were to love our enemies.

Notes

1. The Jallianwala Bagh [garden] had become a public meeting place during the war. It had a limited number of exits and Dyer's forces blocked at least one of the exits so the crowd was essentially trapped.
2. Dr Saifuddin Kitchlu and Dr Satya Pal were both members of the Congress Party and leaders in the nationalist movement.
3. A hartal is an extended demonstration, usually involving a general strike.
4. The Hunter Committee was called by British Secretary of State Edwin Montagu to investigate the circumstances of the military's intervention at the Jallianwala Bagh. It led to General Dyer being relieved of his command.

Study Question

1. If the British had not reacted to the anti-Rowlatt demonstrations with brute force would the movement for Indian independence have been so successful?

Winston Churchill

During the Second World War there was considerable debate in Great Britain regarding the country's future role in India and the possibility of granting full independence. British Prime Minister Winston Churchill (1874–1965) remained adamantly opposed

to granting independence to the 'jewel in Britain's crown'. In the following address to the House of Commons, Churchill addressed some of his concerns regarding India's independence and the future role of the Indian National Congress.

On India

Parliamentary Debates, House of Commons Official Report, 1942

The Prime Minister (Mr Churchill): The course of events in India has been improving and is, on the whole, reassuring. The broad principles of the declaration made by His Majesty's Government which formed the basis of the Mission of the Lord Privy Seal to India, must be taken as representing the settled policy of the British Crown and Parliament. These principles stand in their full scope and integrity. No one can add anything to them, and no one can take anything away. The good offices of the Lord Privy Seal were rejected by the Indian Congress Party.

Mr S.O. Davies[1]: And by every party.

The Prime Minister: This, however, does not end the matter. The Indian Congress Party does not represent all India. It does not represent the majority of the people of India. It does not even represent the Hindu masses. It is a political organisation built around a party machine and sustained by certain manufacturing and financial interests. Outside that party and fundamentally opposed to it are the 90,000,000 Moslems in British India. . . .

Mr S.O. Davies: Nonsense.

The Prime Minister: . . . who have their rights of self-expression; the 50,000,000 Depressed Classes, or the Untouchables as they are called because they are supposed to defile their Hindu co-religionists

by their presence or by their shadow; and the 95,000,000 subjects of the Princes of India with whom we are bound by treaties; in all 235,000,000 in these three large groupings alone, out of about 390,000,000 in all India. This takes no account of large elements among the Hindus, Sikhs, and Christians in British India who deplore the present policy of the Congress Party. It is necessary that these main facts should not be overlooked here or abroad, because no comprehension of the Indian problem or of the relations between Britain and India is possible without the recognition of these basic data.

The Congress Party has now abandoned in many respects the policy of non-violence which Mr Gandhi has so long inculcated in theory, and has come into the open as a revolutionary movement designed to paralyse the communications by rail and telegraph and generally to promote disorder, the looting of shops and sporadic attacks upon the Indian police, accompanied from time to time by revolting atrocities—the whole having the intention or at any rate the effect of hampering the defence of India against the Japanese invader who stands on the frontiers of Assam and also upon the eastern side of the Bay of Bengal. It may well be that these activities by the Congress Party have been aided by Japanese fifth-column work on a widely extended scale and with special direction to strategic points. It is noteworthy, for instance, that the communications of the Indian forces defending Bengal on the Assam frontier have been specially attacked.

In these circumstances the Viceroy and Government of India, with the unanimous support of the Viceroy's Council, the great majority of which are Indians, patriotic and wise men, have felt it necessary to proclaim and suppress the central and Provincial organs of this association which has become committed to hostile and criminal courses. Mr Gandhi and other principal leaders have been interned under conditions of the highest comfort and consideration, and will be kept out of harm's way till the troubles subside.

It is fortunate, indeed, that the Congress Party has no influence whatever with the martial races, on whom the defence of India apart from British Forces largely depends. Many of these races are divided by unbridgeable religious gulfs from the Hindu Congress, and would never consent to be ruled by them. Nor shall they ever be against their will so subjugated. There is no compulsory service in India, but upwards of a million Indians have volunteered to serve the cause of the United Nations in this world struggle. The bravery of the Indian troops has been distinguished in many theatres of war, and it is satisfactory to note that in these last two months when the Congress has been measuring its strength against the Government of India, more than 140,000 new volunteers for the Army have come forward in loyal allegiance to the King-Emperor, thus surpassing all records in order to defend their native land. So far as matters have gone up to the present, they have revealed the impotence of the Congress Party either to seduce or even sway the Indian Army, to draw from their duty the enormous body of Indian officials, or still less to stir the vast Indian masses.

India is a continent, almost as large as and actually more populous than Europe and divided by racial and above all by religious differences far deeper than any that have separated Europeans.

The whole administration of the government of the 390,000,000 who live in India is carried on by Indians, there being under 600 British members of the Indian Civil Service. All the public services are working. In five provinces, including two of the greatest and comprising 110,000,000 people, provincial ministers responsible to their Legislatures stand at their posts. In many places, both in town and country, the population has rallied to the support of the civil power. The Congress conspiracy against the communications is breaking down. Acts of pillage and arson are being repressed and punished with incredibly small loss of life. Less than 500 persons have been killed over this mighty area of territory and population and it has only been necessary to move a few brigades of British troops here and there in support of the civil power. In most cases the rioters have been successfully dealt with by the Indian police. I am sure the House would wish me to pay a tribute to the loyalty and steadfastness of these brave Indian police as well as of the Indian official classes generally whose behaviour has been deserving of the highest praise.

To sum up, the outstanding fact which has so far emerged from the violent action of the Congress Party has been their non-representative character and their powerlessness to throw into confusion the normal peaceful life of India. It is the intention of His Majesty's Government to give all necessary support to the Viceroy and his Executive in the firm but tempered measures by which they are protecting the life of the Indian community and leaving the British and Indian Armies free to defend the soil of India against the Japanese.

I may add that large reinforcements have reached India and that the numbers of white soldiers now in that country, though very small compared with its size and population, are larger than at any time in the British connection. I, therefore, feel entitled to report to the House that the situation in India at this moment gives no occasion for undue despondency or alarm.

Note

1. Siegfried Owen Davies (1886–1972) was elected as a Labour MP in 1934, representing Merthyr, Wales. He remained a lifelong socialist.

Study Question

1. Which of the points raised by Churchill retain some validity?

Caio Prado Júnior

Caio Prado Júnior (1907–90) was a Marxist historian and geographer who lived through much of Brazil's twentieth century instability. He argued that the root of Brazil's development problems could be traced to the period of colonial control and the continuing hold of global capitalism. He was favourably impressed with the Soviet Union of the 1930s, a belief which created conflict between Prado and the government of Getúlio Vargas. The following excerpt is taken from Prado's Economic History of Brazil *(1945).*

The Coffee Cycle in Brazil

Coffee holds the first and sovereign place among all modern Brazilian products. In an earlier phase, under the Empire, we observed its ascendant progress, bringing under its sway the best and most important activities of the country. Now, under the Republic, we see it attaining the zenith of its grandiose course and establishing itself on a level that definitely puts in the shade all other Brazilian products. Even in absolute and world terms, coffee acquired an outstanding position. In the twentieth century it was, if not the first, at least among the first food products of international trade; and Brazil, with 70 per cent of the world's coffee production, enjoyed an undisputed supremacy. . . .

The advance of coffee agriculture in Brazil since the last decade of the nineteenth century, remarkable when regarded as a whole, was nevertheless very irregular if we consider the different regions of the country. There was no uniform and harmonious development; expansion in some sectors coincided with decline and even complete annihilation in others. We noted this

Men, women, and children picking coffee berries in Brazil in the early 1920s. Frank and Frances Carpenter Collection. Courtesy of the Library of Congress, Prints and Photographs Division (LC-USZ62-104097).

cyclical evolution of coffee under the Empire—an evolution in which the space of a few decades saw an ascending phase followed by another of decadence in each producing zone. The great area of progress in the period under discussion was the western portion of São Paulo, an almost desert region that was rapidly conquered and brought under cultivation. . . .

But the quantitative advance of coffee cultivation in Brazil was not accompanied by an equal qualitative progress. By and large, the rudimentary agricultural processes of the past continued to be employed. A certain improvement was evident in the preparation and processing of the product: the cleaning and stripping of the 'berries'. For this purpose better machinery and installations were introduced. But as concerned cultivation proper (the care of the soil and the plant, selection of varieties, etc.), on the whole matters stood as before. And this was the principal reason for the invariable decline in the productivity of plantations, even though they were located in regions of superior soils and highly favorable natural conditions. . . .

Another aspect of coffee production, much more important in its history, as well as in the evolution of the Brazilian economy in general, was its financial vicissitudes in the period that opened with the establishment of the Republic. If the large expansion of production brought the country wealth and progress, it also brought a problem of overproduction that began to plague Brazil's coffee economy only a few years after the start of its great cycle of growth and that has continued to the present day, with profound and varied repercussions on the general evolution of the Brazilian economy. I have already noted that the first signs of disequilibrium appeared in 1896. It was the result of the extensive plantings made during the first years of the Republic, and which now began to bear fruit (let us recall again that the coffee tree is a plant that begins production at the age of four or five years). At

that time appeared the classic symptoms of overproduction: decline in prices, the formation of unsalable stocks. . . .

Commercial speculation intervened in this situation for its own benefit, and this was of great importance, not only in the particular sector of coffee production and commerce but in the economic and financial life of Brazil in general. Dependent as it was on its principal product, the Brazilian economy suffered all the vicissitudes through which coffee passed. I have already indicated how commercial speculation first intervened in the coffee industry in 1896.

From then on, its maneuvers largely conditioned the evolution of the coffee economy. Good harvests were utilized for the formation of reserves that dragged prices down or were doled out later, in years of poor harvests, at advantageous prices. The planters, compelled to dispose of their products without delay in order to pay the costs of production, lost the difference in price to the middlemen, who in the last analysis were large financial houses and international banks operating under cover. Maneuvers of this type were carried out even within the space of a single agricultural year. The coffee harvest in Brazil occupies the relatively short space of four months (May to August), when production flows to the ports, forcing a fall in prices. This is followed by a period of shortages of the product, when prices rise. The commercial middlemen would be buyers in the first phase, sellers in the second. In this way they monopolized the major part of the profits of the business, to the detriment of the producers. . . .

. . . Brazil's weak national finances were inadequate for such a large-scale operation; an appeal for foreign credit was rejected by Brazil's bankers in Europe (the Rothschild House and group). Directly or indirectly, they were too closely tied to established interests to accept any modification of the existing order in the coffee business. Now there entered upon the scene other financial groups, who took advantage of the opportunity (it may even be that they had prepared that opportunity) to change in their favor the control of the coffee trade. First entered a great German exporting firm, Theodor Wille & Co. This marked the simultaneous entrance of German imperialism, which until that time had played only a modest role in Brazilian affairs. Behind Theodor Wille were aligned the principal financial groups of that country: the Discount Gesellschaft and the Dresden Bank. They were joined by English and French bankers who formed an opposition in their countries to the groups that had held Brazilian finances in their hands. They were J. Henry Schroder and Co. of London, and the Société Générale of Paris. The National City Bank of New York also joined this aggregation. It furnished São Paulo with the necessary means to implement the valorization plan, making credits available to the amount of 4,000,000 pounds.

In the face of this development, Rothschild, seeing that his previous refusal had been without effect and unwilling to remain on the outside and compromise his position, hastened to join the group. Through him São Paulo received 3,000,000 pounds more. The Bank of France, representing the established financial and commercial interests in the coffee business, refused to accept coffee warrants calculated on a basis higher than 40 francs a bag (the price reached by coffee at that time fluctuated around 50 francs); in this way it hoped to neutralize the maneuvers of valorization.[1] At the same time the importing firms of Havre, the great French center of the coffee trade, unleashed a powerful campaign to discredit the loans being floated by Brazil in Europe.

But the battle was finally won by the 'bulls'. In order to consolidate the previous loans and carry the operation to a conclusion, fifteen more millions were obtained; intervention in the market continued until 1910, when, tension having eased and prices stabilized, the purchases were finally suspended. During the period 1906–1910 nearly 8,500,000 bags had been withdrawn from the free market.

The financial interests involved in the operation thus won the contest. And it was they, much more than the producers in whose name the operation had been conducted, who reaped its best fruits. . . . While the financial agents of the valorization reaped large profits from the operation, the producers, though enjoying better and more stable prices for some years, later had to bear its entire burden. It was they who assumed the responsibility for the large debts contracted in order to execute the plan. For this purpose there was established a new tax of five gold francs per bag of coffee exported. This tax was used to pay the principal and interest of the debt, which even today, more than thirty years later . . . has not been entirely liquidated.

Note

1. Valorization is a Marxist concept which refers to the increase in the value of an asset when labour is applied to it.

Study Question

1. Is there any way to escape the cycle of debt once a country has become dependent on a single cash crop such as coffee?

W.E.B. DU BOIS

W.E.B. Du Bois (1868–1963) was an historian, sociologist, and activist. Widely travelled and highly educated—Du Bois received a Ph.D. from Harvard in 1895—he devoted his life to the study of the black population of the world. Du Bois was a founding member of the National Association for the Advance- *ment of Colored People NAACP and a strong advocate of Pan-Africanism as a means to achieve the freedom of all black peoples. Du Bois remained interested in socialist and communist movements throughout his life, but was first and foremost a black nationalist. The following excerpt was written in 1915.*

THE NEGRO

What is to be the future relation of the Negro race to the rest of the world? . . . Most persons have accepted that tacit but clear modern philosophy which assigns to the white race alone the hegemony of the world and assumes that other races, and particularly the Negro race, will either be content to serve the interests of the whites or die out before their all-conquering march. This philosophy is the child of the African slave trade and of the expansion of Europe during the nineteenth century.

The Negro slave trade was the first step in modern world commerce, followed by the modern theory of colonial expansion. Slaves as an article of commerce were shipped as long as the traffic paid. When the Americas had enough black laborers for their immediate demand, the moral action of the eighteenth century had a chance to make its faint voice heard. . . .

Finally European capital began to find better investments than slave shipping and flew to them. These better investments were the fruit of the new industrial revolution of the nineteenth century, with its factory system; they were also in part the result of the cheapened price of gold and silver, brought about by slavery and the slave trade to the new world. Commodities other than gold, and commodities capable of manufacture and exploitation in Europe out of materials furnishable by America, became enhanced in value; the bottom fell out of the commercial slave trade and its suppression became possible. . . .

As the emancipation of millions of dark workers took place in the West Indies, North and South America, and parts of Africa at this time, it was natural to assume that the uplift of this working class lay along the same paths with that of European and American whites. This was the *first* suggested solution of the Negro problem. Consequently these Negroes received partial enfranchisement, the beginnings of education, and some of the elementary rights of wage earners and property holders, while the independence of Liberia and Hayti [Haiti] was recognized. However, long before they were strong enough to assert the rights thus granted or to gather intelligence enough for proper group leadership, the new colonialism of the later nineteenth and twentieth centuries began to dawn. The new colonial theory transferred the reign of commercial privilege and extraordinary profit from the exploitation of the European working class to the exploitation of backward races under the political domination of Europe. For the purpose of carrying out this idea the European and white American working class was practically invited to share in this new exploitation, and particularly were flattered by popular appeals to their inherent superiority to 'Dagoes', 'Chinks', 'Japs', and 'Niggers'.

This tendency was strengthened by the fact that the new colonial expansion centered in Africa. Thus in 1875 something less than one-tenth of Africa was under nominal European control, but the Franco-Prussian War and the exploration of the Congo led to new and fateful things. Germany desired economic expansion and, being shut out from America by the Monroe Doctrine, turned to Africa. France, humiliated in war, dreamed of an African empire from the Atlantic to the Red Sea. Italy became ambitious for Tripoli and Abyssinia. Great Britain began to take new interest in her African realm, but found herself largely checkmated by the jealousy of all Europe. Portugal sought to make good her ancient claim to the larger part of the whole southern peninsula. It was Leopold of Belgium who started to make the exploration and civilization of Africa an international movement. This project failed, and the Congo Free State became in time simply a Belgian colony. While the project was under discussion, the international scramble for Africa began. As a result the Berlin Conference and subsequent wars and treaties gave Great Britain control of 2,101,411 square miles of African territory, in addition to Egypt and the Egyptian Sudan with 1,600,000 square miles. This includes South Africa, Bechuanaland and Rhodesia, East Africa, Uganda and Zanzibar, Nigeria, and British West Africa. The French hold 4,106,950 square miles, including nearly all North Africa (except Tripoli) west of the Niger Valley and Libyan Desert, and touching the Atlantic at four points. To this is added the Island of Madagascar. The Germans have 910,150 square miles, principally in Southeast and South-west Africa and the Kamerun. The Portuguese retain 787,500 square miles in Southeast and Southwest Africa. The Belgians have 900,000 square miles, while Liberia (43,000 square miles) and Abyssinia (350,000 square miles) are independent. The Italians have about 600,000 square miles and the Spanish less than 100,000 square miles.

This partition of Africa brought revision of the ideas of Negro uplift. Why was it necessary, the European investors argued, to push a continent of black workers along the paths of social uplift by education, trades-unionism, property holding, and the electoral franchise when the workers desired no change, and the rate of European profit would suffer?

There quickly arose then the *second* suggestion for settling the Negro problem. It called for the virtual enslavement of natives in certain industries, as rubber and ivory collecting in the Belgian Congo, cocoa raising in Portuguese Angola, and diamond mining in South Africa. This new slavery or 'forced' labor was stoutly defended as a necessary foundation for implanting modern industry in a barbarous land; but its likeness to slavery was too clear and it has been modified, but not wholly abolished. . . .

. . . the economic significance of the Negro to-day is tremendous. Black Africa to-day exports annually nearly two hundred million dollars' worth of goods, and its economic development has scarcely begun. The black West Indies export nearly one hundred million dollars' worth of goods; to this must be added the labor value of Negroes in South Africa, Egypt, the West Indies, North, Central, and South America, where the result is blended in the common output of many races. The economic foundation of the Negro problem can easily be seen to be a matter of many hundreds of millions to-day, and ready to rise to the billions tomorrow. . . .

What do Negroes themselves think of these their problems and the attitude of the world toward them? First and most significant, they are thinking. There is as yet no great single centralizing of thought or unification of opinion, but there are centers which are growing larger and larger and touching edges. The most significant centers of this new thinking are, perhaps naturally, outside Africa and in America: in the United States and in the West Indies; this is followed by South Africa and West Africa and then, more vaguely, by South America, with faint beginnings in East Central Africa, Nigeria, and the Sudan.

The Pan-African movement when it comes will not, however, be merely a narrow racial propaganda. Already the more far-seeing Negroes sense the coming unities: a unity of the working classes everywhere, a unity of the colored races, a new unity of men. The proposed economic solution of the Negro problem in Africa and America has turned the thoughts of Negroes toward a realization of the fact that the modern white laborer of Europe and America has the key to the serfdom of black folk, in his support of militarism and colonial expansion. He is beginning to say to these workingmen that, so long as black laborers are slaves, white laborers cannot be free. Already there are signs in South Africa and the United States of the beginning of understanding between the two classes.

In a conscious sense of unity among colored races there is to-day only a growing interest. There is slowly arising not only a curiously strong brotherhood of Negro blood throughout the world, but the common cause of the darker races against the intolerable assumptions and insults of Europeans has already found expression. Most men in this world are colored. A belief in humanity means a belief in colored men. The future world will, in all reasonable probability, be what colored men make it. In order for this colored world to come into its heritage, must the earth again be drenched in the blood of fighting, snarling human beasts, or will Reason and Good Will prevail? That such may be true, the character of the Negro race is the best and greatest hope; for in its normal condition it is at once the strongest and gentlest of the races of men: 'Semper novi quid ex Africa!' [everything new comes out of Africa—Pliny]

> **Study Question**
>
> 1. What were the primary obstacles to movements such as Pan-Africanism?

V.I. LENIN

Vladimir Ilyich Ulyanov ('Lenin') was born in Simbirsk, Russia, in 1870. He died in January 1924 in Gorki, USSR. Lenin was a good student but after the execution of his brother Alexander he was expelled from university for participating in radical student politics. By the 1890s he was studying Marxism in St Petersburg where he was arrested in 1895; he was tried and exiled to Siberia until 1900. After 1900

Lenin was an active member of the Russian Social Democratic Labour Party (RSDLP), eventually leading the Bolshevik faction to break with the more moderate Mensheviks in 1903. In 1907 Lenin left Russia once more, this time for Finland. For the next ten years Lenin travelled throughout Europe meeting with various Social Democratic leaders and writing some of his most important theoretical works.

IMPERIALISM, THE HIGHEST STAGE OF CAPITALISM

. . . For the first time the world is completely divided up, so that in the future only redivision is possible, i.e., territories can only pass from one 'owner' to another, instead of passing as ownerless territory to an owner. . . .

For Great Britain, the period of the enormous expansion of colonial conquests was that between 1860 and 1880, and it was also very considerable in the last twenty years of the nineteenth century. For France and Germany this period falls precisely in these twenty years. We saw above that the development of premonopoly capitalism, of capitalism in which free competition was predominant, reached its limit in the 1860s and 1870s. We now see that it is precisely after that period that the tremendous 'boom' in colonial conquests begins, and that the struggle for the territorial division of the world becomes extraordinarily sharp. It is beyond doubt, therefore, that capitalism's transition to the stage of monopoly capitalism, to finance capital, is connected with the intensification of the struggle for the partitioning of the world.

Hobson, in his work on imperialism, marks the years 1884–1900 as the epoch of intensified 'expansion' of the chief European states. According to his estimate, Great Britain during these years acquired 3,700,000 square miles of territory with 57,000,000 inhabitants; France, 3,600,000 square miles with 36,500,000; Germany, 1,000,000 square miles with 14,700,000; Belgium, 900,000 square miles with 30,000,000; Portugal, 800,000 square miles with 9,000,000 inhabitants. The scramble for colonies by all the capitalist states at the end of the nineteenth century and particularly since the 1880s is a commonly known fact in the history of diplomacy and of foreign policy. . . .

. . . at the end of the nineteenth century the British heroes of the hour were Cecil Rhodes and Joseph Chamberlain, who openly advocated imperialism and applied the imperialist policy in the most cynical manner! . . . It is not without interest to observe that even then these leading British bourgeois politicians saw the connection between what might be called the purely economic and the socio-political roots of modern imperialism. Chamberlain advocated imperialism as a 'true, wise and economical policy', and pointed particularly to the German, American and Belgian competition which Great Britain was encountering in the world market. Salvation lies in monopoly, said the capitalists as they formed cartels, syndicates and trusts. Salvation

lies in monopoly, echoed the political leaders of the bourgeoisie, hastening to appropriate the parts of the world not yet shared out. And Cecil Rhodes, we are informed by his intimate friend, the journalist Stead, expressed his imperialist views to him in 1895 in the following terms: 'I was in the East End of London (a working-class quarter) yesterday and attended a meeting of the unemployed. I listened to the wild speeches, which were just a cry for "bread! bread!" and on my way home I pondered over the scene and I became more than ever convinced of the importance of imperialism. . . . My cherished idea is a solution for the social problem, i.e., in order to save the 40,000,000 inhabitants of the United Kingdom from a bloody civil war, we colonial statesmen must acquire new lands to settle the surplus population, to provide new markets for the goods produced in the factories and mines. The Empire, as I have always said, is a bread and butter question. If you want to avoid civil war, you must become imperialists.'[1]

The principal feature of the latest stage of capitalism is the domination of monopolist associations of big employers. These monopolies are most firmly established when all the sources of raw materials are captured by one group, and we have seen with what zeal the international capitalist associations exert every effort to deprive their rivals of all opportunity of competing, to buy up, for example, ironfields, oilfields, etc. Colonial possession alone gives the monopolies complete guarantee against all contingencies in the struggle against competitors, including the case of the adversary wanting to be protected by a law establishing a state monopoly. The more capitalism is developed, the more strongly the shortage of raw materials is felt, the more intense the competition and the hunt for sources of raw materials throughout the whole world, the more desperate the struggle for the acquisition of colonies. . . .

In order to finish with the question of the division of the world, I must make the following additional observation. This question was raised quite openly and definitely not only in American literature after the Spanish-American War, and in English literature after the Anglo-Boer War, at the very end of the nineteenth century and the beginning of the twentieth; not only has German literature, which has 'most jealously' watched 'British imperialism', systematically given its appraisal of this fact. This question has also been raised in French bourgeois literature as definitely and broadly as is thinkable from the bourgeois point of view. Let me quote Driault, the historian, who, in his book, *Political and Social Problems at the End of the Nineteenth Century*, in the chapter 'The Great Powers and the Division of the World', wrote the following: 'During the past few years, all the free territory of the globe, with the exception of China, has been occupied by the powers of Europe and North America. This has already brought about several conflicts and shifts of spheres of influence, and these foreshadow more terrible upheavals in the near future. For it is necessary to make haste. The nations which have not yet made provision for themselves run the risk of never receiving their share and never participating in the tremendous exploitation of the globe which will be one of the most essential features of the next century (i.e., the twentieth). That is why all Europe and America have lately been afflicted with the fever of colonial expansion, of "imperialism", that most noteworthy feature of the end of the nineteenth century.' And the author added: 'In this partition of the world, in this furious hunt for the treasures and the big markets of the globe, the relative strength of the empires founded in this nineteenth century is totally out of proportion to the place occupied in Europe by the nations which founded them. The dominant powers in Europe, the arbiters of her destiny, are not equally preponderant in the whole world. And, as colonial might, the hope of controlling as yet unassessed wealth, will evidently react upon the relative strength of the European powers, the colonial question—"imperialism", if you will—which has already modified the political conditions of Europe itself, will modify them more and more.'[2]

Notes

1. [Lenin] *Die Neue Zeit*, XVI, 1, 1898, S. 304.
2. [Lenin] J.E. Driault, *Problèmes politiques et sociaux*, Paris, 1900, p. 299.

Study Question

1. Was Lenin correct that imperialism, and its economic rationale, was the primary source of conflict in the world?

TIPS FOR ANALYSIS

Assessing Bias in an Author

A bias is not necessarily a negative or discriminatory belief; it is simply any belief or ideology which influences the way the author approaches the topic. People are biased by their position in society, their knowledge of the world around them, their personal and public interests, and so on. This is why it is necessary to examine the author's background and prior experiences when reading a primary document.

WEB RESOURCES

Internet Resources for Latin America
http://lib.nmsu.edu/subject/bord/laguia
Internet Modern History Sourcebook: Imperialism
http://www.fordham.edu/halsall/mod/modsbook34.html
History in Focus: Empire
http://www.history.ac.uk/ihr/Focus/Empire/web.html
Sources and General Resources on Latin America
http://www.oberlin.edu/faculty/svolk/latinam.htm

RECOMMENDED READING

Joseph Conrad, *Heart of Darkness* (Oxford: Oxford University Press, 2003). Conrad's complex narrative focuses on Charles Marlow's journey up the Congo River to find the reclusive European Kurtz. The novel, written in 1899, has been condemned as a typical nineteenth-century European view of 'the dark continent', but it remains one of the most intriguing commentaries on the dialectical relationship between 'civilization' and 'barbarism'.

E.M. Forster, *Passage to India* (New York: Everyman's Library, 1992). *Passage to India*—the 1924 product of two visits to India in 1912 and 1921—spans a series of key events in the history of British India: the First World War, Gandhi's return, the Rowlatt Acts, and the Amritsar Massacre. Though Forster denied that this was a political novel, it highlights many of the key issues that dominated the struggle for independence.

Amadou Hampate Ba, *The Fortunes of Wangrin* (Bloomington, IN: Indiana University Press, 2000). French West African society in the early part of the twentieth century is the backdrop for Amadou Hampate Ba's examination of the impact of colonization, both on West Africans themselves and on the French citizens of the colonies.

Rudyard Kipling, *Kim* (New York: Penguin Classics, 1992). *Kim*—the story of an Irish soldier's orphan, living on the streets of Lahore amidst the convoluted political and social setting of British India—was created in part from Kipling's memories of his childhood in India. Kipling's novel, originally published in 1901, reflects on the interaction between the British and Indian cultures and the position of those who, like him, had been born in India of European ancestry.

Uwe Timm, *Morenga* (New York: New Directions Publishing, 2003). Historical sources and fictional elements combine in Timm's story of Morenga, the leader of the Nama rebellion against German colonialism in October 1904 (several months after the brutal suppression of the Herero uprising). The novel examines ethnic conflict, colonial prejudices, and the possibility of political freedom in German Southwest Africa.

RECOMMENDED VIEWING

Sanders of the River (UK, 1935). Director: Zoltan Korda (B&W). Based on a book by Edgar Wallace, *Sanders of the River* (also released under the title *Bosambo*) is a British imperialist film set in Nigeria. With strongly propagandistic overtones, the film portrays the heroism of colonial officials and the values of British imperial rule.

Zulu (UK, 1964). Director: Cy Raker Endfield. During the Battle of Rorke's Drift in 1879 just over 100 British soldiers held off an attack by some 4,000 Zulu warriors. Recognized as one of the finest war movies ever made, the film focuses less on the details of British colonialism in southern Africa and more on the impact of war on all of the participants.

Khartoum (UK, 1966). Director: Basil Dearden. *Khartoum* recreates the fate of General Charles Gordon, administrator of the Sudan between 1874 and 1880, who was sent back to Sudan in 1884 to rescue the British garrison. The film portrays the Arab uprising against British-Egyptian rule and the clash between colonial ideals and Arab nationalism.

Breaker Morant (Australia, 1980). Director: Bruce Beresford. *Breaker Morant* is a dramatization of actual events that occurred during the Boer War. Three Australian soldiers serving in the British army were tried for war crimes allegedly committed against Boer POWs and a German missionary. Beresford's film has strong anti-war overtones and illustrates the complex political situation that existed at the turn of the century.

CHAPTER THREE

WAR AND PEACE

Aggressive nationalism, colonial competition, and a resultant arms race combined in the early part of the twentieth century to create a number of conflicts in Europe. By 1914 three crises involving territorial claims had occurred in Eastern Europe, with war being narrowly averted on each occasion. Military strategists across the continent were so certain that war was imminent that they had already prepared elaborate war plans. There was, however, very little resemblance between the war that so many had anticipated, and the war that actually occurred between 1914 and 1918. Far from resembling the short and decisive wars of the late

Soldiers attempt to relax in the cold, cramped trenches of the Western Front on 16 June 1916. Courtesy of the Library of Congress, Prints and Photographs Division (LC-USZ62-55899).

nineteenth century, the First World War rapidly evolved into one of attrition in which all national resources had to be mobilized in order to sustain the war effort. Rationing, conscription, censorship, and an unprecedented level of government control over everyday life were the hallmarks of this conflict. Colonial empires were also drawn in and, in some cases, they experienced even greater levels of privation than their colonial overlords.

The mobilization of colonial empires guaranteed that the effects of the war would be felt in most parts of the world. One consequence of this was that, as imperial powers were weakened economically by the war, independence movements in the colonies gained strength and influence. Several of the extensive multi-ethnic empires in Europe—the Austro-Hungarian, Russian, and Ottoman Empires—collapsed completely during the war, releasing previously suppressed tensions. One by-product of this realignment of power and control was the first twentieth century outbreak of genocide as Turks massacred Armenians beginning in 1915. Another by-product was the creation of numerous small states in Eastern Europe. None of these states was ethnically homogeneous and most contained the basis for future regional conflicts. Meanwhile, in the former Russian Empire the war had ended with the removal of the Tsarist regime and the rise of the Bolshevik Party. Peace with Germany in 1918 led to the secession of vast areas of territory in the west and, ultimately, to war with Russia's former allies.

Perhaps the greatest global impact, however, came from the treaties that formally ended the hostilities: borders were shifted, empires officially dissolved, new leaders were anointed, and colonies redistributed. New tensions emerged out of many of the postwar settlements. The mandate system in the Middle East frustrated the ambitions of both Arabs and Zionists and seemed to disregard promises made during the war; decisions regarding former German colonies antagonized Chinese students and reformers; Indian political leaders remained disappointed by the lack of progress towards home rule; and, throughout Central and Eastern Europe, ethnic minorities remained dissatisfied with the power structure in the new states. Even the architects of the postwar settlement soon expressed doubts regarding their new international order.

Despite widespread disappointment with the peace treaties, there was some hope that the League of Nations and the idea of collective security would prevent a repeat of 'the war to end all wars'. Despite strong congressional opposition in the United States, a great many scholars and diplomats believed genuinely in the power of the League to usher in a new, co-operative era of international relations.

The documents in this section examine the experience of war and the repercussions of the postwar settlement. Excerpts from *All Quiet on the Western Front* reveal some of the horrors of warfare on the Western Front, while 'Russian Women in Combat' shows another side of the conflict. The McMahon Letter and the Balfour Declaration provide an idea of the competing promises made during the war. The Armenian genocide is examined through newspaper reports that appeared in the United States and Britain. Woodrow Wilson's 'Fourteen Points' document illustrates the illusion of a just peace, while John Maynard Keynes outlines the reality of the peace settlement. Marcus Garvey warns the negotiators not to forget the fate of the black peoples of the world. Finally, H.G. Wells and others defend the potential of the League of Nations and Henry Cabot Lodge summarizes the American congressional opposition to the League.

Erich Maria Remarque

Erich Maria Remarque (1898–1970), born Erich Paul Remark, wrote All Quiet on the Western Front *(in German:* Im Westen nichts Neues*—'In the West, Nothing New') in the late 1920s. For many years it was believed that the book was a semi-autobiographical account of Remarque's own wartime experiences; however, much controversy remains with respect to Remarque's military career which was extremely limited. He was conscripted on 21 November 1916, first reached the Western Front on 12 June 1917, and was invalided out of active service on 31 July of the same year. In light of this, much of the story is likely second-hand. Nonetheless, Remarque's fictional account remains one of the most widely accepted accounts of the German trenches during the First World War. In 1933 the Nazi authorities banned the novel. Remarque had already left Germany by this time, living the remainder of his life in New York and Switzerland. Though he continued to write, he refused to answer any questions relating to* All Quiet on the Western Front.

All Quiet on the Western Front

Müller is dead. Someone shot him point-blank in the stomach with a Verey Light.[1] He lived for half an hour, quite conscious, and in terrible pain.

Before he died he handed over his pocket-book to me, and bequeathed me his boots—the same that he once inherited from Kemmerich. I wear them, for they fit me quite well. After me Tjaden will get them, I have promised them to him.

We have been able to bury Müller, but he is not likely to remain long undisturbed. Our lines are falling back. There are too many fresh English and American regiments over there. There's too much corned beef and white wheaten bread. Too many new guns. Too many aeroplanes.

But we are emaciated and starved. Our food is bad and mixed up with so much substitute stuff that it makes us ill. The factory owners in Germany have grown wealthy;—dysentery dissolves our bowels. The latrine poles are always densely crowded; the people at home ought to be shown these grey, yellow, miserable, wasted faces here, these bent figures from whose bodies the colic wrings out the blood, and who with lips trembling and distorted with pain, grin at one another and say:

'It is not much sense pulling up one's trousers again.'

Our artillery is fired out, it has too few shells and the barrels are so worn that they shoot uncertainly, and scatter so widely as even to fall on ourselves. We have too few horses. Our fresh troops are anaemic boys in need of rest who cannot carry a pack, but merely know how to die. By thousands. They understand nothing about warfare, they

A field bakery prepares bread for German troops stationed near the Ypres Salient. George Granthan Bain Collection. Courtesy of the Library of Congress, Prints and Photographs Division (LC-DIG-ggbain-17961).

simply go on and let themselves be shot down. A single flyer routed two companies of them for a joke, just as they came fresh from the train—before they had ever heard of such a thing as cover.

'Germany ought to be empty soon,' says Kat.

We have given up hope that some day an end may come. We never think so far. A man can stop a bullet and be killed; he can get wounded, and then the hospital is his next stop. There, if they do not amputate him, he sooner or later falls into the hands of one of those staff surgeons who, with the War Service Cross in his button-hole, says to him: 'What, one leg a bit short? If you have any pluck you don't need to run at the front. The man is A1. Dismiss!'

Kat tells a story that has traveled the whole length of the front from the Vosges to Flanders;— of the staff surgeon who reads the names on the list, and when a man comes before him, without looking up, says: 'A1. We need soldiers up there.' A fellow with a wooden leg comes up before him,

the staff surgeon again says A1—'And then,' Kat raises his voice, 'the fellow says to him: "I already have a wooden leg, but when I go back again and they shoot off my head, then I will get a wooden head made and become a staff surgeon".' This answer tickles us all immensely.

There may be good doctors, and there are, lots of them; all the same, every soldier some time during his hundreds of inspections falls into the clutches of one of these countless hero-grabbers who pride themselves on changing as many C3's and B3's as possible into A1's.[2]

There are many such stories, they are mostly far more bitter. All the same, they have nothing to do with mutiny or lead-swinging. They are merely honest and call a thing by its name; for there is a very great deal of fraud, injustice, and baseness in the army. It is nothing that regiment after regiment returns again and again to the ever more hopeless struggle, that attack follows attack along the weakening, retreating, crumbling line.

From a mockery the tanks have become a terrible weapon. Armoured they come rolling on in long lines, more than anything else embody for us the horror of war.

We do not see the guns that bombard us; the attacking lines of the enemy infantry are men like ourselves; but these tanks are machines, their caterpillars run on as endless as the war, they are annihilation, they roll without feeling into the craters, and climb up again without stopping, a fleet of roaring, smoke-belching armour-clads, invulnerable steel beasts squashing the dead and the wounded—we shrivel up in our thin skin before them, against their colossal weight our arms are sticks of straw, and our hand-grenades matches.

Shells, gas clouds, and flotillas of tanks—shattering, corroding, death.

Dysentery, influenza, typhus—scalding, choking, death.

Trenches, hospitals, the common grave—there are no other possibilities.

. . .

In one attack our Company Commander, Bertinck, falls. He was one of those superb front-line officers who are foremost in every hot place. He was with us for two years without being wounded, so that something had to happen in the end.

We occupy a crater and get surrounded. The stink of petroleum or oil blows across with the fumes of powder. Two fellows with a flame-thrower are seen, one carries the tin on his back, the other has the hose in his hands from which the fire spouts. If they get so near that they can reach us we are done for, we cannot retreat yet.

We open fire on them. But they work nearer and things begin to look bad. Bertinck is lying in the hole with us. When he sees that we cannot hit them because under the sharp fire we have to think too much about keeping under cover, he takes a rifle, crawls out of the hole, and lying down propped on his elbows, he takes aim. He fires—the same moment a bullet smacks into him, they have

got him. Still he lies and aims again;—once he shifts and again takes aim; at last the rifle cracks. Bertinck lets the gun drop and says: 'Good', and slips back into the hole. The hindmost of the two flame-throwers is hit, he falls, the hose slips away from the other fellow, the fire squirts about on all sides and the man burns.

Bertinck has a chest wound. After a while a fragment smashes away his chin, and the same fragment has sufficient force to tear open Leer's hip. Leer groans as he supports himself on his arm, he bleeds quickly, no one can help him. Like an emptying tube, after a couple of minutes he collapses.

What use is it to him now that he was such a good mathematician at school.

. . .

The months pass by. The summer of 1918 is the most bloody and the most terrible. The days stand like angels in blue and gold, incomprehensible, above the ring of annihilation. Every man here knows that we are losing the war. Not much is said about it, we are falling back, we will not be able to attack again after this big offensive, we have no more men and no more ammunition.

Still the campaign goes on—the dying goes on—

Summer of 1918—Never has life in its niggardliness seemed to us so desirable as now;—the red poppies in the meadows round our billets, the smooth beetles on the blades of grass, the warm evenings in the cool, dim rooms, the black mysterious trees of the twilight, the stars and the flowing waters, dreams and long sleep—O Life, life, life!

Summer of 1918—Never was so much silently suffered as in the moment when we depart once again for the front-line. Wild, tormenting rumours of an armistice and peace are in the air, they lay hold on our hearts and make the return to the front harder than ever.

Summer of 1918—Never was life in the line more bitter and more full of horror than in the hours of the bombardment, when the blanched faces lie in the dirt and the hands clutch at the one thought: No! No! Not now! Not now at the last moment!

Summer of 1918—Breath of hope that sweeps over the scorched fields, raging fever of impatience, of disappointment, of the most agonizing terror of death, insensate question: Why? Why do they make an end? And why do these rumours of an end fly about?

. . .

There are so many airmen here, and they are so sure of themselves that they give chase to single individuals, just as though they were hares. For every one German plane there come at least five English and American. For one hungry, wretched German soldier come five of the enemy, fresh and fit. For one German army loaf there are fifty tins of canned beef over there. We are not beaten, for as soldiers we are better and more experienced; we are simply crushed and driven back by overwhelming superior forces.

Behind us lay rainy weeks—grey sky, grey fluid earth, grey dying. If we go out, the rain at once soaks through our overcoat and clothing;—and we remain wet all the time we are in the line. We never get dry. Those who will wear high boots tie sand bags round the tops so that the mud does not pour in so fast. The rifles are caked, the uniforms caked, everything is fluid and dissolved, the earth one dripping, soaked, oily mass in which lie yellow pools with red spiral streams of blood and into which the dead, wounded, and survivors slowly sink down.

The storm lashes us, out of the confusion of grey and yellow the hail of splinters whips forth the child-like cries of the wounded, and in the night shattered life groans painfully into silence.

Our hands are earth, our bodies clay and our eyes pools of rain. We do not know whether we still live.

Notes:

1. A Verey Light (also Very Light) is a coloured flare fired from a pistol, ordinarily used for signaling.

2. An 'A' designation indicated fitness for service at the front; 'B' indicated fitness only for base service or service on the home front; 'C' indicated fitness only for service on the home front. The numerical designations further qualified the fitness of the soldier.

Study Question

1. Consider the demographic impact of the high casualties suffered during the Great War. In what ways would this impact the postwar world?

NOVOE VREMYA

There has been considerable debate during the past few decades regarding the truthfulness of accounts of Russian women fighting in combat roles during the First World War. These accounts were initially believed to be myths, created to inspire patriotism on the home front. However, there is now substantial research proving that many of these accounts are real.

The first all-female unit was called 'The Battalion of Death' and was commanded by Maria Botchkareva. It participated in the defence of Russia's Provisional Government in the months leading up to the Bolshevik uprising. The following account was first printed in Russian newspapers and then reprinted in the New York Times in 1917.

A photo-montage depicting a Petrograd women's regiment in 1918. Regiments such as this were involved in the Russian Civil War. Courtesy of the Library of Congress, Prints and Photographs Division (LC-USZ62-129088).

RUSSIAN WOMEN IN COMBAT

Stories are filtering in from the various belligerent countries telling of actual fighting in the ranks by women. . . . A correspondent of the *Novoe Vremya*[1] tells an interesting story of the experiences of twelve young Russian girls who fought in the ranks as soldiers of the line. The story was also authenticated by the Petrograd correspondent of the London *Times*.

She was called Zoya Smirnov. She came to our staff straight from the advanced positions, where she had spent fourteen months wearing soldier's clothes and fighting with the foe on even terms with the men. Zoya Smirnov was only 16 years old. Closely cropped hair gave her the appearance of a boy, and only a thin girlish voice involuntarily betrayed her sex.

At the beginning Zoya was somewhat shy; she carefully chose her words and replied confusedly to our questions; but later she recovered and told us her entire history, which brought tears to the eyes of many a case-hardened veteran who heard it.

She and her friends decided to go to the war on the eighth day of mobilization—i.e., at the end of July 1914; and early in August they succeeded in realizing their dream.

Exactly twelve of them assembled; and they were all nearly the same age and from the same high school. Almost all were natives of Moscow, belonging to the most diversified classes of society, but firmly united in the camaraderie of school life.

'We decided to run away to the war at all costs,' said Zoya. 'It was impossible to run away from Moscow, because we might have been stopped at the station. It was therefore necessary to hire *izvozchiks*[2] and ride out to one of the suburban stations through which the military echelons were continually passing. We left home early in the morning without saying a word to our parents and departed. It was a bit terrible at first; we were very sorry for our fathers and mothers, but the desire to see the war and ourselves kill the Germans overcame all other sentiments.'

And so they attained the desired object. The soldiers treated the little patriots quite paternally and properly, and having concealed them in the cars, took them off to the war. A military uniform was obtained for each; they donned these and unobstructed arrived at the Austrian frontier, where they had to detrain and on foot proceed to Lemberg. Here the regimental authorities found out what had happened, but not being able to persuade the young patriots to return home allowed them to march with the regiment.

The regiment traversed the whole of Galicia; scaled the Carpathians,[3] incessantly participating in battle, and the girls never fell back from it a step, but shared with the men all the privations and horrors of the march and discharged the duties of ordinary privates, since they were taught to shoot and were given rifles.

Days and months passed.

The girls almost forgot their past, they hardly responded to their feminine names, for each of them had received a masculine surname, and completely mingled with the men. The soldiers themselves mutually guarded the girls and observed each other's conduct.

The battles in which the regiment engaged were fierce and sanguinary, particularly in the Spring, when the Germans brought up their heavy artillery to the Carpathians and began to advance upon us with their celebrated phalanx.

Our troops underwent a perfect hell and the young volunteers endured it with them.

'Was it terrible?' an officer asked Zoya. 'Were you afraid?'

'I should say so! Who wouldn't be afraid? When for the first time they began to fire with their heavy guns, several of us couldn't stand it and began to cry out.'

'What did you cry out?'

'We began to call "Mamma." Shura was the first to cry, then Lida. They were both 14 years old, and they remembered their mothers all the time. Besides, it seems that I also cried out as well. We all cried. Well, it was frightful even for the men.'

During one of the Carpathian engagements, at night, one of the twelve friends, the sixteen-year-old Zina Morozov, was killed outright by a shell. It struck immediately at her feet, and the entire small body of the girl was torn into fragments.

'Nevertheless, we managed to collect her remains,' Zoya stated with a tender inflexion in her voice. 'At dawn the firing died down and we all—that is, all the remaining high school volunteers—assembled near the spot where Zina had perished, and somehow collected her bones and laid them in a hastily dug grave. In the same grave we laid also all Zina's things, such as she had with her. The grave was then filled up and upon the cross which we erected above it the following inscription was written: "Volunteer of such and such a regiment, Zina Morozov, 16 years old, killed in action on such and such a date in such and such year".'

On the following day we were already far away, and exactly where Zina's grave is I don't remember well. I only know that it is in the Carpathians at the foot of a steep rocky incline.'

After the death of Zina other of her friends were frequently wounded in turn—Nadya, Zhena, and the fourteen-year-old Shura. Zoya herself was wounded twice—the first time in the leg, and the second time in the side. Both wounds were so serious that Zoya was left unconscious on the battlefield, and the stretcher-bearers subsequently discovered her only by accident. After the second wound she was obliged to lie at a base hospital for over a month. On being discharged she again proceeded to the positions, endeavoring to find her regiment, but on reaching the familiar trenches she could no longer find a single regimental comrade, nor a single fellow-volunteer; they had all gone to another front, and in the trenches sat absolute strangers. The girl lost her presence of mind, and for the first time during the entire campaign began to weep, thus unexpectedly betraying her age and sex. Her unfamiliar fellow-countrymen gazed with amazement upon the strange young non-commissioned officer with the Cross of St George medal on her breast, who resembled a stripling and finally proved to be a girl. But the girl had with her all necessary documents, not excepting a certificate giving her the right to wear the St George's Cross received for a brave and dashing reconnaissance, and distrustful glances promptly gave place to others full of respect.

Zoya was finally induced to abandon the trenches, at least for the time being, and to try to engage in nursing at one of the advanced hospitals. She is now working at the divisional hospital of the N—— division, in the village of K., ten versts from the Austrian town of Z.

From her remaining friends whom she left with the regiment which went to another front Zoya has no news whatever.

What has befallen them? Do these amazing Russian girls continue their disinterested and heroic service to the country, or do graves already hold them, similar to that which was dug for the remnants of poor little Zina, who perished so gloriously in the distant Carpathians?

Notes

1. *New Times.*
2. Carriages.
3. Galicia was an Austrian province in east central Europe, which is today divided between Poland and Ukraine. Lemberg was the capital of Galicia. The Carpathians are a range of mountains stretching through eastern Europe, where many battles were fought in the First World War.

Study Question

1. Why would accounts such as this appear in American newspapers?

A. HENRY MCMAHON/ARTHUR JAMES BALFOUR

During the First World War, agents of the British government made numerous contradictory statements regarding the fate of the Middle East. Two documents in particular—the McMahon Letter and the Balfour Declaration—would prove to be an ongoing source of instability in the region.

The Balfour Declaration is a clear indication of support for the creation of a national home for the Jewish people in Palestine. The McMahon Letter, which predates the Balfour Declaration, is a far more detailed blueprint for Arab control in much of the post-war Middle East.

THE McMAHON LETTER

24 October 1915

I have received your letter of the 29th Shawal, 1333,[1] with much pleasure and your expression of friendliness and sincerity have given me the greatest satisfaction.

I regret that you should have received from my last letter the impression that I regarded the question of limits and boundaries with coldness and hesitation; such was not the case, but it appeared to me that the time had not yet come when that question could be discussed in a conclusive manner.

I have realised, however, from your last letter that you regard this question as one of vital and urgent importance. I have, therefore, lost no time in informing the Government of Great Britain of the contents of your letter, and it is with great pleasure that I communicate to you on their behalf the following statement, which I am confident you will receive with satisfaction.

The two districts of Mersina and Alexandretta and portions of Syria lying to the west of the districts of Damascus, Homs, Hama, and Aleppo cannot be said to be purely Arab, and should be excluded from the limits demanded. With the above modification, and without prejudice to our existing treaties with Arab chiefs, we accept those limits. As for those regions lying within those frontiers wherein Great Britain is free to act without detriment to the interests of her ally, France, I am empowered in the name of the Government of Great Britain to give the following assurances and make the following assurances and make the following reply to your letter:

1. Subject to the above modifications, Great Britain is prepared to recognise and support the independence of the Arabs in all the regions within the limits demanded by the Sherif of Mecca.

2. Great Britain will guarantee the Holy Places against all external aggression and will recognise their inviolability.

3. When the situation admits, Great Britain will give to the Arabs her advice and will assist them to establish what may appear to be the most suitable forms of government for those various territories.

4. On the other hand, it is understood that the Arabs have decided to seek the advice and guidance of Great Britain only, and that such European advisers and officials as may be required for the formation of a sound form of administration will be British.

5. With regard to the vilayets of Bagdad and Basra, the Arabs will recognise that the established position and interests of Great Britain necessitate special administrative arrangements in order to secure these territories from foreign aggression to promote the welfare of the local populations and to safeguard our mutual economic interests.

I am convinced that this declaration will assure you beyond all possible doubt of the sympathy of Great Britain towards the aspirations of her friends the Arabs and will result in a firm and lasting alliance, the immediate results of which will be the expulsion of the Turks from the Arab countries and the freeing of the Arab peoples from the Turkish yoke, which for so many years has pressed heavily upon them.

I have confined myself in this letter to the more vital and important questions, and if there are any other matters dealt with in your letters that I have omitted to mention, we may discuss them at some convenient date in the future.

It was with very great relief and satisfaction that I heard of the safe arrival of the Holy Carpet and the accompanying offerings which, thanks to the clearness of your directions and the excellence of your arrangements, were landed without trouble or mishap in spite of the dangers and difficulties occasioned by the present sad war. May God soon bring a lasting peace and freedom of all peoples.

I am sending this letter by the hand of your trusted and excellent messenger, Sheikh Mohammed ibn Arif ibn Uraifan, and he will inform you of the various matters of interest, but of less vital importance, which I have not mentioned in this letter.

(Compliments)

(Signed): A. HENRY MCMAHON

THE BALFOUR DECLARATION

2 November 1917

Dear Lord Rothschild,

I have much pleasure in conveying to you, on behalf of His Majesty's Government, the following declaration of sympathy with Jewish Zionist aspirations, which has been submitted to, and approved by, the Cabinet.

'His Majesty's Government view with favour the establishment in Palestine of a national home for the Jewish people, and will use their best endeavours to facilitate the achievement of this object, it being clearly understood that nothing shall be done which may prejudice the civil and religious rights of existing non-Jewish communities in Palestine, or the rights and political status enjoyed by Jews in any other country.'

I should be grateful if you would bring this declaration to the knowledge of the Zionist Federation.

Yours sincerely,

ARTHUR JAMES BALFOUR

Note

1. McMahon uses the Islamic calendar in his response. The date of the original letter from the Sharif of Mecca was 9 September 1915.

Study Questions

1. Based on your reading of the two documents, which should take precedence?

THE ARMENIAN NATIONAL INSTITUTE:
PRESS REPORTS ON THE ARMENIAN GENOCIDE

In 1915 a number of reports appeared in American and British newspapers regarding a genocide being carried out by the Ottoman government against the Armenians. These reports continued both during and after the First World War; however, the war and its consequences would mean that the genocide committed against the Armenian people between 1915 and 1920 was largely ignored by history. Attempts have been made only recently to study this genocide and its implications. The Turkish government and many other nations continue to deny that a genocide occurred.

500,000 ARMENIANS SAID TO HAVE PERISHED

The New York Times, 24 September 1915
Washington Asked to Stop Slaughter of Christians
by Turks and Kurds
Special to The New York Times

WASHINGTON, Sept. 23. Charles R. Crane of Chicago, a Director of Roberts College, Constantinople, and James L. Burton of Boston, Foreign Secretary of the American Board of Commissioners for Foreign Missions, visited the State Department today and conferred with Acting Secretary of State Polk and other officials regarding the slaughter of Armenians by Turks and Kurds in Asia Minor. They will attend a meeting of a general committee, to be held in New York within a few days, to devise a plan for appealing to the American people for funds and aid for as many of the unfortunate Armenians as can be helped.

It was learned, in connection with the conferences held here today, that general representations have from time to time been made to the Ottoman Government by Ambassador Morgenthau[1] for humane treatment of Armenians. Despite these representations, the slaughter of Armenians has continued.

The records of the State Department are replete with detailed reports from American Consular officers in Asia Minor, which give harrowing tales of the treatment of the Armenian Christians by the Turks and the Kurds. These reports have not been made public. They indicate that the Turk has undertaken a war of extermination on Armenians, especially those of the Gregorian Church,[2] to which about 90 per cent of the Armenians belong. The Turkish Government originally ordered the deportation of all Armenians, but, some time ago, after representations had been made by Ambassador Morgenthau, the Ottoman Government gave assurances that the order would be modified so as not to embrace Catholic and Protestant Armenians.

Reports reaching Washington indicate that about 500,000 Armenians have been slaughtered or lost their lives as a result of the Turkish deportation order and the resulting war of extinction. Turkish authorities drove the Gregorian Armenians out of their homes, ordered them to proceed to distant towns in the direction of Baghdad, which could only be reached by crossing long stretches of desert. During the exodus of Armenians across the deserts they have been fallen upon by Kurds and slaughtered, but some of the Armenian women and girls, in considerable numbers, have been carried off into captivity by the Kurds. The reports that have been sent to the State Department by its agents in Asia Minor fully confirm these statements made in the appeal sent to this country by Viscount Bryce, formerly British Ambassador to the United States, to try to stop the slaughter of the Armenians. Viscount Bryce stated that the horrors through which the Armenians have passed have been unparalleled in modern times.

800,000 ARMENIANS COUNTED DESTROYED

The New York Times, 7 October 1915

LONDON, Oct.6. Viscount Bryce, former British Ambassador to the United States, in the House of Lords today said that such information as had reached him from many quarters showed that the figure of 800,000 Armenians destroyed since May was quite a possible number. Virtually the whole nation had been wiped out, he declared, and he did not suppose there was any case in history of a crime 'so hideous and on so large a scale'.

'The death of these people,' said Lord Bryce, 'resulted from the deliberate and premeditated policy of the gang now in possession of the Turkish Government. Orders for the massacres came in every case direct from Constantinople. In some instances local Governors, being humane, pious men, refused to carry out the orders and at least two Governors were summarily dismissed for this reason.'

'The customary procedure was to round up the whole of the population of a designated town. A part of the population was thrown into prison and the remainder were marched out of town and in the suburbs the men were separated from the women and children. The men were then taken to a convenient place and shot and bayoneted. The women and children were then put under a convoy of the lower kind of soldiers and dispatched to some distant destination.'

They were driven by the soldiers day after day. Many fell by the way and many died of hunger, for no provisions were furnished them. They were robbed of all they possessed, and in many cases the women were stripped naked and made to continue the march in that condition. Many of the women went mad and threw away their children. The caravan route was marked by a line of corpses. Comparatively few of the people ever reached their destination.'

The facts as to the slaughter in Trebizond are vouched for by the Italian Consul. Orders came for the murder of all the Armenian Christians in Trebizond. Many Mussulmans tried to save their Christian friends, but the authorities were implacable and hunted out all the Christians and then drove them down to the sea front. Then they put them aboard sail boats and carried them some distance out to sea and threw them overboard. The whole Armenian population, numbering 10,000, was thus destroyed in one afternoon.' The Lord Mayor at a meeting at the Mansion House on Oct. 15, will start a fund for the aid of Armenian refugees. Among the speakers will be Lord Bryce, Cardinal Bourne and T.P. O'Connor.

ARMENIANS DYING IN PRISON CAMPS

The New York Times, 21 August 1916
Hundreds of Thousands Still in Danger from Turks, Refugees Fund Secretary Says.
GERMANS WON'T INTERFERE
About 1,000,000 Victims Deported and 500,000 Massacred, the Rev. Harold Buxton Reports.
Special Cable to *The New York Times*

LONDON, Monday, Aug. 21. The Rev. Harold Buxton, Secretary of the Armenian Refugees Fund, has just returned to England after devoting three months to relief work in the devastated villages. In an interview the Rev. Mr Buxton gave details which entirely confirm the grave statements made by Lord Bryce some months ago in the House of Lords. Asked whether he had any proof that the deportation of Armenians last summer was due to German instigation, he said:

'All I can say is that the German Government did nothing to stop the massacres. During the whole business German influence was supreme at Constantinople, and German Consuls were at their posts in all the chief centres through Asia Minor. Besides, the people were swept away with a methodical thoroughness which one does not expect from the Turk, who, when left to himself, acts rather with sudden spasms of fury.'

'I have evidence from an American missionary that certain of the German Consuls did their best on behalf of the Armenian people. For instance, the German Consul at Erzerum wired to his Ambassador in Constantinople vigorously protesting at the order of deportation. He received a reply in these words: "We cannot interfere in the internal affairs of Turkey".'

'I don't think there has been any exaggeration as to losses as published in England. The Armenian race numbered over 4,000,000, of whom 2,000,000 were Turkish Armenians, and of these perhaps 1,000,000 have been deported and 500,000 massacred. Only 200,000 escaped into the mountains, and so across to Russian soil. There are some hundreds of thousands in concentration camps between Aleppo and Mosul and in the neighboring regions of Mesopotamia, where Turkey continues to be supreme over their fate.'

'To this considerable population we have no access, and it is still in danger. According to reports which come through, it is being ravaged by sickness, famine, privations of all kinds, outrages, and murder, all of which means high mortality among the victims.'

◇

SHALL ARMENIA PERISH?

The Independent, 28 February 1920
By Henry Morgenthau, Former Ambassador to Turkey, and National Vice-Chairman of Near East Relief

Two hundred and fifty thousand Christian Armenian women enslaved in Turkish harems call to the people of America for liberation! One hundred thousand women already rescued by Near East Relief agents from harems will perish unless support from America is continued! Two hundred and fifty thousand children, orphaned by the unspeakable Turks, are calling in the only English they know, 'Bread, Uncle Sam.' One million two hundred thousand destitute, homeless, clotheless adults look to the giant in the West for the succor that will keep them from annihilation. What shall our answer be?

If they were good enough to fight and die for us when we needed their help so sorely, are they not good enough to be given some crumbs from our plenty?

Since the beginning of the war, the Turkish Armenians have been largely refugees. A simple, agricultural people, they have been exiled from their farms and deprived of all opportunity to support themselves. Now, more than a year after the armistice, they are still living the life of nomads, able to continue alive only by virtue of American philanthropy. If ever unmerited suffering called for succor the plight of the Armenians should be heeded now. A few months more and it may be relief will come too late for those myriads whom only we can save.

Let the American slogan now become—'Serve Armenians for a little while longer with life's necessities that they may be preserved for the day of national freedom and rebirth, which no people more truly and greatly deserves.'

The belief, held by some persons, that Turkey has repented and can do not further harm, is without foundation. The group that led Turkey into the war on the side of Germany is now in the saddle. The Turk has not been disarmed and these leaders are now aiding the Tartars. Kurds and Bolshevists are urging them on to kill and rob the surviving Armenians at every opportunity. The deportations and massacres during the war were not spontaneous uprisings of unorganized mobs, but were the working out of a well-plotted plan of wholesale extermination in which regular Turkish officers and troops took part as if in a campaign against an enemy in the field.

More than 2,000,000 persons were deported. The system was about the same everywhere. The Armenians, men, women and children, would be assembled in the marketplace. Then the able-bodied men would be marched off and killed by being shot or clubbed in cold blood at some spot which did not necessitate the trouble of burial.

Next the women would be sorted out. Agents of the Turk officers picked the youngest and fairest for their masters' harems. Next the civil officials had their pick, and then the remainder either were sold for one medjidi—a silver coin valued at about 80 cents—or were driven forth to be seized by the lower class Turks and Kurds.

As a last step, those who remained, mothers, grandmothers, children, were driven forth on their death pilgrimages across the desert of Aleppo, with no food, no water, no shelter, to be robbed and beaten at every halt, to see children slain in scores before their eyes, and babies dashed to death against rocks or spitted on the bayonets of the soldier guards.

If America is going to condone these offenses, if she is going to permit to continue conditions that threaten and permit their repetition, she is party to the crime. These peoples must be freed from the agony and danger of such horrors. They must not only be saved for the present but either thru governmental action or protection under the League of Nations they must be given assurance that they will be free in peace and that no harm can come to them.

Notes

1. Henry I. Morgenthau was the United States Ambassador at Constantinople from 1913–16.
2. The Gregorian Church dates to the late third century AD. It is an independent Christian Church.

Study Questions

1. Was the war alone responsible for the lack of public scrutiny devoted to the Armenian genocide?

WOODROW WILSON

Woodrow Wilson (1856–1924) held degrees in both law and political science. A social reformer, Wilson entered politics in 1911 and won the governorship of New Jersey on his first attempt. In 1912 a three-way race[1] allowed Wilson to win the presidency of the United States; however, his plans to focus on domestic social reforms were shattered by the outbreak of war in Europe in 1914. Determined to maintain a policy of neutrality, Wilson managed to keep the US out of the war until April 1917, by which time American *commercial interests were being seriously compromised by Germany's unrestricted U-Boat campaign. However, even as the United States was mobilizing for war, Wilson was already envisioning the peace settlement. In 1917 he noted that '[p]unitive damages, and the dismemberment of empire we deem childish and in the end less than futile'. Similar sentiments guided the creation of his 'fourteen points for peace'. In January 1918 Wilson presented the outline of his Fourteen Points to a joint session of Congress.*

FOURTEEN POINTS SPEECH

Gentlemen of the Congress:

It will be our wish and purpose that the processes of peace, when they are begun, shall be absolutely open and that they shall involve and permit henceforth no secret understandings of any kind. The day of conquest and aggrandizement is gone by; so is also the day of secret covenants entered into in the interest of particular governments and likely at some unlooked-for moment to upset the peace of the world. It is this happy fact, now clear to the view of every public man whose thoughts do not still linger in an age that is dead and gone, which makes it possible for every nation whose purposes are consistent with justice and the peace of the world to avow now or at any other time the objects it has in view.

We entered this war because violations of right had occurred which touched us to the quick and made the life of our own people impossible unless they were corrected and the world secured once for all against their recurrence. What we demand in this war, therefore, is nothing peculiar to ourselves. It is that the world be made fit and safe to live in; and particularly that it be made safe for every peace-loving nation which, like our own, wishes to live its own life, determine its own institutions, be assured of justice and fair dealing by the other peoples of the world as against force and selfish aggression. All the peoples of the world are in effect partners in this interest, and for our own part we see very clearly that unless justice be done to others it will not be done to us. The program of the world's peace, therefore, is our program; and that program, the only possible program, as we see it, is this:

I. Open covenants of peace, openly arrived at, after which there shall be no private international understandings of any kind but diplomacy shall proceed always frankly and in the public view.

II. Absolute freedom of navigation upon the seas, outside territorial waters, alike in peace and in war, except as the seas may be closed in whole or in part by international action for the enforcement of international covenants.

III. The removal, so far as possible, of all economic barriers and the establishment of an equality of trade conditions among all the nations consenting to the peace and associating themselves for its maintenance.

IV. Adequate guarantees given and taken that national armaments will be reduced to the lowest point consistent with domestic safety.

V. A free, open-minded, and absolutely impartial adjustment of all colonial claims, based upon a strict observance of the principle that in determining all such questions of sovereignty the interests of the populations concerned must have equal weight with the equitable claims of the government whose title is to be determined.

VI. The evacuation of all Russian territory and such a settlement of all questions affecting Russia as will secure the best and freest cooperation of the other nations of the world in obtaining for her an unhampered and unembarrassed opportunity for the independent determination of her own political development and national policy and assure her of a sincere welcome into the society of free nations under institutions of her own choosing; and, more than a welcome, assistance also of every kind that she may need and may herself desire. The treatment accorded Russia by her sister nations in the months to come will be the acid test of their good will, of their comprehension of her needs as distinguished from their own interests, and of their intelligent and unselfish sympathy.

VII. Belgium, the whole world will agree, must be evacuated and restored, without any attempt to limit the sovereignty which she enjoys in common with all other free nations. No other single act will serve as this will serve to restore confidence among the nations in the laws which they have themselves set and determined for the government of their relations with one another. Without this healing act the whole structure and validity of international law is forever impaired.

VIII. All French territory should be freed and the invaded portions restored, and the wrong done to France by Prussia in 1871 in the matter of Alsace-Lorraine, which has unsettled the peace of the world for nearly fifty years, should be righted, in order that peace may once more be made secure in the interest of all.

IX. A readjustment of the frontiers of Italy should be effected along clearly recognizable lines of nationality.

X. The peoples of Austria-Hungary, whose place among the nations we wish to see safeguarded and assured, should be accorded the freest opportunity of autonomous development.

XI. Rumania, Serbia, and Montenegro should be evacuated; occupied territories restored; Serbia accorded free and secure access to the sea; and the relations of the several Balkan states to one another determined by friendly counsel along historically established lines of allegiance and nationality; and international guarantees of the political and economic independence and territorial integrity of the several Balkan states should be entered into.

XII. The Turkish portions of the present Ottoman Empire should be assured a secure sovereignty, but the other nationalities which are now under Turkish rule should be assured an undoubted security of life and an absolutely unmolested opportunity of an autonomous development, and the Dardanelles should be permanently opened as a free passage to the ships and commerce of all nations under international guarantees.

XIII. An independent Polish state should be erected which should include the territories inhabited by indisputably Polish populations, which should be assured a free and secure access to the sea, and whose political and economic

independence and territorial integrity should be guaranteed by international covenant.

XIV. A general association of nations must be formed under specific covenants for the purpose of affording mutual guarantees of political independence and territorial integrity to great and small states alike.

In regard to these essential rectifications of wrong and assertions of right we feel ourselves to be intimate partners of all the governments and peoples associated together against the Imperialists. We cannot be separated in interest or divided in purpose. We stand together until the end.

For such arrangements and covenants we are willing to fight and to continue to fight until they are achieved; but only because we wish the right to prevail and desire a just and stable peace such as can be secured only by removing the chief provocations to war, which this program does not remove. We have no jealousy of German greatness, and there is nothing in this program that impairs it. We grudge her no achievement or distinction of learning or of pacific enterprise such as have made her record very bright and very enviable. We do not wish to injure her or to block in any way her legitimate influence or power. We do not wish to fight her either with arms or with hostile arrangements of trade if she is willing to associate herself with us and the other peace-loving nations of the world in covenants of justice and law and fair dealing. We wish her only to accept a place of equality among the peoples of the world—the new world in which we now live—instead of a place of mastery.

Neither do we presume to suggest to her any alteration or modification of her institutions. But it is necessary, we must frankly say, and necessary as a preliminary to any intelligent dealings with her on our part, that we should know whom her spokesmen speak for when they speak to us, whether for the Reichstag majority or for the military party and the men whose creed is imperial domination.

We have spoken now, surely, in terms too concrete to admit of any further doubt or question. An evident principle runs through the whole program I have outlined. It is the principle of justice to all peoples and nationalities, and their right to live on equal terms of liberty and safety with one another, whether they be strong or weak. Unless this principle be made its foundation no part of the structure of international justice can stand. The people of the United States could act upon no other principle; and to the vindication of this principle they are ready to devote their lives, their honor, and everything that they possess. The moral climax of this the culminating and final war for human liberty has come, and they are ready to put their own strength, their own highest purpose, their own integrity and devotion to the test.

Note

1. Theodore Roosevelt and William Howard Taft both ran as Republican candidates, allowing Wilson, the only democratic challenger, to win the election.

Study Question

1. Which countries would benefit the most from the ideals established in the Fourteen Points?

MARCUS GARVEY

Marcus Garvey (1887–1940) was one of the strongest advocates of black nationalism in the first half of the twentieth century. Garvey argued for a 're-segregation' of the races as Africans around the world would return to Africa and liberate the continent from colonial rule. In 1919 he founded the Black Star Line to facilitate the movement of African-Americans back to Africa. Garvey hoped that the peace-makers who met in Paris in 1919 would begin the process of decolonizing Africa.

ADVICE OF THE NEGRO TO THE PEACE CONFERENCE

Now that the statesmen of the various nations are preparing to meet at the Peace Conference, to discuss the future government of the peoples of the world, we take it as our bounden duty to warn them to be very just to all those people who may happen to come under their legislative control. If they, representing the classes, as they once did, were alive to the real feeling of their respective masses four and one-half years ago, today Germany would have been intact, Austria-Hungary would have been intact, Russia would have been intact, the spirit of revolution never would have swept Europe, and mankind at large would have been satisfied. But through graft, greed and selfishness, the classes they represented then, as some of them represent now, were determined to rob and exploit the masses, thinking that the masses would have remained careless of their own condition for everlasting.

It is a truism that you 'fool half of the people for half of the time, but you cannot fool all of the people for all of the time'; and now that the masses of the whole world have risen as one man to demand true equity and justice from the 'powers that be', then let the delegates at the Peace Conf[e]rence r[e]alize, just now, that the Negro, who forms an integral part of the masses of the world, is determined to get no less than what other men are to get. The oppressed races of Europe are to get their freedom, which freedom will be guaranteed them. The Asiatic races are to get their rights and a larger modicum of self-government.

We trust that the delegates to the Peace Conference will not continue to believe that Negroes have no ambition, no aspiration. There are no more timid, cringing Negroes; let us say that those Negroes have now been relegated to the limbo of the past, to the region of forgetfulness, and that the new Negro is on the stage, and he is going to play his part good and well. He, like the other heretofore oppressed peoples of the world, is determined to get restored to him his ancestral rights.

When we look at the map of Africa today we see Great Britain with fully five million square miles of our territory, we see France with fully three million five hundred thousand square miles, we see that Belgium has under her control the Congo, Portugal has her sway over Southeast Africa, Italy has under her control Tripoli, Italian Somaliland on the Gulf of Aden and Erythria on the Red Sea. Germany had clamored for a place in the sun simply because she had only one million square miles, with which she was not satisfied, in that England had five millions and France three millions five hundred thousand. It can be easily seen that the war of 1914 was the outcome of African aggrandizement, that Africa, to which the white man has absolutely no claim, has been raped, has been left bleeding for hundreds of years, but within the last thirty years the European powers have concentrated more than ever on the cleaning up of that great continent so as to make it a white man's country. Among those whom they have killed are millions of our people, but the age of killing for naught is passed and the age of killing for something has come. If black men have to die in Africa or anywhere else, then they might as well die for the best of things, and that is liberty, true freedom and true democracy. If the delegates to the Peace Conference would like to see no more wars we would advise them to satisfy the yellow man's claims, the black man's claims and the white man's

A follower of Marcus Garvey stands outside the Harlem, NY, office of the Garvey Club. Library of Congress, Prints and Photographs Division, FSA/OWI Collection (LC-USW3-024005-E).

claims, and let all three be satisfied so that there can be indeed a brotherhood of men. But if one section of the human race is to arrogate to itself all that God gave for the benefit of mankind at large, then let us say human nature has in no way changed, and even at the Peace Conference where from the highest principles of humanity are supposed to emanate there will come no message of peace.

There will be no peace in the world until the white man confines himself politically to Europe, the yellow man to Asia and the black man to Africa. The original division of the earth among mankind must stand, and any one who dares to interfere with this division creates only trouble for himself. This division was made by the Almighty Power that rules, and therefore there can be no interference with the plans Divine.

Cowardice has disappeared from the world. Men have died in this world war so quickly and so easily that those who desire liberty today do not stop to think of death, for it is regarded as the price which people in all ages will have to pay to be free; that is the price the weaker people of Europe have paid; that is the price the Negro must pay some day.

Let the Peace Conference, we suggest, be just in its deliberations and in its findings, so that there can be a true brotherhood in the future with no more wars.

Study Question

1. In what ways did the First World War contribute to the development of Pan-African movements?

J.M. KEYNES

John Maynard Keynes (1883–1946) was educated in mathematics at the University of Cambridge and worked briefly in the British Civil Service's India Office. After lecturing at Cambridge he joined the British Treasury and in 1919 served as the Treasury's representative to the Paris Peace Conference. Keynes soon grew frustrated with what he perceived to be the greed of the major leaders and their lack of concern for the impact of the treaty on the global economy. The excerpt which follows was written after Keynes resigned in protest and returned to Cambridge.

THE ECONOMIC CONSEQUENCES OF THE PEACE

This chapter must be one of pessimism. The treaty includes no provisions for the economic rehabilitation of Europe—nothing to make the defeated Central empires into good neighbours, nothing to stabilise the new states of Europe, nothing to reclaim Russia; nor does it promote in any way a compact of economic solidarity amongst the Allies themselves; no arrangement was reached at Paris for restoring the disordered finances of France and Italy, or to adjust the systems of the Old World and the New.

The Council of Four paid no attention to these issues, being preoccupied with others— Clemenceau to crush the economic life of his enemy, Lloyd George to do a deal and bring home something which would pass muster for a week, the President to do nothing that was not just and right. It is an extraordinary fact that the fundamental economic problem of a Europe starving and disintegrating before their eyes, was the one question in which it was impossible to arouse the interest of the Four. Reparation was their main excursion into the economic field, and they settled it as a problem of theology, of politics, of electoral chicane, from every point of view except that of the economic future of the states whose destiny they were handling.

I leave, from this point onwards, Paris, the conference, and the treaty, briefly to consider the present situation of Europe, as the war and the peace have made it; and it will no longer be part of my purpose to distinguish between the inevitable fruits of the war and the avoidable misfortunes of the peace.

The essential facts of the situation, as I see them, are expressed simply. Europe consists of the densest aggregation of population in the history of the world. This population is accustomed to a relatively high standard of life, in which, even now, some sections of it anticipate improvement rather than deterioration. In relation to other continents Europe is not self-sufficient; in particular it cannot feed itself. Internally the population is not evenly distributed, but much of it is crowded into a relatively small number of dense industrial centres. This population secured for itself a livelihood before the war, without much margin of surplus, by means of a delicate and immensely complicated organisation, of which the foundations were supported by coal, iron, transport, and an unbroken supply of imported food and raw materials from other continents. By the destruction of this organisation and the interruption of the stream of supplies, a part of this population is deprived of its means of livelihood. Emigration is not open to the redundant surplus. For it would take years to transport them overseas, even, which is not the case, if countries could be found which were ready to receive them. The danger confronting us, therefore, is the rapid depression of the standard of life of the European populations to a point which will mean actual starvation for some (a point already reached in Russia and approximately reached in Austria). Men will not always die quietly. For starvation, which brings to some lethargy and a helpless despair, drives other temperaments to the nervous instability of hysteria and to a mad despair. And these in their distress may overturn the remnants of organisation, and submerge civilisation itself in their attempts to satisfy desperately the overwhelming needs of the individual. This is the danger against which all our resources and courage and idealism must now co-operate.

On 13 May 1919 Count Brockdorff-Rantzau addressed to the peace conference of the Allied and Associated Powers the Report of the German economic commission charged with the study of the effect of the conditions of peace on the situation of the German population. 'In the course of the last two generations,' they reported, 'Germany has become transformed from an agricultural state to an industrial state. So long as she was an agricultural state, Germany could feed 40 million inhabitants. As an industrial state she could ensure the means of subsistence for a population of 67 millions; and in 1913 the importation of foodstuffs amounted, in round figures, to 12 million tons. Before the war a total of 15 million persons in Germany provided for their existence by foreign trade, navigation, and the use, directly or indirectly, of foreign raw material.' After rehearsing the main relevant provisions of the peace treaty the report continues: 'After this diminution of her products, after the economic depression resulting from the loss of her colonies, her merchant fleet, and her foreign investments, Germany will not be in a position to import from abroad an adequate quantity of raw material. An enormous part of German industry will, therefore, be condemned inevitably to destruction. The need of importing foodstuffs will increase considerably at the same time that the possibility of satisfying this demand is as greatly diminished. In a very short time, therefore, Germany will not be in a position to give bread and work to her numerous millions of inhabitants, who are prevented from earning their livelihood by navigation and trade. These persons should emigrate, but this is a material impossibility, all the more because many countries and the most important ones will oppose any German immigration. To put the peace conditions into execution would logically involve, therefore, the loss of several millions of persons in Germany. This catastrophe would not be long in coming about, seeing that the health of the population has been broken down during the war by the blockade, and during the armistice by the aggravation of the blockade of famine. No help, however great, or over however long a period it were continued, could prevent these deaths en masse.' 'We do not know, and indeed we doubt,' the Report concludes, 'whether the delegates of the Allied and Associated Powers realise the inevitable consequences which will take place if Germany, an industrial state, very thickly populated, closely bound up with the economic system of the world, and under the necessity of importing enormous quantities of raw material and foodstuffs, suddenly finds herself pushed back to the phase of her development which corresponds to her economic condition and the numbers of her population as they were half a century ago. Those who sign this treaty will sign the death sentence of many millions of German men, women, and children.'

I know of no adequate answer to these words. The indictment is at least as true of the Austrian, as of the German, settlement. This is the fundamental problem in front of us, before which questions of territorial adjustment and the balance of European power are insignificant. Some of the catastrophes of past history, which have thrown back human progress for centuries, have been due to the reactions following on the sudden termination, whether in the course of Nature or by the act of man, of temporarily favourable conditions which have permitted the growth of population beyond what could be provided for when the favourable conditions were at an end.

> **Study Questions**
>
> 1. Do you believe that it would have been possible to gain acceptance for a less punitive peace?

H.G. WELLS, ET AL.

H.G. Wells (1866–46), along with a number of prominent British scholars and diplomats, was a founding member of the League of Free Nations Association, which was formed in 1918 to advance the cause of global unification. Wells and others believed that there could be no more wars as the scale of destruction would devastate the globe. A truly international organization, built on the principle of collective security, could perhaps avoid such a catastrophe. Many of Wells's fictional works explore his fears of a future dominated by increasingly destructive wars.

THE IDEA OF THE LEAGUE OF NATIONS

Unification of human affairs, to the extent at least of a cessation of war and a worldwide rule of international law, is no new idea; it can be traced through many centuries of history. It is found as an acceptable commonplace in a fragment, *De Republica*, of Cicero. It has, indeed, appeared and passed out of the foreground of thought, and reappeared there, again and again

Hitherto, however, if only on account of the limitations of geographical knowledge, the project has rarely been truly world-wide, though in some instances it has comprehended practically all the known world. Almost always there has been an excluded fringe of barbarians and races esteemed as less than men.

. . . at the outbreak of the Great War in August, 1914, Europe and the world awoke out of a dream of intensified nationality to a new system of realities which were entirely antagonistic to the continuance of national separations.

It is necessary to state very plainly the nature of these new forces. Upon them rests the whole case for the League of Nations as it is here presented. It is a new case. It is argued here that these forces give us powers novel in history and bring mankind face to face with dangers such as it has never confronted before. It is maintained that, on the one hand, they render possible such a reasoned coordination of human affairs as has never hitherto been conceivable, and that, on the other, they so enlarge and intensify the scope and evil of war and of international hostility as to give what was formerly a generous aspiration more and more of the aspect of an imperative necessity. Under the lurid illumination of the world war, the idea of world-unification has passed rapidly from the sphere of the literary idealist into that of the methodical, practical man, and the task of an examination of its problems and possibilities, upon the scale which the near probability of an actual experiment demands, is thrust upon the world. . . .

And we live to-day in a time of accelerated inventiveness and innovation, when a decade modifies the material of inter-communication far more extensively than did any century before, in range, swiftness, and intensity alike. Within the present century, since 1900, there have been far more extensive changes in these things than occurred in the ten centuries before Christ. Instead of regarding *Around the World in Eighty Days* as an amazing feat of hurry, we can now regard a flight about the globe in fifteen or sixteen days as a reasonable and moderate performance. The teaching of history compels us to recognize in these new facilities factors which will necessarily work out into equally revolutionary social and political consequences. . . .

While all these things, on the one hand, point plainly now to such possibilities of human unification and world unanimity as no one could have dreamed of a hundred years ago, there has been, on the other hand, a change, an intensification, of the destructive processes of war which opens up a black alternative to this pacific settlement of human affairs. The case as it is commonly stated in the propaganda literature for a League of Nations is a choice between, on the one hand, a general agreement on the part of mankind to organize a permanent peace, and on the other, a progressive development of the preparation for war and the means of conducting war which must ultimately eat up human freedom and all human effort, and, as the phrase goes, destroy civilization.

It is not impossible to adumbrate the general nature of the catastrophe which threatens mankind if war-making goes on. Modern warfare is not congenial to the working masses anywhere. No doubt the primitive form of warfare, a murderous bickering with adjacent tribes, is natural enough to uneducated men; but modern warfare, and still more the preparation for it, involves distresses, strains, and a continuity of base and narrow purpose quite beyond the patience and interest of the millions of ordinary men who find no other profit in it but suffering. The natural man is more apt for chaotic local fighting than for large-scale systematic fighting. Hatred campaigns and a sustained propaganda are needed to keep up the combatant spirit in a large modern state, even during actual hostilities; and in the case of Russia we have a striking example of the distaste a whole population may develop for the war-strain, even during the war and with the enemy at its gates.

What is likely to happen, then, when the working masses of Central and Western Europe, being no longer sustained by the immediate excitement of actual war, find themselves still obliged to go on, year after year, producing vast masses of war-material, pledged to carry a heavy burden of war loan *rentiers* on their backs, and subjected to an exacerbated conscription? Possibly, so far as the *rentier* burden on the worker goes, a great rise in prices and wages will relieve the worker to some extent, but only at the cost of acute disappointment and distress at another social level. There is a dangerously narrowing limit now to the confidence of the common man in the intelligence and good faith of those who direct his affairs; and the probability of a cruel confused class-war throughout Europe, roughly parallel in its methods to the Bolshevik revolution in Russia, and released by a similar loss of faith in leaders and government, appears at the end of the vista of waste of directive energy and natural resources, completing that waste of energy and resources into which the belligerent systems of Europe, the German Empire being the chief and foremost, have led mankind. Systematic force, overstrained and exhausted, will then give place to chaotic force, and general disorganization will ensue. Thereafter the world may welter in confusion for many generations, through such ruinous and impoverished centuries as close the Roman imperial story, before it develops the vitality for an effective reorganization.

Such, roughly, is the idea of the phrase 'downfall of civilization' as used in discussions like these. It is a vision of the world as a social system collapsing chaotically, not under the assault of outer barbarians, but beneath the pressure of this inevitable hypertrophy of war.

> **Study Question**
>
> 1. In retrospect, how accurate was this assessment of a future without a strong commitment to collective security?

HENRY CABOT LODGE

Henry Cabot Lodge (1850–1924) was elected as a Republican member of Congress in 1887. Though he hoped that the United States would play a role in world affairs and he had backed Theodore Roosevelt's ambitions in Latin America, Lodge was best known for his opposition to Woodrow Wilson's policies—in particular, United States participation in the League of Nations. Lodge argued that the League would only weaken the United States by involving it in every minor global conflict.

ON THE LEAGUE OF NATIONS

Mr President:

The independence of the United States is not only more precious to ourselves, but to the world, than any single possession. Look at the United States today. We have made mistakes in the past. We have had shortcomings. We shall make mistakes in the future and fall short of our own best hopes. But none the less is there any country today on the face of the earth which can compare with this in ordered liberty, in peace, and in the largest freedom?

I feel that I can say this without being accused of undue boastfulness, for it is the simple fact, and in making this treaty and taking on these obligations all that we do is in a spirit of unselfishness and in a desire for the good of mankind. But it is well to remember that we are dealing with nations every one of which has a direct individual interest to serve, and there is grave danger in an unshared idealism.

Contrast the United States with any country on the face of the earth today and ask yourself whether the situation of the United States is not the best to be found. I will go as far as anyone in world service, but the first step to world service is the maintenance of the United States.

I have always loved one flag and I cannot share that devotion [with] a mongrel banner created for a League.

You may call me selfish if you will, conservative or reactionary, or use any other harsh adjective you see fit to apply, but an American I was born, an American I have remained all my life. I can never be anything else but an American, and I must think of the United States first, and when I think of the United States first in an arrangement like this I am thinking of what is best for the world, for if the United States fails, the best hopes of mankind fail with it.

I have never had but one allegiance—I cannot divide it now. I have loved but one flag and I cannot share that devotion and give affection to the mongrel banner invented for a league. Internationalism, illustrated by the Bolshevik and by the men to whom all countries are alike provided they can make money out of them, is to me repulsive.

National I must remain, and in that way I like all other Americans can render the amplest service to the world. The United States is the world's best hope, but if you fetter her in the interests and quarrels of other nations, if you tangle her in the intrigues of Europe, you will destroy her power for good and endanger her very existence. Leave her to march freely through the centuries to come as in the years that have gone.

Strong, generous, and confident, she has nobly served mankind. Beware how you trifle with your marvellous inheritance, this great land of ordered liberty, for if we stumble and fall freedom and civilization everywhere will go down in ruin.

We are told that we shall 'break the heart of the world' if we do not take this league just as it stands. I fear that the hearts of the vast majority of mankind would beat on strongly and steadily and without any quickening if the league were to perish altogether. If it should be effectively and beneficently changed the people who would lie awake in sorrow for a single night could be easily gathered in one not very large room but those who would draw a long breath of relief would reach to millions.

We hear much of visions and I trust we shall continue to have visions and dream dreams of a fairer future for the race. But visions are one thing and visionaries are another, and the mechanical appliances of the rhetorician designed to give a

'If We Were in the League of Nations.' A 1920 propaganda poster emphasizes the potential cost to the US of joining the League of Nations. Courtesy of the Library of Congress, Prints and Photographs Division (LC-USZ62-85742).

picture of a present which does not exist and of a future which no man can predict are as unreal and short-lived as the steam or canvas clouds, the angels suspended on wires and the artificial lights of the stage.

They pass with the moment of effect and are shabby and tawdry in the daylight. Let us at least be real. Washington's entire honesty of mind and his fearless look into the face of all facts are qualities which can never go out of fashion and which we should all do well to imitate.

Ideals have been thrust upon us as an argument for the league until the healthy mind which rejects cant revolts from them. Are ideals confined to this deformed experiment upon a noble purpose, tainted, as it is, with bargains and tied to a peace treaty which might have been disposed of long ago to the great benefit of the world if it had not been compelled to carry this rider on its back? *Post equitem sedet atra cura*[1] Horace tells us, but no blacker care ever sat behind any rider than we shall find in this covenant of doubtful and disputed interpretation as it now perches upon the treaty of peace.

No doubt many excellent and patriotic people see a coming fulfilment of noble ideals in the words 'league for peace.' We all respect and share these aspirations and desires, but some of us see no hope, but rather defeat, for them in this murky covenant. For we, too, have our ideals, even if we differ from those who have tried to establish a monopoly of idealism.

Our first ideal is our country, and we see her in the future, as in the past, giving service to all her people and to the world. Our ideal of the future is that she should continue to render that service of her own free will. She has great problems of her own to solve, very grim and perilous problems, and a right solution, if we can attain to it, would largely benefit mankind.

We would have our country strong to resist a peril from the West, as she has flung back the German menace from the East. We would not have our politics distracted and embittered by the dissensions of other lands. We would not have our country's vigour exhausted or her moral force abated, by everlasting meddling and muddling in every quarrel, great and small, which afflicts the world.

Our ideal is to make her ever stronger and better and finer, because in that way alone, as we believe, can she be of the greatest service to the world's peace and to the welfare of mankind.

Note

1. Black care sits behind the rich man on horseback'; i.e., riches and high position bring dark worries.

Study Question

1. Can a nation maintain its independence and yet participate in a meaningful way in organizations based on collective security?

TIPS FOR ANALYSIS

What if I don't know who the author of a document is?

Read the document carefully. Are key events mentioned? Did the author experience these events? If it is clear that the author experienced the events discussed then you have already determined some basic information about the person, as well as the time and place of the document. From this information you can determine potential biases.

WEB RESOURCES

The War to End All Wars
http://www.firstworldwar.com
Canada and the First World War
http://www.collectionscanada.gc.ca/firstworldwar/index-e.html
World War I: Trenches on the Web
http://www.worldwar1.com
Spartacus Educational: First World War Index
http://www.spartacus.schoolnet.co.uk/FWW.htm

RECOMMENDED READING

Vera Brittain, *Testament of Youth* (New York: Penguin, 1994). *Testament of Youth* is an autobiographical story of the author's coming of age in pre-war England and her service as a nurse, both in Malta and in France near the Western Front during the Great War. Personal losses and the lost generation are interwoven into Brittain's memoir, which is based on letters and diaries written at the time.

Robert Graves, *Goodbye to All That* (New York: Anchor, 1958). *Goodbye to All That* is Graves's autobiography. It speaks of a generation raised in late Victorian Britain and sacrificed on the battlefields of France and Belgium. Considered by many to be the best First World War narrative, it contains observations on society, class, nationalism, and above all, the horrors of the trenches.

Ernest Hemingway, *The Sun Also Rises* (London: Scribner, 1995). Set in Paris, Madrid, and Pamploma, Hemingway's 1926 volume, *The Sun Also Rises*, explores the physical and psychological impact of the Great War on 'the lost generation'. Key themes include the search for meaning and fulfillment, and the escape from reality through alcohol, sex, and violence.

Aldous Huxley, *Brave New World* (New York: HarperCollins Perennial Classics, 1998). *Brave New World*, written in 1932, tells of life in the futuristic utopia of the year 632 AF (After Ford). Science and technology provide for all needs and have assumed control of all human functions, including reproduction—humans are now tailored genetically to fit their future jobs. Mood altering drugs and unlimited sexual partners maintain happiness, at the cost of freedom and individuality.

Sinclair Lewis, *Babbitt* (New York: Bantam Classics, 1998). *Babbitt* chronicles American society in the business-driven, capitalist, materialistic, 'normalcy' of the 1920s. Through George E. Babbitt of Zenith, Ohio, the values of 'normalcy' are tested during a brief period of Bohemian experimentation, after which 'normalcy' returns, with Babbitt slightly more tolerant and wiser.

Henry Miller, *Tropic of Cancer* (New York: Grove Press, 1987). *Tropic of Cancer*—banned in the United States from its initial publication in 1934, and for nearly thirty years thereafter due to its graphic sexuality—is Miller's semi-autobiographical account of the economically depressed, bohemian interwar Paris (*Tropic of Capricorn*, 1936, is set in the United States in the same era).

Erich Maria Remarque, *All Quiet on the Western Front* (New York: Ballantine, 1987). Remarque's 1928 antiwar testimony is told through the eyes of Paul Baumer, a German infantryman on the Western Front. The novel captures much of the horror of the war: the senseless slaughter of the trenches and the psychological impact on winners and losers alike.

H.G. Wells, *War of the Worlds* (New York: Signet Books, 1996). Focused on the consequences of a Martian invasion, *War of the Worlds*, written in 1898, remains one of the most famous turn-of-the-century narratives on technological and industrial change, imperialism, war, and destruction.

RECOMMENDED VIEWING

Metropolis (Germany, 1927). Director: Fritz Lang (Silent, B&W). *Metropolis* is considered to be the most important German expressionist film. Set in the year 2000, the film offers Lang's vision of the future, where the elite live in towering skyscrapers and the masses labour beneath the earth, producing for the elite. Though many versions of *Metropolis* exist, a 2003 Kino Video release restored the film to 124 minutes and returned the original orchestral score by Gottfried Huppertz.

All Quiet on the Western Front (USA, 1930). Director: Lewis Milestone (B&W). Based on Erich Maria Remarque's novel, the movie is a classic depiction of the brutality of trench warfare from the German perspective. Considered one of the finest cinematic anti-war statements, this Academy Award winning film recreates the horrific conditions on the Western Front while revealing the intense patriotism of 1914.

Westfront 1918 (Germany, 1930). Director: G.W. Pabst (B&W). A multinational cast recreates the final few months of the First World War. Pabst's film emphasizes the extreme futility of war and briefly examines the desperate state of the German home front by the end of the war. The film is renowned for its exceptional battle scenes.

Paths of Glory (USA, 1957). Director: Stanley Kubrick (B&W). Set in 1917, Kubrick's film condemns the idiocy of the French military leadership during the First World War and highlights the futility of the war itself. The movie, which was banned in France for many years, focuses on the needless sacrifice of French troops and the consequences of refusing to follow orders.

Cabaret (USA, 1972). Director: Bob Fosse. Based on Christopher Isherwood's novel *Goodbye to Berlin*, this movie is a musical recreation of life in Germany during the early 1930s. Fosse's film—a winner of eight Academy Awards—focuses on the cabaret culture of the era, depicting the hedonism and excess of the late Weimar period and the slow descent of German society into fascism.

Gallipoli (Australia, 1991). Director: Peter Weir. *Gallipoli* dramatizes the catastrophic defeat of Australian and New Zealand forces at the Battle of Gallipoli. The second half of the film recreates the battle itself. Like *All Quiet on the Western Front*, Peter Weir's film makes a strong anti-war statement.

Ararat (Canada, 2002). Director: Atom Egoyan. *Ararat* examines the Armenian genocide and its historical impact. Egoyan creates a non-linear depiction of the impact of the genocide on several generations of Armenian émigrés. A number of different plot lines are interwoven, with the genocide itself standing as the unifying theme.

CHAPTER FOUR

THE APPEAL OF REVOLUTIONARY CHANGE

Tsar Nicholas II, the final member of the Romanov dynasty to rule Russia. Tsar Nicholas made what many believe to be a fatal mistake by leaving St Petersburg to command Russian troops at the front. Photograph courtesy of the University of Texas Libraries.

The late nineteenth and early twentieth centuries witnessed profound political, economic, cultural, and social transformations around the world. Both Russia and China experienced revolutionary changes to their traditional political systems which radically altered the lives of the people in those countries. In Russia, a revolutionary process began in the late nineteenth century and reached its climax during the First World War with the rise to power of Vladimir Lenin and the Bolshevik Party. However, Russia's transformation had only just begun in 1917. From the Bolshevik Revolution until the late 1930s Russian society continued to experience massive socio-economic upheavals, first under Lenin and then, perhaps even more profoundly, under Joseph Stalin.

In China, resentment towards foreign control and its social and economic impact increased throughout the late nineteenth and early twentieth centuries, leading to periodic anti-foreign and anti-dynastic uprisings. By 1911 there had been numerous unsuccessful attempts to topple the Qing dynasty, but on 10 October 1911 a fortuitous set of circumstances, including a revolt by elements of the Qing military, allowed the rebels to secure control over a key region in Central China. In 1912, Puyi, the boy Emperor, was forced to abdicate. After several thousand years of monarchical rule China became a republic. Stability, however, would prove to be elusive as the people of China experienced several more decades of revolutionary upheaval before the final victory of the Chinese Communists in 1949.

The appeal of revolutionary change was not limited to China and Russia. European intellectuals such as Rosa Luxemburg saw socialism as a means to end the bloodshed of the First World War while simultaneously initiating the final confrontation between proletariat and bourgeoisie. Socialist ideas also made a powerful impact in the colonial world. Leaders such as Jawaharlal Nehru saw socialism as the key to independence and to a better future for the 400 million people of the Indian subcontinent. The changes initiated in Turkey, where Mustapha Kemal Atatürk set out to transform the last remnant of the Ottoman Empire into a modern, secular, democratic state, were no less revolutionary.

The documents in this chapter highlight the sweeping changes which took place around the world during the 1910s and 1920s. Luxemburg's 'Junius Pamphlet' invokes the power of the European working class to transform their own lives. Documents by Vladimir Lenin and Nikita Khrushchev reveal both the chaotic situation in Russia in the early years of the twentieth century, and the great hope for the future. Sun Yat-sen and Soong Ching-ling propose far-reaching changes for newly republican China. Li Dazhao sees in the triumph of Bolshevism in Russia, the best hope for the future of the world's oppressed classes. Similarly, Nehru reflects on the importance of socialism, both in India and around the world. Finally, Atatürk discusses the transformation of Turkey since the war for independence.

ROSA LUXEMBURG

Rosa Luxemburg (1871–1919) was born in the Polish area of Russia. In 1889 she emigrated to Zurich and joined study groups with other exiled Russian revolutionaries including Alexandra Kollontai and Georgi Plekhanov. In 1898 she joined the German Social Democratic Party (SPD). Between 1907 and 1914 Luxemburg gradually developed a more radical interpretation of Marxist theory, insisting on the necessity of a violent revolution.

'The Junius Pamphlet' was written in early 1915 while Luxemburg was imprisoned for her opposition to the war. It was published in Zurich in February 1916 and was illegally smuggled into Germany for distribution. The ideas Luxemburg expressed in the pamphlet became the core ideals of several important communist groups, including the German Communist Party (KPD). Luxemburg was murdered by right-wing extremists on 15 January 1919.

THE JUNIUS PAMPHLET

The scene has changed fundamentally. The six weeks' march to Paris has grown into a world drama.[1] Mass slaughter has become the tiresome and monotonous business of the day and the end is no closer. Bourgeois statecraft is held fast in its own vice. The spirits summoned up can no longer be exorcised.

Gone is the euphoria. Gone the patriotic noise in the streets, the chase after the gold-coloured automobile, one false telegram after another, the wells poisoned by cholera, the Russian students heaving bombs over every railway bridge in Berlin, the French airplanes over Nuremberg, the spy hunting public running amok in the streets, the swaying crowds in the coffee shops with ear-deafening patriotic songs surging ever higher, whole city neighbourhoods transformed into mobs ready to denounce, to mistreat women, to shout hurrah and to induce delirium in themselves by means of wild rumours. Gone, too, is the atmosphere of ritual murder, the Kishinev air where the crossing guard is the only remaining representative of human dignity.[2]

The spectacle is over. German scholars, those 'stumbling lemurs', have been whistled off the stage long ago. The trains full of reservists are no longer accompanied by virgins fainting from pure jubilation. They no longer greet the people from the windows of the train with joyous smiles. Carrying their packs, they quietly trot along the streets where the public goes about its daily business with aggrieved visages.

In the prosaic atmosphere of pale day there sounds a different chorus—the hoarse cries of the vulture and the hyenas of the battlefield. Ten

An 1890 portrait of Rosa Luxemburg. At this time she was studying in Zurich with prominent Marxist intellectuals. Courtesy of the Library of Congress, Prints and Photographs Division (LC-USZ62-122266).

thousand tarpaulins guaranteed up to regulations! A hundred thousand kilos of bacon, cocoa powder, coffee-substitute—c.o.d, immediate delivery! Hand grenades, lathes, cartridge pouches, marriage bureaus for widows of the fallen, leather belts, jobbers for war orders—serious offers only! The cannon fodder loaded onto trains in August and September is mouldering in the killing fields of Belgium, the Vosges, and Masurian Lakes where the profits are springing up like weeds. It's a question of getting the harvest into the barn quickly. Across the ocean stretch thousands of greedy hands to snatch it up.

Business thrives in the ruins. Cities become piles of ruins; villages become cemeteries; countries, deserts; populations are beggared; churches, horse stalls. International law, treaties, and alliances, the most sacred words and the highest authority have been torn in shreds. Every sovereign 'by the grace of God' is called a rogue and lying scoundrel by his cousin on the other side. Every diplomat is a cunning rascal to his colleagues in the other party. Every government sees every other as dooming its own people and worthy only of universal contempt. There are food riots in Venice, in Lisbon, Moscow, Singapore. There is plague in Russia, and misery and despair everywhere.

Violated, dishonoured, wading in blood, dripping filth—there stands bourgeois society. This is it [in reality]. Not all spic and span and moral, with pretence to culture, philosophy, ethics, order, peace, and the rule of law—but the ravening beast, the witches' sabbath of anarchy, a plague to culture and humanity. Thus it reveals itself in its true, its naked form.

In the midst of this witches' sabbath a catastrophe of world-historical proportions has happened: International Social Democracy has capitulated. To deceive ourselves about it, to cover it up, would be the most foolish, the most fatal thing the proletariat could do. Marx says: '. . . the democrat (that is, the petty bourgeois revolutionary) [comes] out of the most shameful

defeats as unmarked as he naively went into them; he comes away with the newly gained conviction that he must be victorious, not that he or his party ought to give up the old principles, but that conditions ought to accommodate him.' The modern proletariat comes out of historical tests differently. Its tasks and its errors are both gigantic: no prescription, no schema valid for every case, no infallible leader to show it the path to follow. Historical experience is its only school mistress. Its thorny way to self-emancipation is paved not only with immeasurable suffering but also with countless errors. The aim of its journey—its emancipation depends on this—is whether the proletariat can learn from its own errors. Self-criticism, remorseless, cruel, and going to the core of things is the life's breath and light of the proletarian movement. The fall of the socialist proletariat in the present world war is unprecedented. It is a misfortune for humanity. But socialism will be lost only if the international proletariat fails to measure the depth of this fall, if it refuses to learn from it.

The last forty-five year period in the development of the modern labour movement now stands in doubt. What we are experiencing in this critique is a closing of accounts for what will soon be half a century of work at our posts. The grave of the Paris Commune ended the first phase of the European labour movement as well as the First International.[3] Since then there began a new phase. In place of spontaneous revolutions, risings, and barricades, after which the proletariat each time fell back into passivity, there began the systematic daily struggle, the exploitation of bourgeois parliamentarianism, mass organizations, the marriage of the economic with the political struggle, and that of socialist ideals with stubborn defence of immediate daily interests. For the first time the polestar of strict scientific teachings lit the way for the proletariat and for its emancipation. Instead of sects, schools, utopias, and isolated experiments in various countries, there arose a uniform, international theoretical basis which bound countries together like the strands of a rope. Marxist knowledge gave the working class of the entire world a compass by which it can make sense of the welter of daily events and by which it can always plot the right course to take to the fixed and final goal. . . .

One thing is certain. The world war is a turning point. It is foolish and mad to imagine that we need only survive the war, like a rabbit waiting out the storm under a bush, in order to fall happily back into the old routine once it is over. The world war has altered the conditions of our struggle and, most of all, it has changed us. Not that the basic law of capitalist development, the life-and-death war between capital and labour, will experience any amelioration. But now, in the midst of the war, the masks are falling and the old familiar visages smirk at us. The tempo of development has received a mighty jolt from the eruption of the volcano of imperialism. The violence of the conflicts in the bosom of society, the enormousness of the tasks that tower up before the socialist proletariat—these make everything that has transpired in the history of the workers' movement seem a pleasant idyll.

Historically, this war was ordained to thrust forward the cause of the proletariat. . . . It was ordained to drive the German proletariat to the pinnacle of the nation and thereby begin to organize the international and universal conflict between capital and labour for political power within the state.

But to push ahead to the victory of socialism we need a strong, activist, educated proletariat, and masses whose power lies in intellectual culture as well as numbers. These masses are being decimated by the world war. The flower of our mature and youthful strength, hundreds of thousands of whom were socialistically schooled in England, France, Belgium, Germany, and Russia, the product of decades of educational and agitational training, and other hundreds of thousands who could be won for socialism tomorrow, fall and moulder on the miserable battlefields. The fruits of decades of sacrifice and the efforts of generations are destroyed in a few weeks. The key troops of the international proletariat are torn up by the roots.

The blood-letting of the June Days [1848] paralyzed the French workers' movement for a decade and a half. Then the blood-letting of the Commune massacres again retarded it for more than a decade. What is now occurring is an unprecedented mass slaughter that is reducing the adult working population of all the leading civilized countries to women, old people, and cripples. This blood-letting threatens to bleed the European workers' movement to death. Another such world war and the outlook for socialism will be buried beneath the rubble heaped up by imperialist barbarism. . . .

The world war today is demonstrably not only murder on a grand scale; it is also suicide of the working classes of Europe. The soldiers of socialism, the proletarians of England, France, Germany, Russia, and Belgium have for months been killing one another at the behest of capital. They are driving the cold steel of murder into each other's hearts. Locked in the embrace of death, they tumble into a common grave.

'Deutschland, Deutschland über Alles! Long live democracy! Long live the Tsar and Slavdom! Ten thousand tarpaulins guaranteed up to regulations! A hundred thousand kilos of bacon, coffee-substitute for immediate delivery!'. . . Dividends are rising, and the proletarians are falling. And with every one there sinks into the grave a fighter of the future, a soldier of the revolution, mankind's saviour from the yoke of capitalism.

The madness will cease and the bloody demons of hell will vanish only when workers in Germany and France, England and Russia finally awake from their stupor, extend to each other a brotherly hand, and drown out the bestial chorus of imperialist war-mongers and the shrill cry of capitalist hyenas with labour's old and mighty battle cry:

Proletarians of all lands, unite!

Notes

1. Six weeks was the time allotted for victory on the Western Front by the Schlieffen Plan. The German general staff was forced to scrap the plan in October 1914 as the war of movement swiftly evolved into a war of attrition.

2. For three days in April 1903 Kishinev, in the Russian Empire, was the scene of anti-Jewish riots. According to an official report, more than fifty Jews were killed and over 500 injured; hundreds of homes and shops were vandalized.

Local authorities did little to prevent the anti-Semitic violence.

3. At the end of the Franco–Prussian War of 1870–71 Parisians revolted against the French government. For ten weeks representatives of the working class, the Commune, ruled Paris. However, the government retook the capital after violent street fighting. The First International, founded by Karl Marx in 1864, was accused of directing the Commune.

Study Question

1. What do you think were the most important factors which induced soldiers to continue to fight, even when the situation seemed hopeless?

V.I. LENIN

Frustration with Russia's poor performance in the Russo–Japanese war combined with latent tensions created by late industrialization and weak leadership to produce the necessary conditions for a revolutionary uprising in Russia in 1904 and 1905. Bolshevik leaders, including Lenin, saw this as the first salvo in a great proletarian uprising. However, by late 1905 relatively

minor concessions by the Tsar in combination with a strong showing of military power induced many of the more moderate elements of the revolution to surrender. The failure of the 1905 revolution left many of the more radical Bolsheviks disillusioned with the moderate reformers. The following call to arms was written before Lenin's return to Russia in late 1905.

THE BEGINNING OF THE REVOLUTION IN RUSSIA

Geneva, Wednesday, January 25

Events of the greatest historical importance are developing in Russia. The proletariat has risen against tsarism. The proletariat was driven to revolt by the government. There can hardly be any doubt now that the government deliberately allowed the strike movement to develop and a wide demonstration to be started more or less without hindrance in

order to bring matters to a point where military force could be used. Its manoeuvre was successful. Thousands of killed and wounded—such is the toll of Bloody Sunday, January 9, in St Petersburg. The army defeated unarmed workers, women, and children. The army vanquished the enemy by shooting prostrate workers. 'We have taught them a good lesson!' the tsar's henchmen and their

European flunkeys from among the conservative bourgeoisie say with consummate cynicism.

Yes, it was a great lesson, one which the Russian proletariat will not forget. The most uneducated, backward sections of the working class, who naïvely trusted the tsar and sincerely wished to put peacefully before 'the tsar himself' the petition of a tormented people, were all taught a lesson by the troops led by the tsar or his uncle, the Grand Duke Vladimir.

The working class has received a momentous lesson in civil war; the revolutionary education of the proletariat made more progress in one day than it could have made in months and years of drab, humdrum, wretched existence. The slogan of the heroic St Petersburg proletariat, 'Death or freedom!' is reverberating throughout Russia. Events are developing with astonishing rapidity. The general strike in St Petersburg is spreading. All industrial, public, and political activities are paralysed. On Monday, January 10, still more violent clashes occurred between the workers and the military. Contrary to the mendacious government reports, blood is flowing in many parts of the capital. The workers of Kolpino are rising. The proletariat is arming itself and the people. The workers are said to have seized the Sestroretsk Arsenal. They are providing themselves with revolvers, forging their tools into weapons, and procuring bombs for a desperate bid for freedom. The general strike is spreading to the provinces. Ten thousand have already ceased work in Moscow, and a general strike has been called there for tomorrow (Thursday, January 13). An uprising has broken out in Riga. The workers are demonstrating in Lodz, an uprising is being prepared in Warsaw, proletarian demonstrations are taking place in Helsingfors. Unrest is growing among the workers and the strike is spreading in Baku, Odessa, Kiev, Kharkov, Koyno, and Vilna. In Sevastopol, the naval stores and arsenals are ablaze, and the troops refuse to shoot at the mutineers. Strikes in Revel and in Saratov. Workers

W.A. Rogers, an American cartoonist, illustrates Lenin and Trotsky as lizards. Rogers was criticizing the upper class fascination with Bolshevism.

and reservists clash with the troops in Radom.

The revolution is spreading. The government is beginning to lose its head. From the policy of bloody repression it is attempting to change over to economic concessions and to save itself by throwing a sop to the workers or promising the nine-hour day. But the lesson of Bloody Sunday cannot be forgotten. The demand of the insurgent St Petersburg workers—the immediate convocation of a Constituent Assembly on the basis of universal, direct, and equal suffrage by secret ballot—must become the demand of all the striking workers. Immediate overthrow of the government—this was the slogan with which even the St Petersburg workers who had believed in the tsar answered the massacre of January 9; they answered through their leader, the priest Georgi Gapon, who declared after that bloody day: 'We no longer have a tsar. A river of blood divides the tsar from the people. Long live the fight for freedom!'

Long live the revolutionary proletariat! say we. The general strike is rousing and rallying increasing masses of the working class and the urban poor. The arming of the people is becoming an immediate task of the revolutionary moment.

Only an armed people can be the real bulwark of popular liberty. The sooner the proletariat succeeds in arming, and the longer it holds its fighting positions as striker and revolutionary, the sooner will the army begin to waver; more and more soldiers will at last begin to realise what they are doing and they will join sides with the people against the fiends, against the tyrant, against the murderers of defenceless workers and of their wives and children. No matter what the outcome of the present uprising in St Petersburg may be, it will, in any case, be the first step to a wider, more conscious, better organised uprising. The government may possibly succeed in putting off the day of reckoning, but the postponement will only make the next step of the revolutionary onset more stupendous. This will only mean that the Social-Democrats will take advantage of this postponement to rally the organised fighters and spread the news about the start made by the St Petersburg workers. The proletariat will join in the struggle, it will quit mill and factory and will prepare arms for itself. The slogans of the struggle for freedom will be carried more and more widely into the midst of the urban poor and of the millions of peasants. Revolutionary committees will be set up at every factory, in every city district, in every large village. The people in revolt will overthrow all the government institutions of the tsarist autocracy and proclaim the immediate convocation of a Constituent Assembly.

The immediate arming of the workers and of all citizens in general, the preparation and organisation of the revolutionary forces for overthrowing the government authorities and institutions—this is the practical basis on which revolutionaries of every variety can and must unite to strike the common blow. The proletariat must always pursue its own independent path, never weakening its connection with the Social-Democratic Party, always bearing in mind its great, ultimate objective, which is to rid mankind of all exploitation. But this independence of the Social Democratic proletarian party will never cause us to forget the importance of a common revolutionary onset at the moment of actual revolution. We Social-Democrats can and must act independently of the bourgeois-democratic revolutionaries and guard the class independence of the proletariat. But we must go hand in hand with them during the up rising, when direct blows are being struck at tsarism, when resistance is offered the troops, when the bastilles of the accursed enemy of the entire Russian people are stormed.

The proletariat of the whole world is now looking eagerly towards the proletariat of Russia. The overthrow of tsarism in Russia, so valiantly begun by our working class, will be the turning-point in the history of all countries; it will facilitate the task of the workers of all nations, in all states, in all parts of the globe. Let, therefore, every Social-Democrat, every class-conscious worker bear in mind the immense tasks of the broad popular struggle that now rest upon his shoulders. Let him not forget that he represents also the needs and interests of the whole peasantry, of all who toil, of all who are exploited, of the whole people against their enemy. The proletarian heroes of St Petersburg now stand as an example to all.

Long live the revolution!

Long live the insurgent proletariat!

Study Question

1. What were the most important reasons for the failure of the uprising of 1905?

NIKITA KHRUSHCHEV

Nikita Sergeyevich Khrushchev (1894–1971) joined the Bolsheviks in 1918 and became a member of the CPSU Central Committee in 1934. Khrushchev participated in Stalin's purges and earned his complete trust. After 1939 Khrushchev became a full member of the Politburo and remained a loyal supporter until Stalin's death in 1953. In 1956 he emerged victorious from the power struggle that took place after Stalin's death. At the Twentieth Party Congress in 1956 he delivered a secret report denouncing Stalin's policies and personality. The following excerpt from Khrushchev's memoirs recalls the Fifteenth Party Congress in 1927—the final congress before Stalin's consolidation of power.

KHRUSHCHEV REMEMBERS

In 1927 I attended—again, as a delegate from the Yuzovka Party organization—the Fifteenth Party Congress, at which Stalin and his supporters squared off against the Zinovievites[1] or 'Leningrad opposition' as they were then called. I remember we used to say that even the sparrows were chirping the news to the man in the street that a schism had formed in the Party. Our delegation was again quartered in the House of Soviets at Number 3, Karetny Row. Shortly after we arrived in Moscow, we were told that Yakov Arkadyevich Yakovlev was coming by to talk to us about certain developments in the Party and to warn us about the situation that was likely to arise at the Congress. I think Yakovlev was one of Sergo Ordzhonikidze's deputies. We knew Yakovlev must be coming to see us on factional business because we were told not to let anyone into the meeting except members of the Ukrainian delegations. We also realized that Yakovlev was passing on to us confidential information and instructions directly from Stalin himself. Yakovlev explained where we differed with the Zinovievites and told us what we were to do. In other words, he prepared us to carry out factional work against the Zinoviev-Kamenev opposition which was then gathering force. Zinoviev was Chairman of the Comintern, the international Communist organization which steered the course of the world revolution. As the main person in the international Communist movement, Zinoviev commanded much authority and prestige. Yakovlev explained that Zinoviev was to be co-speaker with Stalin at the Congress. (He had given the General Report after Lenin's death and had been co-speaker with Stalin at the previous Party Congress, the Fourteenth, in 1925.) Yakovlev told us that the Leningrad delegation to the Fifteenth Congress had written a letter to the Congress Presidium demanding, on the basis of the Party Statutes, that Zinoviev once again be given equal time with Stalin.

When the Congress began we found that once again we had the central place in the hall. On our left were the Leningraders, and on our right was the Moscow delegation. We were in contact with the Moscow Party workers, coordinating with them our activities against the Leningrad opposition. Discussions and arguments were going on everywhere, formal and informal in large groups and small during the sessions and during the recesses, inside St George's Hall and out in the corridors.

I was distressed to find my old comrade Abramson in the enemy camp. He had been the editor of the newspaper *The Dictatorship of Labour* in Yuzovka when I returned from the army in 1922. Now he was working in Leningrad as the secretary of some district committee. He was a good Communist, but like all Leningraders, he was a Zinovievite. The Zinovievites had also added Badayev and Nikolayeva to their delegation, so that the opposition might swing more weight at the Congress. These were good active Party members. They're all dead now.

Stalin, Rykov, and Bukharin[2] spoke for the Central Committee line—that is, Stalin's line. There was the Central Committee line on one side and the opposition on the other. There was nothing in between.

A word about Bukharin. He was much respected and very popular. I had seen him and heard him speak back in 1919 when I was serving in the Red Army. As Secretary of our unit's Party cell I had been invited to a meeting of the active Party members in Kursk Province at which Bukharin gave a speech. Everyone was very pleased with him, and I was absolutely spellbound. He had an appealing personality and a strong democratic spirit. Later I met some comrades who had worked with him—simple, progressive Communists from Moscow who were more or less at my level of political development. They told me how Bukharin had lived with them in their dormitory and eaten with them at their mess at the same table. This impressed me very much. Bukharin was also the editor of *Pravda*[3]. He was the Party's chief theoretician. Lenin always spoke affectionately of him as 'Our Bukharchik'. On Lenin's instructions he wrote *The A–B–C of Communism*, and everyone who joined the Party learned Marxist-Leninist science by studying Bukharin's work. In short, Bukharin was much beloved in the Party.

During the Fifteenth Party Congress some delegation or other presented the Congress Presidium with a steel broom. Rykov, who was Chairman of the Presidium, made a speech, saying, 'I hereby present this steel broom to Comrade Stalin so that he may sweep away our enemies.' There was a burst of appreciative applause and laughter. Rykov himself broke into a smile and then laughed, too. He obviously trusted Stalin to use the broom wisely, for the good of the Party, against anti-Party elements and opponents of the General Line. Rykov could hardly have foreseen that he, too, would be swept away by this same broom which he handed over to Stalin in 1927.

At the time of the Fifteenth Party Congress we had no doubt in our minds that Stalin and his supporters were right, and that the opposition was wrong. I still think that Stalin's ideological position was basically correct. We realized that a merciless struggle against the opposition was unavoidable. We justified what was happening in a lumberjack's terms: when you chop down a forest, the chips fly. After all, it was no accident that Stalin held the leading position in the Party, and it was no accident that the Party supported him against such powerful opponents as the Trotskyites, Zinovievites and later the right–left bloc of Syrtsov and Lominadze. Stalin was a powerful personality, and he had contributed greatly to the mobilization of the Party's forces for the reconstruction of our industry and agriculture and the strengthening of our army. It shouldn't be overlooked that Stalin's name hadn't been very widely known among the masses in the first years of the Revolution. He had come a long way in a short time, and he had brought our Party and our people with him.

Notes

1. Grigori Zinoviev sided with Lenin in the 1903 Social-Democratic Party split. After the Russian Revolution, he led the Comintern (1919–26) and served in the Politburo (1921–26). In 1935 he was tried for alleged involvement in the death of Sergei Kirov. In 1936 Zinoviev, Lev Kamenev, and others were tried for treason and executed.

2. Aleksei Rykov succeeded Lenin as Prime Minister of the Soviet Union. Nikolai Bukharin was the Party's greatest intellectual and a close friend of Lenin. They were tried in 1938, condemned, and shot.

3. *Truth*—the primary newspaper of the Communist Party of the Soviet Union.

> **Study Question**
>
> 1. Khrushchev argued that Stalin's call for a merciless purge of all opposition was both necessary and valid in the context of preserving the revolution. Was Khrushchev correct?

SUN YAT-SEN

Sun Yat-sen[1] (1866–1925) became familiar with Western ideas and religions at an Anglican boys' school in Honolulu. During the early 1890s Sun became increasingly involved in anti-Qing activities. With the onset of the Sino–Japanese War, Sun felt that the Qing dynasty was vulnerable enough to be overthrown. To achieve this he formed the 'Society for Regenerating China'.[2] However, the Society's 1895 uprising ended in failure. After ten years of fundraising activities among overseas Chinese communities, Sun settled in Japan in 1905, at which time the Revive China Society merged with several other movements to become the Chinese Revolutionary Alliance.[3] Between 1905 and 1911 eight more uprisings failed,[4] but on 10 October 1911 a garrison of soldiers in Wuchang rebelled and declared China to be a republic. At the time of the Wuchang rebellion Sun was in the United States. He returned to China in December 1911 and was sworn in as Provisional President of the Chinese Republic. Within two months Sun resigned his post in favour of Yuan Shikai—a former Qing general. Sun remained as director of the Guomindang, a political party that was founded in 1912 as the political successor of the Revolutionary Alliance. In 1917 Sun established a new government in Canton, but controlled only a small part of China. He wrote Fundamentals of National Reconstruction in 1923.

FUNDAMENTALS OF NATIONAL RECONSTRUCTION

Following China's war with France (1883–84) I made up my mind to devote myself to the revolution. In 1895 I started the first insurrection in Canton and the revolution of 1911 culminated in the establishment of the Republic. Up to the present the task of revolution, however, has not yet been completed. A span of thirty-seven years of my revolutionary work is to be chronicled by future historians from all manner of facts and incidents. An outline sketch is given below.

I. Principles of Revolution. The term Kemin, or revolution, was first used by Confucius. Incidents of a revolutionary nature repeatedly happened in Chinese history after Tang (founder of the Shang Dynasty, 1766 BCE) and Wu (founder of the Zhou Dynasty, 1122 BCE). In Europe revolutionary tides surged in the seventeenth and eighteenth centuries and they have since spread over the whole world. In due course they created republics, they conferred constitutions on monarchies. The principles which I have held in promoting the Chinese revolution were in some cases copied from our traditional ideals, in other cases modeled on European theory and experience, and in still

A US immigration photograph of Sun Yat-sen taken in 1910 upon his arrival in San Francisco from Korea. The immigration department opened an investigation under the Chinese Exclusion Acts. Courtesy of the National Archives at San Francisco.

others formulated according to original and self-developed theories. They are described as follows:

a. Principle of Nationalism. Revelations of Chinese history prove that the Chinese as a people are independent in spirit and in conduct. Coerced into touch with other people, they could at times live in peace with them by maintaining friendly relations and at others assimilate them as the result of propinquity. During the periods when their political and military prowess declined, they could not escape for the time from the fate of a conquered nation, but they could eventually vigorously reassert themselves. Thus the Mongol rule of China (1260–1333 CE), lasting nearly a hundred years was finally overthrown by Tai Tse of the Ming dynasty and his loyal followers. So in our own time was the Manchu yoke thrown off by the Chinese. Nationalistic ideas in China did not come from a foreign source; they were inherited from our remote forefathers. Upon this legacy is based my principle of nationalism, and where

necessary, I have developed it and amplified and improved upon it. No vengeance has been inflicted on the Manchus and we have endeavoured to live side by side with them on an equal footing. This is our nationalistic policy toward races within our national boundaries. Externally, we should strive to maintain independence in the family of nations, and to spread our indigenous civilization as well as to enrich it by absorbing what is best in world civilization, with the hope that we may forge ahead with other nations towards the goal of ideal brotherhood.

b. Principle of Democracy. In ancient China we had the Emperor Yao (2357–2258 BCE) and Emperor Shun (2258–2206 BCE) who departed from the hereditary system and chose their successors. We also had Tang and Wu who overthrew kingdoms by revolution. Preserved in our books are such sayings as 'Heaven sees as the people see'; 'Heaven hears as the people hear'; 'We have heard of a person named Zhou having been slain, we have not heard of a monarch having been murdered'; 'The people are most important, while the king is of the least importance.' All these sayings ring with democratic sentiments. Since we have had only ideas about popular rights, and no democratic system has been evolved, we have to go to Europe and America for a republican form of government. There some countries have become republics and others have adopted constitutional monarchism, under which royal power has shrunk in the face of the rising demand for popular rights. Though hereditary monarchs have not yet disappeared, they are but vestiges and shadows of their former selves.

All through my revolutionary career I have held the view that China must be made a republic. There are three reasons. First, from a theoretical point of view, there is no ground for preserving a monarchical form of government, since it is widely recognized that the people constitute the foundation of a nation and they are all equal in their own country. In the second place, under

Manchu occupation the Chinese were forced into the position of the vanquished and suffered oppression for more than two hundred and sixty years. While a constitutional monarchy may not arouse deep resentment in other countries and can maintain itself for the time being, it will be an impossibility in China. This is from a historical point of view. A third reason may be advanced with an eye on the future of the nation. That in China prolonged periods of disorder usually followed a revolution was due to the desire of every insurgent to be a king and to his subsequent contention for the throne. If a republican government is adopted, there will be no contention. . . .

My second decision is that a constitution must be adopted to ensure good government. The true meaning of constitutionalism was discovered by Montesquieu. The threefold separation of the legislative, judicial, and executive powers as advocated by him was accepted in every constitutional country in Europe. On a tour of Europe and America I made a close study of their governments and laws and took note of their shortcomings as well as their advantages. The shortcomings of election, for instance, are not incurable. In the past China had two significant systems of examination and censoring and they can be of avail where the Western system of government and law falls short. I therefore advocate that the examinative and censorial powers should be placed on the same level with legislative, judicial, and executive, thereby resulting in the five-fold separation of powers. On top of that, the system of the people's direct political powers should be adopted in order that the provision that the sovereign power is vested in the people may become a reality. In this way my principle of democracy may be carried out satisfactorily.

c. Principle of Livelihood. With the invention of modern machines, the phenomenon of uneven distribution of wealth in the West has become all the more marked. Intensified by crosscurrents, economic revolution was flaring up more ferociously than political revolution. This situation was scarcely noticed by our fellow-countrymen thirty years ago. On my tour of Europe and America, I saw with my own eyes the instability of their economic structure and the deep concern of their leaders in groping for a solution. I felt that, although the disparity of wealth under our economic organization is not so great as in the West, the difference is only in degree, not in character. The situation will become more acute when the West extends its economic influence to China. We must form plans beforehand in order to cope with the situation. After comparing various schools of economic thought, I have come to the realization that the principle of state ownership is most profound, reliable, and practical. Moreover, it will forestall in China difficulties that have already caused much anxiety in the West. I have therefore decided to enforce the principle of the people's livelihood simultaneously with the principles of nationalism and democracy, with the hope to achieve our political objective and nip economic unrest in the bud.

To sum up, my revolutionary principles in a nutshell consist in the Three Principles of the People and the Five Power Constitution. Those who have a clear knowledge of the general tendency of the world and the conditions in China will agree that my views are practical and must be put in practice.

II. Fundamentals of Revolution. In the age of autocracy, the masses of the people were fettered in spirit and body so that emancipation seemed impossible. Those who worked for the welfare of the people and were willing to sacrifice themselves for the success of revolution not only did not receive assistance from the people but were also ridiculed and disparaged. Much as they desired to be the guides of the people, they proceeded without followers. Much as they desired to be the vanguards, they advanced without reinforcement.

It becomes necessary that, apart from destroying enemy influence, those engaged in revolution should take care to develop the constructive ability of the people. A revolutionary program is therefore indispensable.

According to my plan, the progress of our revolution should be regulated and divided into three stages: First, military rule; second, political tutelage; third, constitutional government. The first stage is a period of destruction, during which military rule is installed. The revolutionary army is to break down (as it did) Manchu despotism, sweep away official corruptions, and reform vicious customs.

The second stage is a transitional period, during which a provisional constitution (not the present one) will be promulgated. Its object is to build a local self-government system for the development of democracy. The Hsien or district will be unit of self-government. When disbanded troops are disposed of and fighting ceases, every district should accept the provisional constitution, which will regulate the rights and duties of the people and the administrative powers of the revolutionary government. It will be in force for three years, at the end of which period the people will choose their district magistrates. Even before the expiration of the period, the people in a district may be empowered to choose their own magistrate and become a complete self-governing body. . . .

The third stage, which marks the completion of national reconstruction, will usher in constitutional government. During this period the self-governing bodies in the various districts should exercise the direct political powers of the people. In district political affairs citizens should have the rights of universal suffrage, initiative, referendum, and recall. In national political affairs they should, while directly exercising the right of election, delegate the three other rights to their representatives in the People's Congress. This period of constitutional government marks the completion of national reconstruction and the successful conclusion of the revolution.

Notes

1. Sun Chung-Shan/Sun Zhong-shan/Sun Wen (Mandarin).
2. Often referred to simply as the Revive China Society—Hsing Chung Hui/Xing Zhong Hui. The Society was founded in Hawaii but headquartered in Hong Kong.
3. T'ung Meng Hui/Tongmeng Hui.
4. In addition to these, the uprising of 1895 failed, as did an uprising backed by Sun in 1900 during the Boxer Rebellion. Thus the Wuchang uprising of October 1911, which ultimately succeeded, was the eleventh attempt to overthrow the Qing.

Study Question

1. To what extent were Sun's 'Fundamentals' applicable given the state of China in 1923?

SOONG CHING-LING

Soong Ching-ling (1893–1981) was born in Shanghai. After graduation she attended Wesleyan College in the United States and received her degree in 1913. Soong took over her sister Ai-ling's job as secretary to Sun Yat-sen upon returning home. Sun and Soong were married in 1915. Her youngest sister Mei-ling eventually married Sun's deputy Chiang Kai-shek. Soong Ching-ling worked alongside her husband both to preserve and to advance the revolution in China. After Sun's death in 1925 Soong devoted herself to preserving his ideals, a position which brought her into direct opposition to Chiang Kai-shek. Between 1932 and her death in 1981, Soong founded the China League for Civil Rights, the China Defence League, and the China Welfare Institute. In 1981 she was made an honourary Chairman of the People's Republic. The following document was written in August 1927 as Soong and the more radical faction of the Guomindang began to split with Chiang Kai-shek over his recent crackdown on the Chinese Communist Party and its members.

THE STRUGGLE FOR NEW CHINA

If China is to survive as an independent country in the modern struggle of nations, her semi-feudal conditions of life must be fundamentally changed and a modern state created to replace the medieval system that has existed for more than a thousand years. This task needs to be done by the method of revolution, if only because the alternative method of gradualness postulates a period of time which is denied the nation by both the cancerous force of Chinese militarism eating from inside and foreign imperialism ravaging from outside.

To forge a fit instrument of revolution, Sun Yat-sen reorganized the Guomindang on a revolutionary basis in the winter of 1924, and reinforced the 'Three People's Principles' by formulating the 'Three Great Policies' of action. The first of these policies calls for the inclusion and support of the nation's workers and peasants in the work of the revolution. These two massive elements of the national population—one carrying on and sustaining the life of organized society and the other producing food on which man lives—represent nearly 90 per cent of the nation. And, in view of their numerical strength and the fact that the masses ought to be the chief beneficiaries of the revolution, they must be drawn into it if there is to be life and reality in the movement.

The second of the policies laid down by Sun recognizes the necessity of cooperation between the Guomindang and members of the

Soong Ching-ling in 1937 after her break with Chiang Kai-shek and the more right wing elements of the Nationalist Party. New York World-Telegram and the Sun Newspaper Photograph Collection. Courtesy of the Library of Congress, Prints and Photographs Division (LC-USZ62-132824).

Chinese Communist Party during the period of revolutionary struggle with Chinese militarism and foreign imperialism. The Chinese Communist Party is indubitably the most dynamic of all internal revolutionary forces in China; and its influence over the masses and power of propaganda enabled the Guomindang to control its military elements and subordinate them to the civil authorities.

The third of Sun Yat-sen's policies deals with the profoundly important question of the connection of the Soviet Union with the Guomindang. The connection is sometimes justified on the ground that the Soviet Union has no unequal treaties with China. This, however, was a minor consideration in Sun's view of the matter. In formulating the third policy, he was moved by larger reasons. Just as he regarded the Chinese Communist Party as the most active revolutionary force in China, so he envisaged the Soviet Union as the most powerful revolutionary force in the world; and he believed that a right correlation by the Guomindang of these two outstanding revolutionary forces would signally assist the revolution to realize national independence for China. Sun was not afraid or ashamed to avow this revolutionary thesis, since he knew that the revolutionary role played by France, in the person of Lafayette in the American Revolution, was repeated in many a chapter in the history of freedom.

It was a statesmanlike application of these three policies of Sun and the correlation of the forces deriving from them that enabled the Guomindang power to put an end to ten years of disorder and confusion in Canton, and to create and finance revolutionary armies that conquered their way to the historic line of the Yangtze and—after shattering the main force of the Fengtien army[1] in Honan—penetrated to the bank of the Yellow River. Besides its striking administrative work at Canton and the great military achievement of the Northern Expedition, the Guomindang scored memorable successes in a field in which China has always known defeat and humiliation. It raised the international status of China to a point never attained before, compelling the representatives of great powers to meet the foreign minister of Nationalist China as an equal in council, and causing men in high as well as in the scattered places of the earth to heed his statements on

Nationalist aims and aspirations. In those days— it is but three months since—the Guomindang may have been hated and even feared, but none dared to despise it.

Today it is otherwise. The famous name of the Nationalist Government is now sunk to the level of other semi-feudal remnants in the North; and those who have been entrusted by the revolution with leadership are allowing the new militarist clique in the Yangtze to capture and utilize the Guomindang; and they themselves are now becoming or are about to become, the secretaries and clerks of the new Caesar. No one fears and no one respects the Guomindang, which is now despised even by foes who used to blanch and flee at the sound of its armies on the march.

What is the cause for this startling change in values and in men's opinions? The answer is to be found in the work of the reaction in Canton, in Nanking and Shanghai, in Changsha, and lastly in Wuhan. Peasants and their leaders, workers, and their leaders, Communists and their leaders, who laboured in order that the Guomindang power might reach the Yangtze, have been ruthlessly and wantonly killed; and Soviet workers who gave of their best to the Guomindang and who men, in later and juster days, will adjudge to have deserved well of Nationalist China, have been forced to leave, because so-called 'leaders' of the Guomindang—petty politicians reverting to type—believe that they can violate Sun Yat-sen's Three Policies and rely on the new militarism to carry out the stupendous task of the revolution.

They will fail and go the way of those before them who have sought to rule in like fashion. But they must not be permitted to involve in their own ultimate ruin the heritage left to us by Sun. His true followers must seek to rescue the real Guomindang from the degradation of becoming a mere secretariat of the new militarist clique emerging out of the intrigues and disloyalties now afoot.

My own course is clear. Accepting the thesis that the Three Policies are an essential part of the thought and technique of the revolution, I draw the conclusion that real nationalist success in the struggle with Chinese militarism and foreign imperialism is possible only by a right correlation, under Guomindang leadership, of the revolutionary forces issuing from the Three Policies. As the reaction led by pseudo-leaders of the Guomindang endangers the Third Policy, it is necessary for the revolutionary wing of the Guomindang—the group with which Sun would today be identified had he been alive—to leave no doubt in the Soviet mind that, though some have crossed over to reaction and counter-revolution, there are others who will continue true and steadfast to the Three Policies enunciated by him

for the guidance and advancement of the work of the revolution.

I go, therefore, to Moscow to explain this in person.

Note

1. The Fengtien army was controlled by a Manchurian warlord named Zhang Zuolin.

> **Study Question**
>
> 1. Based on your reading of Sun Yat-sen and Soong Ching-ling, did Soong remain faithful to Sun's original ideas?

Li Dazhao

Li Dazhao[1] (1888–1927) was drawn to the study of Marxist theory after the Bolshevik victory in Russia. He is recognized as one of the founding members of the Chinese Communist Party (CCP) (along with Chen Duxiu) and maintained close ties between the CCP and the COMINTERN. Like many

Chinese modernizers Li had studied in Japan. He taught at Beijing University where he is credited with greatly influencing Mao Zedong. In the following essay, written in November 1918, Li discusses the global implications of the Bolshevik victory.

The Victory of Bolshevism

'Victory! Victory! The Allies have been victorious! Surrender! Surrender! Germany has surrendered!' These words are on the national flag bedecking every doorway, they can be seen in colour and can be indistinctly heard in the intonation of every voice. Men and women of the Allied powers run up and down the street in celebration of the victory, and in the city of Peking the soldiers of these nations loudly blast forth their triumphal songs. . . .

But let us think carefully as small citizens of the

world; to whom exactly does the present victory belong? Who has really surrendered? Whose is the achievement this time? And for whom do we celebrate? If we ponder over these questions, then not only will our non-fighting generals' show of strength and our shameless politicians' grasping of credit become senseless, but also the talk of the Allied nations, that the end of the war was brought about by their military forces defeating the military force of Germany. . . .

For the real cause of the ending of the war was not the vanquishing of the German military power by the Allied military power, but the vanquishing of German militarism by German socialism. It was not the German people who surrendered to the armed forces of the Allied powers, but the German Kaiser, militarists and militarism who surrendered to the new tides of the world. It was not the Allied nations, but the awakened minds of the German people that defeated German militarism. . . . The victory over German militarism does not belong to the Allied nations; even less does it belong to our factious military men who used participation in the war only as an excuse [for engaging in civil war], or to our opportunistic, cunningly manipulative politicians. It is the victory of humanitarianism, of pacifism; it is the victory of justice and liberty; it is the victory of Bolshevism; it is the victory of the red flag; it is the victory of the labour class of the world; and it is the victory of the twentieth century's new tide. Rather than give Wilson and others the credit for this achievement, we should give the credit to Lenin, Trotzky [sic], Collontay [Alexandra Kollontai], to Liebknecht, Scheidemann, and to Marx.[2]

Bolshevism is the ideology of the Russian Bolsheviki. . . . it is clear that their ideology is revolutionary socialism; their party is a revolutionary socialist party; and they follow the German socialist economist Marx as the founder of their doctrine. Their aim is to destroy the national boundaries which are obstacles to socialism at present, and to destroy the system of production in which profit is monopolized by the capitalist. Indeed, the real cause of this war was also the destruction of national boundaries. Since the present national boundaries cannot contain the expansion of the system of production brought about by capitalism, and since the resources within each nation are inadequate for the expansion of its productive power, the capitalist nations began depending on war to break down these boundaries, hoping to make all parts of the globe one single, coordinated economic organ.

. . . The Bolsheviki saw through this point; therefore they vigorously protested and proclaimed that the present war is a war of the Tsar, of the Kaiser, of kings and emperors that it is a war of capitalist governments, but it is not their war. Theirs is the war of classes, a war of all the world's proletariat and common people against the capitalists of the world. While they are opposed to war itself, they are at the same time not afraid of it. They hold that all men and women should work. All those who work should join a union, and there should be a central administrative soviet in each union. Such soviets then should organize all the governments of the world. . . . There will be only the joint soviets of labour, which will decide all matters. . . . They will unite the proletariat of the world, and create global freedom with their greatest, strongest power of resistance: first they will create a federation of European democracies, to serve as the foundation of a world federation. This is the ideology of the Bolsheviki. This is the new doctrine of the twentieth-century revolution.

. . . The pattern of the revolutions generally develops along the same line as that in Russia. The red flag flies everywhere, the soviets are established one after another. Call it revolution entirely à la Russe, or call it twentieth-century revolution. Such mighty rolling tides are indeed beyond the power of the present capitalist governments to prevent or to stop, for the mass movement of the twentieth century combines the whole of mankind in one great mass. The efforts of each individual within this great mass, following the example of some of them, will then be concentrated and become a great, irresistible social force. Whenever a disturbance in this worldwide social force occurs among the people, it will produce repercussions all over the earth, like storm clouds gathering before the wind and valleys echoing the mountains. In the course of such a world mass movement, all those dregs of history which can impede the progress of the new movement—such as emperors, nobles, warlords, bureaucrats, militarism, capitalism— will certainly be destroyed as though struck by a thunderbolt. . . . Although the word 'Bolshevism' was created by the Russians, the spirit it embodies can be regarded as that of a common awakening in the heart of each individual among mankind of the twentieth century. The victory of Bolshevism, therefore, is the victory of the spirit of common awakening in the heart of each individual among mankind in the twentieth century.

Notes

1. Li Ta-chao
2. Karl Liebknecht was a founding member of the German Communist Party, along with Rosa Luxemburg; Philipp Scheidemann was the Social Democrat who proclaimed the creation of the Weimar Republic.

Study Question

1. What was the most important factor that prevented revolutionary movements around the world from uniting in the years immediately following the First World War?

JAWAHARLAL NEHRU

Jawaharlal Nehru (1889–1964) was educated in Britain, attending Harrow and Cambridge. He became familiar with socialist doctrines while training to become a lawyer. On his return to India Nehru gradually came to appreciate the value of Gandhi's satyagraha *campaigns, though a number of ideological differences remained between the two men. In the 1920s he visited Moscow, gaining first-hand knowledge of the revolutionary transformation underway in the Soviet Union. In 1936 Nehru was elected to the leadership of the Indian National Congress, having clearly stated his commitment to Indian independence. As the following document indicates, however, his socialism was not universally shared by the Congress.*

THE SOCIALIST CREED

I am convinced that the only key to the solution of the world's problems and of India's problems lies in socialism, and when I use this word I do so not in a vague humanitarian way but in the scientific economic sense. Socialism is, however, something even more than an economic doctrine; it is a philosophy of life and as such also it appeals to me. I see no way of ending the poverty, the vast unemployment, the degradation and the subjection of the Indian people except through socialism. That involves vast and revolutionary changes in our political and social structure, the ending of vested interests in land and industry, as well as the feudal and autocratic Indian states system. That means the ending of private property, except in a restricted sense, and the replacement of the present profit system by a higher ideal of cooperative service. It means ultimately a change in our instincts and habits and desires. In short, it means a new civilization, radically different from the present capitalist order. Some glimpse we can have of this new civilization in the territories of the U.S.S.R. Much has happened there which has pained me greatly and with which I disagree, but

I look upon that great and fascinating unfolding of a new order and a new civilization as the most promising feature of our dismal age. If the future is full of hope it is largely because of Soviet Russia and what it has done, and I am convinced that, if some world catastrophe does not intervene, this new civilization will spread to other lands and put an end to the wars and conflicts which capitalism feeds.

I do not know how or when this new order will come to India. I imagine that every country will fashion it after its own way and fit it in with its national genius. But the essential basis of that order must remain and be a link in the world order that will emerge out of the present chaos.

Socialism is thus for me not merely an economic doctrine which I favor; it is a vital creed which I hold with all my head and heart. I work for Indian independence because the nationalist in me cannot tolerate an alien domination; I work for it even more because for me it is the inevitable step to social and economic change. I should like the Congress to become a socialist organization and to join hands with the other forces that in the world are working for the new civilization. But I realize that the majority in the Congress, as it is constituted today, may not be prepared to go this far. We are a nationalist organization and we think and work on the nationalist plane. It is evident enough now that this is too narrow even for the limited objective of political independence, and so we talk of the masses and their economic needs. But most of us hesitate, because of our nationalist backgrounds, to take a step which might frighten away some vested interests. Most of those interests are already ranged against us and we can expect little from them except opposition even in the political struggle.

Much as I wish for the advancement of socialism in this country, I have no desire to force the issue on the Congress and thereby create difficulties in the way of our struggle for independence. I shall cooperate gladly and with all the strength in me with all those who work for independence even though they do not agree with the socialist solution. But I shall do so stating my position frankly and hoping in course of time to convert the Congress and the country to it, for only thus can I see it achieving independence.

> **Study Question**
>
> 1. Why did socialism hold so much appeal among colonized nations?

Mustapha Kemal Atatürk

Mustapha Kemal Atatürk (1881–1938)[1] first gained prominence as a military leader. He was involved in the 1908 Young Turk uprising which attempted to modernize the Ottoman Empire along western lines. He fought for the Ottoman Empire during the First World War and, subsequently, for Turkish independence in the early 1920s. In 1923 Atatürk became the leader of the new Turkish Republic and launched an ambitious program of domestic reforms with the goal of creating a secular, democratic state. However, this was initially accomplished by one-party rule. The excerpt which follows addressed the decision to exclude the Ottoman Caliph from the political structure of the new state. The original speech was delivered over six days in 1927.

October 1927 Speech

After the proclamation of the Republic there were also persons and journalists in Constantinople who had the idea of making the Caliph[2] play a role. The newspapers published all sorts of rumours and contradictions about the dismissal of the Caliph which had already taken place or was going to. . . .

It was written that the Caliph, 'sitting at his writing desk', had made a statement to an editor of the newspaper 'Watan', that the Caliph enjoyed great popularity amongst all believers; that he received thousands of letters and telegrams from the Mohamedan[3] world, even from the remotest corners of Asia; that numerous delegations from many places came to him; and the attempt was made of giving the people to understand that the authority of the Caliphate was not of a nature easily to be shaken. Then it was affirmed that the Caliph would not abdicate until Islam had declared itself against him. Simultaneously it was said:

> 'The Government being absorbed in numerous interior questions has not yet been able to occupy itself with the rights of the Caliphate.'

> 'The world of Islam undoubtedly knows that the Government is very much occupied with interior questions and naturally finds that it has not yet been able to dedicate itself to the question of defining the rights of the Caliphate.'

Requesting us in such phrases to define the rights of the Caliphate, to a certain degree they threatened us by letting us know that the Mohamedan world, that had hitherto excused us, could act quite differently in future. On the other hand they tried to attract the attention of Islam for the purpose of inducing it to influence us on this question.

This article, which appeared in the journal 'Watan' dated the 9th November 1923, was followed by an open letter to the Caliph, which was published in the newspaper 'Tanin' on the 10th of the same month. In order to prove the extent to which the nation was agitated by the rumours which were circulated about the dismissal of the Caliph, they had invented in this letter, which was signed by Lutfi Fikri Bey, an incident which was said to have happened on board ship. As soon as the passengers heard the rumours they were seized by a feeling of unrest and sadness. Even those who did not know one another had given themselves up to long, frank discussions. A common anxiety had made them friends in a moment.

'I wish with all my heart,' said Lutfi Fikri Bey, 'and with all my soul that this rumour of dismissal were buried for ever; for such an event would be fatal to the whole world.' Lutfi Fikri Bey also tried to instil [sic] the following thoughts in the minds of the nation: 'We must state with surprise and regret that those who attack this moral treasure (he means the Caliphate) are neither strangers nor do they belong to those Mohamedan nations who are jealous of the Turks. It is ourselves, the Turks, who are making attempts that will lead to the loss of this treasure for ever.'

Strangers did not attack the Caliphate; it was the Turkish nation that could not protect itself from attacks. Those who attacked the Caliphate were not Mohamedan nations who were jealous of Turkey, but Mohamedan peoples who had fought under the flags of the English and French against the Turks at the Dardanelles, in Syria and the Irak.

For the purpose of easily attacking the Turkish nation, it was said that the abolition of the Caliphate, the maintenance of which they preferred, would be suicidal for the Turkish world, and they pretended that we Turks in proclaiming the Republic tried to abolish the Caliphate.

Such publications undoubtedly did not remain without effect. . . .

The chief editor of the 'Tanin' expressed his

views and reflections concerning the Caliphate in the following lines:

'No great sagacity is necessary to understand that if we lose the Caliphate, the Turkish State, comprising between five and ten million souls,[4] would have no longer any weight in the Mohamedan world, and that we would degrade ourselves in addition in the eyes of European diplomacy to the rank of a small state without any importance.'

'Is this a national way of thinking? Every Turk who really possesses national feeling must support the Caliphate with all his strength.'

As I have already explained my views concerning the Caliphate, I believe it unnecessary to submit these statements to another analysis. I shall restrict myself simply to saying that great sagacity is by no means required to understand that a form of government demanding an unconditional adherence to the Caliphate could not be a republic.

I now draw your attention to some other passages of the leading article in the 'Tanin'.

'To endanger the Caliphate, the heirdom of the Ottoman dynasty acquired for ever by Turkey, would apparently be an action which could by no means be in accord with reason, patriotism or national sentiment.'

The chief editor of the 'Tanin' had declared himself a republican; but a republican who wanted to see at the head of the republican government a member of the dynasty as Caliph. Without this, he said, the accomplished fact would not be in accord with reason, patriotism or national sentiment.

According to his opinion we were to protect the Caliphate in such a manner that would make it impossible for it ever to escape from us. The manoeuvres undertaken in this spirit had been wrecked . . .

The significance of these articles and the aim of these reasonings are easily to be explained to-day. To-morrow they will be understood still better. Do not suppose that the coming generations will be astonished that at the head of those who relentlessly attacked the Republic on the very day of its proclamation were exactly those who pretended to be republicans! On the contrary!

The enlightened republican sons of Turkey will have no difficulty in analysing and penetrating into the real mentality of these pretended republicans. They will easily understand that it was impossible to maintain a form of government which after having proclaimed itself a republic would have undertaken the obligation of preserving under the title of Caliph at its head a rotten dynasty, and this in a manner which would never have made its removal possible.

Notes

1. The surname 'Atatürk' was bestowed in 1934; it translates approximately to 'father of the Turkish people'.
2. The Caliph, literally 'successor to the prophet', had been the head of the Islamic Ottoman Empire. As Caliph he also claimed authority over all of the Muslim faithful. Thus, Atatürk's decision in 1924 to abolish the powers of the Caliphate was a key step towards the establishment of the secular state which he envisioned. However, the decision was a controversial one for many Muslims.
3. Muslim.
4. [Atatürk] According to the census of 1927, Turkey had nearly 14 million inhabitants.

Study Question

1. Why did Atatürk place so much emphasis on the creation of a secular state?

TIPS FOR ANALYSIS

What type of document is this and what insights does it provide?

The nature of the document very often alters the way in which it is written. An international treaty will be written in a very different way than a personal diary entry, which will likely be written in the first person. Read the document closely. The author will provide specific insights into the time period which will add to your understanding.

WEB RESOURCES

Marxists Internet Archive
http://www.marxists.org
Marx & Engels WWW Library
http://www.eng.fju.edu.tw/Literary_Criticism/marxism/marxism_links.html
Project Gutenberg [numerous Marxist writings in electronic form]
http://www.gutenberg.org/wiki/Main_Page
Internet Modern History Sourcebook: Asia since 1900
http://www.fordham.edu/halsall/mod/modsbook52.html

RECOMMENDED READING

Boris Pasternak, *Doctor Zhivago* (New York: Everyman's Library, 1991). Pasternak was awarded the Nobel Prize for *Doctor Zhivago* in 1958; he declined the honour due to controversy over the book in his homeland. (The book remained banned in the USSR until the Gorbachev era.) The novel, though not overtly critical, provides an honest look at modern Russian history and the upheavals of the revolutionary era through the life of Iurii Zhivago.

Su Tong (Tong Zhonggui), 'Wives and Concubines', in *Raise the Red Lantern: Three Novellas* (New York: Penguin, 1996). 'Wives and Concubines' is an examination of the domestic life and social values in a traditional Chinese household during the Republican era. Tong's novella relates the story of Lotus, a college student who leaves school to become the fourth concubine of a wealthy man.

Rabindranath Tagore, *The Home and the World* (New York: Penguin, 1996). Tagore, a Nobel Prize–winning Bengali author, sets *The Home & the World* in 1908 Bengal during the early years of the Swadeshi movement, exploring the first expressions of radical nationalism and the excitement they generated. Originally published in 1916, Tagore examines the impact of political awakening on traditional Indian society, and foreshadows the violent conflicts that erupted at partition.

Mo Yan, *Red Sorghum* (New York: Penguin, 1994). Set in the 1930s after the Japanese invasion of China, as the Chinese Communist Party (CCP) was fighting both the Guomindang (GMD) and the Japanese, Mo Yan's violent and gloomy novel portrays of one of the most brutal periods in Chinese history. Rather than presenting an idealized vision of the past, or a clear ideological statement, the author focuses simply on the struggle for survival during this period.

Recommended Viewing

Battleship Potemkin (USSR, 1925). Director: Sergei Eisenstein (Silent, B&W). Commissioned by the Soviet government, Eisenstein recreates the revolution of 1905, as told through the story of the crew of the *Potemkin*. Eisenstein ties the mutiny of the sailors on the battleship to the broader events in Odessa. Considered an early masterpiece of cinematography, the film contains a strong political message regarding the people's hatred of tsarism.

Mat [*Mother*] (USSR, 1926). Director: Vsevolod Pudovkin (Silent, B&W). *Mat* is Pudovkin's recreation of the revolution of 1905, told on a more personal level while the historical events unfold, for the most part, in the background. The film recounts the story of one family caught up in the political radicalism of the era.

Lawrence of Arabia (UK/USA, 1962). Director: David Lean. Lean's film recreates the Allied campaign in the Middle East during the First World War, under the leadership of T.E. Lawrence. The film focuses in painstaking detail on the British effort to unite an Arab force to fight against the Ottoman Turks. The script was written, in part, from the diaries of T.E. Lawrence.

Sand Pebbles (USA, 1966). Director: Robert Wise. Set in republican China during the pivotal year of 1926, *Sand Pebbles* highlights the ongoing tensions and open warfare between Chiang Kai-shek and the Chinese communists. This was compounded by the American presence along the Yangzi River to defend American interests in China.

Shanghai Triad (China, 1995). Director: Zhang Yimou. Set in Shanghai in the 1930s, Zhang Yimou recreates the clashes among the many gangs that controlled the city during the Republican era. The film captures the atmosphere of the era though the narrative, told from the perspective of a young boy, is somewhat fragmented.

CHAPTER FIVE

THE AUTHORITARIAN ALTERNATIVE

◇

In the aftermath of the First World War traditional liberal democratic political systems seemed increasingly unable to deal with the complex problems facing their citizens. Multi-party systems became mired in endless disputes, which threatened to render parliament effectively useless. In one nation after another people turned to extra-parliamentary alternatives to provide relief from political infighting and paralysis, economic crises, and too-rapid social and cultural change. By the late 1930s a fundamental political transformation had taken place. In Italy and Germany fascist regimes had risen to power; in the Soviet Union Stalin had launched one of the most rapid and comprehensive transformations of a nation ever seen; in South America fragile democracies had given way to new, authoritarian governments; and in Japan the liberal democratic system was supplanted by an aggressively expansionist regime, dominated by the military.

Italy was the first European nation to abandon its democratic system. At the end of the Great War Italy faced a number of systemic problems including underdevelopment in the South, political fragmentation, ultra-nationalist agitation, and unrest among industrial workers. In the first postwar elections socialist and communist parties made dramatic gains, causing considerable alarm among Italian industrialists and landowners. Unable to create sustainable coalitions, the government lurched from one crisis to the next, paralyzed by internal power struggles and ideological divisions. Perceiving a threat to their livelihood, Italian industrialists began to hire private armies of strike-breakers to force their discontented workers back to the factories. In this chaotic situation it was relatively simple for a new political force advocating hyper-nationalism and aggressive activism to gain a substantial following. Clever political manoeuvring and a good deal of luck allowed the *Fasci* to gain power in Italy in 1922.

In contrast, Germany's democratic system was able to survive the 1920s intact, even showing some growth in support in the latter years of the decade as reconstruction loans began to produce real economic improvements. The economic

A propaganda magazine for young Italian supporters of Fascism. Note the images of strength and militarism evident on the cover. Courtesy of the University of Wisconsin Digital Collections Center.

crises of the 1930s, however, would prove insurmountable. Increasingly the German people turned away from liberal-democratic political parties to embrace the extremes—the Communist Party and the National Socialist German Workers' Party. Though Communist support remained strong throughout the early years of the 1930s, more voters rallied to the aggressively nationalist message of the National Socialists. In the last free election, in November 1932, the communists received almost six million votes; the Nazis, however, received nearly double that number. The German people had clearly expressed their preference. Few, however, could have anticipated the massive social, economic, cultural, and political changes that would follow the National Socialist rise to power.

Lenin's death in 1924 triggered a succession dispute in the Soviet Union, which Stalin successfully manipulated in order to gain power. He then moved rapidly to dismantle the New Economic Policy (NEP) in order to focus on complete collectivization and a hurried program of industrialization. While the economic results were impressive, the human toll was immense. The Soviet State launched artificial famines, elaborate show trials, and draconian purges in order to gain the total co-operation necessary for such a massive transformation.

The appeal of authoritarian governments was not, however, limited to Europe. The political instability of the nineteenth century intensified in South America with the onset of the Great Depression. In nations such as Brazil latent tensions over industrialization and urbanization led to the overthrow of the republican government and the eventual rise of neo-fascist regimes. Meanwhile, in Japan frustration with the wartime settlement, the national debt, and the perceived injustice of the Washington Naval Limitation Treaty (1922) left many in the public questioning the effectiveness of the so-called Taishō Democracy. By 1930 ultra-nationalism was rising and prominent members of the Japanese military were able to monopolize political power.

The documents in this chapter examine the appeal of authoritarian doctrines, as well as some of their consequences. Antonio Cippico addresses the weaknesses of the Italian democratic state and the potential inherent in fascism. Benito Mussolini's interpretation of fascism is outlined in 'Fascist Doctrines'. Francesco Nitti draws attention to the negative consequences of a fascist government. The 'Anniversary Statement' of the Amur (Black Dragon) Society lays out some of the ultra-nationalist beliefs which facilitated the rise of Japanese militarism. Two documents from Joseph Stalin outline his opinions on opposition and Soviet patriotism. Evgeniia Ginzburg describes the descent into the gulags of the Stalinist era. Turning to National Socialist Germany Joseph Goebbels speaks to the role of propaganda in the new Nazi state. Adolf Hitler describes the role of women in the Nazi New Order, and David Buffum describes *Kristallnacht*, one of the early results of Nazi racial policy. Finally, the 'New State' of Getúlio Vargas in Brazil is discussed in an article from *Fortune* magazine.

◇

ANTONIO CIPPICO

Antonio Cippico (1877–1935) graduated with a degree in jurisprudence from the University of Vienna and, after a brief stay in London, settled in Rome. After volunteering for service in the First World War, *Cippico became an ardent supporter of the annexation of the Dalmatian Coast to the postwar Italian nation. By 1919 Cippico was writing for Mussolini's* Popolo d'Italia *in support of a variety of nationalist causes.*

After being appointed a senator in 1923, he went on to serve as the Italian delegate to the League of Nations from 1925 to 1928. Cippico's defence of Mussolini's Italy—Italy: The Central Problem of the Mediterranean—was published by Yale University Press in 1926.

ITALY: THE CENTRAL PROBLEM OF THE MEDITERRANEAN

In the last months of 1919 and the early ones of 1920, a good third of Italy was red. Over two thousand of the most flourishing communes were in the hands of the Communists. Their administration was characterized by violence and waste of public money. The government was incapable of protecting the public against the outrages of the reds, who imposed themselves more and more on the life of the people by means of assaults, strikes, blackmail, usurpation, and occupation of factories and land. It was, therefore, necessary for those who still kept their belief in the nation, in order and in the sanctity of civil rights, to protect themselves by force of arms, i.e., by answering destructive violence with reconstructive violence.

At the beginning the number of these brave defenders of the nation and of order was small. At the end of March 1919, about forty spirited young men of the proletariat and middle classes gathered in Milan—in red Milan—around Mussolini, and founded the famous original new *Fascismo*. This rapidly found adherents, apostles, and willing fighters, from all classes of the nation, in every city and every village, especially in the populous industrial districts of northern and central Italy, where the tyranny was strongest of the Socialist Syndicates and of the Red Councils of workmen founded on the example of Moscow. There was scarcely a factory or a municipality of the rich industrial towns that did not fly a red or black flag, symbol of social war and destruction.

We then witnessed a whole series of just reprisals, which silently and systematically organized the defence of the nation. Here a Communist Cooperative, there a Socialist Chamber of Labour, in another place the offices and printing works of a Bolshevik newspaper, supported by rubles from Moscow, were attacked, besieged, and burnt. Workmen and peasants, who were inscribed in the red leagues and who lorded it over the country, were, rightly, put *hors de combat* by just measures of reprisal. The authors of these assaults were, in turn, attacked and stabbed, often treacherously, by means of ambuscades and mass attacks. War was declared. But it was not civil war in the real meaning of the word: it was the necessary and legitimate individual defence of the trampled-on rights of all the citizens, above all in defence of the vital interests of the country.

It thus comes about that in Romagna, Tuscany, Lombardy, and Piedmont, risings and encounters between armed bands, looting, and killing increase enormously. The struggle seems unequal—as the Chambers of Labour and the Red Syndicates, in addition to a vast organization and the authority which has accrued to them from the powerlessness of the liberal organs of the state against their criminal arrogance, and their systematic coercion and intimidation both of the working and middle classes, seem determined to undermine the state itself and make themselves masters of it.

The attacks and counterattacks became every day more frequent and violent. The *Fascisti* were determined to give no quarter. The mass of the workers, misled by their leaders and organizers, who had promised them shortly the earthly paradise of a communist revolution, rapidly realized the emptiness of such promises, and realized that their leaders were the false and timid prophets of an Asiatic social religion, foreign to Italian civilization and temperament. The workers at last perceived that the Second and Third International were merely organs of disruption, incapable of reconstruction, that internationalism was a lie; that their own interests were identical with those of the nation, till then forgotten and combated.

Incidents of brutal violence occurred, such as the murder at a meeting of the Communal Council of a member of the red municipality of Bologna, Dr Giordani,[1] who had fought bravely in the Great War; such as the bomb thrown in the Diana Theatre at Milan, which killed at least forty harmless work-people; such as the man-hunts carried out by the reds of Empoli against sailors of the Royal Navy; like the sentence executed on the workmen Scimula and Sonzini, who, because they did not agree with their companions, were condemned by the latter to be thrown alive into the blast furnaces of the factory where they worked at Turin. Such incidents necessarily brought the Italian people, so essentially just and moral, to a rebellion against the tyranny of these brutal social-communist organizers.

In the end, the *Fascisti* got the upper hand in the bloody fight. They were by now an admirably organized and disciplined army composed of ex-soldiers, well-educated youths, peasants, and workmen, representatives of the best classes of the Italian people, who had seen through the communist propaganda, who had given everything to their country during the war, and who expected no recompense except the prosperity and moral greatness of their nation. They were men of thought and action who were determined to mould by their sacrifices a new Italy, no longer to be a museum of dead things, a vast and useless political and literary academy, nor a dreamy scientific Arcadia, dealing more in words than in deeds.

The government at that time was the expression of that form of tired and impotent liberalism which

had lost all authority over the people, a political agnosticism incapable of checking or suppressing the deniers of their country, the renouncers, the *saboteurs* of the state. . . .

Italy, even in her periods of blindest anarchy, desired vaguely to be a state, led and governed by a firm hand, with an economic structure worthy of its capacity of industrial initiative and work. This aspiration, at present incarnated in Fascism, has become her will. In order to reach this goal over three thousand *Fascisti*, generous, disinterested youths, from all classes of the nation, have laid down their lives.

The Fascist program of national reconstruction was synthesized by Mussolini in June 1921, when he proposed in Parliament to 'define some historical and political positions'. He then asked that the functions of the state should be limited to the creation of conditions suitable for individual activity, and of advantage to the consumer, in science, art, economic life, agriculture, industry, and commerce. The state must not confer privileges on one class to the detriment of others. It must resign monopolies: it must be neither banker, manufacturer, dealer, cooperative society, nor newspaper owner. It must not encourage unemployment by the palliative of 'doles', nor enrich a favoured few and impoverish the rest of the people by means of state contracts granted because of political protection or as gifts disguised under the name of cooperation. It is the state's business to do away with all that is superfluous and useless in the great bureaucratic machine. Only thus can true liberty—not license—and the equality of the citizens before the state be assured; only thus can the state be in condition to assure rapid justice and protection for life and property, and to safeguard the dignity and interests of its subjects in foreign countries. . . .

The new Fascist government had the task of restoring order where the maddest anarchy had reigned; of giving back to the citizens security for life and property where, owing to the complicity of governments, of parliaments, and sometimes of magistrates, the workmen had tried to take possession of the factories and of the control of industries, the railway men of the railways, tenants of the houses that they occupied, and peasants of the land; where socialistic communal administrations had madly wasted public money. The government's task was to rehabilitate the finances of the state, to balance the budget, to reduce the paper currency, to strengthen the credit of industries, to wipe out the serious deficit of the railways (nearly 1,300,000,000 lire in 1922) of the posts and telegraphs (over 750,000,000 for the same year). The government, as the authority in the country, was bound to reestablish a serious spirit in the schools, law in the courts of justice, and dignity in home and foreign policies. A really immense undertaking which *Fascismo*, in the two and a half years that it has been in power, has almost accomplished. It is rare in the history of civilized nations, and has never before occurred in Italy, that a government has achieved so much in so short a time. . . .

The work carried out by the Fascist government belongs to history. Much of this work will need altering, correcting, and coordinating in the future. But the fact remains that the Italian people will not turn backwards, that the former politicians have been, one by one, swept away by the great wave of Fascism, which is action. Reconstruction of the state, social reforms, Fascist syndicalism, which is to a certain extent contrary to class war, and the national militia are institutions which will not perish; rather, they will evolve for the good of the country. And another thing will not change; the new spirit of Italy, its new political outlook.

This, if it appears today in the life of Italians in general, is clearly revealed by every word and every act of the great representative man of New Italy—by Benito Mussolini, who said recently at a great Fascist meeting in Rome, 'Since it is necessary for every great movement to have a representative man who shall feel all the passion and carry the flame of the movement: return, O comrades, to your land which I love, and cry with a loud voice and a clear conscience that the banner of the Fascist revolution is entrusted to me and that I am prepared to defend it against all comers, even at the price of my life.'

It is with this new point of view and with this new *condottiere*,[2] who from the multiplicity of races and from all the great facts of the past and present history of Italy draws the elements of his deed, that Italy expectantly awaits the conquest of her future and expects that her political and economic problem, the central problem of the Mediterranean and Europe, shall be equitably solved with the good will of the friendly powers.

Notes

1. Dr Giulio Giordani was murdered at a 1920 meeting of the communal council of Bologna.

2. A *condottiere* is a military leader— usually of mercenary forces.

> **Study Question**
>
> 1. Why did so many Europeans believe fascism to be the government of the future?

BENITO MUSSOLINI

Benito Mussolini (1883–1945) was raised in a socialist household and trained to be an elementary school teacher. Because the socialist movement promoted pacifism, he moved to Switzerland in 1902 to avoid mandatory military service; however, once in Switzerland, Mussolini was arrested and expelled to

Italy. Mussolini opposed the First World War when it began, but several months later he abruptly changed his opinion and began to argue in favour of Italian involvement in the war. In November 1914 he founded a new ultra-nationalist newspaper, Il Popolo d'Italia. *In 1917 he served briefly in the army and then returned to Italy and eventually organized the Fasci di Combattimento. By 1922 the domestic situation in Italy was approaching crisis levels and King Vittorio Emmanuele III invited Mussolini to form a new government. In 1932 Mussolini co-wrote the following article with philosopher Giovanni Gentile.*

FASCIST DOCTRINES

Above all, Fascism, in so far as it considers and observes the future and the development of humanity quite apart from the political considerations of the moment, believes neither in the possibility nor in the utility of perpetual peace. It thus repudiates the doctrine of Pacifism—born of a renunciation of the struggle and an act of cowardice in the face of sacrifice. War alone brings up to their highest tension all human energy and puts the stamp of nobility upon the peoples who have the courage to meet it. All other trials are substitutes, which never really put a man in front of himself in the alternative of life or death. A doctrine, therefore, which begins with a prejudice in favour of peace is foreign to Fascism; as are foreign to the spirit of Fascism, even though acceptable by reason of the utility which they might have in given political situations, all internationalistic and socialistic systems which, as history proves, can be blown to the winds when emotional, idealistic, and practical movements storm the hearts of the peoples. Fascism carries over this anti-pacifist spirit even into the lives of individuals. The proud motto of the *Squadrista*, 'Me ne frego' [It doesn't matter], written on the bandages of a wound, is an act of philosophy not only stoical, it is the epitome of a doctrine that is not only political: it is education for combat, the acceptance of the risks which it brings; it is a new way of life for Italy. Thus the Fascist accepts and loves life, he knows nothing of suicide and despises it; he looks on life as duty, ascent, conquest: life which must be noble and full, lived for oneself, but above all for those others near and far away, present and future. . . .

Mussolini at the Turin Air Show in July 1932, during celebrations of the party's tenth anniversary in power. Courtesy of the University of Wisconsin Digital Collections Center.

Such a conception of life makes Fascism the precise negation of that doctrine which formed the basis of the so-called Scientific or Marxian Socialism: the doctrine of historical Materialism, according to which the history of human civilizations can be explained only as the struggle of interest between the different social groups and as arising out of change in the means and instruments of production. That economic improvements—discoveries of raw materials, new methods of work, scientific inventions—should have an importance of their own, no one denies, but that they should suffice to explain human history to the exclusion of all other factors is absurd: Fascism believes, now and always, in holiness and in heroism, that is in acts in which no economic motive—remote or immediate—plays a part. . . . [A]nd above all it is denied that the class struggle can be the primary agent of social changes. . . .

After Socialism, Fascism attacks the whole complex of democratic ideologies, and rejects them, both in their theoretical premises and in their applications of practical manifestations. Fascism denies that the majority, through the mere fact of being a majority, can rule human societies; it denies that this majority can govern by means of a periodical consultation; it affirms the irremediable, fruitful, and beneficent inequality of men, who cannot be leveled by such a mechanical and extrinsic fact as universal suffrage. By democratic regimes we mean those in which from time to time the people is given the illusion of being sovereign, while true effective sovereignty lies in other, perhaps irresponsible and secret, forces. Democracy is a regime without a king, but with very many kings, perhaps more exclusive, tyrannical, and violent than one king even though a tyrant. . . .

In face of Liberal doctrines, Fascism takes up an attitude of absolute opposition both in the field of politics and in that of economics. It is not necessary to exaggerate—merely for the purpose of present controversies—the importance of Liberalism in the past century, and to make of that which was one of the numerous doctrines sketched in that century, a religion of humanity for all times, present and future. Liberalism flourished for no more than some fifteen years. It was born in 1830, as a reaction against the Holy Alliance that wished to drag Europe back to what it had been before 1789, and it had its year of splendour in 1848 when even Pius IX was a Liberal. Immediately afterwards the decay set in. If 1848 was a year of light and of poetry, 1849 was a year of darkness and tragedy. . . .

If it is admitted that the nineteenth century has been the century of Socialism, Liberalism, and Democracy, it does not follow that the twentieth century must also be the century of Liberalism, Socialism, and Democracy: political doctrines pass; peoples remain. It is to be expected that this century may be that of authority, a century of the 'Right', a Fascist century. If the nineteenth was the century of the individual (Liberalism means individualism) it may be expected that this one may be the century of 'collectivism' and therefore the century of the State. That a new doctrine should use the still vital elements of other doctrines is perfectly logical. No doctrine is born quite new, shining, never before seen. No doctrine can boast of an absolute 'originality'. It is bound, even if only historically, to other doctrines that have been, and must develop into other doctrines that will be. . . .

The keystone of Fascist doctrine is the conception of the State, of its essence, of its tasks, of its ends. For Fascism the State is an absolute before which individuals and groups are relative. Individuals and groups are 'thinkable' in so far as they are within the State. The Liberal State does not direct the interplay and the material and spiritual development of the groups, but limits itself to registering the results; the Fascist State has a consciousness of its own, a will of its own, on this account it is called an 'ethical' State. In

1929, at the first quinquennial[1] assembly of the regime, I said: 'For Fascism, the State is not the night-watchman who is concerned only with the personal security of the citizens; nor is it an organization for purely material ends, such as that of guaranteeing a certain degree of prosperity and a relatively peaceful social order, to achieve which a council of administration would be sufficient, nor is it a creation of mere politics with no contact with the material and complex reality of the lives of individuals and the life of peoples. The State, as conceived by Fascism and as it acts, is a spiritual and moral fact because it makes concrete the political, juridical, economic organization of the nation and such an organization is, in its origin and in its development, a manifestation of the spirit. The State is the guarantor of internal and external security, but it is also the guardian and the transmitter of the spirit of the people as it has been elaborated through the centuries in language, custom, faith. . . . It is the State which educates citizens for civic virtue, makes them conscious of their mission, calls them to unity; harmonizes their interests in justice; hands on the achievements of thought in the sciences, the arts, in law, in human solidarity; it carries men from the elementary life of the tribe to the highest human expression of power which is Empire. . . .

A State founded on millions of individuals who recognize it, feel it, are ready to serve it, is not the tyrannical State of the medieval lord. It has nothing in common with the absolutist States that existed either before or after 1789. In the Fascist State the individual is not suppressed, but rather multiplied, just as in a regiment a soldier is not weakened but multiplied by the number of his comrades. The Fascist State organizes the nation,

but it leaves sufficient scope to individuals; it has limited useless or harmful liberties and has preserved those that are essential. It cannot be the individual who decides in this matter, but only the State. . . .

The Fascist State is a will to power and to government. In it the tradition of Rome is an idea that has force. In the doctrine of Fascism Empire is not only a territorial, military, or mercantile expression, but spiritual or moral. One can think of an empire, that is to say a nation that directly or indirectly leads other nations, without needing to conquer a single square kilometre of territory. For Fascism the tendency to Empire, that is to say, to the expansion of nations, is a manifestation of vitality; its opposite, staying at home, is a sign of decadence: peoples who rise or re-rise are imperialist, peoples who die are renunciatory. Fascism is the doctrine that is most fitted to represent the aims, the states of mind, of a people, like the Italian people, rising again after many centuries of abandonment or slavery to foreigners. But Empire calls for discipline, co-ordination of forces, duty, and sacrifice. . . . If every age has its own doctrine, it is apparent from a thousand signs that the doctrine of the present age is Fascism. That it is a doctrine of life is shown by the fact that it has resuscitated a faith. That this faith has conquered minds is proved by the fact that Fascism has had its dead and its martyrs.

Note

1. Five-yearly.

Study Question

1. What did Mussolini mean by 'harmful freedoms'?

FRANCESCO NITTI

In 1904 Francesco Nitti (1868–1953) was elected to the Italian parliament as a liberal-democratic member and subsequently served in government from 1911 to 1914. From 1917 to 1919 Vittorio Orlando appointed Nitti Minister of Finance. In 1919, during the height of postwar social unrest, he succeeded Orlando as Prime Minister. Nitti resigned in 1920 when he was unable to control the chaotic postwar situation and lived in exile during much of the Fascist period. In the following Atlantic Monthly *article Nitti lays out a series of arguments regarding the negative effects of the fascist government in Italy, both for Italian citizens and for the rest of the world.*

PROBABILITIES OF WAR IN EUROPE

Bolshevism and Fascism are the two menaces to the future prosperity of Europe. Both are similar phenomena in that they deny human liberty and involve the exercise of power on the part of an armed minority. Bolshevism sets about establishing the dictatorship of the proletariat—in other words, putting all resources in the hands of the workers and peasants. It attains this end by force. Fascism suppresses all political liberty and all free manifestations, saying that this is necessary to make Italy a great nation and to found an empire. Mussolini has made numerous speeches insulting the decaying corpse of democracy and asserting that liberty is a prejudice of the past. He has announced that Fascism will found an Italian Empire. To found an empire would mean taking some piece of foreign territory—which in this case would be either a French or a British possession, since it would be out of the question to despoil Switzerland, Austria, or Yugoslavia, which lie along the Italian frontiers.

Italy lacks economic resources, and Italian finance is so wretched that public credit has been profoundly shaken. Italy lacks the prime necessities for war—coal, steel, and oil. She also lacks food and cotton. In her present situation, she could not wage war without the support of Great Britain or the United States. Is it possible that these two countries would encourage such absurd, such grotesque, proposals?

Bolshevism has cut down Russia's productive capacity; and her foreign business, which the Government controls, has been utterly disastrous. The truth is that Russia is producing much less than she did before the war—in other words, much less than she did under the deplorable Tsarist regime! Economic production demands above all else order, liberty, and individual initiative—three things that no dictatorship can bring about.

Fascism has seriously weakened Italian production. In spite of appearances Italy has fallen into a state of the greatest economic disorder in the course of the last six years. Fascism has not bent its efforts to obtaining results, but to producing manifestations. All over the country there are celebrations, parades, and processions of Black Shirts. Wheat and rice production has declined; yet great festivals are held in honour of wheat and rice, and there is a special celebration on behalf of bread. Expressed in gold pounds—in other words, without statistical manipulation—the deficit of Italian business has risen from 643 million gold pounds in 1924 to 1259 million gold pounds in 1927. In short, it has almost doubled. Mr MacLean, the American commercial attaché at Rome, has calculated that domestic business has dropped 40 per cent in the last two years. This is a terrible figure. Nevertheless, Mr MacLean is a little too optimistic, for the real decline is nearly 50 per cent. The loans negotiated in America have been used to maintain the lira, though no one knows how long this will last, and to stabilize it at its present level.

This extravagant stabilization, however, has ruined all industrial exporters. Italy now suffers more bankruptcies than any other country in Europe. In actual figures she has suffered twice as many as any other country, and, relatively to her industrial power, nine or ten times as many as any other country. Because of this absurd lira stabilization at a false level, undertaken not as a part of any economic programme, but merely as a piece of political bluff, the Italians are obliged to pay almost the same taxes as the French, whose country is at least three times as rich. In short, Italian taxes are heavier than those of any other country.

Since the Government bases itself on violence, it needs an even greater number of special militia to maintain it than Bolshevism does. These groups include militia to maintain general order, the voluntary Fascist militia, the railway militia, the post and telegraph militia, the harbour militia, the forest militia, and, most recently of all, the highway militia. About 200,000 people thus make their living off the Fascist Government, and it is like maintaining an army to support them. The industrialists and farmers have to pay for these militias. Besides this, all producers, both employers and employees are grouped into corporations which involve still another enormous expense. There are fourteen ministries, but Mussolini scoffs at the rest of the world and occupies seven of them, comprising the office of Prime Minister, of Minister of the Interior, of Foreign Affairs, War, Marine, Aviation, and Corporations—in other words, Minister of Labour. Under these conditions he is able to involve the country in a war before anyone

knows what is happening and before the people can manifest their desires in any way.

All free journals in Italy have been suppressed, and the press is suffering. The amount of paper used for the various daily journals has fallen off about one half or three-fifths during the last two years. The ablest Italians are in exile, having either been deported or retired from public life. Poverty is increasing, and the Government has refused to meet its obligations on the treasury and has forced them to be transformed into a consolidated debt. No criticism is allowed, even the most cordial. The press cannot discuss the economic crisis except to say that everything is going smoothly. Elections have disappeared. Even the Chamber of Deputies is going to be transformed into an assembly named by the Government. The administrators of local government and even the representatives of the chambers of commerce are no longer elected. They are appointed by the Government.

The economic situation is bad, but the financial situation is worse. On the day when Fascism feels itself lost, will it not attempt to distract attention by some international adventure? Is not this what all dictatorships have done in the past?

Fascism and Bolshevism, although apparently direct opposites, act in the same manner. Several centuries before Jesus, Plato, the greatest of Greek philosophers, wrote that dictatorship always ended in war, saying that when the dictator felt himself lost he made war. There is no example in modern history of a dictatorship that has not ended in war, revolution, or both.

Study Question

1. Why does Nitti argue that dictatorial governments inevitably lead their countries to war? Is he correct?

THE AMUR SOCIETY

The Amur Society, also known as the Black Dragon Society, was an ultra-nationalistic group founded in 1901, in part to promote Japanese expansionism throughout greater East Asia.[1] After the Japanese defeat of Russia in 1905, the society turned its attention to the weaknesses of the liberal parliamentary system. In particular, the society objected to the ongoing Westernization of Japan. With the onset of the Great Depression and its impact on the Japanese economy, the Amur Society dedicated itself to the creation of a more aggressive foreign policy. The following statement was issued in 1930 as the society prepared to celebrate its thirtieth anniversary.

ANNIVERSARY STATEMENT

Today our empire has entered a critical period in which great zeal is required on the part of the entire nation. From the first, we members of the Amur Society have worked in accordance with the imperial mission for overseas expansion to solve our overpopulation; at the same time, we have sought to give support and encouragement to the peoples of East Asia. Thus we have sought the spread of humanity and righteousness throughout the world by having the imperial purpose extend to the neighbouring nations.

Earlier, in order to achieve these principles, we organized the Heavenly Blessing Heroes in Korea in 1894 and helped the Tong Hak rebellion there in order to speed the settlement of the dispute between Japan and China. In 1899 we helped Aguinaldo[2] in his struggle for the independence of the Philippines. In 1900 we worked with other comrades in helping Sun Yat-sen start the fires of revolution in South China. In 1901 we organized this Society and became exponents of the punishment of Russia, and thereafter we devoted ourselves to the annexation of Korea while continuing to support the revolutionary movement in China. At all times we have consistently centered our efforts on the solution of problems of foreign relations, and we have not spared ourselves in this cause.

During this period we have seen the fulfillment of our national power in the decisive victories in the two major wars against China and Russia, in the annexation of Korea, the acquisition of Formosa and Sakhalin, and the expulsion of Germany from the Shantung peninsula. Japan's status among the empires of the world has risen until today she ranks as one of the three great powers, and from this eminence she can support other Asiatic nations. While these achievements were of course attributable to the august virtue of the great Meiji emperor, nevertheless we cannot but believe that our own efforts, however slight, also bore good fruit.

However, in viewing recent international affairs it would seem that the foundation established by the great Meiji emperor is undergoing rapid deterioration. The disposition of the gains of the war with Germany was left to foreign powers, and the government, disregarding the needs of national defence, submitted to unfair demands to limit our naval power. Moreover, the failure of our China policy made the Chinese more and more contemptuous of us, so much so that they have been brought to demand the surrender of our essential defence lines in Manchuria and Mongolia. Furthermore, in countries like the United States and Australia our immigrants have been deprived of rights which were acquired only after long years of struggle, and we now face a highhanded anti-Japanese expulsion movement which knows no bounds. Men of purpose and of humanity who are at all concerned for their country cannot fail to be upset by the situation.

When we turn our attention to domestic affairs, we feel more than deep concern. There is a great slackening of discipline and order. Men's hearts are become corrupt. Look about you! Are not the various government measures and establishments a conglomeration of all sorts of evils and abuses? The laws are confusing, and evil grows apace. The people are overwhelmed by heavy taxes, the confusion in the business world complicates the livelihood of the people, the growth of dangerous thought threatens social order, and our national polity, which has endured for three thousand years, is in danger. This is a critical time for our national destiny; was there ever a more crucial day? What else can we call this time if it is not termed decisive?

And yet, in spite of this our government, instead of pursuing a far-sighted policy, casts about for temporary measures. The opposition party simply struggles for political power without any notion of saving our country from this crisis. And even the press, which should devote itself to its duty of guiding and leading society, is the same. For the most part it swims with the current, bows to vulgar opinions, and is chiefly engrossed in money making. Alas! Our empire moves ever closer to rocks which lie before us. Yet the captains and navigators are men of this sort! Truly, is this not the moment for us to become aroused?

Our determination to rise to save the day is the inescapable consequence of this state of affairs. Previously our duty lay in the field of foreign affairs, but when we see internal affairs in disorder how can we succeed abroad? Therefore we of the Amur Society have determined to widen the scope of our activity. Hereafter, besides our interest in foreign affairs, we will give unselfish criticism of internal politics and of social problems, and we will seek to guide public opinion into proper channels. Thereby we will, through positive action, continue in the tradition of our past. We will establish a firm basis for our organization's policy and, through cooperation with other groups devoted to similar political, social, and ideological ideals, we are resolved to reform the moral corruption of the people, restore social discipline, and ease the insecurity of the people's livelihood by relieving the crises in the financial world, restore national confidence, and increase the national strength, in order to carry out the imperial mission to awaken the countries of Asia. In order to clarify these principles, we here set forth our platform to all our fellow patriots:

Principles

We stand for Divine Rulership (*tennō shugi*). Basing ourselves on the fundamental teachings of the foundation of the empire, we seek the extension of the imperial influence to all peoples and places and the fulfillment of the glory of our national polity.

Platform

Developing the great plan of the founders of the country, we will widen the great Way (*tao*) of Eastern culture, work out a harmony of Eastern and Western cultures, and take the lead among Asian peoples.

We will bring to an end many evils, such as formalistic legalism; it restricts the freedom of the people, hampers common sense solutions, prevents efficiency in public and private affairs, and destroys the true meaning of constitutional government. Thereby we will show forth again the essence of the imperial principles.

We shall rebuild the present administrative systems. We will develop overseas expansion through the activation of our diplomacy, further the prosperity of the people by reforms in internal government, and solve problems of labour and management by the establishment of new social policies. Thereby we will strengthen the foundations of the empire.

We shall carry out the spirit of the Imperial Rescript to Soldiers and Sailors and stimulate a martial spirit by working toward the goal of a nation in arms. Thereby we look toward the perfection of national defence.

We plan a fundamental reform of the present educational system which is copied from those of Europe and America; we shall set up a basic study of a national education originating in our national polity. Thereby we anticipate the further development and heightening of the wisdom and virtue of the Yamato race.

Notes

1. The Amur Society (*Kokuryu-kai*) was founded by Ryohei Uchida; in 1901 the group separated from the *Genyōsha* which dated back to 1871.

2. Emilio Aguinaldo y Famy led Philippine resistance against both the Spanish and later the United States. He was briefly declared president of the Philippine Republic in 1899 before the US asserted its control over the Islands.

Study Question

1. How would you best categorize the ideology of groups such as the Black Dragon society?

Joseph Stalin

Josef Vissarionovich Dzhugashvili (1879–1953) sided with Lenin and the Bolshevik faction in 1903. In 1912 he went to St Petersburg, where he was elected to the party's central committee. About this time he took the name Stalin ('steel'). After the Russian Revolution of March 1917, he joined the editorial board of the party paper Pravda. *When the Bolsheviks took power in November 1917 he became the Commissar of Nationalities. In 1922*

Stalin was made general secretary of the party, a relatively minor position at the time. Before his death in 1924, Lenin wrote a testament urging Stalin's removal from the post because of his arbitrary conduct and well-known rudeness; but in the struggle to succeed Lenin, Stalin was victorious. The two passages which follow outline Stalin's views on opposition within the party and on the 'Socialist Fatherland'.

On Opposition, 1927

From Kamenev's speech it is evident that the opposition does not intend to disarm completely. The opposition's declaration of 3 December indicates the same thing. Evidently, the opposition prefers to be outside the Party. Well, let it be

outside the Party. There is nothing terrible, or exceptional, or surprising, in the fact that they prefer to be outside the Party, that they are cutting themselves off from the Party. If you study the history of our Party you will find that always, at certain serious turns taken by our Party, a certain section of the old leaders fell out of the cart of the Bolshevik Party and made room for new people. A turn is a serious thing, comrades. A turn is dangerous for those who do not sit firmly in the Party cart. Not everybody can keep his balance when a turn is made. You turn the cart—and on looking around you find that somebody has fallen out. *(Applause)*

Let us take 1903, the period of the Second Congress of our Party. That was the period of the Party's turn from agreement with the liberals to a mortal struggle against the liberal bourgeoisie, from preparing for the struggle against tsarism to open struggle against it for completely routing tsarism and feudalism. At that time, the Party was headed by the six: Plekhanov, Zasulich, Martov, Lenin, Axelrod, and Potresov. The turn proved fatal to five out of the six. They fell out of the cart. Lenin alone remained. *(Applause)* It turned out that the old leaders of the Party, the founders of the Party (Plekhanov, Zasulich, and Axelrod) plus two young ones (Martov and Potresov) were against one, also a young one, Lenin. If only you knew how much howling, weeping, and wailing there was then that the Party was doomed, that the Party would not hold out, that nothing could be done without the old leaders. The howling and wailing subsided however, but the facts remained. And the facts were that precisely thanks to the departure of the five the Party succeeded in getting on the right road. It is now clear to every Bolshevik that if Lenin had not waged a resolute struggle against the five, if the five had not been pushed aside, our Party could not have rallied as a Bolshevik Party capable of leading the proletarians to the revolution against the bourgeoisie.

. . .

Our Party is a living organism. Like every organism, it undergoes a process of metabolism: the old and obsolete passes away *(Applause)*, the new and growing lives and develops. *(Applause)* Some go away, both at the top and at the bottom. New ones grow, both at the top and at the bottom, and lead the cause forward. That is how our Party grew. This is how it will continue to grow.

The same must be said about the present period of our revolution. We are in the period of a turn from the restoration of industry and agriculture to the reconstruction of the entire national economy, to its reconstruction on a new technical basis, when the building of socialism is no longer merely in prospect, but a living, practical matter, which calls for the surmounting of extremely great difficulties of an internal and external character.

You know that this turn has proved fatal to the leaders of our opposition, who were scared by the new difficulties and intended to turn the Party in the direction of surrender. And if certain leaders, who do not want to sit firmly in the cart, now fall out, it is nothing to be surprised at. It will merely rid the Party of people who are getting in its way and hindering its progress. Evidently, they seriously want to free themselves from our Party cart. Well, if some of the old leaders who are turning into trash intend to fall out of the cart—a good riddance to them! *(Stormy and prolonged applause)*.

THE SOCIALIST FATHERLAND, 1931

It is sometimes asked whether it is not possible to slow down the tempo a bit, to put a check on the movement. No, comrades it is not possible! The tempo must not be reduced! On the contrary, we must increase it as much as is within our powers and possibilities. This is dictated to us by our obligations to the workers and peasants of the USSR. This is dictated to us by our obligations to the working class of the whole world.

To slacken the tempo would mean falling behind. And those who fall behind get beaten. But we do not want to be beaten. No, we refuse to be beaten! One feature of the history of old Russia was the continual beatings she suffered for falling behind, for her backwardness. She was beaten by the Mongol khans. She was beaten by the Turkish beys. She was beaten by the Swedish feudal lords. She was beaten by the Polish and Lithuanian gentry. She was beaten by the British and French capitalists. She was beaten by the Japanese barons. All beat her—for her backwardness: for military backwardness, for cultural backwardness, for political backwardness, for industrial backwardness, for agricultural backwardness. She was beaten because to do so was profitable and could be done with impunity. Do you remember the words of the pre-Revolutionary poet: 'You are poor and abundant, mighty and impotent, Mother Russia.' These words of the old poet were well learned by those gentlemen. They beat her, saying: 'You are abundant,' so one can enrich oneself at your expense. They beat her, saying: 'You are poor and impotent,' so you can be beaten and plundered with impunity. Such is the law of the exploiters—to beat the backward and the weak. It is the jungle law of capitalism. You are backward, you are weak—therefore you are wrong; hence, you can be beaten and enslaved. You are mighty—therefore you are right; hence, we must be wary of you.

That is why we must no longer lag behind. In the past we had no fatherland, nor could we have one. But now that we have overthrown capitalism and power is in the hands of the working class, we have

An Uzbek weaver works at the Stalin Textile Combine in Tashkent during WWII. Stalin's forced industrialization contributed enormously to the Soviet war effort. Courtesy of the Library of Congress, Prints and Photographs Division, FSA/OWI Collection (LC-USW33-024239-C).

a fatherland, and we will defend its independence. Do you want our Socialist fatherland to be beaten and to lose its independence? If you do not want this you must put an end to its backwardness in the shortest possible time and develop a genuine Bolshevik tempo in building up its Socialist system of economy. There is no other way. That is why Lenin said during the October Revolution: 'Either perish, or overtake and outstrip the advanced capitalist countries.'

We are fifty or a hundred years behind the advanced countries. We must make good this distance in ten years. Either we do it, or they crush us.

Study Question

1. Was Stalin correct in his belief that only a ruthless approach could save the Soviet Union from complete destruction at the hands of the capitalist nations?

EVGENIIA GINZBURG

Evgeniia Semenovna Ginzburg's[1] Journey Into the Whirlwind is considered one of the most important first-hand accounts of the Stalinist-era purges in the Soviet Union. Ginzburg was born in 1906 and was, by all accounts, a loyal supporter of Leninism. Ginzburg became a professor at the Teacher Training Institute of Kazan University and later was editor of a local communist newspaper, Red Tartary. *In February 1937 a colleague denounced her for having failed to attack the work of another colleague, whose writings had angered Stalin. This event began*

Evgeniia Ginzburg's eighteen-year descent into the Soviet gulags. Ginzburg was not released from prison until 1955, even though her original sentence was only ten years. Journey Into the Whirlwind *and its sequel,* Within the Whirlwind, *chronicle her entire imprisonment. When Ginzburg was released as part of Nikita Khrushchev's de-Stalinization she continued to express her loyalty to 'the great Leninist truths'.[2] Evgeniia Ginzburg died in 1977. This excerpt covers Ginzburg's experiences during her arrest, 'trial', and sentencing.*

◇

JOURNEY INTO THE WHIRLWIND

I have often thought about the tragedy of those by whose agency the purge of 1937 was carried out. What a life they had! They were all sadists, of course. And only a handful found the courage to commit suicide.

Step by step, as they followed their routine directives, they traveled all the way from the human condition to that of beasts. Their faces, as time went by, defied description. I, at any rate, cannot find words to convey the expression on the faces of these un-men.

But all this happened only gradually. That night, Interrogator Livanov, who had summoned me, looked like any other civil servant with perhaps a little more than the usual liking for red tape. Everything about him confirmed this impression—the placid, well-fed face, the neat writing with which he filled the left-hand side (reserved for questions) of the record sheet in front of him, and his local, Kazan accent. Certain turns of speech, provincial and old-fashioned, reminded me of our nurse Fima and aroused a host of memories of home.

In that first moment I had a flash of hope that the madness might be over, that I had left

it behind me, down there, with the grinding of padlocks and the pain-filled eyes of the golden-haired girl from the banks of the river Sungari. Here, it seemed, was the world of ordinary, normal people. Outside the window was the old familiar town with its clanging streetcars. The window had neither bars nor a wooden screen, but handsome net curtains. And the plate with the remains of Livanov's supper had not been left on the floor but stood on a small table in a corner of the room.

He might be a perfectly decent man, this quiet official who was slowly writing down my answers to his straight-forward, insignificant questions: Where had I worked between this year and that, where and when had I met this or that person. . .? But now the first page had been filled and he gave it to me to sign.

What was this? He had asked me how long I had known Elvov,[3] and I had answered, 'Since 1932.' But here it said, 'How long have you known the Trotskyist Elvov?' and my reply was put down as 'I have known the Trotskyist Elvov since 1932.'

'This isn't what I said.'

He looked at me in amazement, as though it

really were only a question of getting the definition right.

'But he *is* a Trotskyist!'

'I don't know that.'

'But we do. It's been established. The investigators have conclusive evidence.'

'But I can't confirm something I don't know. You can ask me when I met *Professor* Elvov, but whether he is a Trotskyist, and whether I knew him as a Trotskyist—that's a different question.'

'It's for me to ask the questions, if you please. You've no right to dictate to me the form in which I should put them. All you have to do is answer them.'

'Then put the answers down exactly as I give them, and not in your own words. In fact, why don't we have a stenographer to put them down?'

These words, the height of naïveté, were greeted by peals of laughter—not, of course, from Livanov but from the embodiment of lunacy which had just entered the room in the person of State Security Lieutenant Tsarevsky.

'Well, well, what do I see! You're behind bars now, are you?'. . .

'So you're behind bars,' he sneered again, in a tone of hatred as intense as though I had set fire to his house or murdered his child.

'You realize of course,' he went on more quietly, 'that the regional committee has agreed to your arrest. Everything has come out. Elvov gave you away. That husband of yours, Aksyonov—he's been arrested too, and he's come clean. He's a Trotskyist too, of course. . . .'

'Is Elvov here, in this prison?'

'Yes! In the very cell next to yours. And he's confirmed all the evidence against you.'

'Then confront me with him. I want to know what he said about me. Let him repeat it to my face.'

'Like to see your friend, eh?' He added such a scurrilous obscenity that I could hardly believe my ears.

'How dare you! I demand to see the head of your department. This is a Soviet institution where people can't be treated like dirt.'

'Enemies are not people. We're allowed to do what we like with them. People indeed!'

Again he roared with laughter. Then he screamed at me at the top of his voice, banged the table with his fist . . . and told me I'd be shot if I didn't sign the record.

I noticed with amazement that Livanov, so quiet and polite, looked on unmoved. Obviously, he had seen it all before.

'Why do you allow this man to interfere with a case you're in change of?' I asked.

His smile was almost gentle.

'Tsarevsky's right, you know. You can make things better for yourself if you honestly repent and make a clean breast of it. Stubbornness won't help you. The investigators have conclusive evidence.'

'Of what?'

'Of your counter-revolutionary activity as a member of the secret organization headed by Elvov. You'd much better sign the record. If you do you'll be treated decently. We'll allow you to have parcels, and we'll let you see your children and your husband.'

While Livanov spoke Tsarevsky kept quiet in readiness for his next attack. I thought he had just happened to come into Livanov's office. But after the two of them had been at me for three or four hours, I realized that it was part of a deliberate technique.

The blue light of a February dawn was casting its chill on the room by the time Tsarevsky rang for the warder. The same words ended the interrogation as those of Vevers the day before, but Tsarevsky's voice rose to a falsetto:

'Off to the cell with you! And there you'll sit until you sign.'

Going down the stairs, I caught myself hurrying back to my cell. It seemed, after all, that I was better off there, in the human presence of a companion in misfortune—and the grinding of locks was better than the demented screams of un-men.

[Six months passed during which time Ginzburg was subjected to similar treatment. Then, in August, she was summoned to her trial.]

My hour had come. The military tribunal of the Supreme Court—three officers and a secretary—faced me across a table. On either side of me were two warders. Such were the 'fully public'[4] conditions in which my 'trial' was conducted.

I looked intently at my judges' faces and was struck by the fact that they closely resembled one another and also for some reason reminded me of the official at Black Lake who had taken my watch. They all looked alike, although one of them was dark and another's hair was graying. Yes, I saw what it was they had in common—the empty look of a mummy, or a fish in aspic. Nor was this surprising. How could one carry out such duties day after day without cutting oneself off from one's fellow men—if only by that glazed expression?

Suddenly I found that it was easy to breathe. A summer breeze of extraordinary freshness was blowing through the wide-open window. The room was a handsome one, with a high ceiling. So there were, after all, such places in the world!

Outside the windows there were some large, dark-green trees: their leaves were rustling and I was moved by the cool, mysterious sound. I could not remember having heard it before. It was strangely touching—why had I never noticed it?

And the clock on the wall—large and round, its shiny hands like a gray mustache—how long was it since I had seen anything like it?

I checked the time at the beginning and end of the trial. Seven minutes. That, neither more nor less, was the time it took to enact this tragicomedy.

The voice of the president of the court—Dmitriev, People's Commissar for Justice of the Russian Republic—resembled the expression of his eyes. If a frozen codfish could talk, that is undoubtedly what it would sound like. There was not a trace here of the animation, the zest which my interrogators had put into their performances: the judges were merely functionaries earning their pay. No doubt they had a quota, and were anxious to over-fulfill it if they could.

'You have read the indictment?' said the president in tones of unutterable boredom. 'You plead guilty? No? But the evidence shows . . .'

He leafed through the bulky file and muttered through his teeth: 'For instance the witness Kozlov . . .'

'Kozlova. It's a woman—and, I may add, a despicable one.'

'Kozlova, yes. Or again, the witness Dyachenko . . .'

'Dyakanov.'

'Yes. Well, they both state . . .'

But what they stated the judge was too pressed for time to read. Breaking off he asked me: 'Any questions you wish to ask the court?'

'Yes, I do. I am accused under section 8, of Article 58, which means that I am charged with terrorism. Will you please tell me the name of the political leader against whose life I am supposed to have plotted?'

The judges were silent for a while, taken aback by this preposterous question. They looked reproachfully at the inquisitive woman who was holding up their work. Then the one with grizzled hair muttered:

'You know, don't you, that Comrade Kirov[5] was murdered in Leningrad?'

'Yes, but I didn't kill him, it was someone called Nikolayev. Anyway, I've never been in Leningrad. Isn't that what you call an alibi?'

'Are you a lawyer by chance?' said the gray-haired man crossly.

'No, I'm a teacher.'

'You won't get anywhere by quibbling. You may never have been in Leningrad, but it was your accomplices who killed him, and that makes you morally and criminally responsible.'

'The court will withdraw for consultation,'

grunted the president. Whereupon they all stood up, lazily stretching their limbs . . .

I looked at the clock again. They couldn't even have had time for a smoke! In less than two minutes the worshipful assembly was back in session. The president had in his hand a large sheet of paper of excellent quality, covered with typescript in close spacing. The text, which must have taken at least twenty minutes to copy, was my sentence: the official document setting forth my crimes and the penalty for them. It began with the solemn words: 'In the name of the Union of Soviet Socialist Republics,' followed by something long and unintelligible. Oh, yes, it was the same preamble as in the indictment, with its 'restoration of capitalism,' 'underground terrorist organization,' and all the rest. Only wherever that document had said 'accused,' this one said 'convicted'. . . .

Notes

1. Often rendered into English as Eugenia Semyonova Ginzburg.

2. Evgeniia Semyonovna Ginzburg, *Journey Into the Whirlwind*, transl. Paul Stevenson and Max Hayward (New York: Harcourt, Brace, Jovanovich, 1967), 417.

3. Nikolai Naumovich Elvov's history of the Communist Party had angered Stalin.

4. Under Soviet law everyone had the right to a public trial; however, the definition of 'public' was highly suspect.

5. Sergei Kirov was Secretary of the Central Committee of the CPSU. His assassination in December 1934 provided Stalin with an excuse to launch the wave of purges which followed.

Study Question

1. Was there any way under the system described here to demonstrate one's loyalty?

JOSEPH GOEBBELS

Joseph Paul Goebbels (1897–1945) was the foremost German National Socialist propagandist. He was one of the few highly educated members of the Party's elite, having graduated from the University of Heidelberg with a Ph.D. in 1921. He joined the National Socialist Party during its formative years and was appointed district party leader in Berlin in 1926. From this position he founded Der Angriff (The Attack), *one of the Party's most successful newspapers. Goebbels' propaganda techniques were essential to Hitler's rise*

to power. When Hitler came to power in 1933 he made Goebbels Propaganda Minister. This position gave him complete control over radio, press, cinema, and theatre. His most virulent propaganda was directed against the Jews. Goebbels remained loyal to Hitler until the end; in April 1945, he and his family committed suicide while Berlin was falling to Soviet troops. In the following speech, delivered on 15 March 1933, Goebbels discusses the aims of the new Ministry of Popular Enlightenment and Propaganda.

Joseph Goebbels stands in the centre of this photograph of the Nazi hierarchy. From left to right: Hitler, Goering, Goebbels, and Hess. Courtesy of the Franklin D. Roosevelt Library.

THE REICH MINISTRY OF POPULAR ENLIGHTENMENT AND PROPAGANDA

I see in the setting up of the new Ministry of Popular Enlightenment and Propaganda by the Government a revolutionary act in so far as the new Government no longer intends to leave the people to their own devices. This government is in the truest sense of the word a people's government. It arose out of the people and will always execute the will of the people. I reject most passionately the idea that this government stands for reactionary aims, that we are reactionaries. We want to give the people their due, though admittedly in another form than occurred under parliamentary democracy.

In the newly-established Ministry of Popular Enlightenment and Propaganda I envisage the link between regime and people, the living contact between the national government, as the expression of the people's will, and the people

themselves. In the past few weeks we have seen an increasing coordination between Reich policy and the policy of the states, and in the same way I view the first task of the new Ministry as being to establish coordination between the Government and the whole people. If this government is determined never and under no circumstances to give way, then it has no need of the lifeless power of the bayonet, and in the long run will not be content with 52 per cent behind it and with terrorizing the remaining 48 per cent, but will see its most immediate task as being to win over that remaining 48 per cent.

. . . It is not enough for people to be more or less reconciled to our regime, to be persuaded to adopt a neutral attitude towards us, rather we want to work on people until they have capitulated to us, until they grasp ideologically that what is happening in Germany today not only must be accepted but also can be accepted.

Propaganda is not an end in itself, but a means to an end. If the means achieves the end then the means is good. Whether it always satisfies stringent aesthetic criteria or not is immaterial. But if the end has not been achieved then this means has in fact been inadequate. The aim of our movement was to mobilize people, to organize people, to win them for the national revolutionary ideal. This aim—even the most hostile person cannot dispute this—has been achieved and that represents the verdict on our propaganda methods. The new Ministry has no other aim than to unite the nation behind the ideal of the national revolution. If the aim has been achieved then people can pronounce judgment on my methods if they wish; that would be a matter of complete indifference for the Ministry would then by its efforts have achieved its goal. If, however, the aim is not achieved then although I might be able to prove that my propaganda methods satisfied all the laws of aesthetics I would have done better to become a theatre producer or the director of an Academy of Art not the Minister of a Ministry of Popular Enlightenment and Propaganda . . .

The most important tasks of this Ministry must be the following: first, all propaganda ventures and all institutions of public information belonging to the Reich and the states must be centralized in one hand. Furthermore, it must be our task to instill into these propaganda facilities a modern feeling and bring them up to date. We must not allow technology to run ahead of the Reich but rather the Reich must keep pace with technology. Only the latest thing is good enough. We are living in an age when policies must have mass support . . . the leaders of today must be modern princes of the people, they must be able to understand the people but need not follow them slavishly. It is their duty to tell the masses what they want and put it across to the masses in such a way that they understand it too. . . .

> **Study Question**
>
> 1. Does Goebbels' conception of the role of propaganda differ substantially from the role played by advertising in today's society?

ADOLF HITLER

Adolf Hitler (1889–1945) gave the following speech to the National Socialist Women's Section (NS Frauenbund) on 8 September 1934, just eighteen months after assuming the chancellorship of Germany. This was during the period in which the Nazis were attempting to consolidate absolute power over the German state. The speech explains the National Socialist view of male and female roles. Only a small number of women were able to rise to positions of power within the National Socialist women's organizations and very few women were able to retain the powerful positions they had occupied during the Weimar era.

SPEECH TO THE NATIONAL SOCIALIST *FRAUENBUND*

The slogan 'Emancipation of women' was invented by Jewish intellectuals and its content was formed by the same spirit. In the really good times of German life the German woman had no need to

DIE FRAUEN VERTRAUEN IHM:

Der Führer begrüßt Krankenschwestern

Adolf Hitler spricht mit einer Frau aus dem Volke

Women and children figured prominently in propaganda pictures of Hitler. Here, Hitler greets German nurses and 'a woman of the people'. Image courtesy of Randall Bytwerk, Calvin College.

emancipate herself. She possessed exactly what nature had necessarily given her to administer and preserve; just as the man in his good times had no need to fear that he would be ousted from his position in relation to the woman.

In fact the woman was least likely to challenge his position. Only when he was not absolutely certain in his knowledge of his task did the eternal instinct of self and race-preservation begin to rebel in women. There then grew from this rebellion a state of affairs which was unnatural and which lasted until both sexes returned to the respective spheres which an eternally wise providence had preordained for them.

If the man's world is said to be the State, his struggle, his readiness to devote his powers to the service of the community, then it may perhaps be said that the woman's is a smaller world. For her world is her husband, her family, her children, and her home. But what would become of the greater world if there were no one to tend and care for the smaller one? How could the greater world survive if there were no one to make the cares of the smaller world the content of their lives? No, the greater world is built on the foundation of this smaller world. This greater world cannot survive if the smaller world is not stable. Providence has entrusted to the woman the cares of that world which is her very own, and only on the basis of this smaller world can the man's world be formed and built up. The two worlds are not antagonistic. They complement each other, they belong together just as man and woman belong together.

We do not consider it correct for the woman to interfere in the world of the man, in his main sphere. We consider it natural if these two worlds remain distinct. To the one belongs the strength of feeling, the strength of the soul. To the other belongs the strength of vision, of toughness, of decision, and of the willingness to act. In the one case this strength demands the willingness of the woman to risk her life to preserve this important cell and to multiply it, and in the other case it demands from the man the readiness to safeguard life.

The sacrifices which the man makes in the struggle of his nation, the woman makes in the preservation of that nation in individual cases. What the man gives in courage on the battlefield, the woman gives in eternal self-sacrifice, in eternal pain and suffering. Every child that a woman brings into the world is a battle, a battle waged for the existence of her people. And both must therefore mutually value and respect each other when they see that each performs the task that Nature and Providence have ordained. And this mutual respect will necessarily result from this separation of the functions of each.

It is not true, as Jewish intellectuals assert, that respect depends on the overlapping of the spheres of activity of the sexes; this respect demands that neither sex should try to do that which belongs to the sphere of the other. It lies in the last resort in the fact that each knows that the other is doing everything necessary to maintain the whole community. . . .

So our women's movement is for us not something which inscribes on its banner as its programme the fight against men, but something which has as its programme the common fight together with men. For the new National Socialist national community acquires a firm basis precisely because we have gained the trust of millions of women as fanatical fellow-combatants, women who have fought for the common life in the service of the common task of preserving life,

who in that combat did not set their sights on the rights which a Jewish intellectualism put before their eyes, but rather on the duties imposed by nature on all of us in common.

Whereas previously the programmes of the liberal, intellectualist women's movements contained many points, the programme of our National Socialist Women's movement has in reality but one single point, and that point is the child, that tiny creature which must be born and grow strong and which alone gives meaning to the whole life-struggle. . . .

> **Study Question**
>
> 1. Why do you believe that so many women supported the National Socialist Party?

DAVID BUFFUM

On the night of 9–10 November 1938 the National Socialist regime orchestrated a series of attacks on the remaining German-Jewish population. Synagogues were burned, Jewish shops vandalized, and approximately 30,000 Jews were arrested. Ninety-one Jews were killed and the German-Jewish community was forced to pay for the damages. Most of these attacks were carried out by the Sturmabteilung (SA)

and the Scjutzstaffel (SS). Following Kristallnacht (often translated as the Night of Broken Glass due to the number of shop windows broken during the night) there was a substantial increase in the number of Jews attempting to emigrate from Germany. At the time David Buffum was the American Consul in the city of Leipzig. His report on the events of Kristallnacht follows.

ON *KRISTALLNACHT*

The shattering of shop windows, looting of stores and dwellings of Jews, which began in the early hours of 10 November 1938, was hailed subsequently in the Nazi press as a 'spontaneous wave of righteous indignation throughout Germany, as a result of the cowardly Jewish murder of Third Secretary von Rath[1] in the German

Embassy at Paris'. So far as a very high percentage of the German populace is concerned, a state of popular indignation that would spontaneously lead to such excesses, can be considered as nonexistent. On the contrary, in viewing the ruins and attendant measures employed, all of the local crowds observed were obviously benumbed

The synagogue at Aachen after the devastating attacks on *Kristallnacht*, 10 November 1938. Reprinted by permission of the United Holocaust Memorial Museum (29817).

over what had happened and aghast over the unprecedented fury of Nazi acts that had been or were taking place with bewildering rapidity throughout their city. . . .

At 3 AM on 10 November 1938 was unleashed a barrage of Nazi ferocity as had had no equal hitherto in Germany, or very likely anywhere else in the world since savagery began. Jewish buildings were smashed into and contents demolished or looted. In one of the Jewish sections an eighteen-year-old boy was hurled from a three-storey window to land with both legs broken on a street littered with burning beds and other household furniture and effects from his family's and other apartments. This information was supplied by an attending physician. It is reported from another quarter that among domestic effects thrown out of a Jewish building, a small dog descended four

flights on to a cluttered street with a broken spine. Although apparently centered in poorer districts, the raid was not confined to the humble classes. One apartment of exceptionally refined occupants known to this office was violently ransacked, presumably in a search for valuables which was not in vain, and one of the marauders thrust a cane through a priceless medieval painting portraying a biblical scene. Another apartment of the same category is known to have been turned upside down in the frenzied pursuit of whatever the invaders were after. Reported loss by looting of cash, silver, jewellery, and otherwise easily convertible articles, has been apparent.

Jewish shop windows by the hundreds were systematically and wantonly smashed throughout the entire city at a loss estimated at several millions of marks. There are reports that substantial losses have been sustained on the famous Leipzig 'Grühl', as many of the shop windows at the time of the demolition were filled with costly furs that were seized before the windows could be boarded up. In proportion to the general destruction of real estate, however, losses of goods are felt to have been relatively small. The spectators who viewed the wreckage when daylight had arrived were mostly in such a bewildered mood that there was no danger of impulsive acts, and the perpetrators probably were too busy in carrying out their schedule to take off a whole lot of time for personal profit. At all events, the main streets of the city were a positive litter of shattered plate glass. According to reliable testimony, the debacle was executed by SS men and Stormtroopers not in uniform, each group having been provided with hammers, axes, crowbars, and incendiary bombs.

Three synagogues in Leipzig were fired simultaneously by incendiary bombs and all sacred objects and records desecrated or destroyed, in most cases hurled through the windows and burned in the streets. No attempts whatsoever were made to quench the fires, the activity of the fire brigade being confined to playing water on adjoining buildings. All of the synagogues were irreparably gutted by flames, and the walls of the two that are close to the consulate are now being razed. The blackened frames have been centres of attraction during the past week of terror for eloquently silent and bewildered crowds. One of the largest clothing stores in the heart of the city was destroyed by flames from incendiary bombs, only the charred walls and gutted roof having been left standing. As was the case with the synagogues, no attempts on the part of the fire brigade were made to extinguish the fire, although apparently there was a certain amount of apprehension for adjacent property, for the walls of a coffee house next door were covered with asbestos and sprayed by the doughty firemen. It is extremely difficult to believe, but the owners of the clothing store were actually charged with setting the fire and on that basis were dragged from their beds at 6 AM and clapped into prison.

Tactics which closely approached the ghoulish took place at the Jewish cemetery where the temple was fired together with a building occupied by caretakers, tombstones uprooted, and graves violated. Eyewitnesses considered reliable the report that ten corpses were left unburied at this cemetery for a whole week because all gravediggers and cemetery attendants had been arrested.

Ferocious as was the violation of property, the most hideous phase of the so-called 'spontaneous' action has been the wholesale arrest and transportation to concentration camps of male German Jews between the ages of sixteen and sixty, as well as Jewish men without citizenship. This has been taking place daily since the night of horror. This office has no way of accurately checking the numbers of such arrests, but there is very little question that they have run to several thousands in Leipzig alone. Having demolished dwellings and hurled most of the movable effects onto the streets, the insatiably sadistic perpetrators threw many of the trembling inmates into a small

stream that flows through the Zoological Park, commanding horrified spectators to spit at them, defile them with mud, and jeer at their plight. The latter incident has been repeatedly corroborated by German witnesses who were nauseated in telling the tale. The slightest manifestation of sympathy evoked a positive fury on the part of the perpetrators, and the crowd was powerless to do anything but turn horror-stricken eyes from the scene of abuse, or leave the vicinity. These tactics were carried out the entire morning of 10 November without police intervention and they were applied to men, women, and children.

There is much evidence of physical violence, including several deaths. At least half-a-dozen cases have been personally observed, victims with bloody, badly bruised faces having fled to this office, believing that as refugees their desire to emigrate could be expedited here. As a matter of fact this consulate has been a bedlam of humanity for the past ten days, most of these visitors being desperate women, as their husbands and sons had been taken off to concentration camps.

Similarly violent procedure was applied throughout this consular district, the amount of havoc wrought depending upon the number of Jewish establishments or persons involved. It is understood that in many of the smaller communities even more relentless methods were employed than was the case in the cities. Reports have been received from Weissenfels to the effect that the few Jewish families there are experiencing great difficulty in purchasing food. It is reported that three Aryan professors of the University of Jena have been arrested and taken off to concentration camps because they had voiced disapproval of this insidious drive against mankind.

Note

1.   Ernst vom Rath was shot on 7 November 1938 at the German Embassy in Paris; he died on 9 November. Herschel Grynszpan, a seventeen-year-old Polish-

German Jew, was accused of the murder. The Nazis used this event as an excuse to attack the German-Jewish community on the night of 9–10 November. Grynszpan's motives remain a subject of controversy.

Study Question

1. Was the crowd 'powerless' to do anything under the circumstances?

FORTUNE MAGAZINE

Getúlio Vargas (1882–1954) rose to power in Brazil at the end of a long period of republican rule, in which powerful coffee interests dominated politics. Vargas hoped to end Brazil's reliance on the unstable world market for coffee and usher in a more broadly based program of industrialization. However, opposition from the coffee oligarchs led him to consolidate power in 1934. Using dictatorial controls, Vargas promoted Brazilian nationalism and cracked down on all leftist movements. The article which follows discusses the nature and impact of the Vargas regime; it appeared in Fortune *magazine in 1939.*

GETÚLIO VARGAS AND THE *ESTADO NOVO*

The Brazilian Government is a dictatorship, under a constitution that takes effect only as it is implemented by the dictator's decrees. Although there are liberal tendencies in the regime, labor laws, public works, and certain cooperative economic controls—the usual forms of democracy have been abandoned and probably will remain in the discard for some time to come. The reason is quite simple. Brazilian politics are dominated, as are politics in nearly all Latin American countries, by the influence of the leading army officers, whose hold over their troops is based on personal loyalty. In Brazil this group felt a natural affinity for the Integralista movement[1] and its fascist doctrine. They were thoroughly tired of the squabbles and the oratorical displays of the sectional politicians. Getúlio saw early in 1937 that if the choice lay between the Integralistas and a democratic President supported by a popular assembly, then the preponderant weight of the army would be thrown to the Integralistas and Brazil would indeed be delivered over to fascism.

Moved by this perception, and perhaps even more by a politician's desire to hold on to a job, Getúlio took over the government himself. It was the only way to keep the army in line, and how narrowly it succeeded was shown by the Integralista and army plot just described. While putting down fascism with one hand, Getúlio now spares no pains to keep the army happy and to play off its leaders against one another. The new barracks just completed at Recife include a purple swimming pool and a movie auditorium. Integralistas could scarcely do more. The army is kept busy with its own internal feuds and does not have to worry about politics. And so, as long as the threat of fascism remains, Brazil, by ironic circumstance, is being made safe for democracy by dictatorial means.

The man who is preserving this delicate balance came to prominence up the customary political ladder: military academy, law school, small state jobs, deputy in Rio, Cabinet Minister, and Governor of his native state. Now fifty-six years old, Getúlio is physically a little man, with fine eyes, a strong profile, and a corporeal outline that would at once win him the nickname of 'Tubby' in an American university. He laughs often and heartily, and the laughter is not forced. An enthusiastic beginner at golf—he sometimes breaks 110—he gets in a round at least every Sunday. Getúlio has three sons and two daughters, most prominent of whom is the younger daughter, Alzira, who collects a salary for her titular job as lawyer to the Bank of Brazil, works closely with her father, and calls him 'boss', for, unlike Getúlio, she speaks English well. Getúlio is genuinely popular, and although there are many in São Paulo who refer to him as 'that man' or call him by his full name, Getúlio Vargas, rather than the usual Getúlio, the President is widely liked because of his engaging personality and admired for his uncanny political shrewdness. . . .

Naturally enough, the present regime in Brazil is presented to the people as something a good deal more philosophical than a mere political expedient. Indeed the regime arrogates to itself the best features of all popular systems and proudly labels them the New State, Estado Novo. The name came into use just after the golpe (coup d'état) of 10 November 1937, when Getúlio seized power and closed both federal and state legislatures; but subsequently the designation Estado Novo has been used retroactively on the theory that the golpe was a logical, planned step in an evolution that started in 1930. And that evolution presents certain alarming traits: extreme nationalism, Red-baiting, censorship, army control, and the turgid rhetoric of men straining to justify themselves. Let us take up these traits one by one.

The Estado Novo is decidedly nationalistic. Two-thirds of all employees in each job category in a foreign company must be Brazilians. Pilots of planes flying on national lines (as contrasted with international through routes) must be Brazilians. Brazilians must be paid the same salary as foreigners if they hold the same jobs. Waterpower and mineral resources can be exploited today only by companies controlled by Brazilians, and oil can be exploited only by the government. The constitution provides that all banks and insurance companies are to be nationalized (but so far foreign banks and insurance companies still operate as before). Twenty per cent of the coal bought by a factory must be national coal, although the quality is so poor that some factories simply buy it and pile it up in a dump heap. Alcohol made from Brazilian sugar must be mixed with all gasoline, the percentage varying in different states. Manioc flour must be mixed with wheat flour. A bachelor's tax is contemplated.

Getúlio has said: 'The Estado Novo does not recognize individual rights against the collective state. Individuals have no rights, they have duties. The rights belong to the collective state.' The worst sin a Brazilian can commit is to be a Communist; or to be what is known in this country as a 'fellow traveler'. Or even to possess volumes of Karl Marx. A man who is not a Communist may still get a couple of months in jail if someone complains that he is a Communist. . . .

A censor from the police is assigned to every newspaper office and his pencil deletes whatever is construed as prejudicial to the Estado Novo. Often his chore includes international news: he will demand soft pedaling of a renewed Nazi drive against Jews, as last winter, or the final absorption of Czechoslovakia by Germany. Part of this is policy, to avoid the appearance of taking sides on international questions; part of it is laziness, the reluctance of the censor to stand up under the accusations of prejudice leveled at him by local German officials. The censor also has a special interest to see that the military are treated with the utmost respect. Mail is censored to an unknown extent, but most letters from Europe are strictly inspected for communism.

Getúlio has said: 'That negligible minority made up of the spiteful, the malcontents, of those who circulate rumors, of those who have been defeated, and of the saboteurs waste their time, and those who dare to disturb the order, under whatever pretext, will be punished.' Keeping an eye on malcontents is the job of the police, and there are four different kinds of police in Rio, totaling about 10,000 in all. Besides the police, the army, numbering 65,000 effectives, and on the increase, is always available for real trouble. State police, which in the Estado Novo are under federal authority, add at least 30,000 more. The army is trained by a French mission, and the navy, with 12,500 men, has U.S. instruction. Appropriations for the army and navy departments for the current year are officially set at about one-quarter of the total budget, but the amount will probably prove to be an under-statement of actual expenditures. The new armament program, projected for ten years, amounts to some $10,000,000 a year, with large orders in England now for six cruisers and other orders totaling $40,000,000 placed with Krupp for the eventual delivery of arms, which, incidentally, will use up a lot of the bloated compensation-mark balance. Over a period of years Brazil's expenditures on the armed forces have taken as much as 50 per cent of the tax revenue remaining after payments on the debt.

Note

1. The *Ação Integralista Brasileira* was a political party formed in 1932. Some of the party's ideological inspiration was drawn from Mussolini's fascist movement.

Study Question

1. Can dictatorial states such as the '*Estado Novo*' produce genuine socio-economic reforms?

TIPS FOR ANALYSIS

How did the document come to be produced?

Consider if the document was originally a written piece or a transcript of a speech. Speeches are often crafted to influence an audience to favour a certain policy or to support a particular viewpoint. Therefore, always consider what the speaker is leaving out and the ways in which this can manipulate the listener.

WEB RESOURCES

Internet Modern History Sourcebook: Fascism (see also Nazism)
http://www.fordham.edu/halsall/mod/modsbook42.html
Italian Life under Fascism
http://specialcollections.library.wisc.edu/exhibits/Fascism
German Propaganda Archive
http://www.calvin.edu/academic/cas/gpa
University of Washington Libraries: Latin American History
http://www.lib.washington.edu/subject/History/tm/latin.html

Recommended Reading

Hans Fallada, *Little Man, What Now?* (Chicago: Academy Chicago Publishers, 1992). Written in 1932—immediately prior to the Nazi rise to power—Fallada's novel spans the Weimar era. Economic deprivation falls hardest upon the 'little man', leading to radicalization, desperation, and the inevitable political choice between communism and National Socialism.

Gunter Grass, *The Tin Drum* (New York: Vintage, 1990). *The Tin Drum* chronicles the pivotal events of the First World War, the rise of the Nazis, and the National Socialist regime, including *Kristallnacht*, and the war years. Grass was one of the first German authors to condemn the involvement of ordinary Germans in the activities of the National Socialist regime and to point out the inherent danger of refusing to acknowledge guilt.

Christopher Isherwood, *Goodbye to Berlin* (New York: New Directions Publishing, 1963). Published in 1939, and set amidst the cultural decadence of the late Weimar years, *Goodbye to Berlin*—the inspiration for the musical *Cabaret*—was based on Isherwood's visits to Germany between 1929 and 1933. Sexuality, excess, and the bohemian lifestyle of the late Weimar era stand as the backdrop to the looming rise of National Socialism.

Mikhail Bulgakov, *Master and Margarita* (New York: Vintage, 1996). *Master and Margarita* was completed shortly before Bulgakov's death, but remained unpublished for twenty-six years. Through a complex interweaving of two stories, Bulgakov's satirical novel captures the worst aspects of the Stalinist era: forced collectivization, purges, arbitrary use of terror, and forced atheism.

Arthur Koestler, *Darkness at Noon* (New York: Bantam, 1984). Set in 1938, at the height of the Stalinist purges, Koestler's powerful novel tells the story of an innocent man imprisoned for crimes he did not commit, but who was, at the same time, aware that he was guilty of blind loyalty to the system which has now imprisoned him. The novel was based partly on the author's firsthand experiences.

George Orwell, *Animal Farm* and *1984* (New York: Harcourt, 2003). Orwell's fascinating analyses of totalitarianism: the first is told in allegorical form, the second through the eyes of the protagonist Winston Smith, an employee in the 'Ministry of Truth'. *Animal Farm* is the deceptively simple story of animals that, having overthrown their human masters, must create a new social order. The novel begins with the premise of equality, but concludes 'all animals are equal, but some animals are more equal than others.' *1984* is Orwell's meditation on truth, reality, ideology, resistance, and conformity.

Alexander Solzhenitsyn, *One Day in the Life of Ivan Denisovich* (New York: Bantam, 1984). Solzhenitsyn's novel—authorized for publication by Nikita Khrushchev—played a key role in the de-Stalinization era. Based partly on the author's experiences in the Stalinist Russian labour camps, the novel delves into the absurdities of life under a system where everything is relative to the whims of an absolute authority.

John Wray, *Right Hand of Sleep* (New York: Vintage, 2002). After a twenty-year exile in Soviet Ukraine, a deserter from the Austro-Hungarian armies of the Great War returns to Austria in 1938. There he encounters the desperation of interwar Austria and the implications of the Anschluss. Disillusioned with socialism but uncertain about the future, the protagonist watches Nazism spread slowly through the region.

Recommended Viewing

Zemlya [Earth] (USSR/Ukraine, 1930). Director: Alexander Dovzhenko (Silent, B&W). In this highly idealistic vision of collective farming in Ukraine, Dovzhenko demonizes the Kulak class and idealizes life on Stalin's collective farms. The film contains visually stunning imagery. It was created just prior to the artificially induced famines that decimated Ukraine in the early 1930s.

Triumph of the Will (Germany, 1934). Director: Leni Riefenstahl (B&W). *Triumph of the Will* remains both a documentary masterpiece—the template for the modern documentary—and a tremendously controversial film. Set during the Nuremberg Party rally in 1934, the film provides insights into nature of the regime, the atmosphere of the time, and the mind of the senior Nazi leaders.

Alexander Nevsky (USSR, 1938). Director: Sergei Eisenstein (B&W). Ostensibly a retelling of the thirteenth century Russian defeat of the Teutonic knights, *Alexander Nevsky* was designed to inspire the Soviet people against the looming threat from Hitler's Germany. Despite its propagandistic intent, the film remains impressive for its cinematography and for Sergei Prokofiev's score.

The Great Dictator (USA, 1940). Director: Charles Chaplin (B&W). Chaplin's first talking picture launches a comedic attack on Adolf Hitler, Nazi Germany, and Benito Mussolini. Despite its comedic premise, the film raises vital issues such as anti-Semitism, ghettoization, and discrimination. It closes with Chaplin stepping out of character to plead for peace and humanity.

The Conformist (Italy/France/West Germany, 1970). Director: Bernardo Bertolucci. Bertolucci's psychological drama focuses on the transformation of one man into a loyal fascist. The film links fascist support to a particular personality type, rather than socio-economic causes, but Bertolucci also captures the atmosphere of fascist Italy in this production.

Kaigenrai (Japan, 1973). Director: Yoshishige Yoshida (B&W). *Kaigenrai* is a semi-biographical portrait of the life of Kitta Ikki, whose writings are often seen as being responsible for the rise of radical militarism in the 1930s and 1940s. The film addresses the origins of Japanese militarism, the Emperor system, and racism.

CHAPTER SIX

GLOBAL DEPRESSION

By the late 1920s the interconnectedness of the global economy was evident to many observers. Postwar recovery in Europe had been fuelled in large part by ongoing loans from the United States and by American demand for European goods. Latin America's economies were also tied to the United States, largely by neo-colonial trade agreements. The economies of the colonial world remained tightly bound to the economies of the mother countries, and Japan had created an entire network of formal and informal economic ties throughout East Asia. In short, any major economic downturn was bound to have a ripple effect around the globe.

As well, despite the outward appearance of economic stabilization and, in some cases, growth, serious structural weaknesses remained. Agriculture found itself in a perpetual crisis throughout the 1920s. Industry struggled to modernize— which meant to mechanize—and as a result there were substantial job losses as workers were displaced by assembly lines. At the same time the banking and financial sectors in many nations remained dangerously unregulated. The United States government in particular had adopted a hands-off approach to nearly all facets of the economy; the businessmen, after all, knew best what was good for business, or so many believed.

The first signs of serious financial instability came in the United States in the middle of 1929. Rampant speculation, fuelled by lax margin requirements and easy credit, had driven the stock market to impossible heights. The *New York Times* reported in March 1929 that '[p]laying the stock market has become a major American pastime.'[1] Though some well-informed investors were able to pull their profits out of the market in the summer months, most investors stayed in, believing that the market would continue to soar upwards. It did not. The crash came in late October. On the 28th stock prices began to decline precipitously (thirteen per cent over the day's trading); on the 29th prices fell a further twelve per cent. By the

A Dorothea Lange portrait of Florence Thompson, a 32-year old mother of seven living in a makeshift tent—a common fate for the families of migrant labourers. New York World-Telegram and the Sun Newspaper Photograph Collection. Courtesy of the Library of Congress, Prints and Photographs Division (LC-USZ62-58355).

time the bottom was reached in 1932 the market had fallen eighty-nine per cent overall.[2]

The resulting financial crisis in the United States had immediate global repercussions. America called in its loans to Europe and erected an historically high tariff wall which restricted access to the American market. This, in turn, led to retaliatory protectionist measures by its leading trading partners. The net result was a massive decline in global trade: American imports from Europe dropped from $1,334 million in 1929 to $390 million in 1932; exports from the United States had been $2,341 million in 1929 and fell to $809 million in 1932. Total global trade dropped by sixty-six per cent between 1929 and 1934.[3] European nations, such as Germany, whose recovery had been bankrolled by the United States, were thrown into immediate economic chaos. Other nations, such as Britain, whose economy had been suffering throughout the 1920s, found their social support systems overwhelmed. In the colonial world the level of suffering varied according to the degree to which a country's economy was dependent on the mother country. However, few escaped without feeling any of the Depression's consequences. Japan also suffered and, as a result, began to move away from its reliance on the world market and to seek out new, guaranteed sources of raw materials. Meanwhile, in the United States, the government of Herbert Hoover struggled to find new ways to deal with the economic downturn. Ultimately, despite some successful public works projects, Hoover would be decisively defeated in the 1932 election, allowing Franklin D. Roosevelt to sweep into office with an unprecedented mandate for change.

This set of documents focuses, for the most part, on the Depression's impact on ordinary citizens. Heinrich Hauser describes life for Germany's unemployed; George Orwell chronicles life in Depression-era northern England. Roosevelt's inaugural address provides a sense of the condition of the United States in 1933 and the obstacles that had to be overcome. The exploitation of American workers, in some cases created by the Depression and in other cases simply worsened by it, is examined by journalist Paul Comly French. Lázaro Cárdenas provides some sense of the economic damage wrought by the Depression in Mexico as does W.E.B. Du Bois in his discussion of the fate of Liberia. Finally, Neville Chamberlain and W.L. Mackenzie King discuss the contentious policy of appeasement, which was, to a large degree, a product of the economic crises of the 1930s.

Notes

1. Floyd Norris, 'Looking Back at the Crash of 1929', *New York Times*, http://www.nytimes.com/library/financial/index-1929-crash.html.
2. Ibid.
3. 'Smoot-Hawley Tariff', *Bureau of Public Affairs*, US Department of State, http://www.state.gov/r/pa/ho/time/id/17606.htm.

HEINRICH HAUSER

Heinrich Hauser (1901–55) was a journalist and photographer during the Weimar Republic. He left Germany in the late 1930s, fearing for the safety of his Jewish wife, and relocated to the United States (he returned to Germany in 1948). While in the United States, Hauser wrote several novels and travel books.

In the following account he relates the experiences of Germany's unemployed, in particular the psychological impact of poverty, during the worst years of the Depression—the early 1930s. This was the period in which support for both the National Socialist Party and the German Communist Party increased markedly.

WITH GERMANY'S UNEMPLOYED

An almost unbroken chain of homeless men extends the whole length of the great Hamburg–Berlin highway. There are so many of them moving in both directions, impelled by the wind or making their way against it, that they could shout a message from Hamburg to Berlin by word

National Socialist election banners appealed to the desperation of Germans during the Depression era. Here the banner indicates that Hitler will bring work and bread. Reprinted by permission of the United States Holocaust Memorial Museum (98518).

of mouth. It is the same scene for the entire two hundred miles, and the same scene repeats itself . . . all the highways in Germany over which I traveled this year presented the same aspects . . .

. . . Most of the hikers paid no attention to me. They walked separately or in small groups, with their eyes on the ground. And they had the queer, stumbling gait of barefooted people, for their shoes were slung over their shoulders.

Some of them were guild members—carpenters, milkmen, and bricklayers—but they were in a minority. Far more numerous were those whom one could assign to no special profusion or craft—unskilled young people, for the most part, who had been unable to find a place for themselves in any city or town in Germany, and who had never had a job and never expected to have one. There was something else that had never been seen

before—whole families that had piled all their goods into baby carriages and wheelbarrows that they were pushing along as they plodded forward in dumb despair. It was a whole nation on the march.

I saw them—and this was the strongest impression that the year 1932 left with me—I saw them, gathered into groups, of fifty or a hundred men, attacking fields of potatoes. I saw them digging up the potatoes and throwing them into sacks while the farmer who owned the field watched them in despair and the local policeman looked on gloomily from the distance. I saw them staggering toward the lights of the city as night fell, with their sacks on their backs. What did it remind me of? Of the War, of the worst periods of starvation in 1917 and 1918, but even then people paid for the potatoes. . . .

I saw that the individual can know what is happening only by personal experience. I know what it is to be a tramp. I know what cold and hunger are. I know what it is to spend the night outdoors or behind the thin walls of a shack through which the wind whistles. I have slept in holes, under bridges, and under cattle shelters in pastures. But there are two things that I have only recently experienced—begging and spending the night in a municipal lodging house.

I entered the huge Berlin municipal lodging house in a northern quarter of the city . . .

. . . There was an entrance arched by a brick vaulting, and a watchman sat in a little wooden sentry box . . . We stood waiting in the corridor. Heavy steam rose from the men's clothes. Some of them sat down on the floor, pulled off their shoes, and unwound the rags that were bound around their feet. More people were constantly pouring in the door, and we stood closely packed together. Then another door opened. The crowd pushed forward, and people began forcing their way almost eagerly through this door, for it was warm in there. Without knowing it I had caught the rhythm of the municipal lodging house. It means waiting, standing around, and then suddenly jumping up.

We arrange ourselves in long lines, each leading up to one of these men, and the mill begins to grind. . . .

As the line passes in single file the official does not look up at each new person to appear. He only looks at the paper that is handed to him. These papers are for the most part in-valid cards or unemployment certificates. The very fact that the official does not look up robs the homeless applicant of self-respect, although he may look too beaten down to feel any. . . .

Now it is my turn and the questions and answers flow as smoothly as if I were an old hand. But finally I am asked, 'Have you ever been here before?'

'No.'

'No?' The question reverberates through the whole room. The clerk refuses to believe me and looks through his card catalogue. But no, my name is not there. The clerk thinks this strange, for he cannot have made a mistake, and the terrible thing that one notices in all these clerks is that they expect you to lie. They do not believe what you say. They do not regard you as a human being but as an infection, something foul that one keeps at a distance. He goes on. 'How did you come here from Hamburg?'

'By truck.'

'Where have you spent the last three nights?'

I lie coolly.

'Have you begged?'

I feel a warm blush spreading over my face. It is welling up from the bourgeois world that I have come from. 'No.'

'Never mind. The day will come, comrade, when there's nothing else to do.' And the line breaks into laughter again, the bitterest laughter I have ever heard, the laughter of damnation and despair . . .

Again the crowd pushes back in the kind of rhythm is so typical of a lodging house, and we are all herded into the undressing room. I cling to the man who spoke to me. He is a Saxon with a friendly manner and he has noticed that I am a stranger here. A certain sensitiveness, an almost perverse, spiritual alertness makes me like him very much.

Out of a big iron chest each of us takes a coat hanger that would serve admirably to hit somebody over the head with. As we undress the room becomes filled with the heavy breath of poverty. We are so close together that we brush against each other every time we move. Anyone who has been a soldier, anyone who has been to a public bath is perfectly accustomed to the look of naked bodies. But I have never seen anything quite so repulsive as all these hundreds of withered human frames. For in the homeless army the majority are men who have been defeated in the struggle of life, crippled, old, and sick. There is no repulsive disease of which traces are not to be seen here. There is no form of mutilation or degeneracy that is not represented, and the naked bodies of the old men are in a disgusting state.

It is superfluous to describe what follows. Towels are handed out, then nightgowns—long, sack-like affairs made of plain unbleached cotton but freshly washed. Then slippers . . . Distribution of spoons, distribution of enamelware bowls with the words 'Property of the City of Berlin' written on their sides. Then the meal itself. A big kettle is carried in. Men with yellow smocks have brought it and men with yellow smocks ladle out the food. These men, too, are homeless and they have been expressly picked by the establishment and given free food and lodging and a little pocket money in exchange for their work about the house.

Where have I seen this kind of food distribution before? In a prison that I once helped to guard in the winter of 1919 during the German civil war. There was the same hunger then, the same trembling, anxious expectation of rations. Now the men are standing in a long row, dressed in their plain nightshirts that reach to the ground, and the noise of their shuffling feet is like the noise of big wild animals walking up and down the stone floor of their cages before feeding time . . .

My next recollection is sitting at table in another room on a crowded bench that is like a seat in a fourth-class railway carriage. Hundreds of hungry mouths make an enormous noise eating their food. The men sit bent over their food like animals who feel that someone is going to take it away from them. They hold their bowl with their left arm part way around it, so that nobody can take it away, and they also protect it with their other elbow and with their head and mouth, while they move the spoon as fast as they can between their mouth and the bowl. . . .

We shuffle into the sleeping room, where each bed has a number painted in big letters on the wall over it. You must find the number that you have around your neck, and there is your bed, your home for one night. It stands in a row with fifty others and across the room there are fifty more in a row. . . .

. . . Only a few people, very few, move around at all. The others lie awake and still, staring at their blankets, wrapped up in themselves, but not sleeping. Only an almost soldierly sense of

comradeship, an inner self-control engendered by the presence of so many people, prevents the despair that is written on all these faces from expressing itself. The few who are moving about do so with the tormenting consciousness of men who merely want to kill time. They do not believe in what they are doing.

Going to sleep means passing into the unconscious, eliminating the intelligence. And one can read deeply into a man's life by watching the way he goes to sleep. For we have not always slept in municipal lodgings. There are men among us who still move as if they were in a bourgeois bedchamber. . . .

. . . The air is poisoned with the breath of men who have stuffed too much food into empty stomachs. There is also a sickening smell of Lysol. It seems completely terrible to me, animals die, plants wither, but men always go on living.

> **Study Question**
>
> 1. Which of Germany's political parties would attract those people most affected by the Depression?

GEORGE ORWELL

Eric Arthur Blair was born in India in 1903 (d. 1950). His parents worked in the Indian civil service and Blair initially found a job with the Indian Imperial Police in Burma. After growing disillusioned with British imperial policies, he resigned from the civil service. Blair published four novels in the 1930s

under the pen name George Orwell, and three non-fictional works, including The Road to Wigan Pier *(1937). The book was commissioned by the Left Book Club and provides a sympathetic look at the lives of impoverished miners during the Depression in the Lancashire town of Wigan.*

THE ROAD TO WIGAN PIER

The first sound in the mornings was the clumping of the mill-girls' clogs down the cobbled street. Earlier than that, I suppose, there were factory whistles which I was never awake to hear.

There were generally four of us in the bedroom, and a beastly place it was, with that denied impermanent look of rooms that are not serving their rightful purpose. Years earlier the house had been an ordinary dwelling-house, and when the Brookers had taken it and fitted it out as a tripe-shop and lodging-house, they had inherited some of the more useless pieces of furniture and had never had the energy to remove them. We were therefore sleeping in what was still recognizably a drawing-room. Hanging from the ceiling there was a heavy glass chandelier on which the dust was so thick that it was like fur. And covering most of one wall there was a huge hideous piece of junk, something between a sideboard and a hall-stand, with lots of carving and little drawers and strips of looking-glass, and there was a once-gaudy carpet ringed by the slop-pails of years, and two gilt chairs with burst seats, and one of those old-fashioned horsehair armchairs which you slide off when you try to sit on them. The room had been turned into a bedroom by thrusting four squalid beds in among this other wreckage.

My bed was in the right-hand corner on the side nearest the door. There was another bed across the foot of it and jammed hard against it (it had to be in that position to allow the door to open) so that I had to sleep with my legs doubled up; if I straightened them out I kicked the occupant of the other bed in the small of the back. He was an elderly man named Mr Reilly, a mechanic of sorts and employed 'on top' at one of the coal pits. Luckily he had to go to work at five in the morning, so I could uncoil my legs and have a couple of hours' proper sleep after he was gone. In the bed opposite there was a Scotch miner who had been injured in a pit accident (a huge chunk of stone pinned him to the ground and it was a couple of hours before they could lever it off), and had received five hundred pounds compensation. He was a big handsome man of forty, with grizzled hair and a clipped moustache, more like a sergeant-major than a miner, and he would lie in bed till late in the day, smoking a short pipe. The other bed was occupied by a succession of commercial travelers, newspaper-canvassers, and hire-purchase touts who generally stayed for a couple of nights. . . .

The shop was a narrow, cold sort of room. On the outside of the window a few white letters, relics of ancient chocolate advertisements, were scattered like stars. Inside there was a slab upon which lay the great white folds of tripe, and the grey flocculent stuff known as 'black tripe', and the ghostly translucent feet of pigs, ready boiled. It was the ordinary 'tripe and pea' shop, and not much else was stocked except bread, cigarettes, and tinned stuff. 'Teas' were advertised in the window, but if a customer demanded a cup of tea he was usually put off with excuses. Mr Brooker, though out of work for two years, was a miner by trade, but he and his wife had been keeping shops of various kinds as a side-line all their lives. At one time they had had a pub, but they had lost their licence for allowing gambling on the premises. I doubt whether any of their businesses had ever paid; they were the kind of people who run a business chiefly in order to have something to grumble about. Mr Brooker was a dark, small-boned, sour, Irish-looking man, and astonishingly dirty. I don't think I ever once saw his hands clean. As Mrs Brooker was now an invalid he prepared most of the food, and like all people with permanently dirty hands he had a peculiarly intimate, lingering manner of handling things. If he gave you a slice of bread-and-butter there was always a black thumb-print on it. Even in the early morning when he descended into the mysterious den behind Mrs Brooker's sofa and fished out the tripe, his hands were already black. I heard dreadful stories from the other lodgers about the place where the tripe was kept. Blackbeetles were said to swarm there. I do not know how often fresh consignments of tripe were ordered, but it was at long intervals, for Mrs Brooker used to date events by it. 'Let me see now, I've had in three lots of froze (frozen tripe) since that happened,' etc. We lodgers were never given tripe to eat. At the time I imagined that this was because tripe was too expensive; I have since thought that it was merely because we knew too much about it. The

Brookers never ate tripe themselves, I noticed.

The only permanent lodgers were the Scotch miner, Mr Reilly, two old-age pensioners, and an unemployed man on the PAC[1] named Joe—he was the kind of person who has no surname. The Scotch miner was a bore when you got to know him. Like so many unemployed men he spent too much time reading newspapers, and if you did not head him off he would discourse for hours about such things as the Yellow Peril, trunk murders, astrology, and the conflict between religion and science. The old-age pensioners had, as usual, been driven from their homes by the Means Test. They handed their weekly ten shillings over to the Brookers and in return got the kind of accommodation you would expect for ten shillings; that is, a bed in the attic and meals chiefly of bread-and-butter. One of them was of 'superior' type and was dying of some malignant disease—cancer, I believe. He only got out of bed on the days when he went to draw his pension. The other, called by everyone Old Jack, was an ex-miner aged seventy-eight who had worked well over fifty years in the pits. He was alert and intelligent, but curiously enough he seemed only to remember his boyhood experiences and to have forgotten all about the modern mining machinery and improvements. He used to tell me tales of fights with savage horses in the narrow galleries underground. When he heard that I was arranging to go down several coal mines he was contemptuous and declared that a man of my size (six feet two and a half) would never manage the 'travelling'; it was no use telling him that the 'travelling' was better than it used to be. But he was friendly to everyone and used to give us all a fine shout of 'Good night, boys!' as he crawled up the stairs to his bed somewhere under the rafters. What I most admired about Old Jack was that he never cadged; he was generally out of tobacco towards the end of the week, but he always refused to smoke anyone else's. The Brookers had insured the lives of both old-age pensioners with one of the tanner-a-week

companies. It was said that they were overheard anxiously asking the insurance-tout 'how long people lives when they've got cancer'. . . .

Besides these there was a floating clientele of commercial travellers of the poorer sort, travelling actors—always common in the North because most of the larger pubs hire variety artists at the week-ends—and newspaper-canvassers. The newspaper-canvassers were a type I had never met before. Their job seemed to me so hopeless, so appalling that I wondered how anyone could put up with such a thing when prison was a possible alternative. They were employed mostly by weekly or Sunday papers, and they were sent from town to town, provided with maps and given a list of streets which they had to 'work' each day. If they failed to secure a minimum of twenty orders a day, they got the sack. So long as they kept up their twenty orders a day they received a small salary—two pounds a week, I think; on any order over the twenty they drew a tiny commission. The thing is not so impossible as it sounds, because in working-class districts every family takes in a twopenny weekly paper and changes it every few weeks; but I doubt whether anyone keeps a job of that kind long. The newspapers engage poor desperate wretches, out-of-work clerks and commercial travellers and the like, who for a while make frantic efforts and keep their sales up to the minimum; then as the deadly work wears them down they are sacked and fresh men are taken on. I got to know two who were employed by one of the more notorious weeklies. Both of them were middle-aged men with families to support, and one of them was a grandfather. They were on their feet ten hours a day, 'working' their appointed streets, and then busy late into the night filling in blank forms for some swindle their paper was running—one of those schemes by which you are 'given' a set of crockery if you take out a six weeks' subscription and send a two-shilling postal order as well. The fat one, the grandfather, used to fall asleep with his head on a pile of forms. Neither of them could afford the pound a week which the

Brookers charged for full board. They used to pay a small sum for their beds and make shamefaced meals in a corner of the kitchen off bacon and bread-and-margarine which they stored in their suit-cases. . . .

Of course, as I was indoors a good deal, I heard all about the Brookers' woes, and how everyone swindled them and was ungrateful to them, and how the shop did not pay and the lodging-house hardly paid. By local standards they were not so badly off, for, in some way I did not understand, Mr Brooker was dodging the Means Test and drawing an allowance from the PAC, but their chief pleasure was talking about their grievances to anyone who would listen. Mrs Brooker used to lament by the hour, lying on her sofa, a soft mound of fat and self-pity, saying the same things over and over again. 'We don't seem to get no customers nowadays. I don't know 'ow it is. The tripe's just a-laying there day after day—such beautiful tripe it is, too! It does seem 'ard, don't it now?' etc., etc., etc. All Mrs Brookers' laments ended with 'It does seem 'ard, don't it now?' like the refrain of a ballade. Certainly it was true that the shop did not pay. The whole place had the unmistakable dusty, flyblown air of a business that is going down. But it would have been quite useless to explain to them why nobody came to the shop, even if one had had the face to do it; neither was capable of understanding that last year's dead bluebottles supine in the shop window are not good for trade. . . .

On the day when there was a full chamber-pot under the breakfast table I decided to leave. The place was beginning to depress me. It was not only the dirt, the smells, and the vile food, but the feeling of stagnant meaningless decay, of having got down into some subterranean place where people go creeping round and round, just like blackbeetles, in an endless muddle of slovened jobs and mean grievances. The most dreadful thing about people like the Brookers is the way they say the same things over and over again. It gives you the feeling that they are not real people at all, but a kind of ghost for ever rehearsing the same futile rigmarole. In the end Mrs Brooker's self-pitying talk—always the same complaints, over and over, and always ending with the tremulous whine of 'It does seem 'ard, don't it now?'—revolted me even more than her habit of wiping her mouth with bits of newspaper. But it is no use saying that people like the Brookers are just disgusting and trying to put them out of mind. For they exist in tens and hundreds of thousands; they are one of the characteristic by-products of the modern world. You cannot disregard them if you accept the civilization that produced them. For this is part at least of what industrialism has done for us. Columbus sailed the Atlantic, the first steam engines tottered into motion, the British squares stood firm under the French guns at Waterloo, the one-eyed scoundrels of the nineteenth century praised God and filled their pockets; and this is where it all led—to labyrinthine slums and dark back kitchens with sickly, ageing people creeping round and round them like blackbeetles. It is a kind of duty to see and smell such places now and again, especially smell them, lest you should forget that they exist; though perhaps it is better not to stay there too long.

The train bore me away, through the monstrous scenery of slag-heaps, chimneys, piled scrap-iron, foul canals, paths of cindery mud criss-crossed by the prints of clogs. This was March, but the weather had been horribly cold and everywhere there were mounds of blackened snow. As we moved slowly through the outskirts of the town we passed row after row of little grey slum houses running at right angles to the embankment. At the back of one of the houses a young woman was kneeling on the stones, poking a stick up the leaden waste-pipe which ran from the sink inside and which I suppose was blocked. I had time to see everything about her—her sacking apron, her clumsy clogs, her arms reddened by the cold. She looked up as the train passed, and I was almost near enough to catch her eye. She had a round pale face, the usual exhausted face of the slum girl who is twenty-five and looks forty, thanks to miscarriages and drudgery; and it wore, for the second in which I saw it, the most desolate, hopeless expression I have ever seen. It struck me then that we are mistaken when we say that 'It isn't the same for them as it would be for us,' and that people bred in the slums can imagine nothing but the slums. For what I saw in her face was not the ignorant suffering of an animal. She knew well enough what was happening to her—understood as well as I did how dreadful a destiny it was to be kneeling there in the bitter cold, on the slimy stones of a slum backyard, poking a stick up a foul drain-pipe. . . .

Note

1. PACs (Public Assistance Committees) were set up by local governments in the early 1930s to deliver relief payments to the unemployed. Before any assistance was given, however, the recipient had to submit to a humiliating Means Test. 'On the PAC' meant that a person was receiving relief from the local authorities.

Study Question

1. Orwell condemns 'civilization' as leading inevitably to the slums and desperation he witnessed in northern England. Is this an accurate assessment?

FRANKLIN D. ROOSEVELT

When Franklin D. Roosevelt (1882–1945) took office, statistics showed that the economy was already beginning to respond to the measures put in place by Herbert Hoover. However, the confidence of the American people was at an all-time low. In his inaugural address, Roosevelt laid out, step-by-step, the approach he would take to deal with the worst effects of the Depression. Note throughout Roosevelt's inaugural address the degree to which he intended to increase the government's power to intervene in the lives of its citizens, as well as the clear warning to Congress regarding the penalty for inaction in the latter part of the speech.

INAUGURAL ADDRESS OF THE PRESIDENT, 4 MARCH 1933

I am certain that my fellow Americans expect that on my induction into the Presidency I will address them with a candor and a decision which the present situation of our nation impels. This is pre-eminently the time to speak the truth, the whole truth, frankly and boldly. Nor need we shrink from honestly facing conditions in our country today. This great nation will endure as it has endured, will revive and will prosper. So, first of all, let me assert my firm belief that the only thing we have to fear is fear itself—nameless, unreasoning, unjustified terror which paralyzes needed efforts to convert retreat into advance. In every dark hour of our national life a leadership of frankness and vigor has met with that understanding and support of the people themselves which is essential to victory. I am convinced that you will again give that support to leadership in these critical days.

In such a spirit on my part and on yours we face our common difficulties. They concern, thank God, only material things. Values have

Franklin D. Roosevelt during a 1932 speech. Courtesy of the Franklin D. Roosevelt Library.

shrunken to fantastic levels; taxes have risen; our ability to pay has fallen; government of all kinds is faced by serious curtailment of income; the means of exchange are frozen in the currents of trade; the withered leaves of industrial enterprise lie on every side; farmers find no markets for their produce; the savings of many years in thousands of families are gone.

More important, a host of unemployed citizens face the grim problem of existence, and an equally great number toil with little return. Only a foolish optimist can deny the dark realities of the moment.

Yet our distress comes from no failure of substance. We are stricken by no plague of locusts. Compared with the perils which our forefathers conquered because they believed and were not afraid, we have still much to be thankful for. Nature still offers her bounty and human efforts

have multiplied it. Plenty is at our doorstep, but a generous use of it languishes in the very sight of the supply. Primarily this is because rulers of the exchange of mankind's goods have failed, through their own stubbornness and their own incompetence, have admitted their failure, and abdicated. Practices of the unscrupulous money changers stand indicted in the court of public opinion, rejected by the hearts and minds of men.

True they have tried, but their efforts have been cast in the pattern of an outworn tradition. Faced by failure of credit they have proposed only the lending of more money. Stripped of the lure of profit by which to induce our people to follow their false leadership, they have resorted to exhortations, pleading tearfully for restored confidence. They know only the rules of a generation of self-seekers. They have no vision, and when there is no vision the people perish.

The money changers have fled from their high seats in the temple of our civilization. We may now restore that temple to the ancient truths. The measure of the restoration lies in the extent to which we apply social values more noble than mere monetary profit.

Happiness lies not in the mere possession of money; it lies in the joy of achievement, in the thrill of creative effort. The joy and moral stimulation of work no longer must be forgotten in the mad chase of evanescent profits. These dark days will be worth all they cost us if they teach us that our true destiny is not to be ministered unto but to minister to ourselves and to our fellow men.

Recognition of the falsity of material wealth as the standard of success goes hand in hand with the abandonment of the false belief that public office and high political position are to be valued only by the standards of pride of place and personal profit; and there must be an end to a conduct in banking and in business which too often has given to a sacred trust the likeness of callous and selfish wrongdoing. Small wonder that confidence languishes, for it thrives only on honesty, on honor, on the sacredness of obligations, on faithful protection, on unselfish performance; without them it cannot live.

Restoration calls, however, not for change in ethics alone. This Nation asks for action, and action now.

Our greatest primary task is to put people to work. This is no unsolvable problem if we face it wisely and courageously. It can be accomplished in part by direct recruiting by the Government itself, treating the task as we would treat the emergency of a war, but at the same time, through this employment, accomplishing greatly needed projects to stimulate and reorganize the use of our natural resources.

Hand in hand with this we must frankly recognize the overbalance of population in our industrial centers and, by engaging on a national scale in redistribution, endeavor to provide a better use of the land for those best fitted for the land. The task can be helped by definite efforts to raise the values of agricultural products and with this the power to purchase the output of our cities. It can be helped by preventing realistically the tragedy of the growing loss through foreclosure of our small homes and our farms. It can be helped by insistence that the Federal, State, and local governments act forthwith on the demand that their cost be drastically reduced. It can be helped by the unifying of the relief activities which today are often scattered, uneconomical, and unequal. It can be helped by national planning for and supervision of all forms of transportation and of communications and other utilities which have a definitely public character. There are many ways in which it can be helped, but it can never be helped merely by talking about it. We must act and act quickly.

Finally, in our progress toward a resumption of work we require two safeguards against a return of the evils of the old order; there must be a strict supervision of all banking and credits and investments; there must be an end

to speculation with other people's money, and there must be provision for an adequate but sound currency.

There are the lines of attack. I shall presently urge upon a new Congress, in special session, detailed measures for their fulfillment, and I shall seek the immediate assistance of the several States.

Through this program of action we address ourselves to putting our own national house in order and making income balance outgo. Our international trade relations, though vastly important, are in point of time and necessity secondary to the establishment of a sound national economy. I favour as a practical policy the putting of first things first. I shall spare no effort to restore world trade by international economic readjustment, but the emergency at home cannot wait on that accomplishment.

The basic thought that guides these specific means of national recovery is not narrowly nationalistic. It is the insistence, as a first consideration, upon the interdependence of the various elements in and parts of the United States—a recognition of the old and permanently important manifestation of the American spirit of the pioneer. It is the way to recovery. It is the immediate way. It is the strongest assurance that the recovery will endure.

In the field of world policy I would dedicate this nation to the policy of the good neighbor— the neighbor who resolutely respects himself and, because he does so, respects the rights of others— the neighbor who respects his obligations and respects the sanctity of his agreements in and with a world of neighbors.

If I read the temper of our people correctly, we now realize as we have never realized before our interdependence on each other; that we cannot merely take but we must give as well; that if we are to go forward, we must move as a trained and loyal army willing to sacrifice for the good of a common discipline, because without such discipline no progress is made, no leadership becomes effective. We are, I know, ready and willing to submit our lives and property to such discipline, because it makes possible a leadership which aims at a larger good. This I propose to offer, pledging that the larger purposes will bind upon us all as a sacred obligation with a unity of duty hitherto evoked only in time of armed strife.

With this pledge taken, I assume unhesitatingly the leadership of this great army of our people dedicated to a disciplined attack upon our common problems.

Action in this image and to this end is feasible under the form of government which we have inherited from our ancestors. Our Constitution is so simple and practical that it is possible always to meet extraordinary needs by changes in emphasis and arrangement without loss of essential form. That is why our constitutional system has proved itself the most superbly enduring political mechanism the modern world has produced. It has met every stress of vast expansion of territory, of foreign wars, of bitter internal strife, of world relations.

It is to be hoped that the normal balance of executive and legislative authority may be wholly adequate to meet the unprecedented task before us. But it may be that an unprecedented demand and need for undelayed action may call for temporary departure from that normal balance of public procedure.

I am prepared under my constitutional duty to recommend the measures that a stricken nation in the midst of a stricken world may require. These measures, or such other measures as the Congress may build out of its experience and wisdom, I shall seek, within my constitutional authority, to bring to speedy adoption.

But in the event that the Congress shall fail to take one of these two courses, and in the event that the national emergency is still critical, I shall not evade the clear course of duty that will then confront me. I shall ask the congress for the one remaining instrument to meet the crisis—broad Executive power to wage a war against the emergency, as great as the power that would be given to me if we were in fact invaded by a foreign foe.

For the trust reposed in me I will return the courage and the devotion that befit the time. I can do no less.

We face the arduous days that lie before us in the warm courage of national unity; with the clear consciousness of seeking old and precious moral values; with the clean satisfaction that comes from the stern performance of duty by old and young alike. We aim at the assurance of a rounded and permanent national life.

We do not distrust the future of essential democracy. The people of the United States have not failed. In their need they have registered a mandate that they want direct, vigorous action. They have asked for discipline and direction under leadership. They have made me the present instrument of their wishes. In the spirit of the gift I take it.

In this dedication of a Nation we humbly ask the blessing of God. May He protect each and every one of us. May He guide me in the days to come.

Study Question

1. Based upon his inaugural address, what did Roosevelt believe was the key to the Nation's recovery? Was he correct?

PAUL COMLY FRENCH

The exploitation of children and women in the textile industry has long been a feature of industrial nations. However, during the 1930s Franklin Roosevelt's supportive attitude towards trade unions—traditionally weak and ineffective in the United States—encouraged some workers to take a stand against the factory owners who exploited them. The conditions described below were not particularly unusual in this industry and were only peripherally related to the ongoing economic depression.

As early as 1909 protests against child labour were common. This protest in New York included many young workers—the signs were written in both English and Yiddish. George Grantham Bain Collection. Courtesy of the Library of Congress, Prints and Photographs Division (LC-USZ62-22198).

CHILDREN ON STRIKE

Allentown, Pennsylvania, 20 May

Shocking conditions in the sweatshops of Pennsylvania, where 200,000 men, women, and children work long hours for starvation wages, became front-page news through the efforts of the 'baby strikers' of the Lehigh Valley. Aided by the presence of Mrs Gifford Pinchot on their picket line, they won the first skirmish in their fight against intolerable conditions when some of the employers signed an agreement providing for shorter working hours, a minimum-wage scale, and an immediate 10 per cent increase in wages. Unfortunately the agreement does not affect all the mills in Allentown or those in Easton, Northampton, and Catasqua, where the children are still on the picket line.

Another victory against the sweatshop was won in Philadelphia when 5,000 garment workers, encouraged by the public support of the children's strike against the Morris Freezer plant in Allentown and the D. & D. shirt factory in Northampton, a nearby borough, went on strike. Within two days the operators signed an agreement raising wages 10 per cent, establishing a forty-four-hour week in place of the previous fifty-four-hour week, and allowing to complete unionization of the shops.

Meanwhile Governor Pinchot's commission for the investigation of sweatshops will continue its hearings with a view to recommending to the next session of the General Assembly legislation which would abolish sweatshops and child labor in Pennsylvania. These hearings have so far produced tales of hideous working conditions, long hours, and miserable wages, comparable only to those which obtained in the earliest years of the Industrial Revolution. They have also revealed the forces of reaction against which the reformers must contend. Much credit for the limited victory in the children's strike must go to Mayor Fred E. Lewis of Allentown, who has vigorously protested for years against the evils and degradation of the sweatshops. But Charles Fox, burgess of the neighboring borough of Northampton, where the D. & D. plant is located, holds a different view. 'If I had my way,' he told the Governor's commission, 'I'd give no food orders to unemployed persons who urged factory workers to strike.' And his wife, who handles unemployment relief in Northampton, has even more amazing ideas. 'I don't believe the strikers should be entitled to any unemployment relief,' she testified before the commission, 'because they don't have souls.'

According to a quiet survey which Mrs Pinchot has made in every section of Pennsylvania,

sweatshops are not confined to the Lehigh Valley and Philadelphia. And many of the case histories she has collected tell a story of lost youth and saddened childhood. In Gottlieb's Sewing Factory at York the usual wage is $3 or $4 a week, girls in Bernstein's Factory at York reported a payment of $2.90 for two weeks' work—an average of 3 cents an hour. At the York Suit Company button sewers receive from $3 to $4 a week for fifty hours; York tobacco workers said they received $2.50 for a week's work totaling fifty hours, while workers in a second cigar factory in this rich Lancaster County agricultural section said their wages averaged $1.60 for fifty-four hours. A silk mill in York charged girls $10 for 'teaching them how to become operators'. Pressers in the Lehigh Valley Shirt Company in Allentown receive $4 a week as against $14 paid for the same work two years ago. At the Adkins Shirt Company in Allentown only three girls in the place were over fourteen; their pay averaged from $1.30 to $2 a week, while one girl, with seven years' experience, earned the munificent salary of $7 a week. One boy in an Allentown shop earned 10 cents a week for a ten-week period; another Allentown shirt company paid 14 cents a dozen for a complicated operation, a high wage compared with the 8 cents paid for the same operation in another shop. The Caddy Shirt Company of Allentown moved out of town in the night owing four weeks' wages.

Hale A. Guss, borough manager of Northampton, told the Governor's commission that either Harry or Nathan Dashefsky—the two operate one of the worst sweatshops in the Lehigh Valley, the D. & D. Shirt Company—suggested having a gun 'planted' on a union organizer. Another State official, a woman, said that one of the Dashefskys asked her why he couldn't have national guardsmen to protect his mill against the 'baby strikers'.

'Why?' she asked. 'Aren't the police sufficient protection?' 'Yes,' he said, 'but they won't fight.'

One boy said he worked from 7 AM until 5 PM and then returned to the factory three nights each week to work from 7 PM until 3 AM; others told of being ordered to hide in the cellar and on fire escapes when State inspectors came to the mill; many of the girls testified they had been forced to accept the attentions of their employers or face instant dismissal. A titian-haired girl receiving 55 cents a week said the mill superintendent offered her a 100 per cent wage increase if she would accept his attentions at least three times weekly. Others, mere children, told of being taken to New York hotels for week-ends as playthings for the owners of the factories and for the purpose of enticing buyers to purchase shirts made in their mills. State officials, aided by the vigorous demands of Mrs Pinchot, plan criminal action against these men for violation of the Mann Act.

Other testimony, offered by fourteen-year-old Martin Kroboth, a trimmer, explained how the Dashefsky brothers saved the two-cent check tax by assessing each employee. The boy said his last check, for six days' work, was 96 cents. But he did not get all of that. An additional 10 per cent was deducted as a wage cut together with the two cents for the check tax. Another Allentown employer developed an even better system. He deducted 33 cents a week from the pay envelopes of each child to repay a fine of $100 assessed by the State for his failure to carry workmen's compensation insurance. Frank Selthofer, considered the 'fastest' trimmer in the plant, received $1.73 for two weeks' work.

According to figures of the Bureau of Industrial Relations, many of the children are attempting to support entire families on their meager earnings. 'Hours of labor in many of the Pennsylvania sweatshops range from fifty to ninety a week,' said Stephen Raushenbush, of the bureau, 'and the wages start at 50 cents and go to $10. This deplorable condition is responsible for $1.98 silk dresses, 3-for-10-cent cigars, 39-cent silk hosiery, $10 suits and top coats, and 25 cent shirts and neckties.' More than half of the men's garment industry of the State operates on a sweatshop basis. The average in the cigar-making industry is about 70 per cent, while about 85 per cent of the production of men's shirts and pajamas is conducted on a sweatshop basis. 'The State is powerless in many cases,' Mr Raushenbush said, 'because no statutes prevent women from working for $1 a week or men for any figure they'll accept.'

Sweatshop conditions affect workers throughout the Commonwealth, from the anthracite coal miners of northeastern Pennsylvania to the soft-coal miners of the southwest, and from the silk and hosiery mills of the east to the shops, factories, and mills of the west. The opening attack on these conditions by the 'baby strikers' received immediate support from the Philadelphia *Record* and the Pittsburgh *Press*. The *Record* carried editorials and cartoons depicting the plight of the children, while the *Press*, a Scripps-Howard newspaper, devoted columns to its campaign to rid the State of the evils of the sweatshop. The editor of the *Press*, Edward T. Leech, spoke over the radio as part of the paper's fight. The minor victories in Philadelphia and Allentown are encouraging, but the war on the sweatshop has only begun.

Study Question

1. Given the economic situation of the nation in 1933, was there any way to prevent the abuse of workers who lacked even the most basic of rights?

LÁZARO CÁRDENAS

Lázaro Cárdenas (1895–1970) was elected to Mexico's presidency in 1934 on promises of land and labour reform. Cárdenas redistributed millions of hectares of land, most of which were then transformed into communal farms, and he also introduced compulsory primary education. He next announced the nationalization of Mexico's oil industry, an industry that had been developed by British and American interests—most notably Standard Oil—and had returned virtually no benefits to the people of Mexico. Cárdenas's actions were a drastic attempt to change this situation. In the following radio address, given in March 1938, President Cárdenas discussed the problems created by foreign oil companies in Mexico.

SPEECH TO THE NATION

In each and every one of the various attempts of the Executive to arrive at a final solution of the conflict within conciliatory limits, and which include the periods prior to and following the . . . action which has produced the present situation, the intransigence of the companies was clearly demonstrated.

Their attitude was therefore premeditated and their position deliberately taken, so that the Government, in defence of its own dignity, had to

Cárdenas (centre) meets with labour leaders from the oil industry in Tamaulipas State in 1938. Support from labour leaders would be essential to successful reforms in the industry. New York World-Telegram and the Sun Newspaper Photograph Collection.

resort to application of the Expropriation Act, as there were no means less drastic or decision less severe that might bring about a solution of the problem.

For additional justification of the measure herein announced, let us trace briefly the history of the oil companies' growth in Mexico and of the resources with which they have developed their activities.

It has been repeated *ad nauseam* that the oil industry has brought additional capital for the development and progress of the country. This assertion is an exaggeration. For many years, throughout the major period of their existence, the oil companies have enjoyed great privileges for development and expansion, including customs and tax exemptions and innumerable prerogatives; it is these factors of special privilege, together with the prodigious productivity of the oil deposits granted them by the Nation often against public will and law, that represent almost the total amount of this so-called capital.

Potential wealth of the Nation; miserably underpaid native labor; tax exemptions; economic privileges; governmental tolerance—these are the factors of the boom of the Mexican oil industry.

Let us now examine the social contributions of the companies. In how many of the villages bordering on the oil fields is there a hospital, or school or social centre, or a sanitary water supply, or an athletic field, or even an electric plant fed by the millions of cubic meters of natural gas allowed to go to waste?

What centre of oil production, on the other hand, does not have its company police force for the protection of private, selfish, and often illegal interests? These organizations, whether authorized by the Government or not, are charged with innumerable outrages, abuses, and murders, always on behalf of the companies that employ them.

Who is not aware of the irritating discrimination governing construction of the company camps?

Comfort for the foreign personnel; misery, drabness, and insalubrity for the Mexicans. Refrigeration and protection against tropical insects for the former; indifference and neglect, medical service and supplies always grudgingly provided, for the latter; lower wages and harder, more exhausting labor for our people.

The tolerance which the companies have abused was born, it is true, in the shadow of the ignorance, betrayals, and weakness of the country's rulers; but the mechanism was set in motion by investors lacking in the necessary moral resources to give something in exchange for the wealth they have been exploiting.

Another inevitable consequence of the presence of the oil companies, strongly characterized by their anti-social tendencies, and even more harmful than all those already mentioned, has been their persistent and improper intervention in national affairs.

The oil companies' support to strong rebel factions against the constituted government in the Huasteca region of Veracruz and in the Isthmus of Tehuantepec during the years 1917 to 1920 is no longer a matter for discussion by anyone. Nor is anyone ignorant of the fact that in later periods and even at the present time, the oil companies have almost openly encouraged the ambitions of elements discontented with the country's government, every time their interests were affected either by taxation or by the modification of their privileges or the withdrawal of the customary tolerance. They have had money, arms, and munitions for rebellion, money for the anti-patriotic press which defends them, money with which to enrich their unconditional defenders. But for the progress of the country, for establishing an economic equilibrium with their workers through a just compensation of labor, for maintaining hygenic conditions in the districts where they themselves operate, or for conserving the vast riches of the natural petroleum gases from destruction, they have neither money, nor financial possibilities, nor the desire to subtract the necessary funds from the volume of their profits.

Nor is there money with which to meet a responsibility imposed upon them by judicial verdict, for they rely on their pride and their economic power to shield them from the dignity and sovereignty of a Nation which has generously placed in their hands its vast natural resources and now finds itself unable to obtain the satisfaction of the most elementary obligations by ordinary legal means.

As a logical consequence of this brief analysis, it was therefore necessary to adopt a definite and legal measure to end this permanent state of affairs in which the country sees its industrial progress held back by those who hold in their hands the power to erect obstacles as well as the motive power of all activity and who, instead of using it to high and worthy purposes, abuse their economic strength to the point of jeopardizing the very life of a Nation endeavoring to bring about the elevation of its people through its own laws, its own resources, and the free management of its own destinies.

With the only solution to this problem thus placed before it, I ask the entire Nation for moral and material support sufficient to carry out so justified, important, and indispensable a decision.

The Government has already taken suitable steps to maintain the constructive activities now going forward throughout the Republic, and for that purpose it asks the people only for its full confidence and backing in whatever dispositions the Government may be obliged to adopt.

Nevertheless, we shall, if necessary, sacrifice all the constructive projects on which the Nation has embarked during the term of this Administration in order to cope with the financial obligations imposed upon us by the application of the Expropriation Act to such vast interests; and although the subsoil of the country will give us considerable economic resources with which to meet the obligation of indemnization which

we have contracted, we must be prepared for the possibility of our individual economy also suffering the indispensable readjustments, even to the point, should the Bank of Mexico deem it necessary, of modifying the present exchange rate of our currency, so that the whole country may be able to count on sufficient currency and resources with which to consolidate this act of profound and essential economic liberation of Mexico.

It is necessary that all groups of the population be imbued with a full optimism and that each citizen, whether in agricultural, industrial, commercial, transportation, or other pursuits, develop a greater activity from this moment on, in order to create new resources which will reveal that the spirit of our people is capable of saving the nation's economy by the efforts of its own citizens.

And, finally, as the fear may arise among the interests now in bitter conflict in the field of international affairs that a deviation of raw materials fundamentally necessary to the struggle in which the most powerful nations are engaged might result from the consummation of this act of national sovereignty and dignity, we wish to state that our petroleum operations will not depart a single inch from the moral solidarity maintained by Mexico with the democratic nations, whom we wish to assure that the expropriation now decreed has as its only purpose the elimination of obstacles erected by groups who do not understand the evolutionary needs of all peoples and who would themselves have no compunction in selling Mexican oil to the highest bidder, without taking into account the consequences of such action to the popular masses and the nations in conflict.

Study Question

1. Why do you suppose that the US (or any of the other countries) affected by the expropriation decision did not intervene militarily to defend its interests?

W.E.B. Du Bois

Liberia was one of the few nations to escape formal colonial subjugation during the so-called scramble for Africa in the late nineteenth century. However, as W.E.B. Du Bois clearly demonstrates, it was no less affected by the spread of global capitalism. Du Bois reveals the ways in which corporate interests *had gained control of Liberia and focuses on the economic vulnerability which this created during global economic downturns. The essay also reveals the inability of the League of Nations to enforce its authority when confronting the major powers of the era.*

LIBERIA, THE LEAGUE, AND THE UNITED STATES

A 1918 portrait of W.E.B. Du Bois. Shortly after this picture was taken Du Bois began writing on the peace treaty and the proposed League of Nations. Courtesy of the Library of Congress, Prints and Photographs Division (LC-USZ62-16767).

I remember standing once in a West African forest where thin, silver trees loomed straight and smooth in the air. There were two men with me. One was a black man, Solomon Hood, United States Minister to Liberia; a man of utter devotion, whose solicitude for the welfare of Liberia was like a sharp pain driving him on. And he thought he had found the solution. The solution was the white man beside us. He was a rubber expert sent by the Firestone Corporation of the United States to see if rubber could be grown in Liberia.

Those were rather ticklish times in the rubber situation. England was attempting to corner the world's production and prices were shooting up. Henry Ford flew south to seek plantations. Edison experimented with new plants. Firestone sent his representative to Liberia.

Most people cannot easily visualize the peculiarly helpless position of a small outland in the modern world of industry. It seems that a rich country like Liberia ought easily to be self-supporting and to secure machinery, experts and modern luxuries in return for its raw material. But this is much more easily said than done. In the first place, it must raise the raw materials which the world at the moment demands, and it often finds that the price of its product is so manipulated that absolutely no dependence can be put on it. In fact, between changing and disappearing markets, freight carrying monopolies, high cost of machinery, and absence of expert knowledge, Liberia, like many other small, isolated countries, has been in continual financial difficulties. She needs expert advice; but expert advice from white men, accompanied by invested capital, means loss of political power. And Liberia is jealous of her independence—jealous and proud. Indeed, the record of peace, efficiency and ability made by this little poverty-stricken settlement of the rejected and despised, sitting on the edge of Africa and fighting the world in order to be let alone, is, despite querulous criticism, one of the most heartening efforts in human history. . . .

Just before the World War industrial aggression began again. The Sunlight Soap interests in Great Britain tried to get a concession which would monopolize the palm oil. When Liberia resisted, England began to press for payment of Liberian debts which had been defaulted. Sedition spread among the frontier force, and it looked as though France or England was on the point of seizing the country. Liberia moved swiftly. She sent a delegation to America, which appealed to Booker T. Washington. Mr Washington appealed to Theodore Roosevelt. Theodore Roosevelt needed the Negro vote, and he appointed a Liberian commission. The commission went out and made negotiations for a refunding of the Liberian debt. A new loan of $2,000,000 was raised at 5 per cent. It looked as though at last Liberia had got a start, because, while a Financial Adviser with large powers was the string attached to this new loan, nevertheless there was no American disposition to interfere with Liberian independence.

Then suddenly came the World War and smashed all these dreams. Liberia, despite her large German trade, was forced to declare in favor of the Allies. One inducement was a loan promised her by the United States Government. Before this went through, however, the war was over and Congress refused to confirm the loan. Again Liberia was on the rocks. She sent another delegation to the United States, headed by President King, but little was accomplished.

For five or six years Liberia staggered on during the reaction from the World War, but finally began to make progress between 1922 and 1926. 'The economic and financial future of the country looked brighter than for many years.'[1] But she was handicapped. She needed roads, machinery, local industry. She still feared foreign capital, but she needed it.

Then came Solomon Porter Hood, as United States Minister. He knew Firestone slightly. He corresponded with him. The rubber situation developed. King was reelected President, and at his inauguration, as a gesture of good will, I was designated by cable to act as Special Minister Plenipotentiary and Envoy Extraordinary. The appointment was purely ornamental, but I did all I could to cooperate with Hood and Africa and Liberia and tell them of the tremendous interest which American colored people had in them.

Firestone determined to enter into contract with Liberia to start rubber plantations, and began negotiations. On my return to the United States I wrote to him. I know what modern capital does to poor and colored peoples. I know what European imperialism had done to Asia and Africa; but, nevertheless, I had not then lost faith in the capitalistic system, and I believed that it was possible for a great corporation, headed by a man of vision, to go into a country with something more than the mere ideal of profit. I tried to state this to Mr Firestone. I intimated that the one thing above all which he must avoid was taking capital into a small country and putting it under the control of officials who despised the natives and organized ruthless exploitation. I tried to point out that by using trained American Negroes he might avoid this situation in Liberia, and have a more normal development by putting in the hands of people of the same race, local and immigrant, such power over the invested capital as would divert it, at least to some extent, toward ends of social welfare as well as towards profit. I had no reply to my letter. Perhaps it never got by the assistant secretary. When I heard of the terms which Firestone demanded in Liberia my heart began to fall. The Liberians resisted, and if the leading officials had had their way, the contract would never have been signed.

Firestone presented a contract which gave his company the right to select wherever he wished in Liberia one million acres of land at a nominal rental of only 6 cents an acre, and he insisted that because of certain public improvements Liberia must have more money; particularly, a modern harbor must be built, so that passengers and freight would not have to take that gloriously exciting but dangerous and costly ride in the surf boats over the bar. This insistence upon a loan increased the opposition in Liberia, but the Firestone Company refused to come on any other terms. Moreover, Liberia recognized that her only protection against the territorial and economic aggression of France and England lay in the attitude of America, and she was certain that if an American loan were made the United States would protect Liberia in order to safeguard the loan. In spite, therefore, of bitter opposition on the part of many high officials and without the knowledge of even some of the cabinet officers, the Firestone contract was signed in September 1926. Raymond L. Buell says: 'In response to the question why they agreed to this loan in the face of early opposition and manifestly unfavorable terms, all of them gave the same reply: The State Department of the United States told us to accept this loan.'[2] . . . .

The sudden influx of cash to Liberia in 1926 started a boom. The country was stirred as never before by a vision of prosperity. Mr Buell, who was there then, wrote: 'Business has begun to "hum". More hard money is in circulation than ever before. While most of this goes to private interests, the government has already secured a few thousand dollars a year additional revenue. Many American missionaries and educators are enheartened; they now believe that Liberia will survive.'[3]

Hardly had apparent prosperity come to Liberia than the shadow of the Great Depression began to move across the world. The British rubber monopoly broke. The price of rubber fell from 72 cents to 5 cents. Far from needing a million acres, Firestone took only 50,000 and cut wages of his laborers in half, from a shilling to 6 pence a day;

he did practically nothing about the promised $300,000 harbor. As the commercial and industrial situation began to tighten, opposition began to seethe in Liberia. The former opponents of the loan became vocal. It was pointed out by the opposition that President King was getting rich, not simply by his connection with the Firestone project, but by other transactions; and high government officials were implicated with him. . . .

The League of Nations appointed a committee, headed by Dr Cuthbert Christy, an Englishman. A colored American, Dr Charles S. Johnson, appointed by President Hoover, and the grand old man, the Honorable Arthur Barclay, one of the finest products of Liberia, were the other two members. This Commission made its report in 1930.[4] On the whole it was thorough and frank. The Commission made a careful investigation and proved that domestic slavery existed among the more primitive Liberian tribes; that there was pawning of children; and especially that laborers were recruited among the tribes and sent out of the country to the French colony of Gabon and to the Spanish colony of Fernando Po. Military force had been used, and President King, Vice President Yancy and some other officials were involved in the accusations of profit-sharing from the proceeds of this slave-trade. Members of the frontier force were used in obtaining this labor, and also in extortion and illegal taxation.

The Report of the International Commission of Enquiry was filed at Monrovia on 8 September 1930. The legislature met the second Monday of October, and President King gave his annual message October 30. After the report and various petitions had been received, a select committee of the House of Representatives reported December 2, and on adoption of that report President King, Vice President Yancy and other officials were retired from office. Edwin Barclay, Secretary of State, nephew of Arthur Barclay, one of the Commission, was selected to fill out the unexpired term, and took the oath on December 3. . . .

Despite this, the United States refused to recognize President Barclay and united with the British and German legations on 21 January 1931, to present notes to the Government of Liberia demanding that it ask the Council of the League of Nations to appoint an International Governing Commission to take over Liberia and administer the affairs of the country. President Barclay replied that he could not do this without violating his oath of office, but that he would ask the League of Nations to nominate capable persons to help in reorganizing the country. . . .

Meantime, the full force of the depression had struck Liberia. Prices fell. The value of Liberian exports dropped from $1,497,214 in 1927 to $856,759 in 1930. Salaries of Liberian officials were reduced on three occasions (in one case more than 50 per cent), and the Liberian Secretary of State said in 1932 that "most salaries had not been paid at all during the last seventeen months". At the same time, the debt service was absorbing larger and larger proportions of the whole income of the country.

. . . Liberia is not faultless. She lacks training, experience, and thrift. But her chief crime is to be black and poor in a rich, white world; and in precisely that portion of the world where color is ruthlessly exploited as a foundation for American and European wealth. The success of Liberia as a Negro republic would be a blow to the whole colonial slave labor system. Are we starting the United States Army toward Liberia to guarantee the Firestone Company's profits in a falling rubber market or smash another Haiti in the attempt?

Notes

1. [Du Bois] R.L. Buell, 'The Native Problem in Africa', vol. II, p. 836.
2. [Du Bois] Buell, op. cit., p. 845.
3. [Du Bois] Buell, op. cit., p. 836.
4. [Du Bois] League of Nations: International Commission of Enquiry in Liberia. 'Communication by the Government of Liberia', dated December 15, 1930, transmitting the Commission's Report (1930, VI.B.6. Official No. C. 658, 51. 272, 1930, VI).

Study Question

1. Once a country ties its economy to multinational companies is there any way to break the bonds of neo-colonialism?

NEVILLE CHAMBERLAIN / WILLIAM L. MACKENZIE KING

Neville Chamberlain's (1869–1940) policy of appeasement has been widely condemned as a shortsighted and foolhardy strategy—a strategy that guaranteed that Hitler would try to gain even greater concessions in Europe. At the time, however, there was considerable support for Chamberlain's attempt to avert another war. After all, it had been only twenty years since the Great War had claimed millions of European lives and devastated the economies of victors and vanquished alike. With the effects of the Great Depression still evident around the globe, Chamberlain's policy seemed a reasonable approach that, at minimum, brought Great Britain much needed time to prepare its military for a possible future conflict. Foreign leaders, too, hailed Chamberlain's achievement. The second document in this series is a congratulatory telegram sent from Canadian Prime Minister W.L. Mackenzie King to Chamberlain. Readers should keep in mind the situation in Canada at this time. The after-effects of the stock market crash had devastated Canada and the country was still struggling to find the correct response to the economic crisis.

Speech to the House of Commons, 3 October 1938

The Prime Minister:

Before I come to describe the Agreement which was signed at Munich in the small hours of Friday morning last, I would like to remind the House of two things which I think it very essential not to forget when those terms are being considered. The first is this: We did not go there to decide whether the predominantly German areas in the Sudetenland should be passed over to the German Reich. That had been decided already. Czechoslovakia had accepted the Anglo-French proposals. What we had to consider was the method, the conditions and the time of the transfer of the territory. The second point to remember is that time was one of the essential factors. All the elements were present on the spot for the outbreak of a conflict which might have precipitated the catastrophe. We had populations inflamed to a high degree; we had extremists on both sides ready to work up and provoke incidents; we had considerable quantities of arms which were by no means confined to regularly organised forces. Therefore, it was essential that we should quickly reach a conclusion, so that this painful and difficult operation of transfer might be carried out at the earliest possible moment and concluded as soon as was consistent, with orderly procedure, in order that we might avoid the possibility of something that might have rendered all our attempts at peaceful solution useless. . . .

Before giving a verdict upon this arrangement, we should do well to avoid describing it as a personal or a national triumph for anyone. The real triumph is that it has shown that representatives of four great Powers can find it possible to agree on a way of carrying out a difficult and delicate operation by discussion instead of by force of arms, and thereby they have averted a catastrophe which would have ended civilisation as we have known it. The relief that our escape from this great peril of war has, I think, everywhere been mingled in this country with a profound feeling of sympathy.

[*Hon. Members:* Shame.] I have nothing to be ashamed of. Let those who have, hang their heads. We must feel profound sympathy for a small and gallant nation in the hour of their national grief and loss.

Mr Bellenger: It is an insult to say it.

The Prime Minister: I say in the name of this House and of the people of this country that Czechoslovakia has earned our admiration and respect for her restraint, for her dignity, for her magnificent discipline in face of such a trial as few nations have ever been called upon to meet.

The army, whose courage no man has ever questioned, has obeyed the order of their president, as they would equally have obeyed him if he had told them to march into the trenches. It is my hope and my belief, that under the new system of guarantees, the new Czechoslovakia will find a greater security than she has ever enjoyed in the past. . . .

I pass from that subject, and I would like to say a few words in respect of the various other participants, besides ourselves, in the Munich Agreement. After everything that has been said about the German Chancellor today and in the past, I do feel that the House ought to recognise the difficulty for a man in that position to take back such emphatic declarations as he had

Chamberlain with Hitler in Godesberg, Germany, during the meeting that laid the groundwork for the Munich Conference. New York World-Telegram and the Sun Newspaper Photograph Collection.

already made amidst the enthusiastic cheers of his supporters, and to recognise that in consenting, even though it were only at the last moment, to discuss with the representatives of other Powers those things which he had declared he had already decided once for all, was a real and a substantial contribution on his part. With regard to Signor Mussolini, . . . I think that Europe and the world have reason to be grateful to the head of the Italian government for his work in contributing to a peaceful solution.

In my view the strongest force of all, one which grew and took fresh shapes and forms every day war, the force not of any one individual, but was that unmistakable sense of unanimity among the peoples of the world that war must somehow be averted. The peoples of the British Empire were at one with those of Germany, of France and of Italy, and their anxiety, their intense desire for peace, pervaded the whole atmosphere of the conference, and I believe that that, and not threats, made possible the concessions that were made. I know the House will want to hear what I am sure it does not doubt, that throughout these discussions the Dominions, the Governments of the Dominions, have been kept in the closest touch with the march of events by telegraph and by personal contact, and I would like to say how greatly I was encouraged on each of the journeys I made to Germany by the knowledge that I went with the good wishes of the Governments of the Dominions. They shared all our anxieties and all our hopes. They rejoiced with us that peace was preserved, and with us they look forward to further efforts to consolidate what has been done.

Ever since I assumed my present office my main purpose has been to work for the pacification of Europe, for the removal of those suspicions and those animosities which have so long poisoned the air. The path which leads to appeasement is long and bristles with obstacles. The question of Czechoslovakia is the latest and perhaps the most dangerous. Now that we have got past it, I feel that it may be possible to make further progress along the road to sanity.

TELEGRAM FROM PRIME MINISTER WILLIAM L. MACKENZIE KING TO BRITISH PRIME MINISTER NEVILLE CHAMBERLAIN

Ottawa, 29 September 1938
The Right Honourable Neville Chamberlain, PC, MP
Prime Minister of Great Britain
10 Downing Street,
London, England.

The heart of Canada is rejoicing tonight at the success which has crowned your unremitting efforts for peace. May I convey to you the warm congratulations of the Canadian people, and with them, an expression of their gratitude, which is felt from one end of the Dominion to the other.

My colleagues in the Government join with me in unbounded admiration at the service you have rendered mankind. Your achievements in the past month alone will ensure you an abiding and illustrious place among the great conciliators whom the United Kingdom, the British Commonwealth of Nations and the whole world will continue to honour.

On the very brink of chaos, with passions flaming, and armies marching, the voice of Reason has found a way out of the conflict which no people in their heart desired, but none seemed able to avert.

A turning point in the world's history will be reached if, as we hope, tonight's agreement means a halt to the mad race of arms, and a new start in building the partnership of all peoples. May you have health and strength to carry your great work to its completion.

W.L. Mackenzie King

Study Question

1. Why did so many countries support the appeasement policies of Chamberlain and other world leaders?

TIPS FOR ANALYSIS

Firsthand or Secondhand?

Determine whether the document you are reading was a first-hand account (the author witnessed or took part in the events personally) or a second-hand reflection. If the author did not experience the events first-hand, consider how this may have altered his or her perception of the event. If the account was written many years after the event took place, note too the impact of the passage of time.

WEB RESOURCES

American Memory—American Life Histories (from the Works Progress Administration)
http://memory.loc.gov/ammem/wpaintro/wpahome.html
New Deal Network
http://newdeal.feri.org/index.htm

The History Place—Dorothea Lange
http://www.historyplace.com/unitedstates/lange/index.html
A Guide to the Twentieth Century—The Great Depression
http://www.channel4.com/history/microsites/H/history/guide20/part06b.html

RECOMMENDED READING

Harper Lee, *To Kill a Mockingbird* (New York: Warner Books, 1988). A black man is charged with the rape of a white girl in Depression-era Maycomb, Alabama. Harper Lee's 1960 novel examines the prejudice of the American south, intensified by the economic conditions of the Sepression, as well as the conscience, compassion, and justice of the main characters and their hope for the future.

George Orwell, *The Road to Wigan Pier* (London: Victor Gollancz, 1937). A journalistic account based on Orwell's experiences in the 1930s, this text provides a portrait of the Sepression era, of unemployment, and of the resultant desperation in the industrial towns of Lancashire and Yorkshire. The book is told in two parts: the first relates the misery of life in the northern towns, and the second part is a discourse on the irrelevance of socialist theory in this situation.

Gabrielle Roy, *The Tin Flute* (Toronto: New Canadian Library, 1989). Set in the working class industrial slums of Montreal during the latter years of the Sepression, just before the Second World War, this novel provides a compassionate look at lives dominated by poverty and hopelessness, and the effort to find something more.

John Steinbeck, *The Grapes of Wrath* (New York: Penguin, 2002). The Pulitzer Prize–winning *The Grapes of Wrath* was drawn from Steinbeck's experience in the migrant camps of California in 1936. It tells of migrants from the Dust Bowl of Oklahoma who are headed towards an uncertain future in California. Destitution, abandonment, and oppression are contrasted with the basic human dignity of the Joad family.

RECOMMENDED VIEWING

Modern Times (USA, 1936). Director: Charles Chaplin (Silent, B&W). Set during the Great Depression, Chaplin's *Modern Times* attacks mechanization and the inherent dehumanization of the factory system. The film highlights many of the social problems of the time, including worker riots and communist protests.

You Only Live Once (USA, 1937). Director: Fritz Lang (B&W). Fritz Lang's second American feature film depicts much of the injustice and oppression of the Depression era, including society's attitude towards the poor, the criminals, and the downtrodden.

The Grapes of Wrath (USA, 1940). Director: John Ford (B&W). Many critics believe that John Ford's cinematic adaptation of Steinbeck's novel is the best depiction of the impact of the Depression on rural America. The film illustrates the lives of Dust Bowl migrants: migrant camps, hunger, despair, and inequality. Ford's film contains some of the most famous images of the Great Depression.

Love on the Dole (UK, 1941). Director: John Baxter (B&W). Filmed in the north of England during the 1930s, Baxter created a harrowing depiction of the ravages of the Depression and the extent to which families had to go in order to survive. Black humour punctuates the otherwise bleak narrative.

Bonheur d'occasion [*The Tin Flute*] (Canada, 1982). Director: Claude Fournier. Based on the novel by Gabrielle Roy, *The Tin Flute* is set in 1940, in the aftermath of the Depression during the early part of the Second World War. The film focuses on one family caught in the poverty of the era and the numerous obstacles facing family members as they struggle against unemployment, disease, and war.

CHAPTER SEVEN

GLOBAL WAR
AND GENOCIDE

◇

Typical damage from the German bombing during the Blitz in London. Some 43,000 Britons died during the aerial bombardment. Courtesy of the Franklin D. Roosevelt Library.

The ferocity and barbarism of the Second World War was unprecedented in the modern era. Civilians became military targets, entire peoples were targeted for extermination, and new weapons of mass destruction wiped out whole cities in an instant. By the time the war was over more than sixty million people were dead—nineteen million had been soldiers, while the rest were civilian victims of war, famine, disease, and genocide.[1]

Though few military planners openly admitted to targeting the civilian population, there was little doubt that a total war involved all of a nation's peoples in the war effort. Therefore, the line between legitimate military targets and non-combatants became much harder to establish. In some cases, such as the firebombings of Dresden and Tokyo and the atomic bombings of Hiroshima and Nagasaki, entire cities were destroyed, killing men, women, and children indiscriminately. As well, racial wars, which were carried out under the cover of the military conflict in a number of countries, targeted civilians without exception. The net result was a greater number of civilian casualties than military in almost every nation that committed forces to the war. Meanwhile, civilians determined to be 'enemy aliens' were stripped of their property and interned by ostensibly democratic governments.

Genocide was neither an invention of, nor unique to, the Second World War, but the sheer number and intensity of genocidal acts that occurred during the War was remarkable in and of itself. Adolf Hitler set the destruction of the world's Jewish population as one of his primary wartime goals. Japanese forces were instructed to 'kill all captives' when they invaded China. In the former Yugoslavia both the Croats and the Serbs engaged in 'ethnic cleansing'. Frequently these campaigns were given priority over ongoing military actions. Hitler, for example, refused to allocate railway cars to move troops to the West because they were needed for the war against the Jews. Croatian efforts to wipe out the entire Serbian population as quickly as possible created considerable antagonism between the Croatian government and its German allies.

The collection of documents in this chapter attempts to convey some of the viciousness and brutality that marked the conflict. An eyewitness describes the firebombing of the city of Dresden in 1945, while another describes the massacre committed by Japanese forces in Nanjing. An account from the 1960s analyzes the Nanjing massacre in greater detail by using previously undisclosed sources. The Japanese blueprint for control of East Asia is also included here. The impact of the internment of Japanese-Canadians is illustrated in the extract from Muriel Kitagawa's letters. Turning back to Europe, Victor Klemperer explains what life was like in Germany for the surviving German-Jewish population in the 1940s. Stella Wieseltier confronts those responsible for the Holocaust and considers what it means 'to rejoin the human race' in the aftermath of war and genocide. In the former Yugoslavia, a police commander details the activities of the infamous Ustaše in purging the region's Serbian population. The chapter concludes with the observations of the small group of men who witnessed the first A-Bomb test in Alamogordo, New Mexico. The observers reflect on the inconceivable power of the new weapon, along with its potential military application.

Note

1. A further seven million people died in China during the early years of the Sino–Japanese War, and at least two million Germans died after the end of the war as populations were being relocated from Eastern Europe.

MARGARET FREYER

The following document was written by Margaret Freyer, a German civilian who provides one of the few first-hand accounts of the effects of the allied firebombing of the medieval city of Dresden on the night of 13–14 February 1945. On the night of 13 February the British sent two separate waves of Lancaster bombers to Dresden. The first wave bombed for seventeen minutes. The second wave arrived three hours later. Altogether, the British dropped 2,660 tons of bombs. About fifty per cent of the bombs were incendiaries. Ten hours later the Americans dropped 771 tons of explosives on the city's railway stations and marshalling yards. What made the Dresden attack so extraordinarily destructive was the fact that the city had no air defences. The worst fire occurred within an hour of the RAF bombing, when thousands of separate blazes merged into a 1,500-degree firestorm that engulfed most of the city centre, generating winds of tornado force and incinerating everything and everyone in its path. The firestorm was so intense that counting the victims was an impossible task.

EYEWITNESS ACCOUNT OF THE FIRESTORM IN DRESDEN

I stood by the entrance and waited until no flames came licking in, then I quickly slipped through and out into the street. I had my suitcase in one hand and was wearing a white fur coat which by now was anything but white. I also wore boots and long trousers. Those boots had been a lucky choice, it turned out.

Because of the flying sparks and the fire-storm I couldn't see anything at first. A witches' cauldron was waiting for me out there: no street, only rubble nearly a metre high, glass, girders, stones, craters. I tried to get rid of the sparks by constantly patting them off my coat. It was useless. I stopped doing it, stumbled, and someone behind me called out, 'Take your coat off, it's started to burn.' In the pervading extreme heat I hadn't even noticed. I took off the coat and dropped it. . . .

Suddenly I fall into a big hole—a bomb crater, about six metres wide and two metres deep, and I end up down there lying on top of three women. I shake them by their clothes and start to scream at them, telling them they must get out of here—but they don't move any more. I believe I was severely shocked by this incident; I seemed to have lost all emotional feeling. Quickly, I climbed across the women, pulled my suitcase after me, and crawled on all fours out of the crater.

To my left I suddenly see a woman. I can see her to this day and shall never forget it. She carries a bundle in her arms. It is a baby. She runs, she falls, and the child flies in an arc into the fire. It's only my eyes which take this in; I myself feel nothing. The woman remains lying on the ground, completely still. Why? What for? I don't know, just stumble on. The fire-storm is incredible, there are calls for help and screams from somewhere but all around I see one single inferno. I hold another wet handkerchief in front of my mouth, my hands and my face are burning; I feel as if the skin is hanging down in strips.

On my right I see a big, burnt-out shop where lots of people are standing. I join them, but think, 'No, I can't stay here either, this place is completely surrounded by fire.' I leave all these people behind, and stumble on. Where to? But every time towards those places where it is dark, in case there is no fire there. I have no conception of what the street actually looked like. But it is especially from those dark patches that the people come who wring their hands and cry the same

A statue on the cathedral overlooks the destruction of Dresden. New York World-Telegram and the Sun Newspaper Photograph Collection.

thing over and over again: 'You can't carry on there, we've just come from there, everything is burning there!' Wherever and to whomsoever I turn, always that same answer.

In front of me is something that might be a street, filled with a hellish rain of sparks which look like enormous rings of fire when they hit the ground. I have no choice. I must go through. I press another wet handkerchief to my mouth and almost get through, but I fall and am convinced that I cannot go on. It's hot. Hot! My hands are burning like fire. I just drop my suitcase, I am past caring, and too weak. At least, there's nothing to lug around with me any more.

I stumbled on towards where it was dark. Suddenly, I saw people again, right in front of me. They scream and gesticulate with their hands, and then—to my utter horror and amazement—I see how one after the other they simply seem to let themselves drop to the ground. I had a feeling that they were being shot, but my mind

could not understand what was really happening. Today I know that these unfortunate people were the victims of lack of oxygen. They fainted and then burnt to cinders. I fall then, stumbling over a fallen woman and as I lie right next to her I see how her clothes are burning away. Insane fear grips me and from then on I repeat one simple sentence to myself continuously: 'I don't want to burn to death—no, no burning—I don't want to burn!' Once more I fall down and feel that I am not going to be able to get up again, but the fear of being burnt pulls me to my feet. Crawling, stumbling, my last handkerchief pressed to my mouth . . . I do not know how many people I fell over. I knew only one feeling: that I must not burn.

Then my handkerchiefs are all finished—it's dreadfully hot—I can't go on and I remain lying on the ground. Suddenly a soldier appears in front of me. I wave, and wave again. He comes over to me and I whisper into his ear (my voice has almost gone), 'Please take me with you, I don't want to burn.' But that soldier was much too weak himself to lift me to my feet. He laid my two arms crosswise over my breast and stumbled on across me. I followed him with my eyes until he disappears somewhere in the darkness.

I try once more to get up on my feet, but I can only manage to crawl forward on all fours. I can still feel my body, I know I'm still alive. Suddenly, I'm standing up, but there's something wrong, everything seems so far away and I can't hear or see properly any more. As I found out later, like all the others, I was suffering from lack of oxygen. I must have stumbled forwards roughly ten paces when I all at once inhaled fresh air. There's a breeze! I take another breath, inhale deeply, and my senses clear. In front of me is a broken tree. As I rush towards it, I know that I have been saved, but am unaware that the park is the *Burgerwiese*.

I walk on a little and discover a car. I'm pleased and decide to spend the night in it. The car is full of suitcases and boxes but I find enough room on the rear seats to squeeze in. Another stroke of good luck for me is that the car's windows are all broken and I have to keep awake putting out the sparks which drift in. I don't know how long I sat there, when a hand suddenly descended on my shoulder and a man's voice said, 'Hello! You must get out of there.' I got such a fright, because obviously someone was determined to force me away from my safe hiding place. I said, with great fear in my voice. 'Please, allow me to stay here, I'll give you all the money I've got on me.' (If I think about this now it almost sounds like a joke.) But the answer was 'No, I don't want your money. The car is on fire.'

Good God! I leapt out immediately and could see that indeed all four tires were burning. I hadn't noticed because of the tremendous heat.

Now I looked at the man and recognized him as the soldier who had put my arms across my chest. When I asked him, he confirmed it. Then he started to weep. He continued to stroke my back, mumbling words about bravery, Russian campaign . . . but this here, this is hell. . . .

I spent all the daylight hours which followed in the town searching for my fiancé. I looked for him amongst the dead, because hardly any living beings were to be seen anywhere. What I saw is so horrific that I shall hardly be able to describe it. Dead, dead, dead everywhere. Some completely black like charcoal. Others completely untouched, lying as if they were asleep. Women in aprons, women with children sitting in the trains as if they had just nodded off. Many women, many young girls, many small children, soldiers who were wholly identifiable as such by the metal buckles on their belts, almost all of them naked. Some clinging to each other in groups as if they were clawing at each other. . . .

> **Study Question**
>
> 1. When asked about the morality of bombing Dresden, Air Marshall Arthur Harris, who authorized the mission, replied that the attack was a military necessity and wholly justified. Was he correct?

TOTAL WAR RESEARCH INSTITUTE

On 27 January 1942 the Total War Research Institute[1] prepared a draft outlining the creation of the 'Greater East Asia Co-Prosperity Sphere' for the Japanese government. Despite the benevolent language, the Co-Prosperity Sphere proposed to extend the Japanese Empire throughout East Asia, with the vast majority of benefits flowing back to the Japanese mainland. The Sphere itself was made up of an Inner Sphere (Japan, Manchuria,[2] and North China), a Smaller Co-Prosperity Sphere (Eastern Siberia, China, and Southeast Asia), and the Greater East Asia Co-Prosperity Sphere (Australia, India, the Pacific Islands, and New Guinea). The entire Co-Prosperity Sphere would take approximately twenty years to create.

THE GREATER EAST ASIA CO-PROSPERITY SPHERE

Part 1. Outline of Construction
The Plan. The Japanese empire is a manifestation of morality and its special characteristic is the propagation of the Imperial Way. It strives but for the achievement of Hakkō Ichiu,[3] the spirit of its founding. . . . It is necessary to foster the

increased power of the empire, to cause East Asia to return to its original form of independence and co-prosperity by shaking off the yoke of Europe and America, and to let its countries and peoples develop their respective abilities in peaceful cooperation and secure livelihood.

The Form of East Asiatic Independence and Co-Prosperity. The states, their citizens, and resources, comprised in those areas pertaining to the Pacific, Central Asia, and the Indian Oceans formed into one general union are to be established as an autonomous zone of peaceful living and common prosperity on behalf of the peoples of the nations of East Asia. The area including Japan, Manchuria, North China, lower Yangtze River, and the Russian maritime Province, forms the nucleus of the East Asiatic Union. The Japanese empire possesses a duty as the leader of the East Asiatic Union.

The above presupposes the inevitable emancipation of independence of Eastern Siberia, China, Indo-China, the South Seas, Australia, and India.

Regional Division in the East Asiatic Union and the National Defence Sphere for the Japanese Empire. In the union of East Asia, the Japanese empire is at once the stabilizing power and the leading influence. To enable the empire actually to become the central influence in East Asia, the first necessity is the consolidation of the inner belt of East Asia. . . .

Outline of East Asiatic Administration. It is intended that the unification of Japan, Manchoukuo, and China in neighbourly friendship be realized by the settlement of the Sino-Japanese problems through the crushing of hostile influences in the Chinese interior,[4] and through the construction of a new China in tune with the rapid construction of the Inner sphere. Aggressive American and British influences in East Asia shall be driven out of the area of Indo-China and the South Seas, and this area shall be brought into our defence sphere. The war with Britain and America shall be prosecuted for that purpose.

The Russian aggressive influence in East Asia will be driven out. Eastern Siberia shall be cut off from the Soviet regime and included in our defence sphere. For this purpose a war with the Soviets is expected. It is considered possible that this Northern problem may break out before the general settlement of the present Sino-Japanese and the Southern problems if the situation renders this unavoidable. Next the independence of Australia, India, etc. shall gradually be brought about. . . .

The Building of the National Strength. Since the Japanese empire is the center and pioneer of Oriental moral and cultural reconstruction, the officials and people of this country must return to the spirit of the Orient and acquire a thorough understanding of the spirit of the national moral character.

In the economic construction of the country, Japanese and Manchurian national power shall first be consolidated, then the unification of Japan, Manchoukuo, and China, shall be effected. . . . Thus a central industry will be constructed in East Asia, and the necessary relations established with the Southern Seas.

The standard for the construction of national power and its military force, so as to meet the various situations that might affect the stages of East Asiatic administration and national defence sphere, shall be so set as to be capable of driving off any British, American, Soviet, or Chinese counter-influences in the future. . . .

Chapter 3. Political Construction

Basic Plan. The realization of the great ideal of constructing Greater East Asia Co-Prosperity requires not only the complete prosecution of the current Greater East Asia War but also presupposes another great war in the future. Therefore, the following two points must be made the primary starting points for the next twenty years: 1) Preparation for war with the other spheres of the world; and 2) Unification and construction of the East Asia Smaller Co-Prosperity Sphere.

The following are the basic principles for the political construction of East Asia, when the above two points are taken into consideration:

a. The politically dominant influence of European and American countries in the Smaller Co-Prosperity Sphere shall be gradually driven out and the area shall enjoy its liberation from the shackles hitherto forced upon it.

b. The desires of the peoples in the sphere for their independence shall be made for their fulfillment, but proper and suitable forms of government shall be decided for them in consideration of military and economic requirements and of the historical, political, and cultural elements peculiar to each area.

It must also be noted that the independence of various peoples of East Asia should be based upon the idea of constructing East Asia as 'independent countries existing within the New Order of East Asia' and that this conception differs from an independence based on the idea of liberalism and national self-determination.

c. During the course of construction, military unification is deemed particularly important, and the military zones and key points necessary for defence shall be directly or indirectly under the control of our country.

d. The peoples of the sphere shall obtain their proper positions, the unity of the people's minds shall be effected and the unification of the sphere shall be realized with the empire as its center. . . .

Chapter 4. Thought and Cultural Construction

General Aim in Thought. The ultimate aim in thought construction in East Asia is to make East Asiatic peoples revere the imperial influence by propagating the Imperial Way based on the spirit of construction, and to establish the belief that uniting solely under this influence is the one and only way to the eternal growth and development of East Asia.

And during the next twenty years (the period during which the above ideal is to be reached) it is necessary to make the nations and peoples of East Asia realize the historical significance of the establishment of the New Order in East Asia, and in the common consciousness of East Asiatic unity, to liberate East Asia from the shackles of Europe and America and to establish the common conviction of constructing a New Order based on East Asiatic morality.

Occidental individualism and materialism shall be rejected and a moral world view, the basic principle of whose morality shall be the Imperial Way, shall be established. The ultimate object to be achieved is not exploitation but co-prosperity and mutual help, not competitive conflict but mutual assistance and mild peace, not a formal view of equality but a view of order based on righteous classification, not an idea of rights but an idea of service, and not several world views but one unified world view.

General Aim in Culture. The essence of the traditional culture of the Orient shall be developed and manifested. And, casting off the negative and conservative cultural characteristics of the continents (India and China) on the other hand, and taking in the good points of Western culture on the other, an Oriental culture and morality, on a grand scale and subtly refined, shall be created.

Notes

1. The plans drawn up by Japan's Total War Research Institute (Soryokusen Kenkyujo) would form a key part of the prosecution's argument at the Tokyo War Crimes Trial. The draft plan reflected ideas that had been circulating widely since 1938.

2. The Japanese referred to Manchuria as Manchukuo (spelled Manchoukuo in this document).
3. Literally 'all eight corners of the world under one roof'—an idea conveyed through Shintoism that the Japanese emperor was mandated to rule the whole world.
4. A reference to the resistance being waged by the Chinese Communist Party and its army.

> **Study Question**
>
> 1. Was it realistic for Japan to assume it could control the enormous expanse of territory envisioned in the Greater East Asia Co-Prosperity Sphere?

HAROLD TIMPERLEY

The following report was written by Harold Timperley (1898–1954), an Australian who worked as a correspondent for the Manchester Guardian. *As with all accounts of the Nanjing massacre, there is substantial debate surrounding Timperley's report. In particular, revisionists have argued that Timperley was not in Nanjing during the Japanese attack.[1] Thus his information may have been drawn from second-hand sources. However, foreign charitable and religious organizations did remain in the city in December 1937 and Timperley had established very good contacts among these organizations. In October 2002* The Guardian *(formerly the* Manchester Guardian*) published a detailed defence of Timperley's account and his journalistic integrity.[2]*

AN EYEWITNESS ACCOUNT AT NANJING

Friday, 17 December. Robbery, murder, rape continued unabated. A rough estimate would be at least a thousand women raped last night and during the day. One poor woman was raped thirty-seven times. Another had her five months infant deliberately smothered by the brute to stop its crying while he raped her. Resistance means the bayonet. The hospital is rapidly filling up with the victims of Japanese cruelty and barbarity. Bob Wilson, our only surgeon, has his hands more than full and has to work into the night. Rickshaws, cattle, pigs, donkeys, often the sole means of livelihood of the people, are taken from them. Our rice kitchens and rice shop are interfered with. We have had to close the latter.

After dinner I took Bates[3] to the University and McCallum to the hospital where they will spend the night, then Mills and Smythe to Ginling, for one of our group has been sleeping there each night. At the gate of the latter place we were stopped by what seemed to be a searching party. We were roughly pulled from the car at the point of the bayonet, my car keys taken from me, lined up and frisked for arms, our hats jerked off, electric torches held to our faces, our passports and purpose in coming demanded. Opposite us were Miss Vautrin, Mrs Twinem, and Mrs Chen, with a score of refugee women kneeling on the ground. The sergeant, who spoke a little French (about as much as I do), insisted there were soldiers concealed there. I maintained that aside from about fifty domestics and other members of their staff there were no men on the place. This he said he did not believe and said he would shoot all he found beyond that number. He then demanded that we all leave, including the ladies, and when Miss Vautrin refused she was roughly hustled to the car. Then he changed his mind: the ladies were told to stay and we to go. We tried to insist that one of us should stay too, but this he would not permit. Altogether we were kept standing there for over an hour before we were released. The next day we learned that this gang had abducted twelve girls from the school.

Saturday, 18 December. At breakfast Riggs, who lives in the Zone a block away but has his meals with us, reported that two women, one a cousin of a YMCA secretary, were raped in his house while he was having dinner with us. Wilson reported a boy of five years of age brought to the hospital after having been stabbed with a bayonet five times, once through his abdomen; a man with eighteen bayonet wounds, a woman with seventeen cuts on her face and several on her legs. Between four and five hundred terrorized women poured into our headquarters compound in the afternoon and spent the night in the open.

Sunday, 19 December. A day of complete anarchy. Several big fires raging today, started by the soldiers, and more are promised. The American flag was torn down in a number of places. At the American School it was trampled on and the caretaker told he would be killed if he put it up again. The proclamations placed on all American and other foreign properties by the Japanese Embassy are flouted by their soldiers, sometimes deliberately torn off. Some houses are entered from five to ten times in one day and the poor people looted and robbed and the women raped. Several were killed in cold blood, for no apparent reason whatever. Six out of seven of our sanitation squad in one district were slaughtered; the seventh escaped, wounded, to tell the tale.

Toward evening today two of us rushed to Dr Brady's house (he is away) and chased four would-be rapers out and took all women there to the University. Sperling is busy at this game all day. I also went to the house of Douglas Jenkins of our Embassy. The flag was still there; but in the garage his house boy lay dead, another servant, dead, was under a bed, both brutally killed. The house was in utter confusion. There are still many corpses on the streets. All of them civilians as far as we can see. The Red Swastika Society[4] would bury them, but their truck has been stolen, their coffins used for bonfires, and several of their workers bearing their insignia have been marched away.

Smythe and I called again at the Japanese Embassy with a list of fifty-five additional cases of violence, all authenticated, and told Messers Tanaka and Fukui[5] that today was the worst so far. We were assured that they would 'do their best' and hoped that things would be better 'soon', but it is quite obvious that they have little or no influence with the military whatever, and the military have no control over the soldiers. . . .

Notes

1. When Timperley's wife was interviewed in 2000 she indicated that they had moved to Shanghai by December 1937.

2. John Gittings, 'Japanese Re-Write *Guardian* History', *The Guardian* (Friday 2 October 2002); available online at: http://www.guardian.co.uk/japan/story/0,7369,804391,00.html.

3. Most of the Western names refer to American staff members at the University of Nanjing and its hospital.

4. The Red Swastika Society is an organization devoted to educational and charitable projects. In China, Japan, and Tibet the *destroverse* (pointing to

the left) swastika is a symbol of luck and good fortune.

5. Sueo Tanaka was an attaché at the Japanese Embassy; Kiyoshi Fukui, the Consul-General in Nanjing.

Study Question

1. Why do you suppose that the Japanese invaders acted with such ferocity towards the citizens of Nanjing?

GAO XINGZU, WU SHIMIN, HU YUNGONG, AND CHA RUIZHEN

In 1962 the Department of History at Nanjing University produced an account of Japanese imperialism in China that focused on the 1937 massacre at Nanjing. Their information was drawn from a two-year investigation into the crimes committed by Japanese troops. The book was not published in the People's Republic of China; however, in 1995 portions *of the text were transmitted to the United States. The following excerpts have been translated from the original Chinese document. The Japanese government continues to challenge the veracity of these accounts and has continued to provoke outrage in China and elsewhere due to its attitude towards the Nanjing attack.*

THE NANJING MASSACRE

Chapter II: Two Blood-Stained Paths

When the Japanese forces invaded Nanjing, most of those left behind in the city hid in the safety zone. Some people remained behind in order to care for their shops and businesses, while others wanted to guard their houses and property. Thus, very few people were seen wandering the streets. But routed soldiers from the front lines, injured and sick troops, and refugees from many areas accompanied by their families were all driven to flight by the destructive force of the Japanese army and came gushing into the city through Zhongshan and Zhonghua Gates. After these people fled into Nanjing the sounds of enemy artillery and gunfire drew closer and closer. Panic was spreading and everyone hoped to find solace in the refugee hostels located in the safety zone. But all were being turned away from the safety zone. Finally, some of these people planned to storm out of the city gates and cross the Yangtze River. Thus, one group of people rushed to North

Zhongshan Road, which leads to the banks of the Yangtze River, and prepared to force their way out of Yijiang Gate. After passing through the gate they would flee to Zhongshan Wharf at Xiaguan where they would cross the Yangtze. Another group beat a hasty retreat to Central Road and prepared to force its way through Peace Gate and traverse the river from Swallow Cliff.

While the crowds of refugees were making their way along North Zhongshan and Central Roads, the last of the Kuomintang government troops fleeing from Nanjing were gathering like ants on the banks of the River. The soldiers had not yet been able to escape across the river and feared that the swarms of refugees would impede their escape. Thus, to ensure their successful flight across the river and to save their own lives, they locked Yijiang and Peace Gates tightly behind them.

The fleeing crowds, chased by Japanese gunfire from behind and blocked by the locked city gates ahead, cried, cursed, and let out great howls and angry screams which resounded all along the two roads by which they were attempting to escape. These crowds were mostly comprised of injured and sick soldiers along with elderly and weak men and women who had had to endure hunger and freezing cold temperatures for an extended period of time. Trapped in a situation in which neither advance nor retreat was possible, some people attempted to escape by fleeing in various directions while others stayed put. In both cases, thereafter, they lost control of their own fates.

On the afternoon of 13 December 1937, the Japanese forces brought their invasion into the city along three roads leading to Yuhua, Guanghua, and Zhonghua Gates. That same day, the Japanese forces under the command of Tani Hisao 谷寿夫 [1882–1947] entered the city. After entering city, a group of these brutal soldiers immediately occupied each level of the Nanjing government, in addition to banks and warehouses, while another group, like wild animals, searched out and massacred opponents. The crowds of refugees in the streets, especially those along North Zhongshan and Central Roads and the surrounding alleys, became battle targets. Using machine guns, rifles, and revolvers, the Japanese soldiers indiscriminately shot at these people. In this way the Nanjing massacre began to unfold.

The people in one assembled group—including groups of the elderly, women and children, and wounded and sick soldiers—were toppled over in succession in the wake of echoing gunfire. The vast majority of these people died on the spot, though some survived and were left screaming and moaning on the ground. Suddenly, the roads and alleyways were awash with blood and flesh, and corpses were strewn throughout the streets. Devoid of all humanity, the Japanese forces continued to shoot and kill the unarmed people in the crowd. That day marked the beginning of the massacre.

In the early morning of 14 December, with the Japanese tank battalions leading the way, artillery battalions and all kinds of vehicles poured into Nanjing. The Japanese forces came in great numbers and brutally and viciously continued to massacre people who had fled into the streets and alleyways. The sounds of gunfire rang out and the din of exploding grenades lasted the entire day, not ceasing for even one moment. The slaughter continued until not a soul could be found on the streets. At that point, Yijiang and Peace Gates were thrown open and the massacre was extended to the outskirts of the city.

After the two day massacre on the 13th and 14th of December, South and North Zhongshan Road, Central Road, along with the adjacent streets and alleyways, all became hellish paths awash with blood.

Chapter III: Cruel Slaughter Along the River

The slaughter committed by the Japanese outside the city and in the various districts neighboring Nanjing was even more savage and cruel than that which occurred within the city. Refugees fleeing from all over, wounded and sick soldiers, and family members of the military men died in even greater numbers and under even more cruel circumstances.

As the Kuomintang troops had already seized control of every sort of boat available in order to save their own lives, the refugees from Nanjing who were trapped on the banks of the river could do nothing but gaze helplessly across the Yangtze. On 13 December, the sounds of gunfire emanating from within the city caused a stir among the refugees gathered along the river as they came to realize that the Japanese had already occupied the city. The situation along the river became extremely chaotic. Those with even a little strength left, whether they were routed soldiers or fleeing refugees, used every last bit of energy to put up one last fight. In a desperate attempt to flee across the river, some people went to houses and shops and removed wooden doors, planks of wood, bathtubs, long benches, logs, and even old, rotten pieces of wood to serve as make-shift flotation devices. There were too many people and too few adequate implements. In the end, only a small number of people were lucky enough to cross the river successfully, while the majority were left behind in an entirely hopeless situation.

On the afternoon of 14 December, the Japanese troops suddenly threw open Yijiang Gate and charged forward from the city towards Zhongshan Wharf and Xiaguan Station. Wielding machine guns and rifles, they recklessly fired upon the refugees and indiscriminately tossed grenades into the crowds. Panic-stricken, angry and in despair, thousands upon thousands of refugees were toppled. Some refugees who were still able to put up a struggle and were unwilling to allow themselves to be killed by the Japanese tossed themselves in the river and committed suicide. In the end, those left standing on the banks of the river were forced into the water by the Japanese and drowned en masse. After a short while, tens of thousands of people had lost their lives under the murderous blades of the Japanese soldiers.

On 16 December, more than 5,000 people who had taken refuge in the Overseas Chinese Center (now 81 North Zhongshan Road) were bound together in groups and transported on large trucks to Xiaguan Station to be killed. The corpses were disposed of in the river.

There were various places along the river where the killings occurred on a larger scale. These areas included Straw Sandals Gorge, Swallow Cliff, and Goddess of Mercy Gate. Prior to the occupation of Nanjing, those unable to escape to far-off areas scattered in groups to the outskirts of town. Moreover, those fleeing from the frontlines (amongst whom were a large number of wounded and sick soldiers) increasingly attempted to squeeze into the suburban districts and the area along the Yangtze River. For a short while, those without the means to cross the river organized themselves into a refugee village in order to maintain some semblance of order necessary for their survival. But soon after the Japanese forces occupied Nanjing, they began to scour the countryside. They rounded up and bound large numbers of refugees, about 50,000 in total, who were detained for several days without provision of food or drink. A large number of the sick and wounded starved or froze to death. Finally, those who survived the ordeal were driven to Straw Sandals Gorge where they were brutally slaughtered.

Straw Sandals Gorge was formerly the location of a fortress which housed the Kuomintang headquarters as well as a torpedo boat base. The Yangtze River and a nearby highway ran parallel from east to west, and in between them was a piece of farmland referred to as Straw Sandals Gorge. It was to this area that the refugees were driven to be executed by the Japanese army. A government official was there on the day in question to witness the scene, and he recorded detailed notes describing what he saw.

On a certain evening, I had been sleeping in Damao Cave on Tiger Mountain, an area where there were many refugees. . . . On this particular evening, I heard the sounds of dense machine gunfire emanating from Straw Sandals Gorge. There must have been about twenty machine guns firing. I suspected that our army might be staging a counter-offensive. The next day, before dawn, two bloodied men appeared: Squad Leader Feng of the instructional unit; and Mr Guo, a member of the security unit. They described for me what had happened. After the Japanese invaders entered the city, they rounded up more than 57,000 people, including prisoners, men, women, young and old, and refugees, and imprisoned them in several small hamlets at the foot of Mufu Mountain. On the evening of 16 December, lead wire and rope were used to tie everyone up in pairs. Subsequently, they were lined up in four rows and driven to Straw Sandals Gorge where they were riddled with machine gunfire. The victims of this atrocity summoned all of their courage and yelled out, 'Seize the guns! Seize the guns!' . . . The dead fell on each other and accumulated into a mountain of corpses. The enemy then set upon the corpses with their bayonets, stabbing away randomly. Finally, the bodies were doused with kerosene and set ablaze. Feng and Guo, pretending to lie dead on the ground, pulled the corpses over them. Feng's right arm had been wounded from a bayonet stab and both men's clothing had been burned. ('Sources on the Bitter Hatred of the People of Nanjing', Xinhua *Daily*, Nanjing, 10 March 1950)

The area around Swallow Cliff has many ancient temples, a modest rural town, and a small hill facing the river. Ascending this hill, one can see the Yangtze River. Since ancient times, the 'setting sun over Swallow Cliff' has been one of Nanjing's most famous scenic attractions. Before the occupation of Nanjing, over 100,000 people fled to this area hoping to cross the river and seek refuge north of the Yangtze. But due to a serious shortage of boats there was no way to traverse the river. Prior to the Japanese invasion of Nanjing, this section of the Yangtze had already been patrolled by enemy ships and planes which had opened fire upon fleeing civilians. Thus, these refugees were forced to flee to neighbouring villages. While the Japanese army stormed into Nanjing, unexpectedly a group of enemy soldiers was making its way to Swallow Cliff. They forced the fleeing refugees to a nearby beach and gathered them together. Dozens of machine guns were set up and the refugees were shot to death. Some of the corpses were just left to float away along the river, creating a blood-red tide. Other corpses were piled up on the beach and left to rot in the falling rain and hot sun. No one bothered to do anything about the decaying corpses until the end of spring or the beginning of summer of the next year, even though the foul stench spread for miles and miles around.

North of Zhenjiang, in the vicinity of Dragon Pond and Qixia Mountain, the Japanese captured over 30,000 routed soldiers and refugees. They were bound and transported to a low-lying depression in a small forested area of Central University near Goddess of Mercy Gate. They were left there, freezing and without food, for several days. Subsequently, the Japanese set the trees ablaze and the soldiers and refugees were all burned to death.

Study Question

1. Why do you suppose that the massacres that occurred in China during the Pacific War remained so little known in the years following the war's conclusion?

MURIEL KITAGAWA

Tsukiye Muriel Kitagawa (1912–74) was born in Vancouver and spent much of her childhood in New Westminster. After graduation in 1929 Kitagawa grew more conscious of the restrictions, both formal and informal, facing Vancouver's Nisei[1] population. Japanese-Canadians were prohibited from voting and excluded from many professions and government jobs. Awareness led to activism; Kitagawa was *soon writing in community newspapers and participating in Japanese-Canadian organizations dedicated to gaining 'full equal citizenship with the rest of Canada'.[2] The bombing of Pearl Harbor on 7 December 1941 would make this goal all but impossible to achieve. On 24 February 1942 the Government of Canada issued a secret order-in-council that allowed 'the government to remove all persons of Japanese origin from the "protected area," regardless of citizenship. They are restricted in areas of employment, communication and association with other persons, and denied possession of cameras,* *firearms and radios.'[3] Stripped of their possessions, some 21,000 persons (including 17,000 Canadian citizens) were dispersed throughout the interior of British Columbia and across Canada.*

LETTERS TO WES

4 March 1942

Dear Wes:

Just got your air-mail letter. I'll try to tell you as much as I can get down on paper.

We are Israelites on the move. The public is getting bloodthirsty and will have our blood

NOTICE TO ALL JAPANESE PERSONS
AND PERSONS OF JAPANESE RACIAL ORIGIN

TAKE NOTICE that under Orders Nos. 21, 22, 23 and 24 of the British Columbia Security Commission, the following areas were made prohibited areas to all persons of the Japanese race:—

LULU ISLAND (including Steveston)
SEA ISLAND
EBURNE
MARPOLE
DISTRICT OF QUEENSBOROUGH
CITY OF NEW WESTMINSTER

SAPPERTON
BURQUITLAM
PORT MOODY
IOCO
PORT COQUITLAM
MAILLARDVILLE
FRASER MILLS

AND FURTHER TAKE NOTICE that any person of the Japanese race found within any of the said prohibited areas without a written permit from the British Columbia Security Commission or the Royal Canadian Mounted Police shall be liable to the penalties provided under Order in Council P.C. 1665.

AUSTIN C. TAYLOR,
Chairman,
British Columbia Security Commission

Coastal areas of British Columbia were declared off limits to Japanese Canadians. Soon deportations from these areas would begin. Vancouver Public Library, Special Collections, VPL 5879.

Nazi-fashion. Okay we move. But where? Signs up on all highways. . . JAPS KEEP OUT. Curfew. 'My father is dying. May I have permission to go to his bedside?' 'NO!' Like moles we burrow within after dark, and only dare to peek out of the window or else be thrown into the hoosegow with long term sentences and hard labour. Confiscation of radios, cameras, cars, and trucks. Shutdown of all business. No one will buy. No agency yet set up to evaluate. When you get a notice to report to RCMP for orders to move, you report or be interned. 'Who will guard my wife and daughters?' Strong arm reply. Lord, if this was Germany you can expect such things as the normal way, but this is Canada, a Democracy! And the Nisei, repudiated by the only land they know, no redress anywhere. Sure we can move somewhere on our own, but a job? Who will feed the family? Will they hire a Jap? Where can we go that will allow us to come? The only place to go is the Camp the Government will provide when it gets around to it. Ah, but we are bewildered and bitter and uncertain.

As for Eddie and us, the Bank is worried about us. At any rate, there is so much business that he has to clear up for the removees that no hakujin[4] can do, so though we don't know for certain, he may have to stay till the last. We may stay on with him or move first to wherever we have to go, either to Camp or to some other city where there is a Branch big enough to let Ed do routine work behind the counter, but never at the counter as he is doing now. Perhaps we can move together. I don't know. This uncertainty is more nerve-wracking than anything that can happen. I don't know whether to pack all my stuff or sell it. I can take only the irreplaceables. I hope that by the time we go the twins will be big enough to stand the trip in some discomfort. But again I don't know. I may have to cart 12 bottles and 6 dozen diapers. By myself or with Ed, I don't know. Much as I would hate to sell my books I may have to. My wedding presents, all those little things that are more valuable than furniture or $300 radios, what to do with them? If we go to Camp we shall need more blankets, warm clothes, which we haven't got at all . . . winter or summer I wear cotton dresses. In any case, wherever we go will be colder and hotter than Vancouver. We can't even get around to saying good-bye to friends. Our whole way of life is disrupted. My nights are filled with exodus nightmares. My friends are so sorry for me . . . now that I have four kids, twins at that . . . they daren't phone me for fear of hurting me. So I heard. They are so kind. They come and mind them when I want a bit of time for myself. They wash dishes for me too. But now it's every man for himself and devil take the hindmost. Just the same, I am worried about Eiko and Fumi and Uncle and Aunt Toyofuku, Nobi, and the rest of them. When shall we ever meet again if we scatter? *Don't you dare come here!!!* I'll lose you for sure if you do, then where will we be? You sit tight and maybe if Ed isn't transferred, he may find a job where you are, even as a house-servant if he has to. At least we will be together. The Nisei would have been so proud to wear the King's uniform! Even die in it.[5] But not as Helots, tied to the chariot wheels of Democracy. 'Labour within or without Canada' . . . who knows but the 'without' may be the hot sands of Libya, hauled there as front-line ditch-diggers. And you know that most of the people here call this a 'damned shame', this treatment especially of the Canadian-born? It's just the few antis who have railroaded Ottawa into this unfairness. Talk about opportunists. Was there ever a better excuse for them to kick us out lock stock and barrel?

I'll try to salvage as many of your books as possible, but honest Wes, I can't promise. You see, we don't know what's going to happen next. Maybe we can move everything . . . maybe we can take nothing. Just depends on whether we go to Camp or to some other city. So the saga of the Nisei begins. I, too, mean to survive this. This is the furnace where our worth will be tempered to white-hot resilience or not at all.

Pray for us all, you who are in 'safe' areas. For me, whose faith these last few years is sorely tried and wearing thin. Gosh, your first year at school has been a hell of a time. Don't mind my cuss-words . . . we're doing nothing but.

Tommy has bedded down at the NC office since the curfew tolled. We visit in the mornings, and do our housework at night. Every night, when Ed is late getting home and the minute hand gets nearer seven, I sweat blood, wondering whether he'll make it before he's nabbed. He's so busy at the office transferring accounts and helping the Japanese straighten out their affairs, that he stays till the last possible minute. I sweat and sit fuming and helpless. And he can't leave the house before eight either.

So there you have a blurred picture of what life is like here. I'll keep you posted.

Martial law on the coast in the States. 120,000 Japs on the move inland. But there they don't have to join Gangs, or go to Camps . . . which may be better or worse I don't know. The watchword is 'I don't know'.

I'm glad you are in Toronto.

Love,

Mur.

. . .

20 April 1942

Dear Wes:

I went to the Pool[6] yesterday to see Eiko who is working there as steno. I saw Sab too who is working in the baggage . . . old Horseshow Building. Sab showed me his first paycheque as something he couldn't quite believe . . . $11.75. He's been there for an awful long time. Eiko sleeps in a partitioned stall, she being on the staff, so to speak. This stall was the former home of a pair of stallions and boy oh boy, did they leave their odour behind. The whole place is impregnated with the smell of ancient manure and maggots. Every other day it is swept with dichloride of lime or something, but you can't disguise horse smell, cow smell, sheeps, and pigs, and rabbits, and goats. And is it dusty! The toilets are just a sheet metal trough, and up till now they did not have partitions or seats. The women kicked so they put up partitions and a terribly makeshift seat. Twelve-year old boys stay with the women too. The auto show building, where there was also the Indian exhibit, houses the new dining room and kitchens. Seats 3000. Looks awfully permanent. Brick stoves, 8 of them, shining new mugs . . . very very barrack-y. As for the bunks, they were the most tragic things I saw there. Steel and wooden frames with a thin lumpy straw tick, a bolster, and three army blankets of army quality . . . no sheets unless you bring your own. These are the 'homes' of the women I saw. They wouldn't let me into the men's building. There are constables at the doors . . . no propagation of the species . . . you know . . . it was in the papers. These bunks were hung with sheets and blankets and clothes of every hue and variety, a regular gipsy tent of colours, age, and cleanliness, all hung with the pathetic attempt at privacy. Here and there I saw a child's doll and teddy bear . . . I saw babies lying there beside a mother who was too weary to get up . . . she had just thrown herself across the bed . . . I felt my throat thicken . . . an old old lady was crying, saying she would rather have died than have come to such a place . . . she clung to Eiko and cried and cried. Eiko has taken the woes of the confinees on her thin shoulders and she took so much punishment she went to her former rooms and couldn't stop crying. Fumi was so worried about her. Eiko is really sick. The place

has got her down. There are ten showers for 1,500 women. Hot and cold water. The men looked so terribly at loose ends, wandering around the grounds, sticking their noses through the fence watching the golfers, lying on the grass. Going through the place I felt so depressed that I wanted to cry. I'm damned well not going there. They are going to move the Vancouver women first now and shove them into the Pool before sending them to the ghost towns.

I'm getting kind of frantic because we haven't heard yet from the Bank. The manager wrote again on the 17th. If they would only hurry up and say something one way or the other. If they say no, I shall send you a wire and then you know what to do. If only Eddie can get a job that pays enough to make it worthwhile staying out of the work camps, something we can eat on and save a little. He's quick with his hands, but he knows figures best. He's worked 21 years with the Bank of Montreal. If I can, I am going to take Eiko with me as nursemaid. I don't think it would be wise to take Obasan[7] with us because she is a national's wife, and she is going back to Japan anyway as soon as she can, while Eiko and we have no such intentions.

The other day at the Pool, someone dropped his key before a stall in the Livestock Building, and he fished for it with a long wire and brought to light rotted manure and maggots!!! He called the nurse and then they moved all the bunks from the stalls and pried up the wooden floors. It was the most stomach-turning nauseating thing. They got fumigators and tried to wash it all away and got most of it into the drains, but maggots still breed and turn up here and there. One woman with more guts than the others told the nurse (white) about it and protested. She replied: 'Well, there's worms in the garden aren't there?' This particular nurse was a Jap-hater of the most virulent sort. She called them 'filthy Japs' to their faces and Eiko gave her 'what-for' and Fumi had a terrible scrap with her, both girls saying: 'What do you think we are? Are we cattle? Are we pigs you dirty-so-and-so!' You know how Fumi gets. The night the first bunch of Nisei were supposed to go to Schreiber and they wouldn't, the women and children at the Pool milled around in front of their cage, and one very handsome mountie came with his truncheon and started to hit them, yelling at them, 'Get the hell back in there.' Eiko's blood boiled over. She strode over to him and shouted at him: 'You put that stick down! What do you think you're doing! Do you think these women and children are so many cows that you can beat them back into their place?' Eiko was shaking mad and raked him with fighting words. She has taken it on her to fight for the poor people there, and now she is on the black list and reputed to be a trouble-maker. Just like Tommy and Kunio. I wish I too could go in there and fight and slash around. It's people like us who are the most hurt . . . people like us, who have had faith in Canada, and who have been more politically minded than the others, who have a hearty contempt for the whites.

Fujikazu and his bunch are working with what Kunio calls a 'shyster lawyer' who has told his clients one thing and the Commission another, and in front of Tommy and Kunio, got bawled out by Taylor. There has been some sort of pamphlet they put out that has been uncovered by the police and the stink is rising again.[8]

The cop that nabbed Sab was so drunk he had to be propped up by his assistant, and he weaved around and tried to poke Sab. Sab wisely did not retaliate.

By the way, we got a letter from Uncle . . . or rather Auntie got it. He's the gardener, and has to grow vegetables and flowers on the side. Takashima is cook and gets $50 clear. Uncle only nets about $10. All cards and letters are censored, even to the Nisei camps. Not a word about sit-downs, gambaru-ing[9] or anything makes the papers. It's been hushed. Good thing for us. I wondered why I didn't read about it. I haven't been to meetings so long now that I don't know what's going on.

Uncle's camp is 8 miles from the station up into the hills. Men at the first camps all crowd down to the station every time a train passes with the Nationals and hang onto the windows asking for news from home. Uncle said he wept.

But the men are luckier than the women. They are fed, they work, they have no children to look after. Of course the fathers are awfully worried about their families. But it's the women who are burdened with all the responsibility of keeping what's left of the family together. Frances went to Revelstoke, bag and baggage and baby. When I heard that I felt choked with envy, and felt more trapped than ever. Eiko tells me: 'Don't you dare bring the kids into the Pool.' And Mr. Maikawa says Greenwood is worse. They are propping up the old shacks near the mine shaft. Sab went through there and says it's awful. The United Church parson there says of the Japs: 'Kick them all out.' Sab knows his son who had the room next to him at Union College. Vic and George Saito and family went to the beet fields. Sadas are going tonight. They are going to hell on earth, and will be so connected that they cannot leave the place or move. Whites will not go there.

I pray that Kath and Mom are safe. Mom's got to live through this. Now that Japan proper has been bombed they will come here.

Sab told me his father has applied to get to Winnipeg or to Toronto. Sab is hoping to get to Queens.

Eiko, Fumi and I, and all of us, have gotten to be so profane that Tom and the rest of them have given up being surprised. Eiko starts out with 'what the hell' . . . and Fumi comes out with worse. It sure relieves our pent-up feelings. Men are lucky they can swear with impunity. (Hell . . . I can smell horse all of a sudden . . .)

On account of those fool Nisei who have bucked the gov't, everything the JCCL[10] fought for has been lost. Our name is mud. Why they don't arrest Fujikazu[11] I don't know. I kind of feel that the RCMP are just letting us raise such a stink by ourselves . . . that is fools like Fujikazu and his ilk . . . that the rest of us who are really conscientious and loyal will never have a chance to become integrated with this country. It's damnable. All we have fought for and won inch by inch has gone down the drain. More than the Nationals, our name is mud. There's over 140 Nisei loose, and many Nationals. The Commission thinks the Nationals are cleared but oh boy there are a lot of them who have greased enough palms and are let alone.

By the way if you ever write anything for the NC[12] write it to Tom personally.

How are things there? How are the Pannells and everybody? Three Nisei girls are going to Toronto for housework. Maybe you might get to see them, whoever they are. Aki Hyodo is in Hamilton. If Mrs Pannell doesn't mind the typewriter, I think I shall write to her.

I'll write again soon.

With love,

Mur.

Notes

1. The 'Nisei' are second-generation Japanese-Canadians.
2. Muriel Kitagawa, *This Is My Own: Letters to Wes & Other Writings on Japanese Canadians, 1941–1948*, ed. Roy Miki (Vancouver: Talonbooks, 1985), 30.
3. Canada Order-in-Council PC 1486.
4. Literally 'white person'.
5. Miki, ed.: After Pearl Harbor—and until late 1944—Nisei were not allowed to serve in the armed forces. Opposition came from such powerful political figures as BC Premier T.D. Patullo who wrote to Prime Minister Mackenzie King, '. . . if they are called up for service, there will be a demand they be given the franchise, which we in this province can never tolerate'

(Public Archives of Canada, William Lyon Mackenzie King Papers, MG26 J1, vol. 331, T.D. Patullo to W.L.M. King. 25 September 1940).

6. Vancouver's Pacific National Exhibition site—Hastings Park—was rapidly converted from housing livestock into a temporary camp for Japanese-Canadians awaiting transportation to internment camps in the British Columbia interior and elsewhere in Canada. Many were forced into low-paying, menial jobs while living on the PNE grounds.
7. Miki: Japanese for 'Aunt', here a reference to Aunt Sei Toyofuku.
8. Miki: The pamphlet issued by the Nisei Mass Evacuation Group opposed the breakup of families.
9. Miki: 'Gambaru' is a complex Japanese word with many shades of meaning, here 'to hold out' or 'to resist'.
10. The Japanese-Canadian Citizens' League (JCCL) was formed in 1936 to improve relations between the Nisei and other Canadians.
11. Fujikazu Tanaka was the co-founder of a group—the Nisei Mass Evacuation Group (NMEG)—that refused to comply with the separation of families during the deportation process.
12. *New-Canadian* (NC) was a Japanese-Canadian community newspaper.

Study Question

1. Why did so few people speak up against the Japanese-Canadian internment during the war? Why didn't more people speak up in the decades following the war?

VICTOR KLEMPERER

Victor Klemperer (1881–1960) was born into the Jewish faith but at age twenty-two Klemperer broke with Judaism and was baptized a Protestant. In 1906 he married Eva Schlemmer, a Protestant concert pianist. After service during the First World War, Klemperer became a professor of Romance Languages and Literature at Dresden Technical College. However, the Nuremberg Laws of 1935 were also applied to baptized Jews—even those married to 'Aryan' wives. Klemperer was suspended from his job, stripped of most of his possessions, and he and Eva were forced to move into a so-called 'Jews' House' in Dresden. From 1933 onwards, Klemperer recorded every detail of his life under the National Socialists in a series of diaries. Unlike the vast majority of Germans in his situation, Klemperer survived the war and, in 1945, his job and his house were restored to him. He resumed teaching at the universities of Halle, Berlin, and Greifswald until his death in 1960. Klemperer's second wife Dr Hadwig Klemperer prepared the diaries for publication.

◇

I WILL BEAR WITNESS

June 2, Tuesday toward evening [1942]

Two hours ago saw dispatch printed in bold letters in the *Dresdener NN*. Germany has just given Turkey a credit of 100 million rei to buy arms in Germany. And that means: Turkey is on Germany's side, or at least: She will give Germany passage (and has *more* confidence in the latter's victory than in that of its opponents!); that means an offensive against Syria, Palestine, Egypt; it means the endless prolongation of the war. Very, very depressed, and since my heart rebels more and more and since our position is becoming ever more precarious, so my hope of seeing the end of this calamity sinks ever lower.

On Sunday evening, after I had sat at home for 48 hours, short walk to Südhöhe, Toll House. Everything in bloom. The last time I was there, had to fight my way uphill in the cold, against a biting wind, to shovel show. *Then* we still had enough to eat, *then* we had not yet been beaten and spat upon by the Gestapo. And even then we already believed that things were going very badly for us. Perhaps in three months we shall say: In June we could still almost live in comfort. There is a big blue patch on Eva's arm from the recent ill-treatment. . . .

Yesterday toward evening to Steinitz for half an hour. He had written to me that he would no longer be able to call on me on Mondays. The interruption of this tiresome regularity is at least one agreeable consequence of the Gestapo terror. When Steinitz was recently caught up in a house search at friends' and was punched on the neck, he was immediately asked: 'Where are you working?' Someone who is 'working' is supposed to be treated a little more leniently. Steinitz thereupon registered with the Jewish community and is now, like Dr Magnus, employed in an 'honourary' capacity at the Jewish cemetery. I met him after his first day at work, in shirtsleeves and barefoot. His wife, who is not very nice to him, brought him his food and scolded him, because in his blindness he was dribbling on his trousers. He told me that there were a couple of old men under a gardener out there. Each person gets allocated a grave to clean. A whole day is spent killing time like that, but one had an answer to: 'Where are you working?' and perhaps even some cover against the next evacuation. At the moment factory work is no longer given to people over sixty. —For my part I shall keep away from such tedium for as long as I possibly can. One is in danger everywhere, with and without 'work'.

Deportation from the Siedlce Ghetto to Treblinka in August 1942. Many ghettos were emptied in a matter of days, with few surviving the deportations. Reprinted by permission of the United States Holocaust Memorial Museum (18789).

My days at home are not very fruitful either—the terrible tiredness!—but yet not completely sterile. I am now working my way into *The Myth of the Twentieth Century*. I am also reading aloud a great deal, usually very early in the morning, at four or five, and for a while following afternoon tea. [. . .] New decrees *in judaeos*. The choker is being pulled ever tighter; they are wearing us down with ever new tricks. All the things, great and small, that have accumulated in the last few years! And a pinprick is sometimes more agonizing than a blow with a club. I shall list the decrees once and for all: 1) To be home after eight or nine in the evening. Inspection! 2) Expelled from one's own house. 3) Ban on radio, ban on telephone. 4) Ban on theaters, cinemas, concerts, museums. 5) Ban on subscribing to or purchasing periodicals. 6) Ban on using public transport: three phases: a) buses banned, only front platform of tram permitted, b) all use banned, except to work, c) to work on foot, unless one lives 2 1/2 miles away or is sick (but it is a hard fight to get a doctor's certificate). Also ban on taxicabs, of course. 7) Ban on purchasing 'goods in short supply'. 8) Ban on purchasing cigars or any kind of smoking materials. 9) Ban on purchasing flowers. 10) Withdrawal of *milk* ration card. 11) Ban on going to the barber. 12) Any kind of tradesman can be called only after application to the Community. 13) Compulsory surrender of typewriters, 14) of furs and woolen blankets, 15) of bicycles—it is permissible to cycle to work (Sunday outings and visits by bicycle are forbidden), 16) of deck chairs, 17) of dogs, cats, birds. 18) Ban on leaving the city of Dresden, 19) on entering the railway station, 20) on setting foot on the Ministry embankment, in parks, 21) on using Burgerwiese and the roads bordering the Great Garden (Parkstrasse, Lennéstrasse, and Karcherallee). This most recent restriction since only yesterday. Also, since the day before yesterday, a ban on entering the market halls. 22) Since September 19 [last year] the *Jew's star*. 23) Ban on having reserves of foodstuffs at home. (Gestapo also takes away what has been bought with food coupons.) 24) Ban on use of lending libraries. 25) Because of the star all restaurants are closed to us. And in the restaurants one can still get something to eat, some 'dish of the day', if one has nothing at all left at home. Eva says the restaurants are packed.[1] 26) No clothing card. 27) No fish card. 28) No special rations such as coffee, chocolate, fruit, condensed milk. 29) The special taxes. 30) The constantly contracting disposable allowance. Mine at first 600, then 320, now 185 marks. 31) Shopping restricted to *one* hour (three till four, Saturday twelve till one). I think these 31 points are everything. But all together they are nothing as against the constant threat of house searches, of ill-treatment, of prison, concentration camp, and violent death. . . .

June 19, Friday morning

Wednesday, at about seven o'clock in the evening, furious ringing of the doorbell (the bell push remained stuck). Gestapo car. I opened up, Frau Kreidl was there also. Two of our tormentors, as well as an officer in army uniform with the Iron Cross, First Class. I was courteously asked a number of questions. I could go, Frau Kreidl was also treated courteously and not molested, they merely unsealed Friedheim's rooms and rummaged around in them for a while, before sealing them again. —Later I said to Frau Kreidl: Only the lower ranks are really bad, when an officer is present, one has a degree of protection. She responded very emphatically: 'No!' Immediately after these people, Hirschel came for a moment and announced that the funeral service for Friedheim would take place the next day, Thursday afternoon, at five o'clock. He said the officer was Major Schindhelm, head of the Gestapo here, familiar with all their methods and in agreement with them, occasionally also present at beatings.

After supper we now always sit for a while with Frau Pick, who is still very weak (and who gets on badly with Ida Kriedl—both complain about the other to us). The question arose of who would go to Friedheim's funeral service—a long walk, since we are banned from tram and Great Garden and the cemetery is at the end of Fürstenstrasse. Frau Pick is afraid of being alone [if everyone went to the funeral]. ('If *they* come. . .'). We promised to help, and so yesterday morning, after endless discussions with Frau Pick and Ida Kreidl and Kätchen Sara had already taken place over breakfast, I walked over to the Hirschels's. Wiener Strasse 85, very close to the Marckwalds. A very elegant property, owner Frau Hirschel, née Glauber, a very solid, elegant drawing room with two well-filled bookcases. Frau Hirschel, in her mid-thirties, two small boys, received me, it turned out there were curious connections. She had been an assistant to Walzel, with whom she still corresponded [. . .]. Julius Wahle, with whom I edited the Walzel Festschrift, was her uncle, and died in this house a year ago at a very great age. Frau Pick was living with the Hirschels before she moved into our Jews' House. Frau Hirschel's attitude: German, emphatically non-Zionist, emphatically aesthetic, Goethe-German—*we* shall save Goethe!'—but also, no doubt become so under the pressure of the times, emphatically religious, orthodox Jewish. Pleasantly discreet to me. I asked for books. Once she had 'neither loaned nor borrowed' books, but now she was happy if 'there was a bit of life in her library' as a result. She gave me one volume of *Zionist Writings* by Herzl and lent me three volumes of Dubnow's *Jewish History*. —She organized help for Frau Pick for the afternoon. First she herself would come, then be relieved by a tenant. —She was unambiguous on the cause of Friedheim's death: It was, of course, possible that he had really died of heart failure, but . . . [. . .] There had been an old business pending against Friedheim, which they had probably taken up again. (He was the owner of the Bassenge banking house—God knows what he had tried to save.)

In the afternoon to the Jewish cemetery with Ida Kreidl, who complained incessantly. One and a half hours: Strehlener Kirche, Reicker Strasse, Rayskistrasse, Grunaer Weg, Grüne Wiese . . . Haenel Claus Strasse, Borsbergstrasse. Dresden is lovely: the dark hills, the abundance of nursery gardens, the magnificent flowers and aromas, the piece of open countryside with the gas works like a stopper in the middle of it. But Ida Kreidl complained incessantly about the excessive length of the way there and how we were being hounded and had to avoid the Great Garden . . . And on the way back (alone and, on Eva's advice, somewhat shorter, by way of Giesingstrasse—exactly one and a quarter hours) I was also very tired, so that yesterday I did not manage a diary entry. —I had first seen the bare cemetery hall two years ago. This time everything seemed sadder. A dozen old women, a dozen men, some wearing top hats, Reichenbach looked like a plucked bird, the hat kept slipping over his eyes. Seven corpses were being dispatched. I found myself in an orthodox cemetery, the man wearing a gown read a long Hebrew prayer; afterward, after the coffin had been carried out, he recited a second Hebrew prayer while making curious catholic obeisances to the altar wall. I then went outside for a while, Eva arrived, and we went back in together. The clergyman came up to me: He was a grammar-school teacher whom I had once met at the Breits as their tenant. For Sally Friedheim he read two psalms in German, while the covered black box stood in front of him. Of man's mortality, and that God, the Eternal, protects us. It was all very dreary and quite lacking in solemnity. Two people wept: Fräulein Ludwig and Elsa Kreidl (who was thinking of her husband who was shot). There were no relatives of the deceased. His sister had just died in Hildesheim, his brother was deported and has not been heard of. —

At midday on Thursday I had only a very small Gestapo fright: A man who identified himself as being 'from the Geheime Staatspolizei'[2] was courteous apart from that and wanted only to go into Friedheim's rooms. He seemed familiar, and he also asked Ida Kriedl about me: He was one of the group who had gone through my books in Dölzschen and relieved me of some, he was also looking for books in Friedheim's room.

In Shaw's *Saint Joan* there is a wild hunter of heretics, who breaks down in despair when he sees Joan burning. 'I did not know. . .!' He was unable to imagine the horror. Until now I had found our situation *just as literally unimaginable*: I had always been told about being beaten and spat upon, of trembling at the sound of a car, at every ring at the door, of disappearing and not coming back again—I had not known it. Now I know it, now the dread is always inside me, deadened for a couple of hours or become habitual or paralyzed by 'So far things have always turned out well in the end' and then alive and at one's throat again. . . . It is a thousand times more horrible than all my fear in 1915.[3] —And always being afraid, always running to the window, in case a car . . .

Notes

1. As a non-Jew, even though married to Klemperer, Eva still had access to the restaurants.
2. The Gestapo.
3. Klemperer had served in the German army during the First World War.

Study Question

1. Throughout his memoirs Klemperer defends 'Germans' and 'Germany' as a whole. He condemns only the Nazis whom he believed were 'bad Germans'. Yet other authors have condemned the entire German people for the crimes of this era. Whose argument seems more persuasive?

STELLA WIESELTIER

The following excerpt, entitled 'Rejoining the Human Race', tells the story of Stella Wieseltier (Backenroth). It relates her formerly well-to-do family's struggles to survive during the war. The excerpt also tells of her attitude towards the Nazi war criminals who were hanged at the Madjenek Camp after the end of the Second World War. Stella Wieseltier's story was retold in Yaffa Eliach's Hasidic Tales of the Holocaust.

REJOINING THE HUMAN RACE

In Drohobycz,[1] Stella and her family quickly learned that hunger does not discriminate even against a Backenroth. In the Drohobycz of 1941, a table such as Avrumche Backenroth's where the hungry were fed did not exist.

Stella soon realized that her father, Leibele Backenroth, the oil magnate, who returned that night from the pogrom in Schodnica, was a changed man. All his initiative, vigor, and drive were gone. He was a desperate man, unable to cope with the new order of things. Once when Stella scolded her brother for not addressing their father properly, Leibele Backenroth responded: 'The child is right. A father is no longer a father if he cannot provide a slice of bread and a pair of shoes for his children. I do not deserve the respect accorded to a father.'

The burden of the family's survival was now thrust upon Stella's young shoulders. Under the cover of night she and other young girls would sneak out of Drohobycz, make their way across forest and fields back to Schodnica, and pick vegetables from their own gardens. With loads of fifty pounds and more they would return to Drohobycz. Stella even managed to go back to Schodnica and, in broad daylight, bring to Drohobycz the family cow, parading her under the Gestapo windows! Three days later a decree was issued banning Jews from owning livestock. The cow was confiscated by the Gestapo. Stella did not rest. Nothing was too big, too small, or too difficult for her as long as it brought some food for her darling Zygus, her parents, and her mother's parents, the Tenzers, who had come with them. Conditions in the ghetto became more difficult with each passing day. Stella's father was taken away to the labour camp of Dachufka. Aktions[2] against the very young and the aged became more frequent. The lives of her brother, mother, and grandparents were in constant danger. And then it happened. In the summer of 1943, Stella's grandfather and grandmother were taken aboard trucks to Bronica. In the evening the trucks returned to Drohobycz with the victims' clothing. On the fifth day of Sivan, 8 May 1943, her mother and brother were murdered in Bronica. On the twentieth day of Tamuz, 23 July 1943, her father was shot there too.

Stella was on one of the trucks going to Bronica but she was pulled down by a member of the *Judenrat*:[3] 'You are too young to die,' he announced. 'You can still serve the Third Reich.' As she stood there in a daze, a Gestapo man by the name of Landau was practicing target shooting. Instinctively, she bent down. But Stella was not his target that day. He had a pocket full of lollipops. A group of children who were dragged out of hiding were standing around him. He asked them, one by one, if they would like lollipops, and if they wanted one, they should open their mouths. They did. One by one he shot them in their open mouths. Stella fainted. (Until today, she feels faint

Survivors of the Buchenwald concentration camp. This photograph was taken by the American 80th Division on 16 April 1945 as they liberated the camp. Courtesy of the National Archives (NWDNS-208-AA-206K-31).

when she sees dolls. To her, they represent the little, lifeless bodies of the innocent children on that Drohobycz street.)

After the liquidation of the ghetto, Stella somehow made her way back to Schodnica and found refuge with Stanislav and Aniela Nendza there in a cellar under a stable on the premises of the Backenroth oil wells. She lived with four more adults: her uncles, Leon and David Thome, Dr Isidor Friedman, a lawyer, and Luisa Mahler. The cellar was six feet long, about four feet wide, and about five feet high. It was filled with water and rats. Above, in freedom and more spacious quarters, were a pig, a goat, rabbits, and chickens. Never did Avrumche Backenroth dream that his beloved granddaughter would use his oil fields in this manner!

On Tuesday, 8 August 1944, at 7:00 AM, Benek, the sixteen-year-old son of Janiewski, opened the trapdoor to the cellar and brought them the message of freedom: Russian troops had just liberated Schodnica. Stella, with the others, climbed out of the cellar. It was the first time in nine months that she had seen the sky and the sun.

With swollen feet, barely able to walk, Stella decided to see Schodnica once more. The big synagogue was a stable filled with horses. Her own home was occupied by three Ukrainian families. Around Grandfather Backenroth's huge dining-room table were sitting some drunken Ukrainians. Only the Carpathian mountains were as graceful as ever, and the Backenroth pumps were still bringing up oil from the blood-soaked earth of Schodnica. Stella vowed never to return to this cursed town that she had once loved. She left for Warsaw. There she met and married a young man named Mark Wieseltier, an officer in the Polish Army who had spent the war in Siberia. For some time they lived as Christians in a house filled with icons, fearing that they too would join the ever-growing list of Jewish casualties, Jews who survived the war only to be killed by hostile Poles.

In the fall of 1945 there was a hanging of Nazi war criminals in Majdanek.[4] Stella decided to go there for the occasion. She wanted revenge, revenge for every Jew whom she had buried with her own hands, for each child shot in Drohobycz, for her mother, father, grandparents, for her beloved Zygus, for the world of her youth that was so brutally murdered. She traveled all night to assure herself a choice seat. The hanging began. The noose was placed around the neck of each criminal. The chairs were kicked out from underneath, the bodies dangled, the crowd cheered. Stella closed her eyes in horror. 'My God! What am I doing here?' she mumbled to herself.

'Cheering death? Death begets more death, hatred more hatred. It will never bring back Father, Mother, and Zygus.' Her revenge was short-lived, it had lost all its sweetness. All she wanted was to get away, away from Majdanek, from Warsaw, from Poland, away from this accursed soil—once her ancestral home, now the graveyard of her people.

In that moment, Stella sensed that she had once more joined the human race that still must exist somewhere, someplace—a world like that she once knew in Schodnica.

Notes

1. Now Drogobych, Ukraine.
2. Roundups for deportation.
3. The Jewish administration set up by the Nazis within the ghettos.
4. One of the six extermination camps, which the Nazis had established, all on Polish territory.

Study Question

1. Why was it so important for Wieseltier to distance herself from the postwar reprisals against those who had committed genocide?

SINISA DJURIC (TRANSLATOR)

The following document is a report from the commander of the police platoon in Slunj, a Croatian town on the outskirts of Zagreb. In the report he discusses the various fates suffered by the region's Serbian population following the creation of the Independent State of Croatia under Ante Pavelic. The author goes to some lengths to distance himself and the rest of the local police forces from the activities of the Ustaše—Croat fascist paramilitary forces. Though the final part of the document, and the author's identity, is missing the report still provides a comprehensive overview of the Ustaše's activities throughout the region.

POLICE REPORT ON THE CLEANSING OF SERBS

Headquarters of the 1st Croatian Police Regiment

Number: 484/j-S.

Report on general situation in the zone of the regiment, in consideration of Communist-Chetnik[1] activity.

TO THE DIRECTION FOR PUBLIC ORDER AND SECURITY ZAGREB OF THE INDEPENDENT STATE OF CROATIA Dordiceva St., No. 4

Zagreb, 16th of August 1941.

Commander of the police platoon in Slunj, in report Number 89 of 13th of August 1941, reports the following:

'Until the 27th of July of this year conditions were still satisfactory considering the blow for the Serbian population, which they got by the foundation of Independent State of Croatia. A large number of them had already been reconciled with their fate. Many had already asked to convert to Catholicism. It is true that most of them didn't do that out of conviction, but if the goals of real Chetniks were fulfilled—these Serbs who convert to Catholicism would be exposed to even greater danger than the Catholics themselves, because they would be marked as traitors not only nationally but also religiously, therefore it could be concluded that they had good intentions. More importantly, most of them wouldn't act against the state, on the contrary they would in their own benefit work for its preservation.

'The sabotage of railroad tracks in the district Vojnic on the 27th and 30th of July of this year was the work of Communists, and the idea came from Communists from Karlovac, while the execution of these actions was confided to domestic people, but of Communist disposition. The Serbian population was scared knowing that the blame will fall on them as a community, even though the vast majority of them knew nothing of

this, and didn't want it to happen. This may not be out of love for the state of Croatia but in their own benefit, because they knew they would be the ones to pay for this.

'As of the 29th of July of this year the cleansing by Ustaše had begun. This caused panic within Serbian population so that they all ran to the forests in fear of being cleansed. That lasted until the 8th of August of this year, but the last few days they failed, because the people knew the real situation and were hiding in the forests. They were in a state of general fear. From a psychological point of view, out of crawling and cowardice, but from a different point of view, from a bestial bitterness.

'The work of the Ustaše was among other things non-tactical, because they cleansed the less dangerous and least responsible people like many old men, women and children of the youngest age, while those with dark conscience, young and stronger fled to the forests. Described in a single sentence: "NON-FIGHTERS WERE CLEANSED, AND FIGHTERS STAYED IN THE FORESTS." The more naive ones and those with a clear conscience didn't even run away at first, because they thought no harm will come to them.

'The cleansing operation is completely achieved in Slunj and effectively around Slunj, while in more remote places there was little success.

'The present condition cannot be specified with exact data because the remaining people are still in the forests, but it is certain that a large number of families lost a member.

'The planning for the Ustaše cleansing was almost public, which is one of the main reasons that people hid in the forests. They "cleansed" in houses, yards, on roads, in the presence of parents, children or vice versa. They plundered houses and property of people in such way that they competed among themselves over who will get a wealthier house and who will be the one to cleanse a wealthier man. During the last cleansing, they took clothing, there were disputes among Ustaše because of that. There was carousing, savage scenes during the "cleansing" of a child in a cradle, old people, whole families together, sadistic delight in the most horrid tortures before the final cleansing. These kinds of actions caused disfavour even among the honourable and fair Croats and whispers were heard: "THIS IS DISGRACE FOR THE CROAT PEOPLE, CULTURE AND THE CATHOLIC FAITH." The pits were mostly dug earlier. There were cases, that the ones to be cleansed carried the tools for digging pits themselves and the like. The burial of people barely alive, leaving the dead unburied or poorly buried, so that their relatives and the ones who fled to the forests came to see them.

'All this caused fear among people, but also such bitterness that there cannot be even a thought about reconciliation. Even if there were some conditions there could still be a possibility, but there were no conditions here and to this day there still aren't any.

'I—like all policemen in general—was completely powerless. Everything was done without our knowledge and with great distrust towards us. If I would say anything, even insignificant, they would threaten my life, directly or indirectly, there were even words: "Now it's the policemen's turn."

'Maybe the main reason for distrust towards policemen was that they didn't stand out in the cleansing even if they favoured it. I explained to the same, that we are an organ of authority and that we have to preserve the reputation of the state. Among the Croatian population (many of them) there was also noted a disfavour for this kind of cleansing operation, because it was known that many who were cleansed didn't do any harm to Croats, on the contrary they were despised by earlier regimes exactly because of that reason, because they favoured Croats. These people would have been useful now, because through them, those who fled could be influenced.

'The order came to stop the cleansing and that

the people should be called to return to their homes by policemen, the people were called and we are trying to achieve that, but we have had relatively poor success. They've lost all confidence, but then again they had a horrible reason to run to the forest and every one of them is aware of the fact that with just a single mistake (by returning) they could lose everything. Again I would like to point out that a complete return from the forests will hardly succeed.

'There were cases when policemen asked: "Why are you running away?" The reply was: "I am running away, sir, to live half an hour longer." In some houses there were left children alone, even for just one week, in another, an old man alone. Scenes like this are common. Fruits are mostly ruined and the cattle suffered much if they stayed indoors. A lot of cattle were taken away and stolen. Some fugitives claim, even if they would return, to whom would they return and to what would they return.

'These people would have accepted everything: expulsion, concentration camps, forced labour, conversion to Catholicism, but not to be cleansed, and they would have liked best if they could stay at home and become whatever it is required of them to become (this of course not all of them, but the majority). The conversion to Catholicism would be most successful through missionaries, because in that way they would have converted with conviction.'

'Today, when cleansing began in the Vojnic district, the Italian army was leaving Vojnic, and there were cases that when passing by they told the people: "Run Serbs, Ustaše are coming and they slit everyone's throats."

'The situation concerning Communist-Chetnik actions from station to station in the area of this district is as follows:

SLUNJ: The number of them is negligible, because most of them were cleansed, and the rest of them are harmless and returning to their homes. There is no danger from the domestic ones, and the outsiders will probably not react. Patrols are moving undisturbed throughout the area. . . .

PRIMISLJE: In the area of this station there were several attacks on policemen, and on the 7th of August of this year policeman Luka Perkovic was murdered and Mate Stankic was wounded. Part of this area is somewhat cleansed, and the rest are in the forests and only few have returned home. Police patrols are not safe in villages if they are of lesser strength. In the forests there are larger groups, and there are probably some of them from the Plaski area. Catholic settlements are in danger. If the return is not successful, the situation will be more critical.

VELJUN: In the area of this station the most critical condition for now is in Slunj district. The population is mostly of the Greek religion. The most dangerous place is between Veljun and Cvijanovic Brdo. In this area there are larger groups of armed people, and there are probably some of them even from Krstinja. In this area there were three attacks on police patrols and teachers Ivan Sajfar and Martinic have been taken away. Patrols of policemen cannot go to this area without fear for their lives.

CETINGRAD: The area of this station borders with the stations from Krstinja and V. Kladusa, so the situation is never safe even though nothing is happening for now. Patrols from this station cannot go into some villages of this area, because fugitives are in power there. . . .

KRSTINJA: The situation in the area of this station is the most critical. The army barracks was attacked for several days in such way that there was no contact with it for 5 days. Now it is mostly liberated, but the situation is still critical. Patrols cannot move through villages at all, and all people are in the forests, or in their villages, but when the authorities come in greater strength, they run to the forests.

VOJNIC: The same situation as in Krstinja station, except that there were no attacks on army barracks.

KRNJAK: The population is all of the Greek religion. Most of them are fugitives, but some are returning with distrust. Situation is critical even though there were no significant events.

VUKMANIC: There have been frequent sabotages of the railroad tracks and also hand grenades have been thrown at the post office in Tusilovac. This was the work of Communists from Karlovac. Like in other places, the people are fugitives, but police patrols are still in contact with those who are at home.

'In the area of this headquarters (districts Slunj and Vojnic) 350 army rifles with the necessary quantity of ammunition were given to endangered Croatian villages for defence. This could be good on the one hand, but dangerous on the other, if Chetniks attack them and disarm them and in that way get the weapons they need. The weapons were given on request of Ustaše station in Slunj. Besides this, a large number of hunting rifles were given to people. . . .'

Note

1. Chetniks were the Serbian paramilitary fighters; by 1943 they were beginning to separate their activities from those of the Yugoslav communist movement.

Study Question

1. Do you believe that the author was correct when he noted that there could be no reconciliation after what had happened in Croatia?

US War Department

By 1945 scientists were familiar with the theoretical results of detonating a nuclear bomb; however, no one had ever tested such a device successfully. The Trinity Project was created in order to conduct just such a test and from its results to assess the overall effects of a nuclear explosion. The Trinity device was detonated on 16 July 1945 at a bombing range in Alamogordo, New Mexico. Government sources later indicated that the yield of the plutonium-based Trinity device was equivalent to approximately 19 kilotons of TNT. The following War Department report captures the wide range of reactions by those who witnessed the detonation.

Release on the New Mexico Test, 16 July 1945

Mankind's successful transition to a new age, the Atomic Age, was ushered in 16 July 1945, before the eyes of a tense group of renowned scientists and military men gathered in the desert lands of New Mexico to witness the first end results of their $2,000,000,000 effort. Here in a remote section of the Alamogordo Air Base 120 miles southeast of Albuquerque the first man-made atomic explosion, the outstanding achievement of nuclear science, was achieved at 5:30 AM of that day. Darkening heavens, pouring forth rain and lightning immediately up to the zero hour, heightened the drama.

Mounted on a steel tower, a revolutionary weapon destined to change war as we know it, or which may even be the instrumentality to end all wars, was set off with an impact which signalized man's entrance into a new physical world. Success was greater than the most ambitious estimates. A small amount of matter, the product of a chain of huge specially constructed industrial plants, was made to release the energy of the universe locked up within the atom from the beginning of time. A fabulous achievement had been reached. Speculative theory, barely established in pre-war laboratories, had been projected into practicality.

This phase of the Atomic Bomb Project, which is headed by Major General Leslie R. Groves, was under the direction of Dr J.R. Oppenheimer, theoretical physicist of the University of California. He is to be credited with achieving the implementation of atomic energy for military purposes.

Tension before the actual detonation was at a tremendous pitch. Failure was an ever-present

The mushroom cloud generated by the second Atomic Bomb, dropped on Nagasaki, Japan, 8 August 1945. Courtesy of the National Archives (NWDNS-208-N-438888).

possibility. Too great a success, envisioned by some of those present, might have meant an uncontrollable, unusable weapon. . . .

The full significance of these closing moments before the final factual test was not lost on these men of science. They fully knew their position as pioneers into another age. They also knew that one false move would blast them and their entire effort into eternity. Before the assembly started a receipt for the vital matter was signed by Brigadier General Thomas F. Farrell, General Groves' deputy. This signalized the formal transfer of the irreplaceable material from the scientists to the Army. . . .

The ominous weather which had dogged the assembly of the bomb had a very sobering affect on the assembled experts whose work was accomplished amid lightning flashes and peals of thunder. The weather, unusual and upsetting, blocked out aerial observation of the test. It even held up the actual explosion scheduled at 4:00 AM for an hour and a half. For many months the approximate date and time had been set and had been one of the high-level secrets of the best kept secret of the entire war.

Nearest observation point was set up 10,000 yards south of the tower where in a timber and earth shelter the controls for the test were located. At a point 17,000 yards from the tower at a point which would give the best observation the key figures in the atomic bomb project took their posts. These included General Groves, Dr Vannevar Bush, head of the Office of Scientific Research and Development and Dr James B. Conant, president of Harvard University.

Actual detonation was in charge of Dr K.T. Bainbridge of Massachusetts Institute of Technology. He and Lieutenant Bush, in charge of the Military Police Detachment, were the last men to inspect the tower with its cosmic bomb.

At three o'clock in the morning the party moved forward to the control station. General Groves and Dr Oppenheimer consulted with the weathermen.

The decision was made to go ahead with the test despite the lack of assurance of favorable weather. The time was set for 5:30 AM.

General Groves rejoined Dr Conant and Dr Bush, and just before the test time they joined the many scientists gathered at the Base Camp. Here all present were ordered to lie on the ground, face downward, heads away from the blast direction.

Tension reached a tremendous pitch in the control room as the deadline approached. The several observation points in the area were tied in to the control room by radio and with twenty minutes to go, Dr S.K. Allison of Chicago University took over the radio net and made periodic time announcements.

The time signals, 'minus 20 minutes, minus fifteen minutes', and on and on increased the tension to the breaking point as the group in the control room which included Dr Oppenheimer and General Farrell held their breaths, all praying with the intensity of the moment which will live forever with each man who was there. At 'minus 45 seconds', robot mechanism took over and from that point on the whole great complicated mass of intricate mechanism was in operation without human control. Stationed at a reserve switch, however, was a soldier scientist ready to attempt to stop the explosion should the order be issued. The order never came.

At the appointed time there was a blinding flash lighting up the whole area brighter than the brightest daylight. A mountain range three miles from the observation point stood out in bold relief. Then came a tremendous sustained roar and a heavy pressure wave which knocked down two men outside the control center. Immediately thereafter, a huge multi-colored surging cloud boiled to an altitude of over 40,000 feet. Clouds in its path disappeared. Soon the shifting substratosphere winds dispersed the now grey mass.

The test was over, the project a success.

The steel tower had been entirely vaporized. Where the tower had stood, there was a huge sloping crater. Dazed but relieved at the success of their tests, the scientists promptly marshalled their forces to estimate the strength of America's new weapon. To examine the nature of the crater, specially equipped tanks were wheeled into the area, one of which carried Dr Enrico Fermi, noted nuclear scientist. Answer to their findings rests in the destruction effected in Japan today in the first military use of the atomic bomb. . . .

General Farrell's impressions are: 'The scene inside the shelter was dramatic beyond words. In and around the shelter were some twenty odd people concerned with last-minute arrangements. Included were Dr Oppenheimer, the Director who had borne the great scientific burden of developing the weapon from the raw materials made in Tennessee and Washington, and a dozen of his key assistants, Dr Kistiakowsky, Dr Bainbridge, who supervised all the detailed arrangements for the test; the weather expert, and several others. Besides those, there were a handful of soldiers, two or three Army officers and one Naval Officer. The shelter was filled with a great variety of instruments and radios.

'For some hectic two hours preceding the blast, General Groves stayed with the Director. Twenty minutes before the zero hour, General Groves left for his station at the base camp, first because it provided a better observation point and second, because of our rule that he and I must not be together in situations where there is an element of danger which existed at both points.

'Just after General Groves left, announcements began to be broadcast of the interval remaining before the blast to the other groups participating in and observing the test. As the time interval grew smaller and changed from minutes to seconds, the tension increased by leaps and bounds. Everyone in that room knew the awful potentialities of the thing that they thought was about to happen. The scientists felt that their figuring must be right and that the bomb had to go off but there was in everyone's mind a strong measure of doubt.

'We were reaching into the unknown and we did not know what might come of it. It can safely be said that most of those present were praying—and praying harder than they had ever prayed before. If the shot were successful, it was a justification of the several years of intensive effort of tens of thousands of people—statesmen, scientists, engineers, manufacturers, soldiers, and many others in every walk of life.

'In that brief instant in the remote New Mexico desert, the tremendous effort of the brains and brawn of all these people came suddenly and startlingly to the fullest fruition. Dr Oppenheimer, on whom had rested a very heavy burden, grew tenser as the last seconds ticked off. He scarcely breathed. He held on to a post to steady himself. For the last few seconds, he stared directly ahead and then when the announcer shouted 'Now!' and there came this tremendous burst of light followed shortly thereafter by the deep growling roar of the explosion, his face relaxed into an expression of tremendous relief. Several of the observers standing back of the shelter to watch the lighting effects were knocked flat by the blast.

'The tension in the room let up and all started congratulating each other. Everyone sensed "This is it!" No matter what might happen now all knew that the impossible scientific job had been done. Atomic fission would no longer be hidden in the cloisters of the theoretical physicists' dreams. It was almost full grown at birth. It was a great new force to be used for good or for evil. There was a feeling in that shelter that those concerned with its nativity should dedicate their lives to the mission that it would always be used for good and never for evil.

'Dr Kistiakowsky threw his arms around Dr Oppenheimer and embraced him with shouts of glee. Others were equally enthusiastic. All the pent-up emotions were released in those few minutes and all seemed to sense immediately that the explosion had far exceeded the most optimistic expectations and wildest hopes of the scientists. All seemed to feel that they had been present at the birth of a new age—The Age of Atomic Energy—and felt their profound responsibility to help in guiding into right channels the tremendous forces which had been unlocked for the first time in history.

'As to the present war, there was a feeling that no matter what else might happen, we now had the means to insure its speedy conclusion and save thousands of American lives. As to the future, there had been brought into being something big and something new that would prove to be immeasurably more important than the discovery of electricity or any of the other great discoveries which have so affected our existence.

The effects could well be called unprecedented, magnificent, beautiful, stupendous and terrifying. No man-made phenomenon of such tremendous power had ever occurred before. The lighting effects beggared description. The whole country was lighted by a searing light with the intensity many times that of the midday sun. It was golden, purple, violet, gray and blue. It lighted every peak, crevasse and ridge of the nearby mountain range with a clarity and beauty that cannot be described but must be seen to be imagined. It was that beauty the great poets dream about but describe most poorly and inadequately. Thirty seconds after, the explosion came first, the air blast pressing hard against the people and things, to be followed almost immediately by the strong, sustained, awesome roar which warned of doomsday and made us feel that we puny things were blasphemous to dare tamper with the forces heretofore reserved to the Almighty. Words are inadequate tools for the job of acquainting those not present with the physical, mental and psychological effects. It had to be witnessed to be realized.'

Study Question

1. The use of the A-Bomb was often justified in terms of military necessity: the need to end the war with Japan rapidly and with minimal US casualties. Was this an adequate justification?

TIPS FOR ANALYSIS

Official Documents

An 'official document'—often synonymous with 'legal document'—may be issued by a government, an international institution, a religious organization, or simply a person or organization vested with legal authority. It either grants a particular right, or set of rights, or establishes a legal relationship. Examples of official documents include legal codes, contracts, and charters.

WEB RESOURCES

Avalon Project: WWII Documents
www.yale.edu/lawweb/avalon/wwii/wwii.htm
Yad Vashem
http://www.yadvashem.org

US Holocaust Memorial Museum
http://www.ushmm.org
Historical Text Archive: World War II
http://www.historicaltextarchive.com/sections.php?op=listarticles&secid=18
World War II Archives Foundation
http://wwiiarchives.net

RECOMMENDED READING

Louis de Bernieres, *Corelli's Mandolin* (New York: Vintage, 1995). Set on the Greek Island of Cephallonia before and after the Italian occupation during the Second World War, *Corelli's Mandolin* takes a darkly comedic look at the complications brought by the fascist occupation, collaboration, resistance, and the deprivation of war.

Ernest Hemingway, *For Whom the Bell Tolls* (London: Scribner, 1995). Hemingway's story reveals the flaws on both sides of the Spanish Civil War, though it is slightly more sympathetic to the Republican side. *For Whom the Bell Tolls* is a nuanced portrayal of the conflict and is both a war novel and a story of personal honour and love.

Primo Levi, *If Not Now, When?* (New York: Penguin, 1995). Partially based on Levi's experience with the Italian partisans fighting against the Nazi occupation in 1943, this novel confronts the implications of total war and the power of resistance, even in the face of overwhelming odds.

Shohei Ooka, *Fires on the Plain* (Boston: Tuttle Publishing, 2001). Set in Leyte, as Japanese defeat is imminent, *Fires on the Plain* follows one Japanese soldier, abandoned by his unit, as he wanders the island, starving and delirious, and is captured by American forces. The novel's strong antiwar focus is sometimes compared to Remarque's *All Quiet on the Western Front*.

Jean-Paul Sartre, *Iron in the Soul* (London: Penguin, 2002). Sartre's *Iron in the Soul* is set in June 1940, as the Fall of France is imminent. French soldiers, abandoned by their leaders, await their final defeat at the hands of the Nazis. The novel examines thoughts and actions in the face of total loss. This is the third volume of Sartre's *The Roads to Freedom* series, a trilogy based on the author's war experiences.

Elie Wiesel, *The Night Trilogy* (London: Farrar, Strauss and Giroux, 1987). *The Night Trilogy* is Wiesel's exploration of life in the extermination camps and the guilt of survival. *Night* is the autobiographical story of a boy and his father and their struggle to survive in Auschwitz. *Dawn* is set in Palestine, where terrorist acts against the British lead a survivor of the Holocaust to become a potential executioner. In *The Accident*, a Holocaust survivor faces the guilt of having survived while his family died.

RECOMMENDED VIEWING

A Diary for Timothy (UK, 1945). Director: Humphrey Jennings (Short Documentary). *A Diary for Timothy* is constructed around the life of a baby born in the last year of the Second World War. Written by E.M. Forster, the narrative tells the story of ordinary people and how their lives were impacted by the war, in their own words.

Night and Fog (France, 1955). Director: Alain Resnais (B&W/Colour) (Documentary). Drawn from contemporary newsreels, *Night and Fog* conveys all of the horrors of the extermination camps, especially the mechanization of the killing process. The documentary, which was filmed at Auschwitz in 1955, briefly touches on the issue of responsibility and the Nuremberg Trials. The short film provides an important contrast to the approach of Claude Lanzmann's epic documentary, *Shoah*.

Tora! Tora! Tora! (USA, 1970). Directors: Richard Fleischer/Kinji Fukasaku. A $25 million collaboration between American and Japanese filmmakers, *Tora! Tora! Tora!* recreates the attack on Pearl Harbor. The film focuses on Japanese planning and the American refusal to heed warnings that an attack was imminent. The film was recognized for its remarkable battle scenes.

Enemy Alien (Canada, 1975). Director: Jeanette Lerman (Short Documentary). *Enemy Alien* is a Canadian National Film Board documentary focusing on the internment of Japanese-Canadians during the Second World War. The film uses historical news footage and photographs in examining key issues such as immigration, racism, dispossession, and repatriation.

Das Boot (West Germany, 1981). Director: Wolfgang Petersen. This epic film is told entirely from the German perspective. It follows a U-boat captain and his crew as they patrol the Atlantic and Mediterranean, capturing the boredom, monotony, and tension of life on a submarine, punctuated by the brief, intense moments of combat. The 2004 Director's Cut runs almost five hours.

Kuroi Ame [Black Rain] (Japan, 1989). Director: Shohei Imamura (B&W and Colour). Adapted from the novel by Masuji Ibuse, *Kuroi Ame* is set amidst the aftermath of the atomic bombing and the radioactive fallout—so-called black rain. The film opens with a realistic depiction of the bombing and the moments after, then moves to the postwar era to examine both the physical and psychological impact of the bombing.

Schindler's List (USA, 1993). Director: Steven Spielberg (Primarily B&W). Spielberg's powerful recreation of the life of Oskar Schindler and his efforts to protect his Jewish workers from the extermination camps of Poland is noted for its powerful cinematography and attempt to remain historically accurate. The film won seven Academy Awards.

In the Name of the Emperor (USA, 1998). Directors: Christine Choy/Nancy Tong (Documentary). Choy and Tong's 52-minute documentary focuses on the Rape of Nanjing. Using eyewitness accounts and small pieces of film shot at the time, the film also draws much material from the diaries of missionaries who witnessed the atrocities that followed the Japanese occupation of the Nationalist capital.

Unmei No Toki [Pride] (Japan, 1998). Director: Shunya Ito. *Unmei No Toki* remains a highly controversial film because of its sympathetic depiction of Japanese wartime Prime Minister Hideki Tojo. Ignoring any negative elements of Tojo's life (he was sentenced to death by the 1948 Tokyo war crimes trial), Ito portrays Tojo as a passionate nationalist and heroic leader who was motivated by his determination to eliminate the presence of western imperialism in East Asia.

CHAPTER EIGHT

A NEW
WORLD ORDER?

◇

The destruction wrought by the Second World War ushered in a number of profound changes in the postwar era, most importantly to the global balance of power. The once powerful nations of Europe—Britain, France, and Germany—had been utterly devastated. In Asia, Japan lay in ruins, after a sustained campaign of aerial bombardment, culminating in the detonation of Atomic Bombs over Hiroshima and Nagasaki. Perhaps most importantly, the events of the Second World War seemed to have shaken the foundations of the old world order to its core; no longer would a few great powers be able to enforce their political dominance over the vast majority of the earth's inhabitants. Fascism had been decisively defeated and a commitment to new, democratic political systems secured. Thus, the end of the war seemed to offer the promise of a new cooperative world order based, in the words of the Potsdam Proclamation, on 'peace, security, and justice'.

The creation of the United Nations was intended to ensure that such high ideals were translated into practice. The problematic League of Nations was to be replaced by a new organization built on the principle that '[t]he only true basis of enduring peace is the willing cooperation of free peoples in a world in which, relieved of the menace of aggression, all may enjoy economic and social security'.[1] In 1945, fifty-one nations signed the Charter of the United Nations, thereby committing their governments to be guided by its principles. Unlike the League, the United Nations, through the Security Council, would have the ability to summon military forces in order to maintain peace and security and to repel aggression. Five permanent members—the Republic of China, France, Great Britain, the Soviet Union, and the United States—along with ten rotating members were charged with ensuring that the UN Security Council met this obligation.[2]

The reduced power of the major imperial nations—in particular Great Britain and France—seemed to bode well for groups seeking freedom from colonial rule. Though imperialists such as Winston Churchill continued to defend the concept of

Empire, the economic reality of the postwar world would refocus Britain's attention on its internal situation. This provided a window of opportunity for independence movements which had gained strength in the 1920s and 1930s to exploit.

The documents in this section focus on the potential for a postwar world built on co-operative principles. Both the Atlantic Charter and the Potsdam Proclamation speak of a world based on democracy and self-determination, where justice and security would be provided to all. The Universal Declaration of Human Rights asserts the basic freedoms owing to every individual and condemns prejudice based on gender, race, religion, or political viewpoint. Mohandas Gandhi and Ho Chi Minh affirm the right of their peoples to independent development, free of colonial or neo-colonial influence. An Anglo-American Committee of Inquiry was created to balance the interests of both Arabs and Jewish settlers in Palestine. Finally, Lester Pearson reflects both on the potential of the United Nations, and on the frustrations resulting from the UN's early attempts to mobilize the international community in peacekeeping efforts.

Notes

1. The Declaration of St. James Palace, June 1941, http://www.un.org.
2. In practice, the veto power held by the five permanent members often rendered the Security Council impotent in conflicts involving any of the five.

Franklin D. Roosevelt and Winston S. Churchill

In August 1941, American President Franklin D. Roosevelt and British Prime Minister Winston Churchill met to discuss war aims and a possible postwar settlement. The four-day meeting took place aboard the USS Augusta, anchored off the coast of Newfoundland—at that time still a part of the British Empire. Though the United States had not entered the war at this time, Roosevelt played a major role in shaping the document created at these meetings—the 'Atlantic Charter'. Though Stalin was not present during the discussions, the Soviet Union subsequently agreed to the principles embodied in the Atlantic Charter.

The Atlantic Charter

14 August 1941

The President of the United States of America and the Prime Minister, Mr Churchill, representing His Majesty's Government in the United Kingdom, being met together, deem it right to make known certain common principles in the national policies of their respective countries on which they base their hopes for a better future for the world.

AUGUST 14—"TWO YEARS AGO TODAY, PRESIDENT ROOSEVELT AND PRIME MINISTER CHURCHILL SIGNED THE ATLANTIC CHARTER."... NEWS ITEM

"A SECOND EMANCIPATION PROCLAMATION !!"

This sketch likened the signing of the Atlantic Charter to Lincoln's emancipation of American slaves. Courtesy of the National Archives (NWDNS-208-COM-994).

First, their countries seek no aggrandisement, territorial or other.

Second, they desire to see no territorial changes that do not accord with the freely expressed wishes of the peoples concerned.

Third, they respect the right of all peoples to choose the form of government under which they will live; and they wish to see sovereign rights and self-government restored to those who have been forcibly deprived of them.

Fourth, they will endeavour, with due respect for their existing obligations, to further the enjoyment by all States, great or small, victor or vanquished, of access, on equal terms, to the trade and to the raw materials of the world which are needed for their economic prosperity.

Fifth, they desire to bring about the fullest collaboration between all nations in the economic field, with the object of securing for all improved labour standards, economic advancement, and social security.

Sixth, after the final destruction of the Nazi tyranny they hope to see established a peace which will afford to all nations the means of dwelling in safety within their own boundaries, and which will afford assurance that all the men in all the lands may live out their lives in freedom from fear and want.

Seventh, such a peace should enable all men to traverse the high seas and oceans without hindrance.

Eighth, they believe that all the nations of the world, for realistic as well as spiritual reasons, must come to the abandonment of the use of force. Since no future peace can be maintained if land, sea, or air armaments continue to be employed by nations which threaten, or may threaten, aggression outside of their frontiers, pending the establishment of a wider and permanent system of general security, that the disarmament of such nations is essential. They will likewise aid and encourage all other practicable measures which will lighten for peace-loving peoples the crushing burden of armaments.

> **Study Question**
>
> 1. To what extent did the Atlantic Charter provide a practical and workable framework for the postwar era?

HARRY S. TRUMAN, WINSTON CHURCHILL, AND CHIANG KAI-SHEK

By the summer of 1945 the war in Europe was over and the allied forces had refocused their attention on the Pacific War. Harry S. Truman, who had replaced Franklin D. Roosevelt as the American president, had already approved a land invasion of the Japanese mainland, to be coordinated with Soviet forces in the north. However, by the early days of the Potsdam Conference (17 July–2

August), Truman was also aware of the successful Trinity Test in New Mexico. His confidence bolstered, Truman opted to demand unconditional surrender from the Japanese. Most East Asian advisors believed that, if only the Japanese were permitted to retain their emperor, they would immediately surrender. Truman, however, would make no such guarantee.

THE POTSDAM PROCLAMATION

An ultimatum demanding the immediate unconditional surrender of the armed forces of Japan

26 July 1945

We, the President of the United States, the President of the National Government of the Republic of China, and the Prime Minister of Great Britain,[1] representing the hundreds of millions of our countrymen, have conferred and agree that Japan shall be given an opportunity to end the war.

The prodigious land, sea, and air forces of the United States, the British Empire, and China, many times reinforced by their armies and air fleets from the West, are poised to strike the final blows upon Japan. This military power is sustained and inspired by the determination of all the allied nations to prosecute the war against Japan until she ceases to resist.

The result of the futile and senseless German resistance to the might of the aroused free peoples of the world stands forth in awful clarity as an example to the people of Japan.

The time has come for Japan to decide whether she will continue to be controlled by those self-willed militaristic advisers whose unintelligent calculations have brought the Empire of Japan to the threshold of annihilation, or whether she will follow the path of reason.

The following are our terms. We shall not deviate from them. There are no alternatives. We shall brook no delay.

There must be eliminated for all time the authority and influence of those who have deceived and misled the people of Japan into embarking on world conquest, for we insist that a new order of peace, security, and justice will be impossible until irresponsible militarism is driven from the world.

Until such a new order is established and until there is convincing proof that Japan's war-making power is destroyed points in Japanese territory designated by the Allies will be occupied to secure the achievement of the basic objective we are here setting forth.

The terms of the Cairo Declaration shall be carried out, and Japanese sovereignty shall be limited to the islands of Honshu, Hokkaido, Kyushu, Shikoku, and such minor islands as we determine.[2]

The Japanese military forces after being completely disarmed shall be permitted to return to their homes, with the opportunity of leading peaceful and productive lives.

We do not intend that the Japanese shall be enslaved as a race nor destroyed as a nation, but stern justice will be meted out to all war criminals, including those who have visited cruelties upon our prisoners. The Japanese Government shall remove all obstacles to the revival and strengthening of democratic tendencies among the Japanese people. Freedom of speech, of religion, and of thought, as well as respect for fundamental human rights, shall be established.

Japan shall be permitted to maintain such industries as will sustain her economy and allow of the exaction of just reparations in kind, but not those industries which would enable her to rearm for war. To this end access to, as distinguished from control of, raw materials shall be permitted. Eventual Japanese participation in world trade relations shall be permitted.

The occupying forces of the Allies shall be withdrawn from Japan as soon as these objectives have been accomplished, and there has been established, in accordance with the freely expressed will of the Japanese people, a peacefully inclined and responsible Government.

We call upon the Government of Japan to proclaim now the unconditional surrender of all the Japanese armed forces, and to provide proper and adequate assurances of their good faith in such action. The alternative for Japan is complete and utter destruction.

Notes

1. The Soviet Union was not included in the declaration since, at the time they were not at war with Japan. The USSR subsequently declared war on 8 August 1945.

2. The Cairo Declaration stated that 'Japan shall be stripped of all the islands in the Pacific which she has seized or occupied since the beginning of the first World War in 1914, and that all the territories Japan has stolen from the Chinese, such as Manchuria, Formosa, and the Pescadores, shall be restored to the Republic of China. Japan will also

be expelled from all other territories which she has taken by violence and greed. The aforesaid three great powers, mindful of the enslavement of the people of Korea, are determined that in due course Korea shall become free and independent'.

Study Question

1. Which of these provisions do you believe that the Japanese found most egregious?

UNITED NATIONS

In response to the horrific experiences of the Second World War and the era of imperialism, the United Nations set out, in 1948, to create a comprehensive statement of global human rights. The result was embodied in the Universal Declaration of Human Rights. Following the proclamation of the *Declaration, the General Assembly called on all of its member nations 'to cause it to be disseminated, displayed, read, and expounded principally in schools and other educational institutions, without distinction based on the political status of countries or territories'.[1]*

THE UNIVERSAL DECLARATION OF HUMAN RIGHTS

Preamble

WHEREAS recognition of the inherent dignity and of the equal and inalienable rights of all members of the human family is the foundation of freedom, justice and peace in the world,

WHEREAS disregard and contempt for human rights have resulted in barbarous acts which have outraged the conscience of mankind, and the advent of a world in which human beings shall enjoy freedom of speech and belief and freedom from fear and want has been proclaimed as the highest aspiration of the common people,

WHEREAS it is essential, if man is not to be compelled to have recourse, as a last resort, to rebellion against tyranny and oppression, that human rights should be protected by the rule of law,

WHEREAS it is essential to promote the development of friendly relations between nations,

WHEREAS the peoples of the United Nations have in the Charter reaffirmed their faith in fundamental human rights, in the dignity and worth of the human person and in the equal rights of men and women and have determined to promote social progress and better standards of life in larger freedom,

WHEREAS Member States have pledged themselves to achieve, in co-operation with the United Nations, the promotion of universal respect for and observance of human rights and fundamental freedoms,

WHEREAS a common understanding of these rights and freedoms is of the greatest importance for the full realization of this pledge,

Eleanor Roosevelt reads from the Universal Declaration of Human Rights. Roosevelt was instrumental in securing the passage of the declaration. Courtesy of the United Nations Photo Library (23783/UN/DPI).

Now, Therefore, The General Assembly proclaims:

This Universal Declaration of Human Rights as a common standard of achievement for all peoples and all nations, to the end that every individual and every organ of society, keeping this Declaration constantly in mind, shall strive by teaching and education to promote respect for these rights and freedoms and by progressive measures, national and international, to secure their universal and effective recognition and observance, both among the peoples of Member States themselves and among the peoples of territories under their jurisdiction.

Article 1

All human beings are born free and equal in dignity and rights. They are endowed with reason and conscience and should act towards one another in a spirit of brotherhood.

Article 2

Everyone is entitled to all the rights and freedoms set forth in this Declaration, without distinction of any kind, such as race, colour, sex, language, religion, political or other opinion, national or social origin, property, birth or other status.

Furthermore, no distinction shall be made on the basis of the political, jurisdictional or international status of the country or territory to which a person belongs, whether it be independent, trust, non-self-governing or under any other limitation of sovereignty.

Article 3
Everyone has the right to life, liberty and security of person.

Article 4
No one shall be held in slavery or servitude; slavery and the slave trade shall be prohibited in all their forms.

Article 5
No one shall be subjected to torture or to cruel, inhuman or degrading treatment or punishment.

Article 6
Everyone has the right to recognition everywhere as a person before the law.

Article 7
All are equal before the law and are entitled without any discrimination to equal protection of the law. All are entitled to equal protection against any discrimination in violation of this Declaration and against any incitement to such discrimination.

Article 8
Everyone has the right to an effective remedy by the competent national tribunals for acts violating the fundamental rights granted him by the constitution or by law.

Article 9
No one shall be subjected to arbitrary arrest, detention or exile.

Article 10
Everyone is entitled in full equality to a fair and public hearing by an independent and impartial tribunal, in the determination of his rights and obligations and of any criminal charge against him.

Article 11
(1) Everyone charged with a penal offence has the right to be presumed innocent until proved guilty according to law in a public trial at which he has had all the guarantees necessary for his defence.
(2) No one shall be held guilty of any penal offence on account of any act or omission which did not constitute a penal offence, under national or international law, at the time when it was committed. Nor shall a heavier penalty be imposed than the one that was applicable at the time the penal offence was committed.

Article 12
No one shall be subjected to arbitrary interference with his privacy, family, home or correspondence, nor to attacks upon his honour and reputation. Everyone has the right to the protection of the law against such interference or attacks.

Article 13
(1) Everyone has the right to freedom of movement and residence within the borders of each State.
(2) Everyone has the right to leave any country, including his own, and to return to his country.

Article 14
(1) Everyone has the right to seek and to enjoy in other countries asylum from persecution.
(2) This right may not be invoked in the case of prosecutions genuinely arising from non-political crimes or from acts contrary to the purposes and principles of the United Nations.

Article 15
(1) Everyone has the right to a nationality.
(2) No one shall be arbitrarily deprived of his nationality nor denied the right to change his nationality.

Article 16
(1) Men and women of full age, without any limitation due to race, nationality or religion,

have the right to marry and to found a family. They are entitled to equal rights as a marriage, during marriage and at its dissolution.

(2) Marriage shall be entered into only with the free and full consent of the intending spouses.

(3) The family is the natural and fundamental group unit of society and is entitled to protection by society and the State.

Article 17

(1) Everyone has the right to own property alone as well as in association with others.

(2) No one shall be arbitrarily deprived of his property.

Article 18

Everyone has the right to freedom of thought, conscience and religion; this right includes freedom to change his religion or belief, and freedom, either alone or in community with others and in public or private, to manifest his religion or belief in teaching, practice, worship and observance.

Article 19

Everyone has the right to freedom of opinion and expression; this right includes freedom to hold opinions without interference and to seek, receive and impart information and ideas through any media and regardless of frontiers.

Article 20

(1) Everyone has the right to freedom of peaceful assembly and association.

(2) No one may be compelled to belong to an association.

Article 21

(1) Everyone has the right to take part in the government of his country, directly or through freely chosen representatives.

(2) Everyone has the right of equal access to public service in his country.

(3) The will of the people shall be the basis of the authority of the government; this will shall be expressed in periodic and genuine elections which shall be by universal and equal suffrage and shall be held by secret vote or by equivalent free voting procedures.

Article 22

Everyone, as a member of society, has the right to social security and is entitled to realization, through national effort and international co-operation and in accordance with the organization and resources of each State, of the economic, social and cultural rights indispensable for his dignity and the free development of his personality.

Article 23

(1) Everyone has the right to work, to free choice of employment, to just and favourable conditions of work and to protection against unemployment.

(2) Everyone, without any discrimination, has the right to equal pay for equal work.

(3) Everyone who works has the right to just and favourable remuneration ensuring for himself and his family an existence worthy of human dignity, and supplemented, if necessary, by other means of social protection.

(4) Everyone has the right to form and to join trade unions for the protection of his interests.

Article 24

Everyone has the right to rest and leisure, including reasonable limitation of working hours and periodic holidays with pay.

Article 25

(1) Everyone has the right to a standard of living adequate for the health and well-being of himself and of his family, including food, clothing, housing, and medical care and necessary social services, and the right to security in the event of unemployment, sickness, disability, widowhood, old age, or other lack of livelihood in circumstances beyond his control.

(2) Motherhood and childhood are entitled to special care and assistance. All children, whether born in or out of wedlock, shall enjoy the same social protection.

Article 26
(1) Everyone has the right to education. Education shall be free, at least in the elementary and fundamental stages. Elementary education shall be compulsory. Technical and professional education shall be made generally available and higher education shall be equally accessible to all on the basis of merit.
(2) Education shall be directed to the full development of the human personality and to the strengthening of respect for human rights and fundamental freedoms. It shall promote understanding, tolerance and friendship among all nations, racial or religious groups, and shall further the activities of the United Nations for the maintenance of peace.
(3) Parents have a prior right to choose the kind of education that shall be given to their children.

Article 27
(1) Everyone has the right freely to participate in the cultural life of the community, to enjoy the arts and to share in scientific advancement and its benefits.
(2) Everyone has the right to the protection of the moral and material interests resulting from any scientific, literary or artistic production of which he is the author.

Article 28
Everyone is entitled to a social and international order in which the rights and freedoms set forth in this Declaration can be fully realized.

Article 29
(1) Everyone has duties to the community in which alone the free and full development of his personality is possible.
(2) In the exercise of his rights and freedoms, everyone shall be subject only to such limitations as are determined by law solely for the purpose of securing due recognition and respect for the rights and freedoms and others and of meeting the just requirements of morality, public order and the general welfare in a democratic society.
(3) These rights and freedoms may in no case be exercised contrary to the purposes and principles of the United Nations.

Article 30
Nothing in this Declaration may be interpreted as implying for any State, group or person any right to engage in any activity or to perform any act aimed at the destruction of any of the rights and freedoms set forth herein.

Note

1.   http://www.un.org/en/documents/ udhr/index.shtml.

Study Question

1.   Has the Declaration of Human Rights been an effective means of protecting basic human rights and freedoms in the postwar world? Why or why not?

MOHANDAS K. GANDHI

Mohandas Gandhi was born in 1869 in Porbander. After briefly attending Bombay University in 1887, Gandhi travelled to England in 1888 to train as a barrister. He returned only briefly to India in 1891, and then left in 1893 to take up a legal position in South Africa. While in South Africa, Gandhi developed the essential elements of his later campaign for Indian independence— non-violent non-co-operation (Satyagraha). In 1915, during the First World War, he returned to India. Despite his own non-violent philosophy, Gandhi campaigned in support of the British war effort. However, at the end of the war the British curtailed civil liberties in India in order to control the growing independence movement, and these actions culminated in the deaths of hundreds of Indians during the Amritsar Massacre (see Chapter Two). Resistance to British rule gradually escalated until, in 1942, Gandhi demanded that the British 'Quit India'. The document that follows is the text of Gandhi's original 'Quit India' resolution. This draft was rejected by the All-India Congress Working Committee in favour of a more moderate version submitted by Jawaharlal Nehru.

'QUIT INDIA' DRAFT RESOLUTION

Whereas the British War Cabinet proposals by Sir Stafford Cripps have shown up British imperialism in its nakedness as never before, the All-India Congress Committee has come to the following conclusions:

The committee is of the opinion that Britain is incapable of defending India. It is natural that whatever she does is for her own defence. There is the eternal conflict between Indian and British interest. It follows that their notions of defence would also differ.

The British Government has no trust in India's political parties. The Indian Army has been maintained up till now mainly to hold India in subjugation. It has been completely segregated from the general population, who can in no sense regard it as their own. This policy of mistrust still continues, and is the reason why national defence is not entrusted to India's elected representatives.

Japan's quarrel is not with India. She is warring against the British Empire. India's participation in the war has not been with the consent of the representatives of the Indian people. It was purely a British act. If India were freed, her first step would probably be to negotiate with Japan.

A wartime poster uses key images from India's past and present to question its future direction. Courtesy of the Library of Congress, Prints and Photographs Division (LC-USZC2-803).

The Congress is of the opinion that if the British withdrew from India, India would be able to defend herself in the event of the Japanese, or any aggressor, attacking India.

The committee is, therefore, of the opinion that the British should withdraw from India. The plea that they should remain in India for the protection of the Indian princes is wholly untenable. It is an additional proof of their determination to maintain their hold over India. The princes need have no fear from an unarmed India.

The question of majority and minority is the creation of the British Government, and would disappear on their withdrawal.

For all these reasons, the committee appeals to Britain, for the sake of her own safety, for the sake of India's safety and for the cause of world peace, to let go her hold on India, even if she does not give up all her Asiatic and African possessions.

This committee desires to assure the Japanese Government and people that India bears no enmity, either toward Japan or toward any other nation. India only desires freedom from all alien domination. But in this fight for freedom the committee is of the opinion that India, while welcoming universal sympathy, does not stand in need of foreign military aid.

India will attain her freedom through her non-violent strength, and will retain it likewise. Therefore, the committee hopes that Japan will not have any designs on India. But if Japan attacks India, and Britain makes no response to its appeal, the committee will expect all those who look to the Congress for guidance to offer complete non-violent non-cooperation to the Japanese forces, and not to render any assistance to them. It is no part of the duty of those who are attacked to render any assistance to the attacker. It is their duty to offer complete non-cooperation.

It is not difficult to understand the simple principle of nonviolent non-cooperation:

First, we may not bend the knee to an aggressor, or obey any of his orders.

Second, we may not look to him for any favours nor fall to his bribes, but we may not bear him any malice nor wish him ill.

Third, if he wishes to take possession of our fields we will refuse to give them up, even if we have to die in an effort to resist him.

Fourth, if he is attacked by disease, or is dying of thirst and seeks our aid, we may not refuse it.

Fifth, in such places where British and Japanese forces are fighting, our non-cooperation will be fruitless and unnecessary.

At present, our non-cooperation with the British Government is limited. Were we to offer them complete non-cooperation when they are actually fighting, it would be tantamount to bringing our country deliberately into Japanese hands. Therefore, not to put any obstacle in the way of the British forces will often be the only way of demonstrating our non-cooperation with the Japanese.

Neither may we assist the British in any active manner. If we can judge from their recent attitude, the British Government do not need any help from us beyond our non-interference. They desire our help only as slaves.

It is not necessary for the committee to make a clear declaration in regard to a scorched-earth policy. If, in spite of our nonviolence, any part of the country falls into Japanese hands, we may not destroy our crops or water supply, etc., if only because it will be our endeavor to regain them. The destruction of war material is another matter, and may, under certain circumstances, be a military necessity. But it can never be the Congress policy to destroy what belongs, or is of use, to the masses.

Whilst non-cooperation against the Japanese forces will necessarily be limited to a comparatively small number, and must succeed if it is complete and genuine, true building up of swaraj [self-government] consists in the millions of India wholeheartedly working for a constructive program. Without it, the whole nation cannot rise from its age-long torpor.

Whether the British remain or not, it is our duty always to wipe out our unemployment, to bridge the gulf between the rich and the poor, to banish communal strife, to exorcise the demon of untouchability, to reform the Dacoits [armed bandits] and save the people from them. If scores of people do not take a living interest in this nation-building work, freedom must remain a dream and unattainable by either non-violence or violence.

Foreign soldiers: The committee is of the opinion that it is harmful to India's interests, and dangerous to the cause of India's freedom, to introduce foreign soldiers in India. It therefore appeals to the British Government to remove these foreign legions, and henceforth stop further introduction. It is a crying shame to bring foreign troops in, in spite of India's inexhaustible manpower, and it is proof of the immorality that British imperialism is.

Study Question

1. If Britain had removed all foreign soldiers in India, as Gandhi's version of the proposal demanded, how might this have impacted the Indian independence movement?

HO CHI MINH

President Ho Chi Minh[1] (1890–1969) read the following declaration of independence on 2 September 1945 at a meeting of half a million people in Ba Dinh Square in Hanoi. Though defeated Japanese troops remained in Vietnam and French imperialists were attempting to regain control over the region, Ho Chi Minh, who had fought against the Japanese alongside the Vietminh, believed that Vietnam would finally be able to secure its independence. He was reassured by repeated anti-imperialist proclamations by the United States, believing that the United States would not allow the French to reclaim their Indochinese territories.

DECLARATION OF INDEPENDENCE OF THE DEMOCRATIC REPUBLIC OF VIET NAM

All men are created equal. They are endowed by their Creator with certain unalienable Rights; among these are Life, Liberty and the pursuit of Happiness.'

This immortal statement appeared in the Declaration of Independence of the United States of America in 1776. In a broader sense, it means: All the peoples on the earth are equal from birth, all the peoples have a right to live and to be happy and free.

The Declaration of the Rights of Man and the Citizen, made at the time of the French Revolution, in 1791, also states: 'All men are born free and with equal rights, and must always remain free and have equal rights.'

Those are undeniable truths.

Nevertheless, for more than eighty years, the French imperialists, abusing the standard of Liberty, Equality, and Fraternity, have violated our Fatherland and oppressed our fellow-citizens. They have acted contrary to the ideals of humanity and justice.

Politically, they have deprived our people of every democratic liberty.

They have enforced inhuman laws; they have set up three different political regimes in the North, the Centre, and the South of Viet Nam in order to wreck our country's oneness and prevent our people from being united.

They have built more prisons than schools. They

Ho Chi Minh in 1954, after the defeat of French forces in the battle of Dienbienphu. New York World Telegram and the Sun Newspaper Photograph Collection. Couartesy of the Library of Congress, Prints and Photographs Division (LC-USZ62-119630).

have mercilessly massacred our patriots. They have drowned our uprisings in seas of blood.

They have lettered public opinion and practised obscurantism.

They have weakened our race with opium and alcohol. In the field of economics, they have sucked us dry, driven our people to destitution, and devastated our land.

They have robbed us of our ricefields, our mines, our forests, and our natural resources. They have monopolized the issue of bank-notes and the import and export trade.

They have invented numerous unjustifiable taxes and reduced our people, especially our peasantry, to extreme poverty. They have made it impossible for our national bourgeoisie to prosper; they have mercilessly exploited our workers.

In the autumn of 1940, when the Japanese fascists invaded Indochina to establish new bases against the Allies, the French colonialists went down on their bended knees and opened the door of our country to welcome the Japanese in.

Thus, from that date, our people were subjected to the double yoke of the French and the Japanese. Their sufferings and miseries increased. The result was that towards the end of last year and the beginning of this year, from Quang Tri province to the North more than two million of our fellow-citizens died from starvation.

On the 9th of March this year, the French troops were disarmed by the Japanese. The French colonialists either fled or surrendered, showing that not only were they incapable of 'protecting' us, but that, in a period of five years, they had twice sold our country to the Japanese.

Before the 9th of March, how often the Viet Minh had urged the French to ally themselves with it against the Japanese! But instead of this proposal, the French colonialists only intensified their terrorist activities against the Viet Minh. After their defeat and before fleeing, they massacred the political prisoners detained at Yen Bai and Cao Bang.

In spite of all this, our fellow-citizens have always manifested a lenient and humane attitude towards the French. After the Japanese putsch of 9 March 1945, the Viet Minh helped many Frenchmen to cross the frontier, rescued others from Japanese jails, and protected French lives and property. In fact, since the autumn of 1940, our country had ceased to be a French colony and had become a Japanese possession.

When the Japanese surrendered to the Allies, our entire people rose to gain power and founded the Democratic Republic of Viet Nam.

The truth is that we have wrested our independence from the Japanese, not from the French.

The French have fled, the Japanese have capitulated, Emperor Bao Dai has abdicated. Our people have broken the chains which have fettered them for nearly a century and have won independence for Viet Nam. At the same time they have overthrown the centuries-old monarchic regime and established a democratic republican regime.

We, the Provisional Government of the new Viet Nam, republic representing the entire Vietnamese people, hereby declare that from now on we break off all relations of a colonial character with France; cancel all treaties signed by France on Viet Nam, and abolish all privileges held by France in our country.

The entire Vietnamese people are of one mind in their determination to oppose all wicked schemes by the French colonialists.

We are convinced that the Allies, which at the Teheran and San Francisco Conferences uphold the principle of equality among the nations, cannot fail to recognize the right of the Vietnamese people to independence.

A people who have courageously opposed French enslavement for more than eighty years, a people who have resolutely sided with the Allies against the fascists during these last years, such a people must be free, such a people must be independent.

For these reasons, we, the Provisional Government of the Democratic Republic of Viet Nam, solemnly make this declaration to the world:

Viet Nam has the right to enjoy freedom and independence and in fact has become a free and independent country. The entire Vietnamese people are determined to mobilize all their physical and mental strength, to sacrifice their lives and property in order to safeguard their freedom and independence.

Note

1. Ho Chi Minh was a pseudonym meaning 'the Enlightener'; he was born Nguyen Sinh Cung and also used the name Nguyen Ai Quoc (Nguyen the Patriot).

Study Question

1. Based only upon the Declaration of Independence how would you characterize Ho Chi Minh's ideology?

Anglo-American Committee of Inquiry

Faced with growing public awareness of the events of the Holocaust, on 13 November 1945 British Foreign Secretary Ernest Bevin and American President Harry Truman announced the creation of the 'Anglo-American Committee of Inquiry Regarding the Problems of European Jewry & Palestine'. The Committee was to investigate the situation of the remaining Jews of Europe, as well as the current circumstances in Palestine, and to make recommendations to the local British administration. After a series of hearings in April 1946 the Committee recommended that 100,000 Jews be admitted immediately to Palestine, but that the region should become neither an Arab nor a Jewish state. The following excerpts describe the reaction of the Palestinian population, as well as the argument put forth by Chaim Weizmann.

TESTIMONY ON THE CREATION OF THE STATE OF ISRAEL

The Palestinian Arab Case

The Committee heard a brief presentation of the Arab case in Washington, statements made in London by delegates from the Arab States to the United Nations, a fuller statement from the Secretary General and other representatives of the Arab League in Cairo, and evidence given on behalf of the Arab Higher (Committee and the Arab Office in Jerusalem). In addition, subcommittees visited Baghdad, Riyadh, Damascus, Beirut, and Amman, where they were informed of the views of Government and of unofficial spokesmen.

Stopped to the bare essentials, the Arab case is based upon the fact that Palestine is a country which the Arabs have occupied for more than a thousand years, and a denial of the Jewish historical claims to Palestine. In issuing the Balfour Declaration, the Arabs maintain, the British Government were giving away something that did not belong to Britain, and they have consistently argued that the Mandate conflicted with the Covenant of the League of Nations from which it derived its authority. The Arabs deny that the part played by the British in freeing them from the Turks gave Great Britain a right to dispose of their country.[1] Indeed, they assert that Turkish was preferable to British rule, if the latter involves their eventual subjection to the Jews. They consider the Mandate a violation of their right of self-determination since it is forcing upon them an immigration which they do not desire and will not tolerate—an invasion of Palestine by the Jews.

The Arabs of Palestine point out that all the surrounding Arab States have now been granted independence. They argue that they are just as advanced as are the citizens of the nearby States, and they demand independence for Palestine now. The promises which have been made to them in the name of Great Britain, and the assurances concerning Palestine given to Arab leaders by Presidents Roosevelt and Truman, have been understood by the Arabs of Palestine as a recognition of the principle that they should enjoy the same rights as those enjoyed by the neighbouring countries. Christian Arabs unite with Moslems in all of these contentions. They demand that their independence should be recognized at once, and they would like Palestine, as a self-governing country, to join the Arab League. . . .

The suggestion that self-government should be withheld from Palestine until the Jews have acquired a majority seems outrageous to the Arabs. They wish to be masters in their own house. The Arabs were opposed to the idea of a Jewish National Home even before the Biltmore Program and the demand for a Jewish State. Needless to say, however, their opposition has become more intense and more bitter since that program was adopted.

The Arabs maintain that they have never been anti-Semitic; indeed, they are Semites themselves. Arab spokesmen profess the greatest sympathy for the persecuted Jews of Europe, but they point out that they have not been responsible for this persecution and that it is not just that they should be compelled to atone for the sins of Western peoples by accepting into their country hundreds of thousands of victims of European anti-Semitism. Some Arabs even declare that they might be willing to do their share in providing for refugees on a quota basis if the United States, the British Commonwealth and other Western countries would do the same.

The Peel Commission took the view that the enterprise of the Jews in agriculture and industry had brought large, if indirect, benefits to the Arabs in raising their standard of living. Though a very large part of the Jewish purchases of land has been made from absentee landlords, many of them living outside Palestine, it is probable that many Arab farmers who have sold part of their land to the Jews have been able to make use of the money to improve the cultivation of their remaining holdings. The improvement of health conditions in many parts of the country, while due in part to the activities of Government and in part to the efforts of the Arabs themselves, has undoubtedly been assisted by the work of the Jewish settlers. It is also argued that the Jewish population has conferred substantial indirect benefits on the Arabs through its contribution to the public revenue. On the other hand, the Arabs contend that such improvement as there may have been in their standard of living is attributable solely to their own efforts, perhaps with a measure of aid at some points from the Administration. They assert that at least equal improvements have occurred in other Arab countries, and that the action taken by the Government to assist Jewish industry and agriculture has reacted unfavourably on the Arabs. Import duties for the protection of Jewish industries, for example, are said to have confronted Arab consumers with the necessity of buying high priced local products in place of cheaper imported goods. In any event the Arabs declare that, if they must choose between freedom and material improvement, they prefer freedom. . . .

The Arabs of Palestine are overwhelmed by a vague sense of the power of Western capital represented by the Jewish population. The influx of Western capital and the purchase of modern equipment for agriculture and industry excite in the minds of the Arabs a sense of inferiority and the feeling that they are contending against an imponderable force which is difficult to resist. This feeling is accentuated by the fact that they realize that the Jewish case is well understood and well portrayed in Washington and London, and that they have no means comparable in effectiveness of stating their side of the controversy to the Western World. They have

particularly resented the resolutions in favour of Zionist aspirations, adopted respectively by the United States Congress and by the British Labour Party. Although the Arab States have diplomatic representation and five of them are members of the United Nations, the Arabs of Palestine feel nevertheless that they have not succeeded in making their case heard. The Western countries have many Jewish but few Arab citizens, and Arabs are less familiar with modern methods of propaganda. They feel that their case is being judged and their fate is being decided by mysterious forces in the Western World, which they do not understand and which do not understand them.

Testimony by Chaim Weizmann

As a people, as a race, as a collectivity, the Jews are homeless, and this homelessness and the unchanging attachment of the Jews to Palestine did not begin with Hitler. It existed many, many years, many centuries before Hitler was ever thought of, and long before this hideous tragedy was enacted, the tragedy which would have seemed utterly incredible fifteen or twenty years ago. . . . the Jews have a right to collective self-expression, like everybody else—that the existence of a 'national home', if and when it is established and well-founded, would give poise and satisfaction and would render the Jew less unstable, even in the countries where he enjoys equality of treatment. He would feel that he had found collective self-expression in Palestine. They also realized that Palestine appeals powerfully to the Jews because there has been a connection between them and Palestine unbroken for thousands of years—not only in the moral and religious sense, but literally. With the exception of one or two periods—the period of the Crusades, when the Jews were more or less wiped out, and the subsequent Mongol invasion—there were always Jewish communities in Palestine and a certain amount of

Chaim Weizmann and Rabbi Stephen Wise at a May 1942 emergency meeting of Zionist groups, called to discuss the situation of the European Jewish population. Courtesy of the United States Holocaust Memorial Museum (1013).

Jewish agriculture in Galilee. These communities were not sterile; they showed very considerable intellectual activity, spreading far beyond the confines of Palestine. And whenever there was the faintest possibility of going back, there was a movement, a literal, physical movement for return, even in the face of great difficulties. . . .

I am reliably informed by men in whom I have absolute confidence—some of them trusted colleagues who have seen our country and studied it, who I think are unbiased and honest observers who would not mislead us—and they tell us that if the country is developed to the utmost, and the rain waters and the rivers utilized to the fullest extent, there would be room for many hundred of thousands more. Some of them have named a figure of something like 900,000. As Lord Samuel pointed out, there would seem to be room for double or treble the present population of Palestine without—and I would like to emphasize it—without harm to the present population, Jews or Arabs, and without thinking of displacing anybody. . . .

. . . We are sometimes accused by our Arab friends of having got hold of the best land in Palestine; that you can go round the coast and see the flourishing villages of the Jews, leaving only the poor lands and the hills to the Arabs. There is nothing more false than that accusation. It has become the best of land, but it has been marsh, it has been sand, it has been covered with rocks and with stones, and we have had to clean, to drain, to nurture and to build it up. Along with that, we have had to do the building up of the Jew to the soil, changing him from an urban inhabitant into a man who is attached to soil. We had to build up the soil at the same time, and in this process we are all regenerated. The land which we have now was derelict, it is true, twenty-five or thirty years ago. . . . To us it is not merely an agricultural or industrial enterprise. To us it is a question of life and death. Only we could ever have achieved this progress in face of the heavy cost of material and moral effort. . . .

I have witnessed the gradual whittling down of our rights in Palestine, and this culminated in the White Paper, which really, with the exception of 75,000 immigrants, put a stop to the 'national home'. . . .

The British government, in the White Paper of 1939, laid down once and for all that the Jews were to remain a minority of 1/3 until the end of time. . . . This . . . placed urgent problems of survival before us; not merely of salvage but of survival. My brain reels when I think of six million people being killed off in a comparatively short time, and if nothing is done of what can humanly be done to prevent a repetition of such a tragedy, then I fear for the survival of the Jews. . . .

I recognize fully that what I ask for will meet with considerable opposition on the part of the Arabs, and I know there may be Arabs present, opponents or friends or whatever they are—I think probably opponents. But there is no counsel of perfection in this world, and there is no absolute justice in this world. What you are trying to perform, and what we are all trying to do in our small way, is just rough human justice. I think the decision which I should like this committee to take, if I dare to say this, would be to move on the line of least injustice. Injustice there is going to be, but if you weigh up, on the one hand how the Arabs have emerged out of this war—I do not begrudge them—they have emerged with so many kingdoms, at any rate two kingdoms, four republics; they will have six seats in the UNO, one seat in the Security Council. To speak quite frankly, which may be forgiven—for at my age it may be permitted to be frank—I do not know if it is commensurate, what the Arabs have gained during this war. What is the number of their casualties? Have they suffered so much? If you compare it with our suffering, with our casualties,

with our contribution. . . . I say that there may be some slight injustice politically if Palestine is made a Jewish state, but individually the Arabs will not suffer. They have not suffered hitherto. On the contrary, economically, culturally, religiously, the Arabs will not be affected. Not because we are so good—though perhaps something may be said for the character of the Jew who has gone through hell for thousands of years, and it would stultify his own history if, when he gets his slight chance, he started persecuting the Arabs. We know what it is to be a minority, we know it only too well, but there are quite different reasons. The Arabs have a perfect guarantee: whatever Palestine may be, it will only be an island in an Arab sea, and the Arabs will not need to appeal or to have separate guarantees inserted in the treaties; the mere weight of their existence in organized states would prevent any Jew from doing them injustice even if he wanted to, and I am sure he does not want to. The position of the Arabs as a people is secure. Their national sentiments can find full expression in Damascus and in Cairo and in Baghdad and in all the great countries which will, I hope, some day build up an Arab civilization which will equal the ancient glories of their people. Palestine is to the Jews what Baghdad, Cairo and Damascus all rolled together are to the Arabs, and I think the line of least injustice demands that we should be given our chance. When carried out, that will, I am sure, eventually lead to understanding and harmony between our two races, which are, after all, akin.

Note

1. [Note in original document] We have not felt it necessary to enter into the historical arguments based upon undertakings given by the British Government to the Sharif Hussein of Mecca and others during the last war and interpreted by the Arabs as promising among other things that Palestine would become

an independent Arab country. These undertakings, the most important of which preceded the Balfour Declaration, form an essential part of the Arab case and were examined by an Anglo-Arab Committee in London in February 1939. The report of this Committee, containing statements of both the Arab and the British point of view, is to be found in British Command Paper No. 5974. The documents under examination were printed at the same time in Command Papers Nos. 6967 and 69 (all of 1939).

Study Question

1. Assess the claims of both the Palestinian Arabs and the points raised by Chaim Weizmann. Was there a way to resolve the situation without creating the potential for future violence?

LESTER B. PEARSON

Lester B. 'Mike' Pearson was born in Toronto in 1897. After service during the Great War, he studied history at Oxford. In 1928 Pearson joined the Department of External Affairs serving in numerous capacities, which included attending the sessions of the League of Nations. He was an active participant in the discussions that led to the creation of both the United Nations and the North Atlantic Treaty Organization (NATO). Elected to parliament as a Liberal in 1948, Pearson served as Minister for External Affairs for nine years. During the 1956 Suez Crisis, Pearson proposed a multinational force to keep the peace between Israel and Egypt, an act for which he was awarded the Nobel Peace Prize. The following speech was delivered at Temple University in Philadelphia in 1965.

ON PEACEKEEPING

Mr President, honoured guests and members of the Temple University Alumni Association:

With my very deep personal gratitude for this honour go my thanks for the recognition you have given to my country's efforts—as the citation reads—in promoting the cause of peace and understanding among nations and man. I wish also to pay my tribute to the work and the life of the man whom this Award commemorates. . . .

It is an often noted phenomenon that man's inventive ingenuity has out-distanced his sense of moral obligation; that technology and science have left politics and ethics far behind. Like the sorcerer's apprentice, we have set in motion destructive forces we are unable to control. The point, however, can be put another way. It is one thing to conquer space and to perceive, stretching before one without limit, the prospect of unimpeded exploration and advance. It is another to expect, in scientific terms, a quantum jump from immoral men to a world at peace. We must take it as given, I believe, that man's moral nature will continue to be ambiguous, that in Paul Tillich's words: 'In the best will there is an element of bad will.' The reverse is also true. It is not therefore so much a matter of morality catching up with science, of building a new Jerusalem, while there is something left to build on, but of collectively adjusting our habits of mind and our ways of living to the changing world around us. Surely man's capacity for reason can be applied to international politics as well as to international space and, in the application, strengthen our world community against the consequences of man's inhumanity to man.

As for me, and in spite of current headlines, I remain impressed with the elements of hope in our world as it is today. For one thing, there is a *world* community in a sense that no one would have believed possible fifty years ago, despite the apparent paradox that this community is divided into a greater number of political units than ever before. The paradox is more apparent than real, however, because cultural and racial divisions have always existed. For many years they were hidden by the crust of colonial empires. Now that this quite artificial and imposed unity has been broken, the new nations, as well as the old, are able to judge for themselves how they wish to arrange their relations with each other.

The new nations, also, now share with the old the essentially Western belief in, and pursuit of, material progress. Western technology has spread to the ends of the earth, bringing with it new hope for people long chained to a fatalistic acceptance of poverty, disease and ignorance. They may now hope, with an awakened intensity, that opportunities will exist for their children, if not for themselves, to participate in activities and to share in experience that we, in the West, take for granted. They know that nuclear physics means new sources of energy as well as new means of destruction; that rockets may propel communications satellites into space as well as guided missiles. And we know, as the privileged have never known or admitted before, that our own future and well-being depends on our imaginative capacity to help organize the world's resources and skills so that all may share in its wealth more equitably than in the past.

The most significant and hopeful, if at times

the most frustrating, expression of this sense of community is the United Nations. The world organization means different things to different men. It is godparent and mentor to the new nations, some of whom might not be independent if it were not for the United Nations. It is the gangling, awkward child of the old nations who conceived of the United Nations 'to safeguard succeeding generations from the scourge of war' even as the guns were still sounding on the battlefields of World War II. For all, it is a meeting place, a centre, as the Charter puts it, 'for harmonizing the actions of nations', and an instrument for furthering the common purposes of mankind. It often does just this. Out of the push and pull of debate and negotiation between conflicting interests and ambitions there emerges on may issues what may be thought of as a consensus of world opinion; and, ready to interpret this consensus and to give it form, stands an independent and impartial Secretariat. There has never been anything like it before in history. It is now an indispensable part of human development in a new age.

Keeping the peace is the first and most difficult purpose of the United Nations. I have no doubt it will remain the yardstick by which the United Nations stands or falls, however legitimate and even compelling are the economic, social and ethical purposes which it is also called upon to serve. If we cannot manage our affairs peacefully in the short term, our long-term goals will never be reached.

Threats to peace and the danger of local conflict escalating to nuclear destruction have been responsible in large measure for calling into being the series of UN forces, observer groups and presences that have served to implement what the Secretary-General has described as 'the idea of the UN as a representative instrument for promoting and maintaining international order'. It is a remarkable advance in world affairs that many thousands of UN military personnel from more than a dozen countries should be able effectively to represent the concern of the world's peoples that conflict shall be prevented or stopped before it engulfs us all in war. Future threats to the peace will provoke similar appeals to the UN to put out the fire before it spreads. Tonight, with a feeling of fear and foreboding, I wish that there could be such an appeal from North and South Vietnam.

We have now reached a critical stage in the development of the UN's peace-keeping capacity. The organization is quite different from what it was in 1945, or in 1950, when it was able to mobilize under US leadership collective resistance to aggression in Korea. The increase in the membership to more than double the original number, the nature of that increase and the diffusion of power amongst several regional groups have led to a corresponding decrease in the influence and authority of the Western states.

Nevertheless, the leadership in peace-keeping has come from the West, in close co-operation with the Secretary-General and with members of the non-aligned group. I would reject, however, the Soviet charge that, in this leadership, we had some special Western axe to grind. Indeed the Assembly approved by large majorities the assessment resolutions establishing collective financial responsibility for the operations in the Middle East and the Congo. What has happened is that since 1962 the balance of the membership has tended to take a more critical view of Great Power disputes over peace-keeping. They have begun to question whether, in the light of this disagreement, complete collective responsibility is often feasible in practice, however desirable it may always be in principle. . . .

I would like now to turn to peace-keeping outside the United Nations, specifically to Indo-China. Canada has gained much experience in such peace-keeping through its participation, with India and Poland, during nearly eleven years, on the International Supervisory Commissions in

the former Indo-China States of Vietnam, Laos, and Cambodia. This experience has taught us to recognize the practical difficulties confronting peace-keeping operations. It has, however, also shown us the contribution—at times the essential contribution—which can be made to peace and stability by international bodies of this kind. . . .

When a savage war broke out between the two Vietnams, the whole problem entered an even more difficult stage. What had been a Vietnamese war against a colonial power became a Communist attack against a Vietnamese state.

In this tragic conflict, the US intervened to help South Vietnam defend itself against aggression and at the request of the government of the country that was under attack.

Its motives were honourable; neither mean nor imperialistic. Its sacrifices have been great and they were not made to advance any selfish American interest.

The Government and the great majority of the people of Canada have supported whole-heartedly US peace-keeping and peace-making policies in Vietnam. We wish to be able to continue that support. . . .

The universal concern which is being expressed about the tragedy of Vietnam is a reflection both of this fearful possibility and of that sense of world community to which I have referred. All nations watch with deep anxiety the quickening march of events in Vietnam toward a climax which is unknown but menacing. All are seeking solutions to the dilemma confronting us, because all would be involved in the spread of war.

The dilemma is acute and seems intractable. On the one had, no nation—and particularly no newly-independent nation—could ever feel secure if capitulation in Vietnam led to the sanctification of aggression through subversion and spurious 'wars of national liberation'.

On the other hand, the progressive application of military sanctions can encourage stubborn resistance; rather than a willingness to negotiate.

Continued intensification of hostilities in Vietnam could lead to uncontrollable escalation.

A settlement is hard to envisage in the heat of the battle, but it is now imperative to seek one. . . .

In doing so, we should realize that the crisis in Vietnam is, in part at least, a reflection of a broader conflict, and that a lasting resolution of the specific problem may be possible only within the framework of a much broader settlement. But one thing is certain: without a settlement guaranteeing the independence, neutrality and territorial integrity of North Vietnam's neighbours in Southeast Asia and without a willingness by all parties to respect and protect these, a continuation of the present fear and instability will be inescapable.

The problem, therefore, remains the responsibility of the international community. The members of that community will therefore be obliged to make available the means of supervising any settlement and guaranteeing the fulfilment of its terms in spirit and in letter. The world community will also be obliged to assist in establishing the economic, as well as political, foundations of future understanding and security. In this connection, I was encouraged by President Johnson's expression of the willingness of the United States to help in promoting economic and social co-operation in the whole area. This is important. . . .

We in North America have a special duty and a special opportunity in this struggle for peace. We enjoy a high standard of material well-being and security with freedom. Our good fortune carries with it a corresponding obligation.

At the moment, the most immediate obligation facing the international community—not merely the United States of America—is to restore peace, freedom and security to the people of Vietnam.

If we fail here, the consequence may extend far beyond the area directly concerned. If we succeed, it could make possible new and greater progress toward a better world.

Study Question

1. What were the barriers to an international settlement of the type envisioned by Lester Pearson?

TIPS FOR ANALYSIS

Consider the Audience

Writers are affected by the audience for whom they write. They may wish to gain support or sympathy from the audience. The author may choose to highlight issues with which the audience is familiar or they may wish to challenge their readers (or listeners) to consider alternative viewpoints. In either case it is essential to understand the audience in order to read the source effectively.

WEB RESOURCES

United Nations Website
http://www.un.org
The Avalon Project: World War II Conferences
http://avalon.law.yale.edu/subject_menus/wwii.asp

The Pearson Peacekeeping Centre/Centre pour le Maintien de la Paix
http://www.peaceoperations.org
Research Guide to International Law on the Internet
http://www2.spfo.unibo.it/spolfo/PEACE.htm

RECOMMENDED READING

S.Y. Agnon, *Only Yesterday* (Princeton, NJ: Princeton University Press, 2002). *Only Yesterday* focuses on Jewish emigration to Palestine during the early twentieth century. The central character, Isaac Kumer, arrives in Palestine amidst the devotees of Zionism and the ultra-Orthodox Jews who reject Zionist ideology. His own rootlessness, the inability to establish an identity in his new homeland, and absurd twists of fate, lead Kumer to question his long-held beliefs.

Mulk Raj Anand, *Untouchable* (New York: Penguin, 1990). Anand's *Untouchable*, first published in 1935, tells of the life of Bakha, an untouchable, and his struggle against the restrictions of the caste system. The novel stands as a powerful condemnation of caste, and argues that British colonial rule increased the suffering of the 'untouchables'.

Ghassan Kanafani, *Men in the Sun* (Boulder, CO: Lynne Rienner Publishers, 1998). *Men in the Sun*—set in 1958—is the story of three Palestinians who attempt to escape to Kuwait in order to guarantee their survival. Three generations recollect the Palestinian experience beginning with the war in 1948, offering thoughts on national identity, the refugee question, and survival itself.

Wole Soyinka, *Death and the King's Horseman* (New York: W.W. Norton, 2002). Based on events in the Yoruba village of Oyo in 1946, Soyinka's play examines the clash between traditional values and roles in colonial Nigeria. Following the King's death, his horseman must commit suicide and accompany him, but the British authorities prevent the suicide—with dire consequences.

Rabindranath Tagore, *The Home and the World* (New York: Penguin, 1996). Tagore, a Nobel Prize winning Bengali author, sets *The Home and the World* in 1908 Bengal during the early years of the Swadeshi movement, exploring the first expressions of radical nationalism and the excitement they generated. Originally published in 1916, Tagore examines the impact of political awakening on traditional Indian society, and foreshadows the violent conflicts that erupted at partition.

RECOMMENDED VIEWING

Hamsin [Eastern Wind] (Israel, 1982). Director: Daniel Wachsmann. Set in Galilee, the film provides a balanced look at the tensions that developed when the Israeli army requisitioned Arab land. Wachsmann examines both land disputes and the pre-existing relationships between Arab and Jewish neighbours.

Gandhi (UK/India, 1982). Director: Richard Attenborough. This epic recreation of Mohandas K. Gandhi's life follows its subject from his early life in India, through his experiences in colonial South Africa, to the Indian independence struggle, partition, and death. The film won eight Academy Awards and remains notable for its outstanding cinematography.

Chocolat (France, 1988). Director: Claire Denis. Not to be confused with the 2000 film of the same title, Denis' *Chocolat* is set in Cameroon in 1950s, as a young French woman returns to West Africa during the dying days of French colonial control. The film underscores both the injustices of the system and the complex nature of colonial relationships and racism during the earlier period of colonial rule.

Tsahal (Israel/France, 1994). Director: Claude Lanzmann (Documentary). Tashal is one of three films in Lanzmann's trilogy exploring Jewish life in the twentieth century (*Shoah* and *Pourquoi Israel* are the others). This documentary focuses on the founding of the Israeli state and the role of the military in society and politics.

CHAPTER NINE

ORIGINS AND IMPLICATIONS
OF THE COLD WAR

◇

Despite optimistic predictions of a postwar world built on co-operation and justice, responsive to the wishes of all of the world's peoples, escalating conflicts between the Western powers and the Soviet Union rendered this vision increasingly unlikely. In the last few months of the war occupying armies began to impose their own vision of the postwar world in the regions that they controlled. The final two wartime conferences—at Yalta and Potsdam—were marked by tensions among the leaders of the 'Big Three'.

As the war ended, the areas of Europe controlled by the Western nations—Britain, France, and the United States—were designated for rebuilding and reintegration into the capitalist world economy as quickly as possible in order to halt the political trend to the left throughout Western Europe. In the Soviet zones, which included the majority of Eastern Europe and the Balkan states, Communist and Socialist parties tended to dominate weak coalition governments. In all cases, the armies of occupation retained a strong presence in the immediate aftermath of the war.

Meanwhile in Asia, the end of the Pacific War did not bring an end to conflict. Some regions, such as Indochina and India, found themselves embroiled in struggles for national independence. China, on the other hand, slipped rapidly back into a state of civil war between the Nationalist forces of Chiang Kai-shek (Jiang Jieshi) and the Communist forces of Mao Zedong. Other regions, such as the Korean Peninsula, remained occupied by both Soviet and American armies—their future to be determined, once again, by external powers. Japan similarly remained an occupied nation with the American occupation authorities, led by General Douglas MacArthur, determined to remake the country as an outpost of capitalist democracy.

Xenophobic nationalism reached new heights in both the United States and the Soviet Union during the immediate postwar years. In the United States, Joseph McCarthy's crusade against communists in the American government led to a nationwide Red Scare which far surpassed the wave of anti-communist activity which had followed the First World War. America's quest to root out communism throughout the world would soon embroil the nation in complex conflicts beyond its borders—in Latin America, in Southeast Asia, and in China—conflicts that served to shape the development of the United States for years to come.

In the Soviet Union, Stalin's paranoia regarding Western intentions towards the communist world reached new heights. A renewed round of purges was prevented only by Stalin's death in 1953, an event which ushered in an important period of transition in the Soviet Union. At first the USSR was led by a group of men, most of whom were determined to modernize the nation's economy and reduce the use of the terror and the cult of personality which had marked Stalin's rule. The death of Stalin's police chief, Lavrenti Beria—ironically, at the hands of men who wished to lessen the level of violence and terror—signalled the beginning of this new era. Eventually Nikita Khrushchev emerged from the collective leadership to seize control of the Communist Party of the Soviet Union. In 1956 he spoke to the Twentieth CPSU Congress and systematically denounced the 'crimes' of the Stalin era. In the future, he observed, a more moderate, Leninist path would guide the Soviet Union and, indeed, the entire communist bloc. Nonetheless, even as the level of terror decreased in the USSR, the hold of the Party remained as strong as ever under Khrushchev, leading some former supporters to criticize the 'new' Soviet State. Hopes that Cold War tensions might be alleviated by the USSR's new openness largely came to naught as new conflicts continued to create friction between the world's superpowers.

The documents in this section reflect the tensions of the postwar era. Winston Churchill's 'Iron Curtain' speech draws attention to the ongoing division of Europe and intimates that the Soviet Union would not be satisfied with the position that it occupied in 1946. Churchill, however, failed to mention his own culpability in the division of Europe, despite having agreed to divide the continent between the Western powers and the Soviets in the 1944 Moscow Accords. Stalin's response to Churchill was immediate and contemptuous. He accused Churchill of outright warmongering and went on to defend the actions of Soviet forces in Eastern Europe. Joseph McCarthy's speech to the United States Congress initiated much of the anti-communist hysteria that existed in the postwar United States.

In the wake of Stalin's death Nikita Khrushchev rose to power in the Soviet Union. After securing power he launched a sweeping denunciation of the policies of the Stalin era. Contemporary readers should recall, however, the degree to which Khrushchev was complicit in the actions of the Stalin era. The 'Secret Speech' which ushered in the era of 'de-Stalinization' is included here, as is Milovan Djilas's commentary on the new class system which had emerged in the USSR.

Cold War tensions impacted the actions of the US and the USSR in every corner of the globe. In Indochina, the US shifted from a relatively objective assessment of the country's internal situation in 1945 to a policy almost wholly driven by concerns over the regional spread of communism. Documents by G.H. Blakeslee and Robert McNamara clearly reflect this change in direction.

WINSTON CHURCHILL

After the Second World War, despite Winston Churchill's tremendous wartime popularity, Britons voted him out of office and instead chose left-leaning Labour Party leader Clement Attlee. The speech that follows, originally entitled 'The Sinews of Peace,' was delivered in Fulton, Missouri, at Westminster College, *where Churchill was granted an honorary degree. This speech popularized the phrase 'Iron Curtain' to describe the division of Europe between the Western powers and the area controlled by the Soviet Union. Contemporary readers should keep in mind Churchill's own role in establishing the divided world of 1946.*

IRON CURTAIN SPEECH

I am glad to come to Westminster College this afternoon, and am complimented that you should give me a degree. The name 'Westminster' is somehow familiar to me. I seem to have heard of it before. Indeed, it was at Westminster that I received a very large part of my education in politics, dialectic, rhetoric, and one or two other things. In fact we have both been educated at the same, or similar, or, at any rate, kindred establishments. . . .

The United States stands at this time at the pinnacle of world power. It is a solemn moment for the American Democracy. For with this primacy in power is also joined an awe-inspiring accountability to the future. As you look around you, you must feel not only the sense of duty done, but also you must feel anxiety lest you fall below the level of achievement. Opportunity is here now, clear and shining, for both our countries. To reject it or ignore it or fritter it away will bring upon us all the long reproaches of the aftertime. It is necessary that constancy of mind, persistency of purpose, and the grand simplicity of decision shall rule and guide the conduct of the English-speaking peoples in peace as they did in war. We must, and I believe we shall, prove ourselves equal to this severe requirement. . . .

I have, however, a definite and practical proposal to make for action. Courts and magistrates may be set up but they cannot function without sheriffs and constables. The United Nations Organization must immediately begin to be equipped with an international armed force. In such a matter we can only go step by step, but we must begin now. I propose that each of the Powers and States should be invited to delegate a certain number of air squadrons to the service of the world organization. These squadrons would be trained and prepared in their own countries, but would move around in rotation from one country to another. They would wear the uniform of their own countries but with different badges. They would not be required to act against their own nation, but in other respects they would be directed by the world organization. This might be started on a modest scale and would grow as confidence grew. I wished to see this done after

Joseph Stalin and Winston Churchill talk with US President Harry S. Truman at the opening of the Potsdam Conference in July 1945. U.S. Army Signal Corps, Courtesy of the Harry S. Truman Library.

the First World War, and I devoutly trust it may be done forthwith.

It would nevertheless be wrong and imprudent to entrust the secret knowledge or experience of the atomic bomb, which the United States, Great Britain, and Canada now share, to the world organization, while it is still in its infancy. It would be criminal madness to cast it adrift in this still agitated and un-united world. No one in any country has slept less well in their beds because this knowledge and the method and the raw materials to apply it, are at present largely retained in American hands. I do not believe we should all have slept so soundly had the positions been reversed and if some Communist or neo-Fascist State monopolized for the time being these dread agencies. The fear of them alone might easily have been used to enforce totalitarian systems upon the free democratic world, with consequences appalling to human imagination. God has willed that this shall not be and we have at least a breathing space to set our house in order

before this peril has to be encountered: and even then, if no effort is spared, we should still possess so formidable a superiority as to impose effective deterrents upon its employment, or threat of employment, by others. Ultimately, when the essential brotherhood of man is truly embodied and expressed in a world organization with all the necessary practical safeguards to make it effective these powers would naturally be confided to that world organization.

Now I come to the second danger of these two marauders which threatens the cottage, the home, and the ordinary people—namely, tyranny. We cannot be blind to the fact that the liberties enjoyed by individual citizens throughout the British Empire are not valid in a considerable number of countries, some of which are very powerful. In these States control is enforced upon the common people by various kinds of all-embracing police governments. The power of the State is exercised without restraint, either by dictators or by compact oligarchies operating through a privileged party and a political police. It is not our duty at this time when difficulties are so numerous to interfere forcibly in the internal affairs of countries which we have not conquered in war. But we must never cease to proclaim in fearless tones the great principles of freedom and the rights of man which are the joint inheritance of the English-speaking world and which through Magna Carta, the Bill of Rights, the Habeas Corpus, trial by jury, and the English common law find their most famous expression in the American Declaration of Independence.

All this means that the people of any country have the right, and should have the power by constitutional action, by free unfettered elections, with secret ballot, to choose or change the character or form of government under which they dwell; that freedom of speech and thought should reign; that courts of justice, independent of the executive, unbiased by any party, should administer laws which have received the broad assent of large majorities or are consecrated by time and custom. Here are the title deeds of freedom which should lie in every cottage home. Here is the message of the British and American peoples to mankind. Let us preach what we practice—let us practice what we preach. . . .

Now, while still pursuing the method of realizing our overall strategic concept, I come to the crux of what I have traveled here to say. Neither the sure prevention of war, nor the continuous rise of world organization will be gained without what I have called the fraternal association of the English-speaking peoples. This means a special relationship between the British Commonwealth and Empire and the United States. Fraternal association requires not only the growing friendship and mutual understanding between our two vast but kindred systems of society, but the continuance of the intimate relationship between our military advisers, leading to common study of potential dangers, the similarity of weapons and manuals of instructions, and to the interchange of officers and cadets at technical colleges. It should carry with it the continuance of the present facilities for mutual security by the joint use of all Naval and Air Force bases in the possession of either country all over the world. This would perhaps double the mobility of the American Navy and Air Force. It would greatly expand that of the British Empire Forces and it might well lead, if and as the world calms down, to important financial savings. Already we use together a large number of islands; more may well be entrusted to our joint care in the near future. . . .

A shadow has fallen upon the scenes so lately lighted by the Allied victory. Nobody knows what Soviet Russia and its Communist international organization intends to do in the immediate future, or what are the limits, if any, to their expansive and proselytizing tendencies. I have a strong admiration and regard for the valiant Russian people and for my wartime comrade, Marshal Stalin. There is deep sympathy and goodwill in Britain—and I doubt not here also—towards the peoples of all the Russias and a resolve to persevere through many differences and rebuffs in establishing lasting friendships. We understand the Russian need to be secure on her western frontiers by the removal of all possibility of German aggression. We welcome Russia to her rightful place among the leading nations of the world. We welcome her flag upon the seas. Above all, we welcome constant, frequent and growing contacts between the Russian people and our own people on both sides of the Atlantic. It is my duty, however, for I am sure you would with me to state the facts as I see them to you, to place before you certain facts about the present position in Europe.

From Stettin in the Baltic to Trieste in the Adriatic, an iron curtain has descended across the Continent. Behind that line lie all the capitals of the ancient states of Central and Eastern Europe. Warsaw, Berlin, Prague, Vienna, Budapest, Belgrade, Bucharest, and Sofia; all these famous cities and the populations around them lie in what I must call the Soviet sphere, and all are subject, in one form or another, not only to Soviet influence but to a very high and in some cases increasing measure of control from Moscow. Athens alone— Greece with its immortal glories—is free to decide its future at an election under British, American, and French observation. The Russian-dominated Polish Government has been encouraged to make enormous and wrongful inroads upon Germany, and mass expulsions of millions of Germans on a scale grievous and undreamed-of are now taking place. The Communist parties, which were very small in all these Eastern States of Europe, have been raised to preeminence and power far beyond their numbers and are seeking everywhere to obtain totalitarian control. Police governments are prevailing in nearly every case and so far, except in Czechoslovakia, there is no true democracy. . . .

The safety of the world requires a new unity in Europe, from which no nation should be permanently outcast. It is from the quarrels of the strong parent races in Europe that the world wars we have witnessed, or which occurred in former times, have sprung. Twice in our own lifetime we have seen the United States, against their wishes and their traditions, against arguments, the force of which it is impossible not to comprehend, drawn by irresistible forces, into these wars in time to secure the victory of the good cause, but only after frightful slaughter and devastation had occurred. Twice the United States has had to send several millions of its young men across the Atlantic to find the war; but now war can find any nation, wherever it may dwell between dusk and dawn. Surely we should work with conscious purpose for a grand pacification of Europe, within the structure of the United Nations and in accordance with its Charter. That I feel is an open cause of policy of very great importance. . .

. . . [I]n a great number of countries, far from the Russian frontiers and throughout the world, Communist fifth columns are established and work in complete unity and absolute obedience to the directions they receive from the Communist center. Except in the British Commonwealth and in the United States where Communism is in its infancy, the Communist parties or fifth columns constitute a growing challenge and peril to Christian civilization. These are somber facts for anyone to have to recite on the morrow of a victory gained by so much splendid comradeship in arms and in the cause of freedom and democracy; but we should be unwise not to face them squarely while time remains. . . .

From what I have seen of our Russian friends and Allies during the war, I am convinced that there is nothing they admire so much as strength, and there is nothing for which they have less respect than for weakness, especially military weakness. For that reason the old doctrine of a balance of power is unsound. We cannot afford, if we can help it, to work on narrow margins, offering temptations to a trial of strength. If the Western Democracies stand together in strict adherence to the principles of the United Nations Charter, their influence for furthering those principles will be immense and no one is likely to molest them. If however they become divided or falter in their duty and if these all-important years are allowed to slip away then indeed catastrophe may overwhelm us all.

Last time I saw it all coming and I cried aloud to my own fellow-countrymen and to the world, but no one paid any attention. Up till the year 1933 or even 1935, Germany might have been saved from the awful fate which has overtaken her and we might all have been spared the miseries Hitler let loose upon mankind. There never was a war in history easier to prevent by timely action than the one which has just desolated such great areas of the globe. It could have been prevented, in my belief, without the firing of a single shot, and Germany might be powerful, prosperous and honoured today; but no one would listen and one by one we were all sucked into the awful whirlpool. We surely must not let that happen again. This can only be achieved by reaching now, in 1946, a good understanding on all points with Russia under the general authority of the United Nations Organization and by the maintenance of that good understanding through many peaceful years, by the whole strength of the English-speaking world and all its connections. There is the solution which I respectfully offer to you in this Address to which I have given the title 'The Sinews of Peace'.

Let no man underrate the abiding power of the British Empire and Commonwealth. Because you see the 46 millions in our island harassed about their food supply, of which they only grow one half, even in war-time, or because we have difficulty in restarting our industries and export trade after six years of passionate war effort, do not suppose that we shall not come through these dark years of privation as we have come through the glorious years of agony, or that half a century from now you will not see 70 or 80 millions of Britons spread about the world and united in defence of our traditions, our way of life, and of the world causes which you and we

espouse. If the population of the English-speaking Commonwealths be added to that of the United States, with all that such cooperation implies in the air, on the sea, all over the globe, and in science and in industry, and in moral force, there will be no quivering, precarious balance of power to offer its temptation to ambition or adventure. On the contrary there will be an overwhelming assurance of security. If we adhere faithfully to the Charter of the United Nations and walk forward in sedate and sober strength, seeking no one's land or treasure, seeking to lay no arbitrary control upon the thoughts of men, if all British moral and material forces and convictions are joined with your own in fraternal association, the high roads of the future will be clear, not only for us but for all, not only for our time but for a century to come.

Study Question

1. It is possible to distinguish a number of motives in Churchill's speech. What do you believe to be the most important of these?

JOSEPH STALIN

The following interview appeared in the 14 March 1946 edition of Pravda, *the official newspaper of the Communist Party of the Soviet Union (CPSU). The interview deals directly with the issues raised by Winston Churchill in his 'Iron Curtain' speech. In* *reading Stalin's response, keep in mind the position of both Western and Soviet forces in early 1946, as well as all of the prior agreements with respect to the division of Europe.*

RESPONSE TO CHURCHILL, 14 MARCH 1946

Recently one of *Pravda's* correspondents turned to Comrade Stalin, asking for an explanation of a series of questions regarding Mr Churchill's speech. Comrade Stalin had given respective explanations, which we publish below in form of the answers to the correspondent's questions.

Question: How do you assess the recent speech of Mr Churchill, which he gave in the United States of America?

Answer: My assessment is, it is a dangerous act, calculated to breed strife between allied countries and make their cooperation more difficult.

Question: Could Mr Churchill's speech be considered as a harm to the progress of peace and security?

Answer: Absolutely, yes. As a matter of fact Mr Churchill is standing now in the position of a warmonger. And here Mr Churchill is not alone—he has many friends not only in England but also in the United States. It ought to be mentioned that in this matter Mr Churchill and his friends strikingly resemble Hitler and his friends. Hitler started the process of unleashing war from the proclamation of a racist theory, according to which only the German-speaking people are a worthy nation. Mr Churchill is starting his process of unleashing war also from a racist theory, stating that only the English-speaking countries are worthy nations, destined to manage the fate of the world. German racist theory led Hitler and his friends to the conclusion that Germans, as the only worthy nation, should rule the other nations. English racist theory leads Mr Churchill and his friends into the following conclusion: that English-speaking countries, as the only worthy nations, should govern the other nations of the world. As a matter of fact, Mr Churchill and his friends in England and in the United States are presenting the non-English-speaking nations with something like an ultimatum: either voluntarily agree to our rule, and everything will be all right, or a war is unavoidable. But during five years of difficult war nations shed blood for the sake of freedom and independence of their respective countries, and not for the sake of replacing the tyranny of people like Hitler for the tyranny of those like Churchill. Therefore, by all probability, nations which do not speak English, and yet comprise the majority of the world's population,

will not conform to the new slavery. The tragedy of Mr Churchill is that he, as a deep-rooted Tory, can not accept this simple and clear truth. Undoubtedly, Mr Churchill's aim is war, a war with the USSR. It is also clear that such a goal of Mr Churchill's is incompatible with the present alliance treaty between England and the USSR However, Mr Churchill, in order to misguide the readers, has mentioned in between that the term of the Soviet–English Treaty of Mutual Aid and Cooperation could be extended up to 50 years. But how do we combine such a statement of Mr Churchill with his aim to wage war with the USSR, with his prophecy of war against the USSR? It is clear, that those things could not coexist. And if Mr Churchill is simultaneously calling for war against the Soviet Union and mentioning the extension of the Soviet–English treaty for up to 50 years, it means that he is considering this treaty as a piece of paper, needed only as a cover to mask his anti-Soviet position. Therefore, the false announcements of Mr Churchill and his friends in England about extension of the English-Soviet treaty for up to 50 years, and more, could not be taken seriously. Extension of the agreement has no point when one of the sides is violating the treaty and transforming it into only a piece of paper.

Question: How do you assess the part of Mr Churchill's speech where he attacks the democratic governments of our neighboring European countries and where he criticizes good neighborly interrelations established between those countries and the Soviet Union?

Answer: This part of Mr Churchill's speech represents a blend of elements of defamation and elements of rudeness and tactlessness. Mr Churchill states that 'Warsaw, Berlin, Prague, Vienna, Budapest, Belgrade, Bucharest, Sophia, all those renowned cities and inhabitants of respective regions are in a Soviet zone and all submit in one way or another not only to the Soviet influence, but also in large degree to the growing control of Moscow.' Mr Churchill is qualifying all that as the boundless 'expansionist tendencies' of the Soviet Union. There is no need for any special effort to show that Mr Churchill is rudely slandering Moscow and the above-mentioned countries neighboring the USSR. First, it is particularly absurd to talk about the exclusive control of the Soviet Union in Vienna and Berlin, where the Allied Control Councils exist and whose members represent four powers, and where the Soviet Union has only 1/4 of the votes. Occasionally people cannot resist slander, but one must know where to stop. Secondly, the following matters shall not be forgotten. The Germans carried out the invasion into USSR through Finland, Poland, Romania, Bulgaria, and Hungary. Germans were able to carry out the invasion through those countries because at the time, there existed regimes hostile to the Soviet Union. As a result of the German invasion, the Soviet Union irrevocably lost about 7 million people during the conduct of war, German occupation, and due to driving away people for servitude labor. In other words, the Soviet Union lost several times more people than England and United States combined. It is possible that in some places, some are inclined to forget the colossal sacrifices of the Soviet Nation, which ensured the liberation of Europe from Hitler's regime. But the Soviet Union can not forget the sacrifice. Let the question be asked: Is it odd that the Soviet Union, wishing to ensure its safety, in the future works toward having in those countries' governments loyal to the Soviet Union? How could one, in his right mind, qualify those peaceful measures of the Soviet Union as expansionist tendencies of our country? Further Mr Churchill states that the Polish government, being under Russia's rule, was encouraged to greatly and unfairly encroach upon Germany. Here, every single word is rude, offensive slander. Contemporary, democratic Poland is ruled by outstanding people. By their actions they proved their ability to defend the interests and dignity of their Motherland, which their predecessors were unable to do. On what basis does Mr Churchill state that the government of contemporary Poland has allowed their country to be supervised by members of any given foreign regime? Are Mr Churchill's words not slanderous here because he is attempting to breed strife between Poland and the Soviet Union? Mr Churchill is unhappy, because Poland had turned its policy to the direction of friendship and alliance with the Soviet Union. In the past the relationship between Poland and the USSR was marked by elements of conflict and hostility. This situation gave statesmen such as Mr Churchill the opportunity to play on those feelings of animosity, to take up Poland in hand, pretending to defend it from the Russians, to intimidate Russia by the prospect of war between her and Poland, and to secure for themselves the status of arbiters. But those times have past. The place of hostility between Russia and Poland is now occupied by friendship, and Poland, the contemporary, democratic Poland, does not wish to be a ball in the game played by foreigners. I think this particular circumstance irritates Mr Churchill and pushes him to rude, untactful escapades against Poland. Is it not the case that he simply is not allowed to play at the expense of others? As to Churchill's attacks against USSR in spite of the expansion of Poland's Western borders with the territories occupied by Germans in the past, here I think he is clearly trying to confuse us. It is known that the resolution regarding Poland's borders was accepted during the three countries' conference in Berlin based on Poland's needs. The Soviet Union repeatedly announced that it counts Poland's needs as fair and just. It is very likely that Mr Churchill is unhappy with this solution. But why does Mr Churchill, who uses all his cards in his attack against the Russian position on this matter, hide from his readers the fact that this arrangement was unanimously agreed upon during the Berlin conference, that it was voted upon not only by the Russians but also by English and Americans? Why does Mr Churchill feel that it is necessary to mislead the people? Mr Churchill further states that 'communist parties, which used to have tiny minorities in all Eastern European countries, have become an exclusive power, much more superior than the number of their members, and rush to establish totalitarian control; and military rule in almost all those countries tends to prevail; with the exception of Czechoslovakia, there is no genuine democracy whatsoever.' It is known that right now England is ruled by only one party, the Labour Party, and opposition parties have no right to take part in England's government. This Mr Churchill calls true democracy. In Poland, Romania, Yugoslavia, Bulgaria, Hungary, the power is in the hands of a block that is comprised of four to six parties— and opposition, if only it appears more or less loyal, has a secured part in government. This Mr Churchill calls totalitarianism, tyranny, police state. Why? On what basis? Do not expect Mr Churchill to answer. Mr Churchill does not understand what a silly position he put himself in with his loud speeches about totalitarianism, tyranny, and police states. Mr Churchill would like to see Poland ruled by Sosnkowski and Anders, Yugoslavia by Michajlovic and Pavelic, Romania by Prince Stirbey and Radetzky, and Hungary and Austria by some king from the house of Habsburg, and so on. Mr Churchill wants us to believe that those gentlemen with fascist leanings are able to secure 'true democracy'. This is Mr Churchill's way of 'democracy'. Mr Churchill is close to the truth when he speaks about the growing influence of communist parties in Eastern Europe. But it shall be mentioned that he is not exactly correct. Influence of communist parties grew not only in Eastern Europe but almost in all European countries, where fascism once ruled (Italy, Germany, Hungary, Bulgaria, Romania, Ukraine),

or where the German, Italian, or Hungarian occupation took place (France, Belgium, Holland, Norway, Denmark, Poland, Czechoslovakia, Yugoslavia, Greece, Soviet Union, etc.) The growing influence of communists shall not be taken as a coincidence. It represents a fully normal phenomenon. Influence of the communists grows because during the hard years of fascist rule in Europe, communists displayed themselves as dependable, brave, self-sacrificing fighters against the fascist regime, and for freedom of nations. Mr Churchill sometimes mentions in his speeches about 'common people from simple houses' brotherly patting them on their shoulders and pretending to be one of them. But those people are not that simple as first impressions suggest. They, the 'common people', have their needs, their politics, and they know how to stand for their interests. It was they, the millions of 'common people' in England, who balloted out Mr Churchill and his party giving their votes to the Labourites. It was they, the millions of 'common people', who isolated the reactionaries, the supporters of cooperation with fascism, and preferred leftist, democratic parties in Europe. It was they, the millions of 'common people', who tested the communists in flames of war and resistance against fascism and concluded that communists fully deserve the trust of the nation. This is how the influence of communists in Europe has grown. This is the rule of historic development. Of course, Mr Churchill does not like this kind of development, and he sounds the alarm, appealing to the use of power. But he also did not like the emergence of the Soviet regime in Russia after the First World War. Then he also sounded the alarm and organized the campaign of 14 states against Russia, trying to make true his goal of turning back the wheel of history. But history proved to be stronger than Churchill's intervention; and quixotic attempts of Churchill led to the point where he had experienced full defeat. I don't know if after the Second World War Mr Churchill and his friends will succeed with the new campaign against 'Eastern Europe', but even if they succeed—which is not very likely, because millions of 'common people' are on guard for the cause of peace—it can surely be said that they also will be beaten as they were beaten 26 years ago.

Study Question

1. Both Churchill and Stalin rely heavily on propaganda and distortion of the truth in their accounts. Based on what is now known of postwar events, whose analysis now seems to contain more valid points?

JOSEPH MCCARTHY

American suspicions regarding Soviet intentions in the postwar world seemed to be confirmed by the events of the period 1945 to 1949. When, in 1949, Mao Zedong's communist forces defeated Nationalist China, paranoia in the United States ran rampant. Senator Joseph R. McCarthy (1909–57), a Republican from Wisconsin, emerged as one of the most radical anti-communists in the United States government. 'McCarthyism' reached its height in the early 1950s, as politicians, writers, intellectuals, and actors were brought before the House Un-American Activities Committee and accused of being communist sympathizers. In 1954, when McCarthy accused the United States Army of harbouring Communists, the Army fought back and forced McCarthy to defend his groundless accusations. In December 1954 the United States Senate voted 67 to 22 to censure McCarthy. His political career ruined, McCarthy died soon after of complications related to alcoholism. In the following speech, made before the US Senate on 20 February 1950,[1] McCarthy began his crusade against what he believed to be the 'Reds' in the US government.

ON COMMUNISTS IN GOVERNMENT

Ladies and gentlemen, tonight as we celebrate the one hundred and forty-first birthday of one of the greatest men in American history, I would like to be able to talk about what a glorious day today is in the history of the world. As we celebrate the birth of this man who with his whole heart and soul hated war, I would like to be able to speak of peace in our time, of war being outlawed, and of world-wide disarmament. These would be truly appropriate things to be able to mention as we celebrate the birthday of Abraham Lincoln . . .

Five years after a world war has been won, men's hearts should anticipate a long peace, and men's minds should be free from the heavy weight that comes with war. But this is not such a period—for this is not a period of peace. This is a time of the 'cold war'. This is a time when all the world is split into two vast, increasingly hostile armed camps—a time of a great armaments race. . . .

Six years ago, at the time of the first conference to map out the peace—Dumbarton Oaks[2]—there was within the Soviet orbit 180,000,000 people. Lined up on the antitotalitarian side there were in the world at that time roughly 1,625,000,000 people. Today, only 6 years later, there are 800,000,000 people under the absolute domination of Soviet Russia—an increase of over

"I HAVE HERE IN MY HAND ----"

American political cartoonist Herb Block captures the hysterical nature of McCarthy's accusations. A 1954 Herblock Cartoon, copyright by The Herb Block Foundation.

400 per cent. On our side, the figure has shrunk to around 500,000,000. In other words, in less than 6 years the odds have changed from 9 to 1 in our favor to 8 to 5 against us. This indicates the swiftness of the tempo of Communist victories and American defeats in the cold war. As one of our outstanding historical figures once said, 'When a great democracy is destroyed, it will not be because of enemies from without, but rather because of enemies from within.'

The truth of this statement is becoming terrifyingly clear as we see this country each day losing on every front.

At war's end we were physically the strongest nation on earth and, at least potentially, the most powerful intellectually and morally. Ours could have been the honor of being a beacon on the desert of destruction, a shining living proof that civilization was not yet ready to destroy itself. Unfortunately, we have failed miserably and tragically to arise to the opportunity.

The reason why we find ourselves in a position of impotency is not because our only powerful potential enemy has sent men to invade our shores, but rather because of the traitorous actions of those who have been treated so well by this Nation. It has not been the less fortunate or members of minority groups who have been selling this Nation out, but rather those who have had all the benefits that the wealthiest nation on earth has had to offer—the finest homes, the finest college education, and the finest jobs in Government we can give.

This is glaringly true in the State Department. There the bright young men who are born with silver spoons in their mouths are the ones who have been the worst. . . .

Now I know it is very easy for anyone to condemn a particular bureau or department in general terms. Therefore, I would like to cite one rather unusual case—the case of a man who has done much to shape our foreign policy.

When Chiang Kai-shek was fighting our war, the State Department had in China a young man named John S. Service. His task, obviously, was not to work for the communization of China. Strangely, however, he sent official reports back to the State Department urging that we torpedo our ally Chiang Kai-shek and stating, in effect, that communism was the best hope of China.

Later, this man—John Service—was picked up by the Federal Bureau of Investigation for turning over to the Communists secret State Department information. Strangely, however, he was never prosecuted. However, Joseph Grew, the Under Secretary of State, who insisted on his prosecution, was forced to resign. Two days after Grew's successor, Dean Acheson, took over as Under Secretary of State, this man—John Service—who had been picked up by the FBI and who had previously urged that communism was the best hope of China, was not only reinstated in the State Department but promoted. And finally, under Acheson, placed in charge of all placements and promotions.

Today, ladies and gentlemen, this man Service is on his way to represent the State Department and Acheson in Calcutta—by far and away the most important listening post in the Far East. . . .

Then there was a Mrs Mary Jane Kenny, from the Board of Economic Warfare in the State Department, who was named in an FBI report and in a House committee report as a courier for the Communist Party while working for the Government. And where do you think Mrs Kenny is—she is now an editor in the United Nations Document Bureau. . . .

This, ladies and gentlemen, gives you somewhat of a picture of the type of individuals who have been helping to shape our foreign policy. In my opinion the State Department, which is one of the most important government departments, is thoroughly infested with Communists.

I have in my hand 57 cases[3] of individuals who would appear to be either card carrying members or certainly loyal to the Communist Party, but who nevertheless are still helping to shape our foreign policy. . . .

This brings us down to the case of one Alger Hiss who is more important not as an individual any more, but rather because he is so representative of a group in the State Department. . . .

If time permitted, it might be well to go into detail about the fact that Hiss was Roosevelt's chief advisor at Yalta when Roosevelt was admittedly in ill health and tired physically and mentally. . . .

According to the then Secretary of State Stettinius, here are some of the things that Hiss helped to decide at Yalta. (1) The establishment of a European High Commission; (2) the treatment of Germany—this you will recall was the conference at which it was decided that we would occupy Berlin with Russia occupying an area completely circling the city, which, as you know, resulted in the Berlin airlift which cost 31 American lives; (3) the Polish question; . . . 6) Iran; (7) China—here's where we gave away Manchuria; (8) Turkish Straits question; (9) international trusteeships; (10) Korea. . . .

As you hear this story of high treason, I know that you are saying to yourself, 'Well, why doesn't the Congress do something about it?' Actually, ladies and gentlemen, one of the important reasons for the graft, the corruption, the dishonesty, the disloyalty, the treason in high Government positions—one of the most important reasons why this continues is a lack of moral uprising on the part of the 140,000,000 American people. In the light of history, however, this is not hard to explain.

It is the result of an emotional hang-over and a temporary moral lapse which follows every war. It is the apathy of evil which people who have been subjected to the tremendous evils of war feel. As the people of the world see mass murder, the destruction of defenseless and innocent people, and all of the crime and lack of morals which go with war, they become numb and apathetic. It has always been thus after war.

However, the morals of our people have not been destroyed. They still exist. This cloak of numbness and apathy has only needed a spark to rekindle them. Happily, this spark has finally been supplied.

As you know, very recently the Secretary of State proclaimed his loyalty to a man [Hiss] guilty of what has always been considered as the most abominable of all crime—of being a traitor to the people who gave him a position of great trust. The Secretary of State in attempting to justify his continued devotion to the man who sold out the Christian world to the atheistic world, referred to Christ's Sermon on the Mount as a justification and reason therefore, and the reaction of the American people to this would have made the heart of Abraham Lincoln happy.

When this pompous diplomat in striped pants, with a phony British accent, proclaimed to the American people that Christ on the Mount endorsed communism, high treason, and betrayal of a sacred trust, the blasphemy was so great that it awakened the dormant indignation of the American people.

He has lighted the spark which is resulting in a moral uprising and will end only when the whole sorry mess of twisted, warped thinkers are swept from the national scene so that we may have a new birth of national honesty and decency in Government.

Notes

1. McCarthy had already given a more radical version of this speech to the Women's Club in Wheeling, West Virginia, on 9 February.

2. This was the conference that ultimately led to the creation of the United Nations.

3. In the Wheeling speech McCarthy claimed that there were in fact 205 names on his list and brandished a piece of paper as apparent proof. There was, however, no such list and pundits have suggested that he was holding up his laundry list. By 20 February, when the speech was read into the Congressional Record, McCarthy's list of 205 had shrunk to 57.

> **Study Question**
>
> 1. Considering the global events of the early 1950s, how significant was McCarthy's attack on the State Department?

MILOVAN DJILAS

Milovan Djilas (1911–95) fought with Josip Broz's Yugoslav partisans during the Second World War. During that time his loyalty to communism was unquestionable. However, after the war Djilas became increasingly disillusioned with Soviet efforts to impose a single rigidly Stalinist ideology throughout Eastern Europe. By 1953 Djilas was openly critical of the Soviet Union and supported Tito's efforts to keep Yugoslavia independent of Soviet influence. Djilas was jailed in 1956 for his dissident views. In The New Class *Djilas argued that the communist system had failed to create the promised egalitarian society and instead had produced a new all-powerful elite.*

THE NEW CLASS

Earlier revolutions, particularly the so-called bourgeois ones, attached considerable significance to the establishment of individual freedoms immediately following cessation of the revolutionary terror. Even the revolutionaries considered it important to assure the legal status of the citizenry. Independent administration of justice was an inevitable final result of all these revolutions. The Communist regime in the USSR is still remote from independent administration of justice after forty years of tenure. The final results of earlier revolutions were often greater legal security and greater civil rights. This cannot be said of the Communist revolution. . . .

In contrast to other revolutions, the Communist revolution, conducted in the name of doing away with classes, has resulted in the most complete authority of any single new class. Everything else is sham and an illusion. . . .

This new class, the bureaucracy, or more accurately the political bureaucracy, has all the characteristics of earlier ones as well as some new characteristics of its own. Its origin had its special characteristics also, even though in essence it was similar to the beginnings of other classes. . . . The new class may be said to be made up of those who have privileges and economic preference because of the administrative monopoly they hold. . . .

The mechanism of Communist power is perhaps the simplest which can be conceived, although it leads to the most refined tyranny and the most brutal exploitation. The simplicity of this mechanism originates from the fact that one party alone, the Communist Party, is the backbone of the entire political, economic, and ideological activity. The entire public life is at a standstill or moves ahead, falls behind or turns around according to what happens in the party forums. . . .

Communist control of the social machine . . . restricts certain government posts to party members. These jobs, which are essential in any government but especially in a Communist one, include assignments with police, especially the secret police; and the diplomatic and officer corps, especially positions in the information and political services. In the judiciary only top positions have until now been in the hands of Communists. . . .

Only in a Communist state are a number of both specified and unspecified positions reserved for members of the party. The Communist government, although a class structure, is a party government; the Communist army is a party army; and the state is a party state. More precisely, Communists tend to treat the army and the state as their exclusive weapons.

The exclusive, if unwritten, law that only party members can become policemen, officers, diplomats, and hold similar positions, or that only they can exercise actual authority, creates a special privileged group of bureaucrats. . . .

The entire governmental structure is organized in this manner. Political positions are reserved exclusively for party members. Even in non-political governmental bodies Communists hold the strategic positions or oversee administration. Calling a meeting at the party center or publishing

an article is sufficient to cause the entire state and social mechanism to begin functioning. If difficulties occur anywhere, the party and the police very quickly correct the 'error'. . . .

The classes and masses do not exercise authority, but the party does so in their name. In every party, including the most democratic, leaders play an important role to the extent that the party's authority becomes the authority of the leaders. The so-called 'dictatorship of the proletariat', which is the beginning of and under the best circumstances becomes the authority of the party, inevitably evolves into the dictatorship of the leaders. In a totalitarian government of this type, the dictatorship of the proletariat is a theoretical justification, or ideological mask at best, for the authority of some oligarchs. . . .

Freedoms are formally recognized in Communist regimes, but one decisive condition is a prerequisite for exercising them: freedoms must be utilized only in the interest of the system of 'socialism', which the Communist leaders represent, or to buttress their rule. This practice, contrary as it is to legal regulations, inevitably had to result in the use of exceptionally severe and unscrupulous methods by police and party bodies. . . .

It has been impossible in practice to separate police authority from judicial authority. Those who arrest also judge and enforce punishments. The circle is closed: the executive, the legislative, the investigating, the court, and the punishing bodies are one and the same. . . .

Communist parliaments are not in a position to make decisions on anything important. Selected in advance as they are, flattered that they have been thus selected, representatives do not have the power or the courage to debate even if they wanted to do so. Besides, since their mandate does not depend on the voters, representatives do not feel that they are answerable to them. Communist parliaments are justifiably called 'mausoleums' for the representatives who compose them. Their right and role consist of unanimously approving from time to time that which has already been decided for them from the wings. . . .

Though history has no record of any other system so successful in *checking* its opposition as the Communist dictatorship, none ever has *provoked* such profound and far-reaching discontent. It seems that the more the conscience is crushed and the less the opportunities for establishing an organization exist, the greater the discontent. . . . In addition to being motivated by the historical need for rapid industrialization, the Communist bureaucracy has been compelled to establish a type of economic system designed to insure the perpetuation of its own power. Allegedly for the sake of a classless society and for the abolition of exploitation, it has created a closed economic system, with forms of property which facilitate the party's domination and its monopoly. At first, the Communists had to turn to this 'collectivistic' form for objective reasons. Now they continue to strengthen this form—without considering whether or not it is in the interest of the national economy and of further industrialization—for their own sake, for an exclusive Communist class aim. They first administered and controlled the entire economy for so-called ideal goals; later they did it for the purpose of maintaining their absolute control and domination. That is the real reason for such far-reaching and inflexible political measures in the Communist economy. . . .

A citizen in the Communist system lives oppressed by the constant pangs of his conscience, and the fear that he has transgressed. He is always fearful that he will have to demonstrate that he is not an enemy of socialism, just as in the Middle Ages a man constantly had to show his devotion to the Church. . . . Tyranny over the mind is the most complete and most brutal type of tyranny; every other tyranny begins and ends with it. . . .

History will pardon Communists for much, establishing that they were forced into many brutal acts because of the circumstances and the need to defend their existence. But the stifling of every divergent thought, the exclusive monopoly over thinking for the purpose of defending their personal interests, will nail the Communists to a cross of shame in history. . . .

In essence, Communism is only one thing, but it is realized in different degrees and manners in every country. Therefore it is possible to speak of various Communist systems, i.e., of various forms of the same manifestation.

The differences which exist between Communist states—differences that Stalin attempted futilely to remove by force—are the result, above all, of diverse historical backgrounds. . . . When ascending to power, the Communists face in the various countries different cultural and technical levels and varying social relationships, and are faced with different national intellectual characters. . . . Of the former international proletariat, only words and empty dogmas remained. Behind them stood the naked national and international interests, aspirations, and plans of the various Communist oligarchies, comfortably entrenched.

The nature of authority and property, a similar international outlook, and an identical ideology inevitably identify Communist states with one another. Nevertheless, it is wrong to ignore and underestimate the significance of the inevitable differences in degree and manner, and form in which Communism will be realized . . . No single form of Communism, no matter how similar it is to other forms, exists in any way other than as national Communism. In order to maintain itself, it must become national.

The form of government and property as well as of ideas differs little or not at all in Communist states. It cannot differ markedly since it has an identical nature—total authority. However, if they wish to win and to continue to exist, the Communists must adapt the degree and manner of their authority to national conditions. . . .

The Communist East European countries did not become satellites of the USSR because they benefited from it, but because they were too weak to prevent it. As soon as favourable conditions are created, a yearning for independence and for protection of 'their own people' from Soviet hegemony will rise among them.

The subordinate Communist governments in East Europe can, in fact must, declare their independence from the Soviet government. No one can say how far this aspiration for independence will go and what disagreements will result. The result depends on numerous unforeseen internal and external circumstances. However, there is no doubt that a national Communist bureaucracy aspires to more complete authority for itself. This is demonstrated . . . by the current unconcealed emphasis on 'one's own path to socialism', which has recently come to light sharply in Poland and Hungary. The central Soviet government has found itself in difficulty because of the nationalism existing even in those governments which it installed in the Soviet republics (Ukraine, Caucasia), and still more so with regard to those governments installed in the East European countries. Playing an important role in all of this is the fact that the Soviet Union was unable, and will not be able in the future, to assimilate the economies of the East European countries.

The aspirations toward national independence must of course have greater impetus. These aspirations can be retarded and even made dormant by external pressure or by fear on the part of the Communists of 'imperialism' and the 'bourgeoisie', but they cannot be removed. On the contrary, their strength will grow.

Study Question

1. Could the Soviet Union have developed to such a degree without the presence of Djilas's 'New Class' of administrators and bureaucrats?

NIKITA KHRUSHCHEV

Nikita Khrushchev's 'Secret Speech' had a profound impact on the communist world. In the Soviet Union it ushered in the era of de-Stalinization; in Eastern Europe it triggered nationalist uprisings; and, in the United States it led to a brief thaw in relations between the two superpowers. The more than 20,000-word speech was drafted well before the opening of the Twentieth Party Congress in February 1956.

Khrushchev seized the opportunity to develop his own support base by presenting himself as the one man willing to speak out against Stalin. Khrushchev later acknowledged that the 'secret' speech was leaked to several outside Communist Parties, including the Polish Communist Party, which in turn passed the document along to the American intelligence community.

SECRET SPEECH

Comrades! In the report of the Central Committee of the Party at the XXth Congress, in a number of speeches by delegates to the Congress, as also formerly during the plenary CC/CPSU sessions, quite a lot has been said about the cult of the individual and about its harmful consequences.

After Stalin's death the Central Committee of the Party began to implement a policy of explaining

Nikita Khrushchev listens to debates in the United Nations General Assembly in September 1960. U.S. News and World Report Magazine Photograph Collection. Courtesy of the Library of Congress, Prints and Photographs Division (LC-USZ62-134155).

concisely and consistently that it is impermissible and foreign to the spirit of Marxism-Leninism to elevate one person, to transform him into a superman possessing supernatural characteristics akin to those of a god. Such a man supposedly knows everything, sees everything, thinks for everyone, can do anything, is infallible in his behaviour.

Such a belief about a man, and specifically about Stalin, was cultivated among us for many years.

The objective of the present report is not a thorough evaluation of Stalin's life and activity. Concerning Stalin's merits, an entirely sufficient number of books, pamphlets and studies had already been written in his lifetime. The role of Stalin in the preparation and execution of the Socialist Revolution, in the Civil War, and in the fight for the construction of Socialism in our country is universally known. Everyone knows this well. At the present we are concerned with a question which has immense importance for the Party now and for the future—with how the cult

of the person of Stalin has been gradually growing, the cult which became at a certain specific stage the source of a whole series of exceedingly serious and grave perversions of Party principles, of Party democracy, of revolutionary legality . . .

The great modesty of the genius of the revolution, Vladimir Ilyich Lenin, is known. Lenin had always stressed the role of the people as the creator of history, the directing and organizational role of the Party as a living and creative organism, and also the role of the Central Committee. . . .

While ascribing great importance to the role of the leaders and organizers of the masses, Lenin at the same time mercilessly stigmatized every manifestation of the cult of the individual, inexorably combated the foreign-to-Marxism views about a 'hero' and a 'crowd' and countered all efforts to oppose a 'hero' to the masses and to the people. . . .

During Lenin's life the Central Committee of the Party was a real expression of collective leadership of the Party and of the nation. Being a militant Marxist-revolutionist, always unyielding in matters of principle, Lenin never imposed by force his views upon his co-workers. He tried to convince; he patiently explained his opinions to others. Lenin always diligently observed that the norms of Party life were realized, that the Party statute was enforced, that the Party congresses and the plenary sessions of the Central Committee took place at proper intervals.

In addition to the great accomplishments of V.I. Lenin for the victory of the working class and of the working peasants, for the victory of our Party and for the application of the ideas of scientific Communism to life, his acute mind expressed itself also in this, that he detected in Stalin in time those negative characteristics which resulted later in grave consequences. Fearing for the future fate of the Party and of the Soviet nation, V.I. Lenin made a completely correct characterization of Stalin, pointing out that it was necessary to consider the question of transferring

Stalin from the position of the Secretary General because of the fact that Stalin is excessively rude, that he does not have a proper attitude toward his comrades, that he is capricious and abuses his power.

In December 1922 in a letter to the Party Congress Vladimir Ilyich wrote: 'After taking over the position of Secretary General Comrade Stalin accumulated in his hands immeasurable power and I am not certain whether he will be always able to use this power with the required care.'

This letter—a political document of tremendous importance, known in the Party history as Lenin's 'testament'—was distributed among the delegates to the XXth Party Congress. You have read it, and will undoubtedly read it again more than once. You might reflect on Lenin's plain words, in which expression is given to Vladimir Ilyich's anxiety concerning the Party, the people, the State, and the future direction of Party policy.

Vladimir Ilyich said: 'Stalin is excessively rude, and this defect, which can be freely tolerated in our midst and in contacts among us Communists, becomes a defect which cannot be tolerated in one holding the position of the Secretary General. Because of this, I propose that the comrades consider the method by which Stalin would be removed from this position and by which another man would be selected for it, a man, who above all, would differ from Stalin in only one quality, namely, greater tolerance, greater loyalty, greater kindness and a more considerate attitude toward the comrades, a less capricious temper, etc.'. . . .

These negative characteristics of his developed steadily and during the last years acquired an absolutely insufferable character.

As later events have proven, Lenin's anxiety was justified: in the first period after Lenin's death Stalin still paid attention to his advice, but later he began to disregard the serious admonitions of Vladimir Ilyich.

When we analyze the practice of Stalin in regard to the direction of the Party and of the country, when we pause to consider everything which Stalin perpetrated, we must be convinced that Lenin's fears were justified. The negative characteristics of Stalin, which, in Lenin's time, were only incipient, transformed themselves during the last years into a grave abuse of power by Stalin, which caused untold harm to our Party. . . .

Stalin acted not through persuasion, explanation, and patient co-operation with people, but by imposing his concepts and demanding absolute submission to his opinion. Whoever opposed this concept or tried to prove his viewpoint, and the correctness of his position, was doomed to removal from the leading collective and to subsequent moral and physical annihilation. This was especially true during the period following the XVIIth Party Congress, when many prominent Party leaders and rank-and-file Party workers, honest and dedicated to the cause of Communism, fell victim to Stalin's despotism. . . .

It was determined that of the 139 members and candidates of the Party's Central Committee who were elected at the XVIIth Congress, 98 persons, i.e., 70 per cent, were arrested and shot (mostly in 1937–38). (*Indignation in the hall.*). . . .

The same fate met not only the Central Committee members, but also the majority of the delegates to the XVIIth Congress. Of 1,966 delegates with either voting or advisory rights, 1,108 persons were arrested on charges of anti-revolutionary crimes, i.e., decidedly more than a majority. This very fact shows how absurd, wild and contrary to common sense were the charges of counter-revolutionary crimes made out, as we now see against a majority of participants at the XVIIth Congress. (*Indignation in the hall.*)

We should recall that the XVIIth Party Congress is historically known as the Congress of Victors. Delegates to the Congress were active participants in the building of our socialist state, many of them suffered and fought for Party interests during the pre-revolutionary years in the conspiracy and at the Civil War fronts; they fought their enemies valiantly and often nervelessly looked into the face of death. How then can we believe that such people could prove to be 'two-faced' and had joined the camps of the enemies of socialism during the era after the political liquidation of Zinovievites, Trotskyites and rightists and after the great accomplishments of socialist construction?

This was the result of the abuse of power by Stalin, who began to use mass terror against Party cadres. . . .

Comrades: We must abolish the cult of the individual decisively, once and for all; we must draw the proper conclusions concerning both ideological-theoretical and practical work.

It is necessary for this purpose:

First, in a Bolshevik manner to condemn and eradicate the cult of the individual as alien to Marxism-Leninism and not consonant with the principles of Party leadership and the norms of Party life, and to fight inexorably all attempts at bringing back this practice in one form or another.

To return to and actually practice in all our ideological work the most important theses of Marxist-Leninist science about the people as the creator of history and as the creator of all material and spiritual good of humanity, about the decisive role of the Marxist Party in the revolutionary fight for the transformation of society, about the victory of communism.

In this connection we will be forced to do much work in order to examine critically from the Marxist-Leninist viewpoint and to correct the widely spread erroneous views connected with the cult of the individual in the sphere of history, philosophy, economy and of other sciences, as well as in literature and the fine arts. It is especially necessary that in the immediate future we compile a serious textbook of the history of our Party which will be edited in accordance with scientific Marxist objectivism, a textbook of the history of Soviet society, a book pertaining to the events of the Civil War and the Great Patriotic War.

Secondly, to continue systematically and consistently the work done by the Party's Central Committee during the last years, a work characterized by minute observation in all Party organizations, from the bottom to the top, of the Leninist principles of Party leadership, characterized, above all, by the main principle of collective leadership, characterized by the observation of the norms of Party life described in the Statutes of our Party, and finally, characterized by the wide practice of criticism and self-criticism.

Thirdly, to restore completely the Leninist principles of Soviet socialist democracy, expressed in the Constitution of the Soviet Union, to fight willfulness of individuals abusing their power. The evil caused by acts violating revolutionary socialist legality which have accumulated during a long time as a result of the negative influence of the cult of the individual has to be completely corrected. Comrades! The XXth Congress of the Communist Party of the Soviet Union has manifested with a new strength the unshakable unity of our Party, its cohesiveness around the Central Committee, its resolute will to accomplish the great task of building Communism. (*Tumultuous applause*). And the fact that we present in all their ramifications the basic problems of overcoming the cult of the individual which is alien to Marxism-Leninism, as well as the problem of liquidating its burdensome consequences, is an evidence of the great moral and political strength of our Party. (*Prolonged applause*).

We are absolutely certain that our Party, armed with the historical resolutions of the XXth Congress, will lead the Soviet people along the Leninist path to new successes, to new victories. (*Tumultuous, prolonged applause*).

Long live the victorious banner of our Party— Leninism! (*Tumultuous, prolonged applause ending in ovation. All rise.*)

Study Question

1. Why was the denunciation of Stalin so hard for many Soviet citizens to accept?

G.H. BLAKESLEE

As the Pacific War came to an end Ho Chi Minh declared the independence of the Republic of Vietnam (see Chapter Eight). However, the French Government was equally determined to resist any independence movements in the region and to regain control of its former colonies. Before his death US President Franklin Roosevelt had opposed any effort by the French military to re-establish its control in Indochina;

however, bureaucrats in the State Department's Far Eastern Division had a very different opinion. In a draft memorandum on Indochina the Far Eastern Division argued that the Vietnamese were not ready for self-government. Additionally, they felt the potential for conflict among the many ethnic groups in Indochina was another reason for delaying full independence in the region.

DRAFT MEMORANDUM, FAR EASTERN DIVISION, DEPARTMENT OF STATE, APRIL 1945

Possible Solutions

There are three possible solutions for the Problem of the disposition of Indochina. It may be restored to France, with or without conditions; it may be granted independence; or it may be placed under an international trusteeship.

1. Restoration to France
i. Considerations in Favor of Restoration
a. The Global Situation
If France is to be denied her former position in Indochina she will be to that extent weakened as a world power. It will probably be necessary for the United States to take the lead in any move by which France will be denied her former position in Indochina. If the United States, especially in view of its many unequivocal statements favoring the restoration of the French overseas territories, is the spearhead for partial dismemberment of the French Empire, French resentment will be such as to impose a very serious strain upon our relations and thus tend to defeat basic elements underlying our policy towards France. A disgruntled, psychologically sick and sovereign-conscious France will not augur well for postwar

collaboration in Europe and in the world as a whole.

If it is to be the active policy of the United States to seek and insist upon the adoption of measures by which the peoples of dependent areas are to be lifted from their present social condition and are to be given in time opportunity for full self-determination, we should consider whether that aim can best be accomplished in the case of Indochina through cooperation with the French or through denial of any role to France, and operate through an international trusteeship. In reaching that decision we must determine whether it is of more interest to us and the world as a whole to have a strong, friendly, cooperative France, or have a resentful France plus having on our hands a social and administrative problem of the first magnitude.

b. Commitments of the United States Government
'The policy of the Government of the United States has been based upon the maintenance of the integrity of France and of the French Empire and of the eventual restoration of the complete independence of all French territories'

(Department of State Press Release of 2 March 1942 [no. 85] relative to situation in New Caledonia).

'The Government of the United States recognizes the sovereign jurisdiction of the people of France over French possessions overseas. The Government of the United States fervently hopes that it may see the reestablishment of the independence of France and of the integrity of French territory.' (Acting Secretary of State in note to the French Ambassador at Washington, 13 April 1942 with respect to the establishment of a consular post at Brazzaville.)

'It is thoroughly understood that French sovereignty will be reestablished as soon as possible throughout all the territory, metropolitan and colonial, over which flew the French flag in 1939' (Mr Murphy, the Personal Representative of the President, in an unpublished letter of 2 November 1942 to General Giraud.)

'It has been agreed by all French elements concerned and the United States military authorities that French forces will aid and support the forces of the United States and their allies to expel from the soil of Africa the common enemy, to liberate France and restore integrally the French Empire.' (Preamble of unpublished Clark-Darlan Agreement of 22 November 1942.)

ii. Restoration Subject to Conditions Accepted by Other Colonial Power in the Pacific and Far East

Upon the liberation of Indochina and the termination of military operations in that area under the condition that the French Government accepts the following minimum commitments, which it is assumed will also be accepted by the other colonial powers in the Pacific and the Far East: (1) subscription to a colonial charter; (2) membership on behalf of Indochina in a regional commission; and (3) the submission of annual reports on the progress made in Indochina during the year in education, government, and social and economic conditions.

iii. Restoration Subject to Additional Conditions

The considerations which favor placing additional conditions on France are: (1) French administration of Indochina has in general been less satisfactory and less considerate of the interests of the native peoples than have been the administrations of the other leading colonial powers in the Pacific and the Far East, and (2) the French authorities cooperated with the Japanese and permitted them to enter and to effect military control of the colony.

To remedy the more outstanding weaknesses of the French administration of Indochina the United Nations in the Far Eastern area might insist that France be permitted to return to Indochina only after giving commitments to carry out the following reforms:

1. Tariff autonomy for Indochina.
2. The establishment and development of local and central representative institutions; the extension of the franchise as rapidly as possible.
3. Access on equal terms to all occupations and professions by Indo-Chinese; adequate educational and training facilities for all elements of the population.
4. Abolition of compulsory labor and effective supervision of labor contracts.
5. The development of local industries and a more balanced economy.

2. Independence for Indochina

Over 17 million of the 24 million inhabitants of Indochina are Annamites. The Annamites are one of the most highly civilized peoples in southeastern Asia, and it would seem reasonable to suppose that, after a preparatory period, they would prove to be politically not less capable than the Thai, who have successfully governed Thailand for centuries, or than the Burmese who, before the war, had achieved the substance of self-government though not the title.

A nationalist movement of some proportions exists in Indochina. Although the French never favored the growth of an indigenous nationalism, the liberal principles of French political thought inevitably produced a desire for political liberty among educated native people. More particularly, the development of native political consciousness may be traced to grievances against the French rulers. Among these might be listed the contrast between the native standard of living and that of resident Europeans, discrimination in wage levels and in social and professional opportunities, the high cost of living which largely nullified the economic advantages produced by the French regime, inequality before the law, alleged abuses of its privileges by the Roman Catholic Church, unfilled promises of political liberties beyond the limited advisory councils in each colony, failure to train natives for progressive participation in administration, and the thwarted ambitions of the native intelligentsia.

However, a preparatory period for independence is necessary. At the present, the elements necessary for the early establishment of an independent Indochina are lacking. The French policy of permitting only restricted native participation in government has allowed no opportunity for the development of a trained and experienced body of natives capable of assuming full responsibility for the direction of governmental affairs. The nationalist movement has been weakened by factional strife and by lack of solid organization, and has left the great mass of the people unaffected. The antagonism of the Annamites toward the Khmers and Laotians and toward the resident Chinese also limits the possibilities of early native unity. . . .

> **Study Question**
>
> 1. Why was the policy of the United States based on the restoration and maintenance of the French Empire?

ROBERT MCNAMARA

In 1961 President John F. Kennedy appointed Robert McNamara (1916–2009), the newly appointed President of the Ford Motor Company, as his Secretary of Defense. McNamara held the post from 1961 until 1968, during which time he helped to shape America's policy in Vietnam. Like Kennedy, McNamara had virtually no foreign policy experience when he joined the government. Though McNamara would later have serious reservations about American involvement in Vietnam, in 1961, he endorsed many of the common assumptions about the dangers of non-involvement. In particular, McNamara repeated the common argument that non-intervention would lead to the rapid spread of communist influence throughout Southeast Asia.

Secretary of Defense Robert S. McNamara briefs the press on the situation in Vietnam in 1965. U.S. News and World Report Magazine Photograph Collection. Courtesy of the Library of Congress, Prints and Photographs Division (LC-USZ62-134155).

MEMORANDUM FOR THE PRESIDENT, 8 NOVEMBER 1961

The basic issue framed by the Taylor Report is whether the US shall:

a. Commit itself to the clear objective of preventing the fall of South Vietnam to Communism, and

b. Support this commitment by necessary immediate military actions and preparations for possible later actions.

The Joint Chiefs, Mr Gilpatric, and I have reached the following conclusions:

1. The fall of South Vietnam to Communism would lead to the fairly rapid expansion of Communist con-trol, or complete accom-modation to Communism, in the rest of mainland Southeast Asia and in Indonesia. The strategic implications are wide and, particularly in the Orient, would be extremely serious.

2. The chances are against, probably sharply against, preventing that fall by measures short of the introduction of US forces on a substantial scale. We accept General Taylor's judgment that the various measures proposed by him in short are useful but will not in themselves do the job of restoring confidence and setting Diem on the way to winning his fight.

3. The introduction of a US force of the magnitude of an initial 8,000 men in a flood relief context will be of great help to Diem. However, it will not convince the other side (whether the shots are called from Moscow, Peiping[1] or Hanoi) that we mean business. Moreover, it probably will not tip the scales decisively. We would be almost certain to get increasingly mired down in an inconclusive struggle.

4. The other side can be convinced we mean business only if we accompany the initial force introduction by a clear commitment to the full objective stated above, accompanied by a warning through some channel to Hanoi that continued support of the Viet Cong will lead to punitive retaliation against North Vietnam.

5. If we act in this way, the ultimate possible extent of our military commitment must be faced. The struggle may be prolonged and Hanoi and Peiping may intervene overtly. In view of the logistic difficulties faced by the other side, we can assume that the maximum US forces required on the ground in Southeast Asia will not exceed 6 divisions, or about 205,000 men, (CINCPAC Plan 32–59, Phase IV). Our military posture is, or, with the addition of more National Guard or regular Army divisions, can be made, adequate to furnish these forces without serious interference with our present Berlin plans.

6. To accept the stated objective is of course a most serious decision. Military force is not the only element of what must be a most carefully coordinated set of actions. Success will depend on factors many of which are not within our control—notably the conduct of Diem himself and other leaders in the area. Laos will remain a major problem. The domestic political implications of accepting the objective are also grave, although it is our feeling that the country will respond better to a firm initial position than to courses of action that lead us in only gradually, and that in the meantime are sure to involve casualties. The over-all effect on Moscow and Peiping will need careful weighing and may well be mixed; however, permitting South Vietnam to fall can only strengthen and encourage them greatly.

In sum:

a. We do not believe major units of US forces should be introduced in South Vietnam unless we are willing to make an affirmative decision on the issue stated at the start of this memorandum.

b. We are inclined to recommend that we do commit the US to the clear objective of preventing the fall of South Vietnam to Communism and that we support this commitment by the necessary military actions.

c. If such a commitment is agreed upon, we support the recommendations of General Taylor as the first steps toward its fulfillment.

Note

1.   Beijing.

Study Question

1.   Overall, how accurate was McNamara's 1961 assessment of the situation in Indochina?

TIPS FOR ANALYSIS

The Author's Motivation

A critical reading of primary source material must always include an assessment of the author's motivation in writing the document. Was it written for political purposes? For legal purposes? For personal remembrance or as a way to come to terms with an event? Or was the document written for a future audience in order to ensure that an event is not forgotten? The author's motivations will have a substantial impact on the way the document is constructed. Often, there will be more than one motive.

WEB RESOURCES

The Diefenbunker: Canada's Cold War Museum/Musée canadien de la Guerre froide
http://www.diefenbunker.ca/
Harry S. Truman Library & Museum: Ideological Foundations of the Cold War
http://www.trumanlibrary.org/whistlestop/study_collections/coldwar
Cold War International History Project
http://www.wilsoncenter.org/index.cfm?fuseaction=topics.home&topic_id=1409
The National Security Archive: George Washington University
http://www.gwu.edu/~nsarchiv

RECOMMENDED READING

Ray Bradbury, *Fahrenheit 451* (New York: Simon & Schuster, 2003). *Fahrenheit 451* is a futuristic 1953 novel touching on the censorship of thought, the power of the state, and the unquestioning acceptance of authority. It tells of one man's struggle with the temptation to discover the past through his access to banned books, and of the resistance movement that resorts to memorizing books to prevent their contents from being forgotten.

Ha Jin, *War Trash* (New York: Pantheon, 2004). Set in 1951, *War Trash* is based on historical accounts of Chinese POWs held by the Americans during the Korean War. The POWs find themselves longing for home, but that home was being profoundly transformed by Mao's revolution. The main character, Yu Yuan, acts as a translator in the POW camps and finds himself trapped between Communist and Nationalist POW factions.

Arthur Miller, *The Crucible* (New York: Penguin, 2003). Arthur Miller's 1953 play is based on the historical events and people involved in the 1692 Salem witch trials. It stands as a powerful allegory for the McCarthy era anti-Communist paranoia and hysteria; Miller himself was called to testify before the House Un-American Activities Committee (HUAC). *The Crucible* examines the consequences of political policy based on a misplaced sense of good and evil.

B.F. Skinner, *Walden Two* (New York: Prentice Hall, 1976). A fictional work, drawn heavily from the author's theories of behaviourism, *Walden Two* focuses on a modern utopian community where problems are solved through the scientific study of human behaviour.

John Wyndham, *The Day of the Triffids* (Madison, WI: Turtleback Books, 2004). Survivors of an apocalyptic event discover that the earth is now dominated by triffids—human creations that have set out to destroy their human prey. Wyndham's 1951 novel relates to the Cold War, the development of atomic energy, paranoia with respect to Soviet intentions, and the potentially devastating consequences of bio-engineering.

RECOMMENDED VIEWING

Den Pobedivshey Strany [*A Day in the Country of Victory*] (USSR, 1947). Director: Ilya Kopalin/Irina Setkina. This 68-minute documentary-style film was intended to capture a single day, 14 August 1947, in the lives of typical Soviet citizens in order to provide a visual endorsement of life under the Stalinist system, with typical propaganda images of industry, agriculture, and the military.

Red Menace (USA, 1949). Director: R.G. Springsteen. *Red Menace* remains the classic American propaganda film about the horrors of communist infiltration. It demonstrates all of the stereotypes of the era regarding the communist menace to the United States and to the rest of the 'free world'.

Invasion of the Body Snatchers (USA, 1956). Director: Don Siegel (B&W). *Invasion of the Body Snatchers* can be seen both as a reflection and condemnation of the anti-communist blacklisting actions of the McCarthy era, and as a reflection and denunciation of the conformity of 1950s suburbia. Siegel's original bleak ending was replaced by the studio, but can now be seen in restored director's cuts of the film.

Dr Strangelove (UK/USA, 1964). Director: Stanley Kubrick (B&W). An outstanding satire of the Cold War paranoia, Kubrick's classic black comedy captures the essential absurdity of mutual assured destruction. Faced with an imminent Armageddon resulting from the actions of a madman, the film focuses on the resulting attempts to prevent the destruction.

Hearts and Minds (USA, 1974). Director: Peter Davis (Documentary). This controversial documentary was released just as the United States withdrew its forces from Vietnam, prior to the fall of Saigon. It contains news footage and interviews with veterans and politicians and focuses on the disastrous 'hearts & minds' strategy and the reasons for the near-total failure to achieve this.

The Boys in Company C (USA/Hong Kong, 1977). Director: Sidney J. Furie. *The Boys in Company C* is considered to be one of the most accessible Vietnam war movies. Made in 1977, when tensions about the war remained high, its themes include the futility of the war, demoralization of soldiers, war's impact on idealism, weakness of leadership, and problems of strategy and tactics.

The Atomic Café (USA, 1982). Director: Kevin Rafferty (Documentary). *The Atomic Café*—which was created from 1950s American propaganda film clips—exposes the lies and misinformation propagated by the American government. It remains a strongly relevant commentary on the gullibility of citizens in the face of an ongoing government propaganda barrage.

When Father Was Away On Business (Yugoslavia/Spain, 1985). Director: Emir Kusturica. The political tension of the time period after the break between Stalin and Tito is captured through the eyes of a child whose father has been sentenced to hard labour. The film depicts the subsequent struggles of the fatherless family to maintain their reputation and cope with the day-to-day trials of existence. Kusturica received the Palme d'Or at Cannes in 1985 for this film.

CHAPTER TEN

CHINA AND JAPAN: THE RE-EMERGENCE OF ASIAN POWER

◇

At the end of the Pacific War the nation of Japan was utterly devastated. Its economy had been ruined, both by the cost of fighting and by poorly chosen economic policies during the war. Japan had been stripped of its massive colonial empire, had lost most of its army and navy, and was occupied by the United States Army. Subsequently, the Emperor was forced to renounce all claims to divinity—the traditional source of his power and respect—and was reduced to a symbolic figurehead. China, meanwhile, had successfully defeated the Japanese forces that had first entered the country in 1931, only to find itself immediately embroiled in a devastating civil war between the governing Nationalist forces and the increasingly popular Communists, who had contributed significantly to the defeat of the Japanese. Thus, in 1945, neither nation seemed poised to emerge as a major power in the postwar world.

Ultimately the Chinese Communists emerged victorious in their civil war due to a combination of military skill, careful planning, and fortuitous timing; simultaneously poor decision-making and disastrous economic policies undermined the authority of the Nationalist government. Once in power, though, the Communists, under Mao Zedong, faced a multitude of internal and external difficulties. Overt western hostility and a strained relationship with the Soviet Union meant that the Communist Party could count on only irregular external assistance. Meanwhile, the nation had been economically, politically, and socially devastated by nearly two decades of war. An initial move towards rapid heavy industrialization and full collectivization was halted when its toll on the rural areas of China became evident; however, more moderate types of economic reform, though successful in practice, were viewed as a retreat from the revolutionary goals of the Chinese Communist Party (CCP).

The perceived threat to the revolutionary aims of the movement led to the Great Proletarian Cultural Revolution in 1966 and a draconian crackdown on all 'bourgeois' influences. In turn, this led to an additional period of socio-

Mao addresses supporters in December 1944. The CPP had gained tremendous popularity in Northern China by this time. Courtesy of the Franklin D. Roosevelt Library.

economic upheaval as Mao sought to reign in the more extremist elements in the Communist Party. Mao's death in 1976 resulted in a succession struggle that once more postponed any substantial recovery from the disruptions of the late 1960s. The situation stabilized in the late 1970s when Deng Xiaoping announced his intentions to modernize and strengthen the Chinese economy while building closer ties with the nations of the west. In 1980 four coastal cities were designated as special economic zones—areas where capitalist practices were permitted—in order to facilitate this interaction. Deng's successors continued to implement his plan for modernization, and the changes culminated in China's entry into the World Trade Organization in 2001. While China's economic success is indisputable, progress towards a more representative political system has, however, produced fewer concrete results.

The American occupation authorities shaped Japan's postwar development profoundly. Under their supervision a new constitution was created in 1947 that confirmed the status of the Emperor as a symbolic figure and created a British-style parliamentary democracy. Universal suffrage was entrenched, as was a new human rights code. The large monopolies, which had fuelled prewar economic growth and which had benefited greatly from wartime expansionism, were dissolved and the rights of unions were guaranteed. Finally, Japan was prohibited from maintaining anything more than a civil defence force.

With the outbreak of the Korean War in 1950, the United States came to view Japan as the only barrier to the ongoing spread of communism in Asia. This lead to a rapid shift in focus: from punishing Japan for past transgressions to rebuilding the nation as quickly as possible. Restrictions on economic monopolies were lifted and Japan gained access to the massive American market for its exports. Internally, a high savings rate and low labour costs allowed large-scale government investment in production for export, rather than domestic consumption. Despite the oil crisis of the 1970s and a global turn towards economic protectionism, Japan's economy continued to grow. By 1985 nearly ten per cent of the world's exports were produced by Japan. However, despite the 'economic miracle' of the postwar era, by the 1990s Japan's economy began to falter. Productivity declined, unemployment rose, and government deficits soared while successive leaders attempted to shore up unprofitable ventures. By the end of the century the close relationship between government, industry, and banks, which had been so beneficial during the economic boom, became a dangerous liability.

The documents in this section provide an overview of the key developments in both China and Japan. Mao Zedong's views are presented in a speech delivered at the end of the Pacific War, as he contemplated the best approach to defeating the remnants of imperialism and feudalism which continued to restrict China's development. The catastrophic impact of the Cultural Revolution is discussed in Fox Butterfield's interview with Lihua. One woman's view of the failure of the democratic reform movement of the late 1980s is presented in Chai Ling's account of the Tiananmen Square uprising. Finally, Hu Jintao reflects on the impact of Chinese development on the broader Asian region. Turning to Japan, the postwar struggle to come to terms with past actions can be seen in the writings of Kamei Katsuichirō. Chitoshi Yanaga analyzes the reasons behind Japan's rapid economic recovery and success in the 1960s. Finally, Suvendrini Kacuchi assesses the socio-economic impact of the economic collapse of the 1990s.

◇

MAO ZEDONG

The Chinese Communist Party (CCP) experienced a series of setbacks during its rise to power, including Chiang Kai-shek's attacks during the Northern Expedition and the era of the Jiangxi Soviet. However, as the CCP came to be seen as the more effective fighting force during the Sino–Japanese War, its popularity began to increase. Still, Mao Zedong (1893–1976) was aware that the threat of the Guomindang and the foreign imperialists remained. In 1945, even as the Sino–Japanese War continued,

Mao gave the following speech in order to explain the strategy of the Chinese Communist Party with *respect to its two primary enemies: imperialism and feudalism.*

THE FOOLISH OLD MAN WHO REMOVED THE MOUNTAINS

Our aim in propagating the line of the congress is to build up the confidence of the whole Party and the entire people in the certain triumph of the revolution. We must first raise the political consciousness of the vanguard so that, resolute and unafraid of sacrifice, they will surmount every difficulty to win victory. But this is not enough; we must also arouse the political consciousness of the entire people so that they may willingly and gladly fight together with us for victory. We should fire the whole people with the conviction that China belongs not to the reactionaries but to the Chinese people. There is an ancient Chinese fable called 'The Foolish Old Man Who Removed the Mountains'. It tells of an old man who lived in northern China long, long ago and was known as the Foolish Old Man of the North Mountain. His house faced south and beyond his doorway stood the two great peaks, Taihang and Wangwu, obstructing the way. With great determination, he led his sons in digging up these mountains hoe in hand. Another greybeard, known as the Wise Old Man, said derisively, 'How silly of you to do this! It is quite impossible for you few to dig up these two huge mountains.' The Foolish Old Man replied, 'When I die, my sons will carry on; when they die, there will be my grandsons, and then their sons and grandsons, and so on to

Mao Zedong meets with US Ambassador Patrick J. Hurley at Mao's Yanan headquarters, during discussions of the post war CPP/Nationalist relationship, 27 August 1945. Couartesy of the National Archives (NWDNS-111-SC-360599).

infinity. High as they are, the mountains cannot grow any higher and with every bit we dig, they will be that much lower. Why can't we clear them away?' Having refuted the Wise Old Man's wrong view, he went on digging every day, unshaken in his conviction. God was moved by this, and he sent down two angels, who carried the mountains away on their backs. Today, two big mountains lie like a dead weight on the Chinese people. One is imperialism, the other is feudalism. The Chinese Communist Party has long made up its mind to dig them up. Our god is none other than the masses of the Chinese people. If they stand up and dig together with us, why can't these two mountains be cleared away?

Yesterday, in a talk with two Americans who were leaving for the United States, I said that the US government was trying to undermine us and this would not be permitted. We oppose the US government's policy of supporting Chiang Kai-shek against the Communists. But we must draw a distinction, firstly, between the people of the United States and their government and, secondly, within the US government between the policy-makers and their subordinates. I said to these two Americans, 'Tell the policy-makers in your government that we forbid you Americans to enter the Liberated Areas because your policy is to support Chiang Kai-shek against the Communists, and we have to be on our guard. You can come to the Liberated Areas if your purpose is to fight Japan, but there must first be an agreement. We will not permit you to nose around everywhere. . . . '

The US government's policy of supporting Chiang Kai-shek against the Communists shows the brazenness of the US reactionaries. But all the scheming of the reactionaries, whether Chinese or foreign, to prevent the Chinese people from achieving victory is doomed to failure. The democratic forces are the main current in the world today, while reaction is only a counter-current. The reactionary counter-current is trying to swamp the main current of national independence and people's democracy, but it can never become the main current. Today, there are still three major contradictions in the old world, as Stalin pointed out long ago: first, the contradiction between the proletariat and the bourgeoisie in the imperialist countries; second, the contradiction between the various imperialist powers; and third, the contradiction between the colonial and semi-colonial countries and the imperialist metropolitan countries. Not only do these three contradictions continue to exist but they are becoming more acute and widespread. Because of their existence and growth, the time will come when the reactionary anti-Soviet, anti-Communist, and anti-Democratic counter-currents still in existence today will be swept away.

At this moment two congresses are being held in China, the Sixth National Congress of the Kuomintang and the Seventh National Congress of the Communist Party. They have completely different aims: the aim of one is to liquidate the Communist Party and all other democratic forces in China and thus to plunge China into darkness; the aim of the other is to overthrow Japanese imperialism and its lackeys, the Chinese feudal forces, and build a new-democratic China and thus to lead China to light. These two lines are in conflict with each other. We firmly believe that, led by the Chinese Communist Party and guided by the line of its Seventh Congress, the Chinese people will achieve complete victory, while the Kuomintang's counter-revolutionary line will inevitably fail.

Study Question

1. Why do you think that Mao was able to garner so much support for the CCP when the Guomindang (GMD) was so much better funded and equipped?

FOX BUTTERFIELD

As China entered the 1960s Mao Zedong had lost both his position as Head of State and most of his influence over policy-making, though he remained head of the Chinese Communist Party. Under Deng Xiaoping, Zhou Enlai, and Liu Shaoqi, China moved towards a more liberalized economic and social policy. Gradually Mao became convinced that reactionary elements were seizing control of the revolution and that a massive revitalization was necessary. Thus in 1966, Mao launched an all-out war on 'capitalist' elements in the Party and the country. Mao called his battle the Great Proletarian Cultural Revolution. In the process, Party leaders, intellectuals, and professionals found themselves at the mercy of the Red Guards—revolutionary students entrusted to carry out the revitalization of the Chinese Revolution. Families such as that of Lihua found their lives turned upside down as they were forced into the rural areas for 'rehabilitation'. Lihua's story is told by a journalist, Fox Butterfield, who interviewed her over a period of several months in Beijing in 1979.

LIHUA

She was only six years old when it happened. Until then Lihua had lived in a spacious apartment in Peking with her three older brothers, a younger sister, her father, who was a scientist, and her mother, a nurse. They thought of themselves with pride as what the Chinese call intellectuals, the carriers of the great tradition. Her mother used to tell the children about her own grandfather, who had passed one of the imperial exams under the Qing dynasty before the turn of the century and had held a sinecure job in the court in Peking.

But they had a neighbour who was jealous of them. He was a worker and a Communist Party member, in Chinese terms a good class status. But he drank and smoked a lot, his wife was unemployed, and he had a hard time supporting their five children. In 1966, at the start of the Cultural Revolution, the neighbour moved quickly to organize a radical faction in their apartment building in support of Mao. His new position enabled him to examine Lihua's father's confidential dossier in the Party's files; in it he found her father had once been briefly a member of the Kuomintang before 1949 when he was a student. That was enough to convict him. A rally

was held; Lihua's father was judged a 'hidden counterrevolutionary', and he was stripped of his teaching post.

'Red Guards came to search our house, they confiscated everything,' she recalled. 'They took my father's books, my mother's jewelry, her college photo albums, our furniture. Then they built a bonfire in the yard outside and burned everything.'

'That was the end of my childhood,' Lihua said.

Afterward, the Public Security Bureau ordered her entire family to move to a village in a remote part of Hunan province, eight hundred miles south of Peking. It was punishment for her father's supposed past sins. Lihua's ancestors had come from the village, God Mountain, but neither her mother nor father ever lived there, and no one in the family knew how to farm. Six teen-age Red Guards accompanied the family on the three-day train trip to make sure they got there.

'When we arrived, the local cadres took away the few things we had left, our clothes and our bedding. They left us only what we had on our backs.' The family was put in the village

Mao's enemies are publicly shamed by Red Guards, 26 January 1967. New York World-Telegram and Sun Newspaper Photograph Collection.

schoolhouse, a small one-room building with holes in the walls where the windows should have been and a roof that leaked. There was no furniture. Lihua had to learn to sleep on the mud floor. The school had already been closed by the Cultural Revolution. The teacher had been arrested as a reactionary.

'The peasants and the cadres made my parents parade through the streets every day for several weeks,' she related. 'They hung a placard around my father's neck, they made him kneel down to confess his crimes, and they beat both my father and mother with iron bars.'

'A person is made of flesh. If you beat them long enough, they will die.' Within a month her mother was dead and her father was left deaf and unable to use his right arm.

'My mouth is very stupid because I didn't go to school, but these are a few of the facts.'

Lihua recounted this story the first time we met in September 1979 on the steps of the Peking Municipal Party Committee Headquarters, a functional gray-concrete building. I had gone there when I heard there were a number of petitioners from the countryside standing outside the Party office trying to present their grievances to the city authorities. It was one of those periods when China's leaders temporarily relaxed their control.[1] Some young factory workers and students took advantage of the slack to put up wall posters or print unofficial journals criticizing the regime, what we foreign correspondents came to call the 'democracy movement'. Thousands of other people materialized from the countryside asking to have their own personal cases reexamined. The Chinese referred to them as *shang-fang*, meaning they were 'entreating a higher level for help'. Lihua was one of these. . . . She talked in a calm, dispassionate voice, almost as if all this had happened to someone else, but her story soon gathered a crowd. . . .

'I would walk thirty li [ten miles] up to the hills at sunrise every day, then back that evening. Sometimes I had to carry a hundred pounds, almost twice my weight. But I was inexperienced and often cut myself with the ax,' she said. When I looked down at her hands, there were long scars on the backs of both hands and a gash down the middle finger of her left hand from the tip of the nail to the first joint. 'We didn't have enough money to pay for a doctor to stitch it,' she explained. The village, as part of a commune, had a cooperative medical program, but families of landlords[2] were not eligible to join.

'In that first year, our clothes soon became like tattered pieces of paper. I had to teach myself how to sew for the family by taking apart our old clothes and then putting them back together.'

'I was born into the new society,' she went on, using a Chinese expression for the years after the Communists' victory in 1949. 'I grew up under the Red flag and at first I didn't understand how such things could happen. But gradually I came to realize that I represent many thousands of people. It is just like in the old feudal society before Liberation. We Chinese must still *chi-ku*, "eat bitterness". Nothing has really changed.'

'As humans, we should have rights, the right to a job, to get an education, but the cadres often treat us like dogs and pigs,' she said. . . .

Notes

1. The first era of rehabilitations occurred shortly after Deng Xiaoping came to power.

2. Those who were banished from the cities were assumed to be part of the landlord class, that is, bourgeois exploiters of the peasantry.

> **Study Question**
>
> 1. Was Mao's belief—that only a massive revitalization of the revolution could save communism in China—correct?

CHAI LING

As Deng Xiaoping modernized the Chinese economy during the 1980s, introducing a limited measure of capitalism, China's students recognized an opportunity for political reform. University students began to hold demonstrations in favour of greater political freedom and reforms, such as a free press. These protests, which began in 1987, culminated in *May and June 1989 with a massive demonstration at Tiananmen Square. On the night of 4 June 1989 rural army units[1] were brought into Beijing to suppress the students and remove all traces of their protest. Chai Ling (b. 1966) commanded the student headquarters at the Square. The following radio address was delivered on June 8th.*

JUNE FOUR: A CHRONICLE OF THE CHINESE DEMOCRATIC UPRISING

It is now four o'clock in the afternoon of June the eighth, nineteen eighty-nine. My name is Chai Ling. I was the chief commander of the student headquarters in Tiananmen Square. I am still alive.

I think that I am best qualified to relate the happenings in the Square during the time between June 2 and June 4. I feel obliged to tell the truth to everybody here, and through you to every fellow citizen, every Chinese.

About ten o'clock on the night of June 2 came the first signal of the massacre: a police car ran over four innocent people. Three of them died. Then we found some soldiers unloading guns and army uniforms and distributing them to the students and civilians around them. We were very suspicious of their actions, so we collected those materials and forwarded them to the police. We have kept the receipts as evidence. The third signal arrived at 2:10 PM June 3 at Liubukou and Xinhuaman Gate when armed police attacked our students and civilians. The students had been standing on top of carts and crying out through loudspeakers. They were shouting: 'The People's police must love the people!' and 'The People's police do not beat people.' The students had hardly finished the words when one student got kicked in the belly by a policeman who climbed up the cart. The policeman yelled 'Who the hell loves you!' and gave him another blow on the head. The young man fell down at once.

Let me explain our operation in the Square. I was the chief commander. We had set up a broadcasting station that mainly reported the news of the hunger strike. I was always there directing the students' actions in the Square. There were, of course, other people at the station, people like Li Fu, Feng Congde, etc. We constantly received emergency information about students and civilians being beaten and injured in different parts of the Square.

Things became worse and worse as the time dragged from eight, to nine, to ten o'clock. At least ten news reports about people being attacked by the military were received in this period of time. We held a news conference for the reporters on the site. Unfortunately there were very few foreign correspondents, probably because they had been confined to their hotels by the military. We were also told that their rooms had been searched. Only one or two foreign press personnel managed to enter the Square.

The headquarters issued a statement. We put forward one single slogan, which was, 'Overthrow the Li Peng government.'[2]

At nine o'clock, all the students in Tiananmen Square stood up, raised their right hands, and pledged: 'In order to push forward the democratic process of our motherland, to realize prosperity in our country, to avoid a handful of conspirators draining our great motherland, and to save the 1.1 billion Chinese from losing their lives in white terror, I pledge to use my young life to defend Tiananmen and to defend the republic. My head may be cut off, the blood may flow, but Tiananmen Square must not be lost. I will fight until the last person falls.'

. . . .

All of us were very tired. The four hunger strikers went to the military to try to negotiate. They found an officer who claimed to be responsible and told him that the students would withdraw from the Square on the condition that the army guaranteed the safety of the students. Meanwhile, the student leaders in the Square decided to withdraw after asking the opinions of the other students. However, right before we could pass the decision to our students, the troops broke their promise. Armed with helmets and machine guns, they charged onto the third level of the platform of the Monument. Our loudspeakers were crushed instantly. They were now firing at us on the people's monument, the Monument to the People's Heroes. The students came down the monument in tears. We were all crying in retreat.

People shouted at us, 'Don't cry!' The students replied that we would return to the Square again, because it was our square. Later we learned that some of us still held illusions about this government and its troops. They thought the troops mainly wanted to force them to leave the Square. Fatigue had lulled them to sleep in their tents; tanks knocked their tents down and ground their bodies apart. Some estimated a death toll of two hundred; others said four thousand. I simply have no idea how many died in the massacre. But I know for sure that the members of the Worker's Independent Association all got killed. They were about twenty or thirty people.

It was said that while the students were discussing the issue of withdrawing from the Square or not, the armed forces poured gas over the tents, padded coats, and dead bodies of the students and then set them on fire. They planned to wash the Square later so that no trace of killing could be exposed to the public. The symbol of our democratic movement, the Goddess of Liberty, was likewise crushed.

Holding hands together, we walked around the Mao Tse-tung Memorial Hall trying to find an exit on the west or the south side of the Square. We found about ten thousand soldiers in helmets sitting on the ground south of the Memorial Hall. The students shouted 'dogs!' and 'fascists!' at them. When we left toward the west, we saw column after column of troops running together in Tiananmen Square. The civilians shouted to them 'Dogs!' 'Fascists!' 'Beasts!' The soldiers did not even glance at us. They ran as fast as they could toward the centre. When we passed by Liubukou, where one of the first bloody conflicts took place, the student leaders conscientiously walked in the front line. Debris, such as broken and burnt garbage bins, was everywhere. Between Liubukou and Changanjian Street, we saw vehicles damaged by fire, broken bricks and tiles left to remind us of the fierce fight the previous day, but no corpses. Later we learned that the troops collected the bodies that had fallen to the ground while they had forced their way forward. The bodies, some still alive, were dumped onto buses or tricycles, leaving no chance for the injured people to survive. They did their utmost to hide their crimes.

We wanted to stand up, to demonstrate, and to return to the Square again, but all the people around tried to dissuade us. . . .

On the way to Xidan, we saw a woman wailing. Her child had been killed. A little distance further, we saw four corpses, all civilians. Everyone we saw on our way to our schools had tears in his eyes.

One civilian said to us angrily, 'Are we buying state bonds to allow them more funds to manufacture more bullets to kill our own children and innocent people?' More information came to us from different sources, such as fellow students and civilians. It boiled down to one single truth— the government troops were butchers and were slaughtering people. They had fired rocket guns at the residential houses along Changanjie Avenue at about two AM. They were trying to block the tanks. He saw a small girl waving her arms at the tanks that were coming in her direction. The tanks ran over and ground her into pieces. My friend was holding two students by their arms. One bullet hit the student on the right in the arm and he fell down. Shortly afterwards, another hit the student

on the left. My friend said, 'I believe that death was only a tenth of an inch away from me.'

We saw a woman looking for her son. She gave us his name and told us that he was alive yesterday. 'Is he still there?' Many people were looking for relatives and friends. As we walked toward our schools, we found some office buildings hanging big posters supporting the 'right' decisions of the Central Committee of the Communist Party. We got very angry, so some of us tore the slogan down and burned it.

All through the night the radio was broadcasting the message that 'the military forces were moved to Beijing to quell a handful of rioters and to help the capital to restore order.' I think that I am in a position to determine whether we are rioters at all. Now, every Chinese who has a conscience please put your hand on your heart and think about this: How can young students be considered rioters when all they did was sit together on the platform of the monument? If those who shot at us are animals and beasts, those who sit in front of the cameras or on television screens are worse. They have degenerated to such a rotten base that they are not ashamed to tell lies. Just as we were leaving the Square, a tank ran after us with tear gas bombs knocking down several students, but it didn't care. It drove over students' bodies. It crushed their legs and their necks. Their bodies can never be put together again. Now, who are the rioters? You tell me!

We put on cotton masks because the tear gas was drying up our throats. We walked on and on, mourning our friends who had sacrificed their young lives. They are gone forever.

We finally got back to the Beijing University campus. The university had prepared accommodations for the students who came to Beijing to join us. But none of us wanted bed or food. We were very, very sad. We are the survivors. Many of our friends died on the Square. They won't be coming back again. They will stay on Changanjie Avenue forever.

Our return to Beijing University marked the forced ending of the peaceful petition that started in the form of a hunger strike on 13 May 1989, and continued in the form of a sit-down through 4 June 1989. Later information came that, on the night of 3 June, Li Peng issued three mandates: First, the army was authorized to shoot. Second, armoured carriers were to move at full speed, and Tiananmen Square was to be cleared before the dawn of 4 June. Third, every leader and organizer of the movement was to be persecuted without mercy.

Friends, this is a chaotic government, but it is still moving troops to Beijing and it is still ruling the country. The Beijing massacre has just started. Gradually it will spread to the whole of China; it may have started in other parts of China already. Friends, let us have confidence in the future. The darkest period of the night comes right before the dawn. A real people's republic will be born in the awakening to the fascist suppression. This is a life-or-death moment for the Chinese nation. Arise, Chinese people. Arise, every citizen who has a conscience. The last victory surely belongs to you. It will not be long before the downfall comes

to the government headed by Yang Shangkun, Li Peng, Wang Zheng, and Bo Yibo!

Down with fascism!

Down with the military rulers!

Victory to the people!

Long live the Republic!

Notes

1. Rural military units were utilized because of the fear that the troops normally stationed in Beijing would refuse to fire on the demonstrators.

2. Although Deng Xiaoping remained the acknowledged leader of China, protesters widely blamed Premier Li Peng for the crackdown on pro-democracy movements; it was Li Peng who dismissed Communist Party Chairman Zhao Ziyang, who had been sympathetic to the students.

> **Study Question**
>
> 1. What were the most important reasons for the failure of the student uprising?

HU JINTAO

Hu Jintao (b. 1942) became General Secretary of the Communist Party of China in 2002 and added the presidency of the People's Republic in 2003. He was identified by Deng Xiaoping as a potential leader in the early 1990s and has generally followed Deng's principles on modernization in China. Hu has repeatedly used the phrase 'hexie shehui' 和谐社会 —'harmonious society' —to describe his vision of a modern China in which all peoples live in harmony with one another and with the natural environment. Here, Hu extends his vision to the peoples of Asia.

CHINA'S DEVELOPMENT IS AN OPPORTUNITY FOR ASIA

Ladies and gentlemen,

Both in history and the present-day world, a country can emerge victorious from tough international competition and enjoy faster development only when it gets along with the tide of the times, seizes the opportunities for development, blazes a trail suited to its national conditions and relies on the wisdom and resourcefulness of its own people.

In the past 25 years, while pressing ahead with reform and opening up, China has put initially in place a socialist market economy, an economy that is open to the outside world. China's productive forces and overall national strength have been constantly enhanced. With various social undertakings developing in full swing, the Chinese people as a whole have made the historical leap from subsistence to modest prosperity. In the course of 25 years between 1978 and 2003, China's economy grew by an average annual rate of 9.4 per cent, with its GDP, foreign trade and foreign exchange reserves jumping from US$147.3 billion, US$20.6 billion and US$167 million to over US$1.4 trillion, US$851.2 billion and US$403.3 billion respectively. China now is the world's sixth largest economy and the fourth largest trader. The reason why China has produced such tremendous changes is because we have adhered to the road of building socialism with Chinese characteristics and persevered in reform and opening-up, thus galvanizing the Chinese people's initiative, enthusiasm, and creativity.

Though China has achieved impressive results in its development, there are still many acute problems, such as overpopulation, weak economic foundation, underdeveloped productivity, highly uneven development, and a fairly sharp contradiction between the country's ecological environment and natural resources on the one hand and its economic and social development on the other. China's per capita GDP, though reaching the record high of US$1,000 last year, still ranks behind the 100th place in the world. To make China's modernization program a success and deliver a prosperous life for all the Chinese people still requires a long and uphill battle.

We have already set a clear goal for the first 20 years of this century. Namely, in building a well-off society of a higher standard in an all-round way

for the benefit of well over one billion Chinese people, we will quadruple the 2000 GDP to US$4 trillion with a per capita GDP of US$3,000, further develop the economy, improve democracy, advance science and education, enrich culture, foster greater social harmony, and upgrade the texture of life for the people.

To achieve this goal, we will continue to follow the guidance of Deng Xiaoping theory and the important thoughts of the 'Three Represents' and conscientiously act, in an all-round way, on the concept of people-oriented, comprehensive, coordinated, and sustainable development. This scientific concept of development crystallizes the successful experience of China's reform, opening-up and modernization drive in the past 25 years and that of the other countries in their course of development, and reflects a new understanding of the issue of development by the Chinese Government and people. We will take economic development as our top priority, aim ourselves to the all-round development of man, and follow a development path characterized by high productivity, affluent life and sound eco-system by properly balancing urban and rural development, development among regions, economic and social development, development of man and nature, and domestic development and opening to the outside world. . . .

On our road to progress, we are still encountering the multitude of contradictions and problems, and the various risks and challenges. However, the Chinese people have the confidence and the capability to overcome all kinds of hardships and difficulties and make China's modernization and great rejuvenation a reality.

Ladies and gentlemen,

China is an Asian country. China's development is closely related to Asia's prosperity. China has, and will continue to make a positive impact on Asia in the area of development.— A developing China generates important opportunities for Asia. As the world's biggest potential market, China has presided over in the past 25 years a steadily expanding and maturing market with import growing at an average annual rate of over 15 per cent, which has made China the third largest importer globally and the largest importer in Asia. In 2003, China imported from the rest of Asia a total of US$272.9 billion worth of merchandise, up by 42.4 per cent, with imports from ASEAN, Japan, ROK, and India increasing by over 35 per cent. Direct investment in the rest of Asia by China has risen at an average annual rate of 20 per cent in recent years. In 2003, more than 20 million outbound visits were made by Chinese nationals, as more and more Chinese tourists made Asian countries and regions their choice destinations. With China's development, the size of its market and its overseas investment will grow even larger and still more Chinese will travel to the other parts of Asia for sightseeing, business and visit. China's economy will integrate still more closely with the Asian economy, giving rise to a new type of partnership characterized by mutual benefit, mutual complement and mutual assistance.— China's development contributes to peace and stability in Asia. A stable and prosperous China is in itself an important contribution to peace and stability in Asia. China since ancient times has had a fine tradition of sincerity, benevolence, kindness

and trust towards the neighbors. The very purpose of China's foreign policy is to maintain world peace and promote common development. China always practices what it preaches. Persisting in building good-neighborly relationships and partnership with the neighboring countries, we pursue a policy of bringing harmony, security and prosperity to neighbors and dedicate ourselves to strengthening mutual trust and cooperation with the fellow Asian countries, easing up hot spot tensions, and striving to maintain peace and tranquility in Asia. . . .

China's development cannot be achieved in isolation of Asia, and Asia's prosperity also needs China. China will follow a peaceful development path holding high the banners of peace, development and cooperation, join the other Asian countries in bringing about Asian rejuvenation, and making greater contribution to the lofty cause of peace and development in the world.

Thank you.

Study Question

1. Can a country modernize its economy and society, as envisioned by Hu, without accompanying political reforms?

KAMEI KATSUICHIRŌ

During the 1920s and 1930s Kamei Katsuichirō was a member of the Japanese Communist Party. Like many on the far left of the political spectrum he had been an outspoken advocate of modernization in Japan. However, Japan's brutal wartime aggression towards its neighbours provoked a spiritual and ideological *crisis for Kamei, who began to doubt the validity both of Marxist principles and of rapid Westernization. In the aftermath of the war Kamei developed a new ideology that combined traditional Japanese values with what he perceived to be the shared ideals of all Asian nations.*

RETURN TO THE EAST

One of the problems with which Japanese have been burdened since the Meiji Era has been the necessity of examining Japan's place in Asia and our special fate as Asians. Japan, as everyone knows, was the first country in Asia to become 'modernized', but it is not yet clear what meaning this modernization had for Asia. It is also a question whether Asian thought, which possesses strong traditions despite the repeated taste of defeat and a sense of inferiority before Western science, is

Japanese representatives leave the USS *Missouri* after signing the instruments of surrender, 2 September 1945. Japan was now an occupied nation, subject to American political, economic, and military control. Courtesy of the National Archives (NWDNS-80-D-472629).

doomed to perish without further struggle, or if it is capable of reviving in the twentieth century and contributing something which will enable us to surmount the present crisis. We must begin to consider these questions. In contrast with the fervour with which Europeanization has been pursued since the Meiji Era, this aspect of our lives has been extraordinarily neglected. I believe that the neglect—or perhaps one should say ingratitude—shown by Japanese towards Asia is the tragedy of modern Japan, and that to study it has become since the defeat the greatest responsibility incumbent on us.

It is true, of course, that 'Asia' covers an immense area, and undoubtedly contains many 'spiritual kingdoms' with which I am unfamiliar. I myself have never actually journeyed through Asia; I have not so much as glimpsed it with my own eyes. The best I have been able to do is to imagine what Asia is like by means of the books I have read. Nevertheless, looking back on Japanese history has revealed to me that in every age Asia has breathed in the minds of Japanese. We are all familiar with how Asian culture, transformed or more highly refined, became part of the flesh and blood of Japanese culture. However, like most young men of the past sixty or seventy years, I used not to consider Asia as being necessarily primary to us. My ignorance of and indifference to China and India did not trouble me in the least, and I was constantly fascinated by Europe. I thought that to learn from European knowledge was our first task, and I neglected the matter of learning from the wisdom of the East.

There was something even more seriously wrong with my attitude. My ignorance and indifference with respect to China and India might still have been pardoned if they had been no more than that, but to them in fact was joined a feeling of contempt for those countries. Since the defeat I have come to recognize the fact that it was a fatal error for us to have allowed such a feeling to attain the status of a deep-seated national prejudice.

Japan, thanks to the fact that she was the first country in the Orient to become 'modernized' (or perhaps on account of her modern military strength), began from about the time of the Russo–Japanese War to entertain attitudes of extreme superiority towards the peoples of Asia. This feeling, we must remember, was the reverse of the medal of our feeling of inferiority towards the Europeans, and it came to express itself in a kind of brutality towards the other Asian peoples. We cannot deny that we tended to look on them as our slaves. When and how the fate of Japanese as Asians went astray is the most significant problem of our modern history.

'Asia is one. The Himalayas divide, only to accentuate, two mighty civilizations, the Chinese with its communism of Confucius, and the Indian with its individualism of the Vedas. But not even the snowy barriers can interrupt for one moment that broad expanse of love for the Ultimate and Universal, which is the common thought-inheritance of every Asian race, enabling them to produce all the great religions of the world, and distinguishing them from those maritime peoples of the Mediterranean and the Baltic, who love to dwell on the Particular, and to search out the means, not the end, of life.'[1]

'[The average Westerner] was wont to regard Japan as barbarous while she indulged in the gentle arts of peace: he calls her civilized since she began to commit wholesale slaughter on Manchurian battlefields. Much comment has been given lately to the Code of the Samurai—the Art of Death which makes our soldiers exult in self-sacrifice; but scarcely any attention has been paid to Teaism,[2] which represents so much of our Art of Life. Fain we would remain barbarians, if our claim to civilization were to be based on the gruesome glory of war. Fain would we await the time when due respect shall be paid to our art and ideals.'[3]

'What mean these strange combinations which Europe displays—the hospital and the torpedo, the Christian missionary and imperialism, the maintenance of vast armaments as a guarantee of peace? Such contradictions did not exist in the ancient civilization of the East. Such were not the ideals of the Japanese Restoration; such is not the goal of her reformation. The night of the Orient, which had hidden us in its folds, has been lifted, but we find the world still in the dusk of humanity, Europe has taught us war; when shall she learn the blessings of peace?'[4]

These words were pronounced about the time of the Russo–Japanese War. They voice profound doubts and resistance on the part of one Oriental to certain important aspects of the modern European civilization which was then penetrating eastwards. This situation was not confined to Japan. There should have been common outcries made by men in India, China, and Japan, as Orientals. There should at least have been outcries which would have linked Gandhi and Tagore, Sun Yat-sen and Lu Hsün, and Okakura—outcries of surprise and alarm, or of doubt, or of malediction, or of resistance to the European conquest of Asia.

It should certainly be a matter of the profoundest regret to the Orient that these outcries uttered in the nineteenth and twentieth centuries as Asians, in inflections which varied with the particular features of the different countries of Asia, should never have achieved full expression, but should have died out without reinforcing one another. To us Japanese the most important fact is that the responsibility for causing these voices to die out rests with us. The cause of the tragedy lies in our vigorous, precipitous modernization. We tried with desperate efforts to master European civilization, and in the act of acquiring it we lost something very precious—what I should like to call the characteristic 'love' of Asia.

We cannot ignore the fact that this responsibility is connected with the singularity of our racial transformation. The period between the appearance of Perry's 'black ships' at the end of the shogunate, and the completion of the battleship

Yamato was a period when Japan was changing with extraordinary rapidity into 'the West within the East'. Indeed, if one were asked for what Japan poured out her strength most lavishly, and to what she devoted the finest flower of her scientific abilities during the years following the Meiji Restoration, one would have to answer that it was for warships. This emphasis on armaments must certainly have had its origins in the profound anxiety of our grandfathers who had seen before their eyes the nations of Asia being colonized, one after the other.

It undoubtedly represented an astonishing burst of energy displayed for the sake of national independence and self-defence, but, as fate would have it, the raw materials of the continent were necessary to it. One gets the feeling that in the matter of raw materials and the acquisition of markets Japan was hastily and sometimes crudely imitating the colonial policies of the European nations. We, first among the Asians, mastered the weapons which modern European civilization had employed to invade Asia in pursuit of its colonial policies, and we turned the points of these weapons on Asians. The modernization of Japan would have been impossible had we not victimized China and estranged ourselves from her. Japan has experienced this contradiction at least as an historical fact. The high development of the intellectual curiosity of the Japanese has often been mentioned, but this virtue has been accompanied on the Asian mainland by deadly vice.

This is not the only contradiction. There were during this same period quite a few men like Okakura Kakuzō who preached love for Asia. Indeed, one thing which surprises us when we read the history of Japan during the past half-century is how often the phrase 'to secure the peace of Asia' was used by statesmen. The invasion of China, in fact, was carried out in the name of this principle. In the midst of the so-called Greater East Asia War, I myself believed in Okakura's words and approved of the war because of them. What can this mean?

Every war, inevitably, has its fine slogans which serve as its intellectual adornment. But in my case this was not the whole story. As I have already mentioned, there was in me a deep-seated contempt for the other Asian peoples, a contempt nourished in Japan from about the time of the Russo–Japanese War; one may say that I had become imbued with the conqueror mentality. I could as an overlord of Asia preach with equanimity the love of Asia. And yet it was of course true that Okakura's words were meaningful only so long as Japan did not invade any Asian country.

Japan carried out the European method of conquest: confronting other countries with weapons in one hand and a gospel of love in the other. Warships and Christianity were indivisible elements in the European conquest of Asia; Japan slaughtered people while preaching the love of Asia and the Way of the Gods.

What was the result? Japan became in the East the stepchild of the West, and as a consequence seems now to be fated to become this time the stepchild of the East. The intellectual energy which the Japanese showed when once they had received the baptism of modern Europe was undoubtedly the wonder of Asia, but it imposed strange contradictions on Japan.

One of these, it may be imagined, results from the fact that Japan is an island nation. Japan is assuredly a part of Asia, but it is a special area separated from the continent and, perhaps, though Asian should not really be called Asian at all. Sometimes I have found myself wondering along these lines. Of course Japan is not the West either. While on the one hand preserving in a uniquely assimilated form the various systems of thought and arts of the East, she has an insatiable intellectual curiosity which would make all of the West her own. Has ever a people harboured such frantic contradictions: impetuosity and

caution, confusion and harmony, division and unity—and all of them changing at every instant? I have sometimes wondered whether Japan may not be the unique example in the world of a kind of 'nation in the experimental stage'. It was this island nation's knowledge which, in response to a ceaseless impulsion towards Europe, perpetrated the multi-sided betrayal of Asia.

At the same time—and one may also speak of this as a result—the defeat of Japan brought about the independence of the nations of Asia. The long European rule of Asia either collapsed or was shaken at its very roots. This, together with the revolution in China, represents the greatest event occasioned by the Second World War; one may indeed say that it effected an immense upheaval in world history. A further result, one can probably say, was the ironic one that European capitalism, after playing its part in Japan, should have met this fate in the other countries of Asia because of Japan. Japan, it needs hardly be mentioned, lost all the territory she had gained through aggression.

However, an important factor came into being at this juncture. Now, for the first time in modern Japanese history, Japan was furnished with the conditions of being able to deal with the nations of Asia on terms of equality—not as conqueror or conquered, but on a genuinely equal footing. I should like to lay emphasis on this factor for which our defeat was responsible. The basis for Japanese independence is to be found here—by which I mean that it is the only ethical basis we have for independence.

The true meaning of what I am attempting to discuss under the theme of 'return to the East' may be said in the final analysis to be the product of a sense of guilt towards the East. The only qualification we have for a 'return' is a sense of guilt, particularly towards China and Korea. This is not a question of who holds political power in these countries. A more fundamental question is the recognition of guilt for former aggression towards the peoples of Asia. We must abandon completely the consciousness of being 'leaders' in Asia. I should like to consider the return to Asia as an ethical rather than as a political question.

As a basis for this return Japanese traditions must be scrutinized afresh: how has what Okakura called the 'common inheritance of every Asiatic race' been transmitted from ancient times to the present, and should it be passed on in the future? A re-examination of Buddhism, Confucianism, and Taoism as they exist in Japan, together with a general re-examination of the characteristically Japanese types of learning and art as they have been influenced by these teachings, must be undertaken. I should like to call attention to the steady achievements of men in the fields of anthropology, Japanese literature, Chinese studies, and Buddhist studies. It is a question of the *roots* of the tree onto which European culture has been grafted, and this re-examination is essential if we are to discover the 'individuality' of modern Japan which gives a native character to all our thought.

At the same time there has never been a greater need than today for intellectual interchange among the nations of Asia. Some interchange, however slight, has begun with India, but Japan must seek out opportunities throughout the whole of Asia to discover what the possibilities are of 'Eastern spirit'. However long it may take, I believe that a deepening of intellectual interchange should be made a basic policy. And may we not say, the primary goal should be the discovery of a possibility of common spiritual association in the East. This is the prerequisite for the establishment of a new image of the Asian.

There are in Asia Buddhism, Mohammedanism, Christianity, Communism. European influence also remains powerful. Various systems of thinking thus exist, but they are backed by a characteristically Asian quality, and there is unquestionably one way of thought in which they are all unified through a process of 'Asianization'. This is what we must look for. However, in so doing we must free ourselves from any infantile notions such as the simple schematization formerly in vogue here, according to which the East stood for the spirit and the West for material things. Indeed, the return to the East must not be accompanied by prejudices directed again the West or any form of xenophobia. In fact, it should result in the destruction of the very sense of opposition between East and West which figured so prominently in our former ideas.

Notes

1. Okakura Kakuzō, *The Ideals of the East*, 1; Okakura Kakuzō (1862–1913) lived for many years in the United States; however, his writings on Japanese development advocated a celebration of traditional Japanese values.
2. The cult of the tea ceremony.
3. Okakura, *The Book of Tea*, 7–8.
4. Okakura, *The Awakening of Japan*, 223.

Study Question

1. If Japan had, in 1868, followed the course Kamei advocates, what might the outcome have been?

CHITOSHI YANAGA

Chitoshi Yanaga (1903–85) was born in Hawaii but was sent to Japan to study as a child. As a result he witnessed one of the most important eras *in Japan's modernization—the era of massive industrialization and the onset of imperial conquests. Returning to the United States in his twenties, Yanaga earned a doctoral degree in political science from Berkeley. After the Second World War, Yanaga taught at Yale while studying the relationship between Japanese business, education, and politics. His 1968 study on the role of big business during the Japanese 'economic miracle' influenced American policy towards Japan. In the following excerpt Yanaga discusses the interrelationship among business, politics, education, and banking in Japan.*

BIG BUSINESS IN JAPANESE POLITICS

One of the characteristics of Japanese society is the existence of a number of rather exclusive groupings. . . . Such cliques or groups provide the oasis of the power structure. In the prewar period, power was exercised by three distinct cliques, the financial (*zaibatsu*), bureaucratic (*kambatsu*), and military (*gumbatsu*), but in the postwar period the military and the financial cliques have ceased to exist. Only the bureaucratic clique has retained its power. Zaibatsu has been superseded by *zaikai* (the business leader clique). Two other groups. . .

have come into prominence, namely, the extended family clique (*keibatsu*) and the university clique (*gakubatsu*). . . .

Although no longer recognized as a basic legal unit, the family is still the touchstone of social success. The importance of family background or connections in achieving success in almost any field has not diminished. On the contrary, it seems to have increased greatly. More than ever, family status (*iegara*) and pedigree (*kenami*) are necessary qualifications for membership in high

The postwar relationship between Japan and the US was symbolized by this 1971 visit by Emperor Hirohito and Empress Nagaka to the United States during the Nixon presidency. Courtesy of National Archives, Richard Nixon Library.

society and for achieving a position of prestige and influence in business and politics, even in academic life.

Candidates for important posts are judged on the basis of family ties. When a new governor of the Bank of Japan was appointed in late 1964, press and public approval was on the basis of the appointee's family background rather than on his ability, which was widely recognized. If one's pedigree is not the best, it is always possible to improve it by marrying into the right family. Such ties are widely sought, especially in the business community. Chances for such marriages are greatly enhanced for men who have acquired a quality education, such as graduation from the prestigious Tokyo University, which is open to all solely on the basis of ability. Bright young graduates of the best universities are always in demand as husbands for daughters of influential business and political leaders. When one already has a good pedigree, it is possible to improve it socially and financially by acquiring a degree from an elite school. Marital ties are often established to enhance the position, prestige, and power of the families as well as the individuals involved. . . .

The unique character of the university clique is responsible for the influence wielded by the graduates of Tokyo University in business, politics, and government as well as in higher education, science, technology, and medicine. Ever since its establishment in 1886, Tokyo University has inculcated in its students a strong sense of elitism and leadership. In light of the incredibly difficult entrance examinations, it is not surprising that its graduates feel superior, even though in many instances such an attitude is not justified in terms of academic achievement. The university was founded specifically for the purpose of training government officials. Upon graduation, its early graduates were given the privilege of immediate appointment, without examination, to the newly created higher civil service. This established a tradition of administrative elitism; until the end

of World War I the cream of the Tokyo Imperial University graduates went into government service. In no time the university had established undisputed supremacy in higher education. It attracted the best students from all over the nation, and students have been flocking to it ever since.

Tōdai—as Tokyo University is commonly known—is in a sense a most exclusive club, membership in which establishes eligibility for the highest positions in the realm. Of the ten postwar prime ministers between 1945 and 1965, seven were Tōdai graduates (Shidehara, Katayama, Ashida, Yoshida, Hatoyama, Kishi, and Satō). . . .

One of the most distinctive features of Japan's power structure is the extraordinarily high concentration of power wielders in Tokyo. Here, in the world's largest city, a supermetropolis of over eleven million people and the seat of the national government, are located the main offices of practically all the major corporations, making it the business, banking, financial, transportation, communication, publishing, and mass media center of Japan. All political parties, labour unions, and trade associations have their national headquarters here. The leading universities, research institutes, museums, art galleries, theatres, radio and television broadcasting systems, and the country's six largest newspapers are located in Tokyo. All major political and economic decisions are made in this city. It is as if Washington, DC, New York, Chicago, Philadelphia, Pittsburgh, Boston, and Detroit were rolled into one.

Such a concentration of power is unknown in the United States. To create an analogous situation, it would be necessary to locate the head offices of America's hundred largest corporations in Washington, DC, together with their presidents, board chairmen, and directors, many of whom would be related by marriage not only to each other but to influential political leaders and government administrators. Furthermore these top-level executives would, for the most part, claim the same alma mater, belong to the same country clubs, have ready access to government offices, maintain daily contact with government officials by phone or over the luncheon table, enjoy intimate relations with influential senators and congressmen, and also serve on government advisory bodies and administrative commissions. The impact of this sort of concentration of political, economic, and social power on the governing process can indeed be far-reaching. . . .

Unlike the old zaibatsu, which dominated the prewar economic scene under a system of highly centralized family control through holding companies, the new postwar big business structure is composed of enterprise groups. These groups are of two kinds: those organized around the former zaibatsu and using the old names (Mitsubishi with thirty-eight separate corporations and a research institute; Mitsui with twenty-two corporations; Sumitomo with fifteen corporations) and those held together by large banks (Fuji, formerly Yasuda; Dai Ichi; and the Industrial Bank of Japan, through which the enterprises in both groups manage their financing).

These groups, known as *keiretsu*, cannot be described in American business terms. They are not really monopolies, since they compete with each other strongly and no one group completely dominates a given field. Actually they are horizontal groups of companies, each group containing many varied industries as well as a bank, a trust company, insurance companies, a trade company (or companies), and a real estate company. Member companies tend to cooperate with other companies within the group and to compete with companies outside the group. When entering new fields such as atomic energy or petrochemicals, where investment requirements are beyond the capability of any one company in the group, several or most members will combine to finance the venture jointly. The groups vary in cohesiveness. With each group, the bank is the primary though not the sole source of banking support. The group's trading company handles the sales, particularly export trading, and the purchase of raw materials, but not exclusively. Policy coordination is achieved through presidents' clubs which meet periodically.

These enterprise groups represent the postwar restructuring of big business on the basis of common interests, the better to cope with common problems in such fields as production, sales, and financing.

> **Study Question**
>
> 1. Why was the interlocking system of *batsu* so effective in the late 1950s and 1960s? What are the dangers of such a system?

SUVENDRINI KAKUCHI

Suvendrini Kakuchi began her career in journalism in her native Sri Lanka. She moved to Japan to study Japanese culture and language, after which she worked as a correspondent for a number of publications, reporting on events related to Japan and the broader East Asian region. In 1997 she was awarded a Nieman Fellowship in order to study the impact of civil war on children. Here, Kakuchi reports on the social impact of the economic collapse in Japan at the end of the 1990s.

AMID RECESSION THE NEW POOR DEMAND SAFETY NETS

TOKYO, Sep 11 (IPS)—Raita Taguchi, an economics graduate from prestigious Keio University, thought he had embarked on a stable career when he joined Kankaku, a leading securities company, 10 years ago.

But he lost his job three years after starting work as the firm reeled from the drastic fall of the Nikkei, Japan's stock market, from a high of 38,000 in 1987 to less than 20,000 five years later.

'I was asked to politely leave in 1991 as part of the company's restructuring programme to meet revenue losses,' he recalled.

Still, Taguchi was luckier than others and landed a job at the computer section of Ebara Corp, which deals with machinery and plant equipment.

Almost eight years later, Japan's grim economic picture has upset Taguchi's life once more. As Asian economies collapsed around Japan, Ebara, which has manufacturing firms in six of them, got the jitters. Taguchi lost his job in January.

But this time, Taguchi is not content to just sit by. In April he joined Network Union, a trade union formed to help Japan's increasing number of unemployed young people, and is suing Ebara for unfair dismissal.

'People must be treated differently from commodities. Hard workers must not be forced to take the brunt of a recession that is caused by bad management and unfair policies that were enforced as a result of greed,' Taguchi explained.

He argues that the company could have cut back on other sectors first before resorting to lay-offs. Taguchi considers himself a victim of Japan's high-growth policies, which often included bureaucrat-led excessive production and consumption, and bred corruption.

Today, people like him feel Japan is in an economic rut, the subject of desperate efforts at revival but locked in recession and headed, many say, for a deflationary cycle.

Amid recession, distressed companies need more credit but banks are unable to respond because their client firms are in turn unable to repay loans. Firms are hard pressed too because demand is falling and people are holding on to their savings, forcing companies to cut back on investments and fire staff.

These form a destructive cycle that weakens Japan's economy further, and is starting to take a toll on a population that for a long time did not have to worry about hard times.

Taguchi, part of the growing ranks of the unemployed, is quite a new social phenomenon in the world's second richest country.

In May, the Management and Coordination Agency reported that unemployment stood at 4.2 per cent, or 2.93 million in a country of 126 million people. That is Japan's highest jobless level since the Pacific War.

The worst hit are workers between 45 and 54 years of age, but the report cites a new phenomenon in the rise of unemployment among younger workers. The media estimates this number to be almost 8.4 per cent, up from 7.1 per cent last year.

Last week, Hitachi, one of Japan's largest manufacturers of electric machinery and semiconductors, said it expects a group loss of 1.8 billion U.S. dollars for the fiscal year ending March 1999, its first loss ever.

This is the largest crisis since Hitachi was established in 1920, President Tsutomu Kanai said. The company plans to lay off 4,000 workers, bringing to 66,000 the number of staff it has fired.

Likewise, Japan has just seen the biggest collapse of a manufacturer since the Pacific War—in the fall of Toa Steel Co which said it would liquidate at the end of this fiscal year.

Japan's slump is extremely severe, said Taichi Sakaiya, the new head of the Economic Planning

Agency. He predicted growth for 1998 at between 0.5 per cent and minus 0.5 per cent.

Japan is in the throes of an eight-year recession. Production fell by 5.3 per cent last year and personal and corporate bankruptcies are rising. In June alone, reports the private Tokyo Shoko Research company, the number of corporate collapses was 1,736, a 36 per cent rise from May.

Domestic demand remains stagnant despite government attempts to stimulate spending. Household spending in July was around 2,448.59 dollars, down by 3.4 per cent, marking the ninth straight year-on-year decline.

Small and medium firms that comprise [the] majority of bankruptcies are folding up since banks do not [have] enough resources to lend. Interest rates were cut further on Wednesday, but some analysts fear the economy is in such bad shape it is not responding as expected by picking up consumption.

With more trouble coming, more people in this affluent society are realising the need for social safety nets and are calling for a review of the same growth policies largely responsible for Japan's progress since the Pacific War.

'What we need is a new concept,' said Yasuhiko Shibata, a senior fellow at the Yomuiri Research Institute. 'It's important to establish a system that would enable us to survive in the next century and develop mechanisms to prevent further environmental destruction and to use our limited resources efficiently.'

Faced with the social costs of this economic depression, the government of Prime Minister Keizo Obuchi is having to struggle with new proposals that no longer focus solely on growth.

While the government has promised to revitalise the economy by the year 2000 by enacting reform that would hasten deregulation, it is also introducing measures to ease the burden on the public.

Japan's system is sometimes called Japanese socialism, because it seeks to give economic security to everyone, for instance through the system of seniority in wage systems.

But this is likely to change as Japan ... undertakes more privatisation and deregulation under the label of economic reforms. In fact, Japanese media have been airing public concern about the risks of failure due to cut-throat competition.

The government has proposed an income tax as a way of dealing with growing economic burdens, but critics find this a stopgap measure at best.

Recent media surveys show that people want improved social infrastructure, criticising Tokyo's emphasis on public works when they say the need is for housing, education and welfare.

The government's role is to ensure social fairness for the sake of social stability. It is imperative to ensure that in a period of low economic growth, no one falls through the cracks, the *Asahi Shimbun* daily argued recently, reflecting how high social concerns have climbed amid recession.

Study Question

1. Can a country provide economic security to all of its citizens and still remain competitive in the global economy?

TIPS FOR ANALYSIS

What information was available to the author?

It is very difficult to read an historical document without applying the benefit of hindsight. We know far more than the author did regarding the circumstances and the outcome of the event under discussion. However, it is also important to ask yourself, What could the author have known at the time? Was there a resolution to the situation about which he or she writes? Or was the author writing in the middle of a series of events? In both cases, the information available to the author will have a direct impact on the nature of the document.

WEB RESOURCES

John Fairbank Memorial Chinese History Virtual Library
http://www.cnd.org/fairbank
Mao Tse-tung (Zedong) Internet Library
http://www.marx2mao.com/Mao/Index.html
Historical Text Archive: Japan
http://historicaltextarchive.com/links.php?action=links&cid=5&sid=13
World History Archives: The History of East Asia
http://www.hartford-hwp.com/archives/55/index.html

RECOMMENDED READING

China

Dai Sijie, *Balzac and the Little Chinese Seamstress* (New York: Anchor, 2002). *Balzac and the Little Chinese Seamstress* is the tale of two friends who have been exiled to a remote mountain village for re-education. The novel, set during the Cultural Revolution, examines the survival skills that the friends develop as well as the lessons they learn from their horrific experience. The author himself experienced re-education and was exiled to France in 1984.

Mo Yan, *Big Breasts and Wide Hips* (New York: Arcade Publishing, 2004). Mo Yan's controversial novel covers a broad sweep of Chinese history, from the late Qing years to the post-Mao era. The book—divided into seven chapters, representing each major time period—focuses on strong female characters, including the central character of Mother. The book won awards in the People's Republic, but was quickly banned for its 'immorality'.

Wang Meng, *Bolshevik Salute* (Washington, DC: University of Washington Press, 1990). *Bolshevik Salute* is a fictionalized version of Wang's life as a devoted follower of the revolution in Mao's China. Wang was purged in the anti-Rightist Campaign of 1957 and rehabilitated in 1979; the story explores alienation, political identity, and betrayal. After his rehabilitation Wang served as China's Minister of Culture, but was removed in 1989 following the Tiananmen Square demonstrations.

Yu Hua, *To Live: A Novel* (New York: Anchor, 2003). Set during the revolutionary transformation of Chinese society, *To Live* follows one ordinary man, Fugui, through his life as a member of the landlord class, then as a soldier, then a simple farmer, as the turmoil of China's transformation impacts him and his family over some thirty years.

Japan

Saiichi Maruya, *Singular Rebellion* (New York: Kodansha America, 1990). Set in 1969, the year of student rebellions, *Singular Rebellion* tells the story of one businessman whose single act of rebellion is to marry a younger woman. Maruya examines the consequences that follow from that one decision.

Haruki Murakami, *The Wind-up Bird Chronicle* (New York: Vintage, 1998). Murakami's novel explores postwar Japanese society and the pivotal issue of identity. The author examines the underside of modern Japan, reflecting back through the prewar period and the experience of war, to the repressed memory, the guilt, and the general state of modern society.

RECOMMENDED VIEWING

China

River Without Buoys (China, 1983). Director: Wu Tianming. Filmed in the early years of the Deng Xiaoping era, as the aftereffects of the Cultural Revolution were still being felt, Wu's film deals with the devastation caused by the Cultural Revolution. The film's symbolic story focuses on a group of refugees fleeing persecution by raft only to be faced by a series of challenges from the river itself.

The Blue Kite (China/Hong Kong, 1993). Director: Tian Zhuangzhuang. Focusing on the fate of one family between the early 1950s and late 1960s, Tian Zhuangzhuang shows the human impact of the campaigns to remake China including the Rectification Movement, the Great Leap Forward, and the Cultural Revolution.

Good Men, Good Women (Japan/Taiwan, 1995). Director: Hou Hsiao-Hsien. *Good Men, Good Women*—loosely based on actual events—is set in Taiwan, after Chiang Kai-shek fled Mainland China. It highlights the US-backed anti-Communist campaign launched by Chiang Kai-shek in the early 1950s, and the subsequent unwillingness of the Taiwanese government to address this period in its history.

Zhantai (Hong Kong/Japan/France, 2000). Director: Jia Zhang Ke. *Zhantai* captures the uncertainty of the transition from Maoism to economic liberalization under Deng, revealing the clash between traditional values and the introduction of western elements.

Japan

Night and Fog in Japan (Japan, 1960). Director: Nagisa Oshima. *Night and Fog in Japan* is an examination of left-wing politics in Japan, centred on opposition to the US–Japan Security Treaty. It reveals the divisions inherent on the left and their inability to bring about real changes in Japanese society. It also provides insights into postwar Japanese politics and society, as well as the complex reactions to American occupation.

Asia Rising (UK/USA, 1999). Director: Bill Treharne Jones/WGBH Boston/BBC (Documentary). This documentary examines the postwar rise of Korea and Japan to global economic power, focusing on the economic 'miracles' in both countries and the path taken to achieve that success in the 1950s and 1960s.

CHAPTER ELEVEN

ANTI-COLONIAL MOVEMENTS AND INDEPENDENCE

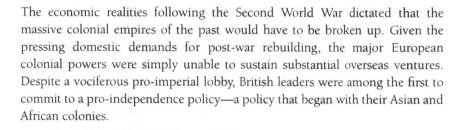

The economic realities following the Second World War dictated that the massive colonial empires of the past would have to be broken up. Given the pressing domestic demands for post-war rebuilding, the major European colonial powers were simply unable to sustain substantial overseas ventures. Despite a vociferous pro-imperial lobby, British leaders were among the first to commit to a pro-independence policy—a policy that began with their Asian and African colonies.

Road construction in Congo after independence. Projects such as this demonstrated the UN's desire to ensure a successful transition to independence. Courtesy of the United Nations Photo Library (74797/UN/DPI/B. Zarov).

French and Belgian leaders, on the other hand, remained reluctant to acknowledge colonial demands for independence and preferred to view their colonies, and their inherent economic obligations, as an integral part of their territorial sovereignty. As a result, France became embroiled in a series of costly wars of independence, most importantly in Indochina and Algeria, the combination of which would eventually lead to the collapse of the Fourth Republic.

In the colonies the early decolonization movement was viewed, for the most part, with enthusiasm. Western educated elites would assume control and govern largely in the traditions established by the former colonizers. This enthusiasm, however, did not last. The colonial era had created and magnified a series of barely contained tensions. After the colonizers left, economic grievances, boundary disputes, problems of ethnicity often related to the post-colonial distribution of power, and any number of related issues served to destabilize the newly independent governments. Military intervention intended to contain these conflicts often undermined any chance for successful civilian governance.

Several regions of the world, despite the trend towards independence, remained under colonial domination. South Africa was the most obvious example. Though Great Britain had granted South Africa dominion status in 1910, power had ultimately passed to the Afrikaner minority—descendents of the region's original Dutch settlers—rather than to the black African majority. This left the vast majority of South Africa's population under what was perceived as colonial rule. Stubbornly resisting demands to moderate their policy of apartheid, or legal segregation, South Africa's leaders withdrew from the British Commonwealth in 1961 and imposed increasingly draconian restrictions on their black African, Asian, and racially mixed populations. The refusal of either superpower to intervene actively, combined with South Africa's tremendous economic resources, enabled the apartheid system to sustain itself—with dire consequences for the indigenous population—until the 1990s.

The documents in this chapter begin with the United Nations Declaration on Colonial Independence, which was issued in 1960. The Declaration called upon all nations to relinquish their colonial possessions immediately. However, it was not at all clear that decolonization would be the order of the day. Men such as Paul Ramadier, Prime Minister of France, argued vehemently that colonialism must continue because it provided innumerable benefits to the colonized peoples. In response, groups such as the National Liberation Front (FLN) in Algeria emerged, determined to fight for freedom from colonial rule. Sekou Touré assesses the aftermath of the French colonial era in Guinea.

In Britain, despite a limited, if vocal, core of support for continued colonial ventures, Labour Prime Minister Clement Attlee set his nation firmly on the road to decolonization. India would be the first British territory to gain full independence in the postwar era. Jawaharlal Nehru's speech on the eve of Indian independence captures both the excitement of the hour and the challenges ahead. Kwame Nkrumah speaks of the necessity of unity in order to recover from the damage of the colonial era. The final documents in this chapter focus upon South Africa and the evolution, and eventual destruction, of the apartheid regime. A.L. Geyer puts forward arguments in defence of the policy, while Desmond Tutu argues for its destruction.

UNITED NATIONS

On 14 December 1960 the United Nations General Assembly adopted Resolution 1514: Declaration on the Granting of Independence to Colonial Countries and Peoples. Though the process of decolonization was well underway by 1960, numerous peoples remained under colonial or neo-colonial rule. Thus the Declaration has been invoked on many occasions in support of nascent independence movements. The contemporary reader should recall, however, that a General Assembly resolution carries little weight under international law.

UN DECLARATION ON COLONIAL INDEPENDENCE

The General Assembly

Mindful of the determination proclaimed by the peoples of the world in the Charter of the United Nations to reaffirm faith in fundamental human rights, in the dignity and worth of the human person, in the equal rights of men and women and of nations large and small, and to promote social progress and better standards of life in larger freedom,

Conscious of the need for the creation of conditions of stability and well-being and peaceful and friendly relations based on respect for the principles of equal rights and self-determination of all peoples, and of universal respect for, and observance of, human rights and fundamental freedoms for all without distinction as to race, sex, language, or religion,

Recognizing the passionate yearning for freedom in all dependent peoples and the decisive role of such peoples in the attainment of their independence,

Aware of the increasing conflicts resulting from the denial of or impediments in the way of the freedom of such peoples, which constitute a serious threat to world peace,

Considering the important role of the United Nations in assisting the movement for independence in Trust and Non-Self-Governing Territories,

Recognizing that the people of the world ardently desire the end of colonialism in all its manifestations,

Convinced that the continued existence of colonialism prevents the development of international economic co-operation, impedes the social, cultural, and economic development of dependent peoples and militates against the United Nations ideal of universal peace,

Affirming that peoples may, for their own ends, freely dispose of their natural wealth and resources without prejudice to any obligations arising out of international economic co-operation, based upon the principle of mutual benefit, and the international law,

Believing that the process of liberation is irresistible and irreversible and that, in order to avoid serious crises, an end must be put to colonialism and all practices of segregation and discrimination associated therewith,

Welcoming the emergence in recent years of a large number of dependent territories into freedom and independence, and recognizing the increasingly powerful trends towards freedom in such territories which have not yet attained independence,

Convinced that all peoples have an inalienable right to complete freedom, the exercise of their sovereignty and the integrity of their national territory,

Solemnly proclaims the necessity of bringing to a speedy and unconditional end colonialism in all its forms and manifestations;

And to this end

Declares that:

1. The subjection of peoples to alien subjugation, domination, and exploitation constitutes a denial of fundamental human rights, is contrary to the Charter of the United Nations and is an impediment to the promotion of world peace and co-operation.

2. All peoples have the right to self-determination; by virtue of that right they freely determine their political status and freely pursue their economic, social and cultural development.

3. Inadequacy of political, economic, social, or educational preparedness should never serve as a pretext for delaying independence.

4. All armed action or repressive measures of all kinds directed against dependent peoples shall cease in order to enable them to exercise peacefully and freely their right to complete independence, and the integrity of their national territory shall be respected.

5. Immediate steps shall be taken, in Trust and Non-Self-Governing Territories or all other territories which have not yet attained independence, to transfer all powers to the peoples of those territories, without any conditions or reservations, in accordance with their freely expressed will and desire, without any distinction as to race, creed, or colour, in order to enable them to enjoy complete independence and freedom.

6. Any attempt aimed at the partial or total disruption of the national unity and the territorial integrity of a country is incompatible with the purposes and principles of the Charter of the United Nations.

7. All States shall observe faithfully and strictly the provisions of the Charter of the United Nations, the Universal Declaration of Human Rights, and the present Declaration on the basis of equality, noninterference in the internal affairs of all States, and respect for the sovereign rights of all peoples and their territorial integrity.

Study Question

1. The Declaration affirms 'all peoples have the right to self-determination'. In what ways could this be seen as a potential source of instability in the post-colonial era?

PAUL RAMADIER

Most nations in postwar Europe considered imperial obligations to be a cost that they could no longer afford. However, postwar French governments, *including those on the left, stridently defended their right to re-occupy their colonial possessions. The following speech to the National Assembly was made by Socialist Prime Minister Paul Ramadier (1888–1961). There are various references throughout the speech to 'applause from the right' and so on. In the French National Assembly deputies are seated from right to left (from conservative to communist) according to their political ideology. Shortly after this speech deputies from the French Communist Party (PCF) were expelled from government.*

◇

Speech to the National Assembly, 18 March 1947

The Prime Minister (Ramadier): Ladies and gentlemen, two things are certain, affirmed by all and should be considered as unanimous conclusions of this debate.

The first is that France must stay in Indochina, that her succession there is not in question and that she must carry out there her civilizing work. *(Applause from the left, centre, and right.)*

The second is that the old ways are over. They have been criticized; they have been praised. There have assuredly been excesses. There have also been glorious pages written. A work has been accomplished which no one can deny, least of all probably those in the ranks of our opponents who came to gain their culture from our hands. *(Applause from the same benches.)* These are two certain facts, two established principles. Faced with the situation in Indochina we have wanted to have a policy of understanding. . . . Perhaps we have been carried away too quickly by the events; we have treated, we have negotiated. For almost a year, from March 6 until the morning of December 19, we have not ceased to negotiate.

The Overseas Minister (Moutet): Very good!

The Prime Minister: And then, on the 19th of December, we were obliged to recognize that the negotiations, even the accords, did not settle everything and that certain acts of violence, of savagery, tore up all the accords and ruined any thought of conciliation.

I have here, ladies and gentlemen, photographs of the mutilated bodies found in the burned-out houses of Hanoi. But perhaps more than any other act of savagery, the total destruction of the Pasteur Institute is the symbol of a wild, destructive will which is not, I am sure, that of the Vietnamese people, but of certain men.[1]

We were then obliged to fight.

Everyone has accepted this struggle, from the time of Léon Blum's Government just as at the moment, on January 21, when I made my declaration before the National Assembly.[2] *(Applause from the left, centre, and right.)*

At that time I said: 'We cannot accept that the peace be disturbed. We must protect the life and the goods of those Frenchmen, foreigners and our Indochinese friends who put their confidence in French liberty. We must assure the security of our forts, reestablish essential communications and insure the security of the people who seek refuge with us.'

This we have done.

The Government has sent the necessary reinforcements. We have sent them in force and as fast as we could. Not all have yet left. The departures continue. But already we can confirm the results.

And it is here that I want to render homage to our Far East Expeditionary Forces, to those soldiers who fight in a climate they are not used to, with a French faith which allows them to hold and to advance under the most difficult circumstances.

They have shown their heroism. France should express her gratitude. *(Prolonged applause from the left, centre, and right. The deputies seated on those benches rise.)*

(Numerous voices from the right and centre call to the extreme left [i.e., to the Communists] 'Get up!' From the centre: 'It is a disgrace to remain seated!')

René Pleven: I see that the Minister of Defence [Billoux, a Communist] has not risen. (*Exclamations from the extreme left.*)

Florimond Bonte [Communist]: It is we who defend the lives of our soldiers. We are not at your command! (*Exclamations from the right.*)

The President: The Prime Minister has the floor. It is to him alone at this time to express the sentiment of the Assembly and the country.

The Prime Minister: France should render homage to those who have fallen. France should render homage to those who fight and who continue to fight. (*Applause from the left, centre, and right. The deputies seated on those benches rise again.*)

Fernand Bouxom: France rises!

The Prime Minister: She can proudly recognize the results obtained. We were speaking of forts it was necessary to open, of communication lines to reestablish along the Chinese border between Langson and the sea. Communications have been reestablished. From Hanoi to Haiphong, the road is open. A clever and audacious operation launched by troops from Tourane and a detachment from Savanaket have permitted us to rejoin the Mekong to the sea. Recently, on Government orders, Nam-Dinh has been cleared of the enemy. (*Applause to the left, centre, and right.*)

There is no solution but a political solution. Now we must build. And we know what it is we must build. We know because the Constitution says it. . . . Within the framework of the French Union we are going to create and organize an association of nations and peoples who will put or coordinate in common their resources and their efforts in order to develop their respective civilizations, increase their well-being, and insure their security. Not domination, not subjugation: association. We are not masters who have spoken as masters. We want to be instructors and counsellors. We are associates. This implies that we respect the independence of peoples. The preamble of the Constitution prescribes it: 'Faithful to her traditional mission, France intends to guide the peoples for whom she has responsibility into freedom to administer themselves and conduct their own affairs democratically.'

That is why, last 21 January, I stated before you: independence within the framework of the French Union, that is the right to conduct and administer democratically their own affairs, to choose their government, to fix the framework in which the Vietnamese people want to live. We expressed no preference. We were not going to impose our views. We recognize, we proclaim, we assure liberty—entirely and completely.

I also said: union of the three Vietnamese countries if the Vietnamese people wish, and I should have added, in the manner they wish. We know without question that the Vietnamese peoples have a feeling of their common culture and history, as well as of their differences, and that they want at once a certain unity and a certain flexibility within this unity. We want to respect their will just as we want to have respected the will of those other peoples, the Cambodians, the Laotians and the Montagnards.[3] Here we are the servants of liberty, and the cause of the French Union and of French influence is tied to this cause of liberty. . . .

From xenophobia, that mindless hatred of the foreigner, we have everything to fear because it is negative and rests upon hatred. But from patriotism we have nothing to fear so long as we remember to respect the liberty of others. In Vietnam we will see new republics built with new liberties knowing, after all, that if the word liberty can be spoken in the Far East it is because France spoke it there first. (*Applause from the left, centre, and right.*) But this cannot be realized except within the framework of the French Union which, in addition to such broad freedom, implies mutual obligations as well. The 62nd Article of the French Constitution states that 'the members of the French Union will pool all their resources in order to guarantee the defence of the entire Union. The Government of the Republic shall see to the coordination of these resources and to the direction of the policy appropriate to prepare and assure this defence.'

That is to say that all these countries share a common foreign policy and military defence and that the French Republic is charged in the interest of all to direct them.

Most probably this was not clearly indicated in the Treaty of March 6. The Constitution had not then been approved; it had not even been written. Today there is no longer any question of the framework of the Treaty of March 6.[4] We can only be bound by the framework of the new Constitution which offers the possibility of a constructive effort. . . .

In order for this work to be accomplished, it is first of all necessary that France—that all of France—wants it and that it not be the policy of a majority against a minority, but the policy of France, wanted by her Assembly, wanted by her Parliament. . . . I address [the Communists]: this is our policy. It is the policy of freedom. It is the policy of the French Union. You accept this policy or you refuse it: here is the issue. (*Sharp applause from the left, centre, and right*.). . . .

Notes

1. The acts of violence to which Ramadier refers occurred in December 1946 following the 23 November bombardment of Haiphong by the French fleet in November. The French actions caused several thousand civilian casualties.

2. The Declaration was made when Ramadier was sworn in as Prime Minister.

3. Aboriginal peoples of the Central Highlands of Vietnam.

4. The Treaty of 6 March 1946 recognized the Republic of Vietnam under Ho Chi Minh as a free state, but within the French Union.

Study Question

1. Did countries that gained their independence through violent struggle gain any advantages over those countries whose independence was granted peacefully?

FRONT DE LIBÉRATION NATIONALE (FLN)

French involvement in Algeria dated back to the 1830s, though total control over the country was not achieved until much later. During this period many European settlers had arrived in Algeria exacerbating tensions with the country's predominantly Muslim population. As in many colonized countries, resistance movements had emerged in the 1920s and 1930s, often led by French-educated Algerians. By 1954 several earlier resistance movements had combined into the National Liberation Front (FLN). Guided by an ideology that combined Algerian nationalism with a strongly socialist orientation, the FLN was eventually successful in its quest for independence. In 1958 the new French government of Charles de Gaulle indicated that it would consider the possibility of granting greater autonomy to Algeria. In 1962 a referendum produced almost unanimous support for independence; however, over one million people who were not sympathetic to the FLN subsequently fled to France.

Proclamation, 1 November 1954

To the Algerian people

To the Militants of the National Cause

To you who are called upon to judge us, the Algerian people in a general way, the militants more particularly, our purpose in distributing this proclamation is to enlighten you concerning the profound reasons which have impelled us to act by revealing to you our program, the meaning of our action, and the cogency of our views, the goal of which remains National Independence within the North African framework. Our wish as well is to help you avoid the confusion maintained by imperialism and its corrupt political and administrative agents.

Before all else, we consider that after decades of struggle the National Movement has reached its final stage of realization. In fact, as the goal of the revolutionary movement is to create all the favorable conditions needed for the launching of operations for liberation, we believe that internally the people are united behind the sign of independence and action; and externally the climate of détente is favorable for the settling of minor problems (among them ours) with the support of our Arab and Muslim brothers above all. The events in Morocco and Tunisia are significant in this regard, and profoundly mark the process of the liberation struggle in North Africa. It is worth noting that for quite some time we have been, in this regard, precursors in the unity of action, unfortunately never realized among the three countries.

Today, many are resolutely engaged on this path and we, relegated to the rear, suffer the fate of those who events have passed by. It is thus that our national movement, overwhelmed by years of *immobilisme* and routine, poorly oriented, deprived of the indispensable support of public opinion, and overtaken by events, has progressively disintegrated, to the great satisfaction of colonialism, which thinks it has carried off its greatest victory in its struggle against the Algerian vanguard. The hour is serious.

Facing this situation, which risks becoming irreparable, a group of young leaders and conscious activists, rallying around it the majority of the healthy and decisive elements, has judged that the moment has arrived to move the National Movement out of the impasse into which it was backed by personal struggles and fights over influence, in order to launch it, at the side of the Moroccan and Tunisian brothers, into the true revolutionary struggle.

To this end, we insist on specifying that *we are independent of the two clans* that are fighting over power. Placing national interest above all petty and erroneous considerations of personality and prestige, in conformity with revolutionary principles, our action is directly solely against colonialism, our only blind and obstinate enemy, which has always refused to grant the least freedom by peaceful means.

These are, we think, sufficient reasons for a movement of renewal to present itself under the name of NATIONAL LIBERATION FRONT, releasing itself in this way from all possible compromises, and offering the possibility to all Algerian patriots of all social classes, of all the purely Algerian parties and movements, to integrate themselves into the struggle for liberation, without any other consideration. . . .

In order to reach these objectives, the National Liberation Front will have two essential tasks to carry out simultaneously: an internal action, on the fronts of politics and action, and an external action, with the goal of the making of the Algerian problem a reality for the entire world, with the support of all our natural allies.

This is a heavy task which necessitates the mobilization of all national energy and resources. It is true that the struggle will be long, but the result is certain.

In the last place, in order to avoid all false interpretations and subterfuges, in order to prove our real desire for peace, to limit the number of human lives lost and the amount of blood spilled, we propose to French authorities an honorable platform of discussion, if these latter are animated by good faith and recognize once and for all in the people they subjugate the right to dispose of themselves:

1. The opening of negotiations with the authorized spokesmen of the Algerian people on the basis of the recognition of sovereignty through Algerian liberation, one and indivisible.
2. The creation of a climate of confidence through the liberation of all political prisoners, the lifting of all measures of exception, and the ceasing of all pursuit of the fighting forces.
3. The recognition of Algerian nationality by an official declaration abrogating the edicts, decrees and laws making Algeria a 'French land', which is a denial of the History, the geography, the language, the religion, and the mores of the Algerian people.

In return:

1. French cultural and economic interests, honestly acquired, will be respected, as will persons and families.

2. All Frenchmen wishing to remain in Algeria will have the choice between their nationality of origin, in which case they will be considered foreigners vis-à-vis the laws in place, or they will opt for Algerian nationality, in which case they will be considered such in rights and obligations.
3. The bonds between France and Algeria will be defined and will be the object of an agreement between the two powers on the basis of equality and mutual respect.

Algerian[s]! We invite you to think over our above Charter. Your obligation is to join with it in order to save our country and restore to it its freedom. The National Liberation Front is your front. Its victory is yours.

As for us, resolved to pursue the struggle, sure of your anti-imperialist sentiments, we give the best of ourselves to the Fatherland.

The Secretariat

Study Question

1. References within this proclamation hint at the problems which would beset Algeria after independence. Which of these problems stand out?

SEKOU TOURÉ

Sekou Touré (1922–84) was born in French West Africa at the height of French colonial domination of the region. He was educated in a French school and was familiar with the works of Marx and Lenin (note his comments below regarding the loss of identity which accompanied his French education). After gaining a leading position in the movement for independence,

Touré was able to convince his fellow Guineans to reject an offer of autonomy within the French Union, and successfully obtained full independence for his country. As President, Touré was criticized for the authoritarian manner by which he ruled his country; however, he was highly regarded by leaders of the more radical civil rights organizations in the United States.

THE REPUBLIC OF GUINEA

Guinea's President Sekou Touré addresses the United Nations in 1962 on the issue of permanent African representation on the Security Council. Bettmann/CORBIS

The African problem is both simple and complex, and many nations, groups, and parties are facing the kind of new problems with which Guinea is now faced. Africa is a geographical and a human entity but, both morally and spiritually, it is more diverse than any other. It is therefore essential to discuss the problems that have to be solved in that context. It is impossible for me, either in writing or in lectures, to present these problems objectively. But it is possible to present a context, though it will necessarily contribute an incomplete image of my country, a country that some of you probably knew before I was born.

The essential factor that I want to bring out is the extent to which we, in Africa, are conditioned by our way of life. Our country is backward and has gone through three distinct stages. First, there was the stage of pre-colonization, in which our organization was communal. Each group had its own customs, its own concepts of economic organization, its own philosophy. It had its own sketchy form of civilization. But the important thing is that this civilization was our own. Like other parts of the world, our countries knew insecurity and famine and went through the kind of struggle which is common to the whole human race. To satisfy their material and moral needs people had to use what means they found at hand. They had few contacts with the outside world.

In the second stage, with the arrival of outsiders, these contacts were established. At first they were economic, then social, cultural, and political. During this period our original way of life was interrupted and modified by our contact with other civilizations. Sometimes the evolution characteristic of the first stage was arrested, sometimes it became more dynamic; in any case life was changed. Above all, it was diverted from its normal course. In my grandparents' time, ethnic, language, and tribal divisions gave way to divisions on a territorial basis. African lands became colonies whose frontiers no longer respected the natural divisions which, though not watertight, had formerly—whether, for instance, in Senegal, in Sudan, or in Guinea—had a real existence.

These countries are inhabited by the same races and have the same civilization. Their essential characteristics are those of the entire African continent. But the colonizers had their own methods. The first change that they made, the modification of frontiers, was a negative contribution. The second, the linking of the African economy to the world economy, was more dynamic. It brought many changes. It helped to increase markets and provided more social opportunities. Yet social development could not progress very far, because the natural basis, the popular basis, was lacking. The new social organization also created new problems. Education brought us into contact with new cultures. A certain number of us assimilated the civilization of other countries, and the result was that Africa became culturally divided. May I quote a personal example? I find myself more at home with French friends than with my own elder brother who has never been to school. Colonization meant that opportunities of advancement were open to a small African élite, but the cost was the creation of deep divisions between us.

Materially, there was progress. But the happiness of man does not come merely from material things. It comes from the harmonious development of material and spiritual elements. The risk was that a moral vacuum would be created, that we should become *déclasseés*, educated, but at home nowhere.

This is the negative contribution of Colonialism. Evolution, which in the pre-colonial era was vertical, now became horizontal. The different areas of Africa evolved inharmoniously, along different lines. It was a period of unification, military, administrative, and cultural unification, when laws were applied throughout a whole territory. The result was to create a positive sense of belonging to a larger community than that of the family or the tribe. But it also had the negative result that the unified system was ill-adapted to meet the real diversity of needs. There was a consequent distortion.

During this phase, individual Africans benefited from new possibilities of evolution. At first, they welcomed assimilation, because education revealed new horizons. But these horizons were always receding. The original aim was to achieve equality between rulers and ruled. But, too often, Africans found, say, when elected to the Assembly, that their problems were as far as ever from a solution. Another phase followed, during which trade unions, students' associations, ex-servicemen's organizations, cultural organizations, and political parties were formed. They constituted an affirmation of the African personality.

This is not a complete picture, but it is a picture of something that we feel deeply, even if we cannot always express these feelings articulately.

There followed a third stage, in which we realized that individual expressions of our personality were not enough. We had to find collective forms of association because, as individuals, we could not achieve our objective, which was the expression of the African personality. This stage is the most important, but the most difficult to describe. Africans believe that the dynamic period of colonialism gave Africa a positive means of action. Our struggle for independence is not negative. We want to retain the positive contribution of colonialism, the increased contacts and the increased possibilities of exchange that it brought. But we want to eliminate its negative aspects. Africa has, we believe, potentialities for economic expansion, and we believe that independence will be a factor making for stabilization. We do not believe that independence will bring a Paradise on earth. We are conscious of our need to unite, and independence is, for us, a means to that end. We are realists. We want to increase our understanding of, and our co-operation with, other peoples, to liquidate the disequilibrium that has been created in Africa.

Man, as a human being, must fulfil himself. If we cannot create the necessary conditions for ourselves, we must create them for those who will come after us. This is the real moving force of African nationalism. You can afford to oppose nationalism, because you have gone through this stage. We have not. That is the tragedy of our situation. What we want is to have laws that are the expression of our own people, and this they have not always been. An imposed system, however good it may be, is never valued as much as one that one has created for oneself. What is lacking is human dignity.

Of course, we in Guinea have our problems. Our country includes many tribes, speaking some twenty different languages. This is a problem which has to be tackled. It is no good shutting one's eyes to the fact of our internal divisions; it is better to tackle them head on. We must organize the country. At first there has naturally been opposition, but in two, or three, or five years our people will have forgotten this.

We want to be responsible for our own lives. One can always give one's brother good advice, but he may prefer to make his own mistakes. That is the African psychology, and it is another reason why we are nationalists. Whatever people may say, nationalism is psychologically inevitable and we are all nationalists. What we Africans are seeking is justice and equality. Let me give you an example of what I mean. An employer may decide to pay a wage of 1,000 francs, even though he knows that the minimum wage is only 500 francs. Everybody will be happy at getting double the rate. But if there is inequality between one worker and another the whole relationship within the group will be affected. This is a human problem that the employer does not understand. He sees only that he is paying double rates. But what the African is interested in is equality.

> **Study Question**
>
> 1. Touré views integration into the wider world economy as a positive contribution of colonialism. With the benefit of hindsight, was he correct?

CLEMENT ATTLEE

Great Britain was devastated at the end of the Second World War. The nation was deeply in debt and many areas had been destroyed by wartime bombardment. Domestic needs had to take precedence over international commitments. Thus, on 15 March 1946 Labour Prime Minister Clement Attlee (1883–1967) announced that Britain was granting India's wish for independence. In the following speech before the House of Commons, Attlee summarized the problems and the potential inherent in an independent India. Within Britain, especially among Conservative MPs, a substantial degree of opposition remained to granting India complete independence.

DEBATES OF THE HOUSE OF COMMONS, 15 MARCH 1946

Prime Minister Attlee: . . . I have had a fairly close connection with this problem now for nearly 20 years, and I would say there have been faults on all sides, but at this time we should be looking to the future rather than harking back to the past. This alone I would say to hon. Members, that it is no good applying the formulae of the past to the present position. The temperature of 1946 is not the temperature of 1920 or of 1930 or even of 1942. The slogans of an earlier day are discarded. Indeed, sometimes words that seemed at that time to Indians to express the height of their aspirations are now set on one side, and other words, other ideas, are substituted. Nothing increases more the pace of public opinion than a great war. Everyone who had anything to do with this question in the early days between the wars knows what an effect the war of 1914–18 had on Indian aspirations and Indian ideals. A tide which runs slowly in peace becomes in wartime vastly accelerated, and especially directly after a war, because that tide is to some extent banked up during the war.

I am quite certain that at the present time the tide of nationalism is running very fast in India and, indeed, all over Asia. One always has to remember that India is affected by what happens elsewhere in Asia. I remember so well, when I was on the Simon Commission,[1] how it was borne in upon us what an effect the challenge that had been thrown out by Japan at that time had had on the Asiatic people. The tide of nationalism that at one time seemed to be canalized among a comparatively small proportion of the people of India—mainly a few of the educated classes—has tended to spread wider and wider. I remember so well, indeed, I think we put it in the Simon Commission Report, that although there were great differences in the expression of nationalist sentiment between what are called the extremists and the moderates, and although in many circumstances there might be such a stress on communal claims as might seem almost to exclude the conception of nationalism, yet we found that Hindu, Muslim, Sikh or Mahrattah,[2] the politician or civil servant—among all of them that conception of nationalism had been growing stronger and stronger. Today I think that national idea has spread right through and not least, perhaps, among some of those soldiers who have given such wonderful service in the war. I should like today therefore, not to stress too much the differences between Indians. Let us all realize that whatever the difficulties, whatever the divisions may be, there is this underlying demand among all the Indian peoples. . . .

The right hon. Gentleman stressed the great part India played during the war. It is worthwhile recording that twice in 25 years India has played a great part in the defeat of tyranny. Is it any wonder that today she claims—as a nation of 400 million people that has twice sent her sons to die for freedom—that she should herself have freedom to decide her own destiny? My colleagues are going to India with the intention of using their utmost endeavours to help her to attain that freedom as speedily and fully as possible. What form of Government is to replace the present regime is for India to decide; but our desire is to help her to set up forthwith the machinery for making that decision. There we are met sometimes with the initial difficulty of getting that machinery set up. We are resolved that machinery shall be set up

and we seek the utmost cooperation of all Indian leaders to do so. . . .

India herself must choose what will be her future Constitution; what will be her position in the world. I hope that the Indian people may elect to remain within the British Commonwealth. I am certain that she will find great advantages in doing so. In these days the demand for complete, isolated nationhood apart from the rest of the world, is really outdated. Unity may come through the United Nations, or through the Commonwealth, but no great nation can stand alone without sharing in what is happening in the world. But if she does so elect, it must be by her own free will. The British Commonwealth and Empire is not bound together by the chains of external compulsion. It is a free association of free peoples. If, on the other hand, she elects for independence, in our view she has the right to do so. It will be for us to help to make the transition as smooth and easy as possible.

We should be conscious that the British have done a great work in India. We have united India and given her that sense of nationalism which she so very largely lacked over the previous centuries. She has learned from us principles of democracy and justice. When Indians attack our rule, they base their attack, not on Indian principles, but on the basis of standards derived from Britain. I was struck the other day in the United States, at a dinner where I met a number of distinguished Americans, including a very distinguished Indian, where the talk was turning on the way in which principles worked out here, have been applied to the continent of America. It was pointed out that America had a great heritage from Britain. My Indian friend said to me, 'You know the Americans sometimes forget there is another great nation that has also inherited these principles and traditions, and that is India. We feel that we have a duty, a right, and a privilege because we also bring to the world and work those very principles that you evolved in Britain.'

I am well aware, when I speak of India, that I speak of a country containing a congeries[3] of races, religions, and languages, and I know well all the difficulties thereby created. But those difficulties can only be overcome by Indians. We are very mindful of the rights of minorities and minorities should be able to live free from fear. On the other hand, we cannot allow a minority to place a veto on the advance of the majority. . . .

In conclusion, may I stress again the crucial nature of the task before us? This problem is of vital importance not only to India and the British Commonwealth and Empire, but to the world. There is this immense nation, set in the midst of Asia, an Asia which has been ravaged by war. Here we have the one great country that has been seeking to apply the principles of democracy. I have always hoped myself that politically India might be the light of Asia. It is a most unfortunate circumstance that, just at the time when we have to deal with these great political issues, there should be grave economic difficulties and, in particular, very grave anxiety over India's food supply.[4] The House knows that His Majesty's Government are deeply concerned in this problem, and my right hon. Friend the Minister of Food is at the present time in the United States with an Indian delegation. We shall do our utmost to help her. At the present moment I do not think I should say anything on the social and economic difficulties

to which the right hon. Gentleman referred except this: I believe that those economic and social difficulties can only be solved by the Indians themselves, because they are so closely bound up with the whole Indian way of life and outlook. Whatever we can do to assist, we shall do. My right hon. Friends are going out to India resolved to succeed and I am sure everyone will wish them 'God speed'. . . .

Notes

1. The Simon Commission was dispatched to India in 1927 to report upon the state of government at the time and to suggest a future constitution for India. The Commission contained no Indian members.
2. The Mahrattah are descendants of an ethnic group that once ruled the southern tip of India (the Tamil region).
3. Congeries: a mass, or collection.
4. The food supply problem in India was a dual result of a cash crop economy and rationing during wartime.

Study Question

1. Did Britain have any option other than to grant independence to India?

JAWAHARLAL NEHRU

By the end of the Second World War, Jawaharlal Nehru had emerged as the clear leader of the Indian National Congress. With the decision to partition the country into predominantly Hindu and Muslim areas under the Mountbatten Plan, Nehru was poised to become the first prime minister of India on *15 August 1947. The following speech was delivered on the evening before independence became official. Even as he spoke Nehru was aware that tremendous violence had broken out as a result of the rapid partition of the country and the resulting movement of population.*

TRYST WITH DESTINY, 14 AUGUST 1947

Long years ago we made a tryst with destiny, and now the time comes when we shall redeem our pledge, not wholly or in full measure, but very substantially.

At the stroke of the midnight hour, when the world sleeps, India will awake to life and freedom. A moment comes, which comes but rarely in history, when we step out from the old to the new, when an age ends, and when the soul of a nation, long suppressed, finds utterance.

It is fitting that at this solemn moment we take the pledge of dedication to the service of India and her people and to the still larger cause of humanity.

At the dawn of history India started on her unending quest, and trackless centuries are filled with her striving and the grandeur of her success and her failures. Through good and ill fortune alike she has never lost sight of that quest or forgotten the ideals which gave her strength. We end today a period of ill fortune and India discovers herself again.

The achievement we celebrate today is but a step, an opening of opportunity, to the greater triumphs and achievements that await us. Are we brave enough and wise enough to grasp this opportunity and accept the challenge of the future?

Freedom and power bring responsibility. The responsibility rests upon this assembly, a sovereign body representing the sovereign people of India. Before the birth of freedom we have endured all the pains of labour and our hearts are heavy with the memory of this sorrow. Some of those pains continue even now. Nevertheless, the past is over and it is the future that beckons to us now.

That future is not one of ease or resting but of incessant striving so that we may fulfil the pledges we have so often taken and the one we shall take today. The service of India means the service of the millions who suffer. It means the ending of

Indian Prime Minister Jawaharlal Nehru visits the United States in 1949, two years after India gained its independence. Future Prime Minister Indira Gandhi, Nehru's daughter, stands to the right of her father. Department of State. Courtesy of the Harry S. Truman Library.

poverty and ignorance and disease and inequality of opportunity.

The ambition of the greatest man of our generation has been to wipe every tear from every eye. That may be beyond us, but as long as there are tears and suffering, so long our work will not be over.

And so we have to labour and to work, and work hard, to give reality to our dreams. Those dreams are for India, but they are also for the world, for all the nations and peoples are too closely knit together today for anyone of them to imagine that it can live apart.

Peace has been said to be indivisible; so is freedom, so is prosperity now, and so also is disaster in this one world that can no longer be split into isolated fragments.

To the people of India, whose representatives we are, we make an appeal to join us with faith and confidence in this great adventure. This is no time for petty and destructive criticism, no time for ill will or blaming others. We have to build the noble mansion of free India where all her children may dwell.

The appointed day has come—the day appointed by destiny—and India stands forth again, after long slumber and struggle, awake, vital, free and independent. The past clings on to us still in some measure and we have to do much before we redeem the pledges we have so often taken. Yet the turning point is past, and history begins anew for us, the history which we shall live and act and others will write about.

It is a fateful moment for us in India, for all Asia and for the world. A new star rises, the star of freedom in the east, a new hope comes into being, a vision long cherished materialises. May the star never set and that hope never be betrayed!

We rejoice in that freedom, even though clouds surround us, and many of our people are sorrow-stricken and difficult problems encompass us. But freedom brings responsibilities and burdens and we have to face them in the spirit of a free and disciplined people.

On this day our first thoughts go to the architect of this freedom, the father of our nation, who, embodying the old spirit of India, held aloft the torch of freedom and lighted up the darkness that surrounded us.

We have often been unworthy followers of his and have strayed from his message, but not only we but succeeding generations will remember this message and bear the imprint in their hearts of this great son of India, magnificent in his faith and strength and courage and humility. We shall never allow that torch of freedom to be blown out, however high the wind or stormy the tempest.

Our next thoughts must be of the unknown volunteers and soldiers of freedom who, without praise or reward, have served India even unto death.

We think also of our brothers and sisters who have been cut off from us by political boundaries and who unhappily cannot share at present in the freedom that has come. They are of us and will remain of us whatever may happen, and we shall be sharers in their good and ill fortune alike.

The future beckons to us. Whither do we go and what shall be our endeavour? To bring freedom and opportunity to the common man, to the peasants and workers of India; to fight and end poverty and ignorance and disease; to build up a prosperous, democratic and progressive nation, and to create social, economic and political institutions which will ensure justice and fullness of life to every man and woman.

We have hard work ahead. There is no resting for any one of us till we redeem our pledge in full, till we make all the people of India what destiny intended them to be.

We are citizens of a great country, on the verge of bold advance, and we have to live up to that high standard. All of us, to whatever religion we may belong, are equally the children of India with equal rights, privileges and obligations. We cannot encourage communalism or narrow-mindedness, for no nation can be great whose people are narrow in thought or in action.

To the nations and peoples of the world we send greetings and pledge ourselves to cooperate with them in furthering peace, freedom and democracy.

And to India, our much-loved motherland, the ancient, the eternal and the ever-new, we pay our reverent homage and we bind ourselves afresh to her service. Jai Hind.

Study Question

1. What was the single greatest problem facing India in 1947?

KWAME NKRUMAH

Kwame Nkrumah (1909–72) became deeply involved in the struggle for African decolonization during his studies in the US and Great Britain. Despite being arrested by the British in 1950, he won election to the Ghanaian parliament while in prison. In 1951, after the British had determined that Ghana would obtain independence, he was released and allowed to take his seat in parliament.

In 1952 Nkrumah became the country's first prime minister. Nkrumah declared Ghana's independence in 1957 and, in 1960, proclaimed the nation a republic. In the following excerpt from I Speak of Freedom, Nkrumah argues that African unity will be necessary in order to repair the damage of the colonial era and to move forward in the modern world.

I SPEAK OF FREEDOM

For centuries, Europeans dominated the African continent. The white man arrogated to himself the right to rule and to be obeyed by the non-white; his mission, he claimed, was to 'civilize' Africa. Under this cloak, the Europeans robbed the continent of vast riches and inflicted unimaginable suffering on the African people.

All this makes a sad story, but now we must be prepared to bury the past with its unpleasant memories and look to the future. All we ask of the former colonial powers is their goodwill and co-operation to remedy past mistakes and injustices and to grant independence to the colonies in Africa. . . .

It is clear that we must find an African solution to our problems, and that this can only be found in African unity. Divided we are weak; united, Africa could become one of the greatest forces for good in the world.

Although most Africans are poor, our continent is potentially extremely rich. Our mineral resources, which are being exploited with foreign capital only to enrich foreign investors, range from gold and diamonds to uranium and petroleum. Our forests contain some of the finest woods to be grown anywhere. Our cash crops include cocoa, coffee, rubber, tobacco and cotton. As for power, which is an important factor in any economic development, Africa contains over 40 per cent of the potential water power of the world, as compared with about 10 per cent in Europe and 13 per cent in North America. Yet so far, less than 1 per cent has been developed. This is one of the reasons why we have in Africa the paradox of poverty in the midst of plenty, and scarcity in the midst of abundance.

Never before have a people had within their grasp so great an opportunity for developing a continent endowed with so much wealth. Individually, the independent states of Africa, some of them potentially rich, others poor, can do little for their people. Together, by mutual help, they can achieve much. But the economic development of the continent must be planned and pursued as a whole. A loose confederation designed only for economic co-operation would not provide the necessary unity of purpose. Only a strong political union can bring about full and effective development of our natural resources for the benefit of our people.

The political situation in Africa today is heartening and at the same time disturbing. It is heartening to see so many new flags hoisted in place of the old; it is disturbing to see so many countries of varying sizes and at different levels of development, weak and, in some cases, almost helpless. If this terrible state of fragmentation is allowed to continue it may well be disastrous for us all.

Kwame Nkrumah is inaugurated as the first president of the Republic of Ghana in 1960. New York World-Telegram and Sun Newspaper Photograph Collection.

There are at present some twenty-eight states in Africa, excluding the Union of South Africa, and those countries not yet free. No less than nine of these states have a population of less than three million. Can we seriously believe that the colonial powers meant these countries to be independent, viable states? The example of South America, which has as much wealth, if not more than North America, and yet remains weak and dependent on outside interests, is one which every African would do well to study.

Critics of African unity often refer to the wide differences in culture, language, and ideas in various parts of Africa. This is true, but the essential fact remains that we are all Africans, and have a common interest in the independence of Africa. The difficulties presented by questions of language, culture, and different political systems are not insuperable. If the need for political union is agreed by us all, then the will to create it is born; and where there's a will there's a way.

The present leaders of Africa have already shown a remarkable willingness to consult and seek advice among themselves. Africans have, indeed, begun to think continentally. They realize that they have much in common, both in their past history, in their present problems and in their future hopes. To suggest that the time is not yet ripe for considering a political union of Africa is to evade the facts and ignore realities in Africa today.

The greatest contribution that Africa can make to the peace of the world is to avoid all the dangers inherent in disunity, by creating a political union which will also by its success, stand as an example to a divided world. A Union of African states will project more effectively the African personality. It will command respect from a world that has regard only for size and influence. The scant attention paid to African opposition to the French atomic tests in the Sahara, and the ignominious spectacle of the UN in the Congo quibbling about constitutional niceties while the Republic was tottering into anarchy, are evidence of the callous disregard of African Independence by the Great Powers.

We have to prove that greatness is not to be measured in stockpiles of atom bombs. I believe strongly and sincerely that with the deep-rooted wisdom and dignity, the innate respect for human lives, the intense humanity that is our heritage, the African race, united under one federal government, will emerge not as just another world bloc to flaunt its wealth and strength, but as a Great Power whose greatness is indestructible because it is built not on fear, envy and suspicion,

nor won at the expense of others, but founded on hope, trust, friendship and directed to the good of all mankind.

The emergence of such a mighty stabilizing force in this strife-worn world should be regarded not as the shadowy dream of a visionary, but as a practical proposition, which the peoples of Africa can, and should, translate into reality. There is a tide in the affairs of every people when the moment strikes for political action. Such was the moment in the history of the United States of America when the Founding Fathers saw beyond the petty wranglings of the separate states and created a Union. This is our chance. We must act now. Tomorrow may be too late and the opportunity will have passed, and with it the hope of free Africa's survival.

> **Study Question**
>
> 1. To date African unity has been virtually impossible to obtain, despite its obvious advantages. Why?

A.L. (Albertus Lourens) Geyer

Dr A.L. Geyer (1894–1969) was a journalist and diplomat. Between 1950 and 1954 he served as the High Commissioner for the Union of South Africa in Britain. This speech, to the Rotary Club in London, discusses the apartheid policy of the National Party under Daniel Malan and provides Geyer's

interpretation of the future benefits of the policy. The speech was given in August 1953 at which time the British government was already expressing opposition to the racial policies of the South African government. In 1961 South Africa left the British Commonwealth and declared itself a republic.

The Case for Apartheid

As one of the aftermaths of the last war, many people seem to suffer from a neurotic guilt-complex with regard to colonies. This has led to a strident denunciation of the Black African's wrongs, real or imaginary, under the white man's

rule in Africa. It is a denunciation, so shrill and emotional, that the vast debt owed by Black Africa to those same white men is lost sight of (and, incidentally, the Black African is encouraged to forget that debt). Confining myself to that area of which I know at least a very little, Africa south of the Equator, I shall say this without fear of reasonable contradiction: every millimetre of progress in all that vast area is due entirely to the White Man.

You are familiar with the cry that came floating over the ocean from the West—a cry that 'colonialism' is outmoded and pernicious, a cry that is being vociferously echoed by a certain gentleman in the East. [This refers to Jawaharlal Nehru, Prime Minister of India.] May I point out that African colonies are of comparatively recent date. Before that time Black Africa did have independence for a thousand years and more and what did she make of it? One problem, I admit, she did solve most effectively. There was no overpopulation. Interminable savage intertribal wars, witchcraft, disease, famine, and even cannibalism saw to that.

Let me turn to my subject, to that part of Africa south of the Sahara which, historically, is not part of Black Africa at all—my own country. Its position is unique in Africa, as its racial problem is unique in the world.

1. South Africa is no more the original home of its black Africans, the Bantu, than it is of its white Africans. Both races went there as colonists and, what is more, as practically contemporary colonists. In some parts the Bantu arrived first, in other parts the Europeans were the first comers.

2. South Africa contains the only independent white nation in all Africa. The only South African nation which has no other homeland to which it could retreat; a nation which has created a highly developed modern state, and which occupies a position of inestimable importance.

3. South Africa is the only independent country in the world in which white people are outnumbered by black people. Including all coloured races or peoples the proportion in Brazil is 20 to 1. In South Africa it is 1 to 4.

This brings me to the question of the future. To me there seems to be two possible lines of development: *Apartheid* or Partnership. Partnership means cooperation of the individual citizens within a single community, irrespective of race. . . . (It) demands that there shall be no discrimination whatsoever in trade and industry, in the professions, and the Public Service. Therefore, whether a man is black or a white African, must according to this policy be as irrelevant as whether in London a man is a Scotsman or an Englishman. I take it: that Partnership must also aim at the eventual disappearance of all social segregation based on race. This policy of Partnership admittedly does not envisage immediate adult suffrage. Obviously, however, the loading of the franchise in order to exclude the great majority of the Bantu could be no more than a temporary expedient. . . . (In effect) 'There must one day be black domination, in the sense that power must pass to the immense African majority. Need I say more to show that this policy of Partnership could, in South Africa, only mean the eventual disappearance of the white South African nation? And will you be greatly surprised if I tell you that this white nation is not prepared to commit national suicide, not even by slow poisoning?'

The only alternative is a policy of *apartheid*, the policy of separate development. The germ of this policy is inherent in almost all of our history, implanted there by the force of circumstances. . . . *Apartheid* is a policy of self-preservation. We make no apology for possessing that very natural urge. But it is more than that. It is an attempt at self-preservation in a manner that will enable the Bantu to develop fully as a separate people.

We believe that, for a long time to come, political power will have to remain with the whites, also in the interest of our still very immature Bantu. But we believe also, in the words of a statement by the Dutch Reformed Church in 1950, a Church that favours *apartheid*, that 'no people in the world worth their salt would be content indefinitely with no say or only indirect say in the affairs of the State or in the country's socioeconomic organization in which decisions are taken about their interests and their future.'

The immediate aim is, therefore, to keep the races outside the Bantu areas apart as far as possible, to continue the process of improving the conditions and standards of living of the Bantu, and to give them greater responsibility for their own local affairs. At the same time the long-range aim is to develop the Bantu areas both agriculturally and industrially, with the object of making these areas in every sense the national home of the Bantu—

areas in which their interests are paramount, in which to an ever greater degree all professional and other positions are to be occupied by them, and in which they are to receive progressively more and more autonomy.

> **Study Question**
>
> 1. Why did British, and later global, opposition to the imposition of apartheid have little effect?

DESMOND TUTU

Desmond Tutu (b. 1931) entered the Anglican priesthood in 1960, serving as a parish priest and lecturing at a theological seminary in Johannesburg. By 1975 he had become an outspoken member of the anti-apartheid movement, calling for global economic sanctions against the apartheid government. The following year he was consecrated as Bishop of Lesotho. His anti-apartheid work was recognized by the Nobel Prize Committee in 1984, and he was awarded the Nobel Prize for Peace; however, the South African government refused to acknowledge the award. By 1986, Tutu had been elected the first black archbishop of Cape Town, making him the head of the Anglican Church in South Africa. He would serve in this post, continuing the fight against apartheid and its after-effects, until 1996 when he resigned to become the full-time head of the Truth and Reconciliation Commission. The following excerpt outlines Tutu's vision for a post-apartheid South Africa.

MY VISION FOR SOUTH AFRICA

We should all have the freedom to become fully human. That is basic to my understanding of society—that God created us without any coercion, freely for freedom. Responsibility is a nonsense except in the context of freedom—freedom to accept or reject alternative options, freedom to obey or disobey. God, who alone has the perfect right to be a totalitarian, has such a tremendous respect for our freedom to be human, that he would much rather see us go freely to hell than compel us to go to heaven.

According to the Bible, a human being can be a human being only because he belongs to a community. A person is a person through other persons, as we say in our African idiom. And so separation of persons because of biological accidents is reprehensible and blasphemous. A person is entitled to a stable community life, and the first of these communities is the family. A stable family life would be of paramount importance in my South Africa.

There would be freedom of association, of thought, and of expression. This would involve freedom of movement as well. One would be free to go wherever one wanted, to associate with whomsoever one wished. As adult humans we

Segregated seating, such as this in Bloemfontein, South Africa, was common at all public events during the apartheid era. Courtesy of the United Nations Photo Library (177913 UN/DPI/H. Vasai).

would not be subject to draconian censorship laws. We can surely decide for ourselves what we want to read, what films to view, and what views to have. We must not be frog-marched into puritanism.

Because we are created in the image of God one of our attributes is creativity. South Africa is starved of the great things many of her children can create and do, because of artificial barriers, and the refusal to let people develop to their fullest potential. When one has been overseas and seen for example the Black Alvin Abbey dance group, which performed modern ballet to standing room only crowds at Covent Garden, then one weeps for how South Africa has allowed herself to be cheated of such performances by her own inhabitants.

How many potentially outstanding people are being denied the opportunity to get on?

When I think of the splendid young people I have met, who despite some horrendous experiences at the hands of the system, have emerged quite unscathed with bitterness, and who have a tremendous humanity and compassion, then I weep because we are so wantonly wasteful of human resources. We need a course on human ecology.

I lay great stress on humanness and being truly human. In our African understanding, part of Ubantu—being human—is the rare gift of sharing. This concept of sharing is exemplified at African feasts even to this day, when people eat together from a common dish, rather than from individual dishes. That means a meal is indeed to have communion with one's fellows. Blacks are beginning to lose this wonderful attribute because we are being inveigled by the excessive individualism of the West. I loathe Capitalism because it gives far too great play to our inherent selfishness. We are told to be highly competitive, and our children start learning the attitudes of the rat-race quite early. They mustn't just do well at school—they must sweep the floor with their rivals. That's how you get on. We give prizes to such persons, not so far as I know to those who know how best to get on with others, or those who can coax the best out of others. We must delight in our ulcers, the symbols of our success.

So I would look for a socio-economic system that placed the emphasis on sharing and giving, rather than on self-aggrandizement and getting. Capitalism is exploitative and I can't stand that. We need to engage the resources that each person has. My vision includes a society that is more compassionate and caring, in which 'superfluous appendages'[1] are unthinkable, where young and old are made to feel wanted, and that they belong and are not resented. It is a distorted community that trundles its aged off into soulless institutions. We need their accumulated wisdom and experience. They are splendid for helping the younger to feel cared for; certainly that has been the experience in the extended family.

I believe too that in a future South Africa we must be supportive of the family. The nuclear family is not geared to stand all the strains placed on it by modern day pressures. There are things we can survive better in a group than singly. I know there are pressures in the extended family, but I need to be persuaded that these are greater than those presently haunting the nuclear family.

Basically I long and work for a South Africa that is more open and more just; where people count and where they will have equal access to the good things of life, with equal opportunity to live, work, and learn. I long for a South Africa where there will be equal and untrammeled access to the courts of the land, where detention without trial will be a thing of the hoary past, where bannings and other such arbitrary acts will no longer be even so much as mentioned, and where the rule of law will hold sway in the fullest sense. In addition, all adults will participate fully in political decision making, and in other decisions which affect their lives. Consequently they will have the vote and be eligible for election to all public offices. This South Africa will have integrity of territory with a common citizenship, and all the rights and privileges that go with citizenship, belonging to all its inhabitants.

Clearly, for many people, what I have described is almost a Utopia, and we cannot reach that desired goal overnight. Black leaders would, I feel, be willing to go back to the black community, and say: 'Hold on—things are moving in the right direction' if certain minimum conditions were pledged and met, even in stages, by the white powers that be. These are:

a. Abolition of the Pass Laws.

b. The immediate halting of population removals.

c. The scrapping of Bantu Education, and a move towards a unitary educational system.

d. A commitment to call a National Convention.

These would be significant steps towards realizing the vision.

Note

1. The South African government referred to black workers as 'superfluous appendages'.

> **Study Question**
>
> 1. Until the late-1980s official western support for ending apartheid was minimal at best. Why did so few western governments support the views put forward by Desmond Tutu and others?

Tips for Analysis

'Accuracy'

Is the document comparable to other writings on the same topic? While opinions and interpretations may vary widely it is usually possible to judge the degree of accuracy within the document. Compare the facts presented by the author to other accounts of similar events in order to judge the reliability of the source.

WEB RESOURCES

African History on the Internet: Colonial Period
http://www-sul.stanford.edu/depts/ssrg/africa/history/hiscolonial.html
Internet African History Sourcebook
http://www.fordham.edu/halsall/africa/africasbook.html
History in Focus: Empire
http://www.history.ac.uk/ihr/Focus/Empire/index.html
Political Discourse: Theories of Colonialism and Postcolonialism
http://www.postcolonialweb.org/poldiscourse/discourseov.html

RECOMMENDED READING

Andre Brink, *A Dry White Season* (New York: Penguin, 1984). Brinks is an Afrikaner author whose powerful novel exposes many of the injustices of the apartheid system. *A Dry White Season*—set against the Soweto Riots in 1976—tells the story of a white Afrikaner who attempts to explain the disappearance of a black friend.

Graham Greene, *The Quiet American* (New York: Penguin, 1996). American involvement in Indochina, particularly during the final days of French rule, forms the backdrop for the 1955 novel, *The Quiet American*. The novel is sympathetic towards the Vietminh guerrillas and seems prophetic in its look at the consequences of early American activities in the region.

Khushwant Singh, *Train to Pakistan* (New York: Grove Press, 1990). In 1947 a small village on the proposed border with Pakistan finds itself immersed in the panic of partition. Traditionally peaceful relations between Hindu and Muslim are strained as the devastating consequences of forcible separation become clear. Singh's novel provides a sensitive look at the tension and violence wrought by the decision to partition India.

Rohinton Mistry, *A Fine Balance* (New York: Vintage, 2001). Mistry's Giller Prize–winning novel takes place in India in 1975–6 during the state of emergency declared by Indira Gandhi. Social policies, including forced sterilization, corruption, violence, and caste discrimination, form the backdrop as the characters try to find a 'fine balance between hope and despair'.

V.S. Naipaul, *A Bend in the River* (New York: Vintage, 1989). Set in Kisangani on the Congo River, a young merchant of Indian descent sets out to make his fortune in post-colonial Zaire. The novel takes place during Mobutu's attempt to forge a new identity for Zaire as the country experienced spiralling poverty, ethnic conflict, and government corruption. *A Bend in the River* raises complex questions of identity, traditional values, modernity, and post-colonial power structures.

M.G. Vassanji, *The In-Between World of Vikram Lall* (New York: Knopf, 2003). The story of a third-generation Indian child growing up in East Africa, caught between the world of Africans and the world of Europeans, experiences the Mau Mau rebellion, post-independence government, the colonial legacy, corruption, and finally, exile.

RECOMMENDED VIEWING

Cry, the Beloved Country (UK, 1951). Director: Zoltan Korda (B&W). Shot on location in South Africa when the apartheid system was consolidating its grip on the country, Korda provides a powerful examination of systemic racism and its consequences in the 1940s.

The Battle of Algiers (Algeria/Italy, 1966). Director: Gilberto Pontecorvo. This film provides a highly sympathetic account of the FLN's struggle to liberate Algeria from French rule. The film, which was banned in France for several years, captures the motivations and radical tactics utilized by the FLN, and later adopted by many other groups around the world.

Cry Freedom (UK/USA, 1987). Director: Richard Attenborough. In *Cry Freedom* Attenborough recreates the friendship between white South African journalist Donald Woods and the black anti-apartheid activist Stephen Biko, the struggle to investigate Biko's death, and the difficulty of keeping Biko's anti-apartheid message alive.

Long Night's Journey Into Day (USA, 2000). Directors: Frances Reid/Deborah Hoffmann. (Documentary). This 90-minute documentary examines the workings of the Truth and Reconciliation Commission in South Africa. It follows four of the Commission's cases as the perpetrators attempt to reconcile with the families of their victims.

The Quiet American (USA/Australia, 2002). Director: Phillip Noyce. Much of the history in *The Quiet American* is played out in the background, but this adaptation of Graham Greene's novel still offers an interesting look at the level of American involvement prior to the French defeat in Indochina. In particular, the film exposes the early years of CIA involvement in Vietnamese politics.

CHAPTER TWELVE

TECHNOLOGY AND
THE ENVIRONMENT

───────◇───────

In the aftermath of the Second World War the power of technology to transform human existence—even to destroy human existence—was evident as never before. Entire nations lay in ruins, devastated by 'conventional' aerial bombardment and, in the case of Hiroshima and Nagasaki, by atomic weapons. At the same time, the war had provided a tremendous impetus to the development of the earliest computer technology, which had been created initially to perform code-breaking functions and then was gradually extended to additional military and, eventually, civilian applications.

Once the Soviets successfully tested an atomic bomb in 1949—several years ahead of the schedule predicted by US military analysts—the nuclear arms race began in earnest. New, more powerful weapons such as the Hydrogen Bomb soon followed, some designed for tactical use, as in the case of the neutron bomb, which was intended to target humans while leaving buildings and infrastructure intact. The stability attained when the US and Soviets achieved a state of Mutual Assured Destruction (MAD) did little to reassure the ordinary citizen living in a bipolar world.

In many ways the space race can be seen as an outgrowth of the Cold War arms race and the need for more efficient, long-range delivery systems. The Soviet Union's launch of the Sputnik satellite in October 1957 intensified fears (fears that were largely incorrect) of a missile gap and led the US to pursue an increasingly ambitious space program. This culminated in the 20 July 1969 landing of the manned *Eagle* module on the moon and the historic first steps by Neil Armstrong on the lunar surface.

Even as military advances created new and more efficient ways of destroying human life and the environment which supports it, awareness of the fragility of the global environment began to develop. Rachel Carsen's seminal work *Silent Spring* first focused attention on the potentially harmful results of the use of DDT. The end of the war in Vietnam brought concerns over the widespread use of defoliants such as Agent Orange and their impact on human health.

Astronaut Edwin 'Buzz' Aldrin walks on the surface of the moon, July 1969. Courtesy of NASA.

Organizations such as Greenpeace were founded to focus the world's attention on the dangers of nuclear weapons. Subsequently, many of these organizations broadened their focus to other pressing environmental issues.

As the twenty-first century dawned, however, no one issue attracted greater public and scientific attention than concerns over global climate change. Numerous scientific studies pointed to a pattern of climate change beginning during the industrial revolution and accelerating during the twentieth century. Critics countered that the global climate has always passed through cycles of heating and warming, but the alarming melting of polar ice caps at the turn of the century gave new weight to scientific claims regarding climate change.

The documents in this chapter deal with the transformative role of technology in the modern world as well as the growing awareness of mankind's impact on the environment. John F. Kennedy's 1962 speech in Houston promised Americans that the US could put a man on the moon. Valentina Tereshkova, the Soviet Union's first female cosmonaut, discusses the current state of the Russian space program and recalls her own achievements in 1963. Marshall McLuhan reflects on the broader impact of technological change in the modern world. Turning to the environment, the first chapter of *Silent Spring* introduces the reader to Rachel Carson; Rex Wyler recalls the early days of Greenpeace; and Al Gore discusses the environmental challenges facing the twenty-first century in his 2007 Nobel Prize acceptance speech. Finally, British physicist Stephen Hawking argues for a return to space in the very near future.

JOHN F. KENNEDY

John F. Kennedy (1917–63) was elected US president in November 1960 as the Cold War entered a new phase. The paranoia of the McCarthy era had begun to recede, but tensions with the Soviets, under Nikita Khrushchev, remained high. In 1961 alone, Kennedy faced crises in Berlin, Cuba, and Vietnam, none of which were resolved to his satisfaction. Thus,

Kennedy's determination to take the lead in space exploration and to put a man on the moon—first proposed to Congress in May 1961—can be tied to his need for a clear foreign policy victory over the Soviets. The following speech was delivered in September 1962 at Rice University in Houston, Texas.

ON THE SPACE RACE

. . . .We meet at a college noted for knowledge, in a city noted for progress, in a state noted for strength, and we stand in need of all three, for we meet in an hour of change and challenge, in a decade of hope and fear, in an age of both knowledge and

President John F. Kennedy, Jackie Kennedy, and Vice-President Lyndon Johnson watch *Mercury* astronaut Alan Shepard travel into space.

ignorance. The greater our knowledge increases, the greater our ignorance unfolds.

Despite the striking fact that most of the scientists that the world has ever known are alive and working today, despite the fact that this Nation's own scientific manpower is doubling every 12 years in a rate of growth more than three times that of our population as a whole, despite that, the vast stretches of the unknown and the unanswered and the unfinished still far outstrip our collective comprehension.

No man can fully grasp how far and how fast we have come, but condense, if you will, the 50,000 years of man's recorded history in a time span of but a half-century. Stated in these terms, we know very little about the first 40 years, except at the end of them advanced man had learned to use the skins of animals to cover them. Then about 10 years ago, under this standard, man emerged from his caves to construct other kinds of shelter. Only five years ago man learned to write and use a cart with wheels. Christianity began less than two years ago. The printing press came this year, and then less than two months ago, during this whole 50-year span of human history, the steam engine provided a new source of power. Newton explored the meaning of gravity. Last month electric lights and telephones and automobiles and airplanes became available. Only last week did we develop penicillin and television and nuclear power, and now if America's new spacecraft succeeds in reaching Venus, we will have literally reached the stars before midnight tonight.

This is a breathtaking pace, and such a pace cannot help but create new ills as it dispels old, new ignorance, new problems, new dangers. Surely the opening vistas of space promise high costs and hardships, as well as high reward.

So it is not surprising that some would have us stay where we are a little longer to rest, to wait. But this city of Houston, this state of Texas, this country of the United States was not built by those who waited and rested and wished to look behind them. This country was conquered by those who moved forward—and so will space. . . .

Those who came before us made certain that this country rode the first waves of the industrial revolution, the first waves of modern invention, and the first wave of nuclear power, and this generation does not intend to founder in the backwash of the coming age of space. We mean to be a part of it—we mean to lead it. For the eyes of the world now look into space, to the moon and to the planets beyond, and we have vowed that we shall not see it governed by a hostile flag of conquest, but by a banner of freedom and peace. We have vowed that we shall not see space filled with weapons of mass destruction, but with instruments of knowledge and understanding.

Yet the vows of this Nation can only be fulfilled if we in this Nation are first, and, therefore, we intend to be first. In short, our leadership in science and industry, our hopes for peace and security, our obligations to ourselves as well as others, all require us to make this effort, to solve these mysteries, to solve them for the good of all men, and to become the world's leading space-faring nation.

We set sail on this new sea because there is new knowledge to be gained, and new rights to be won, and they must be won and used for the progress of all people. For space science, like nuclear science and all technology, has no conscience of its own. Whether it will become a force for good or ill depends on man, and only if the United States occupies a position of pre-eminence can we help decide whether this new ocean will be a sea of peace or a new terrifying theater of war. I do not say that we should or will go unprotected against the hostile misuse of space any more than we go unprotected against the hostile use of land or sea, but I do say that space can be explored and mastered without feeding the fires of war, without repeating the mistakes that man has made in extending his writ around this globe of ours.

There is no strife, no prejudice, no national conflict in outer space as yet. Its hazards are hostile to us all. Its conquest deserves the best of all mankind, and its opportunity for peaceful cooperation may never come again. But why, some say, the moon? Why choose this as our goal? And they may well ask why climb the highest mountain? Why, 35 years ago, fly the Atlantic? Why does Rice play Texas?

We choose to go to the moon. We choose to go to the moon in this decade and do the other things, not because they are easy, but because they are hard, because that goal will serve to organize and measure the best of our energies and skills, because that challenge is one that we are willing to accept, one we are unwilling to postpone, and one which we intend to win, and the others, too.

It is for these reasons that I regard the decision last year to shift our efforts in space from low to high gear as among the most important decisions that will be made during my incumbency in the office of the Presidency. . . .

To be sure, we are behind, and will be behind for some time in manned flight. But we do not intend to stay behind, and in this decade, we shall make up and move ahead.

The growth of our science and education will be enriched by new knowledge of our universe and environment, by new techniques of learning and mapping and observation, by new tools and computers for industry, medicine, the home as well as the school. Technical institutions, such as Rice, will reap the harvest of these gains.

And finally, the space effort itself, while still in its infancy, has already created a great number of new companies, and tens of thousands of new jobs. Space and related industries are generating new demands in investment and skilled personnel, and this city and this state, and this region, will share greatly in this growth. What was once the furthest outpost on the old frontier of the West will be the furthest outpost on the new frontier of science and space. Houston, your city of Houston, with its Manned Spacecraft Center, will become the heart of a large scientific and engineering community. During the next five years the National Aeronautics and Space Administration expects to double the number of scientists and engineers in this area, to increase its outlays for salaries and expenses to $60 million a year; to invest some $200 million in plant and laboratory facilities; and to direct or contract for new space efforts over $1 billion from this center in this city. . . .

. . . I think we're going to do it, and I think that we must pay what needs to be paid. I don't think we ought to waste any money, but I think we ought to do the job. And this will be done in the decade of the Sixties. It may be done while some of you are still here at school at this college and university. It will be done during the terms of office of some of the people who sit here on this platform. But it will be done. And it will be done before the end of this decade.

And I am delighted that this university is playing a part in putting a man on the moon as part of a great national effort of the United States of America.

Many years ago the great British explorer George Mallory, who was to die on Mount Everest, was asked why did he want to climb it. He said, 'Because it is there.'

Well, space is there, and we're going to climb it, and the moon and the planets are there, and new hopes for knowledge and peace are there. And, therefore, as we set sail we ask God's blessing on the most hazardous and dangerous and greatest adventure on which man has ever embarked.

Thank you.

Study Question

1. Some have argued that Kennedy's determination to put a man on the moon represented a massive waste of funds that were desperately needed in other areas. Do you agree? Why or why not?

VALENTINA TERESHKOVA

In June 1963 Valentina Tereshkova (b. 1937) became the first woman in space when she completed a three-day, forty-eight-orbit mission in Vostok 6. She later completed a graduate degree in engineering and became a key member of the Soviet government in the 1970s and 1980s. Despite the fall of the Soviet Union, Tereshkova remains a highly respected figure in Russia and, in 2008, disclosed to Pravda *that she would like to complete a final mission to Mars. In the interview which follows, Tereshkova's patriotism remains clear.*

ON THE SOVIET SPACE PROGRAMME

Q: You are the head of the Russian Center for International Scientific and Cultural Cooperation. In your opinion, how much interest is there in Russian science and technology in the rest of the world?

A: There is great interest and that is only natural. In the second half of the 20th century our country launched the first artificial space satellite and sent the first man into space, built the first-ever passenger jet, the first nuclear reactor and the first quantum generator. Such a research potential cannot dissipate overnight no matter how adverse the circumstances. Even today our scientists and engineers get impressive results. Take the SU and MIG planes which have no analogies in the world and epitomize the most advanced and innovative engineering trends of our day. . . .

Q: I understand that one of the Center's main activities is spreading the Russian language. How popular is Russian in the world today? What language programs does the Center support?

A: Interest in the Russian language abroad has always been quite high. People want to read the masterpieces of Russian literature in the original and many are keen to learn the language for their professional careers. According to the International Association of Teachers of the Russian Language and Literature, there are 27 million students of Russian in the world. Our Center has its own Russian language courses and a staff of experienced teachers who regularly deliver lectures and conduct methodological seminars in universities and other schools in foreign countries. In quite a few countries the Center's missions support local associations of Russian scholars as well.

Lately, intense short-term courses running from three weeks to a year have been the most popular. They fit the needs of business people, journalists, all sorts of government officials, such as customs officers, for example, and tourist guides. We also run crash courses—12 to 20 hours long—for tourists. We also provide individual tutors for business people and, at the same time, prepare people who are planning to enroll in Russian universities.

Some 20,000 students attend the Russian language courses operated by the Center in 40 foreign countries. These courses have been very popular for years. We also have classes for school and even preschool children. For example, last year the Center's office in Mongolia launched a school for kindergarten children where they can study not only Russian but also the Mongolian language, music and basic math.

We also conduct contests for students of Russian in many countries, and some of the winners win trips to Russia. Last year such trips were organized for students from Yugoslavia, Rumania, Poland, Hungary and several other countries. Finally, on the eve of the 200th birthday anniversary of Pushkin, our national poet, the centers are organizing literary parties, exhibitions and conferences aimed at familiarizing the public with the poet's life and work.

Q: What about the Center's work in the field of higher education? How many foreign students come to Russia to get a higher education? Which professions are in most demand?

A: Some 60,000 undergraduate and graduate students and trainees study in Russian universities. Most of them pay their own expenses. But our country offers scholarships to some of the foreign students. As a rule, the recipients are those who major in fields which are most important in cooperation between Russia and other countries. As for the professions which are in special demand among foreigners, I can mention architecture and civil engineering, machine-building, medicine and jurisprudence. As a matter of fact, many graduates of Russian schools have become prominent politicians, scientists and entrepreneurs in their countries.

Our center in Moscow and its offices in other countries are keeping the public abreast of the system of Russian higher education, its research and pedagogical potential at exhibitions and presentations for various schools of higher learning.

Together with diplomats working at Russian embassies abroad, the Center's staffers decide whom among the applicants to give state scholarships to study in Russian universities. Incidentally, we have a good tradition of helping maintain contacts between alumni of Russian schools and their alma maters. . . .

Q: Ms. Tereshkova, this summer will be the 35th anniversary of your historic space flight. Many people today are speaking about the hard times that have fallen on the Russian space program. What do you think about it?

A: It would be more correct to say that the conditions in which Russian space science is developing now are not the best. But Russia has not yielded its lead in space research, and there is much proof of this. Just take the work of the Mir orbital station. It is a unique experiment in the 20th-century engineering practice. A tremendous amount of research has been performed on the Mir station, including the longest space flight—up to 438 days. Cosmonauts from Afghanistan, Austria, Bulgaria, France, Germany, Great Britain, Japan, India, Syria and the US have worked on board the Mir. I am convinced that the modular structure of the Mir will be the main trend in manned orbital stations development in the next century.

Furthermore, Russia is an active participant in major international commercial space projects. It is playing a leading role in the development of the Maritime Start platform in the Atlantic from which earth satellites will be launched and is collaborating with the US, Japan, Canada and the European Space Union in the construction of the Alpha international space station, where it is responsible for eight of the 18 modules.

Therefore Russia is still the leader in world space exploration. But its position of leader involves great responsibility—we have no right to lag behind. We can and we must move constantly forward.

Q: Do you remember what you felt at the moment your space flight was over and you were again among us here on Earth? What was the hardest thing for you during those several days in outer space?

A: First of all I felt that I had done my duty and had become convinced that men and women could work in space. Throughout the flight I was so preoccupied with the desire to cope with my assignment that it overshadowed the natural feeling of risk I was taking. But I was aware of the risk involved. So when I landed, I was simply overwhelmed with joy that it was all over and behind—the weightlessness, the closed space of the ship, and all sorts of extraordinary situations which, theoretically, might have happened. And when I was back among people, I repeated the words of Frederic Jolios after the flight of Yuri Gagarin[1]: 'Mankind is no longer chained to its planet.'

Q: Do you ever see your colleagues from the first cosmonaut unit?

A: Of course, I do. We are all great friends. We have lived together through triumphs and failures and the death of our comrades. I also have professional ties with the 'Zvezdnyi gorodok'.[2] Last year we celebrated the anniversary of the launching of the first earth satellite by holding an international symposium featuring Russia's accomplishments in space exploration and international cooperation in space. . . . It was held at the Berlin headquarters of the Russian Center for Scientific and Cultural Cooperation.

Notes

1.   Yuri Gagarin (1934–68) was the first man in space, in April 1961.
2.   Star City, the site of the Gagarin Russian

State Scientific-Research Test Center for Cosmonaut Training and location of the majority of the Soviet space programme from the 1960s onwards.

Study Question

1. Why did the Soviet Union place such great emphasis on the space race?

MARSHALL McLUHAN

An Edmonton native, Herbert Marshall McLuhan (1911–80) was drawn to the study of culture and communication in the 1940s. In 1951 he published The Mechanical Bride, *which is viewed by many to have established 'popular culture' as a legitimate field of study.*

Much of McLuhan's work focused on the impact of various media technologies on communication among people. In the interview below, McLuhan comments on the impact of a number of media technologies, focusing in particular on the television.

THE PLAYBOY INTERVIEW, MARCH 1969 (CONDUCTED BY ERIC NORDEN)

PLAYBOY: To borrow Henry Gibson's oft-repeated one-line poem on Rowan and Martin's Laugh-In—'Marshall McLuhan, what are you doin'?'

MCLUHAN: Sometimes I wonder. I'm making explorations. I don't know where they're going to take me. My work is designed for the pragmatic purpose of trying to understand our technological environment and its psychic and social consequences. But my books constitute the process rather than the completed product of discovery; my purpose is to employ facts as tentative probes, as means of insight, of pattern recognition, rather than to use them in the traditional and sterile sense of classified data, categories, containers. I want to map new terrain rather than chart old landmarks. . . .

PLAYBOY: Will you trace [the impact of media technologies] for us—in condensed form?

MCLUHAN: It's difficult to condense into the format of an interview such as this, but I'll try

to give you a brief rundown of the basic media breakthroughs. You've got to remember that my definition of media is broad; it includes any technology whatever that creates extensions of the human body and senses, from clothing to the computer. And a vital point I must stress again is that societies have always been shaped more by the nature of the media with which men communicate than by the content of the communication. All technology has the property of the Midas touch; whenever a society develops an extension of itself, all other functions of that society tend to be transmuted to accommodate that new form; once any new technology penetrates a society, it saturates every institution of that society. New technology is thus a revolutionizing agent. We see this today with the electric media and we saw it several thousand years ago with the invention of the phonetic alphabet, which was just as far-reaching an innovation—and had just as profound consequences for man. . . .

The age of print, which held sway from approximately 1500 to 1900, had its obituary tapped out by the telegraph, the first of the new electric media, and further obsequies were registered by the perception of 'curved space' and non-Euclidean mathematics in the early years of the century, which revived tribal man's discontinuous time–space concepts—and which even Spengler dimly perceived as the death knell of Western literate values. The development of telephone, radio, film, television and the computer have driven further nails into the coffin. Today, television is the most significant of the electric media because it permeates nearly every home in the country, extending the central nervous system of every viewer as it works over and molds the entire sensorium[1] with the ultimate message. It is television that is primarily responsible for ending the visual supremacy that characterized all mechanical technology, although each of the other electric media have played contributing roles.

PLAYBOY: But isn't television itself a primarily visual medium?

MCLUHAN: No, it's quite the opposite, although the idea that TV is a visual extension is an understandable mistake. Unlike film or photograph, television is primarily an extension of the sense of touch rather than of sight, and it is the tactile sense that demands the greatest interplay of all the senses. The secret of TV's tactile power is that the video image is one of low intensity or definition and thus, unlike either photograph or film, offers no detailed information about specific objects but instead involves the active participation of the viewer. The TV image is a mosaic mesh not only of horizontal lines but of millions of tiny dots, of which the viewer is physiologically able to pick up only 50 or 60 from which he shapes the image; thus he is constantly filling in vague and blurry images, bringing himself into in-depth involvement with the screen and acting out a constant creative dialog with the iconoscope. The contours of the resultant cartoonlike image are fleshed out within the imagination of the viewer, which necessitates great personal involvement and participation; the viewer, in fact, becomes the screen, whereas in film he becomes the camera. By requiring us to constantly fill in the spaces of the mosaic mesh, the iconoscope is tattooing its message directly on our skins. Each viewer is thus an unconscious pointillist painter like Seurat, limning new shapes and images as the iconoscope washes over his entire body. . . .

PLAYBOY: Even if, as you contend, the medium is the ultimate message, how can you entirely discount the importance of content? Didn't the content of Hitler's radio speeches, for example, have some effect on the Germans?

MCLUHAN: By stressing that the medium is the message rather than the content, I'm not suggesting that content plays no role—merely that it plays a distinctly subordinate role. Even if Hitler had delivered botany lectures, some other demagog [sic] would have used the radio to retribalize the Germans and rekindle the dark atavistic side of the tribal nature that created European fascism in the Twenties and Thirties. By placing all the stress on content and practically none on the medium, we lose all chance of perceiving and influencing the impact of new technologies on man, and thus we are always dumfounded by—and unprepared for—the revolutionary environmental transformations induced by new media. Buffeted by environmental changes he cannot comprehend, man echoes the last plaintive cry of his tribal ancestor, Tarzan, as he plummeted to earth: 'Who greased my vine?'. . .

PLAYBOY: How is television reshaping our political institutions?

MCLUHAN: TV is revolutionizing every political system in the Western world. For one thing, it's creating a totally new type of national leader, a man who is much more of a tribal chieftain than a politician. Castro is a good example of the new tribal chieftain who rules his country by a mass-participational TV dialog and feedback; he governs his country on camera, by giving the Cuban people the experience of being directly and intimately involved in the process of collective decision making. Castro's adroit blend of political education, propaganda and avuncular guidance is the pattern for tribal chieftains in other countries. The new political showman has to literally as well as figuratively put on his audience as he would a suit of clothes and become a corporate tribal image—like Mussolini, Hitler and F.D.R. in the days of radio, and Jack Kennedy in the television era. All these men were tribal emperors on a scale theretofore unknown in the world, because they all mastered their media.

PLAYBOY: How did Kennedy use TV in a manner different from his predecessors—or successors?

MCLUHAN: Kennedy was the first TV President because he was the first prominent American politician to ever understand the dynamics and lines of force of the television iconoscope. As I've explained, TV is an inherently cool medium, and Kennedy had a compatible coolness and indifference to power, bred of personal wealth, which allowed him to adapt fully to TV. Any political candidate who doesn't have such cool, low definition qualities, which allow the viewer to fill in the gaps with his own personal identification, simply electrocutes himself on television—as Richard Nixon did in his disastrous debates with Kennedy in the 1960 campaign. Nixon was essentially hot; he presented a high-definition, sharply-defined image and action on the TV screen that contributed to his reputation as a phony—the 'Tricky Dicky' syndrome that has dogged his footsteps for years. 'Would you buy a used car from this man?' the political cartoon asked—and the answer was no, because he didn't project the cool aura of disinterest and objectivity that Kennedy emanated so effortlessly and engagingly. . . .

PLAYBOY: A number of experimental projects are bringing both TV and computers directly into the classrooms. Do you consider this sort of electronic educational aid a step in the right direction?

MCLUHAN: It's not really too important if there is ever a TV set in each classroom across the country, since the sensory and attitudinal revolution has already taken place at home before the child ever reaches school, altering his sensory existence and his mental processes in profound ways. Book learning is no longer sufficient in any subject; the children all say now, 'Let's talk Spanish,' or 'Let the Bard be heard,' reflecting their rejection of the old sterile system where education begins and ends in a book. What we need now is educational crash programming in depth to first understand and then meet the new challenges. Just putting the present classroom on TV, with its archaic values and methods, won't change anything; it would be just like running movies on television; the result would be a hybrid that is neither. We have to ask what TV can do, in the instruction of English or physics or any other subject, that the classroom cannot do as presently constituted. The answer is that TV can deeply involve youth in the process of learning, illustrating graphically the complex interplay of people and events, the development of forms, the multileveled interrelationships between and among such arbitrarily segregated subjects as biology, geography, mathematics, anthropology, history, literature and languages.

If education is to become relevant to the young of this electric age, we must also supplant the stifling, impersonal and dehumanizing multiversity with a multiplicity of autonomous colleges devoted to an in-depth approach to learning. This must be done immediately, for few adults really comprehend the intensity of youth's alienation from the fragmented mechanical world and its fossilized educational system, which is designed in their minds solely to fit them into classified slots in bureaucratic society. To them, both draft card and degree are passports to psychic, if not physical, oblivion, and they accept neither. A new generation is alienated from its own 3,000-year heritage of literacy and visual culture, and the celebration of literate values in home and school only intensifies that alienation. If we don't adapt our educational system to their needs and values, we will see only more dropouts and more chaos.

Note

1.   Sensorium: all of the senses combined.

> **Study Question**
>
> 1.   Do you agree with McLuhan's assertion that technology has introduced a revolutionary environmental transformation?

RACHEL CARSON

Rachel Carson (1907–64) was a biologist and naturalist by training. Her work on river and ocean ecosystems in the 1940s led to an increasing awareness of the impact of synthetic pesticide use. Carson's concern for the environment was crystallized in 1957 by a US Department of Agriculture (USDA) campaign to eliminate fire- *ants. Carson argued that the effects of the pesticides used had been inadequately researched. Her 1962 monograph* Silent Spring *assessed the human and animal toll of widespread pesticide use. Despite widespread attacks from chemical companies and their political representatives, the book contributed to the successful ban on the pesticide* DDT *in 1972.*

A FABLE FOR TOMORROW

There was once a town in the heart of America where all life seemed to live in harmony with its surroundings. The town lay in the midst of a checkerboard of prosperous farms, with fields of grain and hillsides of orchards where, in spring, white clouds of bloom drifted above the green fields. In autumn, oak and maple and birch set up a blaze of color that flamed and flickered across a backdrop of pines. Then foxes barded in the hills and deer silently crossed the fields, half hidden in the mists of the fall mornings.

Along the roads, laurel, viburnum and alder, great ferns and wildflowers delighted the traveler's eye through much of the year. Even in winter the roadsides were places of beauty, where countless birds came to feed on the berries and on the seed heads of the dried weeds rising above the snow. The countryside was, in fact, famous for the abundance and variety of its bird life, and when the flood of migrants was pouring through in spring and fall people traveled from great distances to observe them. Others came to fish the streams, which flowed clear and cold out of the hills and contained shady pools where trout lay. So it had been from the days many years ago when the first settlers raised their houses, sank their wells, and built their barns.

Then a strange blight crept over the area and everything began to change. Some evil spell had settled on the community: mysterious maladies swept the flocks of chickens; the cattle and sheep sickened and died. Everywhere was a shadow of death. The farmers spoke of much illness among their families. In the town the doctors had become more and more puzzled by new kinds of sickness appearing among their patients. There had been several sudden and unexplained deaths, not only among adults but even among children, who would be stricken suddenly while at play and die within a few hours.

There was a strange stillness. The birds, for example—where had they gone? Many spoke of them, puzzled and disturbed. The feeding stations in the backyards were deserted. The few birds seen anywhere were moribund; they trembled violently and could not fly. It was a spring without voices. On the mornings that had once throbbed with the dawn chorus of robins, catbirds, doves, hays, wrens, and scores of other bird voices there was now no sound; only silence lay over the fields and woods and marsh.

On the farms the hens brooded, but no chicks hatched. The farmers complained that they were unable to raise any pigs—the litters were small and the young survived only a few days. The apple trees were coming into bloom but no bees droned among the blossoms, so there was no pollination and there would be no fruit.

The roadsides, once so attractive, were now lined with browned and withered vegetation as though swept by fire. These, too, were silent, deserted by all living things. Even the streams were now lifeless. Anglers no longer visited them, for all the fish had died.

In the gutters under the eaves and between the shingles of the roofs, a white granular powder still showed a few patches; some weeks before it had fallen like snow upon the roofs and the lawns, the fields and streams.

No witchcraft, no enemy action had silenced the rebirth of new life in this stricken world. The people had done it themselves.

This town does not actually exist, but it might easily have a thousand counterparts in America or elsewhere in the world. I know of no community that has experienced all the misfortunes I

Rachel Carson collecting specimens of marine life in the Florida Keys in 1955. Courtesy US Fish and Wildlife Service National Digital Library.

describe. Yet every one of these disasters has actually happened somewhere, and many real communities have already suffered a substantial number of them. A grim specter has crept upon us almost unnoticed, and this imagined tragedy may easily become a stark reality we all shall know.

What has already silenced the voices of spring in countless towns in America? . . .

Study Question

1. Carson came under attack for branding all pesticides as evil. Was this a fair criticism?

REX WEYLER

Rex Weyler (b. 1947) is a journalist and activist who has been involved in the Canadian environmental movement since the early 1970s. He took part in many of the early campaigns of Greenpeace and served on the board of the Greenpeace Foundation. *In the article which follows, Weyler recalls the context in which concern for the environment first emerged, as well as the events leading to the creation of the Greenpeace Foundation.*

WAVES OF COMPASSION

I arrived in Vancouver, on the west coast of Canada, in the spring of 1972 as a fugitive of American justice, a draft-resister with the FBI on my trail and intimidating my family to give me up. I faced 25 years in prison had they caught me. My wife of 6 months, Glenn, and I slept by the furnace in the cellar of a Vancouver shelter set up for war objectors on 7th Avenue near Fir Street. We had our sleeping bags, a change of clothes, forty-seven dollars, and a wrinkled piece of paper with the names of Canadian peace activists who might help us.

Unitarian minister and University librarian Mac Elrod and his wife Norma took us in and introduced us to the local pacifist crowd. I found a job as reporter and photographer at the *North Shore News* community newspaper. While covering a local story, I met Bree Drummond who was sitting in a platform, high in a cottonwood tree to save it from being felled for a parking lot by North Vancouver maintenance crews. Her boyfriend, Rod Marining, was a wild Yippie environmentalist who had helped stop the construction of a Four Seasons Hotel at the entrance to Vancouver's magnificent Stanley Park by declaring the land 'All Season Park' and camping out on the site until the developers gave up. He also had sailed for the Aleutian Island of Amchitka to protest a US atomic bomb test there as a member of the Don't Make A Wave

Committee that had changed its name to the 'Greenpeace Foundation' that spring.

Rod introduced me to Bob Hunter from Winnipeg, clearly the hippest young journalist in the city, writing a daily column in the Vancouver *Sun* in which he explained Gestalt Therapy, described peyote ceremonies, introduced edgy psychologists like R.D. Laing, and quoted famed ecologist Rachel Carson. Hunter had written a brilliant novel, *Erebus*, and a profound, post-McLuhan analysis of media and social consciousness, *Storming of the Mind*. He had also sailed on the protest boat with the Don't Make a Wave Committee. He had a beard, long hair, and a large leather bag over his shoulder, filled with newspaper clippings, books, and his own journal in which he wrote incessantly. I liked him right away, traveled in similar media circles, and began sharing beer and philosophy with him at the Cecil Hotel pub. Now, three decades later, the Cecil is a glitzy strip bar, but in the early 1970s it was a pool hall and hangout for Vancouver radicals and intelligencia. Greenpeace had no public office at this time. We sat near the pay-phone to conduct both our journalist and activist business. . . .

It was here in the pub that Dr Paul Spong, a scientist at the Vancouver Aquarium, appeared in 1974 promoting his radical idea that we should put our lives on the line to save the whales. The anti-war activists were skeptical at first, but

Preparing to sail from Vancouver to Amchitka Island to protest nuclear testing in 1971. From left to right: Jim Bohlen, John Cormack, Erving Stowe, and Paul Cote. © Bettman/CORBIS.

Spong's idea would soon change the face of this little band of radicals.

On an Ocean Named for Peace

In 1969 in Vancouver hippies and revolutionaries mixed gleefully in the redbrick coffee houses of Gastown, and in the rainbow-painted organic juice bars of tree-lined Kitsilano near the University of British Columbia. 'Revolutions,' says Hunter, 'start at the outer fringes of the empire, in this case the American Empire.' When the US announced that summer that they were going to test a 1.2 megaton nuclear bomb on the Aleutian Island of Amchitka, Vancouver peaceniks, love children, American draft dodgers, and Marxist revolutionaries began to agitate. In September 1969 Hunter warned in his newspaper column of 'a distinct danger that the tests might set in motion earthquakes and tidal waves which could sweep from one end of the Pacific to the other'. This image of the tidal wave captured the imagination of Canadians opposed to the US bomb test.

Three decades later Hunter recalls 'In Vancouver at that time there was a convergence of hippies, draft dodgers, Tibetan monks, seadogs, artists, radical ecologists, rebel journalists, Quakers, and expatriate Yanks in the one major city that happened to be closest to Amchitka Island, where the U.S. wanted to explode a bomb. Greenpeace was born of all of this.'

Vancouver lawyer Hamish Bruce read Hunter's columns and called the reporter. Bruce wanted to start an organization called the 'Green Panthers'. Hunter and Bruce became fast friends. They plotted to establish the Green Panthers as the ecological equivalent of the Black Panthers, whose leader, Fred Hampton, Hunter had interviewed in Chicago. 'Our idea,' says Bruce today, 'was that ecology was the sleeping giant, the issue that was ultimately going to rock the world.'

At that time, Hunter was writing his third book, *Storming of the Mind*, about the 'new holistic consciousness', in which he declares 'In ecology we see the new consciousness finding its roots'. Hunter predicted that continued environmental deterioration would lead to the rise of 'the Green Panthers or their equivalent', and he advocated 'the hoisting of the green flag'.

On October 2, when the US detonated the bomb at Amchitka, a mob from Vancouver stormed the US border, closing it to traffic for two hours. A banner placed at the border crossing read: 'Don't Make a Wave' in reference to the potential tidal wave. In January 1970 the protestors moved to the US Embassy and 'liberated' Granville Street in downtown Vancouver. The seeds of Greenpeace were in these crowds. Hippies on bicycles milled among the anti-bomb protestors, stopping cars and delivering speeches about ecology.

Among the protestors was freelance journalist Ben Metcalfe, who had a radio program on the CBC. Metcalfe, on his own initiative, had placed 12 billboard signs in Vancouver that read:

Ecology
Look it up. You're involved.

'It's hard to imagine now,' says Metcalfe, 'but in those days most people had no idea what the word ecology meant. I was doing environmental stories on my radio program and I started a campaign to stop the Skagit River Dam. In the winter of 1969 and 1970, the US bomb tests were the hot story. The night we closed the US border, Hunter and Hamish Bruce were there, and Jim and Marie Bohlen.' . . .

. . . Marie Bohlen, inspired by the Quaker boat the Golden Rule, suggested to Jim one morning over coffee that someone should 'just sail a boat up there and confront the bomb'. Moments later, in one of the synchronous events that would

characterize the evolution of Greenpeace, a Vancouver *Sun* reporter phoned for an update on the Sierra Club's plans to protest the bomb. 'Before I knew it,' recalls Jim Bohlen, 'I was telling them we were sailing a boat into the test zone.'

The next day, the *Sun* ran the story, but the Sierra Club had not officially ratified the action, so at the next Don't Make a Wave meeting, the ad hoc group adopted the plan. Typical of those days, the anti-war crowd parted with the V-sign, saying 'peace'. A quiet 23-year-old Canadian carpenter, union organizer, and ecologist, Bill Darnell, who rarely spoke at the meetings, added sheepishly 'Make it a green peace.'

'The term had a nice ring to it,' Hunter recalls. 'It worked better in a headline than The Don't Make a Wave Committee. We decided to find a boat and call it Greenpeace'. . . .

These twelve souls headed off across the Gulf of Alaska for Amchitka Island, making landfall on Akutan Island on September 26. The Greenpeace was immediately seized by the US Coast Guard for landing without permission and escorted back to Sand Point, Alaska, where they paid a fine and were released. The bomb test was then postponed until November, but the boat charter with Captain Cormack ran out at the end of October.

'We found out in Sand Point,' recalls Metcalfe, 'that the voyage was getting media attention in Canada and the US. Demonstrations had occurred in every major Canadian city.' Twenty members of the Coast Guard vessel Confidence, which seized the Greenpeace boat, signed a letter saying 'what you are doing is for the good of all mankind'. The protestors sensed that they were having an impact, but there was a fierce battle among the crew. Hunter wanted to continue on to Amchitka, while Bohlen and Metcalfe felt they had done their job and should head home. Bohlen took charge and instructed Cormack to head for Vancouver. At Kodiak Fineberg left the boat and Rod Marining joined. In the meantime, the Don't Make A Wave Committee chartered a larger, faster Canadian minesweeper, renamed Greenpeace Too. The two boats met in Union Bay, BC where, Simmons, Cummings, Marining, and Birmingham joined the second boat, headed for Amchitka.

'During the voyage,' Hunter remembers, 'Metcalfe, Bohlen, and I discussed replacing Irving Stowe as the leader. But Stowe had control of Don't Make a Wave, so I suggested we start a new organization called Greenpeace.' When they returned, Hunter, Moore, and Bruce founded The Whole Earth Church, using the Greenpeace emblem and Moore's now famous line from the voyage, 'A flower is your brother'. The Whole Earth Church espoused that 'all forms of life are inter-related. Any form of life which goes against the natural laws of interdependency has fallen from the State of Grace known as ecological harmony.' Members of the Church were asked to 'assume their rightful role as Custodians of the Earth'.

It was during this voyage that Hunter read *Warriors of the Rainbow* by William Willoya and Vinson Brown, which recounts the Cree Indian prophecy that one day, when the earth was poisoned by humans, a group of people from all nations would band together to defend nature. 'Well, this is us, I thought right away,' Hunter remembers. 'We're the Warriors of the Rainbow.'

> **Study Question**
>
> 1. How effective have radical ecology groups such as Greenpeace been?

ALBERT GORE

In 2007 Al Gore (b. 1948) and the Intergovernmental Panel on Climate Change were named joint recipients of the Nobel Peace Prize for their efforts to raise awareness of man-made global climate change. Gore's environmental activism dates back to the mid-1970s, but he was able to reach a wider audience in the 1990s when he served as US President Bill Clinton's vice-president (1993–2001). After his failed bid for the presidency in 2000, Gore devoted himself with increasing urgency to environmental causes.

NOBEL LECTURE

We, the human species, are confronting a planetary emergency—a threat to the survival of our civilization that is gathering ominous and destructive potential even as we gather here. But there is hopeful news as well: we have the ability to solve this crisis and avoid the worst—though not all—of its consequences, if we act boldly, decisively and quickly.

However, despite a growing number of honorable exceptions, too many of the world's leaders are still best described in the words Winston Churchill applied to those who ignored Adolf Hitler's threat: 'They go on in strange paradox, decided only to be undecided, resolved to be irresolute, adamant for drift, solid for fluidity, all powerful to be impotent.'

So today, we dumped another 70 million tons of global-warming pollution into the thin shell of atmosphere surrounding our planet, as if it were an open sewer. And tomorrow, we will dump a slightly larger amount, with the cumulative concentrations now trapping more and more heat from the sun.

As a result, the earth has a fever. And the fever is

rising. The experts have told us it is not a passing affliction that will heal by itself. We asked for a second opinion. And a third. And a fourth. And the consistent conclusion, restated with increasing alarm, is that something basic is wrong.

We are what is wrong, and we must make it right.

Last September 21, as the Northern Hemisphere tilted away from the sun, scientists reported with unprecedented distress that the North Polar ice cap is 'falling off a cliff'. One study estimated that it could be completely gone during summer in less than 22 years. Another new study, to be presented by US Navy researchers later this week, warns it could happen in as little as seven years.

Seven years from now.

In the last few months, it has been harder and harder to misinterpret the signs that our world is spinning out of kilter. Major cities in North and South America, Asia and Australia are nearly out of water due to massive droughts and melting glaciers. Desperate farmers are losing their livelihoods. Peoples in the frozen Arctic and on low-lying Pacific islands are planning evacuations of places they have long called home. Unprecedented wildfires have forced a half million people from their homes in one country and caused a national emergency that almost brought down the government in another. Climate refugees have migrated into areas already inhabited by people with different cultures, religions, and traditions, increasing the potential for conflict. Stronger storms in the Pacific and Atlantic have threatened whole cities. Millions have been displaced by massive flooding in South Asia, Mexico, and 18 countries in Africa. As temperature extremes have increased, tens of thousands have lost their lives. We are recklessly burning and clearing our forests and driving more and more species into extinction. The very web of life on which we depend is being ripped and frayed.

We never intended to cause all this destruction, just as Alfred Nobel never intended that dynamite be used for waging war. He had hoped his invention would promote human progress. We shared that same worthy goal when we began burning massive quantities of coal, then oil and methane. . . .

We also find it hard to imagine making the massive changes that are now necessary to solve the crisis. And when large truths are genuinely inconvenient, whole societies can, at least for a time, ignore them. Yet as George Orwell reminds us: 'Sooner or later a false belief bumps up against solid reality, usually on a battlefield.'

In the years since this prize was first awarded, the entire relationship between humankind and the earth has been radically transformed. And still, we have remained largely oblivious to the impact of our cumulative actions.

Indeed, without realizing it, we have begun to wage war on the earth itself. Now, we and the earth's climate are locked in a relationship familiar to war planners: 'Mutually assured destruction.'

More than two decades ago, scientists calculated that nuclear war could throw so much debris and smoke into the air that it would block life-giving sunlight from our atmosphere, causing a 'nuclear winter'. Their eloquent warnings here in Oslo helped galvanize the world's resolve to halt the nuclear arms race.

Now science is warning us that if we do not quickly reduce the global warming pollution that is trapping so much of the heat our planet normally radiates back out of the atmosphere, we are in danger of creating a permanent 'carbon summer'.

As the American poet Robert Frost wrote, 'Some say the world will end in fire; some say in ice.' Either, he notes, 'would suffice'.

But neither need be our fate. It is time to make peace with the planet.

We must quickly mobilize our civilization with the urgency and resolve that has previously been seen only when nations mobilized for war. These prior struggles for survival were won when leaders found words at the 11th hour that released a mighty surge of courage, hope and readiness to sacrifice for a protracted and mortal challenge.

These were not comforting and misleading assurances that the threat was not real or imminent; that it would affect others but not ourselves; that ordinary life might be lived even in the presence of extraordinary threat; that Providence could be trusted to do for us what we would not do for ourselves.

No, these were calls to come to the defense of the common future. They were calls upon the courage, generosity and strength of entire peoples, citizens of every class and condition who were ready to stand against the threat once asked to do so. Our enemies in those times calculated that free people would not rise to the challenge; they were, of course, catastrophically wrong.

Now comes the threat of climate crisis—a threat that is real, rising, imminent, and universal. Once again, it is the 11th hour. The penalties for ignoring this challenge are immense and growing, and at some near point would be unsustainable and unrecoverable. For now we still have the power to choose our fate, and the remaining question is only this: Have we the will to act vigorously and in time, or will we remain imprisoned by a dangerous illusion?

Mahatma Gandhi awakened the largest democracy on earth and forged a shared resolve with what he called 'Satyagraha'—or 'truth force'.

In every land, the truth—once known—has the power to set us free.

Truth also has the power to unite us and bridge the distance between 'me' and 'we', creating the basis for common effort and shared responsibility.

There is an African proverb that says, 'If you want to go quickly, go alone. If you want to go far, go together.' We need to go far, quickly.

We must abandon the conceit that individual, isolated, private actions are the answer. They can and do help. But they will not take us far enough without collective action. At the same time, we must ensure that in mobilizing globally, we do not invite the establishment of ideological conformity and a new lock-step 'ism'.

That means adopting principles, values, laws, and treaties that release creativity and initiative at every level of society in multifold responses originating concurrently and spontaneously.

This new consciousness requires expanding the possibilities inherent in all humanity. The innovators who will devise a new way to harness the sun's energy for pennies or invent an engine that's carbon negative may live in Lagos or Mumbai or Montevideo. We must ensure that entrepreneurs and inventors everywhere on the globe have the chance to change the world.

When we unite for a moral purpose that is manifestly good and true, the spiritual energy unleashed can transform us. The generation that defeated fascism throughout the world in the 1940s found, in rising to meet their awesome challenge, that they had gained the moral authority and long-term vision to launch the Marshall Plan, the United Nations, and a new level of global cooperation and foresight that unified Europe and facilitated the emergence of democracy and prosperity in Germany, Japan, Italy and much of the world. One of their visionary leaders said, 'It is time we steered by the stars and not by the lights of every passing ship.' . . .

We have everything we need to get started, save perhaps political will, but political will is a renewable resource.

So let us renew it, and say together: 'We have a purpose. We are many. For this purpose we will rise, and we will act.'

Study Question

1. Why does Gore warn that the establishment of a 'lock-step-ism' such as 'environmentalism' is the wrong approach to solve the global environmental crisis?

STEPHEN HAWKING

Stephen Hawking (b. 1942) is a world-renowned theoretical physicist from Great Britain. He has worked on questions relating to cosmology and quantum gravity for over forty years and has also authored a number of popular works, *including* A Brief History of Time, *aimed at making his theories accessible to a lay audience. The speech which follows was part of NASA's 50th Anniversary Lecture Series and was delivered in April 2008.*

WHY WE SHOULD GO INTO SPACE

Why we should go into space. What is that justification for spending all that effort and money on getting a few lumps of moon rock? Aren't there better causes here on Earth?

Stephen Hawking visits the Kennedy Space Center in 2007 in preparation for a zero gravity flight. NASA//Kim Shiflett.

In a way, the situation was like that in Europe before 1492. People might well have argued that it was a waste of money to send Columbus on a wild goose chase. Yet, the discovery of the new world made a profound difference to the old. Just think, we wouldn't have had a Big Mac or a KFC. *[Laughter.]*

Spreading out into space will have an even greater effect. It will completely change the future of the human race and maybe determine whether we have any future at all.

It won't solve any of our immediate problems on Planet Earth, but it will give us a new perspective on them and cause us to look outwards and inwards. Hopefully, it would unite us to face a common challenge.

This would be a long-term strategy, and by long term, I mean hundreds or even thousands of years. We could have a base on the Moon within 30 years or reach Mars in 50 years and explore the moons of the outer planets in 200 years. By 'reach', I mean with man or, should I say, person space flight.

We have already driven Rover and landed a probe on Titan, a moon of Saturn, but if one is considering the future of the human race, we have to go there ourselves.

Going into space won't be cheap, but it will take only a small proportion of world resources. NASA's budget has remained roughly constant in real terms since the time of the Apollo landings, but it has decreased from 0.3 per cent of US GDP in 1970 to 0.12 per cent now.

Even if we were to increase the international budget 20 times to make a serious effort to go into space, it would only be a small fraction of world GDP.

There will be those who argue that it would be better to spend our money solving the problems of this planet, like climate change and pollution, rather than wasting it on a possibly fruitless search for a new planet.

I am not denying the importance of fighting climate change and global warming, but we can do that and still spare a quarter of a percent of world GDP for space. Isn't our future worth a quarter of [a] per cent?

We thought space was worth a big effort in the '60s. In 1962, President Kennedy committed the US to landing a man on the Moon by the end of the decade. This was achieved just in time by the Apollo 11 mission in 1969.

The space race helped to create a fascination with science and led to great advances in technology, including the first large-scale integrated circuits which are the basis of all modern computers.

However, after the last Moon landing in 1972, with no future plans for further manned space flight, public interest in space declined. This went along with a general dissention with science in the West because, although it had brought great benefits, it had not solved the social problems that increasingly occupied public attention.

A new manned space flight program would do a lot to restore public enthusiasm for space and for science generally.

Robotic missions are much cheaper and may provide more scientific information, but they don't catch the public imagination in the same way, and they don't spread the human race into space which I am arguing should be our long-term strategy.

A goal of a base on the Moon by 2020 and of a man landing on Mars by 2025 would reignite a space program and give it a sense of purpose in the same way that President Kennedy's Moon target did in the 1960s.

A new interest in space would also increase the public standing of science generally. The low esteem in which science and scientists are held is having serious consequences. We live in a society that is increasingly governed by science and technology, yet fewer and fewer young people long to go into science. . . .

Can we exist for a long time away from the Earth? Our experience with the ISS, the International Space Station, shows that it is possible for human beings to survive for many months away from Planet Earth. However, the zero gravity aboard it causes a number of undesirable physiological changes and weakening of the bones, as well as creating practical problems with liquids, et cetera.

One would, therefore, want any long-term base for human beings to be on a planet or moon. By digging into the surface, one would get thermal insulation and protection from meteors and cosmic rays. The planet or moon could also serve as a source of the raw materials that would be needed if the extraterrestrial community was to be self-sustaining independently of Earth.

What are the possible sites of a human colony in the solar system? The most obvious is the Moon. It is close by and relatively easy to reach. We have already landed on it and driven across it in a buggy.

On the other hand, the Moon is small and without atmosphere or a magnetic field to deflect the solar radiation particles, like on Earth. There is no liquid water, but there may be ice in the craters at the north and south poles. A colony on the Moon could use this as a source of oxygen with power provided by nuclear energy or solar panels. The Moon could be a base for travel to the rest of the solar system.

Mars is the obvious next target. It is half as far, again, as the Earth from the Sun and so receives half the warmth. It once had a magnetic field, but it decayed 4 billion years ago, leaving Mars without protection from solar radiation. It stripped Mars of most of its atmosphere, leaving it with only 1 per cent of the pressure of the Earth's atmosphere.

However, the pressure must have been higher in the past because we see what appear to be runoff channels and dried-up lakes. Liquid water cannot exist on Mars now.

It would vaporize in the near-vacuum. This suggests that Mars had a warm wet period during which life might have appeared either spontaneously or through panspermia.[1] There is no sign of life on Mars now, but if we found evidence that life had once existed, it would indicate that the probability of life developing on a suitable planet was fairly high. . . .

What about beyond the solar system? Our observations indicate that a significant fraction of stars have planets around them. So far, we can detect only giant planets like Jupiter and Saturn, but it is reasonable to assume that they will be accompanied by smaller Earth-like planets. Some of these will lay in the [inaudible] zone where the distance from the stars is the right range for liquid water to exist on their surface.

There are around a thousand stars within 30 lightyears of Earth. If 1 per cent of each had Earth-size planets in the [inaudible] zone, we would have 10 candidate new worlds. We can revisit it with current technology, but we should make interstellar a long-term aim. By long term, I mean over the next 200 to 500 years. The human race has existed as a separate species for about 2 million years. Civilization began about 10,000 years ago, and the rate of development has been steadily increasing.

If the human race is to continue for another million years, we will have to boldly go where no one has gone before.

Thank you for listening.

Note

1. Panspermia: microorganisms with the potential to generate life under favourable conditions.

Study Question

1. What is the basis for Hawking's claim that the colonization of space will be essential to human survival?

TIPS FOR ANALYSIS

Question Every Source

No matter whether you are reading a primary document or a secondary analysis of a situation, always question the source. Few interpretations are truly balanced; most provide evidence in a selective manner in order to reinforce their own argument. Ask yourself whether or not the author has considered other viewpoints. If not, consider them yourself as part of your evaluation of the source.

WEB RESOURCES

The Eisenhower Archives: Sputnik and the Space Race
http://eisenhower.archives.gov/Research/Digital_Documents/Sputnik/
    Sputnikdocuments.html
NASA (National Aeronautics and Space Administration)
http://www.nasa.gov
Library of Congress: The Environment
http://www.loc.gov/rr/scitech/selected-internet/environment.html
Intergovernmental Panel on Climate Change
http://www.ipcc.ch

RECOMMENDED READING

Rachel Carson, *Silent Spring* (Boston: Houghton Mifflin, 2002). Carson's ground breaking work examines the consequences of the uncontrolled use of pesticides on the natural environment. The book is considered to be one of the seminal works of the 1960s environmental movement.

Isaac Asimov, *I, Robot* (New York: Bantam Spectra, 2008). Originally nine short stories published in 1950, Asimov's *I, Robot* considers questions of morality, responsibility, and humanity through the lens of robotic 'life'.

Frank Herbert, *Dune* (New York: Ace Books, 1999). Herbert's 1965 novel, which takes place thousands of years in the future after humans have populated much of the universe, raises questions about the relationship between humans and animals, greed, expansionism, ecology, and human nature.

Kim Stanley Robinson, *The Mars Trilogy* (New York: Spectra, 1993). Written in three volumes (*Red Mars*, *Green Mars*, *Blue Mars*), Robinson's trilogy focuses on the first settlement of Mars and the resulting consequences of transforming the natural environment of Mars to make it suitable for human habitation.

Michael Crichton, *State of Fear* (New York: HarperCollins, 2005). Crichton's *State of Fear* focuses on an environmental organization planning a series of eco-terrorist attacks around the world in order to bring environmental issues to global attention. The book openly challenges the theory of man-made climate change.

Amulya Malladi, *A Breath of Fresh Air* (New York: Ballantine Books, 2002). Malladi's novel takes place in the aftermath of the 1984 release of toxic methyl isocyanate gas in Bhopal, India. The novel confronts the reader with both the immediate and long term effects of the disaster.

RECOMMENDED VIEWING

Silkwood (US, 1983). Director: Mike Nichols. Nichols's film retells the true story of Karen Silkwood, who was killed under mysterious circumstances in 1974 just before she was scheduled to meet with a *New York Times* reporter about conditions at the Kerr-McGee plutonium fuel plant in Oklahoma where she worked. The plant closed in 1975 but the site remained contaminated for many years.

The Rainbow Warrior Conspiracy (Australia, 1989). Director: Chris Thomson. This Australian drama examines the events leading up to the sinking of the Greenpeace flagship by agents of the French intelligence service in 1985.

Who Killed the Electric Car (US, 2006). Director: Chris Paine. Paine's documentary focuses on the electric cars developed in the 1990s and the chain of events which led to their elimination by the mid-2000s.

An Inconvenient Truth (US, 2006). Director: Davis Guggenheim. The documentary based on Al Gore's environmental slide show. Though attacked for bias and over-simplification by elements of the popular media, Gore's film resonated with its audience in a way that few documentaries ever have before, bringing worldwide attention to the climate crisis.

Flow: For Love of Water (US/France, 2008). Director: Irena Salina. Salina's film focuses on the commoditization of water in the twenty-first century and the resulting impact on politics, economics, and human rights. The film addresses the potential outcome of corporate ownership of water rights.

WALL-E (US, 2008). Director: Andrew Stanton. Stanton's animated film presents a world abandoned by its inhabitants after being rendered uninhabitable by mounds of discarded trash. WALL-E is the robot tasked with cleaning up the planet so that humans—who have become almost immobilized by the technologies that make their lives easier—can return.

CHAPTER THIRTEEN

POST-COLONIAL
LEGACIES

◇

A young Fidel Castro during the guerilla campaign in Cuba's
Sierra Maestra mountains. Courtesy of the Library of Congress,
Prints and Photographs Division (LC-USZ62-72042).

The vast majority of nationalist leaders who led their countries to independence
in the 1950s and 1960s were firmly committed to the promotion of rapid
economic modernization. Prompted by economic advisors from the former
colonial powers, a number of leaders envisioned their nations following the same

path to economic prosperity as the western nations before them: modernization and industrialization would bring future prosperity, even if they required short-term sacrifices.

However, a number of obstacles needed to be overcome if the newly independent nations were to achieve economic success. The economic infrastructure left over from the colonial era was frequently outdated and, even if it could be modernized, had been designed to suit the needs of the colonizer, not the colonized peoples. In addition, a majority of former colonies still relied on the production of cash crops and had developed little in the way of secondary or tertiary economic sectors. Neither the United States nor the Soviet Union encouraged the recently independent nations to change their economic orientation. In fact, both superpowers encouraged the development of subservient or neo-colonial relationships in the formerly colonized regions of the world.

Even in nations such as India, where genuine economic development did take place, additional factors frequently prevented any substantial progress. Most importantly, population growth often became an insurmountable obstacle to national prosperity. The conditions for massive population growth had been established in the colonial era: internal warfare had largely ended, nutrition and health-care had improved, and the food supply had become more consistent. Thus death rates declined while birth rates, for the most part, remained high. In the immediate post-colonial period, inexperienced leaders struggled to address the demands of an ever-increasing population. As population growth in the rural areas outstripped the available land and employment opportunities, mass migrations to urban areas ensued. Because the cities generally lacked the rapidly expanding industrial sectors that had absorbed a similar influx during the Industrial Revolution in the west, the cities often became dead ends for rural migrants. Impoverished urban areas then became a further drain on the already over-taxed rural economies that people were attempting to escape. The net effect was a general decline in the standard of living and increasing unpopularity for the governments that seemed unable, or unwilling, to redress the worsening situation.

The documents in this chapter address some of the issues discussed above, primarily from the perspective of the formerly colonized peoples. Kwame Nkrumah, the post-independence leader of Ghana, blamed the majority of his nation's troubles on the persistence of neo-colonialism in the region. Frantz Fanon, in contrast, blamed indigenous leaders who had been too anxious to please their former colonial overlords by retaining their basic economic structures. Zizwe Poe provides a more recent analysis of Nkrumah's contribution to the development of Pan-Africanism. Turning to Latin America Fidel Castro assesses the net effect of years of foreign neo-colonial intervention in Cuba. Richard Behrendt weighs the advantages that American companies brought to Guatemala against the impact on the nation's uprooted workers. Finally, Ché Guevara comments on the successful Cuban Revolution and his vision for the future of Cuba.

KWAME NKRUMAH

After more than a decade as his country's prime minister, Kwame Nkrumah had seen many of his development policies fail, oftentimes blocked by intransigent parliaments that were divided along ethnic lines. In 1964 he declared himself 'President for Life' and began to rule in an increasingly authoritarian *manner. In the excerpt below, from 1965, Nkrumah argued that Ghana's lack of success, and the problems facing other post-colonial states, was due primarily to the persistence of neo-colonialism in sub-Saharan Africa. Nkrumah was overthrown by the military in 1966 and lived the remainder of his life in exile.*

NEO-COLONIALISM: THE LAST STAGE OF IMPERIALISM

The neo-colonialism of today represents imperialism in its final and perhaps its most dangerous stage. In the past it was possible to convert a country upon which a neo-colonial regime had been imposed—Egypt in the nineteenth century is an example—into a colonial territory. Today this process is no longer feasible. Old-fashioned colonialism is by no means entirely abolished. It still constitutes an African problem, but everywhere on the retreat. Once a territory has become nominally independent it is no longer possible, as it was in the last century, to reverse the process. Existing colonies may linger on, but no new colonies will be created. In place of colonialism as the main instrument of imperialism we have today neo-colonialism.

The essence of neo-colonialism is that the State which is subject to it is, in theory, independent and has all the outward trappings of international sovereignty. In reality its economic system and thus its political policy is directed from the outside.

The methods and form of this direction can take various shapes. For example, in an extreme case the troops of the imperial power may garrison the territory of the neo-colonial State and control the government of it. More often, however, neo-colonialist control is exercised through economic or monetary means. The neo-colonial State may be obliged to take the manufactured products of the imperialist power to the exclusion of competing products from elsewhere. Control over government policy in the neo-colonial State may be secured by payments towards the cost of running the State, by the provision of civil servants in positions where they can dictate policy, and by monetary control over foreign exchange through the imposition of a banking system controlled by the imperial power.

Where neo-colonialism exists the power exercising control is often the State which formerly ruled the territory in question, but this is not necessarily so. For example, in the case of South Vietnam the former imperial power was France, but neo-colonial control of the State has now gone to the United States. It is possible that neo-colonial control may be exercised by a consortium of financial interests which are not specifically identifiable with any particular State. The control of the Congo by great international financial concerns is a case in point.

The result of neo-colonialism is that foreign capital is used for the exploitation rather than for the development of the less developed parts of the world. Investment under neo-colonialism increases rather than decreases the gap between the rich and the poor countries of the world.

The struggle against neo-colonialism is not aimed at excluding the capital of the developed world from operating in less-developed countries. It is aimed at preventing the financial power of

American Vice-President Richard Nixon attends Ghana's independence ceremonies in 1957. Courtesy of the National Archives (306-rnt-12-16).

the developed countries being used in such a way as to impoverish the less developed.

Nonalignment, as practiced by Ghana[1] and many other countries, is based on cooperation with all States whether they be capitalist, socialist, or have a mixed economy. Such a policy, therefore, involves foreign investment from capitalist countries, but it must be invested in accordance with a national plan drawn up by the government of the nonaligned State with its own interests in mind. The issue is not what return the foreign investor receives on his investments. He may, in fact, do better for himself if he invests in a non-aligned country than if he invests in a neo-colonial one. The question is one of power. A State in the grip of neo-colonialism is not master of its own destiny. It is this factor which makes neo-colonialism such a serious threat to world peace. The growth of nuclear weapons has made out-of-date the old-fashioned balance of power which rested upon the ultimate sanction of a major war. Certainty of mutual destruction effectively prevents either of the great power blocs from threatening the other with the possibility of a worldwide war, and military conflict has thus become confined to 'limited war'. For these neo-colonialism is the breeding ground.

Such wars can, of course, take place in countries which are not neo-colonialist controlled. Indeed their object may be to establish in a small but independent country a neo-colonialist regime. The evil of neo-colonialism is that it prevents the formation of those large units which would make impossible 'limited war'. To give one example: if Africa was united, no major power bloc would attempt to subdue it by limited war because from the very nature of limited war, what can be achieved by it is itself limited. It is only where small States exist that it is possible, by landing a few thousand marines or by financing a mercenary force, to secure a decisive result.

The restriction of military action of 'limited wars' is, however, no guarantee of world peace and is likely to be the factor which will ultimately involve the great power blocs in a world war, however much both are determined to avoid it.

Limited war, once embarked upon, achieves a momentum of its own. Of this, the war in South Vietnam is only one example. It escalates despite the desire of the great power blocs to keep it limited. While this particular war may be prevented from leading to a world conflict, the multiplication of similar limited wars can only have one end—world war and the terrible consequences of nuclear conflict.

Neo-colonialism is also the worst form of imperialism. For those who practice it, it means power without responsibility and for those who suffer from it, it means exploitation without redress. In the days of old-fashioned colonialism, the imperial power had at least to explain and justify at home the actions it was taking abroad. In the colony those who served the ruling imperial power could at least look to its protection against any violent move by their opponents. With neo-colonialism neither is the case.

Above all, neo-colonialism, like colonialism before it, postpones the facing of the social issues which will have to be faced by the fully developed sector of the world before the danger of world war can be eliminated or the problem of world poverty resolved.

Neo-colonialism, like colonialism, is an attempt to export the social conflicts of the capitalist countries. The temporary success of this policy can be seen in the ever-widening gap between the richer and the poorer nations of the world. But the internal contradictions and conflicts of neo-colonialism make it certain that it cannot endure as a permanent world policy. How it should be brought to an end is a problem that should be studied above all, by the developed nations of the world, because it is they who will feel the full impact of the ultimate failure. The longer it continues the more certain it is that its inevitable collapse will destroy the social system of which they have made it a foundation.

Note

1. The policy of non-alignment was pioneered by Nehru's India and Nkrumah's Ghana; the idea was to side with neither the United States nor the Soviet Union during the Cold War in the hopes of creating a powerful third bloc.

Study Question

1. Is neo-colonialism primarily to blame for the problems facing the less-developed world in the post-colonial era, or are the actions of indigenous elites equally or more responsible?

FRANTZ FANON

In The Wretched of the Earth, *Frantz Fanon (1925–61), a French-trained psychiatrist and opponent of colonial control, addressed the issue of neo-colonialism and its impact upon newly independent nations. Fanon, however, defined neo-colonialism in much broader* terms *than many of his contemporaries, indicting not only the former colonial overlords, but also many of the new indigenous leaders who had replaced them.* The Wretched of the Earth *was published in 1961, the year of Fanon's death.*

THE COLLABORATING CLASS IN NEO-COLONIALISM

History teaches us clearly that the battle against colonialism does not run straight away along the lines of nationalism. For a very long time the native devotes his energies to ending certain definite abuses: forced labour, corporal punishment, inequality of salaries, limitation of political rights, etc. This fight for democracy against the oppression of mankind will slowly leave the confusion of neo-liberal universalism to emerge, sometimes laboriously, as a claim to nationhood. It so happens that the unpreparedness of the educated classes, the lack of practical links between them and the mass of the people, their laziness, and, let it be said, their cowardice at the decisive moment of the struggle will give rise to tragic mishaps. . . .

This traditional weakness, which is almost congenital to the national consciousness of underdeveloped countries, is not solely the result of the mutilation of the colonized people by the colonial regime. It is also the result of the intellectual laziness of the national middle class, of its spiritual penury, and of the profoundly cosmopolitan mould that its mind is set in.

The national middle class which takes over power at the end of the colonial regime is an underdeveloped middle class. It has practically no economic power, and in any case it is in no way commensurate with the bourgeoisie of the mother country which it hopes to replace. In its willful narcissism, the national middle class is easily convinced that it can advantageously replace the middle class of the mother country. But that same independence which literally drives it into a corner will give rise within its ranks to catastrophic reactions, and will oblige it to send out frenzied appeals for help to the former mother country. The university and merchant classes which make up the most enlightened section of the new state are in fact characterized by the smallness of their number and their being concentrated in the capital, and the type of activities in which they are engaged: business, agriculture, and the liberal professions. Neither financiers nor industrial magnates are to be found within this national middle class. The national bourgeoisie of underdeveloped countries is not engaged in production, nor in invention, nor building, nor labour; it is completely canalized into activities of the intermediary type. Its innermost vocation seems to be to keep in the running and to be part of the racket. The psychology of the national bourgeoisie is that of the businessman, not that of a captain of industry; and it is only too true that the greed of the settlers and the system of embargoes set up by colonialism has hardly left them any other choice.

Under the colonial system, a middle class which accumulates capital is an impossible phenomenon. Now, precisely, it would seem that the historical vocation of an authentic national middle class in an underdeveloped country is to repudiate its own nature insofar as it is bourgeois, that is to say insofar as it is the tool of capitalism, and to make itself the willing slave of that revolutionary capital which is the people.

In an underdeveloped country an authentic national middle class ought to consider as its bounden duty to betray the calling fate has marked out for it, and to put itself to school with the people; in other words to put at the people's disposal the intellectual and technical capital that it has snatched when going through the colonial universities. But unhappily we shall see that very often the national middle class does not follow this heroic, positive, fruitful, and just path; rather, it disappears with its soul set at peace into the shocking ways—shocking because anti-national—of a traditional bourgeoisie, of a bourgeoisie which is stupidly, contemptibly, cynically bourgeois.

The objective of nationalist parties as from a certain given period is, we have seen, strictly national. They mobilize the people with slogans of independence, and for the rest leave it to future events. When such parties are questioned on the economic program of the State that they are clamoring for, or on the nature of the regime which they propose to install, they are incapable of replying, because, precisely, they are completely ignorant of the economy of their own country.

The economy has always developed outside the limits of their knowledge. They have nothing more than an approximate, bookish acquaintance with the actual and potential resources of their country's soil and mineral deposits; and therefore they can only speak of these resources on a general and abstract plane. After independence this underdeveloped middle class, reduced in numbers and without capital, which refuses to follow the path of revolution, will fall into deplorable stagnation. It is unable to give free rein to its genius, which formerly it was wont to lament, though rather too glibly, was held in check by colonial domination. The precariousness of its

resources and the paucity of its managerial class forces it back for years into an artisanal economy. From its point of view, which is inevitably a very limited one, a national economy is an economy based on what may be called local products. Long speeches will be made about the artisan class. Since the middle classes find it impossible to set up factories that would be more profit-earning both for themselves and for the country as a whole, they will surround the artisan class with a chauvinistic tenderness in keeping with the new awareness of national dignity, and which moreover will bring them in quite a lot of money. This cult of local products and this incapability to seek out new systems of management will be equally manifested by the bogging down of the national middle class in the methods of agricultural production which were characteristic of the colonial period.

The national economy of the period of independence is not set on a new footing. It is still concerned with the ground-nut harvest, with the cocoa crop, and the olive yield. In the same way there is no change in the marketing of basic products, and not a single industry is set up in the country. We go on sending out raw materials; we go on being Europe's small farmers, who specialize in unfinished products.

. . . .

As regards internal affairs and in the sphere of institutions, the national bourgeoisie will give equal proof of its incapacity. In a certain number of underdeveloped countries the parliamentary game is faked from the beginning. Powerless economically, unable to bring about the existence of coherent social relations, and standing on the principle of its domination as a class, the bourgeoisie chooses the solution that seems to it the easiest, that of the single party. It does not yet have the quiet conscience and the calm that economic power and the control of the state machine alone can give. It does not create a State that reassures the ordinary citizen, but rather one that rouses his anxiety.

The State, which by its strength and discretion ought to inspire confidence and disarm and lull everybody to sleep, on the contrary seeks to impose itself in spectacular fashion. It makes a display, it jostles people and bullies them, thus intimating to the citizen that he is in continual danger. The single party is the modern form of the dictatorship of the bourgeoisie, unmasked, unpainted, unscrupulous, and cynical.

It is true that such a dictatorship does not go very far. It cannot halt the processes of its own contradictions. Since the bourgeoisie has not the economic means to ensure its domination and to throw a few crumbs to the rest of the country; since, moreover, it is preoccupied with filling its pockets as rapidly as possible but also as prosaically as possible, the country sinks all the more deeply into stagnation. And in order to hide this stagnation and to mask this regression, to reassure itself and to give itself something to boast about, the bourgeoisie can find nothing better to do than to erect grandiose buildings in the capital and to lay out money on what are called prestige expenses.

The national bourgeoisie turns its back more and more on the interior and on the real facts of its undeveloped country, and tends to look towards the former mother country and the foreign capitalists who count on its obliging compliance. As it does not share its profits with the people, and in no way allows them to enjoy any of the dues that are paid to it by the big foreign companies, it will discover the need for a popular leader to whom will fall the dual role of stabilizing the regime and of perpetuating the domination of the bourgeoisie. The bourgeois dictatorship of underdeveloped countries draws its strength from the existence of a leader. We know that in the well-developed countries the bourgeois dictatorship is the result of the economic power of the bourgeoisie. In the underdeveloped countries on the contrary the leader stands for moral power, in whose shelter the thin and poverty-stricken bourgeoisie of the young nation decides to get rich. The people who for years on end have seen this leader and heard him speak, who from a distance in a kind of dream have followed his contests with the colonial power, spontaneously put their trust in this patriot. Before independence, the leader generally embodies the aspirations of the people for independence, political liberty, and national dignity. But as soon as independence is declared, far from embodying in concrete form the needs of the people in what touches bread, land, and the restoration of the country to the sacred hands of the people, the leader will reveal his inner purpose: to become the general president of that company of profiteers impatient for their returns which constitutes the national bourgeoisie.

Study Question

1. Whose argument seems the most convincing, Fanon's or the previous argument of Kwame Nkrumah?

D. ZIZWE POE

Daryl Zizwe Poe is a professor of African-American studies at Lincoln University in Pennsylvania. His work focuses on Nkrumah's legacy, particularly his contribution to the development of a regional strategy for combating the aftermath of colonialism in Africa.

AFROCENTRIC SUMMARY OF NKRUMAH'S MAJOR CONTRIBUTIONS

. . . . For Nkrumah, following in the path of those who educated him in West Africa, the immediate optimal level was that of West Africa. He would later amend his thought and advocate against a 'regional first' approach. His conclusion from his experience was that the optimal level of African agency was a continental socialist union government. The influence of Garvey as well as his educational experience in the USA and England helped to expand Nkrumah's vision on a united Africa and its descended populations.

Nkrumah's participation in the 1945 Manchester Congress[1] elevated his stature to the inner-circle of Pan-African activists. It was from this point that Nkrumah vanguarded the Pan-African nationalist movement. Two years after that famous congress Nkrumah was involved in liberating an African territory from which he could assist with the prosecution of the Pan-African Nationalist Movement. That movement, as Nkrumah was to become keenly aware of, eventually distinguished itself from nationalists concerned solely with liberation in their territory. This latter force opposed Nkrumah's efforts.

For Nkrumah, Pan-African Nationalism required liberated territories organized along socialist lines with a population growing in the awareness of Pan-Africanism. To Nkrumah that awareness needed to be formatted with an ideology of the African revolution. Those who worked with Nkrumah would later come to name that ideology 'Nkrumahism'. Nkrumah did not wait for the official naming of the ideology to begin his campaign of massive political education. From his return to the Gold Coast colony until his overthrow, Nkrumah used all media available to him to impress on all who would listen or read his messages, the need for a totally liberated and unified socialist Africa.

Nkrumah strategically set out to organize women and youth as key sectors in the battle to radically transform the African landscape. He also paid meticulous attention to reconstructing the institutions of higher learning within Ghana for it was these institutions that would ensure the methodical dissemination of Nkrumahism: the ideology of the African revolution.

Nkrumah was not the first to use the phrase 'African Personality' but he was the first in modern times to give that concept the resources of an official government. He completed some of the aspects of Garvey's program and some of Garvey's symbols became part of everyday Ghana. The most famous of these symbols was the Black Star, which Nkrumah attached to his shipping lines and a public square in Accra. His most important contribution to the memory of Garvey was his organization of millions of Africans toward the redemption of African glory. In this way Nkrumah became the conduit of Pan-African agency, which was apparent in Garvey and others like Du Bois. The efforts of both, however, required synthesis and at that, Nkrumah was extraordinary.

Synthesis became a major theme in Nkrumah's quest to enthrone the agents of Pan-African nationalism. Nkrumah used this approach to both remove the presence of the British Empire from Ghana and to unite African peoples with themselves and their cultural experiences. Nkrumah advocated a philosophy that sought to harmonize the materiality of the world and the spirituality of humanity. Nkrumah also sought to harmonize the Christian and Islamic impacts with the traditional African base. He also advocated certain ethical principals which he claimed were African at root and which urged African societies along the path of socialist development. Finally, Nkrumah demanded an Afrocentric approach to the study of African phenomenon. He saw knowledge as a conditioner of purposeful practice.

. . . [O]nly Nkrumah can claim to have had the opportunity to implement what to others remained dreams and declarations. In summarizing Nkrumah's contribution to Pan-African agency from 1945–1966, the attempt here was not to prove uniqueness but to prove effectiveness. In that light, six major points can be summarized:

1. Nkrumah linked the traditions of West African nationalism and Pan-African nationalism.
2. Nkrumah initiated and developed the first Pan-African liberated state in modern history.
3. Nkrumah elevated Pan-African agency to the level of nation-states.
4. Nkrumah developed the concept of socialist African union as the optimal level for the African personality, genius, community, and agency.
5. Nkrumah offered a formal philosophy to defend the ideology of the African Revolution.

6. Nkrumah initiated the first African state sponsored effort for Afrocentric research.

Note

1. The 5th Pan-African Congress was held in Manchester, England, in October 1945. It brought together leading figures in the struggle for independence such as Nkrumah and Jomo Kenyatta as well as representatives from the United States and the African diaspora. Marcus Garvey's wife also attended to represent her husband's legacy.

Study Question

1. Do the achievements enumerated above justify Nkrumah's use of dictatorial methods in governing Ghana?

FIDEL CASTRO

The following speech was delivered by Fidel Castro (b. 1926) to a massive gathering of Cuban people in Havana in September 1960. A little over eighteen months had elapsed since Castro's forces had toppled the Batista regime, during which time his policy towards the United States had remained relatively moderate.

However, this speech marked the first clear statement of Castro's new socialist policy and his increasingly hostile view of American attempts to undermine the Cuban revolution. The speech provides an overview of the desperate situation facing the people of Cuba and its new government in 1960.

ON THE EXPLOITATION OF THE CUBAN NATION

Citizens: It is obvious that each of you, from where you are sitting, is completely unable to see the vast size of the crowd which has gathered this afternoon. It is a true sea of humanity which stretches into the distance on both sides of the Civic Plaza.

For us, the men of the revolutionary government, who have seen many popular gatherings, this one

is so huge that it impresses us deeply and helps to show us the vast responsibility which you and we carry upon our shoulders.

The people have gathered today to discuss important matters, particularly those of an international nature. But why has no one remained at home? Why has this been the largest gathering our people have held since the triumph of the

Cuban men and women working on a sugar plantation in the 1910s. Conditions were little improved when Castro took power in Cuba in 1959. National Photo Company Collection. Courtesy of the Library of Congress, Prints and Photographs Division (LC-DIG-ncc-19915).

revolution? Why? Because our people know what they are defending, our people know what battle they are waging. And as our people know that they are waging a great struggle for their survival and triumph, and since our people are a combative and a courageous people—that is why Cubans are present here.

And it is said that today, when we are going to discuss the same questions as were discussed in Costa Rica, the 21 American foreign ministers are not seated here. It is very sad that they are not present, so that they could have a chance to see the people they condemned at the Costa Rica meeting. It is sad that they are not here, so they could see how different the diplomatic language of the foreign ministries and the language of the peoples are!

There, however, our foreign minister spoke on behalf of our people. But those who heard him,

the majority of those who were gathered there, did not represent their peoples. If there, in Costa Rica, men representing the true interests and feelings of the peoples of America, particularly the peoples of Latin America, had gathered there, never could a statement such as that issued against the interests of an American people and against the interests of all the brotherly peoples of America have been drafted.

And what were they discussing there? There they were playing with the destiny of our country, there they were whitewashing the aggressions against our country. There they were sharpening the dagger which the criminal hand of Yankee imperialism wants to drive into the heart of the Cuban fatherland!

But why did they want to condemn Cuba? What has Cuba done to be condemned? What has our people done to merit the Costa Rica Declaration?

Our people have done nothing but break their chains! Our people have done nothing, harming no other people and taking nothing from any other people, than to fight for a better destiny. Our people have wanted only to be free, our people have wanted only to live from their own works, and our people have wanted nothing but to live from the fruits of their efforts. Our people have wanted nothing except to have what is theirs, that what is produced from their land, that what is produced with their blood, that what is produced with their sweat should be theirs.

The Cuban people have only wanted the decisions guiding their conduct to be theirs, that the flag with the solitary star which flutters over our fatherland should be theirs and theirs alone! They wanted their laws to be their own, their natural wealth to be their own, their democratic and revolutionary institutions to be their own. They wanted their fate to be their own, a fate in which no interest, no oligarchy and no government, however powerful it might be, would have a right to interfere.

And it must be our freedom, because it has cost us much sacrifice to win it. Sovereignty must be ours and complete, because our people have been fighting for sovereignty for a century. The wealth of our land and the fruits of our labour must be ours, because our people have had to sacrifice much for this and all that has been created has been created by the people, and all there is here of wealth has been produced by our people, through their sweat and their labour.

Our people had a right to be a free people one day. Our people had a right to govern their own destiny one day. Our people had a right to expect one day to have a government which would not defend the foreign monopolies, which would not defend the privileged interests, which would not defend the exploiters, but which would put the interests of the people and their fatherland above the interests of the greedy foreigners, a government which would put the interests of the

people, the interests of the peasants, the interests of the workers, the interests of the young people and children, the interests of the women and the old people above the interests of the privileged and the exploiters.

When the revolution came to power on 1 January 1959, just a little more than a year and a half ago, what was there in our country? What was there in our fatherland but tears, blood, misery, and sweat? What was there for the peasants in our country? What was there for the children? What was there for the workers here? What was there in Cuba for the humble families? What prevailed in our fatherland until that day?

The most inhuman exploitation, abuse, injustice, systematic plunder of public funds by greedy politicians, had prevailed, the systematic exploitation of our national wealth by foreign monopolies, inequality and discrimination, lies and deceit, submission to foreign ambitions and poverty had prevailed. Hundreds and hundreds of thousands of families lived without hope in their humble huts. Hundreds and hundreds of thousands of children were without schools. More than a half a million Cubans were without work. And black Cubans had less opportunity than anyone to find work. The rural people lived in compounds. The sugar cane workers were employed only a few months a year and they and their children suffered hunger the rest of the time. Vice, gambling and all that goes with it prevailed in our country. The farmer was exploited, the fisherman was exploited, the worker was exploited—the vast majority of the people were exploited.

Nothing was ever done for the people. No measures of justice were ever undertaken to free the people from hunger, from their poverty, from their pain and suffering, to free you, the Cuban citizens, to free you, men and women, old people and children, to free you, this vast multitude which has gathered here, to free the Cuban nation, to do something for it, to make something good of it—absolutely nothing was done.

And the people, helpless, had to tolerate it. The people had to pay the highest rents in the world in our fatherland. The people had to pay the highest electrical rates in the world in our fatherland. The people had to pay for telephone services as dictated by the interests of a foreign company which extracted concessions from a tyrannical government, while the blood of our heroic student youth was still warm in the courtyards of the Presidential Palace.

The monetary reserves of the nation were down to only 70 million. Our country, in unequal trade with the United States, had paid out a billion dollars more than we had been paid for our goods in ten years. There were no factories. Who would establish factories for the hundreds of thousands of Cubans who were without work? There were no plans for agriculture, no plans for industry. Who would concern himself with establishing industries? And the people, what could they do? What could the sugar worker do? What could the sugar cane farmer do? What could the worker do? The worker had only his miserable wage, the piece of bread which he could not always provide to his starving children. The profits were carried off by the foreign monopolies, the profits were accumulated by the owners. The profits were accumulated by the interests which grew fat off the labor of the people. And this money was either kept indefinitely in the banks or was spent on all kinds of luxuries. Mainly, it went abroad.

Who would establish factories for the hundreds of thousands of Cubans who were without work? And as the Cuban population was growing, and as each year more than 50,000 young people came of age, what were they to live on? What was the growing population of our fatherland to live on? How were the peasants, the children of the peasants, to live when they had neither work nor land? How was a people which was growing, and whose growth was much more rapid than the increase in its industry and its economy supposed to live?

The people lacked every kind of opportunity. The son of a peasant, or of a worker, or of any humble family, could hardly hope to become a professional one day—a doctor, an engineer, an architect, or a university technician. There were children of poor families who by dint of great sacrifice managed to complete higher studies, but the vast majority of the children of our families often even lacked the opportunity to learn their letters, and there were entire regions in Cuba where there had never been a teacher. Our people had access to nothing but work, if they could find it! For our people, only the worst was available. For our people, there were never any sports fields, never any streets, never any parks, and there were many places where if there was a park, some citizens—the black ones—were not allowed.

This was what the revolution inherited when it came to power: an economically underdeveloped country, a people which had been the victim of every kind of exploitation. This was what the revolution found at the end of its heroic and bloody struggle. And revolutions are not undertaken to leave things as they were. Revolutions are undertaken to correct all the injustices. Revolutions are not undertaken to protect and promote privileges. Revolutions are undertaken to aid those who need to be aided. Revolutions are undertaken to establish justice, to put an end to abuse, to put an end to exploitation. And our revolution was undertaken for this, and to this end those who fall gave their lives, and to achieve this goal so many sacrifices were made.

The revolution came to correct matters in our fatherland. The revolution came to do what each Cuban had been asking to have done for so long. When any helpless Cuban citizen analyzed life in our country and the picture presented by national life, he said: 'This must be corrected. This needs correcting, one day this must be changed.' And the more optimistic said: 'One day this will be changed.'

To correct matters in their country, Cubans had been fighting for a long time. But there was a greater force which prevented us from correcting things in our country. This force was the imperialist penetration of the United States in our fatherland. It was this force which frustrated our full independence. It was this force which prevented Calixto Garcia and his brave soldiers in Santiago de Cuba from succeeding. It was this force which prevented the liberation army from undertaking revolution in the early days of the republic. It was this force which determined the destiny of our fatherland from the very first. It was this force which permitted the seizure of the natural resources and the best lands of our fatherland by foreign interests. It was this force which appropriated the right to intervene in our country's affairs. It was this force which crushed so many revolutionary efforts. It was this force which was always associated with everything negative, everything reactionary, and everything abusive in our country. It was this force which prevented an earlier revolution in our fatherland, and it is this force which is trying to prevent us from correcting things in our country now. This is the force which maintained the tyranny. This is the force which trained the hired ruffians of the tyranny, which armed the soldiers of the tyrant, which provided weapons, planes, and bombs to the tyrant's regime, in order to keep our people under the worst kind of oppression. This force has been the main enemy of development and progress in our country. This force has been the main cause of our evils. This force has dedicated itself to the failure of the Cuban revolution. This force is trying to ensure that the war criminals will return, that the exploiters will return, that the monopolies will return, that the large estate owners will return, that misery will return, that oppression will return to our country.

Cubans must see with full clarity that imperialism is the force to which we refer, that it is trying to prevent our people from achieving full development. They must understand that this force does not want you, the Cubans, to achieve a higher standard of living. It does not want your children educated, it does not want our workers to profit from the fruits of their labour. It does not want our peasants to enjoy the fruits of their land. It does not, in a word, want our people to be able to grow, to be able to work, and to have a better destiny.

Our people have not had an opportunity in the past to understand these great truths. The truth was concealed from our people. Our people were miserably deceived. Our people were kept divided and confused. Our people have never had an opportunity to discuss these matters of an international nature. The people did not know a word of what was being said by the American Ambassador to the government leaders. The people did not know a word of what the foreign ministers were saying, the people counted for nothing. The people were not gathered together to learn about their problems. The people were not gathered together to be guided or to be told the truth. The destinies of our peoples were decided by the US Foreign Minister, our people counted for nothing in the destiny of the country.

Could Cuba continue to resign itself to this fate? Could Cubans continue to tolerate this system? What have the Cubans done? All they have done is to rebel against all this. All the Cubans have done is to free themselves from all this.

> **Study Question**
>
> 1. Could Cuba and the United States have created an amicable relationship, rather than an antagonistic one?

RICHARD F. BEHRENDT

Richard Behrendt (1908–73) was a German sociologist and economist. He travelled throughout South and Central America during the 1940s and early 1950s, working with the International Bank for Reconstruction and Development *(part of the World Bank Group) and the United Nations Organization. In the 1949 article which follows, Behrendt examined the impact of the movement of labour on the indigenous population of Guatemala.*

THE UPROOTED: A GUATEMALA SKETCH

Esteban Pazuj was an Indian carpenter in Guatemala. He made chairs and tables from a poor type of pine, fitted together without nails. In order to find customers, he had to take them from Totonicapán to Guatemala City, one hundred and twenty miles of mountain road at altitudes ranging down from eight thousand to four thousand feet. He carried on his shoulders and back the table and six chairs suspended from a tump-strap pressed against his forehead. He had to take his food along and would spend the nights in caves or under trees near the road. It took him eight days to reach the capital, several days to sell his goods on a special market, and another week to return home. He used to get three dollars for the table and the chairs or forty cents for each chair if sold separately. He charged for the lumber and his work only, not for the time spent en route. When he returned home, he had usually just enough left to buy more lumber and sustain himself and his family until his next sale.

During a few weeks every year, Esteban and his family used to go down to the western slopes of the volcanic mountain range, at about 3000 feet altitude, to pick coffee beans on a large plantation owned by Germans. He received twenty cents a day and his children, who were working with him in the field, ten cents a day. They lived in a large shack together with dozens of other families of seasonal workers. Each family prepared its meals, consisting mostly of corn and beans, over open fires inside the building. They slept on homemade woolen blankets spread on the dirt floor. There was no furniture of any kind. The women got their water from a brook half a mile away. Nature served as an open-air toilet. The Indian workers greeted the German administrators or their families, when these happened to cross their path, with bare heads and folded arms. If the workers broke any of the rules they were denied payment or put in the stocks for a night or longer.

Four years ago, an agent of the United Fruit Company came to Esteban's home town near Totonicapán to hire workers for the banana plantations around Tiquisate, in the lowlands of the west coast. He offered seventy cents a day, free housing, food at lower prices than it could be had in the stores, and the use of a plot of land for any worker who wanted to grow food of his own. It sounded fantastic to Esteban, and he accepted.

Now he loads banana stems on railway lorries from six o'clock in the morning to two o'clock in the afternoon. Sometimes he works overtime and is paid fifty per cent extra. In the afternoon he works for a few hours on his lot, if he feels like it. He and his family occupy a medium-sized room in a low, long wooden building housing several families. They have a kitchen of their own and share a toilet with their neighbors. They have electric light. They can buy rations of staple foods in the company commissary, at prices lower than those in regular stores. Their children go to a nearby school provided by the company, as required by the law of the country. The company fights the malaria-carrying mosquitoes and provides safe water supply. The company hospital, the second largest in the country, gives free service to the workers and their families.

But Esteban is not happy. For one thing, he and his family have never liked the hot, humid climate of the lowlands. He knows that he, his wife, and his children have more things to eat and a better place to live than before. However, to get these things he had to leave his village where generations of his family had spent their lives. His neighbors are comparative strangers, not related to him by blood, custom or even language. Esteban does not speak Spanish very well and his neighbors, having come from other parts of the country, do not speak his language, which is Quiché. He had to discard his aboriginal dress, with its patterns and colors distinctive of his native village. He now lives on an outlying *finca*, very different from his old, tight little home town whose people had been organized for centuries in kinships, *cofradías* (civic hereditary fraternities), and parishes. There everybody knew—although not necessarily spoke to—everybody else, and there everyone's position in the community was strictly defined by tradition.

Tiquisate is very different indeed from those parts of Guatemala where Esteban spent his earlier life. There are no old buildings; everything seems to him too new. In fact, the entire town and the outlying plantations were established only fifteen years ago when the fruit company shifted part of its operations from the Atlantic to the Pacific coast, because of plant diseases and soil exhaustion. There was then very little population and very little of anything—except climate and soil. Workers like Esteban had to be hired in the highlands where too many people try to eke out a living from thin soil on steep hillsides. Housing, transportation, communications, sanitation, irrigation, schools, hospital, entertainment had

to be provided by the company. People from various countries, speaking different languages, professing even different religions, having different traditions and customs—and very different living standards—came to live here.

Esteban, and some ten thousand workers like him, with their families, changed from a form of life which had remained essentially fixed for centuries, almost unaffected by outside influences, in which people had obeyed traditional institutions and leaders, to a new, planned form of life which was organized by a foreign corporation for the one purpose of producing and marketing a profitable commodity. The company is an anonymous entity of which they know nothing except that it is controlled by an indefinite number of foreigners, somewhere in the United States, nobody knows exactly how. They have never seen those people and never will. Some foreigners they do see: the North Americans who manage and supervise local operations. The Guatemalan workers do not bow with folded arms to them. Nor are they put in the stocks for infractions. Still they are not closer to them than they were to their German bosses. The americanos live in a small town of their own, divided from the 'native' town by a barbed wire fence. They have their own school, commissary, club house, swimming pool, and pleasant one-family bungalows on well-kept grounds. Esteban and most of his fellow workers do not see much of the americanos, because the time keepers and foremen are Guatemalans; but they know that those americanos are the bosses. Or, rather, that they represent the real bosses who live in a faraway country where everything seems to be plentiful, and whence they send orders which may mean great changes for every one of the thirty thousand or more people of Tiquisate, even the loss of their jobs. Formerly, Esteban had lived in his own house, poor as it was, and most of the time he had been his own boss, engaged in a fairly steady trade, even if it paid him only a barest living.

Thus, Esteban is torn between gratification and dissatisfaction. He is bewildered. He is not sure that the advantages of his new life outweigh its disadvantages. In spite of the fact that he earns more than he ever did before, he sometimes feels that he is not paid enough. He knows of neighbors who earn as much as one quetzal (equal to a dollar) or one quetzal and forty cents a day. They were skilled workers: sprayers, or banana pickers, or mechanics, or drivers. They have mastered certain techniques and know how to handle some of the innumerable tools and machines which were unknown to them and most of their fellows until they came to work for the North Americans. These better paid skilled workers have gone to school and can read, write, and use elementary arithmetic. Their number is increasing steadily, as more efficient, more highly mechanized methods of production and transportation are being introduced and elementary school instruction is becoming more common. Esteban's children will probably belong to them.

Strangely enough, the skilled workers are more dissatisfied than Esteban. It is they who are most active in the labor unions which were founded during the last few years, taking advantage of the liberal laws adopted after the overthrow of the dictatorship in 1944. It is they who demand higher wages, better working conditions, free transportation on vacation trips, more school facilities, and many other things of which Esteban would never have dreamed a few years ago in his highland village. Some of these people have even learned English so that they can read the company's reports on its earnings. They now claim that the foreign owners of the company are taking too much money out of the country and they should be forced to leave greater benefits to the nationals, by paying higher wages and offering more social services of all kinds. They are not impressed with the arguments that the company already pays the best wages in the country, and that Esteban and his fellows would still be living

the miserable, unhealthy, undernourished, and illiterate life of the past if it had not been for the many millions of dollars of North American capital invested by the company's stockholders. Some of the leaders of the union of which Esteban is a member, though not a very active one, even say that they, the Guatemalans, can take over the banana industry if the North Americans want to pull out of the country—just as the Guatemalans have taken charge of the German coffee and sugar plantations since the last war.

Esteban and his fellow workers have moved from a stationary way of life to a way of life where change—technological, economic, social, geographic—is the rule. They are not yet adjusted to it, but they are becoming accustomed to change. In fact, they may want to operate changes of their own, against the powerful corporation which has exposed them to this new way of life. Up to now, change has been planned and administered by the businessmen and engineers from the United States. New techniques, machinery, and skills were taught by these people to the natives of an economically backward country. Material inducements were offered to them for working in new places and unaccustomed enterprises. Now the principle of change is going farther than its original sponsors had intended. Social status and income are no longer determined by tradition and the accident of birth and, therefore, no longer accepted without criticism or ambition for improvement, as they were for centuries. On the other hand, the new factors on which one's place in life now depends are uncertain and not clearly understood.

If ambition and change are good and should take the place of conformity and tradition, for the sake of progress and a better life, why not push change until Esteban and all Guatemalans will enjoy the good things which are now reserved to the gringos and a few Guatemalans? If children of illiterate Guatemalan peasants can learn how to operate a railway engine, repair a truck, service an airplane, and do double-entry bookkeeping, things which only foreigners did thirty years ago, why can't they also learn to run all of Tiquisate— for their own benefit? And if the ability to operate machines and to plan and administer the work of many men is not limited to the members of certain master races or superior nations or ruling classes—why not change the traditional division of property under which a few families have owned most of the good lands and exploited the majority of the landless people who have had to work for them? Why put up any longer with the rule of privileged cliques in politics and public administration? If Esteban's children can learn things he never learned, as they do right now in school and shops, things which until recently were considered the prerogative of the overlords, what will stop them, or their children, from taking the place of those overlords?

Esteban Pazuj is representative not only of

some thousands of fellow workers on the banana plantations of Guatemala but of millions of people working in many parts of the world. They are all going through essentially the same experience. Soon there will be even more Estebans.

Someone in a discussion of the evils of cultural displacement uttered this baroque epigram which sums up aptly the risks of the situation: 'The uprooted and the roots of the uprooted are roots of revolution.'

> **Study Question**
>
> 1, In 1949 Behrendt predicted a revolutionary overthrow of foreign interests as countries continued along the path of modernization. Revolutions have occurred; however, the hold of foreign corporations remains strong. Why?

ERNESTO CHÉ GUEVARA

K'ung Mai and Ping An, two journalists from the People's Republic of China, interviewed Ché Guevara (1928–67) on 18 April 1959. At this time Guevara was the second-most powerful man in Cuba, after Fidel Castro, and had been *appointed head of both the National Institute for Agrarian Reform and of Cuba's new national bank. This interview was summarized on Beijing Radio and a few excerpts appeared in Chinese newspapers.*

A NEW OLD INTERVIEW

Reporter: Will you please tell us how Cuba achieved her revolutionary victory?

Guevara: Certainly. Let us begin at the time I joined the 26th of July Movement in Mexico. Before the dangerous crossing on the Granma[1] the views on society of the members of this organisation were very different. I remember, in a frank discussion within our family in Mexico, I suggested we

ought to propose a revolutionary program to the Cuban people. I have never forgotten how one of the participants in the attack on the Moncada army camp responded at that time. He said to me: 'Our action is very simple. What we want to do is initiate a coup d'état. Batista pulled off a coup and in only one morning took over the government. We must make another coup and expel him from power. . . . Batista has made a hundred concessions to the Americans, and we will make one hundred and one.' At that time I argued with him, saying that we had to make a coup on the basis of principle and yet at the same time understand clearly what we would do after taking over the government. That was the thinking of a member of the first stage of the 26th of July Movement. Those who held the same view and did not change left our revolutionary movement later and adopted another path.

From that time on, the small organisation that later made the crossing on the Granma encountered repeated difficulties. Besides the never-ending suppression by the Mexican authorities, there was also a series of internal problems, like those people who were adventurous in the beginning but later used this pretext and that to break away from the military expedition. Finally at the time of the crossing on the Granma there remained only eighty-two men in the organisation. The adventurous thought of that time was the first and only catastrophe encountered within the organisation during the process of starting the uprising. We suffered from the blow. But we gathered together again in the Sierra Maestra. For many months the manner of our life in the mountains was most irregular. We climbed from one mountain peak to another, in a drought, without a drop of water. Merely to survive was extremely difficult.

The peasants who had to endure the persecution of Batista's military units gradually began to change their attitude toward us. They fled to us for refuge to participate in our guerrilla units. In this way our rank and file changed from city people to peasants. At that same time, as the peasants began to participate in the armed struggle for freedom of rights and social justice, we put forth a correct slogan—land reform. This slogan mobilised the oppressed Cuban masses to come forward and fight to seize the land. From this time on the first great social plan was determined, and it later

Ernesto Ché Guevara in 1964. Guevara was involved with revolutionary groups around the world by 1964. New York World-Telegram and Sun Newspaper Photograph collection.

became the banner and primary spearhead of our movement.

It was at just this time that a tragedy occurred in Santiago de Cuba; our Comrade Frank País was killed. This produced a turning point in our revolutionary movement. The enraged people of Santiago on their own poured into the streets and called for the first politically oriented general strike. Even though the strike did not have a leader, it paralysed the whole of Oriente Province. The dictatorial government suppressed the incident. This movement, however, caused us to understand that working class participation in the struggle to achieve freedom was absolutely essential! We then began to carry out secret work among the workers, in preparation for another general strike, to help the Rebel Army seize the government.

The victorious and bold secret activities of the Rebel Army shook the whole country; all of the people were stirred up, leading to the general strike on April 9 last year. But the strike failed because of a lack of contact between the leaders and the working masses. Experience taught the leaders of the 26th of July Movement a valuable truth: the revolution must not belong to this or that specific clique, it must be the undertaking of the whole body of the Cuban people. This conclusion inspired the members of the movement to work their hardest, both on the plains and in the mountains. At this time we began to educate our forces in revolutionary theory and doctrine. This all showed that the rebel movement had already grown and was even beginning to achieve political maturity. . . .

Every person in the Rebel Army remembered his basic duties in the Sierra Maestra and other areas: to improve the status of the peasants, to participate in the struggle to seize land, and to build schools. Agrarian law was tried for the first time; using revolutionary methods we confiscated the extensive possessions of the officials of the dictatorial government and distributed to the peasants all of the state-held land in the area. At this time there rose up a peasant movement, closely connected to the land, with land reform as its banner. . . .

To carry out thoroughly the law providing for the abolition of the latifundia[2] system will be the concern of the peasant masses themselves. The present State Constitution provides for mandatory monetary compensation whenever land is taken away, and land reform under it will be both sluggish and difficult. Now after the victory of the revolution, the peasants who have achieved their freedom must rise up in collective action and democratically demand the abolition of the latifundia system and the carrying out of a true and extensive land reform.

Reporter: What problems does the Cuban Revolution now face, and what are its current responsibilities?

Guevara: The first difficulty is that our new actions must be engaged in on the old foundations. Cuba's anti-people regime and army are already destroyed, but the dictatorial social system and economic foundations have not yet been abolished. Some of the old people are still working within the national structure. In order to protect the fruits of the revolutionary victory and to enable the

unending development of the revolution we need to take another step forward in our work to rectify and strengthen the government. Second, what the new government took over was a rundown mess. When Batista fled he cleaned out the national treasury, leaving serious difficulties in the national finances. . . . Third, Cuba's land system is one in which latifundistas hold large amounts of land, while at the same time many people are unemployed. . . . Fourth, there is still racial discrimination in our society which is not beneficial to efforts to achieve the internal unification of the people. Fifth, our house rents are the highest in the world; a family frequently has to pay over a third of its income for rent. To sum up, the reform of the foundations of the economy of the Cuban society is very difficult and will take a long time.

In establishing the order of society and in democratising the national life, the new government has adopted many positive measures. We have exerted great effort to restore the national economy. For example, the government has passed a law lowering rents by fifty per cent. Yesterday a law regulating beaches was passed to cancel the privileges of a small number of people who occupy the land and the seashores. . . .

Most important is the land reform law, which will soon be promulgated. Moreover, we will found a National Land Reform Institute. Our land reform here is not yet very penetrating; it is not as thorough as the one in China. Yet it must be considered the most progressive in Latin America. . . .

Reporter: How will Cuba struggle against domestic and foreign reactionary enemies? What are the prospects of the revolution?

Guevara: The Cuban Revolution is not a class revolution, but a liberation movement that has overthrown a dictatorial, tyrannical government. The people detested the American-supported Batista dictatorial government from the bottoms of their hearts and so rose up and overthrew it. The revolutionary government has received the broad support of all strata of people because its economic measures have taken care of the requirements of all and have gradually improved the livelihood of the people. The only enemies remaining in the country are the latifundistas and the reactionary bourgeoisie. They oppose the land reform that goes against their own interests. These internal reactionary forces may get in league with the developing provocations of the foreign reactionary forces and attack the revolutionary government.

The only foreign enemies who oppose the Cuban Revolution are the people who monopolise capital and who have representatives in the United States State Department. The victory and continuous development of the Cuban Revolution has caused these people to panic. They do not willingly accept defeat and are doing everything possible to maintain their control over the Cuban government and economy and to block the great influence of the Cuban Revolution on the people's struggles in the other Latin American countries. . . .

Our revolution has set an example for every other country in Latin America. The experience and lessons of our revolution have caused the mere talk of the coffee houses to be dispersed like smoke. We have proved that an uprising can begin even when there is only a small group of fearless men with a resolute will; that it is only necessary to gain the support of the people who can then compete with, and in the end defeat, the regular disciplined army of the government. It is also necessary to carry out a land reform. This is another experience that our Latin American brothers ought to absorb. On the economic front and in agricultural structure they are at the same stage as we are.

The present indications are very clear that they are now preparing to intervene in Cuba and destroy the Cuban Revolution. The evil foreign enemies have an old method. First they begin a political offensive, propagandising widely and saying that the Cuban people oppose Communism. These false democratic leaders say that the United States cannot allow a Communist country on its coastline. At the same time they intensify their economic attack and cause Cuba to fall into economic difficulties. Later they will look for a pretext to create some kind of dispute and then utilise certain international organisations they control to carry out intervention against the Cuban people. We do not have to fear an attack from some small neighbouring dictatorial country, but from a certain large country, using certain international organisations and a certain kind of pretext in order to intervene and undermine the Cuban Revolution. . . .

Notes

1. The boat that carried Ché Guevara, Fidel Castro, and their allies to Cuba was named the *Granma*. The vessel ran aground off the coast of Cuba forcing Castro's men into the water and leading to heavy casualties from Batista's forces on the shoreline.

2. The system of landholding in Cuba before the revolution. The latifundia system was characterized by an intensive concentration of land in the hands of a few landowners.

Study Question

1. Was Guevara correct to assume that the Cuban Revolution must begin with a complete reform of the landholding system?

TIPS FOR ANALYSIS

Where Was the Document Written?

Try to determine where the document was produced. Was the author in the country about which he or she writes? Was he or she there during the events discussed? Or, was the document written from another location? If so, ask yourself what was taking place in that location that might have influenced the way the author views the events.

WEB RESOURCES

Internet Modern History Sourcebook: Decolonization
http://www.fordham.edu/halsall/mod/modsbook51.html
University of Pennsylvania: African Studies Center
http://www.africa.upenn.edu/AS.html
Latin American Network Information Center
http://www1.lanic.utexas.edu
Handbook of Latin American Studies Online
http://lcweb2.loc.gov/hlas/hlashome.html

RECOMMENDED READING

Isabel Allende, *The House of the Spirits* (New York: Bantam, 1986). Allende's novel, set in an unidentified Latin American country, spans several generations of the Trueba family and their struggles: between landlords and tenants, rich and poor, Marxist and Conservative. Throughout, the constant role of the military in government is evident.

Graham Greene, *Our Man in Havana* (New York: Penguin, 1991). Set in Havana prior to the fall of the Batista government, a cynical British émigré involved in activities of MI5 creates an accidental diplomatic crisis by inventing situation reports. The novel shows considerable sympathy toward the anti-Batista opposition in Cuba.

Gabriel Garcia Marquez, *The Autumn of the Patriarch* (New York: HarperCollins Perennial Classics, 1999). Garcia Marquez's 1975 novel takes place in a Caribbean country following the death of a dictator and the subsequent end of his long reign. The novel examines the mythical status attained by some dictators, the ever-present military junta, corruption, and the oppression of nations living under a carefully constructed system of terror.

David Landau, *Death is Not Always the Winner* (Los Angeles, CA: PurePlay Press, 2002). Landau's fictionalized history of the early years after the Castro victory in Cuba examines the consolidation of power and the disillusionment of Castro's supporters who soon find themselves fighting against the new regime. Landau also looks at the failure of the Bay of Pigs invasion and CIA involvement in the region.

Recommended Viewing

Noch Nad Chili [*Night Over Chile*] (Chile/USSR, 1977). Director: Sebastian Alarcon. This Soviet-made docudrama examines the situation surrounding the overthrow of Salvador Allende by recreating the key elements of the coup, based on interviews with Chileans who experienced the events first-hand.

The Killing Fields (UK, 1984). Director: Roland Joffé. Set in Cambodia during the genocidal era of the Khmer Rouge, *The Killing Fields* is based on the true story of Dith Pran, who was captured by the Khmer Rouge and imprisoned in the 're-education camps'. The film also tells some of the political history of the notorious Khmer Rouge.

The Official Story (Argentina, 1985). Director: Luis Puenzo. *The Official Story* is a fictionalized look at the aftermath of Argentina's 'dirty war' and the consequences of the murders and disappearances orchestrated by the Argentine military government. Puenzo's film provides some insight into the depth of the cover-ups and their consequences for ordinary citizens and perpetrators alike.

Thirteen Days (USA, 2000). Director: Roger Donaldson. *Thirteen Days* recreates the events surrounding the thirteen days in October when the United States and the Soviets clashed over the placement of missiles in Cuba. The film captures the extreme tension of the era, the conflict between 'doves' and 'hawks', and the very real possibility of nuclear war.

Comandante (USA, 2003). Director: Oliver Stone (Documentary). Unprecedented access to Fidel Castro—over thirty hours of interviews—allowed Stone to create this 90-minute documentary. Despite the restrictions placed on Stone, the film still provides an excellent look at life in Cuba today. *Comandante* saw limited release in the United States due to Stone's perceived sympathy for Castro.

Ché (USA/France/Spain, 2008). Director: Steven Soderbergh. Soderbergh's two-part bio-pic covers the planning for and ultimate success of the Cuban Revolution and Ché's capture and death in Bolivia.

CHAPTER FOURTEEN

PATHS TO MODERNIZATION

———◇———

As an increasing number of countries gained their independence in the 1960s and 1970s, many post-colonial leaders looked to regional co-operation as the key to future development. Conflict would need to be reduced, if not eliminated, in order to provide the stability necessary to modernize. Few leaders were willing to reject outright the systems imposed by the colonizers, because all could see the necessity of modern technologies in order to ensure economic viability.

However, the immediate post-colonial years were marked by increasingly destructive conflicts, including genocide in Rwanda, civil wars in Congo and Nigeria, and a prolonged battle for control in the former Portuguese colonies. The victims of these struggles included some of the early advocates of a co-operative approach, including Congo's Patrice Lumumba. In such a setting some leaders, such as Julius Nyerere, looked to their own national strengths and advocated self-sufficiency as the key to future development. Others, such as Leopold Senghor stayed as close as possible to the traditions of the former colonizer.

In reading the documents which follow, the reader should once again keep in mind the global constraints facing post-colonial leaders. Though most advocated non-alignment, this did little to shield them from the effects of the superpower rivalry. The Congolese independence struggle, for example, saw the Soviets offer aid to Lumumba's Congolese National Movement (MNC), which, in turn, led the Americans to brand Lumumba a Communist, and to plot his overthrow and assassination. Thus, every leader faced a severely limited range of options when it came to post-colonial development.

Perhaps most difficult, however, was the need to come to terms with the legacy of colonization. In the documents below, Leopold Senghor reflects on the relationship between colonizers and colonized and proposes a hybrid state created from the best values of both systems. Congolese Prime Minister Patrice Lumumba looked to a collaborative approach to independence and development

Female prisoners chained at the neck during the colonial era in Tanganyika, between 1890 and 1927. Frank and Frances Carpenter Collection. Courtesy of the Library of Congress, Prints and Photographs Division (LC-USZ62-91959).

in Congo; yet the tensions unleashed at independence would end in Lumumba's death in 1961.

Julius Nyerere, the post-independence president of Tanzania, believed he had found a solution to the problems of development in a policy of economic self-sufficiency. The American political commentator, P.J. O'Rourke, analyzes both the successes and failures of this approach, while outlining additional problems created by ongoing external intervention in Tanzanian development. The complex web of problems confronting newly independent nations is detailed in a 1964 *Atlantic Monthly* country report on the nation of Rwanda. Finally, Huey Newton calls for a unified liberation struggle that would free both black Africans and African-Americans.

◇

LEOPOLD SENGHOR

Leopold Senghor (1906–2001) was born in Senegal but educated entirely in the French tradition, both in his homeland and in France. He has been called one of the most important French language poets of the twentieth century. After serving with French forces during the Second World War he was elected to the French National Assembly as a Socialist deputy for Senegal-Mauritania. Senghor was a strong advocate of co-operative development among African states. At independence, in 1960, he was elected president of Senegal, a position he would hold until 1980. During his tenure Senegal retained very close ties to France and played a key role in the development of the Francophonie*—the community of French-speaking nations. The essay below was published in 1962.*

SOME THOUGHTS ON AFRICA

I am always glad to be in London, where, just after the last war, I took part in a series of Pan-African discussions whose importance for the future of Afro-European relations needs no stressing now.[1]

These discussions brought together African intellectuals of English and French culture. That was a foretaste of the Africa we want to build, of diverse but complementary elements. Despite the well-founded resentment we may have felt at that time, we have never wanted to place Africa outside the current of history, to cut her off from the other continents. It serves no purpose to deny facts that are incontrovertible. We have always been conscious of the fact that colonialism is a transitory stage, like feudalism, like capitalism. Colonialism has had its dark moments and its moments of light. If it destroyed some of the values of our civilization, Europe sometimes brought us substitutes, almost always fertile ones: *complementary* ones. The clash between two civilizations has always been an arduous experience for the weaker of the two. In fact, what matters is that from this encounter, inhuman though it may be at first, a new civilization should arise, grafting the skills of the colonizer on to the living stock of the colonized.

Certainly Europe brought destruction to Africa, but she also brought values which we lacked: technical skill and method. Here in London it was in English and French that we discussed the future, as, for example, in the 'Old Africa Congress', convened under the initiative of Mr Nkrumah. It is not by chance that the idea of the Commonwealth came from London, or that the concept of the Communauté was born on the banks of the Seine. In both cases it was a question of an association founded on equality, friendship, and co-operations, born of life and memories in common, of mutual and familiar interests, an association founded on mutual respect and solidarity. The only difference between the Commonwealth and the Communauté lies in the traditions of the two ancient Motherlands. . . .

All of us in Africa are fully aware of our 'situation', in Sartre's sense of the word. Our countries need developing. They can be developed thanks to the efforts of our peoples, but also thanks to the helpful understanding of our friends in Europe. Our progress is a continuation of the Negro-African tradition of authenticity, firmly rooted in reality. We must be forgiven for refusing to utter violent threats or brandish violent weapons, for refusing to renounce our friends. In doing so we have kept faith with Africa, which favours the peaceful voice of discussion and venerates loyalty and friendship. For what should our final aim be but to create the *civilization of the universal*, for which all men and all continents must strive, otherwise it will not come into existence? Everyone may rest assured that our contribution to that civilization of the universal will not be measured by the destructive potential of our weapons. We are living in an unsettled age, in which man's passion for violence seems to be in the ascendancy. Never in our history has mankind been in such danger of annihilation. European technical skill to which man owes so many of the discoveries which have transformed his life, now holds over his head bombs capable of obliterating him.

Faced with this divided world on the brink of catastrophe, it is our duty to bring back the antagonists to a more reasonable state of mind. We must call on them for more humanity. The countries of the Brazzaville group and the Monrovia group have stated their position on the grave problems which beset our world. These countries represent neither destructive military power nor outstanding industrial potential.[2] They are simply countries aware of their situation and of the part they can play in bringing back a greater sense of humanity and greater peace to the rest of the world. Our wish is quite simple to reduce the tension between the two opposing blocs. We have no wish to remonstrate with anyone, nor to blackmail anyone. We are neither neutral nor uncommitted. You must forgive us. You must also forgive our own way of tackling our problems. In this, as in other matters, we have opted for courage and clear-sightedness, and shunned demagogy. Faced with the grave problems of peace, decolonization, and the fostering of internationalism, we stand for a policy of non-alignment: non-alignment along with our friends, for a concerted policy, and non-alignment along with those who have not yet become our friends.

In this way we shall remain faithful to the Negro-African tradition of wisdom. We shall remain faithful to an *ideal* which is not an *ideology*. Our ideal is the creation of the Civilization of the Universal, in which our complementary differences will be fused and live on together in symbiosis. We know how easy it is to be partisan in this world of unbridled passions. We, for our part, remain partisans of progress, peace, and friendship. As we have often said, we are not Communists. But we refuse to take part in anti-Communist activities. We have chosen the African way to Socialism, which will be a synthesis of Negro-African cultural values, of Western methodological and spiritual values, and Socialist technical and social values. Man is the constant factor in all our calculations; we want to make him happier by setting him free from contradictions and from all forms of slavery; we want to put an end to his 'alienation' in the real world.

Notes

1.   Senghor refers to the Fifth Pan-African Congress in Manchester in October 1945.

2.   The Brazzaville Group included the countries of Chad, Dahomey, Gabon, Upper Volta, Cameroon, the Republic of Congo, Niger, the Malagasy Republic, Mauritania, the Central African Republic, Senegal, and the Ivory Coast. The Monrovia Group included Ethiopia, Libya, Liberia, Nigeria, Sierra Leone, Somalia, Togo, and Tunisia.

Study Question

1.   Could the synthesis of values of which Senghor speaks in the final paragraph be achieved? Why or why not?

PATRICE LUMUMBA AND GRAHAM HEATH

Patrice Lumumba (1925–61) was part of a very small Congolese middle class by virtue of his education at a Protestant school and his job as a postal clerk. He emerged as a key figure in the movement for greater independence from Belgian rule in the 1950s. Unlike his rivals, Lumumba emphasized a common Congolese nationalism, as well as a Pan-African focus. At independence, in 1960, Lumumba was elected the country's first prime minister, but was immediately faced with a Belgian-backed secessionist movement in the wealthy Katanga province. Despite UN intervention the situation in Congo spiralled out of control and, facing a political stalemate, Lumumba eventually accepted aid from the Soviet Union. Shortly thereafter the US authorized a plot to assassinate Lumumba. In the end, however, he was captured by Belgian forces and turned over to his Congolese rivals who executed him. The excerpt which follows was published posthumously in 1962.

◇

CONGO: MY COUNTRY

To My Congolese Compatriots

What should be our attitude towards the complex and agonising problems which confront us and which involve the future of our country? It must be one of calm, level-headedness, correct behaviour, impartiality, objectivity, justice, patience, perseverance, constant faith and continuity of effort and action. We must not give way to discouragement if we are to complete our difficult journey with its many hazards, disappointments and rebuffs.

Problems exist, and will continue to exist, as long as the world exists. The solution of these problems often depends on many factors which are not always evident to us. Let us not always jump to the conclusion that these problems are due to ill-will on the part of the authorities or of our rulers.

Every time that we évolués[1] discuss these problems, we must think of the mass of our fellow-Africans, for our task, like that of the Government of the country, is to concern ourselves not with a single class but with the population as a whole.

Let us not stand aloof from our brothers because they are less educated, less cultured, less fortunate than ourselves; this would create an unfortunate gulf between us. We want to bridge the gulf which separates us from the Whites but we must not create another one behind us. Who will work for them if we abandon them? May they not one day turn against us? Our concern must be not to satisfy personal ambitions but to achieve the harmonious development of all Africans. We must give up any activities which may cause cleavages within our society.

Our success depends above all on our unity. This can only be achieved if we manage to rid our minds of excessive clannishness, to face up together to our patriotic duty and, above all, to be aware of the absolute necessity for each one of us to achieve the harmonious development of the Congo by means of a united and unselfish effort.

The reforms which we are seeking must be achieved in a spirit of agreement and harmony. Anyone who plans rebellion or conspiracy will endanger the country and bring it into disrepute.

It is easy enough to shout slogans, to sign manifestos, but it is quite a different matter to build, manage, command, spend days and nights seeking the solution of problems.

Some Europeans of the less desirable kind exploit the credulity of the still largely uneducated Africans by urging them to claim immediate independence; they go so far as to suggest that autonomy will never be obtained without the spilling of blood, that all the Western countries had to fight in order to obtain their independence and that the Congolese must do the same if they wish to free themselves from the Belgians. This is indeed a sad state of mind!

We must reject these ideas, from whatever source they may come. The Congo will obtain its independence with dignity and not with barbarism. Civilisation and war are incompatible.

Some nations may have obtained their independence by means of atom bombs and bloody wars, but we shall obtain ours by words, by intelligence, by reason. It would be an act of the greatest barbarism, an act of banditry, to sacrifice human lives, the lives of our fellow-countrymen who are so dear to us, in our zeal for independence. No, the Congo shall not be kept on apron strings. Let us spare our country this misfortune, which humanity would hold against us. Instead of imitating other warlike nations, we shall give them an object lesson.

This is no childish phrase. There is no moral justification for war, with its slaughter and pillage, and those who commit such barbarous acts, except under extreme provocation, do not deserve the name of civilised people whether they be white, yellow or red. . . .

Let us tell the Belgians frankly what we want, opening our hearts to them and they will do the same to us. Frankness and sincerity must be the keynote of our mutual relations in this freely contracted Belgo-Congolese marriage, because those qualities are indispensable if the union is to be a lasting one. Let us give up all tendencies to hypocrisy in dealing with Europeans. Many Congolese tell the Europeans not what they think or feel in the depths of their heart but what they think the Europeans would like them to say. We must realise that the Europeans who devote themselves to our problems have no desire for flattery or excessive and hypocritical praise, nor is this in their interest. On the contrary, they want to be told frankly what our problems are. How can they get to know us, find a solution for our troubles or correct our judgments (many of us do in fact still lack reasoning powers) if we conceal our true thoughts from them? There are many people who say that one should never tell the truth to a European because this will not be appreciated and your frankness will later cost you dear. It is, of course, a fact that some of us have suffered and still do sometimes suffer for our frankness and sincerity, either because we have boldly put forward a valid point of view which

is not accepted by the Europeans concerned, or because we have defended a just cause; but that is no reason to lose heart, to take refuge in silence or, worst of all, to dull our wits by hypocrisy . . . This dumbness is a serious handicap to the liberation of our minds because, instead of discovering the truth and correcting our false judgments, we remain prisoners of ignorance and fear—very often imaginary fear.

There is no question of saying everything that comes into our heads; that would be stupid. The essential point is not to violate truth and commonsense. We must set ourselves to search ceaselessly for truth in all its forms. Truth is the only means by which we can contribute to our spiritual and intellectual development. . . .

Let us not always have our hands outstretched to receive, but always make a personal effort to obtain what we want. We shall achieve nothing by folding our arms, indulging in perpetual lamentations and recriminations or philosophising over a glass of beer. We shall never achieve anything except by working feverishly, struggling fiercely for our existence, and searching for constructive solutions. Life on this earth is hard, very hard, and bristles with difficulties; it often requires sacrifices.

Civilisation is not handed out like alms; nor can it be poured into men as one pours water into a bottle; it must be acquired by personal effort.

We must sacrifice all that we have in order to teach and educate our children, for the future of the Congo is in their hands; we must be very exacting in regard to them, watching over their studies, their outings and their walks, keeping in close touch with their teachers, so as to bring to light and remedy in good time any difficulties in their school life, and we must subject them to very severe discipline. . . .

We must not continue to live like spoilt children, always awaiting magnificent gifts. We must take action so that the Congo shall not lag behind the other countries of Africa in regard to education and political emancipation; we must realise that this emancipation depends on a real maturity of its citizens.

When the Congo has its own technicians in every trade, its doctors, agricultural specialists, engineers, businessmen, geologists, administrators, contractors, skilled workers (this does not mean that we have no skilled workers at present; I am referring here to highly qualified workers like those to be found in the big factories in Europe), social workers, nurses and mid-wives, then and then only can we talk of independence or autonomy, because we shall then be strong enough, intellectually, technically, and materially, to administer the country on our own if necessary.

Some Congolese like to keep on recalling past errors. But what is gained by this? Virtually nothing. Let us leave to the past what belongs to the past and look at the future from another angle.

No one denies that these mistakes have been made. They were errors due to inexperience. But we must remember that those who made these mistakes, the pioneers of colonisation, were not saints and had not the gift of infallibility. Yet it is to these brave pioneers of the Free State, these heroes who obtained little or no benefit from their labours, that we owe our present position.

These pioneers of the Free State left their fair country to answer the call of conscience; they left behind them their families, their closest friends, their pleasures, in order to cross the seas and rescue us from chaos and from the yoke of the man-hunting pirates; they crossed trackless and perilous country to establish lines of communication. These humanitarians, who lived in the greatest discomfort and shared our sorrows and our food, were closer to us than the 'modernists' of the epoch of refrigerators and American cars.

Some of them, worn out and demoralised by countless disappointments, undoubtedly made some mistakes, but are not those mistakes outweighed by the immense amount of good which has been achieved and is in the process of achievement?

No human activity is entirely free from blemishes and mistakes. It is often these blemishes and mistakes which show the correct route to be followed in the future. . . . people who claim that the Whites are in Africa solely to exploit the Blacks seem to be mistaken in their judgment. There are, of course, some who exploit the Blacks but it is wrong to claim that all Europeans exploit the Blacks.

Is the African to show ingratitude by reviling the pioneers of the civilising process who sleep their last sleep in this country which they loved and served? Certainly not. We must not lay ourselves open to such a charge.

When we pass the graves of these heroes who gave their lives for our safety, and thanks to whom we can now utter the words 'independence—autonomy', let us be silent for a few moments and bow our heads respectfully in their memory. Together with our fellow countrymen they gave their lives for the defence of the country. May the mingled blood of the Belgians and Congolese, which was spilt in their common struggle and formed an undying bond of friendship, cement Belgo-Congolese friendship for ever.

Note

1. Africans who had received a European education and who had been integrated into the European colonial system.

> **Study Question**
>
> 1. To what extent do the sentiments expressed here support or undermine the claims made by Frantz Fanon in the previous chapter?

JULIUS NYERERE

In February 1967, Tanzanian President Julius Nyerere (1922–99) announced a new policy direction. Tanzania would become an egalitarian socialist society, based upon co-operative agriculture. Nyerere emphasized self-sufficiency, the need to break away from foreign aid and investment, and placed new emphasis on education and literacy. Economic co-operation, racial and tribal harmony,

and self-sacrifice would characterize Nyerere's Tanzania. Despite his vision for his country, when Nyerere retired in 1985, Tanzania was still one of the most impoverished nations in the world. Some people might consider this a failure on Nyerere's part; however, Tanzania was also politically and socially stable and had one of the highest literacy rates in sub-Saharan Africa.

◇

THE ARUSHA DECLARATION

It is obvious that in the past we have chosen the wrong weapon for our struggle, because we chose money as our weapon. We are trying to overcome our economic weakness by using the weapons of the economically strong—weapons which in fact we do not possess. By our thoughts, words,

East African Heads of Government Conference in 1964. Left to right: Julius Nyerere (Tanzania), Milton Obote (Uganda), and Jomo Kenyatta (Kenya). © Bettman/CORBIS.

and actions it appears as if we have come to the conclusion that without money we cannot bring about the revolution we are aiming at. It is as if we have said, 'Money is the basis of development. Without money there can be no development.'. . .

It is stupid to rely on money as the major instrument of development when we know only too well that our country is poor. It is equally stupid, indeed it is even more stupid, for us to imagine that we shall rid ourselves of our poverty through foreign financial assistance rather than our own financial resources. . . .

Let us therefore always remember the following. We have made a mistake to choose money, something which we do not have, to be our major instrument of development. We are mistaken when we imagine that we shall get money from foreign countries, firstly because, to say the truth, we cannot get enough money for our development and, secondly, because even if we could get it, such complete dependence on outside help would have endangered our independence and the other policies of our country.

Because of our emphasis on money, we have made another big mistake. We have put too much emphasis on industries. Just as we have said 'Without money there can be no development', we also seem to say 'industries are the basis of development'. This is true. The day when we have lots of money we shall be able to say we are a developed country.

The mistake we are making is to think that development begins with industries. It is a mistake because we do not have the means to establish many modern industries in our country. We do not have either the necessary finances or the technical know-how. It is not enough to say that we shall borrow the finances and the technicians from other countries to come and start the industries. The answer to this is the same one we gave earlier, that we cannot get enough money, and borrow enough technicians to start all the industries we need. And even if we could get the necessary assistance, dependence on it could interfere with our policy of socialism. The policy of inviting a chain of capitalists to come and establish industries in our country might succeed in giving us all the industries we need, but it would also succeed in preventing the establishment of socialism unless we believe that without first building capitalism, we cannot build socialism. . . .

The development of a country is brought about by people, not by money. Money, and the wealth it represents, is the result and not the basis of development. . . .

A great part of Tanzania's land is fertile and gets sufficient rains. Our country can produce various crops for home consumption and for export. We can produce food crops (which can be exported if we produce in large quantities) such as maize, rice, wheat, beans, and groundnuts. And we can produce such cash crops as sisal, cotton, coffee, tobacco, pyrethrum, and tea. Our land is also good for grazing cattle, goats, sheep, and for raising chickens; we can get plenty of fish from our rivers, lakes, and from the sea. All of our farmers are in areas which can produce two or three or even more of the food and cash crops enumerated above, and each farmer could increase his production so as to get more food or more money. And because the main aim of development

is to get more food, and more money for our other needs, our purpose must be to increase production of these agricultural crops. This is in fact the only road through which we can develop our country—in other words, only by increasing our production of these things can we get more food and more money for every Tanzanian.

Everybody wants development, but not everybody understands and accepts the basic requirements for development. The biggest requirement is hard work. Let us go to the villages and talk to our people and see whether or not it is possible for them to work harder.

In towns, for example, the average paid worker works seven and a half or eight hours a day for six or six and a half days a week. This is about 45 hours a week, excluding two or three weeks leave every year. This means that an urban worker works for 45 hours a week in 48 to 50 weeks a year.

For a country like ours, these are really quite short working hours. In other countries, even those which are more developed than we are, people work for more than 45 hours a week. It is not normal for a young country to start with such a short working week. The normal thing is to begin with long working hours and decrease them as the country becomes more and more prosperous. By starting with such short working hours and asking for even shorter hours, we are in fact imitating the more developed countries. And we shall regret this imitation. . . .

It would be appropriate to ask our farmers, especially the men, how many hours a week and how many weeks a year they work. Many do not even work for half as many hours as the wage earner does. The truth is that in the villages the women work very hard. At times they work for 12 or 14 hours a day. They even work on Sundays and public holidays. Women who live in the villages work harder than anybody else in Tanzania. But the men who live in villages (and some of the women in towns) are on leave for half of their life. The energies of the millions of men in the villages and thousands of women in the towns which are at present wasted in gossip, dancing, and drinking, are a great treasure which could contribute more toward the development of our country than anything we could get from rich nations. . . .

The second condition of development is the use of intelligence. Unintelligent hard work would not bring the same good results as the two combined. Using a big hoe instead of a small one; using a plough pulled by oxen instead of an ordinary hoe; the use of fertilizers; the use of insecticides; knowing the right crop for a particular season or soil; choosing good seeds for planting; knowing the right time for planting, weeding, etc.; all these things show the use of knowledge and intelligence. And all of them combine with hard work to produce more and better results.

The money and time we spend on passing on this knowledge to the peasants are better spent and bring more benefits to our country than the money and the great amount of time we spend on other things which we call development. . . .

None of this means that from now on we will not need money or that we will not start industries or embark upon development projects which require money. Furthermore, we are not saying that we will not accept, or even that we shall not look for, money from other countries for our development. This is not what we are saying. We will continue to use money; and each year we will use more money for the various development projects than we used the previous year because this will be one of the signs of our development.

What we are saying, however, is that from now on we shall know what is the foundation and what is the fruit of development. Between money and people it is obvious that the people and their hard work are the foundation of development, and money is one of the fruits of that hard work.

From now on we shall stand upright and walk forward on our feet rather than look at this problem upside down. Industries will come and money will come, but their foundation is the people and their hard work, especially in agriculture. This is the meaning of self-reliance.

Study Question

1. Was complete self-reliance, as envisioned by Nyerere, a realistic objective?

P.J. O'ROURKE

P.J. O'Rourke was born in 1947; he is an American essayist and political satirist. Politically, O'Rourke leans to the right (though he claims to be a communist and tends to be critical of all organized political parties). This piece, based upon his travels throughout Tanzania, considers the problems of development in Africa and in particular the problems related to foreign aid and foreign investment. Note the references to Julius Nyerere's policies and their after effects.

INSIDE TANZANIA

The Hotels on the northern Tanzania 'safari circuit' had been good. None was as splendid as the Ngorongoro Serena Lodge, but all were posh and efficient, until I got to the Tarangire, another huge chunk of Tanzania set aside as a game park. The hotel there was 'Albanian tropical'. The rooms were squatty stucco cylinders topped with whimsically shaped toupees of faux thatch—intended, no doubt, to evoke local peasant housing but actually reminiscent of a 50-per-cent-off-bad-lamps sale at Pier One.

There was a fountain in the basement. The waiters dressed in dashiki pajama suits worn with the combination flair and embarrassment more usually seen in black American politicians campaigning in kinte cloth. So I went to the bar. Nobody was in there but tourists. I know, I'm one too, but even so. . . . The United States should just face that fact that its national costume is a man's undershirt with a humiliating stencil, a clip-on gut pouch, Playskool-colored cellulite-length shorts, dark socks, and Reeboks the size of Easter hams. Let's celebrate this. Let's wear it to weddings and funerals. Let's make the president dress this way on solemn national occasions—to the extent that he doesn't already.

But a person who thinks that American tourists are obnoxious has not seen the harem pants, micro-halter tops, tuna-net scarves, high-heeled hiking boots and hats you wouldn't buy for Mardi Gras worn by the Italians and French on holiday. That person hasn't heard the mai-tai-churning shrieks, rude bellowing at employees and nauseating, phlegmy chortles of the vacationing British. Or listened to the loud, monotonic droning of traveling Germans recounting to each other exactly what they did all day together.

I wound up asking Charles the bartender why Tanzania was so poor. He said, 'lack of education', and then held forth with a 15-minute mathematical explication concerning the exchange rate that left me massively shortchanged and in some doubt about his theory. I gathered an armload of Serengeti beer . . . and went to sit on the small terrace of my cisternlike room, meditatively drinking. . . .

We drove to Arusha. . . . A derelict bus sat by the side of the road. It hadn't been there 10 days ago. The blackened frame and spars were stripped so clean, they looked like an abandoned buffalo carcass.

Seeing the people in Arusha going about their business—or lack thereof—should have been even more depressing than it was. Describing the English poor of 150 years ago, George Eliot noted 'the leaden, blank-eyed gaze of unexpectant want'. But with Tanzanians, there's always a twinkle in that gaze. The women walked down the roads bearing all the burden of Tanzanian material possessions. These are few enough—but still a lot to carry on your head. And more often than not, the women were smiling. Their kangas swayed and billowed. The printed cloths are embellished with slogans and catch phrases such as PENYE KUKU WENGI HAKUMWAGWIMTAMA: 'Don't dry the millet where the chickens are.' Children rushed home from school as gleefully as if they were headed for rec-rooms full of Sega games and *Little Mermaid* videos. (Tanzanian kids all wear school uniforms in case you think that regulation is the answer to all of society's ills.) Arusha's merchants are nice to the point of chagrin over any commercial aspect of your visit to their store. One shop had an apologetic sign posted in the window:

You are my friend
Yes
You are my relative
Yes thank you
But my business does not know you

And yet when I returned to Arusha from the safari circuit, the poverty was a greater shock than it had been when I arrived in Arusha on a jet from America. Then, you think you've come to a separate universe. Now, you think, 'No such luck; it's the same universe. Just one big game park. . . .'

I assume that on the great global SAT test of life, the question 'Why is Tanzania so poor?' must be answered with a wild guess as 'all of the above'. Let's do what the SAT people do when scores are too low and change the question. It's Eurocentric, anyway, and, for all I know, gender biased. 'How can Tanzania get rich?' That looks more positive on a quiz plus it requires an answer, so we can bullshit.

Well, there's 'improvements in agricultural yield', always a favorite with development-aid types. The British Labour Government tried this after World War II in what became known as 'the groundnut scheme'. The Labourites decided that Tanzania, then called Tanganyika, was going to become the world's foremost producer of groundnuts, that is to say, peanuts. They selected three huge sites and cleared the land by running a chain between two tractors, pulling the chain through the bush and destroying thousands of acres of wilderness. Thirty-six and a half million British pounds were invested, an amount equal to the whole Tanganyikan government budget from 1946 to 1950. It was then discovered that peanuts won't grow in Tanganyika.

The Tanzanian government budget contains more pages on agriculture than would ever be read by anyone. . . . But in this document the only mentions of land ownership are an admission that buying land entails 'lengthy and bureaucratic procedures' and this weasel sentence: 'A new law being formulated proposes to introduce different structural arrangements.' Julius Nyerere, the repentant socialist who ruled Tanzania from 1962 to 1985, said it was a mistake to collectivize the small farms, the *shambas*. But it's a mistake that hasn't been corrected. Farms must be bought—as my guide John, who owns one, put it—'informally'.

(Another fun fact not from the budget: 'Fisheries—the sector still faces problems from dynamite fishing.')

I did see one prosperous coffee plantation, Gibb's Farm, at the foot of the Ngorongoro Crater, above the Mosquito River. This is run by English people and has thousands of neatly clipped coffee bushes lined in parade file, a smoothly raked dirt road winding up through the property with woven-stick barriers stuck in the drain gullies to hinder erosion and a profusion of blossoms around the main house. The very picture of a Cotswold cottage year has been somehow created from weird, thorny African plants that need to be irrigated every minute. The English will garden the ash heaps of Hades if Hell lets them.

I suppose the farms of Tanzania could all look like Gibb's Farm, but it turns out that Gibb's Farm doesn't make any money as a farm but prospers because a bunch of upscale tourist lodgings have been installed. So there's tourism.

According to the US State Department's *Commercial Guide*, 'Tourism is currently the second-largest foreign-currency earner for Tanzania, after coffee.' (Actually the largest foreign-currency earner for Tanzania is foreign aid. But never mind, with Republicans running Congress, foreign aid is not likely to be a growth industry.) All the tourists I talked to were voluble in their praise of Tanzania, as soon as they'd recovered enough from their Jeep trips to form words. Tanzania's tourist hotels produced $205 million in revenue in 1995. But that's only 6.7 per cent of the country's gross domestic product. This compared to the 6 per cent of the GDP produced by Tanzania's transport and communications sector. 'Tanzania doesn't have any communication.' As for transport, according to the same State Department guide that talks up tourism, 'It takes approximately three days to travel by road from the capital, Dar es Salaam, to the second largest city, Mwanza.'

People will pay to look at Tanzania. Its face is its fortune—like Kate Moss. But it's easier to make a buck off Kate. She's portable and doesn't need to be fed often.

I talked to the manager of a luxury hotel near Lake Manyara, a Kenyan whom I'll call Shabbir, and his friend, a Tanzanian named, let's say, Mwambande, who ran the plush tented camp down the road. Shabbir said it was difficult to get these resorts to function. What was going on in his kitchen right now 'was hell'. And at another hotel in Tanzania, I did watch a waiter just arrived from rural climes being utterly confounded by a soda-can pop-top. I asked Shabbir and Mwambande if tourism could make a country like Tanzania rich. Shabbir didn't think so. He was leaving for better opportunities in Vietnam. Mwambande didn't think so, either, but more optimistically. 'Tourism acts as a showcase,' he said. 'It helps people come see a place for them to invest.'

They explained that tourism doesn't make much for Tanzania because so much of what's spent is 'yo-yo money'. The foreigners arrive via foreign-owned airlines in planes built by foreigners. They stay at hotels constructed with foreign building materials, ride around in foreign made cars and eat food imported from foreign places. The money rolls in, pauses for a moment, and rolls back out.

Some of the foreigners are indeed rich people. 'Is the Tanzanian government giving them any incentive to invest?' I asked.

'Oh, yes,' said Mwambande. 'If you build a plant here, you get a five-year tax holiday.'

'But,' I said, 'it normally takes a new enterprise five years to make a profit.' Mwambande and Shabbir laughed. 'And what about after the tax holiday?' I asked. 'What are the taxes like then?' Mwambande and Shabbir laughed and laughed.

In a 10 February 1997 story about a Tanzanian crackdown on illegal tour operators, *The East African* newspaper mentioned these taxes just in passing: 'a hotel levy (20 per cent), sales tax on food (15 per cent), sales tax on fresh juices and cakes (30 per cent), stamp duty (1 per cent of turnover), withholding tax on goods and

services (2 per cent), training levy (10 percent on expatriate-employees' taxable income), payroll levy (4 per cent on gross taxable income of all employees), vocational-education training-agency tax (2 per cent on gross taxable income of all employees).'

Forget about tourism. . . . I talked to a man who owned Safari Barn, whom I'll call Nisar. By his faintly Middle Eastern speech and pallor (and wow of a wristwatch), I judged him to be a foreigner. But, though Europeans were rare, Tanzanians cover all skin-color bases. There is a sizeable population with roots in India, Persia, and Oman, plus people of mixed African-Arab and whatever-whichever ancestry. Nisar's family had been in Tanzania for six generations.

Nisar said that Julius Nyerere's 'economics were no good'. The British tradition of understatement survives in Tanzania. Although only sometimes. 'I have queued for a loaf of bread for two weeks,' said Nisar. 'Under Nyerere, even if I had enough money for a dozen Rolls-Royces, if I drove a Mercedes I'd go to jail for seven years—languish in jail.' So he hated Nyerere's guts? No. 'Nyerere destroyed tribalism in Tanzania,' Nisar said and claimed that he encountered no prejudice for being non-African. He praised Nyerere's insistence that everyone speak Kiswahili: 'It unified the nation.'

Safari Barn was successful, said Nisar, because 'I poured money into Tanzania when others were afraid to spend a shilling.' It was hard getting Safari Barn built. Nisar's description of working with Tanzanian contractors was the same as Shabbir's description of work in the Lake Manyara kitchen. Nisar had gotten no tax holidays, no subsidies. The government always wanted him to go to Dar es Salaam and hang around. He explained, '"the minister is here." "The minister is there." "The minister is gone for a week." It could take a month to see the right guy. I'm a one-man show here.' Then Nisar said (without a *but* or a *however* or an *even so*) 'Tanzania is the best country in Africa. And I have traveled all over. If there is a food shortage in Tanzania, people won't riot. There has never been that tradition here. They will get through it. They will share, help each other. They will organize to complain. They will have meetings. They are very political. But not violent. This is not a violent country.' He paused and thought that over for a second. 'Tanzanian people,' said Nisar, 'are so damn lazy.'

[So how does Tanzania get rich?]

The Tanzanian government has an idea, a slight inkling, of what to do—or, rather what not to do. With governments, doing nothing is sometimes the most important thing. That brings us back to what we should do. We should do nothing, too.

Not the cheap, easy kind of nothing. There are plenty of charities and causes in Tanzania that ought to be supported—and lavishly, if we're the kind, decent Americans we like to say we are. People can be helped. But can you 'help a nation'?

Official Development Assistance has funded disasters and fostered attitudes of gross dependence. Yoweri Museveni, the president of Uganda, says his country 'needs just two things. We need infrastructure and we need foreign investment. That is what we need. The rest we shall do by ourselves.' This is the, 'If we had ham, we could have ham and eggs, if we had eggs' philosophy. . . .

Delivering our cash to dictatorial and silly governments was bad, but even worse was delivering our big ideas about centralization, economic planning, and social justice to a country that had 120 university graduates at the time of independence. Not that the Tanzanians didn't understand our big ideas; they understood them too well. They just had no experience with how bad most big ideas are. They hadn't been through Freudianism, Keynesianism, liberalism, and www.heavensgate.com. They don't have 10,000 unemployed liberal-arts majors sitting around Starbucks with nose rings.

There's even some evidence that getting ahead in the world comes from a lack of big ideas. Call this the Bell-Dip Theory. The United States is arguably the most successful nation in history but not—by any argument—the smartest. Japan is an economic miracle, but we're talking about a people in love with Hello Kitty.

Progress does not come from thinking immense thoughts and forming grandiose designs. Real improvement in material existence—the kind that gives most people comfortable lives and all people opportunities—is the result of exercising the most mundane responsibilities and privileges. Progress comes from practical application, forethought, self-restraint, and lots of dull, plodding work. Progress comes from what our dull, plodding parents called 'being grown-up'. There's nothing childish about Tanzanians themselves, but the same cannot yet be said for the political and economic structures in which they live.

Tanzania is one of those places called a 'developing country', as if the family of nations had teens, as if various whole geographical regions were callow, inarticulate, clumsy—but endearing, of course. You know, going through an awkward phase.

And that's about right. Every 24 hours in Tanzania is like a crib sheet on adolescence. There's the dewy-aired, hopeful dawn. All is beautiful. All is fresh. Then, as the day goes on, the dust rises. The noise builds. Everything is seen in a too vivid light. The glaring inadequacies of life are revealed. Enormous confusion develops. There's a huge stink. And just when you've really had it—when you're ready to call for the International Monetary Fund's equivalent of 'grounding', when you're about to take the keys to the goat or something—the whole place goes to sleep for 18 hours.

Study Question

1. According to O'Rourke, foreign aid in almost any form is counter-productive, especially when grandiose political ideologies and blueprints accompany it. Is this an accurate assessment?

THE ATLANTIC MONTHLY

In June 1964 The Atlantic Monthly *published a country report on Rwanda. It contained a detailed overview of Rwanda's twentieth century history and offered insights into the tensions between Rwanda's competing ethnic groups. The report concluded by identifying ongoing sources of conflict* *that would continue throughout the 1960s. Many of the claims in this report have since been challenged by Africanists who argue that the tribal divisions enumerated below were much more a creation of the colonial period than they were a product of earlier African history.*

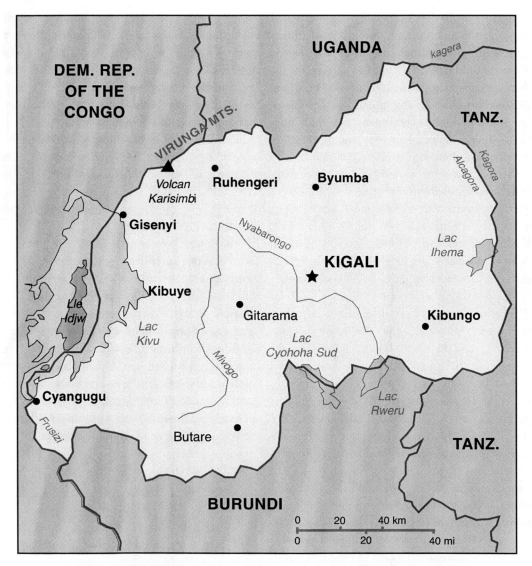

Rwanda's main tribal groups cross many of the national boundaries depicted in this map.

Rwanda 1964

The Central African Republic of Rwanda lies isolated and landlocked between the Nile and Congo River basins some 1,000 miles from the Indian Ocean and 1,600 miles from the Atlantic. It is roughly the size of Vermont and has the highest population density in Africa South of the Sahara (245 persons per square mile) and the lowest per capita income ($50 per year).

Rwanda has always known population pressure on scant resources; yet, in the midst of this scarcity one sector of its population evolved a highly intricate society, which has today fallen apart. The consequences of the destruction of that society and the attempt to replace it with another lie at the root of Rwanda's present tragic situation.

The population of Rwanda is divided into three distinct tribal groups sharing a common language. The pygmoid Twa constitute less than one per cent of the population and are rarely seen, being hunters and forest dwellers. The short, stocky, Bantu, Negroid Hutu represent 85 per cent of the population. They were the first to fell Rwanda's forest, to clear the brush, and to cultivate. They never evolved a centralized political system, and their reliance on small units formed around clan chiefs made them highly vulnerable to invasion.

Some four centuries ago a tall, slender, haughty, exquisitely aristocratic people known as the Tutsi conquered Rwanda through a combination of force and persuasion.[1] Although they never constituted more than 15 per cent of the population, their hierarchical organization, built around a king known as the Mwami, their development of specialized warrior castes, and above all their possession of cattle enabled them to dominate the Hutu. Reputed to have originated in Ethiopia or the Nile Valley, the Tutsis were the outer fringe of a great southbound pastoral migration.

The Tutsi Sacred Cows

The Tutsi promised protection and cattle to individual Hutu, who in turn accepted the Tutsi as their lords to whom they owed personal services and a portion of their crops, and who eventually secured possession of all cattle and land. Each Tutsi was the client of another Tutsi patron, the Mwami being at the pinnacle.

This feudal system was justified by an elaborate ideology which had as its essential premise the fundamental inequality of human beings. . . .

This legend reflects the reality of four centuries of Tutsi domination whereby a small and highly self-conscious minority indulged in the pleasures of a distinct leisure class through the exploitation of the Hutu majority. The basis of this exploitation was the cow. The highly exotic, sleek long-horned *Ndanga* cattle were the only recognized form of wealth, and Hutus could obtain them only by serving their Tutsi masters, who could at any time break the relationship and regain all the cattle they had lent to their clients.

It was not until 1894 that the first European entered Rwanda. Four years later Rwanda and the neighboring Tutsi kingdom of Burundi came under German rule. Both countries had first been allotted to Germany at the Berlin Conference in 1885, during the colonial scramble for Africa.

At the end of the First World War Belgium acquired a League of Nations mandate for Rwanda as partial compensation for war reparations which Germany would be unlikely to be able to pay. The Belgians continued the German system of indirect rule, relying upon the Mwami and the Tutsi officialdom and confining administrative posts and education to the Tutsi elite.

While never directly attacking the basis of Tutsi rule, the colonial period set in motion forces which led to its eventual destruction. Foremost among these forces was Christianity, which preached the equality of all men in the eyes of Christ. The Catholics took an early lead and soon converted the Mwami and his court; through the Church the Hutus could aspire to status, education, and authority, which were denied them elsewhere. The introduction of cash cropping and cultivation of Arabica coffee provided Hutu peasants with an income and lessened their reliance on their Tutsi masters. Finally, because of population pressures, thousands of Hutus migrated to neighboring territories, where some were exposed to and returned with ideas of democracy and majority rule.

The sudden attainment of political independence by the former Belgian Congo, and United Nations pressure on the Belgians, who exercised a trusteeship for Rwanda, caused political activity in Rwanda to spurt. It was obvious that unless the Hutus seized power before the Belgians left, an independent Rwanda in Tutsi hands would forever enslave the Hutu. Yet the Hutus were handicapped by their lack of education and experience and their inborn submissiveness.

The Rise of the Hutus

On 24 July 1959, the forty-six-year-old Mwami Rudahigwa died suddenly under mysterious circumstances without having designated his successor. This proved the occasion for the decisive clash between the Tutsi and the embryonic Parmehutu, the political organization of the Hutu, led by Gregoire Kayibanda, former seminary student, guide at the Brussels World's Fair, and editor of the Catholic newspaper. While the Tutsis quickly installed the Mwami's nephew as the new king and prepared a terrorist campaign against leading Hutu politicians, the Hutu masses staged an uprising under Parmehutu direction. The Mwami was deposed and fled the country along with thousands of other Tutsi refugees, and a provisional Hutu government was installed.

Two extremely bitter years followed, during which a United Nations-supervised referendum

resulted in an 80 per cent victory for the Parmehutu Party and the decisive rejection of the monarchy. Periodic fighting between Hutus and Tutsis continued, and additional thousands of refugees fled the country.

Meanwhile, in neighbouring Burundi, to which Rwanda was linked by a customs and monetary union, the sixty-four-year-old Mwami Mwambutsa used the political skills garnered through fifty years on the throne to hold his country and Tutsi rule together. While Rwanda achieved independence on 1 July 1962, as a republic, Burundi remained a monarchy, and ideological strains caused relations between the two countries to deteriorate rapidly.

Among the 100,000 Tutsis who fled Rwanda prior to its independence and the 250,000 who remained behind, there are many who refuse to face a life of permanent exile or to accept Hutu rule. Four centuries of domination have led them to believe that they are superior to the humble, submissive, and physically inferior Hutu. Among the hard-core exiles a secret terrorist organization known as the Inyenzi was formed. This became the focus of counterrevolutionary activity directed at overthrowing the Rwanda government and restoring the monarchy. . . .

Invasion by Refugees

This period of calm has been rudely and decisively shattered by three invasion attempts mounted by the Inyenzi. The first of these occurred on 25 November 1963, when 3,000 Tutsi refugees in Burundi began a march toward the Rwanda border to 'return to their homeland'. The marchers included old men, women, and children, as well as three truckloads of arms. The marchers were spotted by missionaries and UN refugee officials, and the Burundi government intervened to turn them back.

The second invasion attempt occurred on 20 December 1963, one day after the conclusion of a conference between the Rwanda and Burundi governments in which they agreed to dissolve their customs and monetary union. The invaders struck this time at Nemba on the Rwanda–Burundi border. They were armed only with homemade rifles, spears, and bows and arrows, and first attacked a Rwanda military base under construction, where they seized light arms and two jeeps. The invaders then proceeded north toward Kigali, the smallest and probably worst-defended capital in the world, with a population of 4,500 and one paved street. They advanced to within twelve miles of Kigali before they were intercepted by the Rwanda Garde Nationale. The invaders fled, suffering heavy losses, after a battle waged with modern weapons but highly reminiscent of an intertribal skirmish.

The Rwanda government was panic-stricken by the news of the second invasion attempt. Rwanda's mountainous terrain, lack of village life, and open borders make it ideal for terrorist operations. The one-thousand-man Garde Nationale had its hands full defending the capital and the border posts, and the defence of the country would have had to rely on the civilian Hutu population taking up arms.

The government took two measures to guard the country against further invasion and internal subversion (the second group of invaders had made contact with local Tutsis). Prominent Tutsis throughout Rwanda were arrested and herded to government prisons, where after severe beatings the majority were released. However, all those whose names had been found on a list of people whom the invaders planned to install as government officials were shot. This list had been taken off the body of a Congolese mercenary killed while fighting with the invaders.

The second measure was to send a minister to each of Rwanda's ten prefectures to organize the 'self-defense' of the civilian population with the aid of the local prefect and the elected burgomasters. The individual situation in each prefecture and the attitude of local officials, rather than government policy, caused the subsequent massive reprisals

and massacres of the local Tutsi population which have been so widely reported.

The worst slaughter took place in Gikongoro prefecture, where the dense tropical forest provides an open border with Burundi. Here, word had been received that Kigali had fallen and the former Mwami restored. Local Tutsis had for several days prior to the invasion been boasting of their hopes of returning to power and had been congregating around the former royal residence, located in this prefecture. Whether spontaneously or upon the orders of local officials, the Hutu population arose against the Tutsis in this prefecture.

The most reliable estimates of the numbers killed are between 10,000 and 14,000. The population used any weapons nearby, mostly hoes and long knives for cutting grass, resulting in hideous atrocities. Bodies were dumped into rivers and streams, left alongside roads to be scavenged by wild animals, and buried in mass graves.

Elsewhere in Rwanda timely action averted tragedy. Thus, in Kibungo prefecture on the Tanganyikan border the Catholic White Fathers prevailed upon the local authorities not to excite the Hutu population. The result was relative calm; Hutu and Tutsi celebrated Christmas mass together, and local Tutsis turned over to the authorities an Inyenzi invader hiding among them. Yet the White Fathers were convinced that had a single Tutsi hut been burned, all the Tutsis in the prefecture would have fled.

There was never a government policy of genocide against the Tutsi. Beginning on Christmas Eve, 6,000 Tutsis, including 5,300 women and children, fled into Uganda, with 13,000 head of cattle. No attempt was made by the Rwanda government to interfere with this defenseless horde or even larger masses of refugees who fled into Burundi, the Congo, and Tanganyika. Other thousands of Tutsis took refuge in Catholic mission stations within Rwanda, where they believed they would be safe because of Catholic influence in the government.

While the government tried to induce these internal refugees to return to their homes, it took no action against them.

A third invasion attempt occurred at Kizinga on the Uganda border on December 27. At this point 500 well-armed Tutsis, coming mostly from the Congo, were met by a force of the Rwanda Garde Nationale, which had been alerted for several days to expect an attack. The invaders were repulsed; more than 300 were killed, and the others were taken prisoner by Ugandan officials.

A Call for UN Help

This invasion attempt prompted the Rwanda government to cable U Thant for UN assistance. Max Dorsinville, personal representative of U Thant in the Congo, arrived in Kigali on January 1 and spent several days in the country before going on to Burundi. His failure to protest vociferously or threaten international action enabled the reprisals to continue, and they were not brought under control until mid-January, largely as a result of pressure from Catholic and Protestant authorities and foreign embassies within Rwanda. Meanwhile, the world remained almost totally uninformed since Radio Rwanda is too weak to be heard outside the Country and Rwanda has no newspapers except a monthly bulletin in Kinyarwanda.

Today Rwanda remains in a state of constant military alert, with passes required for traveling within the Country and military roadblocks maintained on the principal roads. The effects of the invasions and of the security situation have been disastrous for the Rwanda economy. The cash sector, dependent almost entirely on exports of coffee, is dying, and the standard of living has fallen markedly. The subsistence sector continues to supply adequate foodstuffs, although malnutrition is widespread. Rwanda hopes to create its own currency, although its foreign-exchange reserves are depleted and its balance-of-payments deficit is chronic. Only Belgian and other external aid and technicians are keeping the non-subsistence sector of the economy alive.

The 150,000 Tutsi refugees huddled along Rwanda's borders provide a constant security threat and a fertile ground for Inyenzi agitation. Their presence makes life impossible for the Tutsis remaining in Rwanda, who are regarded as suspect by the Rwanda government.

Urgent measures are required to prevent Rwanda from erupting again into violence and to restore hope to its crippled economy. Among these are military measures to control the refugees and prevent further invasion attempts by the Inyenzi. The neighbouring governments of Uganda, Tanganyika, and the Congo are using the limited military means at their disposal toward these ends, and the Burundi government is under pressure to do likewise. Also required is external assistance to enable the permanent resettlement of the refugees in the neighbouring countries, where fortunately there is ample unused arable land.

Finally, even if the Tutsi question is resolved, Rwanda still faces a galloping population increase threatening its meagre resources. The strength of Catholicism within Rwanda and the traditional high regard for children rule out artificial methods of population control. Meanwhile, at the present rate the population will double within twenty-three years, and unless a long-term economic plan is implemented to increase agricultural productivity and bring additional lands into cultivation, the only alternative will be a return to pre-colonial Malthusian methods of population control. This can be averted if economic planning, technical assistance, and external aid to the total sum of $8 to $10 million a year are forthcoming. Otherwise, Rwanda is likely to remain on the world's conscience.

Note

1. The physical differences between Hutu and Tutsi are overstated in the article.

Study Question

1. Given Rwanda's past history, was there any way to avoid the genocide that occurred in 1994?

◇

HUEY P. NEWTON

The struggle to end colonialism in Africa coincided with the civil rights movement in the United States, leading many American civil rights advocates to call for a joint liberation effort. Huey Newton (1942–89), one of the founders of the Black Panther movement,[1] drew his inspiration from the teachings of Marx,

Lenin, Ché Guevara, and Mao Zedong. The following excerpt ties the northern civil rights movement to the independence struggle in Mozambique. It was written in October 1971, a period in which the Panther movement, under constant attack by the FBI, began to split into factions.

◇

UNITING AGAINST A COMMON ENEMY

On the continent of Africa there are people who look like us. They are Black. We are brothers because our struggle is common. We have both suffered under White racism and under oppression. This is why we should not let the reactionaries of the world be the only ones communicating across the waters and masses of land. We have a common interest to serve, and therefore, we can learn from each other. What happens here affects our brothers in Africa; what happens in Africa affects us. The United States has seen to this. But this is good. We can learn to fight together, though separated.

There is a place in Africa called Mozambique. It lies on Africa's eastern shore, in the southern portion of the continent. It is a rich land, like most in Africa. In 1498 (six years after Columbus' famous 'discovery') the Portuguese invaders (if you remember, your elementary school books credit him as an 'explorer') Vasco da Gama violated the shores of Mozambique. The rest of the troops landed seven years later, in 1505. From that point on the Portuguese have dominated the economy and lives and the culture of the Mozambican

people. Their national language became, and still is, Portuguese. To this day, the Portuguese lay claim to Mozambique, referring to 'Portuguese' Mozambique.

This, of course, is not in agreement with our brothers and sisters in Mozambique. Mozambique is their home. They are not the invaders. Of course, the people of Mozambique have made many attempts throughout their long history of Portuguese colonial oppression to rid themselves of their chains. However, the most powerful and successful struggle is presently being waged under the guidance of the revolutionary organization FRELIMO (Front for the Liberation of Mozambique). The people support FRELIMO, for FRELIMO is of the people and is organizing struggle in the true interest of all the people. . . .

Today, FRELIMO, under the wise leadership of President Machel,[2] is guiding the people of Mozambique toward greater and final victory. But today, naturally, the attacks of the combined forces of the United States, Portugal, Germany, France, and Britain are even more fierce: constant bombings and many ground attacks take place. However, there is a more intricate, but ultimately more vicious, plan in the making, headed primarily by the United States. They plan to build, for the Portuguese, a large hydroelectric dam. The site for the dam is in the liberated Tete Province in Cabora Bassa, along the Zambesi [sic] River, bordering racist Rhodesia. Its purpose is to not only give financial aid to impoverished Portugal but to be used as a key part in a plot with South Africa to launch a political, diplomatic, and military offensive upon all of Africa. A familiar name to us is General Electric. The General Electric Company has spent millions to aid in building the Cabora Bassa Dam. Altogether, the United States and others have agreed to invest 500 million dollars in the dam, which is capable of producing 18.4 billion kilowatts of electricity. Also, in regard to this Cabora Bassa Dam, late FRELIMO President Mondlane[3] once said, 'They say it will enable them to settle one million Whites in Mozambique within 10 years . . . to form a great white barrier across Southern Africa.'

If we believe that we are brothers with the people of Mozambique, how can we help? They need arms and other material aid. We have no weapons to give. We have no money for materials. Then how do we help? Or, how can they help our struggle? They cannot fight for us. We cannot fight in their place. We can each narrow the territory that our common oppressor occupies. We can liberate ourselves, learning from and teaching each other along the way. But the struggle is one; the enemy is the same. Eventually, we and our brothers in Mozambique, in all of Africa, throughout the world, can discuss a world without boundaries or national ties. We will have a human culture, a human language, the earth will be all our territory, serving all our interests; serving the interest of all people.

Notes

1. The group's full name was the Black Panther Party for Self-Defense.
2. Samora Machel (1933–86) was a revolutionary leader who played a key role in FRELIMO'S fight for independence. He was named the country's first president at independence in 1975.
3. Eduardo Mondlane (1920–69).

Study Question

1. Newton called the United States government the primary enemy of black liberation. To what degree did this claim have validity in the early 1970s?

TIPS FOR ANALYSIS

Was the document sent somewhere other than where it was written?

Consider if the document was intended to be sent to a person or group, either inside the country in which it was written, or outside the country's borders. If it was sent somewhere else, evaluate the ways in which this might have affected both the tone of the document and its reliability.

WEB RESOURCES

Voice of the Shuttle: Postcolonial (and Colonial) Studies
http://vos.ucsb.edu/browse.asp?id=2089
Colonial and Postcolonial Studies Resources
http://myweb.uiowa.edu/sessions/ColStudies.htm
Vistas Internet Links
http://www.smith.edu/vistas/vistas_web/links.htm
Internet Archive: 'Postcolonial'
http://www.archive.org/search.php?query=subject%3A%22postcolonial%22

RECOMMENDED READING

Chinua Achebe, *Anthills of the Savannah* (London: Heinemann, 1987). Achebe's first novel to be set in post-colonial Africa provides a fictionalized look at the problems of nation-building, the corrupting nature of political power, and the persistence of tradition amidst a rapidly modernizing world.

Chimamanda Ngozi Adichie, *Half of a Yellow Sun* (New York: Anchor, 2007). Adichie's novel is set during the Biafran civil war, between 1967 and 1970. The book has been called 'a searing history lesson in fictional form' (*Publisher's Weekly*, September 2006).

Shimmer Chinodya, *A Harvest of Thorns* (Bedminster, NJ: Baobab Books, 1989). Chinodya's novel gives a balanced look at both sides of the Zimbabwean independence struggle, showing the brutalities committed by the Rhodesian army as well as by the guerrillas. The novel also provides insight into life in a Rhodesian black township in the 1960s and 1970s.

Ngugi wa Thiong'o, *Petals of Blood* (Harmondsworth: Penguin, 2005). Written in the 1970s, *Petals of Blood* is set in post-colonial Kenya and examines the frustrations and disappointments that followed the granting of independence. The novel touches on greed and corruption, as well as the pressures of globalization.

RECOMMENDED VIEWING

Guelwaar (Senegal/France, 1993). Director: Ousmane Sembene. *Guelwaar* illustrates the complexities of life in post-colonial Senegal, highlighting the religious conflicts between Catholics and Muslims, bureaucratic corruption and its impact on the nation, and the nature of foreign aid and its impact. Underlying the film is the story of AIDS in Africa.

Une republique devenue folle: Rwanda, 1894–1994 (Belgium/Canada/France, 1996). Director: Luc De Heusch. This historical documentary examines 100 years of Rwandan history, seeking to understand the impact of colonialism and the roots of the 1994 genocide.

Lumumba (France/Belgium/Germany/Haiti, 2000). Director: Raoul Peck. *Lumumba* is a dramatization of the life and work of Patrice Lumumba. The film focuses on Lumumba's struggles to organize resistance in Congo and then to control the forces that had been unleashed. The film ends with Congo's destructive civil war, the events of which laid the foundation for the region's disastrous state today.

The Huey P. Newton Story (USA, 2001). Director: Spike Lee. This documentary, based on a one-man stage play, retells the story of Newton's life, the founding of the Black Panthers, his struggles with the FBI, his death, and his legacy.

Un chant nègre, Léopold Sédar Senghor (France, 2006). Director: Jean-Denis Bonan. Bonan's documentary chronicles Senghor's life and influence. The film was commissioned to celebrate the hundredth anniversary of Senghor's birth.

CHAPTER FIFTEEN

THE POSTWAR ERA
IN THE MIDDLE EAST

$\diamond$

Postwar development in the Middle East must be understood in the context of prewar policy, as well as the events of the Second World War. The creation of League of Nations Mandates throughout the region, in the wake of the First World War, had intensified pre-existing conflicts and created new ones. The British White Paper of 1939 endeavoured to contain some of these tensions by severely limiting emigration to the Mandate of Palestine. In retrospect the timing of these emigration restrictions could not have been worse. Hitler was poised to begin his expansion into Eastern Europe and had already predicted in January 1939 that, in the event of another war, it would be the Jews of Europe who would pay the ultimate price.

By 1945, Soviet and American troops had liberated the remaining concentration and extermination camps and the pressure to settle Jewish survivors and refugees was growing. In the Mandate of Palestine anti-British sentiment was becoming increasingly violent, with organizations such as Irgun using increasingly effective terror tactics against the British authorities. The British government, facing problems at home and in its empire, chose to hand the situation off to the United Nations, which ultimately devised a proposal to create two states—one Arab and one Jewish—in the area. The immediate result was the 1948 Arab–Israeli War, the end of which saw the State of Israel substantially strengthened and the Arab forces weakened and divided. At least 700,000 refugees fled the area during the 1948 war, creating an ongoing conflict over the right of those refugees to return to Palestine. Meanwhile the remaining League Mandates in the area, including Transjordan, Syria, and Lebanon, also broke free of their mandatory overlords in the immediate aftermath of the Second World War.

The events taking place in the postwar Middle East also played out in the context of the Cold War. Though both the US and the Soviet Union supported the creation of the State of Israel, over the years the Americans increasingly supported the Israelis, whereas the Soviets backed the Arab States. Thus, periodic conflicts in the region threatened to evolve into catastrophic superpower clashes, particularly in the 1950s and 1960s.

The documents in this chapter focus primarily on the impact of the creation of the State of Israel and the subsequent regional conflicts. The MacDonald White Paper of 1939 sets the stage for the events which followed in the second half of the twentieth century. The reader can also refer to the documents in Chapter Eight for more on the discussions which led to the creation of the State of Israel. Few events have been as important in the Middle East as the 1967 Six-Day War and the seizure of the Occupied Territories. UN Resolution 242 discusses the international opinion on the war; the Palestine National Charter presents the opinions of some of the inhabitants of the occupied territories.

Some of the optimism of the mid-1970s is captured in Golda Meir's remarks on Egyptian President Anwar Sadat's visit to Israel in 1977. As well, the joint US/USSR statement on peace in the Middle East provides insight into the pressure exerted by both superpowers to resolve the endless cycle of violence in the region. However, despite the achievement of peace between Egypt and Israel in 1978, the major concerns of the Palestinians remained unresolved. This led to the creation of increasingly radical groups, such as Hamas, in the 1980s. Excerpts from the Hamas Covenant provide insight into the organization's ideology in 1988. Finally, the late Edward Said speaks of the possibility of 'truth and reconciliation' between Israel and the Palestinians in the wake of the accords of the early 1990s.

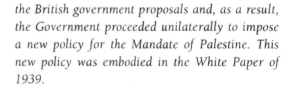

GOVERNMENT OF GREAT BRITAIN

In late 1938 the British Government invited representatives of both the Arab and Jewish populations of Palestine to a discussion of future British policy in the region. Neither the Arab nor the Jewish representatives were willing to accept the British government proposals and, as a result, the Government proceeded unilaterally to impose a new policy for the Mandate of Palestine. This new policy was embodied in the White Paper of 1939.

THE WHITE PAPER OF 1939

The Mandate for Palestine, the terms of which were confirmed by the Council of the League of Nations in 1922, has governed the policy of successive British Governments for nearly 20 years. It embodies the Balfour Declaration and imposes on the Mandatory four main obligations. . . . There is no dispute regarding the interpretation of one of these obligations, that touching the protection of and access to the Holy Places and religious buildings or sites. The other three main obligations are generally as follows:

To place the country under such political, administrative, and economic conditions as will secure the establishment in Palestine of a national home for the Jewish People. To facilitate Jewish immigration under suitable conditions, and to encourage, in cooperation with the Jewish Agency, close settlement by Jews on the Land.

To safeguard the civil and religious rights of all inhabitants of Palestine, irrespective of race and religion, and, whilst facilitating Jewish immigration and settlement, to ensure that the rights and position of other sections of the population are not prejudiced.

To place the country under such political, administrative, and economic conditions as will secure the development of self-governing institutions.

The Royal Commission and previous commissions of Enquiry have drawn attention to the ambiguity of certain expressions in the Mandate, such as the expression 'a national home for the Jewish people', and they have found in this ambiguity and the resulting uncertainty as to the objectives of policy a fundamental cause of unrest and hostility between Arabs and Jews. His Majesty's Government are convinced that in the interests of the peace and well-being of the whole people of Palestine a clear definition of policy and objectives is essential. The proposal of partition recommended by the Royal Commission would have afforded such clarity, but the establishment of self-supporting independent Arab and Jewish States within Palestine has been found to be impracticable. It has therefore been necessary for His Majesty's Government to devise an alternative policy which will, consistent with their obligations to Arabs and Jews, meet the needs of the situation in Palestine. Their views and proposals are set forth below under three heads, Section I, 'The Constitution'; Section II, 'Immigration'; and Section III, 'Land'.

Section I. 'The Constitution'

It has been urged that the expression 'a national home for the Jewish people' offered a prospect that Palestine might in due course become a Jewish State or Commonwealth. His Majesty's Government do not wish to contest the view, which was expressed by the Royal Commission,

that the Zionist leaders at the time of the issue of the Balfour Declaration recognised that an ultimate Jewish State was not precluded by the terms of the Declaration. But, with the Royal Commission, His Majesty's Government believe that the framers of the Mandate in which the Balfour Declaration was embodied could not have intended that Palestine should be converted into a Jewish State against the will of the Arab population of the country. That Palestine was not to be converted into a Jewish State might be held to be implied in the passage from the Command Paper of 1922, which reads as follows:

> Unauthorized statements have been made to the effect that the purpose in view is to create a wholly Jewish Palestine. Phrases have been used such as that 'Palestine is to become as Jewish as England is English.' His Majesty's Government regard any such expectation as impracticable and have no such aim in view. Nor have they at any time contemplated . . . the disappearance or the subordination of the Arabic population, language, or culture in Palestine. They would draw attention to the fact that the terms of the (Balfour) Declaration referred to do not contemplate that Palestine as a whole should be converted into a Jewish National Home, but that such a Home should be founded IN PALESTINE.

But this statement has not removed doubts, and His Majesty's Government therefore now declare unequivocally that it is not part of their policy that Palestine should become a Jewish State. They would indeed regard it as contrary to their obligations to the Arabs under the Mandate, as well as to the assurances which have been given to the Arab people in the past, that the Arab population of Palestine should be made the subjects of a Jewish State against their will. . . .

In the recent discussions the Arab delegations have repeated the contention that Palestine was included within the area in which Sir Henry

McMahon, on behalf of the British Government, in October 1915, undertook to recognise and support Arab independence. The validity of this claim, based on the terms of the correspondence which passed between Sir Henry McMahon and the Sharif of Mecca, was thoroughly and carefully investigated by the British and Arab representatives during the recent conferences in London. Their report, which has been published, states that both the Arab and the British representatives endeavoured to understand the point of view of the other party but that they were unable to reach agreement upon an interpretation of the correspondence. There is no need to summarize here the arguments presented by each side. His Majesty's Government regret the misunderstandings which have arisen as regards some of the phrases used. For their part they can only adhere, for the reasons given by their representatives in the Report, to the view that the whole of Palestine west of Jordan was excluded from Sir Henry McMahon's pledge, and they therefore cannot agree that the McMahon correspondence forms a just basis for the claim that Palestine should be converted into an Arab State.

His Majesty's Government are charged as the Mandatory authority 'to secure the development of self-governing institutions' in Palestine. Apart from this specific obligation, they would regard it as contrary to the whole spirit of the Mandate system that the population of Palestine should remain forever under Mandatory tutelage. It is proper that the people of the country should as early as possible enjoy the rights of self-government that are exercised by the people of neighbouring countries. His Majesty's Government are unable at present to foresee the exact constitutional forms which government in Palestine will eventually take, but their objective is self government, and they desire to see established ultimately an independent Palestine State. It should be a State in which the two peoples in Palestine, Arabs, and Jews, share authority in government in such a way that the essential interests of each are shared.

The establishment of an independent State and the complete relinquishment of Mandatory control in Palestine would require such relations between the Arabs and the Jews as would make good government possible. Moreover, the growth of self-governing institutions in Palestine, as in other countries, must be an evolutionary process. A transitional period will be required before independence is achieved, throughout which ultimate responsibility for the Government of the country will be retained by His Majesty's Government as the Mandatory authority, while the people of the country are taking an increasing share in the Government, and understanding and cooperation amongst them are growing. It will be the constant endeavour of His Majesty's Government to promote good relations between the Arabs and the Jews.

In the light of these considerations His Majesty's Government make the following declaration of their intentions regarding the future government of Palestine:

The objective of His Majesty's Government is the establishment within 10 years of an independent Palestine State in such treaty relations with the United Kingdom as will provide satisfactorily for the commercial and strategic requirements of both countries in the future. The proposal for the establishment of the independent State would involve consultation with the Council of the League of Nations with a view to the termination of the Mandate.

The independent State should be one in which Arabs and Jews share government in such a way as to ensure that the essential interests of each community are safeguarded.

The establishment of the independent State will be preceded by a transitional period throughout which His Majesty's Government will retain responsibility for the country. During the transitional period the people of Palestine will be given an increasing part in the government of their country. Both sections of the population will have an opportunity to participate in the machinery of government, and the process will be carried on whether or not they both avail themselves of it.

As soon as peace and order have been sufficiently restored in Palestine steps will be taken to carry out this policy of giving the people of Palestine an increasing part in the government of their country, the objective being to place Palestinians in charge of all the Departments of Government, with the assistance of British advisers and subject to the control of the High Commissioner. Arab and Jewish representatives will be invited to serve as heads of Departments approximately in proportion to their respective populations. The number of Palestinians in charge of Departments will be increased as circumstances permit until all heads of Departments are Palestinians, exercising the administrative and advisory functions, which are presently performed by British officials. When that stage is reached consideration will be given to the question of converting the Executive Council into a Council of Ministers with a consequential change in the status and functions of the Palestinian heads of Departments. . . .

Section II. 'Immigration'

Under Article 6 of the Mandate, the Administration of Palestine, 'while ensuring that the rights and position of other sections of the population are not prejudiced,' is required to 'facilitate Jewish immigration under suitable conditions.' Beyond this, the extent to which Jewish immigration into Palestine is to be permitted is nowhere defined in the Mandate. But in the Command Paper of 1922 it was laid down that for the fulfilment of the policy of establishing a Jewish National Home:

> it is necessary that the Jewish community in Palestine should be able to increase its numbers by immigration. This immigration cannot be so great in volume as to exceed whatever may be the economic capacity of the country at the time to absorb new arrivals. It is essential to ensure that the immigrants should not be a burden upon the people of Palestine as a whole, and that they should not deprive any section of the present population of their employment.

In practice, from that date onwards until recent times, the economic absorptive capacity of the country has been treated as the sole limiting factor, and in the letter which Mr Ramsay MacDonald, as Prime Minister, sent to Dr Weizmann in February 1931 it was laid down as a matter of policy that economic absorptive capacity was the sole criterion. This interpretation has been supported by resolutions of the Permanent Mandates Commissioner. But His Majesty's Government do not read either the Statement of Policy of 1922 or the letter of 1931 as implying that the Mandate requires them, for all time and in all circumstances, to facilitate the immigration of Jews into Palestine subject only to consideration of the country's economic absorptive capacity. Nor do they find anything in the Mandate or in subsequent Statements of Policy to support the view that the establishment of a Jewish National Home in Palestine cannot be effected unless immigration is allowed to continue indefinitely. If immigration has an adverse effect on the economic position in the country, it should clearly be restricted; and equally, if it has a seriously damaging effect on the political position in the country, that is a factor that should not be ignored. Although it is not difficult to contend that the large number of Jewish immigrants who have been admitted so far have been absorbed economically, the fear of the Arabs that this influx will continue indefinitely until the Jewish population is in a position to dominate them has produced consequences which are extremely grave for Jews and Arabs alike and for the peace and prosperity of Palestine. . . .

Jewish immigration during the next five years will be at a rate, which, if economic absorptive capacity permits, will bring the Jewish population up to approximately one third of the total population of the country. Taking into account the expected natural increase of the Arab and Jewish populations, and the number of illegal Jewish immigrants now in the country, this would allow the admission, as from the beginning of April this year, of some 75,000 immigrants over the next five years. These immigrants would, subject to the criterion of economic absorptive capacity, be admitted as follows:

For each of the next five years a quota of 10,000 Jewish immigrants will be allowed on the understanding that a shortage one year may be added to the quotas for subsequent years, within the five year period, if economic absorptive capacity permits.

In addition, as a contribution towards the solution of the Jewish refugee problem, 25,000 refugees will be admitted as soon as the High Commissioner is satisfied that adequate provision for their maintenance is ensured, special consideration being given to refugee children and dependents.

The existing machinery for ascertaining economic absorptive capacity will be retained, and the High Commissioner will have the ultimate responsibility for deciding the limits of economic capacity. Before each periodic decision is taken, Jewish and Arab representatives will be consulted.

After the period of five years, no further Jewish immigration will be permitted unless the Arabs of Palestine are prepared to acquiesce in it.

His Majesty's Government are determined to check illegal immigration, and further preventive measures are being adopted. The numbers of any Jewish illegal immigrants who, despite these measures, may succeed in coming into the country and cannot be deported will be deducted from the yearly quotas. . . .

Study Question

1. Would the Palestinian state envisioned by the creators of the White Paper have produced a workable solution to the ongoing regional instability?

Map of the Middle East.

UNITED NATIONS SECURITY COUNCIL/
PALESTINE NATIONAL COUNCIL

During the course of the Six-Day War in June 1967, Israeli forces moved into a number of Palestinian territories, including the Golan Heights, East Jerusalem, the West Bank, and the Gaza Strip. Both the Americans and the Soviets—concerned primarily with the stability of the Middle East—backed a resolution in the United Nations Security Council calling for the withdrawal of Israeli occupation forces to pre-1967 lines. To date Resolution 242 has not been enforced. Given the ineffectiveness of Resolution 242, the Palestinian people found themselves surrounded by a vastly strengthened Israeli State. As well, thousands of additional refugees had been forced to flee across the borders into neighbouring Arab states. A number of movements dedicated to liberating the Palestinian people from Israeli occupation formed among these refugees. The Palestinian National Charter summarized the basic aims of many such groups in July 1968. The Charter itself follows Resolution 242.

RESOLUTION 242, 22 NOVEMBER 1967

The Security Council,

Expressing its continuing concern with the grave situation in the Middle East,

Emphasizing the inadmissibility of the acquisition of territory by war and the need to work for a just and lasting peace in which every state in the area can live in security.

Emphasizing further that all member states in their acceptance of the Charter of the United Nations have undertaken a commitment to act in accordance with Article 2 of the Charter,

1. *Affirms* that the fulfillment of Charter principles requires the establishment of a just and lasting peace in the Middle East which should include the application of both the following principles:

(i) Withdrawal of Israeli armed forces from territories of recent conflict;

(ii) Termination of all claims or states of belligerency, and respect for and acknowledgement of the sovereignty, territorial integrity and political independence of every state in the area and their right to live in peace within secure and recognized boundaries free from threats or acts of force;

2. *Affirms* further the necessity

(a) For guaranteeing freedom of navigation through international waterways in the area;

(b) For achieving a just settlement of the refugee problem;

(c) For guaranteeing the territorial inviolability and political independence of every state in the area, through measures including the establishment of demilitarized zones;

3. *Requests* the Secretary General to designate a special representative to proceed to the Middle East to establish and maintain contacts with the states concerned in order to promote agreement and assist efforts to achieve a peaceful and accepted settlement in accordance with the provisions and principles in this resolution.

4. *Requests* the Secretary General to report to the Security Council on the progress of the efforts of the special representative as soon as possible.

The Khan Younis refugee camp in Gaza was established in 1949 for Palestinian refugees. The UN estimates its population today at more than 180,000. Courtesy of the United Nations Photo Library (20758 UN/DPI).

THE PALESTINIAN NATIONAL CHARTER

1. Palestine is the homeland of the Arab Palestinian people; it is an indivisible part of the Arab homeland, and the Palestinian people are an integral part of the Arab nation.

2. Palestine, with the boundaries it had during the British Mandate, is an indivisible territorial unit.

3. The Palestinian Arab people possess the legal right to their homeland and have the right to determine their destiny after achieving the liberation of their country in accordance with their wishes and entirely of their own accord and will.

4. The Palestinian identity is a genuine, essential, and inherent characteristic; it is transmitted from parents to children. The Zionist occupation and the dispersal of the Palestinian Arab people, through the disasters which befell them, do not make them lose their Palestinian identity and their membership in the Palestinian community, nor do they negate them.

5. The Palestinians are those Arab nationals who, until 1947, normally resided in Palestine regardless of whether they were evicted from it or have stayed there. Anyone born, after that date, of a Palestinian father—whether inside Palestine or outside it—is also a Palestinian.

6. The Jews who had normally resided in Palestine until the beginning of the Zionist invasion will be considered Palestinians.

7. That there is a Palestinian community and that it has material, spiritual, and historical connection with Palestine are indisputable facts. It is a national duty to bring up individual Palestinians in an Arab revolutionary manner. All means of information and education must be adopted in order to acquaint the Palestinian with his country in the most profound manner, both spiritual and material, that is possible. He must be prepared for the armed struggle and ready to sacrifice his wealth and his life in order to win back his homeland and bring about its liberation.

8. The phase in their history, through which the Palestinian people are now living, is that of national struggle for the liberation of Palestine. Thus the conflicts among the Palestinian national forces are secondary, and should be ended for the sake of the basic conflict that exists between the forces of Zionism and of imperialism on the one hand, and the Palestinian Arab people on the other. On this basis the Palestinian masses, regardless of whether they are residing in the national homeland or in Diaspora (*mahajir*) constitute—both their organizations and the individuals—one national front working for the retrieval of Palestine and its liberation through armed struggle.

9. Armed struggle is the only way to liberate Palestine. Thus it is the overall strategy, not merely a tactical phase. The Palestinian Arab people assert their absolute determination and firm resolution to continue their armed struggle and to work for an armed popular revolution for the liberation of their country and their return to it. They also assert their right to normal life in Palestine and to exercise their right to self-determination and sovereignty over it.

10. Commando action constitutes the nucleus of the Palestinian popular liberation war. This requires its escalation, comprehensiveness, and the mobilization of all the Palestinian popular and educational efforts and their organization and involvement in the armed Palestinian revolution. It also requires the achieving of unity for the national (*watani*) struggle among the different groupings of the Palestinian people, and between the Palestinian people and the Arab masses, so as to secure the continuation of the revolution, its escalation, and victory.

11. The Palestinians will have three mottoes: national (*wataniyya*) unity, national (*qawmiyya*) mobilization, and liberation.

12. The Palestinian people believe in Arab unity. In order to contribute their share toward the attainment of that objective, however, they must, at the present stage of their struggle, safeguard their Palestinian identity and develop their consciousness of that identity, and oppose any plan that may dissolve or impair it.

13. Arab unity and the liberation of Palestine are two complementary objectives, the attainment of either of which facilitates the attainment of the other. Thus, Arab unity leads to the liberation of Palestine, the liberation of Palestine leads to Arab unity; and work toward the realization of one objective proceeds side by side with work toward the realization of the other.

14. The destiny of the Arab nation, and indeed Arab existence itself, depend upon the destiny of the Palestine cause. From this interdependence spring the Arab nation's pursuit of, and striving for, the liberation of Palestine. The people of Palestine play the role of the vanguard in the realization of this sacred national goal.

15. The liberation of Palestine, from an Arab viewpoint, is a national duty and it attempts to repel the Zionist and imperialist aggression against the Arab homeland, and aims at the elimination of Zionism in Palestine. Absolute responsibility for this falls upon the Arab nation—peoples and governments—with the Arab people of Palestine in the vanguard. Accordingly, the Arab nation must mobilize all its military, human, moral and spiritual capabilities to participate actively with the Palestinian people in the liberation of Palestine. It must, particularly in the phase of the armed Palestinian revolution, offer and furnish

the Palestinian people with all possible help, and material and human support, and make available to them the means and opportunities that will enable them to continue to carry out their leading role in the armed revolution, until they liberate their homeland.

16. The liberation of Palestine, from a spiritual point of view, will provide the Holy Land with an atmosphere of safety and tranquility, which in turn will safeguard the country's religious sanctuaries and guarantee freedom of worship and of visit to all, without discrimination of race, colour, language, or religion. Accordingly, the people of Palestine look to all spiritual forces in the world for support.

17. The liberation of Palestine, from a human point of view, will restore to the Palestinian individual his dignity, pride, and freedom. Accordingly the Palestinian Arab people look forward to the support of all those who believe in the dignity of man and his freedom in the world.

18. The liberation of Palestine, from an international point of view, is a defensive action necessitated by the demands of self-defence. Accordingly the Palestinian people, desirous as they are of the friendship of all people, look to freedom-loving, and peace-loving states for support in order to restore their legitimate rights in Palestine, to re-establish peace and security in the country, and to enable its people to exercise national sovereignty and freedom.

19. The partition of Palestine in 1947 and the establishment of the state of Israel are entirely illegal, regardless of the passage of time, because they were contrary to the will of the Palestinian people and to their natural right in their homeland, and inconsistent with the principles embodied in the Charter of the United Nations; particularly the right to self-determination.

20. The Balfour Declaration, the Mandate for Palestine, and everything that has been based upon them, are deemed null and void. Claims of historical or religious ties of Jews with Palestine are incompatible with the facts of history and the true conception of what constitutes statehood. Judaism, being a religion, is not an independent nationality. Nor do Jews constitute a single nation with an identity of its own; they are citizens of the states to which they belong.

21. The Arab Palestinian people, expressing themselves by the armed Palestinian revolution, reject all solutions which are substitutes for the total liberation of Palestine and reject all proposals aiming at the liquidation of the Palestinian problem, or its internationalization.

22. Zionism is a political movement organically associated with international imperialism and antagonistic to all action for liberation and to progressive movements in the world. It is racist and fanatic in its nature, aggressive, expansionist, and colonial in its aims, and fascist in its methods. Israel is the instrument of the Zionist movement, and a geographical base for world imperialism placed strategically in the midst of the Arab homeland to combat the hopes of the Arab nation for liberation, unity, and progress. Israel is a constant source of threat vis-à-vis peace in the Middle East and the whole world. Since the liberation of Palestine will destroy the Zionist and imperialist presence and will contribute to the establishment of peace in the Middle East, the Palestinian people look for the support of all the progressive and peaceful forces and urge them all, irrespective of their affiliations and beliefs, to offer the Palestinian people all aid and support in their just struggle for the liberation of their homeland.

Study Questions

1. To what extent was Resolution 242 a realistic solution to the situation in the Middle East after the Six-Day War?
2. Is 'armed struggle the only way to liberate Palestine'? Why or why not?

GOLDA MEIR

Golda Meir (1898–1978) served in a number of capacities in the Israeli government, including minister of labour, foreign minister, and, eventually, prime minister from 1969 until 1974. Although Israel emerged victorious in the Yom Kippur War in 1973, Meir's leadership in the weeks leading up to the war was criticized by many in the country. However, she remained a prominent figure in politics even after her resignation. In 1977 she delivered the first speech in the Israeli parliament (the Knesset), marking the historic visit of Egyptian president Anwar Sadat (1918–81).

REMARKS TO PRESIDENT SADAT

Mr President, I'm sure that from the moment your plane landed at Lydda Airport, and as you drove through the streets of Jerusalem, you must have felt, in all your encounters with the many people who turned out to meet you—the little children; the mothers with babies in their arms; the old people; the people who were born in this country, the second, third, fourth and fifth generations, and those who have come recently—that all, without exception, were overjoyed to see you in our Land.

When asked, many years ago, when I thought that peace would come to this region to our country and to our neighbouring countries—I said: I do not know the date, but I do know under what conditions it will come—when there will be a leader, a great leader of an Arab country. He will wake up one morning and feel sorry for his own people, for his own sons who have fallen in battle, and that day will be the beginning of peace between us.

Mr President, we have a saying in Hebrew: 'zchut rishonim'. In English, this means 'the privilege of being the first'. I congratulate you, Mr President, that you are privileged to be the first great Arab leader of the greatest country among our neighbours to come to us, with courage and determination, despite so many difficulties, for the sake of your sons, as well as for the sake of our; for the sake of all mothers who mourn sons that fell in battle. No mother should have to give birth to a son in the fear that he may fall in battle. For the sake of all our sons and all our children, not only those who are alive today but also those to be born in future generations—you have come to us and said: let us have peace; let the war of 1973 be the last war between us.

You have come telling us that, from now on, you are prepared to live in peace with us. I can assure you, Mr President, that as far as we are concerned, the desire for peace, the hope of peace and the dream of peace have never left the hearts of a single one of us. We have come back to this country to live in peace. We have come back to this country to live. We have come back to this country to create. In this room, you will see people who, for the first time in their lives, have climbed hills and planted trees in this country; who, for the first time, have gone down to the desert—it was considered a desert, a God-forsaken land and have made it green, so that our children can live and play everywhere in it. Many of these children—very many of them—also enjoy the privilege of having been the first, after centuries upon centuries, to bring life to the desert, to the swamps and to the hills of this country. All this we have done for peace—to live in peace; to live, but to live in peace.

Mr President, we listened to you last night and we heard your appeal for peace. When I was in office, and I am sure this was true for everyone who preceded me and for those who succeeded me

Egyptian President Anwar Sadat and Israeli Prime Minister Menachem Begin in 1978 at the announcement of the successful outcome of the Camp David Accords. U.S. News and World Report Magazine Photograph Collection. Courtesy of the Library of Congress, Prints and Photographs Division (LC-DIG-ppmsca-09792).

in office—I hoped that the day would come when we could meet with a leader of one of the Arab countries and hold a discussion with him. Not that we ever imagined that, at the very first meeting, we would come with pens in our hands, ready to sign a peace treaty. But our hope was that we would hold discussions on points of disagreement, and that we would discuss these points face-to-face, rather than through intermediaries for, no matter how successfully intermediaries may report to both of us, it is not the same. As I sit here and look at you, and as I heard you in person last night, it is not the same.

Of course, we must all realize that the path leading to peace may be a difficult one, but not as difficult as that path which leads to war. What Israel wants—what this group with which you are meeting today has wanted, from the very beginning, is territorial compromise, in accordance with the programme it adopted immediately after the war of 1967. As a matter of fact, Israel has made and accepted compromises ever since 1947. I can say, in all sincerity, that we have desired additional territory. We have always been prepared to live within our existing boundaries.

We will not go into history today, but what we want to tell you is that we were, and are, prepared for territorial compromise on all our borders—with one condition: these borders will give us security, and protect us from danger, so that we will never be in need, God forbid, at any time, of help from abroad in order to defend ourselves. We have never sought such help from others; nobody has ever come to defend us. The blood that has been shed, to our sorrow, has been our own. We don't want to shed the blood of others.

With us today is Mr Rabin. After the war of 1967, he was awarded an Honorary degree by the

Hebrew University of Jerusalem and, in his words of acceptance, as Chief of Staff, he said: 'Here is the Israeli army that came back victorious. It came back a sad army, despite its victory; sad because of our men who fell, but also because of our sons who were compelled to shoot others.' These two things we do not want: we do not want to be shot at—and, believe me—we do not want to shoot others.

Therefore, we want borders within which, when we do sign peace treaties, all Israelis will be assured that they live in security, without having to rely on international guarantees. I do not think we will need these when we have peace—neither we shall need them, nor you. But we must have borders that will enable us—if, God forbid, something should happen in the future—to defend ourselves. Territorial compromise—yes, but not compromise with our security! Each country, each nation, will decide its security requirements. When we talk of territorial compromise, it is essential that we remember this.

Mr President. We, the People of Israel, are the last to be insensitive to the sorrow of others. We have never said that we want the Palestinian Arabs to remain as they are—in camps, in misery, dependent on charity. We do not wish to be dependent upon others, nor do we wish them to be dependent upon others. Had it been within our power, there would never have been a problem of this kind. Of course, we realize that there are Palestinian Arabs and we believe there is a solution, one that is both good for them and safe for us.

Because we believe this, we believe also that there is no connection between our opposition to another state between us and Jordan—a Palestinian state which would be small, probably not viable and perhaps forced to expand—and between our awareness of the need to solve the problem of the Palestinian Arabs. Our opposition to another state is based on Israel's most vital security requirements. Mr President, should we agree to

the establishment of such a state, there would be only ten miles between the Mediterranean and the borders of this state. You cannot expect us to feel secure within such borders.

Of course, we favour a solution for the Palestinian Arabs, and believe that in the programme of this group gathered here today with you, such a solution exists. This programme, formulated prior to the elections and still valid to this day, states that in our peace treaty with Jordan, there must be a solution for the Palestinian Arabs, so the camps may be wiped out and become a thing of the past. But not at the expense of Israel's security. If there were no solution, it would be a terrible problem for us. But there is a solution to this problem too.

Therefore, we say to you, Mr President, that, while we do not agree with everything you said last night—surely, this does not surprise you—we deeply appreciate your call for peace, and believe in your sincere desire for it, just as I hope you believe in our sincere desire for it. Now, let us go forward. Even if we do not reach agreement on everything this morning, let us, at least, conclude one thing: the beginnings that you have made, with such courage and with such hope for peace, must go on, continuing face-to-face between ourselves and you, so that even an old lady like myself will live to see the day—yes, you always call me an old lady—and regardless of whoever signs on Israel's behalf, I want to live to see that day—that peace reigns between you and us, peace between ourselves and all our neighbours.

And, Mr President, as a grandmother to a grandfather, may I give you a little present for your new grand-daughter, and thank you for the present you have given me.

Study Question

1. Under what circumstances could Israel enjoy the security of which Golda Meir speaks here?

Joint US/Soviet Statement on Peace in the Middle East, September 1977

By 1977 several wars had been fought over the presence of the State of Israel—in 1948, 1956, 1967, and 1973. All had threatened to embroil the superpowers, due to the nature of the Cold War alliance system. The framework below reflects the determination of both the United States, under President Jimmy Carter, and the Soviet Union, under Leonid Brezhnev, to avoid further conflicts in the region.

---◇---

Having exchanged views regarding the unsafe situation which remains in the Middle East, United States Secretary of State Cyrus Vance and member of the Politburo of the Central Committee of the CPSU, Minister for Foreign Affairs of the USSR, A.A. [Andrei] Gromyko have the following statement to make on behalf of their countries, which are Co-chairmen of the Geneva Peace Conference[1] on the Middle East:

1. Both governments are convinced that vital interests of the peoples of this area as well as the interests of strengthening peace and international security in general urgently dictate the necessity of achieving as soon as possible a just and lasting settlement of the Arab–Israeli conflict. This settlement should be comprehensive, incorporating all parties concerned and all questions.

The United States and the Soviet Union believe that, within the framework of a comprehensive settlement of the Middle East problem, all specific questions of the settlement should be resolved, including such key issues as withdrawal of Israeli armed forces from territories occupied in the 1967 conflict; The resolution of the Palestinian question including ensuring the legitimate rights of the Palestinian people; Termination of the state of war and establishment of normal peaceful relations on the basis of mutual recognition of the principles of sovereignty, territorial integrity, and political independence.

The two governments believe that, in addition to such measures for ensuring the security of the borders between Israel and the neighboring Arab states as the establishment of demilitarized zones and the agreed stationing in them of UN troops or observers, international guarantees of such borders as well as of the observance of the terms of the settlement can also be established, should the contracting parties so desire. The United States and the Soviet Union are ready to participate in these guarantees, subject to their constitutional processes.

2. The United States and the Soviet Union believe that the only right and effective way for achieving a fundamental solution to all aspects of the Middle East problem in its entirety is negotiations within the framework of the Geneva Peace Conference, specially convened for these purposes, with participation in its work of the representatives of all the parties involved in the conflict including those of the Palestinian people, and legal and contractual formalization of the decisions reached at the conference.

In their capacity as Co-Chairmen of the Geneva Conference, the US and the USSR affirm their intention through joint efforts and in their contacts with the parties concerned to facilitate in every way the resumption of the work of the conference not later than December 1977. The Co-Chairmen note that there still exist several questions of a procedural and organizational nature which remain to be agreed upon by the participants to the conference.

3. Guided by the goal of achieving a just political

settlement in the Middle East and of eliminating the explosive situation in this area of the world, the US and the USSR appeal to all the parties in the conflict to understand the necessity for careful consideration of each other's legitimate rights and interests and to demonstrate mutual readiness to act accordingly.

Note

1. The Geneva Peace Conference was convened in 1973 to reach a solution to the conflict between Israel and the Arab States. Though the Geneva process failed, it did set the stage for the successful Israeli–Egyptian accord signed at Camp David in 1978.

> **Study Question**
>
> 1. Why were both the United States and the Soviet Union determined to push Israel and Egypt towards a peace settlement in the mid-1970s?

HAMAS

Hamas was founded in 1987 in the wake of repeated failures to achieve a peaceful resolution to conflicts between Israelis and Palestinians. Unlike organizations such as the Palestine Liberation Organization (PLO), which include strongly secular elements, Hamas calls for the creation of an Islamic Palestinian State. In 2006, in an election deemed by international observers to be both free and fair, Hamas gained a majority of seats in the Palestinian National Authority. Hamas is viewed by many Palestinians to be less corrupt than Fatah, its major rival, and more reliable in terms of providing basic social services in the West Bank and Gaza. Most western nations, however, regard Hamas as a terrorist organization.

COVENANT OF THE ISLAMIC RESISTANCE MOVEMENT, 1988

In The Name Of The Most Merciful Allah

'Ye are the best nation that hath been raised up unto mankind: ye command that which is just, and ye forbid that which is unjust, and ye believe in Allah. And if they who have received the scriptures had believed, it had surely been the better for them: there are believers among them, but the greater part of them are transgressors. They shall not hurt you, unless with a slight hurt; and if they fight against you, they shall turn their backs to you, and they shall not be helped. They are smitten with vileness wheresoever they are found; unless they obtain security by entering into a treaty with Allah, and a treaty with men; and they draw on themselves indignation from Allah, and they are afflicted with poverty. This they suffer, because they disbelieved the signs of Allah, and slew the prophets unjustly; this, because they were rebellious, and transgressed' (Al-Imran, verses 109–111).

'Israel will exist and will continue to exist until Islam will obliterate it, just as it obliterated others before it' (The Martyr, Imam Hassan al-Banna, of blessed memory).

'The Islamic world is on fire. Each of us should pour some water, no matter how little, to

Residents of Gaza check voters lists in advance of the 2006 election which brought Hamas to power. © Shawn Baldwin/ Corbis.

extinguish whatever one can without waiting for the others.' (Sheikh Amjad al-Zahawi, of blessed memory).

In The Name Of The Most Merciful Allah

Introduction

Praise be unto Allah, to whom we resort for help, and whose forgiveness, guidance and support we seek; Allah bless the Prophet and grant him salvation, his companions and supporters, and to those who carried out his message and adopted his laws—everlasting prayers and salvation as long as the earth and heaven will last. Hereafter: O People:

Out of the midst of troubles and the sea of suffering, out of the palpitations of faithful hearts and cleansed arms; out of the sense of duty, and in response to Allah's command, the call has gone out rallying people together and making them follow the ways of Allah, leading them to have determined will in order to fulfill their role in life, to overcome all obstacles, and surmount the difficulties on the way. Constant preparation has continued and so has the readiness to sacrifice life and all that is precious for the sake of Allah.

Thus it was that the nucleus (of the movement) was formed and started to pave its way through the tempestuous sea of hopes and expectations, of wishes and yearnings, of troubles and obstacles, of pain and challenges, both inside and outside.

When the idea was ripe, the seed grew and the plant struck root in the soil of reality, away from passing emotions, and hateful haste. The Islamic Resistance Movement emerged to carry out its role through striving for the sake of its Creator, its arms intertwined with those of all the fighters for the liberation of Palestine. The spirits of its fighters meet with the spirits of all the fighters who have sacrificed their lives on the soil of Palestine, ever since it was conquered by the companions of the Prophet, Allah bless him and grant him salvation, and until this day.

This Covenant of the Islamic Resistance Movement (Hamas), clarifies its picture, reveals its identity, outlines its stand, explains its aims, speaks about its hopes, and calls for its support, adoption and joining its ranks. Our struggle against the Jews is very great and very serious. It needs all sincere efforts. It is a step that inevitably should be followed by other steps. The Movement is but one squadron that should be supported by more and more squadrons from this vast Arab and Islamic world, until the enemy is vanquished and Allah's victory is realised.

Thus we see them coming on the horizon 'and you shall learn about it hereafter' 'Allah hath written, Verily I will prevail, and my apostles: for Allah is strong and mighty' (The Dispute, verse 21).

'Say to them, This is my way: I invite you to Allah, by an evident demonstration; both I and he who followeth me; and, praise be unto Allah! I am not an idolator' (Joseph, verse 107).

Hamas (means) *strength and bravery* (according to) Al-Mua'jam al-Wasit: c1.

. . .

Article Four

The Islamic Resistance Movement welcomes every Moslem who embraces its faith, ideology, follows its programme, keeps its secrets, and wants to belong to its ranks and carry out the duty. Allah will certainly reward such one.

Article Six

The Islamic Resistance Movement is a distinguished Palestinian movement, whose allegiance is to Allah, and whose way of life is Islam. It strives to raise the banner of Allah over every inch of Palestine, for under the wing of Islam followers

of all religions can coexist in security and safety where their lives, possessions and rights are concerned. In the absence of Islam, strife will be rife, oppression spreads, evil prevails and schisms and wars will break out.

How excellent was the Moslem poet, Mohamed Ikbal, when he wrote: 'If faith is lost, there is no security and there is no life for him who does not adhere to religion. He who accepts life without religion, has taken annihilation as his companion for life.'

Article Seven

. . . The Islamic Resistance Movement is one of the links in the chain of the struggle against the Zionist invaders. It goes back to 1939, to the emergence of the martyr Izz al-Din al Kissam and his brethren the fighters, members of Moslem Brotherhood. It goes on to reach out and become one with another chain that includes the struggle of the Palestinians and Moslem Brotherhood in the 1948 war and the Jihad operations of the Moslem Brotherhood in 1968 and after.

Moreover, if the links have been distant from each other and if obstacles, placed by those who are the lackeys of Zionism in the way of the fighters obstructed the continuation of the struggle, the Islamic Resistance Movement aspires to the realisation of Allah's promise, no matter how long that should take. The Prophet, Allah bless him and grant him salvation, has said: 'The Day of Judgement will not come about until Moslems fight the Jews (killing the Jews), when the Jew will hide behind stones and trees. The stones and trees will say O Moslems, O Abdulla, there is a Jew behind me, come and kill him. Only the Gharkad tree, (evidently a certain kind of tree) would not do that because it is one of the trees of the Jews' (related by al-Bukhari and Moslem).

Article Eight

Allah is its target, the Prophet is its model, the

Koran its constitution: Jihad is its path and death for the sake of Allah is the loftiest of its wishes. . . .

Article Fifteen

The day that enemies usurp part of Moslem land, Jihad becomes the individual duty of every Moslem. In face of the Jews' usurpation of Palestine, it is compulsory that the banner of Jihad be raised. To do this requires the diffusion of Islamic consciousness among the masses, both on the regional, Arab and Islamic levels. It is necessary to instill the spirit of Jihad in the heart of the nation so that they would confront the enemies and join the ranks of the fighters.

It is necessary that scientists, educators and teachers, information and media people, as well as the educated masses, especially the youth and sheikhs of the Islamic movements, should take part in the operation of awakening (the masses). It is important that basic changes be made in the school curriculum, to cleanse it of the traces of ideological invasion that affected it as a result of the orientalists and missionaries who infiltrated the region following the defeat of the Crusaders at the hands of Salah el-Din (Saladin). The Crusaders realised that it was impossible to defeat the Moslems without first having ideological invasion pave the way by upsetting their thoughts, disfiguring their heritage and violating their ideals. Only then could they invade with soldiers. This, in its turn, paved the way for the imperialistic invasion that made Allenby declare on entering Jerusalem: 'Only now have the Crusades ended.' General Guru stood at Salah el-Din's grave and said: 'We have returned, O Salah el-Din.' Imperialism has helped towards the strengthening of ideological invasion, deepening, and still does, its roots. All this has paved the way towards the loss of Palestine.

It is necessary to instill in the minds of the Moslem generations that the Palestinian problem is a religious problem, and should be dealt with

on this basis. Palestine contains Islamic holy sites. In it there is al-Aqsa Mosque which is bound to the great Mosque in Mecca in an inseparable bond as long as heaven and earth speak of Isra (Mohammed's midnight journey to the seven heavens) and Mi'raj (Mohammed's ascension to the seven heavens from Jerusalem).

'The bond of one day for the sake of Allah is better than the world and whatever there is on it. The place of one's whip in Paradise is far better than the world and whatever there is on it. A worshipper's going and coming in the service of Allah is better than the world and whatever there is on it' (As related by al-Bukhari, Moslem, al-Tarmdhi and Ibn Maja).

'I swear by the holder of Mohammed's soul that I would like to invade and be killed for the sake of Allah, then invade and be killed, and then invade again and be killed' (As related by al-Bukhari and Moslem). . . .

Article Twenty-Seven

The Palestinian Liberation Organization is the closest to the heart of the Islamic Resistance Movement. It contains the father and the brother, the next of kin and the friend. The Moslem does not estrange himself from his father, brother, next of kin or friend. Our homeland is one, our situation is one, our fate is one and the enemy is a joint enemy to all of us.

Because of the situations surrounding the formation of the Organization, of the ideological confusion prevailing in the Arab world as a result of the ideological invasion under whose influence the Arab world has fallen since the defeat of the Crusaders and which was, and still is, intensified through orientalists, missionaries and imperialists, the Organization adopted the idea of the secular state. And that is how we view it.

Secularism completely contradicts religious ideology. Attitudes, conduct and decisions stem from ideologies.

That is why, with all our appreciation for The

Palestinian Liberation Organization—and what it can develop into—and without belittling its role in the Arab–Israeli conflict, we are unable to exchange the present or future Islamic Palestine with the secular idea. The Islamic nature of Palestine is part of our religion and whoever takes his religion lightly is a loser.

'Who will be adverse to the religion of Abraham, but he whose mind is infatuated?' (The Cow, verse 130).

The day The Palestinian Liberation Organization adopts Islam as its way of life, we will become its soldiers, and fuel for its fire that will burn the enemies.

Until such a day, and we pray to Allah that it will be soon, the Islamic Resistance Movement's

stand towards the PLO is that of the son towards his father, the brother towards his brother, and the relative to relative, suffers his pain and supports him in confronting the enemies, wishing him to be wise and well-guided.

'Stand by your brother, for he who is brotherless is like the fighter who goes to battle without arms. One's cousin is the wing one flies with—could the bird fly without wings?'

Study Question

1. What is the greatest obstacle to Israeli–Palestinian peace: Israeli/Palestinian differences or differences among Palestinian factions?

EDWARD SAID

Edward Said (1935–2003) received his early education in Jerusalem and Cairo, continuing on to Princeton and Harvard to pursue both undergraduate and graduate work. Said claimed to have become a political activist in 1969 when Golda Meir declared that there 'are no Palestinian people'. He immediately set out to prove her wrong. Thereafter Said became *one of the foremost spokesmen for the Palestinian cause. Yet, as the following article demonstrates, he was most certainly not an uncritical supporter of the ambitions of the Palestinian Authority. Before his death in 2003, Said was professor of English and Comparative Literature at Columbia University in New York.*

TRUTH AND RECONCILIATION

Given the collapse of the Netanyahu government over the Wye peace agreement, it is time once again to question whether the entire peace process begun in Oslo in 1993 is the right instrument for bringing peace between Palestinians and Israelis. It is my view that the peace process has in fact put off the real reconciliation that must occur if the 100-year war between Zionism and the Palestinian people is to end. Oslo set the stage for separation, but real peace can come only with a

bi-national Israeli–Palestinian state.

This is not easy to imagine. The Zionist–Israeli narrative and the Palestinian one are irreconcilable. Israelis say they waged a war of liberation and so achieved independence; Palestinians say their society was destroyed, most of the population evicted. And, in fact this irreconcilability was already quite obvious to several generations of early Zionist leaders and thinkers, as of course it was to all the Palestinians.

'Zionism was not blind to the presence of Arabs in Palestine,' writes the distinguished Israeli historian Zeev Sternhell in his recent book, *The Founding Myths of Israel*. 'Even Zionist figures who had never visited the country knew that it was not devoid of inhabitants. At the same time, neither the Zionist movement abroad nor the pioneers who were beginning to settle the country could frame a policy toward the Palestinian national movement. The real reason for this was not a lack of understanding of the problem but a recognition of the insurmountable contradictions between the basic objectives of the two sides. If Zionist intellectuals and leaders ignored the Arab dilemma, it was chiefly because they knew that this problem had no solution within the Zionist way of thinking.'

Ben Gurion, for instance, was always clear: 'There is no example in history,' he said in 1944, 'of a people saying we agree to renounce our country, let another people come and settle here and outnumber us.' Another Zionist leader, Berl Katznelson, also had no illusions that the opposition between Zionist and Palestinian aims could ever be surmounted. And binationalists like Martin Buber, Judah Magnes, and Hannah Arendt were fully aware of what the clash would be like, if it ever came to fruition, as of course it did.

Vastly outnumbering the Jews, Palestinian Arabs during the period after the 1917 Balfour Declaration and the British Mandate always refused anything that would compromise their dominance. It's unfair to berate the Palestinians retrospectively for not accepting partition in 1947. Until 1948, Zionists held only about seven per cent of the land. Why, the Arabs said when the partition resolution was proposed, should we concede 55 per cent of Palestine to the Jews who were a minority in Palestine? Neither the Balfour Declaration nor the mandate ever specifically conceded that Palestinians had political, as opposed to civil and religious, rights in Palestine. The idea of inequality between Jews and Arabs was therefore built into British, and subsequently Israeli and United States, policy from the start.

The conflict appears intractable because it is a contest over the same land by two peoples who believed they had valid title to it and who hoped that the other side would in time give up or go away. One side won the war, the other lost, but the contest is as alive as ever. We Palestinians ask why a Jew born in Warsaw or New York has the right to settle here (according to Israel's Law of Return) whereas we, the people who lived here for centuries, cannot. After 1967, the issue between us was exacerbated. Years of military occupation have created in the weaker party anger, humiliation, and hostility.

To its discredit, Oslo did little to change the situation. Arafat and his dwindling number of supporters were turned into enforcers of Israeli security, while Palestinians were made to endure the humiliation of dreadful and noncontiguous 'homelands' that make up only about nine per cent of the West Bank and 60 per cent of Gaza. Oslo required us to forget and renounce our history of loss, dispossessed by the very people who have taught everyone the importance of not forgetting the past. Thus we are the victims of the victims, the refugees of the refugees. Israel's raison d'être as a state has always been that there should be a separate country, a refuge, exclusively for Jews. Oslo itself was based on the principle of separation between Jews and others, as Yitzhak Rabin tirelessly repeated. Yet over the past 50 years, especially since Israeli settlements were first implanted on the Occupied Territories in 1967, the lives of Jews have become more and more entwined with those of non-Jews.

The effort to separate has occurred simultaneously and paradoxically with the effort to take more and more land, which in turn has meant that Israel has acquired more and more Palestinians. In Israel proper, Palestinians number about one million, almost 20 per cent of the population. Among Gaza, East Jerusalem, and the West Bank, which is where the settlements are the thickest, there are almost 2.5 million more Palestinians. Israel has built an entire system of 'by-passing' roads, designed to go around Palestinian towns and villages, connecting settlements and avoiding Arabs. But so tiny is the land area of historical Palestine, so closely intertwined are Israelis and Palestinians, despite their inequality and antipathy, that clean separation simply won't, can't really occur or work. It is estimated that by 2010 there will be demographic parity. What then?

Clearly, a system of privileging Israeli Jews will satisfy neither those who want an entirely homogenous Jewish state nor those who live there but are not Jewish. For the former, Palestinians are an obstacle to be disposed of somehow; for the latter, being Palestinians in a Jewish polity means forever chafing at inferior status. But Israeli Palestinians don't want to move; they say they are already in their country and refuse any talk of joining a separate Palestinian state, should one come into being. Meanwhile, the impoverishing conditions imposed on Arafat are making it difficult to subdue the highly politicised people of Gaza and the West Bank. These Palestinians have aspirations for self-determination that, contrary to Israeli calculations, show no sign of withering away. It is also evident that as an Arab people— and, given the despondently cold peace treaties between Israel and Egypt and Israel and Jordan, this fact is important—Palestinians want at all costs to preserve their Arab identity as part of the surrounding Arab and Islamic world.

For all this, the problem is that Palestinian self-determination in a separate state is unworkable, just as unworkable as the principle of separation between a demographically mixed, irreversibly connected Arab population without sovereignty and a Jewish population with it. The question, I believe, is not how to devise means for persisting in trying to separate them but to see whether it is possible for them to live together as fairly and peacefully as possible.

What exists now is a disheartening, not to say, bloody, impasse. Zionists in and outside Israel will not give up on their wish for a separate Jewish state; Palestinians want the same thing for themselves despite having accepted much less from Oslo. Yet in both instances the idea of a state for 'ourselves' simply flies in the face of the facts: short of ethnic cleansing or mass transfer as in 1948 there is no way for Israel to get rid of the Palestinians or for Palestinians to wish Israelis away. Neither side has a viable military option against the other, which, I am sorry to say, is why both opted for a peace that so patently tries to accomplish what war couldn't.

The more that current patterns of Israeli settlement and Palestinian confinement and resistance persist, the less likely it is that there will be real security for either side. It was always patently absurd for Netanyahu's obsession with security to be couched only in terms of Palestinian compliance with his demands. On the one hand, he and Ariel Sharon crowded Palestinians more and more with their shrill urgings to the settlers to grab what they could. On the other hand, Netanyahu expected such methods to bludgeon Palestinians into accepting everything Israel did, with no reciprocal Israeli measures.

Arafat, backed by Washington, is daily more repressive. Improbably citing the 1936 British Emergency Defence Regulations against Palestinians, he has recently decreed, for example, that it is a crime to incite not only violence, racial or religious strife but also to criticize the peace process. There is no Palestinian constitution or basic law. Arafat simply refuses to accept limitations on his power in light of American and Israeli support for him. Who actually thinks all this can bring Israel security and permanent Palestinian submission?

Violence, hatred, and intolerance are bred out of injustice, poverty, and a thwarted sense of political fulfillment. Last fall, hundreds of acres of Palestinian land were expropriated by the Israeli army from the village of Umm Al-Fahm, which isn't in the West Bank but inside Israel. This drove home the fact that, even as Israeli citizens, Palestinians are treated as inferior, as basically a sort of underclass existing in a condition of apartheid. . . .

In the West Bank, Jerusalem, and Gaza, the situation is deeply unstable and exploitative. Protected by the army, Israeli settlers (almost 350,000 of them) live as extraterritorial, privileged people with rights that resident Palestinians do not have. (For example, West Bankers cannot go to Jerusalem, and in 70 per cent of the territory is still subject to Israeli military law, with their land available for confiscation). Israel controls Palestinian water resources and security, as well as exits and entrances. Even the new Gaza Airport is under Israeli security control. One doesn't need to be an expert to see that this is a prescription for extending, not limiting, conflict. Here the truth must be faced, not avoided or denied.

There are Israeli Jews today who speak candidly about 'post-Zionism', insofar as, after 50 years of Israeli history, classic Zionism has neither provided a solution to the Palestinian presence, nor an exclusively Jewish presence. I see no other way than to begin now to speak about sharing the land that has thrust us together, sharing it in a truly democratic way, with equal rights for each citizen. There can be no reconciliation unless both peoples, two communities of suffering, resolve that their existence is a secular fact, and that it has to be dealt with as such. This does not mean a diminishing of Jewish life as Jewish life or surrendering Palestinian Arab aspirations and political existence. On the contrary, it means self-determination for both peoples. But that does mean being willing to soften, lessen, and finally give up special status for one people at the expense of the other. The Law of Return for Jews and the right of return for Palestinian refugees have to be considered and trimmed together. Both the notions of Greater Israel as

the land of the Jewish people given to them by God and of Palestine as an Arab land that cannot be alienated from the Arab homeland need to be reduced in scale and exclusivity. Interestingly, the millennia-long history of Palestine provides at least two precedents for thinking in such secular and more modest terms. First, Palestine is and always has been a land of many histories; it is a radical simplification to think of it as principally, or exclusively Jewish or Arab. While the Jewish presence is long-standing, it is by no means the main one. Other tenants have included Canaanites, Moabites, Jebusites, and Philistines in ancient times, and Romans, Ottomans, Byzantines, and Crusaders in the modern ages. Palestine is multicultural, multi-ethnic, multi-religious. There is as little historical justification for homogeneity as there is for notions of national or ethnic and religious purity today.

Second, during the inter-war period, a small but important group of Jewish thinkers (Judah Magnes, Buber, Arendt, and others) argued and agitated for a binational state. The logic of Zionism naturally overwhelmed their efforts, but the idea is alive today here and there among Jewish and Arab individuals frustrated with the evident insufficiencies and depredations of the present. The essence of that vision is coexistence and sharing in ways that require an innovative, daring and theoretical willingness to get beyond the arid stalemate of assertion and rejection. Once the initial acknowledgment of the other as an equal is made, I believe the way forward becomes not only possible but attractive.

The initial step, however, is a very difficult one to take. Israeli Jews are insulated from the Palestinian reality; most of them say that it does not really concern them. I remember the first time I drove from Ramallah into Israel: it was like going straight from Bangladesh into southern California. Yet reality is never that near. My generation of Palestinians, still reeling from the shock of losing everything in 1948, find it nearly impossible to accept that their homes and farms were taken over by another people. I see no way of evading the fact that in 1948 one people displaced another, thereby committing a grave injustice. Reading Palestinian and Jewish history together not only gives the tragedy of the Holocaust and of what subsequently happened to the Palestinians their full force but also reveals how, in the course of interrelated Israeli and Palestinian life since 1948, one people, the Palestinians, have borne a disproportional share of the pain and loss.

Religious and right-wing Israelis and their supporters have no problem with such a formulation. Yes, they say, we won, but that's how it should be. This land is the land of Israel not of anyone else. I heard those words from an Israeli soldier guarding a bulldozer that was destroying a West Bank Palestinian field (its owner helplessly watching) in order to expand a by-pass road.

But they are not the only Israelis. For others, who want peace as a result of reconciliation, there is dissatisfaction both with the religious parties' increasing hold on Israeli life and Oslo's unfairness and frustrations. Many such Israelis demonstrate energetically against their government's Palestinian land expropriations and house demolitions. So one senses a healthy willingness to look elsewhere for peace than in land-grabbing and suicide-bombs.

For some Palestinians, because they are the weaker party, the losers, giving up on a full restoration of Arab Palestine is giving up on their own history. Most others, however, especially my children's generation, are sceptical of their elders and look more unconventionally toward the future, beyond conflict and unending loss. Obviously, the establishments in both communities are too tied to present 'pragmatic' currents of thought and political formations to venture anything more risky, but a few others (Palestinian and Israeli) have begun to formulate radical alternatives to the status quo. They refuse

to accept the limitations of Oslo, what one Israeli scholar has called 'peace with Palestinians', while others tell me that the real struggle is over equal rights for Arabs and Jews, not a separate, necessarily dependent and weak, Palestinian entity.

The beginning is to develop something entirely missing from both Israeli and Palestinian realities today: the idea and practice of citizenship, not of ethnic or racial community, as the main vehicle for coexistence. In a modern state, all its members are citizens by virtue of their presence and the sharing of rights and responsibilities. Citizenship therefore entitles an Israeli Jew and a Palestinian Arab to the same privileges and resources. A constitution and a bill of rights thus become necessary for getting beyond square one of the conflict, since each group would have the same right to self-determination; that is, the right to practice communal life in its own (Jewish or Palestinian) way, perhaps in federated cantons, a joint capital in Jerusalem, equal access to land and inalienable secular and juridical rights. Neither side should be held hostage to religious extremists.

Yet, feelings of persecution, suffering and victimhood are so ingrained that it is nearly impossible to undertake political initiatives that hold Jews and Arabs to the same general principles of civil equality while avoiding the pitfalls of us-versus-them. Palestinian intellectuals need to express their case directly to Israelis in public forums, universities, and the media. The challenge is both to and within civil society which long has been subordinate to a nationalism that has developed into an obstacle to reconciliation. Moreover, the degradation of discourse— symbolized by Arafat and Netanyahu trading charges while Palestinian rights are compromised by exaggerated 'security' concerns—impedes any wider, more generous perspective from emerging.

The alternatives are unpleasantly simple: either

the war continues (along with the onerous cost of the current peace process) or a way out, based on peace and equality (as in South Africa after apartheid) is actively sought, despite the many obstacles. Once we grant that Palestinians and Israelis are there to stay, then the decent conclusion has to be the need for peaceful coexistence and genuine reconciliation. Real self-determination. Unfortunately, injustice and belligerence don't diminish by themselves: they have to be attacked by all concerned.

Study Question

1. Said notes that, '[t]he conflict appears intractable because it is a contest over the same land by two peoples who believed they had valid title to it and who hoped that the other side would in time give up or go away.' Given this, how does one approach 'peace and reconciliation'?

TIPS FOR ANALYSIS

When was the document written?

The time period in which the document was written is one of the most important keys to reading a document critically. If the document was written as the events happened the author had only a limited amount of information. If it was written many years after the fact the author would have had more information to work with, but would have been influenced by intervening events and the benefit of hindsight. No authors can remove themselves entirely from the influences of the time period in which they are writing.

WEB RESOURCES

Columbia University Libraries: Middle East and Islamic Studies
http://www.columbia.edu/cu/lweb/indiv/mideast/cuvlm
Yale University Library: Research Guide to Middle East Politics
http://www.library.yale.edu/neareast/politics2.html
University of Exeter: Arabic, Islamic, and Middle Eastern Resources
http://library.exeter.ac.uk/internet/arabic.html
Harvard University Center for Middle Eastern Studies
http://cmes.hmdc.harvard.edu/outreach/resources

RECOMMENDED READING

S.Y. Agnon, *Only Yesterday* (Princeton, NJ: Princeton University Press, 2002). *Only Yesterday* focuses on Jewish emigration to Palestine during the early twentieth century. The central character, Isaac Kumer, arrives in Palestine amidst the devotees of Zionism and the ultra-Orthodox Jews who reject Zionist ideology. His own rootlessness, the inability to establish an identity in his new homeland, and absurd twists of fate lead Kumer to question his long-held beliefs.

Ghassan Kanafani, *Men in the Sun* (Boulder, CO: Lynne Rienner Publishers, 1998). *Men in the Sun*—set in 1958—is the story of three Palestinians who attempt to escape to Kuwait in order to guarantee their survival. Three generations recollect the Palestinian experience beginning with the war in 1948, offering thoughts on national identity, the refugee question, and survival itself.

Abdelrahman Munif, *Cities of Salt* (New York: Vintage, 1989). Set in an unidentified Gulf State that the author calls Mooran, *Cities of Salt* is often seen as a veiled allusion to the history of Saudi Arabia. The novel traces the development of 'Mooran' from Bedouin times to the discovery of oil and its consequences, including the negative effects of Western influence in the Gulf region.

A.B. Yehoshua, *Mr Mani* (Fort Washington, PA: Harvest Books, 1993). The story of six generations of the Mani family, from 1848 to 1982, is told through a series of conversations. Yehoshua's novel touches on many of the key events in European and Israeli Jewish history, with numerous intersecting plot lines, as it moves backwards from contemporary Israel to nineteenth century Athens.

RECOMMENDED VIEWING

Occupied Palestine (Palestine, 1981). Director: David Koff (Documentary). *Occupied Palestine* is an Israeli-made documentary that focuses on the Palestinian plight from the perspective of the Palestinians. The film was intended to balance what the director believed to be the one-sided depiction of Palestinians in the American media.

Hamsin [*Eastern Wind*] (Israel, 1982). Director: Daniel Wachsmann. Set in Galilee, the film provides a balanced look at the tensions that developed when the Israeli army requisitioned Arab land. Wachsmann examines both land disputes and the pre-existing relationships between Arab and Jewish neighbours.

Tsahal (Israel/France, 1994). Director: Claude Lanzmann (Documentary). *Tashal* is one of three films in Lanzmann's trilogy exploring Jewish life in the twentieth century (*Shoah* and *Pourquoi Israel* are the others). This documentary focuses on the founding of the Israeli state and the role of the military in society and politics.

Munich (USA, 2005). Director: Stephen Spielberg. Speilberg's film focuses on the five Mossad agents chosen to assassinate the surviving members of Black September who perpetrated the massacre of Israeli athletes at the 1972 Munich Olympics.

CHAPTER SIXTEEN

IDEOLOGICAL CHANGE

◇

The founder of *Ms* Magazine, Gloria Steinem became one of the key voices of the women's liberation movement in the 1970s. US News & World Report Magazine Photograph Collection/Photo by Warren K. Leffler. Courtesy of the Library of Congress, Prints and Photographs Division (LC-U9-25332-25).

The postwar era was characterized by a series of revolts against established authorities. The civil rights movement in the United States was the first of these revolts to attain global prominence. Beginning in the mid-1950s all forms of segregation came under attack across the southern states. Influential leaders such as Dr Martin Luther King, Jr, and Malcolm X focused global media attention on the plight of African-Americans. Ill-considered and violent reprisals by southern authorities soon brought the weight of worldwide disapproval against southern segregationists. Eventually federal legislation against the discriminatory practices in the South was imposed. The attention of the civil rights leaders turned next to the desperate economic conditions of African-Americans in the northern urban ghettos. However, the civil rights movements made far less progress in this area.

Young activists who rejected the assumptions and prejudices of the previous generation proved to be one of the most important driving forces of the civil rights movement. The youth movement quickly evolved into a much broader protest against false democracy, false gods, capitalist exploitation, imperialism, the military-industrial complex, and many other issues. Spurred on by intellectual theories on alienation and the absence of meaning in modern existence, the protest movements spread to Britain, France, West Germany, Canada, Japan, and other countries. By May 1968 a student occupation of the main campus at the University of Paris led to a sympathy strike by more than half of the French workforce. Though the student movements eventually subsided they contributed greatly to discrediting, albeit temporarily, the conservative postwar political elites and their governments.

Alongside the youth and civil rights movement, the 1960s and 1970s also saw the emergence of a substantial women's movement. Because of the economic changes that led to an increasing number of women joining the workforce and seeking higher education, the women's movement focused, initially, on basic civil rights: equal pay for equal work, the right to contraception, and equality under the law. More radical women's groups, often inspired by Marxist ideals, called for an end to all gender-based exploitation and the punishment of those who continued to inflict such abuse. Divisions among conservative, liberal, and radical feminists often served to undermine the effectiveness of the women's movement, though substantial changes were accomplished in some areas. One of the most important aims of the American women's movement, however, the Equal Rights Amendment to the United States Constitution, did not secure enough state support to become law.

The documents in this chapter look at the evolution of the women's movement, new currents of thought in the postwar era, and one of the most important speeches in the history of the civil rights movement. Eleanor Roosevelt was one of the earliest advocates of an activist role for women. In 1928 she argued that 'women must learn to play the game as men do'. Alexandra Kollontai, who had been involved in the Russian revolutionary movement since the 1890s, argued that the rights for which western women struggled had finally been realized in the postwar Soviet Union. Finally, one of the more radical statements of 1960s feminist theory is included in the 'Redstockings Manifesto'. Jean-Paul Sartre's early postwar writings on the meaning of existence in the wake of war and genocide are contained in the excerpt from *Existentialism*. The platform of the 1960s protest movement, the Yippies, is revealed in a portion of the transcript from the trial of the Chicago Seven. Dr Martin Luther King, Jr's famous 'I Have a Dream' speech, made at the height of the civil rights movement during the 1963 March on Washington reflects the ambitions of the mainstream civil rights movement. Finally, Kwame Anthony Appiah reflects on questions of race and identity in a modern, multicultural world.

ELEANOR ROOSEVELT

Eleanor Roosevelt (1884–1962) would eventually become known as one of the most activist first ladies in American history. As early as the 1920s, she was involved in the struggle for women's rights. Politically, Eleanor Roosevelt remained devoted to her husband's causes, but after his death in 1945 she moved into a public role in her own right—as American representative to the United Nations. In her capacity at the UN she was instrumental in securing the passage of the Universal Declaration of Human Rights. The following article was written for The Red Book Magazine. *In it, Eleanor Roosevelt argues that women must take an active role in the political process, in the process learning to 'play the game like men do'.*

WOMEN MUST LEARN TO PLAY THE GAME AS MEN DO

Women have been voting for ten years. But have they achieved actual political equality with men? No. They go through the gesture of going to the polls; their votes are solicited by politicians; and they possess the external aspect of equal rights. But it is mostly a gesture without real power. With some outstanding exceptions, women who have gone into politics are refused serious consideration by the men leaders. Generally they are treated most courteously, to be sure, but what they want, what they have to say, is regarded as of little weight. In fact, they have no actual influence or say at all in the consequential councils of their parties.

In small things they are listened to; but when it comes to asking for important things they generally find they are up against a blank wall. This is true of local committees, State committees, and the national organizations of both major political parties.

From all over the United States, women of both camps have come to me and their experiences are practically the same. When meetings are to be held at which momentous matters are to be decided, the women members often are not asked. When they are notified of formal meetings where important matters are to be ratified, they generally find all these things have been planned and prepared, without consultation with them, in secret confabs of the men beforehand. If they have objections to proposed policies or candidates,

Eleanor Roosevelt visits the GM Aircraft Division in February 1943 to urge the acceleration of wartime production. Office of War Information Photograph Collection. Courtesy of the Library of Congress, Prints and Photographs Division (LC-USE6-D-011025).

they are adroitly overruled. They are not allowed to run for office to any appreciable extent and if they propose candidates of their own sex, reasons are usually found for their elimination which, while diplomatic and polite, are just pretexts nevertheless.

In those circles that decide the affairs of national politics, women have no voice or power whatever. On the national committee of each party there is a woman representative from every State, and a woman appears as vice-chairman. Before national elections they will be told to organize the women throughout the United States, and asked to help in minor ways in raising funds. But when it comes to those grave councils at which possible candidates are discussed, as well as party policies, they are rarely invited in. At the national conventions

no woman has ever been asked to serve on the platform committee.

Politically, as a sex, women are generally 'frozen out' from any intrinsic share of influence in their parties.

The machinery of party politics has always been in the hands of men, and still is. Our statesmen and legislators are still keeping in form as the successors of the early warriors gathering around the campfire plotting the next day's attack. Yes, they have made feints indicating they are willing to take women into the high councils of the parties. But, in fact, the women who have gone into the political game will tell you they are excluded from any actual kind of important participation. They are called upon to produce votes, but they are kept in ignorance of noteworthy plans and affairs.

Their requests are seldom refused outright, but they are put off with a technique that is an art in itself. The fact is that generally women are not taken seriously. With certain exceptions, men still as a class dismiss their consequence and value in politics, cherishing the old-fashioned concept that their place is in the home. While women's votes are a factor to be counted upon, and figure largely in any impending campaign, the individual women who figure in party councils are regarded by their male confrères as having no real power in back of them. And they haven't.

Men who work hard in party politics are always recognized, or taken care of in one way or another. Women, most of whom are voluntary workers and not at all self-seeking, are generally expected to find in their labour its own reward. When it comes to giving the offices or dealing out favors, men are always given precedence. They will ask women to run for office now and then, sometimes because they think it politic and wise to show women how generous they are, but more often because they realize in advance their ticket cannot win in the district selected. Therefore they will put up a woman, knowing it will injure the party less to have a woman defeated, and then they can always say it was her sex that defeated her. Where victory is certain, very rarely can you get a woman nominated on the party ticket.

Of course there are women all over the United States who have been elected to high and important offices. There are three women in Congress; there have been two woman governors; and women sit in various State legislatures and hold State offices. In New York City one could cite several who have not only been elected but who have conducted themselves in office with ability and distinction. But does that indicate any equal recognition of share in political power? Infinitely more examples come to mind of women who were either denied a nomination or who were offered it only when inevitable defeat stared the party leaders in the face. . . .

Beneath the veneer of courtesy and outward show of consideration universally accorded women, there is a widespread male hostility—age-old, perhaps—against sharing with them any actual control.

How many excuses haven't I heard for not giving nominations to women! 'Oh, she wouldn't like the kind of work she'd have to do!' Or, 'You know she wouldn't like the people she'd have to associate with—that's not a job for a nice, refined woman'. Or more usually: 'You see, there is so little patronage nowadays. We must give every appointment the most careful consideration. We've got to consider the good of the party.' 'The good of the party' eliminates women!

When no women are present at the meetings, the leaders are more outspoken. 'No, we're not going to have any woman on the ticket,' declared one leader according to a report once made to me. 'Those fool women are always making trouble, anyway. We won't have any we don't have to have, and if we have to have one, let's get one we understand.

It is a strong and liberal man, indeed, who speaks on behalf of the women at those secret conclaves, and endeavours to have them fairly treated.

To many women who fought so long and so valiantly for suffrage, what has happened has been most discouraging. For one reason or another, most of the leaders who carried the early fight to success have dropped out of politics. This has been in many ways unfortunate. Among them were women with gifts of real leadership. They were exceptional and high types of women, idealists concerned in carrying a cause to victory, with no idea of personal advancement or gain. In fact, attaining the vote was only part of a program for equal rights—an external gesture toward economic independence, and social and spiritual equality with men.

When the franchise was finally achieved, their interest was not held by any ambition for political preferment or honours. To learn the intricate machinery of politics and play the men's game left them cold. The routine of political office held no appeal. One of the most prominent of those early crusaders today gives her energies to campaigning for world peace. By nature a propagandist, it would be impossible to interest her in either of the major parties. Another woman, who donated hundreds of thousands of dollars to the cause, frankly admits she has never even cast a vote. She considers the situation, with women coping with men in the leading parties, utterly hopeless. Like many others, she regards suffrage as an empty victory, equal rights a travesty, and the vote a gesture without power.

An extreme point of view, in my opinion. There is a method—and not the one advocated by certain militants who hold aloof from party politics—by which, I believe, the end of a fair representation and share in control may be attained.

Personally, I do not believe in a Woman's Party. A woman's ticket could never possibly succeed. And to crystallize the issues on the basis of sex-opposition would only further antagonize men, congeal their age-old prejudices, and widen the chasm of existing differences.

How, then, can we bring the men leaders to concede participation in party affairs, adequate representation and real political equality?

Our means is to elect, accept, and back women political bosses.

To organize as women, but within the parties, in districts, counties, and States just as men organize, and to pick efficient leaders—say two or three in each State—whom we will support and by whose decisions we will abide. With the power of unified women voters behind them, such women bosses would be in a position to talk in terms of 'business' with the men leaders; their voices would be heard, because their authority and the elective power they could command would have to be recognized.

Women are today ignored largely because they have no banded unity under representative leaders and spokesmen capable of dealing with the bosses controlling groups of men whose votes they can 'deliver'. These men bosses have the power of coordinated voters behind them. Our helplessness is that of an incoherent anarchy . . .

If women believe they have a right and duty in political life today, they must learn to talk the language of men. They must not only master the phraseology, but also understand the machinery which men have built up through years of practical experience. Against the men bosses there must be women bosses who can talk as equals, with the backing of a coherent organization of women voters behind them.

Voters who are only voters, whether men or women, are only the followers of leaders. The important thing is the choosing of leaders.

We must be fair, and admit the blame for our present ineffectuality in politics does not lie wholly with the men. If we are still a negligible factor, ignored and neglected, we must be prepared to admit in what we have ourselves failed.

The trouble with many women is that they won't work. They won't take up their jobs as men do and put in seven or eight real working hours a day. They lack knowledge, and at that many won't take the pains to study history, economics, political methods, or get out among human beings. If they take a volunteer political job, it is a thing of constant interruptions, with no sense of application, concentration, business efficiency, or order. One of the reasons why men leaders so often do not consider as important what a woman says is that they do not feel sure she has been active among the mass of women voters and has learned what they want. In fact, many women do make the mistake of 'talking out of a blue sky' instead of going about, mixing with women, and getting their point of view from close personal contact and practical experience. When a man leader says his following want certain things, the men higher up realize that he knows what he is talking about, and that he has gone through his district . . .

Women are different. Many of them have no professional careers. If they go into politics it is usually because of some interest which they realize is dependent on government action. I know women who are interested in education, in health conditions, in the improvement of rural life, in social problems, in housing, and all active in politics because they have come to realize by that way they may further their particular cause. Politics is less of a game to them because they haven't had the same training for games as men, and their first contact with great groups of people is an exciting and disturbing experience, not to be taken lightly but almost prayerfully.

In this I am not speaking of the small army of women who are trained in some profession, some of whom hold minor political offices, and a few of whom hold minor positions of importance in the parties. Some of these have attained the attitude of men, and meet them on the same ground. Then there are women, as there are men, who frankly are in politics for what they can get out of it. I remember well one woman who had worked hard in an organization and was denied recognition in the tangible way she desired—namely, a paid job. Whereupon she announced she was going over to the opposing political party, where, when they wished to reward a worker, they created a job if one was not available at the time! . . .

I should not want the average woman, or the exceptional woman for that matter, who for one reason or another could not do a public job well, to take one at present. For just now a woman must do better than a man, for whatever she does in the public eye reflects on the whole cause of women. There are women in the United States I would gladly see run for any office. But if we cannot have the best I should prefer to wait and prepare a little longer until women are more ready to make a fine contribution to public life in any office they might hold.

An old politician once objected, 'Don't you think these women lose their allure, that the bloom is just a little gone? Men are no longer interested?'

Frankly, I don't know. I imagine the answer is individual. It was once said that men did not marry women who showed too much intelligence. In my youth I knew women who hid their college degrees as if they were one of the seven deadly sins. But all that is passing, and so will pass many other prejudices that have their origin in the ancient tradition that women are a by-product of creation.

Remember, women have voted just ten years. They have held responsible positions in big business enterprises only since the war, to any great extent. The men at the head of big business or controlling politics are for the most part middle-aged men. Their wives grew up in an era when no public question was discussed in a popular manner, when men talked politics over their wine or cigars, and pulled their waistcoats down, on joining the ladies, to talk music, or the play or the latest scandal. Can you blame them if the adjustment to modern conditions is somewhat difficult?

Certain women profess to be horrified at the thought of women bosses bartering and dickering in the hard game of politics with men. But many more women realize that we are living in a material world, and that politics cannot be played from the clouds. To sum up, women must learn to play the game as men do. If they go into politics, they must stick to their jobs, respect the time and work of others, master a knowledge of history and human nature, learn diplomacy, subordinate their likes and dislikes of the moment and choose leaders to act for them and to whom they will be loyal. They can keep their ideals; but they must face facts and deal with them practically.

Study Question

1. To what extent do you believe that the early American women's movement would agree with the principles espoused by Eleanor Roosevelt?

ALEXANDRA KOLLONTAI

Alexandra Kollontai (1872–1952) became a member of the Russian Social Democratic movement in the 1890s; her work laid the foundation for a mass women's movement in Russia. Exiled for her revolutionary activities, she returned to Russia in early 1917. After the October Revolution, Kollontai was elected Commissar for Social Welfare but differences over a number of issues led to tensions *with the Russian Communist Party. In 1922 she was appointed advisor to the Soviet Legation in Norway. A variety of other diplomatic posts served to keep her out of the Soviet Union from 1922 until 1946 when she became an advisor to the Soviet Ministry of Foreign Affairs. Kollontai reflected on the status of women in the USSR in the following 1946 article.*

THE SOVIET WOMAN—A FULL AND EQUAL CITIZEN OF HER COUNTRY

It is a well-known fact that the Soviet Union has achieved exceptional successes in drawing women into the active construction of the state. This generally accepted truth is not disputed even by our enemies. The Soviet woman is a full and equal citizen of her country. In opening up to women access to every sphere of creative activity, our state has simultaneously ensured all the conditions necessary for her to fulfil her natural obligation—that of being a mother bringing up her children and mistress of her home.

From the very beginning, Soviet law recognised that motherhood is not a private matter, but the social duty of the active and equal woman citizen. This proposition is enshrined in the Constitution. The Soviet Union has solved one of the most important and complex of problems how to make active use of female labour in any area without this being to the detriment of motherhood.

A great deal of attention has been given to the organisation of public canteens, kindergartens, Young Pioneer camps, playgrounds and crèches—those institutions which, as Lenin wrote, facilitate in practice the emancipation of women and are able, in practice, to reduce the female inequality vis-à-vis men. More than seven thousand women's and children's consultation centres have been established in the USSR, of which half are in rural areas. Over 20 thousand crèches have been organised. It should be pointed out here that in tsarist Russia in 1913 there existed only 19 crèches and 25 kindergartens, and even these were not maintained by the state, but by philanthropic organisations.

The Soviet state provides increasing material assistance to mothers. Women receive allowances and paid leave before and after the birth of the child and their post is kept open for them until they return from leave.

Large and one-parent families receive state allowances to help them provide for and bring up their children. In 1945 the state paid out more than two thousand million roubles in such allowances. The title 'Mother-Heroine' has been awarded to more than 10 thousand women in the RSFSR alone, while the order of 'Maternal Glory' and the 'Medal of Motherhood' have been awarded to 1,100 thousand women.

Soviet women have justified the trust and concern shown to them by their state. They have shown a high degree of heroism both in peaceful, creative labour before the war, during the years of armed battle against the Nazi invaders, and now, in the efforts to fulfil the monumental tasks set by the new five-year plan. Many branches of industry in which female labour is predominant are among the first to fulfil their plans. Equally worthy of mention are the enormous achievements of the Soviet peasant women, who bore on their shoulders the greater part of the burden of agricultural labour during the war years.

Our women have mastered professions that have long been considered the exclusive domain of men. There are women engine-drivers, women mechanics, women lathe operators, women fitters, well-qualified women workers in charge of the most complex mechanisms.

The women of the Soviet Union work on an equal footing with men to advance science, culture and the arts; they occupy an outstanding place in the national education and health services.

In a country where, 30 years ago, out of 2,300 thousand working women 1,300 thousand worked as servants in the towns and 750 thousand as farm labourers in the countryside, in a country where there were almost no women engineers, almost no scientists, and appointment to a teaching post was accompanied by conditions insulting to female dignity, in that country there are now 750 thousand women teachers, 100 thousand women doctors, and 250 thousand women engineers. Women make up one half of the student body in institutions of higher education. Over 33 thousand women are working in laboratories and in research institutes, 25 thousand women have academic titles and degrees, and 166 women have been awarded the State Prize for their achievements in science and work.

The women of the Soviet Union are implementing their political rights in practice. The Supreme Soviet of the USSR has 277 women deputies, while 256 thousand women have been elected to rural, urban, regional, and republican organs of state power . . .

The women of the Soviet Union do not have to demand from their government the right to work, the right to education, the right to the protection of motherhood. The state itself, the government itself, draws women into work, giving them wide access to every sphere of social life, assisting and rewarding mothers.

During the years of invasion by Nazi aggressors, Soviet women, and the women of other democratic countries, saw with their own eyes the need to wage a tireless battle against Nazism until every trace of it had been removed. Only this will spare the world the threat of new wars.

The struggle for democracy and lasting peace, the struggle against reaction and fascism, is the main task we face today. To cut women off from this basic and important task, to attempt to confine them within 'purely female', feminist organisations, can only weaken the women's democratic movement. Only the victory of democracy can ensure women equality.

We, the women of the Land of Soviets, are devoting all our energy to creative labour, to the fulfilment of the monumental tasks set by the five-year plan, knowing that in so doing we are strengthening the bulwark of peace throughout the world—the Union of Soviet Socialist Republics.

At the same time we must be on the alert for intrigues by the reactionaries and expose their plans and intentions, their attempts to divide the ranks of democracy.

The unity of all the forces of democracy is our most reliable weapon in the struggle against reaction, in the struggle for freedom and peace throughout the world.

Study Question

1. Was Kollontai correct that the Soviet Union had far surpassed the nations of the capitalist world in terms of women's equality?

REDSTOCKINGS

In the 1960s and 1970s feminism incorporated a wide range of ideological positions around the world. In the United States and Europe a number of groups adopted Marxist theories; yet rather than see economic exploitation as the root of all social and political relationships, radical feminist groups saw gender exploitation as the foundation of all other relationships. The Redstockings group was founded in 1969 in New York City by Shulamith Firestone and Ellen Willis; in 1970 Redstockings expanded to San Francisco.[1] Firestone would go on to write one of the most influential Marxist-inspired feminist tracts, The Dialectic of Sex: The Case for Feminist Revolution. In it she argued that childbearing was the crux of women's oppression and that technological advances could eventually free women from this enslavement. The 1969 Redstockings manifesto clearly demonstrates the reworking of Marxist ideology and its resulting radical implications.

A FEMINIST MANIFESTO

Opponents of the Equal Rights Amendment rally outside the White House in Washington, DC, February 1977. U.S. News and World Report Magazine Photograph Collection. Courtesy of the Library of Congress, Prints and Photographs Division (LC-U9-33889A-31/31A).

I. After centuries of individual and preliminary political struggle, women are uniting to achieve this final liberation from male supremacy. Redstockings is dedicated to building their unity and winning our freedom.

II. Women are an oppressed class. Our oppression is total, affecting every facet of our lives. We are exploited as sex objects, breeders, domestic servants, and cheap labour. We are considered inferior beings, whose only purpose is to enhance men's lives. Our humanity is denied. Our prescribed behaviour is enforced by the threat of physical violence.

Because we have lived so intimately with our oppressors, in isolation from each other, we have been kept from seeing our personal suffering as a political condition. This creates the illusion that a woman's relationship with her man is a matter of interplay between two unique personalities, and can be worked out individually. In reality, every such relationship is a *class* relationship, and the conflicts between individual men and women are *political* conflicts that can only be solved collectively.

III. We identify the agents of our oppression as men. Male supremacy is the oldest, most basic form of domination. All other forms of exploitation and oppression (racism, capitalism, imperialism, and the like) are extensions of male supremacy: men dominate women, a few men dominate the rest. All power structures throughout history have been male-dominated and male-oriented. Men have controlled all political, economic, and cultural institutions and backed up this control with physical force. They have used their power to keep women in an inferior position. *All men receive economic, sexual, and psychological* benefits from male supremacy. *All men* have oppressed women.

IV. Attempts have been made to shift the burden of responsibility from men to institutions or to women themselves. We condemn these arguments as evasions. Institutions alone do not oppress; they are merely tools of the oppressor. To blame institutions implies that men and women are equally victimized, obscures the fact that men benefit from the subordination of women, and gives men the excuse that they are forced to be oppressors. On the contrary, any man is free to renounce his superior position provided that he is willing to be treated like a woman by other men.

We also reject the idea that women consent to or are to blame for their own oppression. Women's submission is not the result of brainwashing, stupidity, or mental illness but of continual, daily pressure from men. We do not need to change ourselves, but to change men.

The most slanderous evasion of all is that women can oppress men. The basis for this illusion is the isolation of individual relationships from their political context and the tendency of men to see any legitimate challenge to their privileges as persecution.

V. We regard our personal experience, and our feelings about that experience, as the basis for an analysis of our common situation. We cannot rely on existing ideologies as they are all products of male supremacist culture. We question every generalization and accept none that are not confirmed by our experience.

Our chief task at present is to develop female class consciousness through sharing experience and publicly exposing the sexist foundation of all our institutions. Consciousness-raising is not 'therapy', which implies the existence of individual solutions and falsely assumes that the male-female relationship is purely personal, but the only method by which we can ensure that our program for liberation is based on the concrete realities of our lives.

The first requirement for raising class consciousness is honesty, in private and in public, with ourselves and other women.

VI. We identify with all women. We define our best interest as that of the poorest, most brutally exploited woman.

We repudiate all economic, racial, educational, or status privileges that divide us from other women. We are determined to recognize and eliminate any prejudices we may hold against other women.

We are committed to achieving internal democracy. We will do whatever is necessary to ensure that every woman in our movement has an equal chance to participate, assume responsibility, and develop her political potential.

VII. We call on all our sisters to unite with us in struggle.

We call on all men to give up their male privileges and support women's liberation in the interests of our humanity and their own.

In fighting for our liberation we will always take the side of women against their oppressors. We will not ask what is 'revolutionary' or 'reformist', only what is good for women.

The time for individual skirmishes has passed. This time we are going all the way.

Note

1. In 1973 Redstockings incorporated as a non-profit, educational, and scientific organization for the furtherance of the women's liberation movement.

Study Question

1. Were groups such as Redstockings a help or a hindrance to the women's liberation movements of the late 1960s and early 1970s? Why?

JEAN-PAUL SARTRE

Philosopher Jean-Paul Sartre (1905–80) is best known for his theories of existentialism. His 1938 novel Nausea (La Nausée) *explored the extreme alienation of mankind, a concept that he proceeded to develop more fully in his non-fictional work,* Being and Nothingness (L'Être et le néant) *in 1943. During the Second World War,*

Sartre was imprisoned by the Germans but he continued to write. The result was a series of essays primarily exploring the negative aspects of the human experience. The essay 'Existentialism Is a Humanism' ('L'existentialisme est un humanisme') was written in 1946 both to explain and defend his philosophical views.

EXISTENTIALISM

I should like on this occasion to defend existentialism against some charges which have been brought against it.

First, it has been charged with inviting people to remain in a kind of desperate quietism because, since no solutions are possible, we should have to consider action in this world as quite impossible. We should then end up in a philosophy of contemplation; and since contemplation is a luxury, we come in the end to a bourgeois philosophy. The communists in particular have made these charges.

On the other hand, we have been charged with dwelling on human degradation, with pointing up everywhere the sordid, shade, and slimy, and neglecting the gracious and beautiful, the bright side of human nature; for example, according to Mlle Mercier, a Catholic critic, with forgetting the smile of a child. Both sides charge us with having ignored human solidarity, with considering man as an isolated being. The communists say that the main reason for this is that we take pure subjectivity, the Cartesian *I think*, as our starting point; in other words, the moment in which man becomes fully aware of what it means to him to be an isolated being; as a result, we are unable to return to a state of solidarity with the men who are not ourselves, a state which we can never reach in the *cogito*.

From the Christian standpoint, we are charged with denying the reality and seriousness of human undertakings, since, if we reject God's commandments and the eternal verities, there no longer remains anything but pure caprice, with everyone permitted to do as he pleases and incapable, from his own point of view, of condemning the points of view and acts of others.

Actually, it [existentialism] is the least scandalous, the most austere of doctrines. It is intended strictly for specialists and philosophers. Yet it can be defined easily. What complicates matters is that there are two kinds of existentialist; first, those who are Christian, among whom I would include Jaspers and Gabriel Marcel, both Catholic; and on the other hand the atheistic existentialists, among whom I class Heidegger, and then the French existentialists, and myself. What they have in common is that they think that existence precedes essence, or, if you prefer, that subjectivity must be the starting point.

Atheistic existentialism states that if God does not exist, there is at least one being in whom existence precedes essence, a being who exists before he can be defined by any concept, and that this being is man, or, as Heidegger says, human reality. What is meant here by saying that existence precedes essence? It means that, first of all, man exists, turns up, appears on the scene, and, only afterwards, defines himself. If man, as the existentialist conceives him, is indefinable, it is because at first he is nothing. Only afterward will he be something, and he himself will have made what he will be. Thus, there is no human nature, since there is no God to conceive it. Not only is man what he conceives himself to be, but he is also only what he wills himself to be after this thrust toward existence.

Man is nothing else but what he makes of himself. Such is the first principle of existentialism. It is also what is called subjectivity, the name we are labeled with when charges are brought against us. But what do we mean by this, if not that man has a greater dignity than a stone or table? For we mean that man first exists, that is, that man first of all is the being who hurls himself towards a future and who is conscious of imagining himself as being in the future. Man is at the start of a plan which is aware of itself, rather than a patch of moss, a piece of garbage, or a cauliflower; nothing exists prior to this plan; there is nothing in heaven; man will be what he will have planned to be. Not what he will want to be. Because by the word 'will' we generally mean a conscious decision, which is subsequent to what we have already made of ourselves. I may want to belong to a political party, write a book, get married; but all that is only a manifestation of an earlier, more spontaneous choice that is called 'will'. But if existence really does precede essence, man is responsible for what he is. Thus, existentialism's first move is to make every man aware of what he is and to make the full responsibility of his existence rest on him. And when we say that a man is responsible for himself, we do not only mean that he is responsible for his own individuality, but that he is responsible for all men.

If existence precedes essence, and if we grant that we exist and fashion our image at one and the same time, the image is valid for everybody and for our whole age. Thus, our responsibility is much greater than we might have supposed, because it involves all mankind. To take an individual matter, if I want to marry, to have children; even if this marriage depends solely on my own circumstances or passion or wish, I am involving all humanity in monogamy and not merely myself. Therefore, I am responsible for myself and for everyone else. I am creating a certain image of man of my own choosing. In choosing myself, I choose man.

This helps us understand what the actual content is of such rather grandiloquent words as anguish, forlornness, despair. As you will see, it's all quite simple.

First, what is meant by anguish? The existentialists say at once that man is anguish. What that means is this: The man who involves himself and who realizes that he is not only the person he chooses to be, but also a lawmaker who is, at the same time, choosing all mankind as well as himself, cannot help escape the feeling of his total and deep responsibility. Of course, there are many people who are not anxious; but we claim that they are hiding their anxiety, that they are fleeing from it. Certainly, many people believe that when they do something, they themselves are the only ones involved, and when someone says to them, 'What if everyone acted that way?' they shrug their shoulders and answer, 'Everyone doesn't act that way.' But really, one should always ask himself, 'What would happen if everybody looked at things that way?' There is no escaping this disturbing thought except by a kind of double-dealing. A man who lies and makes excuses for himself by saying 'not everybody does that,' is someone with an uneasy conscience, because the act of lying implies that a universal value is conferred upon the lie.

When we speak of forlornness, a term Heidegger was fond of, we mean only that God does not exist and that we have to face all the consequences of this.

The existentialist thinks it very distressing that God does not exist, because all possibility of finding values in a heaven of ideas disappears along with Him; there can no longer be an *a priori* Good, since there is no infinite and perfect consciousness to think it. Nowhere is it written that the Good exists, that we must be honest, that we must not lie; because the fact is we are on a plane where there are only men. Dostoyevsky said, 'If God didn't exist, everything would be possible.' That is the very starting point of existentialism. Indeed, everything is permissible if God does not exist, and as a result man is forlorn, because neither within him nor without does he find anything to cling to. He can't start making excuses for himself.

If existence really does precede essence, there is no explaining things away by reference to a fixed and given human nature. In other words, there is no determinism, man is free, man is freedom. On the other hand, if God does not exist, we find no values or commands to turn to which legitimize our conduct. So, in the bright realm of values, we have no excuse behind us, nor justification before us. We are alone, with no excuses.

That is the idea I shall try to convey when I say that man is condemned to be free. Condemned, because he did not create himself, yet in other respects is free; because, once thrown into the world, he is responsible for everything he does. The existentialist does not believe in the power of passion. He will never agree that a sweeping passion is a ravaging torrent which fatally leads a man to certain acts and is therefore an excuse. He thinks that man is responsible for his passion.

The existentialist does not think that man is going to help himself by finding in the world some omen by which to orient himself. Because he thinks that man will interpret the omen to suit himself. Therefore, he thinks that man, with no support and no aid, is condemned every moment to invent man. Ponge, in a very fine article, has said 'Man is the future of man.' That's exactly it.

From these few reflections it is evident that nothing is more unjust than the objections that have been raised against us. Existentialism is nothing else than an attempt to draw all the consequences of a coherent atheistic position. It isn't trying to plunge man into despair at all. But if one calls every attitude of unbelief despair, like the Christians, then the word is not being used in its original sense. Existentialism isn't so atheistic that it wears itself out showing that God doesn't exist. Rather, it declares that even if God did exist, that would change nothing. There you've got our point of view. Not that we believe that God exists, but we think the problem of His existence is not the issue. In this sense existentialism is optimistic, a doctrine of action, and it is plain dishonesty for Christians to make no distinction between their own despair and ours and then to call us despairing.

Study Question

1. What are the implications of Sartre's claim that 'man is nothing else but what he makes of himself'?

THE CHICAGO SEVEN TRIAL TRANSCRIPT

By 1968, antiwar movements, civil rights movements, and protest groups had combined to create an explosive atmosphere in the United States. During the 1968 Democratic Party Convention in Chicago, protesters clashed violently with massive numbers of police and national guardsmen called out by Chicago mayor Richard Daley. A number of high-profile protesters were arrested and charged with crossing state lines for the purpose of inciting a riot. The ensuing 'Chicago Seven Trial' made a mockery of the American judicial system, as this excerpt from the testimony of Abbie Hoffman (1936–89) demonstrates. In February 1970 the defendants were found guilty and sentenced to five years in prison. On appeal all of the sentences were overturned and a subsequent inquiry blamed police over-reaction for all of the violence that took place at the convention.

ABBIE HOFFMAN

Mr Weinglass: Will you please identify yourself for the record?

The Witness: My name is Abbie. I am an orphan of America.

Mr Schultz: Your Honor, may the record show it is the defendant Hoffman who has taken the stand?

The Court: Oh, yes. It may so indicate. . . .

Mr Weinglass: Where do you reside?

The Witness: I live in Woodstock Nation.

Mr Weinglass: Will you tell the Court and jury where it is?

The Witness: Yes. It is a nation of alienated young people. We carry it around with us as a state of mind in the same way as the Sioux Indians carried the Sioux nation around with them. It is a nation dedicated to cooperation versus competition, to the idea that people should have better means of exchange than property or money, that there should be some other basis for human interaction. It is a nation dedicated to—

The Court: Just where it is, that is all.

The Witness: It is in my mind and in the minds of my brothers and sisters. It does not consist of property or material but, rather, of ideas and certain values. We believe in a society—

The Court: No, we want the place of residence, if he has one, place of doing business, if you have a business. Nothing about philosophy or India, sir. Just where you live, if you have a place to live. Now you said Woodstock. In what state is Woodstock?

The Witness: It is in the state of mind, in the mind of myself and my brothers and sisters. It is a conspiracy. Presently, the nation is held captive, in

The Chicago Seven: Lee Weiner, John Froines, Abbie Hoffman, Rennie Davis, Jerry Rubin, Tom Hayden, Dave Dellinger, Chicago, 5 November 1969. Photograph Richard Avedon. © 2009 The Richard Avedon Foundation.

the penitentiaries of the institutions of a decaying system.

Mr Weinglass: Can you tell the Court and jury your present age?

The Witness: My age is 33. I am a child of the 60s.

Mr Weinglass: When were you born?

The Witness: Psychologically, 1960.

Mr Schultz: Objection, if the Court please. I move to strike the answer.

Mr Weinglass: What is the actual date of your birth?

The Witness: 30 November 1936.

Mr Weinglass: Between the date of your birth, 30 November 1936, and 1 May 1960, what if anything occurred in your life?

The Witness: Nothing. I believe it is called an American education.

Mr Schultz: Objection.

The Court: I sustain the objection.

The Witness: Huh.

Mr Weinglass: Abbie, could you tell the Court and jury—

Mr Schultz: His name isn't Abbie. I object to this informality.

Mr Weinglass: Can you tell the Court and jury what is your present occupation?

The Witness: I am a cultural revolutionary. Well, I am really a defendant—full-time.

Mr Weinglass: What do you mean by the phrase 'cultural revolutionary'?

The Witness: Well, I suppose it is a person who tries to shape and participate in the values, and the mores, the customs and the style of living of new people who eventually become inhabitants of a new nation and a new society through art and poetry, theater, and music.

Mr Weinglass: What have you done yourself to participate in that revolution?

The Witness: Well, I have been a rock and roll singer. I am a reporter with the Liberation News Service. I am a poet. I am a film maker. I made a movie called 'Yippies[1] Tour Chicago or How

I Spent My Summer Vacation'. Currently, I am negotiating with United Artists and MGM to do a movie in Hollywood. I have written an extensive pamphlet on how to live free in the city of New York. I have written two books, one called *Revolution for the Hell of It* under the pseudonym Free, and one called, *Woodstock Nation*.

Mr Weinglass: Taking you back to the spring of 1960, approximately May 1, 1960, will you tell the Court and jury where you were?

Mr Schultz: 1960?

The Witness: That's right.

Mr Schultz: Objection.

The Court: I sustain the objection.

Mr Weinglass: Your Honor, that date has great relevance to the trial. May 1, 1960, was this witness's first public demonstration. I am going to bring him down through Chicago.

The Court: Not in my presence, you are not going to bring him down. I sustain the objection to the question.

The Witness: My background has nothing to do with my state of mind?

The Court: Will you remain quiet while I am making a ruling? I know you have no respect for me.

Mr Kunstler: Your Honor, that is totally unwarranted. I think your remarks call for a motion for a mistrial.

The Court: And your motion calls for a denial of the motion. Mr Weinglass, continue with your examination.

Mr Kunstler: You denied my motion? I hadn't even started to argue it.

The Court: I don't need any argument on that one. The witness turned his back on me while he was on the witness stand.

The Witness: I was just looking at the pictures of the long hairs up on the wall. . . .

The Court: . . . I will let the witness tell about this asserted conversation with Mr Rubin on the occasion described.

Mr Weinglass: What was the conversation at that time?

The Witness: Jerry Rubin told me that he had come to New York to be project director of a peace march in Washington that was going to march to the Pentagon in October, October 21. He said that the peace movement suffered from a certain kind of attitude, mainly that it was based solely on the issue of the Vietnam war. He said that the war in Vietnam was not just an accident but a direct by-product of the kind of system, a capitalist system in the country, and that we had to begin to put forth new kinds of values, especially to young people in the country, to make a kind of society in which a Vietnam war would not be possible. And he felt that these attitudes and values were present in the hippie movement and many of the techniques, the guerrilla theater techniques that had been used and many of these methods of communication would allow for people to participate and become involved in a new kind of democracy. I said that the Pentagon was a five-sided evil symbol in most religions and that it might be possible to approach this from a religious point of view. If we got large numbers of people to surround the Pentagon, we could exorcize it of its evil spirits. So I had agreed at that point to begin working on the exorcism of the Pentagon demonstration. . . .

Mr Weinglass: Now, drawing your attention to the first week of December 1967, did you have occasion to meet with Jerry Rubin and the others?

The Witness: Yes.

Mr Weinglass: Will you relate to the Court and jury what the conversation was?

The Witness: Yes. We talked about the possibility of having demonstrations at the Democratic Convention in Chicago, Illinois, that was going to be occurring that August. I am not sure that we knew at that point that it was in Chicago. Wherever it was, we were planning on going. Jerry Rubin, I believe, said that it would be a good idea to call it the Festival of Life in contrast to the Convention of Death, and to have it in some kind of public area, like a park or something, in Chicago. One

thing that I was very particular about was that we didn't have any concept of leadership involved. There was a feeling of young people that they didn't want to listen to leaders. We had to create a kind of situation in which people would be allowed to participate and become in a real sense their own leaders. . . .

Mr Weinglass: The document that is before you, D-222 for identification, what is that document?

The Witness: It was our initial call to people to describe what Yippie was about and why we were coming to Chicago.

Mr Weinglass: Now, Abbie, could you read the entire document to the jury.

The Witness: It says: 'A STATEMENT FROM YIP! "Join us in Chicago in August for an international festival of youth, music, and theater. Rise up and abandon the creeping meatball! Come all you rebels, youth spirits, rock minstrels, truth-seekers, peacock-freaks, poets, barricade-jumpers, dancers, lovers and artists! It is summer. It is the last week in August, and the NATIONAL DEATH PARTY meets to bless Lyndon Johnson. We are there! There are 50,000 of us dancing in the streets, throbbing with amplifiers and harmony. We are making love in the parks. We are reading, singing, laughing, printing newspapers, groping, and making a mock convention, and celebrating the birth of FREE AMERICA in our own time. Everything will be free. Bring blankets, tents, draft-cards, body-paint, Mr. Leary's Cow, food to share, music, eager skin, and happiness. The threats of LBJ, Mayor Daley, and J. Edgar Freako will not stop us. We are coming! We are coming from all over the world! The life of the American spirit is being torn asunder by the forces of violence, decay, and the napalm-cancer fiend. We demand the Politics of Ecstasy! We are the delicate spores of the new fierceness that will change America. We will create our own reality, we are Free America! And we will not accept the false theater of the Death Convention. We will be in Chicago. Begin preparations now! Chicago is yours! Do it!". . . .'

Mr Weinglass: Now, will you read for the Court and jury the eighteen demands [of the Yippie Movement] first, then the postscript.

The Witness: I will read it in the order that I wrote it. 'Revolution toward a free society, Yippie, by A. Yippie. This is a personal statement. There are no spokesmen for the Yippies. We are all our own leaders. We realize this list of demands is inconsistent. They are not really demands. For people to make demands of the Democratic Party is an exercise in wasted wish fulfillment. If we have a demand, it is simply and emphatically that they, along with their fellow inmates in the Republican Party, cease to exist. We demand a society built along the alternative community in Lincoln Park, a society based on humanitarian cooperation and equality, a society which allows and promotes the creativity present in all people and especially our youth.

'Number one. An immediate end to the war in Vietnam and a restructuring of our foreign policy which totally eliminates aspects of military, economic and cultural imperialism; the withdrawal of all foreign based troops and the abolition of military draft.

'Two. An immediate freedom for Huey Newton of the Black Panthers and all other black people; adoption of the community control concept in our ghetto areas; an end to the cultural and economic domination of minority groups.

'Three. The legalization of marijuana and all other psychedelic drugs; the freeing of all prisoners currently imprisoned on narcotics charges.

'Number four. A prison system based on the concept of rehabilitation rather than punishment.

'Five. A judicial system which works towards the abolition of all laws related to crimes without victims; that is, retention only of laws relating to crimes in which there is an unwilling injured party: i.e. murder, rape, or assault.

'Six. The total disarmament of all the people beginning with the police. This includes not only guns but such brutal vices as tear gas, Mace, electric prods, blackjacks, billy clubs, and the like.

'Seven. The abolition of money, the abolition of pay housing, pay media, pay transportation, pay food, pay education, pay clothing, pay medical health, and pay toilets.

'Eight. A society which works towards and actively promotes the concept of full unemployment, a society in which people are free from the drudgery of work, adoption of the concept "Let the machines do it."

[Nine is missing from the trial transcript]

'Number ten. A program of ecological development that would provide incentives for the decentralization of crowded cities and encourage rural living.

'Eleven. A program which provides not only free birth control information and devices, but also abortions when desired.

'Twelve. A restructured educational system which provides a student power to determine his course of study, student participation in over-all policy planning; an educational system which breaks down its barriers between school and community; a system which uses the surrounding community as a classroom so that students may learn directly the problems of the people.

'Number thirteen. The open and free use of the media; a program which actively supports and promotes cable television as a method of increasing the selection of channels available to the viewer.

'Fourteen. An end to all censorship. We are sick of a society that has no hesitation about showing people committing violence and refuses to show a couple fucking.

'Fifteen. We believe that people should fuck all the time, any time, wherever they wish. This is not a programmed demand but a simple recognition of the reality around us.'

'Sixteen. A political system which is more streamlined and responsive to the needs of all the people regardless of age, sex, or race; perhaps a national referendum system conducted via television or a telephone voting system; perhaps a decentralization of power and authority with many varied tribal groups, groups in which people exist in a state of basic trust and are free to choose their tribe.

'Seventeen. A program that encourages and promotes the arts. However, we feel that if the free society we envision were to be sought for and achieved, all of us would actualize the creativity within us; in a very real sense we would have a society in which every man would be an artist.

'And eighteen was left blank for anybody to fill in what they wanted. It was for these reasons that we had come to Chicago, it was for these reasons that many of us may fight and die here. We recognize this as the vision of the founders of this nation. We recognize that we are America; we recognize that we are free men. The present-day politicians and their armies of automatons have selfishly robbed us of our birthright. The evilness they stand for will go unchallenged no longer. Political pigs, your days are numbered. We are the second American Revolution. We shall win.

'YIPPIE.'

Mr Weinglass: When you used the words 'fight and die here', in what context were you using those words?

The Witness: It is a metaphor. That means that we felt strongly about our right to assemble in the park and that people should be willing to take risks for it. It doesn't spell it out because people were capable of fighting in their own way and making their own decisions and we never would tell anyone specifically that they should fight, fistfight.

Mr Weinglass: Did you during the week of the Convention and the period of time immediately before the Convention tell any person singly or in groups that they should fight in the park?

Mr Schultz: Objection.

The Court: I sustain the objection. . . .

Mr Weinglass: Abbie Hoffman, prior to coming to Chicago, from April 1968 on to the week of the Convention, did you enter into an agreement with David Dellinger, John Froines, Tom Hayden, Jerry Rubin, Lee Weiner, or Rennie Davis, to come to the city of Chicago for the purpose of encouraging and promoting violence during the Convention week?

The Witness: An agreement?

Mr Weinglass: Yes.

The Witness: We couldn't agree on lunch.

Mr Weinglass: I have no further questions.

Note

1. 'Yip' or 'Yippies' was short for the 'Youth International Party'.

Study Question

1. What do you believe was accomplished by the more radical protest movements such as the Yippies?

MARTIN LUTHER KING, JR

Martin Luther King, Jr (1929–68), was born in Atlanta, Georgia, at the height of racial segregation. He graduated from Morehouse College with a BA and went on to study theology at Crozer Theological Seminary in Pennsylvania. He ultimately graduated from Boston University in 1955 with a doctoral degree *in theology. An ordained minister since 1948, King became pastor of the Dexter Avenue Baptist Church in Montgomery, Alabama, in 1954. It was during this time that King became actively involved in the civil rights movement, participating in the Montgomery Bus Boycott, the Selma to Montgomery March,* and eventually founding the Southern Christian Leadership Conference (SCLC). He headed the SCLC, which advocated non-violent social change, until his death in 1968. The following speech was one of King's most famous, delivered at the March on Washington in 1963.

Coretta Scott King and Martin Luther King meet New York City mayor Robert Wagner in 1964. New York World-Telegram and the Sun Newspaper Photograph Collection. Courtesy of the Library of Congress, Prints and Photographs Division (LC-USZ62-120210).

I Have a Dream

I am happy to join with you today in what will go down in history as the greatest demonstration for freedom in the history of our nation.

Five score years ago, a great American, in whose symbolic shadow we stand today, signed the Emancipation Proclamation. This momentous decree came as a great beacon light of hope to millions of Negro slaves who had been seared in the flames of withering injustice. It came as a joyous daybreak to end the long night of captivity.

But one hundred years later, the Negro still is not free. One hundred years later, the life of

Copyright 1963 Martin Luther King Jr, copyright renewed 1991 Coretta Scott King. Reprinted by arrangement with the Estate of Martin Luther King Jr, c/o Writers House as agent for the proprietor, New York, NY.

the Negro is still sadly crippled by the manacles of segregation and the chains of discrimination. One hundred years later, the Negro lives on a lonely island of poverty in the midst of a vast ocean of material prosperity. One hundred years later, the Negro is still languished in the corners of American society and finds himself in exile in his own land. So we have come here today to dramatize a shameful condition.

In a sense we've come to our nation's Capital to cash a check. When the architects of our republic wrote the magnificent words of the Constitution and the Declaration of Independence, they were signing a promissory note to which every American was to fall heir.

This note was a promise that all men, yes, black men as well as white men, would be guaranteed the unalienable rights of life, liberty, and the pursuit of happiness.

It is obvious today that America has defaulted on this promissory note insofar as her citizens of color are concerned. Instead of honoring this sacred obligation, America has given the Negro people a bad check; a check which has come back marked 'insufficient funds'.

But we refuse to believe that the bank of justice is bankrupt. We refuse to believe that there are insufficient funds in the great vaults of opportunity of this nation. So we have come to cash this check—a check that will give us upon demand the riches of freedom and the security of justice.

We have also come to this hallowed spot to remind America of the fierce urgency of now. This is no time to engage in the luxury of cooling off or to take the tranquilizing drug of gradualism.

Now is the time to make real the promises of democracy. Now is the time to rise from the dark and desolate valley of segregation to the sunlit path of racial justice. Now is the time to lift our nation from the quicksands of racial injustice to the solid rock of brotherhood. Now is the time to make justice a reality for all of God's children.

It would be fatal for the nation to overlook the urgency of the moment. This sweltering summer of the Negro's legitimate discontent will not pass until there is an invigorating autumn of freedom and equality. Nineteen sixty-three is not an end, but a beginning. Those who hope that the Negro needed to blow off steam and will now be content will have a rude awakening if the nation returns to business as usual. There will be neither rest nor tranquility in America until the Negro is granted his citizenship rights. The whirlwinds of revolt will continue to shake the foundations of our nation until the bright day of justice emerges.

But there is something that I must say to my people who stand on the warm threshold which leads into the palace of justice. In the process of gaining our rightful place we must not be guilty of wrongful deeds. Let us not seek to satisfy our thirst for freedom by drinking from the cup of bitterness and hatred. We must forever conduct our struggle on the high plane of dignity and discipline. We must not allow our creative protest to degenerate into physical violence. Again and again we must rise to the majestic heights of meeting physical force with soul force.

The marvelous new militancy which has engulfed the Negro community must not lead us to a distrust of all white people, for many of our white brothers, as evidenced by their presence here today, have come to realize that their destiny is tied up with our destiny. And they have come to realize that their freedom is inextricably bound to our freedom. We cannot walk alone.

And as we walk, we must make the pledge that we shall march ahead. We cannot turn back. There are those who are asking the devotees of civil rights, 'When will you be satisfied?'

We can never be satisfied as long as the Negro is the victim of the unspeakable horrors of police brutality.

We can never be satisfied as long as our bodies, heavy with the fatigue of travel, cannot gain lodging in the motels of the highways and the hotels of the cities.

We cannot be satisfied as long as the Negro's basic mobility is from a smaller ghetto to a larger one.

We can never be satisfied as long as our children are stripped of their selfhood and robbed of their dignity by signs stating 'for whites only'.

We cannot be satisfied as long as a Negro in Mississippi cannot vote and a Negro in New York believes he has nothing for which to vote.

No, no, we are not satisfied, and we will not be satisfied until justice rolls down like waters and righteousness like a mighty stream.

I am not unmindful that some of you have come here out of great trials and tribulations. Some of you have come fresh from narrow jail cells. Some of you have come from areas where your quest for freedom left you battered by the storms of persecution and staggered by the winds of police brutality. You have been the veterans of creative suffering. Continue to work with the faith that unearned suffering is redemptive.

Go back to Mississippi, go back to Alabama, go back to South Carolina, go back to Georgia, go back to Louisiana, go back to the slums and ghettos of our northern cities, knowing that somehow this situation can and will be changed. Let us not wallow in the valley of despair.

I say to you today, my friends, so even though we face the difficulties of today and tomorrow, I still have a dream. It is a dream deeply rooted in the American dream.

I have a dream that one day this nation will rise up and live out the true meaning of its creed: 'We hold these truths to be self-evident; that all men are created equal.'

I have a dream that one day on the red hills of Georgia the sons of former slaves and the sons of former slave owners will be able to sit down together at the table of brotherhood.

I have a dream that one day even the state of Mississippi, a state sweltering with the heat of injustice, sweltering with the heat of oppression, will be transformed into an oasis of freedom and justice.

I have a dream that my four little children will one day live in a nation where they will not be judged by the color of their skin but by the content of their character.

I have a dream today.

I have a dream that one day down in Alabama, with its vicious racists, with its governor having his lips dripping with the words of interposition and nullification, that one day right down in Alabama little black boys and black girls will be able to join hands with little white boys and white girls as sisters and brothers.

I have a dream today.

I have a dream that one day every valley shall be exalted, every hill and mountain shall be made low, the rough places will be made plain, and the crooked places will be made straight, and the glory of the Lord shall be revealed, and all flesh shall see it together.

This is our hope. This is the faith that I will go back to the South with. With this faith we will be able to hew out of the mountain of despair a stone of hope. With this faith we will be able to transform the jangling discords of our nation into a beautiful symphony of brotherhood.

With this faith we will be able to work together, to pray together, to struggle together, to go to jail together, to stand up for freedom together, knowing that we will be free one day.

This will be the day when all of God's children will be able to sing with new meaning, 'My country 'tis of thee, sweet land of liberty, of thee I sing. Land where my fathers died, land of the Pilgrims' pride, from every mountainside, let freedom ring.'

And if America is to be a great nation, this must become true. So let freedom ring from the prodigious hilltops of New Hampshire. Let freedom ring from the mighty mountains of New York. Let freedom ring from the heightening Alleghenies of Pennsylvania.

Let freedom ring from the snow-capped Rockies of Colorado. Let freedom ring from the curvaceous slopes of California. But not only that; let freedom ring from the Stone Mountain of Georgia. Let freedom ring from Lookout Mountain of Tennessee.

Let freedom ring from every hill and molehill of Mississippi. From every mountainside, let freedom ring.

And when this happens, and when we allow freedom ring, when we let it ring from every village and every hamlet, from every state and every city, we will be able to speed up that day when all of God's children, black men and white men, Jews and gentiles, Protestants and Catholics, will be able to join hands and sing in the words of the old Negro spiritual, 'Free at last! Free at last! Thank God Almighty, we are free at last!'

Study Question

1. King's vision of non-violent social change was often frustrated by groups that argued that non-violence would accomplish little against such powerful opponents. Whose assessment was more accurate?

KWAME ANTHONY APPIAH

Categories of collective identity such as African-American, Chinese-Canadian, gay, straight, and many others have, since the 1950s and 1960s, come to be widely accepted in contemporary culture. However, the work of Kwame Anthony Appiah (b. 1954) challenges these conventions and calls on educated people to move beyond such categories and to embrace 'cosmopolitanism'—a genuine dialogue across cultures that embraces the diversity of global experience. In this excerpt he discusses the origins and the problems of narrowly defined identities.

IDENTITY, AUTHENTICITY, SURVIVAL

The large collective identities that call for recognition come with notions of how a proper person of that kind behaves: it is not that there is one way that gays or blacks should behave, but that there are gay and black modes of behavior. These notions provide loose norms or models, which play a role in shaping the life plans of those who make these collective identities central to their individual identities.[1] Collective identities, in short, provide what we might call scripts: narratives that people can use in shaping their life plans and in telling their life stories. . . .

This is not just a point about modern Westerners: crossculturally it matters to people that their lives have a certain narrative unity; they want to be able to tell a story of their lives that makes sense. The story—my story—should cohere in the way appropriate by the standards made available in my culture to a person of my identity. In telling that story, how I fit into the wider story of various collectivities is, for most of us, important. It is not just gender identities that give shape (through, for example, rites of passage into woman- or manhood) to one's life: ethnic and national identities too fit each individual story into a larger narrative. And some of the most individualist of individuals value such things. Hobbes spoke of the desire for glory as one of the dominating impulses of human beings, one that was bound to make trouble for social life. But glory can consist in fitting and being seen to fit into a collective history, and so, in the name of glory, one can end up doing the most social things of all.

In our current situation in the multicultural West, we live in societies in which certain individuals have not been treated with equal dignity because they were, for example, women, homosexuals, blacks, Catholics. Because . . . our identities are dialogically shaped, people who have these characteristics find them central—often negatively so—to their identities. Nowadays there is a widespread agreement that the insults to their dignity and the limitations of their autonomy imposed in the name of these collective identities are seriously wrong. One form of healing the self that those who have these identities participate in is learning to see these collective identities not as sources of limitation and insult but as a valuable part of what they centrally are. Because the ethics of authenticity requires us to express what we centrally are, they further demand recognition in social life as women, homosexuals, blacks, Catholics. Because there was no good reason to treat people of these sorts badly, and because the culture continues to provide degrading images of them nevertheless, they demand that we do cultural work to resist the stereotypes, to challenge the insults, to lift the restrictions.

These old restrictions suggested life-scripts for the bearers of these identities, but they were negative ones. In order to construct a life with dignity, it seems natural to take the collective identity and construct positive life-scripts instead. An African-American after the Black Power movement takes the old script of self-hatred, the script in which he or she is a nigger, and works, in community with others, to construct a series of positive Black life-scripts. In these life-scripts, being a Negro is recoded as being Black, and this requires, among other things, refusing to assimilate to white norms of speech and behavior. And if one is to be Black in a society that is racist then one has to deal constantly with assaults on one's dignity. In this context, insisting on the right to

live a dignified life will not be enough. It will not even be enough to require being treated with equal dignity despite being Black, for that will require a concession that being Black counts naturally or to some degree against one's dignity. And so one will end up asking to be respected as a Black.

The same example holds for gay identity. An American homosexual after Stonewall and gay liberation takes the old script of self-hatred, the script of the closet, the script in which he is a faggot, and works, in community with others, to construct a series of positive gay life-scripts. In these lifescripts, being homosexual, is recoded as being gay, and this requires, among other things, refusing to stay in the closet. And if one is to be out of the closet in a society that deprives homosexuals of equal dignity and respect then one has to deal constantly with assaults on one's dignity. In this context, the right to live as an 'open homosexual' will not be enough. It will not even be enough to be treated with equal dignity despite being homosexual, for that will require a concession that being homosexual counts naturally or to some degree against one's dignity. And so one will end up asking to be respected as a homosexual.

. . . I think we need to go on to the next necessary step, which is to ask whether the identities constructed in this way are ones we—I speak here as someone who counts in America as a gay black man—can be happy with in the longer run. Demanding respect for people as blacks and as gays requires that there are some scripts that go with being an African-American or having same-sex desires. There will be proper ways of being black and gay, there will be expectations to be met, demands will be made. It is at this point that someone who takes autonomy seriously will ask whether we have not replaced one kind of tyranny with another. If I had to choose between the world of the closet and the world of gay liberation, or between the world of Uncle Tom's Cabin and Black Power, I would, of course, choose in each case the latter. But I would like not to have to choose. I would like other options. The politics of recognition requires that one's skin color, one's sexual body, should be acknowledged politically in ways that make it hard for those who want to treat their skin and their sexual body as personal dimensions of the self. And personal means not secret, but not too tightly scripted. I think . . . that the desire of some Québécois to require people who are 'ethnically' francophone to teach their children in French steps over a boundary. I believe . . . that this is, in some sense, the same boundary that is crossed by someone who demands that I organize my life around my 'race' or my sexuality.

It is a familiar thought that the bureaucratic categories of identity must come up short before the vagaries of actual people's lives. But it is equally important to bear in mind that a politics of identity can be counted on to transform the identities on whose behalf it ostensibly labors.[2]

Between the politics of recognition and the politics of compulsion, there is no bright line.

Notes

1. [Appiah] I say 'make', here, not because I think there is always conscious attention to the shaping of life plans or a substantial experience of choice, but because I want to stress the antiessentialist point that there are choices that can be made.

2. [Appiah] This is another point essentialists are ill-equipped to see.

> **Study Question**
>
> 1. What does Appiah mean by 'the politics of identity'?

TIPS FOR ANALYSIS

The Author's Age

When in the author's life was the document written? If the document was written early in a person's life consider their experiences to that point. If the document was written very late in a person's life consider the issue of memory and the impact of the events which have intervened between the writing of the document and the events under discussion.

WEB RESOURCES

The King Center (Martin Luther King, Jr)
http://www.thekingcenter.org
Sixties Project: Primary Document Archive
http://www2.iath.virginia.edu/sixties/HTML_docs/Resources/Primary.html
Library of Congress: Civil Rights Resource Guide
http://www.loc.gov/rr/program/bib/civilrights/external.html
Internet Women's History Sourcebook
http://www.fordham.edu/halsall/women/womensbook.html

RECOMMENDED READING

Anthony Burgess, *A Clockwork Orange* (New York: W.W. Norton, 1986). In a futuristic London, where gangs of teenage 'droogs' commit random unspeakably violent acts, the central character, Alex, is captured and imprisoned. An experimental hospital treatment modifies his behaviour in such a way as to 'free' him from his violent nature; however, the cost of freedom is the loss of free will. The conditioning is eventually reversed. Note that the 1962 British version of the novel contains a final, optimistic chapter in which Alex turns twenty-one and, having escaped adolescence, freely chooses to abandon his violent ways. This ending was omitted from most American editions of the novel, as well as from the film.

Joseph Heller, *Catch-22* (New York: Simon & Schuster, 1996). Set in Second World War Italy, *Catch-22* (written in 1961) is a satirical and surrealist commentary on the essential insanity of war. The war is seen through the eyes of bombardier John Yossarian as he struggles to stay alive in the face of the omnipresent bureaucracy that demands he demonstrate his insanity—the precondition of getting out of the military—by continuing to fly dangerous missions.

Hermann Hesse, *Steppenwolf* (New York: Picador, 2002). Although written in 1927, the 1960s counterculture movement idolized Hesse's *Steppenwolf*. The novel tells the story of one man's struggle between a life of bourgeois peace and order, and one of action, instinct, and impulse. Hesse's central message concerns the need to focus on one's inner voice, and reject the dictates of the external world: 'There is no reality except the one contained within us.'

Jack Kerouac, *On the Road* (New York: Penguin, 1991). The classic novel of the Beat Generation, written in 1957, tells a fictionalized version of Kerouac's cross-country travels and his meetings with counter-culture icons such as Allen Ginzberg and William Burroughs. Kerouac's themes include dropping out, sex, drugs, mysticism, energy, speed, and freedom.

J.D. Salinger, *The Catcher in the Rye* (New York: Little, Brown and Company, 1991). Considered the essential novel of youth alienation and coming of age, Holden Caulfield runs away to 1940s New York with its jazz scene, ambivalent sexuality, alcohol, prostitution, and violence. Loneliness and alienation are intensified by his experiences, leading to a complete breakdown.

Kurt Vonnegut. 1969. *Slaughterhouse Five* (New York: Delacorte Press, 1994). *Slaughterhouse Five* is a science fiction/fantasy novel drawn, in part, from the author's experiences as a POW during the firebombing of Dresden. (Vonnegut survived, sheltered under a slaughterhouse.) The novel recounts Billy Pilgrim's journey through time, over the course of which he encounters the dangers of technology, the butchery of war, and the risk of blind obedience.

RECOMMENDED VIEWING

In the Year of the Pig (USA, 1968). Director: Emile de Antonio (Documentary). This controversial 1968 documentary—often considered the forerunner of contemporary investigative documentaries—attempted to uncover the truth behind the ongoing war in Vietnam. The film, using archival footage and interview, is both intensely anti-war and anti-American.

Easy Rider (USA, 1969). Director: Dennis Hopper. Perhaps the best known of the 1960s 'anti-establishment' films, *Easy Rider* highlights the youth culture, hippies, drug culture, and music of the era. Shot on location in documentary style, the film also touches on the rampant poverty and prejudice of 1960s America.

Stammheim (West Germany, 1986). Director: Reinhard Hauff. Hauff's fictionalized account of the West German Baader–Meinhof group (Red Army Faction) of the late 1960s and early 1970s tackles the issue of anti-military, anti-corporate terrorism and its consequences. It also reveals the complexities of German–American relations during the Cold War and the level of support for radical groups using terrorist tactics.

Mississippi Burning (USA, 1988). Director: Alan Parker. *Mississippi Burning* is a highly fictionalized dramatization of the 1964 Klu Klux Klan murders of three white civil rights activists. It captures the climate of hatred in the southern United States and the determination to prevent the civil rights movement from gaining any ground.

The Laramie Project (USA, 2002). Director: Moisés Kaufman. *The Laramie Project* is the film version of Kaufman's stage play about the vicious murder of gay university student Matthew Sheppard. The film re-enacts some of the events leading to Sheppard's murder, the town's reaction, and the subsequent debates about hate crime legislation.

CHAPTER SEVENTEEN

THE END OF THE COLD WAR AND ITS AFTERMATH

Gorbachev and Reagan at the White House on 8 December 1987, signing the INF treaty to reduce immediate-range nuclear weapons. Courtesy of the Ronald Reagan Library.

Eastern European countries made several failed attempts to break away from the control of the Soviet Union throughout the 1950s and 1960s; Poland and Hungary rebelled in 1956, Czechoslovakia in 1968. On each occasion the Soviet Union used its military superiority to re-impose control over the rebellious satellite states. However, even as the Soviets re-asserted control, some concessions—particularly on economic matters—were made to the defiant Eastern bloc nations. These compromises, and the potential for greater freedoms in the future, sustained an active underground opposition movement in the region.

The mere presence of dissent would likely never have achieved independence for Eastern Europe. However, by the late 1970s, the economy of the Soviet Union was severely overburdened by the accelerated military spending necessary to keep pace with the United States. Increasingly the Soviets sacrificed the basic needs of their own citizens in order to maintain their global commitments. By the early 1980s alarming statistics showed that infant mortality was increasing and longevity declining. The Soviet economy was simply no longer able to deliver essential services such as health care and, as a result, the quality of Soviet life declined. Meanwhile, nepotism and corruption grew, especially within the massive Communist Party bureaucracy. The death of Leonid Brezhnev in 1982 brought few immediate changes, but it was clear that the present situation could not continue.

By March 1985 the situation in the Soviet Union was desperate. The aged leaders of the Communist Party had little choice but to move in a new direction under the leadership of the Politburo's youngest member, the then fifty-four-year-old Mikhail Gorbachev. Gorbachev had long since concluded that the time for small changes was past and that only radical reforms could preserve the Leninist system while moving the USSR into the post-industrial age. Over the next three years Gorbachev unleashed the widest array of reforms that the Soviet Union had seen since the 1920s. Peaceful co-existence was sought with the West through arms limitation talks, new economic initiatives were designed to make Soviet goods competitive in the world markets, political openness was encouraged, and it was made clear that the Soviets would no longer invest monies in propping up the unpopular governments of Eastern Europe.

The immediate result of the latter decision was open demonstrations of dissatisfaction throughout Eastern Europe. Lacking Soviet military backing, communist governments across the region crumbled. Unpopular governments were overthrown in Poland, Hungary, East Germany, Bulgaria, Czechoslovakia, Rumania, and Yugoslavia. The early jubilation, however, proved short-lived, as the end of single-party states did not automatically solve the major problems facing the former Soviet satellites. The collapse of communism saw a resurgence of multi-party democratic systems that tended to form along traditional ethnic and religious lines. The conflicts that ensued were sufficient to destroy both Czechoslovakia and Yugoslavia. Elsewhere, weak coalition governments struggled with the transition to capitalism and suffered hyperinflation, massive unemployment, and social dislocation as the conversion proceeded.

Meanwhile, few of Gorbachev's reforms were unfolding as planned in the Soviet Union. Angry consumers resented the removal of subsidies from basic foodstuffs, managers resented the new requirements to demonstrate profitability, advocates of democratic political reforms demanded Gorbachev move faster while old-guard communists argued that he had already gone too far. Gradually it became evident that Gorbachev was unable to control the forces he had unleashed and few in the Soviet Union were distressed when a coup d'état in August 1991 left

Gorbachev with vastly reduced powers. In his place, Boris Yeltsin, the newly elected president of the Russian Republic, assumed greater control. By the end of 1991 the Soviet Union had been dissolved and in its place the more loosely affiliated Commonwealth of Independent States emerged. In Russia itself, Yeltsin struggled to contain inflation, criminal activity, and rebellious ethnic minorities. Though relations with the West improved during his presidency, a series of economic crises and rampant corruption, combined with questions regarding Yeltsin's health, forced him to relinquish office on 31 December 1999 in favour of his hand-picked successor, Vladimir Putin.

The documents in this section introduce the views of Eastern European dissidents, including Ludvík Vaculík and Václav Havel. As well, we see Mikhail Gorbachev's analysis of the situation facing the Soviet Union in the mid-1980s and Aleksandr Solzhenitsyn's suggestions for rebuilding Russia. The chapter concludes with two documents that focus on the fragmentation of nation-states in the wake of the Cold War: an excerpt from Benjamin Barber's *Jihad versus McWorld* and Robert Kaplan's analysis of the situation in the former Yugoslavia and in Moldova.

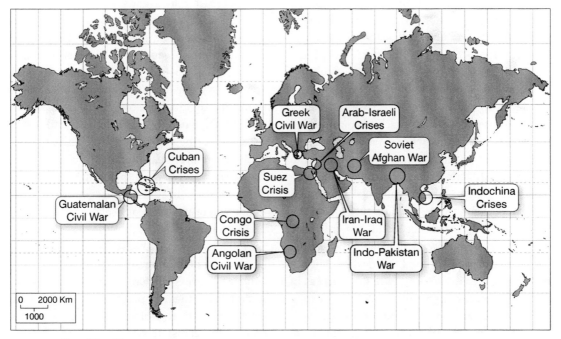

Proxy Wars Map

Ludvík Vaculík

Ludvík Vaculík (b. 1926) was a well-known novelist and journalist in postwar Czechoslovakia. Inspired by the events of the Prague Spring, during which Czechoslovakian Communist leader Aleksandr Dubček attempted to create a more humane form of socialism, Vaculík wrote, 'Two Thousand Words to Workers, Farmers, Scientists, Artists, and Everyone'. The essay was published in a number of Prague newspapers on 27 June 1968. Vaculík condemned the Communist Party and urged the reformers to accelerate their pace. However, far from advancing the cause of reform, the essay in fact helped to convince Soviet leader Leonid Brezhnev that the reform movement in Czechoslovakia had to be stopped. On 21 August 1968 Warsaw Pact troops invaded Czechoslovakia, occupied Prague and other major cities, and restored a more Orthodox pro-Soviet regime under the leadership of Gustav Husak.

Two Thousand Words to Workers, Farmers, Scientists, Artists, and Everyone

After the war people had great confidence in the Communist party, but it gradually preferred to have official positions instead of the people's trust, until it had only official positions, and nothing else. . . . The incorrect line of the leadership turned the party from a political party and ideological grouping into a power organization which became very attractive to power-hungry egotists, reproachful cowards, and people with bad consciences. When they came into the party, its character and behaviour began to be affected. Its internal organization was such that good people, who might have maintained its development for it to have fitted into the modern world, could not wield any influence at all without shameful incidents occurring. Many communists opposed this decline, but not in one single case did they have any success in preventing what happened.

The conditions in the Communist party were the model for and the cause of an identical situation in the state. . . . There was no criticism of the activity of the state and economic organizations. Parliament forgot how to debate: The government forgot how to govern and the directors how to direct. Elections had no significance, and the laws lost their weight. We could not trust representatives on any committee, and even if we did, we could not ask them to do anything, because they could not ask them to do anything, because they could accomplish nothing. What was still worse was that we could hardly trust each other any more. There was a decline of individual and communal honour. You didn't get anywhere by being honest, and it was useless expecting ability to be appreciated. Most people, therefore, lost interest in public affairs; they worried only about themselves and about their money. . . . To sum up, the country reached a point where its spiritual health and character were both threatened. . . .

In the future, we shall have to display personal initiative and determination of our own.

Above all, we shall have to oppose the view, should it arise, that it is possible to conduct some sort of democratic revival without the communists or possibly against them. This would be both unjust and unreasonable. The communists have well-constructed organizations, and we should support the progressive wing within them. They have experienced officials, and last but not least, they also have in their hands the decisive levers

'Out, Out, Brief Candle!' © 1969 by Herblock in *The Washington Post.* Cartoonist Herbert Block depicts Leonid Brezhnev snuffing out the flame of the Prague Spring. A 1969 Herblock Cartoon, copyright by The Herbert Block Foundation.

and buttons. Their Action Program has been presented to the public. It is a program for the initial adjustment of the greatest inequalities, and no one else has any similarly concrete program. We must demand that local Action Programs be submitted to the public in each district and each community. By doing so, we shall have suddenly taken very ordinary and long-expected steps in the right direction. . . .

The practical quality of the future democracy depends on what becomes of the [factories] and what will happen to them. . . . We have to find good managers and back them up. It is true that, in comparison with the developed countries, we are all badly paid, and some are worse off than others.

We can demand more money—but although it can be printed, it will be worth less. We should instead demand that directors and chairmen explain to us the nature and extent of the capital they want for production, to whom they want to sell their products and for how much, what profit they can expect to make, and the percentage of this profit that is to be invested in the modernization of production and the percentage to be shared out.

Under quite superficially boring headlines, a very fierce struggle is going on in the press about democracy and who leads the country. Workers can intervene in this struggle by means of the people they elect to [factory] administrations and councils. As employees, they can do what is best for themselves by electing as their representatives on trade union organs their natural leaders, capable and honest people no matter what their party affiliation is.

If at the moment we cannot expect any more from the central political organs, we must achieve more in the districts and smaller communities. We should demand the resignation of people who have misused their power, who have damaged public property, or who have acted in a dishonest or brutal way. We have to find ways and means to persuade them to resign, through public criticism, for instance, through resolutions, demonstrations, demonstrating work brigades, collections for retirement gifts for them, strikes, and picketing their houses. . . . And let us set up special citizens' committees and commissions to deal with subjects that nobody is yet interested in. It's quite simple, a few people get together, elect a chairman, keep regular minutes, publish their findings, demand a solution, and do not allow themselves to be intimidated.

We must turn the district and local press, which has degenerated into a mouthpiece for official views, into a platform for all the positive political forces. . . . Let us establish committees for the defence of the freedom of the press. Let us organize our own monitoring services at meetings. If we hear strange news, let's check on it ourselves, and let's send delegations to the people concerned and, if need be, publish their replies . . .

This spring, as after the war, we have been given a great chance. We have once again the opportunity to take a firm grip on a common cause, which has the working title of socialism, and to give it a form which will much better suit the once good reputation that we had and the relatively good opinion that we once had of

ourselves. The spring has now come to an end, and it will never return. By winter we will know everything.

> **Study Question**
>
> 1. To what extent did 'Two Thousand Words' represent a threat to the Soviet Union's control of its satellite states?

VÁCLAV HAVEL

Václav Havel (b. 1936) rose to prominence during the 1960s as an opponent of the Soviet system imposed upon Czechoslovakia after the Second World War. He played an active role during the Prague Spring (1968) and his writings in defence of Eastern European independence would lead to numerous arrests and a four-and-a-half year prison term. Havel continued to publish anti-Soviet literature throughout the 1970s and 1980s.

In 1989, when the USSR granted full independence to the satellite states, Havel was elected as the first president of Czechoslovakia. He remained president during the peaceful separation of the Czechoslovakian Federation into two states and served until February 2003. In the following excerpt, originally published in 1986, Havel responds to questions regarding the potential for reform in the 1980s.

DISTURBING THE PEACE

Hvízd'ala: Do you see a grain of hope anywhere in the 1980s?

Havel: I should probably say first that the kind of hope I often think about (especially in situations that are particularly hopeless, such as prison) I understand above all as a state of mind, not a state of the world. Either we have hope within us or we don't; it is a dimension of the soul, and it's not essentially dependent on some particular observation of the world or estimate of the situation. Hope is not prognostication. It is an orientation of the spirit, an orientation of the heart; it transcends the world that is immediately experienced, and is anchored somewhere beyond its horizons. . . .

Hope, in this deep and powerful sense, is not the same as joy that things are going well, or willingness to invest in enterprises that are obviously headed for early success, but, rather, an ability to work for something because it is good, not just because it stands a chance to succeed. The more unpropitious the situation in which we demonstrate hope, the deeper that hope is. Hope is definitely not the same thing as optimism. It is not the conviction that something will turn out well, but the certainty that something makes sense, regardless of how it turns out. . . .

That was by way of introduction; now to answer your question about the state of the world and the kind of hopeful phenomena I see in it. Here too,

I think you can find modest grounds for hope. I leave it to those more qualified to decide what can be expected from Gorbachev and, in general, 'from above'—that is, from what is happening in the sphere of power. I have never fixed my hopes there; I've always been more interested in what was happening 'below', in what could be expected from 'below', what could be won there, and what defended. All power is power over someone, and it always somehow responds, usually unwittingly rather than deliberately, to the state of mind and the behavior of those it rules over. One can always find in the behavior of power a reflection of what is going on 'below'. No one can govern in a vacuum. The exercise of power is determined by thousands of interactions between the world of the powerful and that of the powerless, all the more so because these worlds are never divided by a sharp line: everyone has a small part of himself in both.

Having said that, if I try to look unbiasedly at what is going on 'below', I must say that here too I find a slow, imperceptible, yet undoubted and undoubtedly hopeful movement. After seventeen years of apparent stagnation and moribundity, the situation is rather different now. If we compare how society behaves now, how it expresses itself, what it dares to do—or, rather, what a significant minority dares to do—with how it was in the early seventies, those differences must be obvious. People seem to be recovering gradually, walking straighter, taking a renewed interest in things they had so energetically denied themselves before. New islands of self-awareness and self-liberation are appearing, and the connections between them, which were once so brutally disrupted, are multiplying. A new generation, not traumatized by the shock of the Soviet occupation, is maturing: for them, the invasion is history and Dubček is what Kramář,[1] for example, was to my generation. Something is happening in the social awareness, though it is still an undercurrent as yet, rather than something visible.

And all of this brings subtle pressure to bear on the powers that govern society. I'm not thinking now of the obvious pressure of public criticism coming from dissidents, but of the invisible kinds of pressure brought on by this general state of mind and its various forms of expression, to which power unintentionally adapts, even in the act of opposing it. One is made aware of these things with special clarity when one returns from prison and experiences the sharp contrast between the situation as he had fixed it in his mind before his arrest, and the new situation at the moment of his return. I have observed this in my own case, and others have had the same experience. Again and again, we were astonished at all the new things that were going on, the greater risks people were taking, how more freely they were behaving, how much greater and less hidden was their hunger for truth, for a truthful word, for genuine values. . . .

But things are different now from the way they were a few years ago, right in the midst of the so-called dissident or Chartist milieu as well. And although those in power have not altered their view of the Charter, they have still had to get used to it. Today it is a firm part of social life here, even though its position is marginal, one that society perceives more as the final horizon of its relationships or the final focus of various values than as an immediate challenge, something to be emulated. Today it is hard to imagine a time when the Charter did not exist, and when one does try to imagine it, it evokes a feeling of vacuum and moral relativity.

Or take VONS.[2] Few of us were arrested and sent to prison for working in the 'antistate center'. When that happened, VONS did not cave in; others immediately filled in and continued the work. We didn't cave in either; we served our sentences, and VONS is here to this day, working energetically on, and apparently no one thinks anymore of prosecuting it for what it does. It still officially remains an 'antistate organization' (an epithet those in power are too vainglorious to withdraw), but by insisting on it, they have turned it into a worthless phrase: what kind of an 'antistate organization' is it that can go on publicly functioning for nine years? In a sense, our jail sentences gained us the right to run VONS.

To outside observers, these changes may seem insignificant. 'Where are your ten-million-strong trade unions?' they may ask. 'Where are your members of parliament? Why does Husák not negotiate with you? Why is the government not considering your proposals and acting on them?' But for someone from here who is not completely indifferent, these are far from insignificant changes; they are the main promise of the future, since he has long ago learned not to expect it from anywhere else.

I can't resist concluding with a question of my own. Isn't the reward of all those small but hopeful signs of movement this deep, inner hope that is not dependent on prognoses, and which was the primordial point of departure in this unequal struggle? Would so many of those small hopes have 'come out' if there had not been this great hope 'within', this hope without which it is impossible to live in dignity and meaning, much less find the will for the 'hopeless enterprise' which stands at the beginning of most good things?

Notes

1. Karel Kramář (1860–1937) was instrumental in gaining Czech independence from the Austro-Hungarian Empire.
2. VONS: The Committee for the Defence of the Unjustly Prosecuted (*Vybor na obranu nespravedlive stihanych*).

> **Study Question**
>
> 1. Was it the 'small but hopeful' signs that achieved Czechoslovakia's freedom from Soviet rule, or a 'revolution from above'?

MIKHAIL GORBACHEV

Mikhail Gorbachev (b. 1931) joined the Communist Party of the Soviet Union in 1952 and then rose steadily through the ranks of the party bureaucracy. With degrees in law and agriculture, Gorbachev joined the Central Committee of the CPSU in 1971 and became the youngest member in the history of the Politburo in 1980. The death of Konstantin Chernenko in March 1985 and the desperate social and economic situation in the Soviet Union opened the way for Gorbachev to be elected General Secretary of the Communist Party of the Soviet Union. This speech, given at the closing of the 27th Congress of the Communist Party in 1986, was one of Gorbachev's most candid regarding the many challenges facing the USSR in the mid-1980s.

ON THE CLOSING OF THE 27TH CONGRESS OF THE CPSU

Dear Comrades,

The 27th Congress is about to close.

It is up to history to give an objective evaluation of its importance. But already today we can say: the Congress has been held in an atmosphere of Party fidelity to principle, in a spirit of unity, exactingness, and Bolshevik truth; it has frankly pointed out shortcomings and deficiencies, and made a profound analysis of the internal and external conditions in which our society develops. It has set a lofty moral and spiritual tone for the Party's activity and for the life of the entire country.

US President Ronald Reagan stands with Mikhail Gorbachev in Red Square, May 1988, during the Moscow Summit. Courtesy of the Ronald Reagan Library.

Coming to this rostrum, delegates put all questions frankly, and did not mince words in showing what is impeding our common cause, what is holding us back. Not a few critical statements were made about the work of all links of the Party, of government and economic organizations, both at the centre and locally. In fact, not a single sphere of our life has escaped critical analysis. All this, comrades, is in the spirit of the Party's finest traditions, in the Bolshevik spirit.

More than sixty years ago, when summing up the discussion on the Political Report of the RCP(B) Central Committee to the 11th Party Congress, Lenin expressed a thought that is of fundamental importance. He said: 'All the revolutionary parties that have perished so far, perished because they became conceited, because they failed to see the source of their strength and were afraid to discuss their weaknesses. We, however, shall not perish, because we are not afraid to discuss our weaknesses and will learn to overcome them.'

It is in this way, in Lenin's way, that we have acted here at our Congress. And that is the way we shall continue to act!

The Congress has answered the vital questions that life itself has put before the Party, before society, and has equipped every Communist, every Soviet citizen, with a clear understanding of the coming tasks. It has shown that we were right when we advanced the concept of socioeconomic acceleration at the April 1985 Plenary Meeting. The idea of acceleration imbued all our pre-Congress activity. It was at the centre of attention at the Congress. It was embodied in the Political Report of the Central Committee, the new edition of the Party Programme, and the amendments to the Party Rules, as well as in the Guidelines for the Economic and Social Development of the USSR for the 12th Five-Year Plan Period and for the Period Ending in the Year 2000. These documents were wholeheatedly endorsed and approved by the delegates to the Congress.

The adopted and approved general line of the Party's domestic and foreign policy—that of the country's accelerated socioeconomic development, and of consolidating world peace—is the main political achievement of the 27th CPSU Congress. From now on it will be the law of life for the Party, for its every organization, and a guide to action for Communists, for all working people.

We are aware of the great responsibility to history that the CPSU is assuming, of the huge load it has taken on by adopting the strategy of acceleration. But we are convinced of the vital necessity of this strategy. We are confident that this strategy is a realistic one. Relying on the inexhaustible potentials and advantages of socialism, on the vigorous creative activity of the people, we shall be able to carry out all the projected objectives.

To secure the country's accelerated socio-economic development means to provide new powerful stimuli to the growth of the productive forces and to scientific and technological progress through the improvement of socialism's economic system, and to set in motion the tremendous untapped potentials of our national economy.

To secure acceleration means conducting an active and purposeful social policy by closely linking the improvement of the working people's well-being with the efficiency of labour, and by combining all-round concern for people with the consistent implementation of the principles of social justice.

To secure acceleration means to provide scope for the initiative and activity of every working person, every work collective, by deepening democracy, by steadily developing the people's socialist self-government, and by ensuring more openness in the life of the Party and society.

To secure acceleration means to bring ideological and organizational work closer to the people and direct it towards the elimination of difficulties and the practical solution of our tasks by associating this work more closely with the actual problems of life, by getting rid of hollow verbiage and didacticism, and by increasing people's responsibility for their job.

Comrades, we can and must accomplish all this! The CPSU is entering the post-Congress period better organized, more cohesive, more efficient, with a well-considered long-term policy. It is determined to act with purpose, aware of all the complexity, the great scope and novelty of the tasks it faces, undaunted by difficulties and obstacles.

It is up to us to reach every Soviet citizen and bring home the essence and spirit of the Congress decisions. Not only must we explain the basic concepts of the Congress; we must also organize in practice all work in line with present-day demands.

Very many interesting proposals were made and many profound thoughts expressed at our Congress and in the pre-Congress period. They must be carefully examined, and everything valuable and useful should be put into effect.

The most important thing now is to convert the energy of our plans into the energy of concrete action. This idea was very well expressed by a delegate to our Congress, Vasily Gorin, chairman of a Belgorod collective farm.

'All over the country,' he said, 'in every work collective, a difficult but, we are sure, irreversible process of renovation and reconstruction is now under way. It passes through the hearts and minds of Soviet people and calls for complete dedication on the part of each and everyone. Above all in their work.'

Yes, comrades, acceleration and radical changes in all spheres of our life are not just a slogan but a course that the Party will follow firmly and undeviatingly.

Many delegates noted that departmentalism, localism, paper work, and other bureaucratic practices are a big obstacle to what is new and progressive. I wish to assure you, comrades, that the Central Committee will resolutely eliminate all the obstacles standing in the way of accelerating socioeconomic progress, strengthen discipline and order, and create the organizational, moral, and material pre-requisites for the maximum development of creative activity, bold search, and socialist enterprise. I am confident that this will meet with broad and active support on the part of the entire Party and of all working people.

The Party committees, from top to bottom, are the organizers of the work of implementing the instructions of the Congress. What we now need are a concrete, businesslike, and consistent style of work, unity of words and deeds, use of the most effective ways and means, a thorough consideration of people's opinions, and efficient coordination of the actions of all social forces.

Sluggishness, formalism, indifference, the habit of letting good ideas get bogged down in empty, and endless roundabout discussions and attempts to 'adjust to readjustment' must be completely overcome.

One of the main conclusions of the Congress

is that all Party committees should act as genuine bodies of political leadership. In the final analysis, the success of all our efforts to implement the general line of the 27th Party Congress will be determined by the conscious participation of the broadest masses of the people in building communism. Everything depends on us, comrades! The time has come for vigorous and united actions. The Party calls on every Communist, every Soviet citizen, to join actively in the large-scale work of putting our plans into practice, of perfecting Soviet society, of renovating our socialist home.

Comrades, the Congress has strongly reaffirmed that socialism and peace, and peace and constructive endeavour, are indivisible. Socialism would fail to carry out its historic mission if it did not lead the struggle to deliver mankind from the burden of military threats and violence. The main goal of Soviet policy is security and a just peace for all nations. We regard the struggle against war and military preparations, against the propagation of hatred and violence as an inseparable part of the democratization of all international relations, of the genuine normalization of the political climate in the world.

In one respect the nuclear danger has put all states on an equal footing: in a big war nobody will be able to stand aside or to profit from the misfortunes of others. Equal security is the imperative of the times. Ensuring this security is becoming increasingly a political issue, one that can be resolved only by political means. It is high time to replace weapons by a more stable foundation for the relations among states. We see no alternative to this, nor are we trying to find one.

Unfortunately, however, in the international community there are still some who lay claims to a special security, one that is suited only to themselves. This is illustrated by the thinking in Washington. Calls for strength are still in fashion there, and strength continues to be regarded as the most convincing argument in world politics. It looks as though some people are simply afraid of the possibility that has appeared for a serious and long-term thaw in Soviet-American relations and in international relations as a whole.

This is not the first time we have come up against this kind of situation. Now, too, the militaristic, aggressive forces would of course prefer to preserve and perpetuate the confrontation. But what should we do, comrades? Slam the door? It is possible that this is just what we are being pushed into doing. But we very clearly realize our responsibility for the destinies of our country and for the destinies of the world. We do not intend, therefore, to play into the hands of those who would like to force mankind to get used to the nuclear threat and to the arms race.

Soviet foreign policy is oriented towards a search for mutual understanding, towards dialogue, and the establishment of peaceful coexistence as the universal norm in relations among states. We have both a clear idea of how to achieve this and a concrete programme of work for maintaining and consolidating peace.

The Soviet Union is acting and will continue to act in the world arena in an open and responsible way, energetically and in good faith. We intend to work persistently and constructively to eliminate nuclear weapons, radically to limit the arms race, and to build reliable international security that is equal for all countries. A mandate to preserve peace and to curb the arms race resounded forcefully in speeches by delegates to our Congress. The Party will unswervingly carry out this mandate.

We call on the leaders of countries that have a different social system to take a responsible approach to the key issue of world politics today: the issue of war and peace.

The leadership of the CPSU and the Soviet state will do its utmost to secure for our people the opportunity to work under the conditions of freedom and a lasting peace. As reaffirmed by the

Congress, our Party and the Soviet Union have many allies, supporters and partners abroad in the struggle for peace, freedom, and the progress of mankind.

We are sincerely happy to see here the leaders of the socialist countries. Allow me, on behalf of the Congress, wholeheartedly to thank the Communist Parties and peoples of these countries for their solidarity with the CPSU and the Soviet Union!

For a number of the fraternal parties in socialist countries this is also a congress year. The problems and tasks that the very course of history has set before the ruling Communist Parties are similar in many respects. And by responding to them, each party contributes to the treasure-chest of world socialism's combined experience. We wish you every success, dear friends!

The CPSU is grateful for the warm greetings addressed to it by the representatives of communist, revolutionary-democratic, socialist and social-democratic parties, of democratic, liberation, and anti-war forces, and movements. We highly appreciate their understanding and support of the idea advanced by the Congress of establishing a

comprehensive system of international security and the plan for eliminating nuclear arms before the end of the century. The CPSU is convinced that they are consonant with the true interests of all nations, all countries and all humanity.

Comrades, our Congress has shown that at the present stage, which is a turning point in our country's social development, the Leninist Party is equal to its historic tasks. On behalf of the delegates representing our entire Party I should like to say from this rostrum that we Communists set great store by the confidence placed in us by the workers, the farmers, the intelligentsia, by all Soviet people. We put above all else the interests of the people, of our Motherland, of socialism, and peace. We will spare neither effort nor energy to translate into life the decisions of the 27th Congress of the Communist Party of the Soviet Union.

Study Question

1. Was Gorbachev's vision of reform within a socialist framework achievable? If so, how?

ALEKSANDR SOLZHENITSYN

Aleksandr Solzhenitsyn (1918–2008) was one of the best-known critics of the Soviet system. The Gulag Archipelago—published in 1973—chronicled his own experiences in the gulags and work camps of the USSR between 1945 and 1956. Solzhenitsyn sought

to expose the devastating effects of the Stalinist era throughout his career. He was awarded the Nobel Prize for Literature in 1970. Rebuilding Russia, his blueprint for reviving the Russian nation, was published as a pamphlet in the Soviet Union in 1990.

REBUILDING RUSSIA

Time has finally run out for communism.

But its concrete edifice has not yet crumbled.

And we must take care not to be crushed beneath its rubble instead of gaining liberty.

At the End of Our Endurance

Can there still be anyone among us who is unaware of our troubles, covered up though they are by mendacious statistics? For seventy

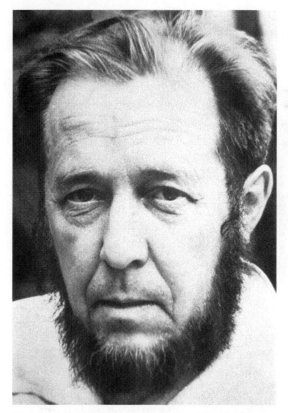

Alexksandr Solzhenitsyn remains one of the best-known critics of the Stalinist regime. Photo by Sergei Guneyev/Time Life Pictures/Getty Images.

years in labored pursuit of a purblind and malignant Marxist-Leninist utopia, we have lost a full third of our population—lives yielded up to the executioner or squandered in the ineptly, almost suicidally waged 'Patriotic War'. We have forfeited our earlier abundance, destroyed the peasant class together with its settlements, deprived the raising of crops of its whole purpose and the soil of its ability to yield a harvest, while flooding the land with man-made seas and swamps. The environs of our cities are befouled by the effluents of our primitive industry, we have poisoned our rivers, lakes, and fish, and today we are obliterating our last resources of clean water, air, and soil, speeding the process by the addition of nuclear death, further supplemented by the storage of Western radioactive wastes for money. Depleting our natural wealth for the sake of grandiose future conquests under a crazed leadership, we have cut down our luxuriant forests and plundered our earth of its incomparable riches—the irreplaceable inheritance of our great-grandchildren—in order to sell them off abroad with uncaring hand. We have saddled our women with backbreaking, impossibly burdensome labor, torn them from their children, and have abandoned the children themselves to disease, brutishness, and a semblance of education. Our health care is utterly neglected, there are no medicines, and we have even forgotten the meaning of a proper diet. Millions lack housing, and a helplessness bred of the absence of personal rights permeates the entire country. And throughout all this we cling to only one thing: that we not be deprived of unlimited drunkenness.

Human beings are so constituted that we can put up with such ruination and madness even when they last a lifetime, but God forbid that anyone should dare to offend or slight our *nationality*! Should that occur, nothing can restrain us in our state of chronic submission: with furious courage we snatch up stones, clubs, spears, and guns and fall upon our neighbors, intent on murder and arson. Such is man: nothing has the capacity to convince us that our hunger, our poverty, our early deaths, the degeneration of our children— that any of these misfortunes can take precedence over national pride.

And that is why, in this attempt to propose some tentative steps toward our recovery and reconstruction, we are forced to begin, not with our unendurable wounds or debilitating suffering, but with a response to such questions as: How will the problem of the nationalities be approached? And within what geographical boundaries shall we heal our afflictions or die? And only thereafter shall we turn to the healing process itself.

Urgent Measures for the Russian Union

After three-quarters of a century we have all grown so poor, so tainted, and so filled with despair, that many of us are ready to give up, and it seems that the intercession of heaven alone can save us.

But miracles do not descend upon those who make no effort on their own behalf.

The fate of our children, our will to live, our millennial history, and the spirit of our ancestors, which must surely have been transferred to us in some fashion—all these things together will help us find the strength to prevail.

We may have been granted no time for reflecting upon the best-suited paths of development, no time to put together a reasoned program, and we may have no choice other than racing around frantically, plugging leaks, while imperative demands close in upon us, each one clamoring for priority. Yet we must preserve presence of mind and the wisdom of circumspection in our choice of initial measures.

I cannot presume to enumerate all these steps by myself; this must be done by a council drawing on the clearest practical minds and the best available energies. All things cry out for help in our present-day economy, and we simply cannot go on without pointing them in the right direction. Our people must urgently be made aware of the meaning of work, after half a century when no one could see any advantage to putting forth an effort—which is why nobody is available to raise crops or tend the cattle. Millions are inhabiting spaces that cannot be called homes, or are forced to spend decades in filthy dormitories. Dire poverty stalks the elderly and the handicapped. Our once magnificent expanses are befouled by industrial dumps and scarred by vehicle tracks due to lack of roads. Nature, disdained so ungratefully by us, is taking its revenge, and the radioactive blotches from Chernobyl and elsewhere are spreading ominously.

On top of all this, must we now prepare to resettle those compatriots who are losing their places of residence? Yes, unavoidably so.

Wherever shall we find the money?

But, then, how long shall we continue supplying and propping up the tyrannical regimes we have implanted the world over, regimes which are incapable of supporting themselves and which are nothing if not insatiable squanderers of our wealth: Cuba, Vietnam, Ethiopia, Angola, North Korea. We mind everyone's business, after all, and the above list is far from complete, with thousands of our 'advisers' roaming about in all sorts of unlikely places. And after all the blood spilled in Afghanistan, isn't it a shame to let that country go? So, should we not dole out money there as well?. . . All this adds up to tens of billions each year.

He who cuts off *all this* at one fell stroke will deserve to be called a patriot and a true statesman.

How long and for what purpose must we keep producing ever more types of offensive weapons? And why the naval presence in all the world's oceans? Do we wish to seize the planet? The cost of all this escalates to hundreds of billions yearly. This, too, must be cut off without delay. The space program can also wait.

There is, furthermore, the preferential supplying of Eastern Europe with our ever-exploited raw materials. But we've had our stint of living together as a 'socialist camp', and enough is enough. We rejoice for the countries of Eastern Europe, may they thrive in freedom, but let them pay for everything at world prices.

But what if this is not enough? Then we must stop reckless capital investment in industries that do not show signs of recovery.

There are, finally, the unimaginably huge assets of the Communist Party, a topic of much recent discussion. They certainly did manage to appropriate a lot of goods from the population over seventy years, and to use it for their pleasure. Of course, there is no way to get back all that has been wasted, scattered, and plundered, but let them at least return what is left: the buildings, resorts, special farms, and publishing houses. . . .

And the whole army of appointive bureaucrats, that parasitic multimillion-strong governing apparatus which inhibits all living forces in the nation—with their high salaries, various benefits, and special stores—we shall feed no more! Let them earn what they can by engaging in useful labor. Under the new order, eighty percent of the ministries and committees will also become unnecessary.

So that the money will come from all these sources.

> **Study Question**
>
> 1. Would the reforms Solzhenitsyn suggested have substantially helped the former Soviet Union to recover?

◇

BENJAMIN BARBER

Benjamin R. Barber, born in 1939, is currently the Kekst Professor of Civil Society at the University of Maryland. He has been active in a number of non-governmental organizations dedicated to supporting democracy. From 1969–2001, he was a member of the Department of Political Science at Rutgers University. He was also an external advisor to President Bill Clinton and Vice-President Al Gore, and has consulted on and directed a number of pieces for television on political topics. Barber is the author of fifteen books, including Strong Democracy *and* An Aristocracy of Everyone. Jihad versus McWorld *was published as a monograph in 1995.*

UN Protection Force in Vukovar, Croatia, July 1992. The limited mandate of the UN force crippled its ability to contain the ethnic unrest in the Balkans. Courtesy of the United Nations Photo Library (159206 UN/DPI/S. Whitehouse).

Jihad versus McWorld

Just beyond the horizon of current events lie two possible political futures—both bleak, neither democratic. The first is a retribalization of large swaths of humankind by war and bloodshed: a threatened Lebanonization of national states in which culture is pitted against culture, people against people, tribe against tribe—a Jihad in the name of a hundred narrowly conceived faiths against every kind of interdependence, every kind of artificial social cooperation and civic mutuality. The second is being borne in on us by the onrush of economic and ecological forces that demand integration and uniformity and that mesmerize the world with fast music, fast computers, and fast food—with MTV, Macintosh, and McDonald's, pressing nations into one commercially homogenous global network: one McWorld tied together by technology, ecology, communications, and commerce. The planet is falling precipitantly apart AND coming reluctantly together at the very same moment.

These two tendencies are sometimes visible in the same countries at the same instant: thus Yugoslavia, clamoring just recently to join the New Europe, is exploding into fragments; India is trying to live up to its reputation as the world's largest integral democracy while powerful new fundamentalist parties like the Hindu nationalist Bharatiya Janata Party, along with nationalist assassins, are imperiling its hard-won unity. States are breaking up or joining up: the Soviet Union has disappeared almost overnight, its parts forming new unions with one another or with like-minded nationalities in neighboring states. The old interwar national state based on territory and political sovereignty looks to be a mere transitional development.

The tendencies of what I am here calling the forces of Jihad and the forces of McWorld operate with equal strength in opposite directions, the one driven by parochial hatreds, the other by universalizing markets, the one re-creating ancient subnational and ethnic borders from within, the other making national borders porous from without. They have one thing in common: neither offers much hope to citizens looking for practical ways to govern themselves democratically. If the global future is to pit Jihad's centrifugal whirlwind against McWorld's centripetal black hole, the outcome is unlikely to be democratic—or so I will argue.

McWorld, or the Globalization of Politics

Four imperatives make up the dynamic of McWorld: a market imperative, a resource imperative, an information-technology imperative, and an ecological imperative. By shrinking the world and diminishing the salience of national borders, these imperatives have in combination achieved a considerable victory over factiousness and particularism, and not least of all over their most virulent traditional form—nationalism. It is the realists who are now Europeans, the utopians who dream nostalgically of a resurgent England or Germany, perhaps even a resurgent Wales or Saxony. Yesterday's wishful cry for one world has yielded to the reality of McWorld.

THE MARKET IMPERATIVE. Marxist and Leninist theories of imperialism assumed that the quest for ever-expanding markets would in time compel nation-based capitalist economies to push against national boundaries in search of an international economic imperium. Whatever else has happened to the scientistic predictions of Marxism, in this domain they have proved farsighted. All national economies are now vulnerable to the inroads of larger, transnational markets within which trade is free, currencies are convertible, access to banking is open, and contracts are enforceable under law. In Europe, Asia, Africa, the South

Pacific, and the Americas such markets are eroding national sovereignty and giving rise to entities—international banks, trade associations, transnational lobbies like OPEC and Greenpeace, world news services like CNN and the BBC, and multinational corporations that increasingly lack a meaningful national identity—that neither reflect nor respect nationhood as an organizing or regulative principle.

The market imperative has also reinforced the quest for international peace and stability, requisites of an efficient international economy. Markets are enemies of parochialism, isolation, fractiousness, war. Market psychology attenuates the psychology of ideological and religious cleavages and assumes a concord among producers and consumers—categories that ill fit narrowly conceived national or religious cultures. Shopping has little tolerance for blue laws, whether dictated by pub-closing British paternalism, Sabbath-observing Jewish Orthodox fundamentalism, or no-Sunday-liquor-sales Massachusetts puritanism. In the context of common markets, international law ceases to be a vision of justice and becomes a workaday framework for getting things done—enforcing contracts, ensuring that governments abide by deals, regulating trade and currency relations, and so forth.

Common markets demand a common language, as well as a common currency, and they produce common behaviors of the kind bred by cosmopolitan city life everywhere. Commercial pilots, computer programmers, international bankers, media specialists, oil riggers, entertainment celebrities, ecology experts, demographers, accountants, professors, athletes—these compose a new breed of men and women for whom religion, culture, and nationality can seem only marginal elements in a working identity. Although sociologists of everyday life will no doubt continue to distinguish a Japanese from an American mode, shopping has a common

signature throughout the world. Cynics might even say that some of the recent revolutions in Eastern Europe have had as their true goal not liberty and the right to vote but well-paying jobs and the right to shop (although the vote is proving easier to acquire than consumer goods). The market imperative is, then, plenty powerful; but, notwithstanding some of the claims made for 'democratic capitalism', it is not identical with the democratic imperative.

THE RESOURCE IMPERATIVE. Democrats once dreamed of societies whose political autonomy rested firmly on economic independence. The Athenians idealized what they called autarky, and tried for a while to create a way of life simple and austere enough to make the polis genuinely self-sufficient. To be free meant to be independent of any other community or polis. Not even the Athenians were able to achieve autarky, however: human nature, it turns out, is dependency. By the time of Pericles, Athenian politics was inextricably bound up with a flowering empire held together by naval power and commerce—an empire that, even as it appeared to enhance Athenian might, ate away at Athenian independence and autarky. Master and slave, it turned out, were bound together by mutual insufficiency.

The dream of autarky briefly engrossed nineteenth-century America as well, for the underpopulated, endlessly bountiful land, the cornucopia of natural resources, and the natural barriers of a continent walled in by two great seas led many to believe that America could be a world unto itself. Given this past, it has been harder for Americans than for most to accept the inevitability of interdependence. But the rapid depletion of resources even in a country like ours, where they once seemed inexhaustible, and the maldistribution of arable soil and mineral resources on the planet, leave even the wealthiest societies ever more resource-dependent and many other nations in permanently desperate straits.

Every nation, it turns out, needs something

another nation has; some nations have almost nothing they need.

THE INFORMATION-TECHNOLOGY IMPERATIVE. Enlightenment science and the technologies derived from it are inherently universalizing. They entail a quest for descriptive principles of general application, a search for universal solutions to particular problems, and an unswerving embrace of objectivity and impartiality.

Scientific progress embodies and depends on open communication, a common discourse rooted in rationality, collaboration, and an easy and regular flow and exchange of information. Such ideals can be hypocritical covers for power-mongering by elites, and they may be shown to be wanting in many other ways, but they are entailed by the very idea of science and they make science and globalization practical allies.

Business, banking, and commerce all depend on information flow and are facilitated by new communication technologies. The hardware of these technologies tends to be systemic and integrated—computer, television, cable, satellite, laser, fiber-optic, and microchip technologies combining to create a vast interactive communications and information network that can potentially give every person on earth access to every other person, and make every datum, every byte, available to every set of eyes. If the automobile was, as George Ball once said (when he gave his blessing to a Fiat factory in the Soviet Union during the Cold War), 'an ideology on four wheels', then electronic telecommunication and information systems are an ideology at 186,000 miles per second—which makes for a very small planet in a very big hurry. Individual cultures speak particular languages; commerce and science increasingly speak English; the whole world speaks logarithms and binary mathematics.

Moreover, the pursuit of science and technology asks for, even compels, open societies. Satellite footprints do not respect national borders; telephone wires penetrate the most closed societies. With photocopying and then fax machines having infiltrated Soviet universities and samizdat literary circles in the eighties, and computer modems having multiplied like rabbits in communism's bureaucratic warrens thereafter, glasnost could not be far behind. In their social requisites, secrecy and science are enemies. . . .

THE ECOLOGICAL IMPERATIVE. The impact of globalization on ecology is a cliché even to world leaders who ignore it. We know well enough that the German forests can be destroyed by Swiss and Italians driving gas-guzzlers fueled by leaded gas. We also know that the planet can be asphyxiated by greenhouse gases because Brazilian farmers want to be part of the twentieth century and are burning down tropical rain forests to clear a little land to plough, and because Indonesians make a living out of converting their lush jungle into toothpicks for fastidious Japanese diners, upsetting the delicate oxygen balance and in effect puncturing our global lungs. Yet this ecological consciousness has meant not only greater awareness but also greater inequality, as modernized nations try to slam the door behind them, saying to developing nations, 'The world cannot afford your modernization; ours has wrung it dry!'

Each of the four imperatives just cited is transnational, transideological, and transcultural. Each applies impartially to Catholics, Jews, Muslims, Hindus, and Buddhists; to democrats and totalitarians; to capitalists and socialists. The Enlightenment dream of a universal rational society has to a remarkable degree been realized—but in a form that is commercialized, homogenized, depoliticized, bureaucratized, and, of course, radically incomplete, for the movement toward McWorld is in competition with forces of global breakdown, national dissolution, and centrifugal corruption. These forces, working in the opposite direction, are the essence of what I call Jihad.

Jihad, or the Lebanonization of the World

OPEC, the World Bank, the United Nations, the International Red Cross, the multinational corporation . . . there are scores of institutions that reflect globalization. But they often appear as ineffective reactors to the world's real actors: national states and, to an ever greater degree, subnational factions in permanent rebellion against uniformity and integration—even the kind represented by universal law and justice. The headlines feature these players regularly: they are cultures, not countries; parts, not wholes; sects, not religions; rebellious factions and dissenting minorities at war not just with globalism but with the traditional nation-state. Kurds, Basques, Puerto Ricans, Ossetians, East Timoreans, Québécois, the Catholics of Northern Ireland, Abkhasians, Kurile Islander Japanese, the Zulus of Inkatha, Catalonians, Tamils, and, of course, Palestinians—people without countries, inhabiting nations not their own, seeking smaller worlds within borders that will seal them off from modernity.

A powerful irony is at work here. Nationalism was once a force of integration and unification, a movement aimed at bringing together disparate clans, tribes, and cultural fragments under new, assimilationist flags. But as Ortega y Gasset noted more than sixty years ago, having won its victories, nationalism changed its strategy. In the 1920s, and again today, it is more often a reactionary and divisive force, pulverizing the very nations it once helped cement together. The force that creates nations is 'inclusive', Ortega wrote in *The Revolt of the Masses*. 'In periods of consolidation, nationalism has a positive value, and is a lofty standard. But in Europe everything is more than consolidated, and nationalism is nothing but a mania.' . . .

This mania has left the post-Cold War world smoldering with hot wars; the international scene is little more unified than it was at the end of the Great War, in Ortega's own time. There were more than thirty wars in progress last year, most of them ethnic, racial, tribal, or religious in character, and the list of unsafe regions doesn't seem to be getting any shorter. Some new world order!

The aim of many of these small-scale wars is to redraw boundaries, to implode states and resecure parochial identities: to escape McWorld's dully insistent imperatives. The mood is that of Jihad: war not as an instrument of policy but as an emblem of identity, an expression of community, an end in itself. Even where there is no shooting war, there is fractiousness, secession, and the quest for ever smaller communities. Add to the list of dangerous countries those at risk: In Switzerland and Spain, Jurassian and Basque separatists still argue the virtues of ancient identities, sometimes in the language of bombs. Hyperdisintegration in the former Soviet Union may well continue unabated— not just a Ukraine independent from the Soviet Union but a Bessarabian Ukraine independent from the Ukrainian republic; not just Russia severed from the defunct union but Tatarstan severed from Russia. Yugoslavia makes even the disunited, ex-Soviet, non-socialist republics that were once the Soviet Union look integrated, its sectarian fatherlands springing up within factional motherlands like weeds within weeds within weeds. Kurdish independence would threaten the territorial integrity of four Middle Eastern nations. . . .

The passing of communism has torn away the thin veneer of internationalism (workers of the world unite!) to reveal ethnic prejudices that are not only ugly and deep-seated but increasingly murderous. Europe's old scourge, anti-Semitism, is back with a vengeance, but it is only one of many antagonisms. It appears all too easy to throw the historical gears into reverse and pass from a Communist dictatorship back into a tribal state.

Among the tribes, religion is also a battlefield. ('Jihad' is a rich word whose generic meaning is 'struggle'—usually the struggle of the soul to avert evil. Strictly applied to religious war, it is used only in reference to battles where the faith is under assault, or battles against a government that denies the practice of Islam. My use here is rhetorical, but does follow both journalistic practice and history.) Remember the Thirty Years War? Whatever forms of Enlightenment universalism might once have come to grace such historically related forms of monotheism as Judaism, Christianity, and Islam, in many of their modern incarnations they are parochial rather than cosmopolitan, angry rather than loving, proselytizing rather than ecumenical, zealous rather than rationalist, sectarian rather than deistic, ethnocentric rather than universalizing. As a result, like the new forms of hypernationalism, the new expressions of religious fundamentalism are fractious and pulverizing, never integrating. This is religion as the Crusaders knew it: a battle to the death for souls that if not saved will be forever lost. . . .

> ### Study Question
>
> 1. Based upon recent events, which scenario—'Jihad' or 'McWorld'—seems more likely in the twenty-first century?

ROBERT KAPLAN

Balkan Ghosts *was the product of Robert Kaplan's extensive travels throughout the region in the 1980s and early 1990s. The following excerpt comprises two separate extracts from his monograph. The first recounts a conversation between Kaplan (b. 1952) and 'Mother Tatiana', a Serbian nun at the monastery of Grachanitsa, in 1989. Mother Tatiana's comments predate the Yugoslavian crises of the 1990s. The second extract from Kaplan's book examines the complex history of Moldova. Here the author focuses on the deep hatreds that exist in this region, and attempts to understand their origin.*

OLD SERBIA AND ALBANIA: BALKAN 'WEST BANK'

Because the Serbs were spread out over wooded and mountainous land that was difficult to subdue, and because they were geographically farther removed from Turkey than either Bulgaria or Greece, the Ottoman yoke was never as complete in Serbia as it was in those countries. Moving pockets of resistance always existed, particularly in the black granite fastnesses of neighboring Montenegro. But Serbia was still not far enough away.

In Serbian legend, the Nemanjic kingdom sacrificed itself to the Turkish hordes in order to gain a new kingdom in heaven; meanwhile, here on earth, Serbia's sacrifice allowed Italy and Central Europe to stay alive and to continue to develop.

'The greatness of Italy and the other nations of Europe was constructed over our bones,' said Mother Tatiana bitterly. 'Come,' she said, beckoning, 'I will tell you about our suffering.'

I entered a typical Turkish building, with madder roof tiles, yellow stone walls, and overhanging wooden balconies adorned with plants. Mother Tatiana labeled it 'typical Serbian' architecture. In Bulgaria, such buildings were considered 'typical Bulgarian revivalist' architecture; in

Greece, 'typical Greek' architecture. The salon was dark. I sat freezing with my coat on, my feet on a Turkish-style rug. Mother Tatiana's black nun's habit appeared in silhouette against white curtains. Another sister poured thick, heavily sugared Turkish coffee from a cylindrical gold metal beaker. Next, the sister poured the monastery's clear homemade plum brandy into glasses. Mother Tatiana slugged back a brandy. Then her large peasant's hands once more came up out of the darkness:

'I am not the Prophet Samuel, but it would be better to die honestly than to live in shame. . . . '

'I am a good Christian, but I'll not turn the other cheek if some Albanian plucks out the eyes of a fellow Serb, or rapes a little girl, or castrates a twelve-year-old Serbian boy.' She knifed the air over her thighs with her hand. 'You know about that incident, don't you?'

I did not but I nodded anyway.

Mother Tatiana put her elbows on the table and leaned closer to me. My eyes adjusted to the darkness, and for the first time I got a good look at her face. She had a strong lusty appearance, with high cheekbones and fiery, maternal eyes. She was a handsome old woman who clearly was once quite attractive. Her eyes, while fiery, also appeared strangely unfocused, as though blotted out by superstition, like the saints' eyes in the church. Her white fingertips flickered to the rhythm of her words. I recalled what John Reed wrote after a journey through Serbia in 1915: 'The rapid, flexible eloquence of the Serbian language struck on our ears like a jet of fresh water.'

'Did you know,' said Mother Tatiana, 'that these young Albanian boys actually dropped their pants in front of the other sisters?'

I nodded again.

'Serbia is being bled dry by these people. It's a lie that they are poor and unemployed. Why, they list their dying grandfathers as out of work. They are all smugglers and they have lots of foreign exchange stashed away. They only dress poor and dirty because that is their habit.

'The Albanians, you know, want to conquer the world by outbreeding us. You know that no *hodja* [an Albanian Moslem cleric] will come to the house of a family that doesn't have at least five children? And that Azen Vlasi [an Albanian political leader], he is just a lecher who screws with the local whore.

'And what is your nationality?' she asked me suddenly.

'I'm an American,' I answered.

'I know that, but all Americans are something else. What are you? You're dark. You don't look like real Americans are supposed to look.'

'I'm a Jew.'

'Hah, ha. I like Jews, but I still want to baptize you.' She laughed, her face exuding a protective kindness. 'I admire the ladies of Israel who carry guns. If I were only forty again I'd carry a gun. There is no faith in Yugoslavia. Only here in Serbia is there real faith. . . . I know that I am a strong Serbian nationalist. Things will get worse between us and the Albanians—you'll see. There can be no reconciliation.'

. . .

To Mother Tatiana and to many other Serbs, Tito's Yugoslavia signified—like the former Turkish Empire—just another anti-Serbian plot. This was because Yugoslav nationalism, as Tito (a half-Croat, half-Slovene) defined it, meant undercutting the power of the numerically dominant Serbs in order to placate other groups, particularly the Croats and the Albanians.

By giving the Albanians their own autonomous province, Kossovo, and by placing this province within the Yugoslav Republic of Serbia, Tito thought he had reconciled the aspirations of both the Albanians and the Serbs. The Serbs thought differently. *Why should these Muslim foreigners, who came only 300 years ago to Old Serbia, the historic heartland of our nation, have autonomy there? Never!*

Communism poured acid in this wound. It dictated that the Serbs must feel ashamed of everything in their collective past that came before the rise of Tito; that such personages as Milutin,[1] Dushan,[2] and Lazar[3] were 'imperialists'; that the Serbs killed along with Lazar at Kossovo Polje were guilty of 'reactionary nationalism'.

On the eve of battle, Knez Lazar warned:

Whoever is a Serb and of Serbian birth,
And who does not come to Kossovo Polje
to do battle against the Turks,
Let him have neither a male
nor a female offspring,
Let him have no crop, . . .

I saw these words were written on a block of grim, blood-colored stone, about 100 feet high,

well-socketed on a wind-swept hill overlooking Kossovo Polje. The monument rested on a platform surrounded by bullet-shaped cement towers inscribed with a sword and the numbers '1389–1989'. Atop each tower was a fresh laurel wreath.

In 1987 an ambitious Serbian Communist party leader, Slobodan Milosevic, came to this area on the 28 June anniversary of Lazar's defeat. He pointed his finger in the distance— at what Mother Tatiana labeled *out there*—and, as legend now has it, pledged: 'They'll never do this to you again. Never again will anyone defeat you.'

At that moment, as the crowd roared, the Serbian revolt against the Yugoslav federation began.

Moldova: 'Conditioned to Hate'

Jassy often appears on maps as 'Iasi', pronounced '*YASH*' by Romanians. Sitwell [Sacheverell Sitwell, author of the travel narrative *Roumanian Journey*] noted that 'Jassy is the town, in all Roumania, which occurs most often in history.'

Since the Middle Ages, Jassy has been the most important town in Moldavia,[4] a territory that stands lengthwise against the Ukrainian steppe with barely a foothill for protection, as though it were a line of naked prisoners facing an icy wind. Jassy witnessed six invasions by Russians in the eighteenth and nineteenth centuries. In the 1850s, when Bucharest was still a small town, Jassy was a hotbed of Romanian nationalism. Here, in 1859, Alexandru Ion Cuza proclaimed the first Romanian state of modern times. In the 1870s and 1880s, Romania's greatest poet, Mihai Eminescu, lived in Jassy and wrote 'Satire III', about 'long and hook-nosed' foreigners:

This poison froth, this dung-heap, this foul and filthy brood
Have they indeed inherited our nation's masterhood!

Nicholae Iorga, Romania's greatest intellectual, who in his old age would be tortured to death by the fascist Legionnaires for not being sufficiently nationalistic and anti-Semitic, grew up in Jassy at the same time Eminescu was writing his poetry. And Lupescu grew up here a short time later, at the turn of the century. During World War I, Queen Marie and the other members of the royal family took refuge in Jassy after the Germans captured Bucharest. Between 1916 and 1918, Jassy served as the capital of free Romania. After the war, Professor A.L. Cuza (no relation to the Cuza who had declared independence in 1859) taught at the university in Jassy. Professor Cuza would later brag that he had given the first anti-Semitic speech the year Hitler was born (1889).

One of Professor Cuza's disciples was Corneliu Zelea Codreanu, the founder of the fascist Legion of the Archangel Michael. Codreanu began his political career in Jassy in the 1920s, organizing anti-Semitic demonstrations on the campus of Cuza University (named after the Cuza who had proclaimed independence).

Behind much of this hate lay a lingering fear and sense of vulnerability. Until 1918, Jassy lay only ten miles from the Russian border of the Prut River. On the other bank of the Prut lay the eastern half of Moldavia, known as Bessarabia. . . In the peace settlement that followed World War I, Romania reclaimed not only Bessarabia, but also a northern fragment of Moldavia from the dismembered Austro-Hungarian Empire. But the fact of having an additional fifty miles of territory between it and the Soviet border—now demarcated by the Dniester River instead of the Prut—was not enough to dampen the nationalist fires that burned in Jassy, after World War I, stoked as they were by the democratization of Romanian party politics, the worldwide economic depression, the rise of fascism across Europe, and the misrule of King Carol II in the 1930s.

In June 1940, Stalin grabbed back Bessarabia; for the next five decades, the border was once again moved to the Prut, just over Jassy's horizon. In the wake of the December 1989 revolution, Jassy's residents were finally free—for the first time in half a century—to express their feelings about all of this. . . .

'Romania is too far off to be helped by the West. The messier and bloodier the disintegration of the Russian Empire is, the better for us. That's the only way for us to become democratic and to be reunited with our brothers in Bessarabia.'

Petru Bejan was an editor of *Timpul* (The *Times*), a weekly newspaper born a few weeks after the December 1989 revolution and published by students at Jassy's Cuza University. *Timpul's* masthead bore the religious pronouncement *Adverat a inviat* ('Truly He has risen'). The issue

Bejan gave me to inspect contained several articles about the addition of Bessarabia to Romania in 1918 and about the 'cultural genocide' perpetrated by the Russians in Bessarabia since World War II. There was also an article about Orthodox saints and a column devoted to Eminescu's poetry.

Bejan told me that a 'second revolution' was necessary in Romania, in order to root out 'all traces of coercion, bureaucracy, and socialism. They can't buy us off with coffee, eggs, and meat.' Bejan claimed that General Ion Antonescu, the pro-Nazi Conducator[5] and World War II ruler of Romania, was a patriot who had always acted in Romania's best interests. . . .

Because of the country's obscure geographical position in Europe's back-of-beyond, events in Romania, no matter how terrible, have always assumed a remote, sideshow quality to people in the West. The Holocaust in Romania was no exception to this rule. Countess Waldeck and the other journalists left the Athenee Palace in January 1941, but history here continued its sinister march, even though there were no longer Western observers to write about it.

Having used his troops and tanks to smash the putsch attempted by the Legion of the Archangel Michael in Bucharest in January 1941, Conducator Antonescu's next order of business was to recover Bessarabia, which Stalin had unilaterally annexed seven months before, in June 1940, under Carol II's watch. This could only be done through an alliance with Nazi Germany. Antonescu made it clear to Hitler that Romanian troops would enthusiastically join in an invasion of the Soviet Union if liberating Bessarabia were part of the deal. The Nazi invasion of the Soviet Union began on 22 June 1941. On June 25, as the Romanian army crossed the Prut to liberate Bessarabia, some Romanian soldiers deserted and took refuge in local houses—including, perhaps, some Jewish houses. A wild rumor spread through Jassy that, in fact, all the deserting soldiers were being protected by Jewish families. Furthermore, these soldiers were said to be not Romanians at all, but Soviet paratroopers who had landed during the night on the outskirts of the city. The rumor, false in every particular, ignited a pogrom. Over the next few days, the Romanian army killed 4,000 Jews in Jassy and the surrounding villages. The army then evacuated an additional 8,000 Jews from the Jassy region. The soldiers crammed them all into padlocked cattle cars, which, in the general confusion, and absence of clear orders, rolled around the Moldavian countryside for several days, until all 8,000 occupants died of thirst and asphyxiation. . . .

In 1941 and 1942, Antonescu oversaw the deportation of 185,000 Jews from Bessarabia and the northern tip of Moldavia (also recently liberated from the Russians) to Transdniestria, where forward units of the Romanian army were setting up the only non-German-run extermination camps in Europe.[6] From late 1941 until the middle of 1942, in this obscure and remote theater of the war, the Romanian army murdered every one of these people, stripping them naked, and shooting them in subzero temperatures. On a few occasions, when soldiers were low on bullets, they shot only the adults and buried the children alive.

It was too much even for Adolf Eichmann, the SS officer in charge of carrying out the extermination of European Jewry. In early 1942, Eichmann pleaded with Antonescu to halt the killings temporarily so that the job could be done more cleanly by Einsatzgruppen (special mobile SS murder squads) after the Nazis completed the conquest of Ukraine, which Eichmann assumed would take only a few more months. But the Romanians were in a killing frenzy. Unfortunately for the Jews of Bessarabia and the extreme north of Moldavia, Antonescu ignored Eichmann.

By the late summer of 1942, however, the Romanian-run extermination camps in Transdniestria began to close down. Antonescu, whatever his faults, always had a sharp nose

for the political winds just over the horizon. He had early understood the necessity for an alliance with Nazi Germany. And later, in 1944, he would foresee his own downfall. Now, just as the siege of Stalingrad was getting underway in September 1942—a turning point in the war—Antonescu began considering the possibility that Hitler might not win after all. Building bridges to the West required introducing a radical shift in Romania's Jewish policy, Antonescu realized. As the Soviet army, in 1943, was rolling back all the territory it had lost to Romania, first in Transdniestria and then in Bessarabia, Antonescu began building a reputation among international Jewish organizations as a pro-Nazi leader who would cooperate with attempts to save Jews and would even help smuggle them to Palestine.

Political considerations, though, cannot adequately explain this incredible behavioral leap. The historian Raul Hilberg, who documented the Holocaust in Romania in his 1961 book, *The Destruction of the European Jews*, asserted that in no other country during World War II, except Germany itself, did national character play such a role in determining the fate of the Jews as in Romania.

Sadly, Romanian history has been a long and continuing hustle—the making of one desperate deal over the head of another in order to stave off disaster. Antonescu's pattern of actions toward the Jews differed little from the one he and his countrymen exhibited toward the Nazis and the Russians. As Hilberg pointed out, Romanian soldiers quickly earned a reputation within the Nazi military hierarchy as brave and, indeed, ferocious troops. But in 1944, when victorious Russian troops crossed the Prut into Romania proper, Romania not only switched sides to fight the Nazis, but did so with enthusiasm. Romanian troops quickly impressed Allied officials with their aggressiveness in fighting their former German and Hungarian allies in Transylvania, a territory the Romanians now sought desperately to recover: just as they had earlier sought to recover Bessarabia. . . .

Whatever their views on World War II history, Petru Bejan . . . and the other students at Cuza University in Jassy that I interviewed displayed no current animosity toward Jews. Their anger was now directed against Arabs. . . .

'We hate the Arab students. We know that our civilization—despite the regime—is a European one. But the Arabs come from a lesser civilization and have no respect for ours. They just bought and humiliated us and our women. They buy off their professors, too. Everybody at the university knows that the Arabs are the weakest students. . . .'

I pointed out that Romanians should not judge Arab culture by the students who were sent to Romania, since Arab countries have always sent their best students to the West, and the weakest and least serious ones to Eastern Europe.

I was not believed. 'The Arabs oppress us,' one student shouted back at me.

Adrian Poruciuc, an assistant professor at Cuza University and an expert on Romanian folklore [explained]. . . .

'In Moldavia especially,' Poruciuc went on, 'Romanians have been caught in the pincers of three empires: Austria-Hungary, Ottoman Turkey, and Russia—czarist or Communist, it made no difference. The people here have been conditioned to hate.'

Notes

1. King Milutin expanded Serbia into a substantial Orthodox Christian empire at the beginning of the fourteenth century. Milutin financed the building of churches and monasteries across the Balkans, including the monasteries of Pec and Grachanitsa.

2. Stefan Dushan ascended the Serbian throne in 1331. Dushan extended the kingdom to the Croatian border in the north, the Adriatic in the west, and the Aegean Sea in the south.

3. Knez Lazar was chosen to lead Serbia in 1371. Meanwhile the Turkish advance into the Balkans continued, culminating in the battle at Kossovo Polje in 1389. Lazar was executed during the Turkish conquest but Serbian legend holds that Lazar chose to build a new Serbian kingdom in heaven. His death thus preserved the Serbian kingdom for all eternity.

4. The historical territory of Moldavia is now divided between Ukraine, Romania, and the Republic of Moldova—a land-locked country in Eastern Europe. Iasi is in Romania, close to the Moldovan border.

5. The title 'Conducator' means 'leader'.

6. The Jasenovac concentration camp complex, created by the Croat Ustaše in August 1941, was also non-German-run.

Study Question

1. Is it possible to overcome generations of hatred, such as those described above, in order to build a unified, functioning society?

TIPS FOR ANALYSIS

Chronological Context

What other events were taking place as the author was writing the document? Of which of these events would the author have been readily aware? The context in which a document is written is a vitally important factor, both in understanding the author's motivation and the influences shaping the events under discussion.

WEB RESOURCES

US Intelligence and the End of the Cold War
https://www.cia.gov/library/center-for-the-study-of-intelligence/kent-csi/docs/v44i3a02p.htm
Cold War International History Project
http://wilsoncenter.org/index.cfm?topic_id=1409&fuseaction=topics.home
Communism: End of an Era
http://news.bbc.co.uk/hi/english/static/special_report/1999/09/99/iron_curtain/default.htm
Harvard Project on Cold War History
http://www.fas.harvard.edu/~hpcws

RECOMMENDED READING

Milan Kundera, *Ignorance: A Novel* (New York: Perennial, 2003). The central themes of *Ignoranc*, set in post-communist Prague, concern the experience of exile and homecoming, and the nature of memory and identity. As in his other works, Kundera focuses on the nature of perceptions and their impact on reality.

Andrei Makine, *Requiem for a Lost Empire* (Washington, DC: Washington Square Press, 2003). Makine's novel spans the entire history of the Soviet Empire, from the Bolshevik Revolution in 1917 to the fall of communism. The narrative is told over three generations of fathers and sons and their experiences of collectivization, the Second World War, the Cold War and its intrigues, and finally, the last years of the USSR.

Ralph Peters, *Flames of Heaven* (Mechanicsburg, PA: Stackpole Books, 2003). Peters's novel examines life during the final years of the failing Soviet Union through the eyes of a disaffected Latvian artist and a decorated veteran of the Afghan war. The story moves from East Germany to Latvia to Uzbekistan amidst political turmoil and the potential threat of Islamic fundamentalism.

Irene Zabytko, *The Sky Unwashed* (Chapel Hill, NC: Algonquin Books, 2000). *The Sky Unwashed* is a documentary novel set amidst the 1986 disaster at Chernobyl and the chaos that followed in small villages across Ukraine. Disorganized evacuations lead many survivors to return home to the contaminated villages, frustrated with the bureaucratic response and struggling to find a way to survive.

RECOMMENDED VIEWING

Czlowiek Z Zelaza [*Man of Iron*] (Poland, 1981). Director: Andrzej Wajda. In a combination of documentary and fictional footage, actors and real political figures (Lech Walesa appears briefly) tell the story of the Gdansk shipyard labour activists and the formation of the Solidarity movement.

Red Dawn (USA, 1984). Director: John Milius. *Red Dawn*, though built on an absurd plot involving a joint Soviet–Cuban invasion of the United States, captures much of the renewed anti-communist paranoia of the Reagan era.

Wag the Dog (USA, 1997). Director: Barry Levinson. In the post–Cold War world an American president attempts to divert attention from an impending scandal by creating a fictitious war with Albania. Levinson's film provides a powerful commentary on the power of media spin-doctors, the gullibility of the average citizen, and the nation's general lack of geopolitical knowledge.

People Power (UK/USA, 1999). Director: Angus McQueen/WGBH/BBC (Documentary). This documentary begins in the 1970s as the weaknesses of communism became evident. It also looks at the rise of the Solidarity Movement, as well as the emergence of Mikhail Gorbachev and his decision not to resist the popular uprisings in the Eastern bloc.

Good Bye Lenin (Germany, 2002). Director: Wolfgang Becker. This insightful film is set in East Germany during the fall of communism. As Westernization rushes into the East Bloc, one man attempts to maintain the illusion of life under the old socialist regime in order to preserve his mother's health. Becker underscores the divide between East and West, while reflecting on the complex question of identity in newly reunified Germany.

The Fog of War (USA, 2003). Director: Errol Morris (Documentary). This documentary, based in part on Robert McNamara's memoir *In Retrospect*, tells the story of President John F. Kennedy's former Secretary of Defense. The film reflects on the beliefs of the early 1960s on Vietnam, the subsequent realization that the United States had made a number of key mistakes, and the lessons that must be learned from this and applied to future foreign policy.

CHAPTER EIGHTEEN

STATE BUILDING
AND ITS DISCONTENTS

◇

In the latter part of the twentieth century, numerous obstacles to economic prosperity and social and political stability remained. In the southern hemisphere, population growth undermined the achievements of even the most successful of states. In many areas of the world, the political systems imposed by western colonizers came to be seen as increasingly inadequate by the new generation of leaders who rose to power in the 1970s and 1980s. However, the quest for new, more authentic political structures created civil wars, governmental instability, and often led to repeated foreign interventions. Elsewhere, old antagonisms re-emerged in the wake of the Cold War, new conflicts were generated by the pressures of failed development schemes, and new diseases took a tremendous toll on the most productive part of the population—young, working aged adults.

After the end of the Cold War, alliance partners shifted and resources were reallocated, leaving many nations economically unstable. The political consequences of this could be seen clearly in nations such as Yugoslavia where competing nationalisms, fuelled by historical hatreds, eventually tore the country apart. Even states with ample resources, global support, and immense promise—such as the newly independent South African state—soon ran into the problems created by the need to address the tremendous imbalance of political and economic power in the country in the wake of the *Apartheid* era.

The documents in this section examine some of the challenges of the latter part of the twentieth century, as well as some of the solutions proposed by political leaders and their consequences. Indira Gandhi discusses the impact of over-population and some possible, if controversial, programs to deal with India's burgeoning population. Syed Abul A'ala Maududi contemplate the replacement of the western political and economic system imposed on Pakistan with a modern Islamic state. Mu'ammar Qadhafi's *Green Book* proposes a socialist system of land ownership as a means to overcome both the inequitable distribution of resources as well as basic human greed.

HIV/AIDS infection rate in Africa, 2003. Note the profound impact on sub-Saharan Africa. Reprinted by permission of the African Renewal. UN.

Turning to sub-Saharan Africa, Nelson Mandela's State of the Nation Address in 1994 captures both the optimism and the challenges facing the South African state as it broke free of *Apartheid* and entered into an era of majority rule. Philip Gourevitch chronicles the descent of the Rwandan state into a period of genocide and civil war. Stephen Lewis provides insight into the depth of the HIV/AIDS epidemic. Finally, Robert Kaplan predicts a bleak future for nations where underdevelopment, civil war, overpopulation, and a lack of resources predominate.

◇

RAMI CHHABRA

Rami Chhabra is a prominent Indian journalist who has been a strong advocate for the rights of women. She reported on many of Indira Gandhi's press *conferences and was appointed by Prime Minister Rajiv Gandhi to the Ministry of Health and Family Welfare in 1986. She has also served on a number of committees on population control. The interview which follows took place in September 1980 after Indira Gandhi returned for a third term as prime minister and after her highly controversial attempt to impose a program of mandatory sterilization in the mid-1970s.*

AN INTERVIEW WITH INDIRA GANDHI

Q. Madam Prime Minister, what priorities does your Government accord to the Family Planning Programme?

A. Our Government was the very first in the whole world which took it up as an official programme and that shows how important it is to us. As you know our population has grown enormously; we add an Australia every year.

Q. Mrs Gandhi, do you see any alternative for economic viability for the nation in the face of failure to curb population growth rate to a manageable proportion?

A. The real answer, of course, is development from both angles: first the development to provide what the people need, to open up areas, and, secondly, because development itself curbs families. I mean people who reach a particular standard are more conscious of their duty to the child. That is, they want something more for their children than they had; and, therefore, they themselves think about smaller families. But ultimately, of course, size of the population has to be tackled at various levels not just through development, but through persuasion of the people.

Q. Because development itself would be denied if we cannot control the situation to the manageable proportions.

A. Well, it is a bit of a circle. But, for instance, take places like Punjab where there has been agricultural progress or industrial areas or even a place like Kerala which has educational progress, there the birth-rate has gone down.

Q. Mrs Gandhi, would you say that even more important in its place within the economic perspective is the question of family planning being the primary concern of the fundamental right of the woman not to be denied options in her life and of the child not to be born into a situation where it is just in a position of neglect?

A. Why leave out the father? I agree with the view that [the] human rights aspect of it is very important, especially of course for the woman because she has the entire burden of child bearing and child rearing and yet her opinion is hardly ever asked for; nor is there much consideration for her welfare. And, unfortunately the child is [the] one who suffers from this. Today birth should be a matter of choice [by] both parents so that they feel responsible for the child and give it its due rights.

US President Richard Nixon meets with Indira Gandhi in August 1969. Courtesy of the National Archives, Richard Nixon Library.

Q. But, given the importance of family planning, would you say, like national security, it should be part of the minimum national consensus, i.e. above party politics and we should be willing to promote this national consensus for the country?

A. Well, obviously a subject like family planning should be above any controversy. But, as you have noticed in the past years, there have been certain parties and groups which have done tremendous propaganda against this, telling people of one religion that they will be exterminated and the others that their numbers were going down and they will be in difficulty; besides, of course, all the propaganda that was done about sterilization. Because we do not believe in coercion; we think that there should be persuasion. But this must be done on a massive educational scale and unless everybody is in favour it will take a very long time and may defeat the whole purpose of it.

Q. But, knowing the very low, totally ineffective performance that there has been in the Family Planning Programme in the last few years, what steps is your Government now proposing to take to revitalize the programme?

A. I think we have to involve not just the department that is in charge of this, but the whole population, specially [especially] schools, the whole youth movement, women's organizations, other institutions which are concerned with any type of social welfare. I mean everybody gets into it to create the right atmosphere; and you find that village women are ready or any woman for that matter, not just one. One part which is very important is that we must ensure better health, because if there is any chance of children dying more, then people will not be willing to risk that. So, they must be ensured better health, education, and of course, even employment later on. It is part of national planning as a whole.

Q. Madam Prime Minister, would you be in favour of systematically linking emphasis on family planning incentives? You know the tax structure on the one hand and all the collective inputs on the other so that a system of reciprocal responsibility can be established between the State and the people.

A. Well, this idea is a very complicated matter and it has been discussed many times; and previously we did give some incentives and some disincentives. I do not know how well it worked. It has to be gone into.

Q. Are you willing to examine the issue?

A. I am willing to examine it.

Q. And also would you feel there is a need for review of the law in order to see how it can be made more supporting to the family planning effort? You know a moral framework can be created within which incentives for family planning are decided upon and not struck down as discriminatory.

A. I do not know whether you can create a moral climate legally. That is a question of changing attitudes to life.

Q. And finally, Mrs Gandhi, may I ask you, since a great deal of research has pointed out women's education, women's employment, raising of women's status is important for fertility decline to take place, quite apart from the fact that this is badly needed in the country itself. Is your Government contemplating any particular steps for bringing up the status of women?

A. We are doing a great deal. We have to start at the bottom, i.e., the girls; and I think a great deal is being done now to help girls to continue with their education and not drop out as they have been doing.

Study Question

1. Is population control a necessary corollary of development?

SYED ABUL A'ALA MAUDUDI

Syed Abul A'ala Maudui (1903–79) was a Pakistani political theorist and the founder of Jamaat-e-Islami, a party dedicated to the creation of an Islamic state in Pakistan. Maudui travelled widely and his works have been translated into a number of languages. For Maudui, an Islamic state was a necessary defence against the imposition of western culture and western ideas, both during and after the colonial ear. The imposition of sharia law would be essential to the creation of a modern Islamic state, despite the problems discussed below.

REPLACING WESTERN FORMS WITH ISLAMIC LAW

If we really wish to see our Islamic ideals translated into reality, we should not overlook the natural law that all stable changes in the collective life of a people come about gradually. The more sudden a change, the more short-lived it is. For a permanent change it is necessary that it should be free from extremist bias and unbalanced approach.

The best example of this gradual change is the revolution brought about by the Holy Prophet (peace be on him) in Arabia. One who is acquainted even superficially with the history of the Prophet's achievements knows that he did not enforce the entire body of Islamic laws with one stroke. Instead, the society was prepared gradually for their enforcement. The Prophet (peace be on him) uprooted the practices of the 'Age of Ignorance' one by one and substituted for them new, moderate principles of human conduct. He started his efforts for reformation by inculcating belief in the fundamentals of Islam, namely, the unity of God, the Life Hereafter and the Institution of Prophethood and by inducing the people to live a life of righteousness and piety. Those who accepted this message were trained by him to believe in and practice the Islamic Way of Life. When this was achieved to a considerable degree, the Prophet (peace be on him) went a step further and established an Islamic State in Medina with the sole object of making the social life of the country conform to the Islamic pattern . . . .

Coming to our own times and our own country, Pakistan, if we wish to promulgate Islamic Law here, it would mean nothing less that the demolition of the entire structure built by your British masters and the erection of a new one in its place. It is obvious that this cannot be achieved by just an official proclamation or a parliamentary bill, because it is a stupendous task and demands a good deal of hard and systematic work on the basis of an all-embracing program. For instance, we need a thorough reorientation of our educational system. At present, we find two kinds of educational institutions running simultaneously in our country, namely, the old, religious 'madrasahs' and the modern, secular universities and colleges. None of them can produce people needed to run a modern Islamic State. The old-fashioned schools are steeped in conservatism to such an extent that they have lost all touch with the modern world. Their education has been disconnected from the practical problems of life and has thus become barren and lifeless. It cannot, therefore, produce people who might be able to serve, for instance, as judges and magistrates of a progressive modern state. As for our modern, secular institutions, they produce people who are ignorant of even a rudimentary knowledge of Islam and its laws. Moreover, we can hardly find such persons among those whose mentality has not been affected by the poisonous content and the thoroughly materialistic bias of modern, secular education.

There is yet another difficultly. The Islamic law has not been in force for the last century or so. Consequently our legal code has become stagnant and has lagged behind the march of time, while our urgent need is to bring it abreast of the latest developments of the modern age. Obviously, this would require a considerable amount of hard work.

There is, however, an even bigger hurdle. Living as slaves of an alien power and deprived of the Islamic influence for a long time, the pattern of our moral, cultural, social, economic, and political life has undergone a radical change, and is today far removed from Islamic ideals. Under such circumstances it cannot be fruitful, even if it were possible, to change the legal structure of the country all at once, because then the general pattern of life and the legal structure will be poles apart, and the legal change will have to suffer the fate of a sapling planted in an uncongenial soil and facing hostile weather. It is, therefore, inevitable that the required reform should be gradual and the changes in the laws should be effected in such a manner as to balance favorably the change in the moral, educational, social, cultural, and political life of the nation. . . .

There are some people who take a few provisions of the Islamic Penal Code [*sharia*] out of their context and jeer at them. But they do not realize that those provisions are to be viewed with the background of the whole Islamic system of life covering the economic, social, political, and educational spheres of activity. If all these departments are not working, then those isolated provisions of our Penal Code can certainly work no miracles.

For example, we all know that Islam imposes the penalty of amputating the hand for the commitment of theft. But this injunction is meant to be promulgated in a full-fledged Islamic society wherein the wealthy pay *zakat* to the state

and the state provides for the basic necessities of the needy and the destitute; wherein every township is enjoined to play host to visitors at its own expense for a minimum period of three days; wherein all citizens are provided with equal privileges and opportunities to seek economic livelihood; wherein monopolistic tendencies are discouraged; wherein people are God-fearing and seek His pleasure with devotion; wherein the virtues of generosity, helping the poor, treating the sick, providing the needy are in the air to the extent that even a small boy is made to realize that he is not a true Muslim if he allows his neighbour to sleep hungry while he has taken his meal. In other words it is not meant for the present-day society where you cannot get a single penny without having to pay interest; where in place of *Baitul Mal* there are implacable money-lenders and banks which, instead of providing relief and succour to the poor and the needy, treat them with callous disregard, heartless refusal, and brutal contempt: where the guiding motto is: 'Everybody for himself and devil takes the hindmost'; where there are great privileges for the privileged ones while others are deprived even of their legitimate rights. . . . Under such conditions, it is doubtful if theft should be penalised at all, not to speak of cutting off the thief's hands! Because to do so would, as a matter of fact, amount to protecting the ill-gotten wealth of a few blood-suckers rather than awarding adequate punishment to the guilty.

On the other hand, Islam aims at creating a society in which none is compelled by the force of circumstances to steal. For, in the Islamic social order, apart from the voluntary help provided by individuals, the state guarantees the basic *necessities of life to all. But, after providing all that,* Islam enjoins a severe and exemplary punishment for those who commit theft, as their action shows that they are unfit to live in such a just, generous, and healthy society and would cause greater harm to it, if left unchecked.

Study Question

1. What are the largest obstacles to the creation of a modern Islamic State, such as that envisioned by Maududi?

MU'AMMAR AL-QADHAFI

Mu'ammar al-Qadhafi (b. 1942) took part in a coup that overthrew the Libyan monarchy in 1969; he has led Libya since that time, despite numerous changes of title. Qadhafi has been a strong supporter of pan-Arabism and a political ideology that he refers to as 'Islamic socialism'. In the 1970s and 1980s Qadhafi's Libya was a strong supporter of *international terrorist organizations, leading to both UN and US sanctions. Recently, however, Qadhafi has paid large sums in compensation to victims of terrorism, in order to free his country from these restrictions. The following excerpt from Qadhafi's Green Book discusses the importance of socialist ownership.*

THE GREEN BOOK

Land

Land is no one's property. But everyone has the right to use it, to benefit from it by working, farming or pasturing. This would take place throughout a man's life and the lives of his heirs, and would be through his own effort without using others with or without wages, and only to the extent of satisfying his own needs.

If possession of land is allowed, only those who are living there have a share in it. The land is permanently there, while, in the course of time, users change in profession, in capacity and in their presence.

The purpose of the new socialist society is to create a society which is happy because it is free. This can be achieved through satisfying the material and spiritual needs of man, and that, in turn, comes about through the liberation of these needs from outside domination and control.

Satisfaction of these needs must be attained without exploiting or enslaving others, or else, it will contradict the purpose of the new socialist society.

Man in the new society works for himself to guarantee his material needs, or works for a socialist corporation in whose production he is a partner, or performs a public service to the society which provides his material needs.

Economic activity in the new socialist society is productive activity for the satisfaction of material needs. It is not unproductive activity or an activity which seeks profit in order, after satisfying material needs, to save the surplus. That is impossible under the rules of the new socialism.

The legitimate purpose of the individual's economic activity is solely to satisfy his needs. For the wealth of the world has limits at each stage as does the wealth of each individual society. Therefore no individual has the right to carry out economic activity in order to acquire more of that wealth than is necessary to satisfy his needs, because the excess amount belongs to other individuals. He has the right to save from his needs and from his own production but not from the efforts of others nor at the expense of their needs. For if we allow economic activity to extend beyond the satisfaction of needs, one person will only have more than his needs by preventing another from obtaining his. The savings which are in excess of one's needs are another person's share of the wealth of society.

To allow private production for the purpose of acquiring savings that exceed the satisfaction of needs is exploitation itself, as in permitting the use of others to satisfy your own needs or to get more than your own needs. This can be done by exploiting a person to satisfy the needs of others and making savings for others at the expense of his needs.

Work for a wage is, in addition to being an enslavement of man as mentioned before, work without incentives because the producer is a wage-worker rather than a partner.

Whoever works for himself is certainly devoted to his productive work because his incentive to production lies in his dependence on his private work to satisfy his material needs. Also whoever works in a socialist corporation is a partner in its production. He is, undoubtedly, devoted to his productive work because the impetus for devotion to production is that he gets a satisfaction of his needs through production. But whoever works for a wage has no incentive to work.

Work for wages failed to solve the problem of increasing and developing production. Work, either in the form of services or production, is continually deteriorating because it rests on the shoulders of wage-workers.

Examples of Labour for Wages for Society, of Labour for Wages for a Private Activity, and Labour for No Wage

First Example:
(a) A worker who produces ten apples for society. Society gives him one apple for his production. The apple fully satisfies his needs.

(b) A worker who produces ten apples for society. Society gives him one apple for his production. The apple is not enough to satisfy his needs.

Second Example:
A worker who produces ten apples for another person and gets a wage of less than the price of one apple.

Third Example:
A worker who produces ten apples for himself.

The Conclusion
The first (a) will not increase his production for whatever the increase might be, he will only get an apple for himself. It is what satisfies his needs. Thus all those working for such a society are always psychologically apathetic.

The first (b) has no incentive to production itself, for he produces for the society without obtaining satisfaction of his needs. However he has to continue to work without incentive because he is forced to submit to the general conditions of work throughout the society. That is the case with members of that society.

The second does not initially work to produce. He works to get wages. Since his wages are not enough to satisfy his needs, he will either search for another master and sell him his work at a better price or he will be obliged to continue the same work just to survive. The third is the only one who produces without apathy and without coercion. In the socialist society, there is no possibility for private production exceeding the satisfaction of individual needs, because satisfaction of needs at the expense of others is not allowed.

As the socialist establishments work for the satisfaction of the needs of society, the third example explains the sound basis of economic production. However, in all conditions, even in bad ones, production continues for survival. The best proof is that in capitalist societies production accumulates and expands in the hands of a few owners who do not work but exploit the efforts of toilers who are obliged to produce in order to survive. However, *The Green Book* not only solves the problem of material production but also prescribes the comprehensive solution of the problems of human society so that the individual may be materially and spiritually liberated . . . a final liberation to attain his happiness. . . .

Study Question

1. Consider the logic of Qadhafi's three examples. What are the flaws in the logic? What are the strengths?

NELSON MANDELA

Nelson Rolihlahla Mandela (b. 1918) graduated in 1942 with a law degree and soon after joined the African National Congress (ANC). Beginning in 1948 Mandela was active in the fight against the segregation policies introduced by Daniel Malan's National Party. Mandela was first arrested, then acquitted in the 1950s. He was arrested again in 1962 and sentenced to hard labour. A 1964 trial on charges of treason brought a sentence of life in prison. Rather than disappearing into the South African penal system, *Mandela gained a wide international audience during his years in jail. In February 1990 he was released and in 1991 he assumed the leadership of the ANC. In 1993 he accepted the Nobel Peace Prize on behalf of all South Africans. On 24 May 1994, just three weeks after winning the first open election in South African history, Nelson Mandela addressed the parliament in Cape Town, summarizing both the state of the nation and the changes needed to ensure a successful transition to majority rule in South Africa.*

STATE OF THE NATION ADDRESS, 1994

Madame Speaker and Deputy Speaker, President of the Senate and Deputy President, Deputy Presidents, Chief Justice, Distinguished members of the National Assembly and the Senate, Provincial Premiers, Commanders of the Security Forces, Members of the Diplomatic Corps, Esteemed guests, Comrades, Ladies and gentlemen.

The time will come when our nation will honour the memory of all the sons, the daughters, the mothers, the fathers, the youth and the children who, by their thoughts and deeds, gave us the right to assert with pride that we are South Africans, that we are Africans and that we are citizens of the world.

The certainties that come with age tell me that among these we shall find an Afrikaner woman who transcended a particular experience and became a South African, an African and a citizen of the world. Her name is Ingrid Jonker.

She was both a poet and a South African. She was both an Afrikaner and an African. She was both an artist and a human being.

In the midst of despair, she celebrated hope. Confronted with death, she asserted the beauty of life.

In the dark days when all seemed hopeless in our country, when many refused to hear her resonant voice, she took her own life.

To her and others like her, we owe a debt to life itself. To her and others like her, we owe a commitment to the poor, the oppressed, the wretched and the despised.

Nelson Mandela's Inaugural Address, 1994. The ANC had dominated the first free election in South Africa's modern history, gaining 63 per cent of the vote. Courtesy of the United Nations Photo Library (186835 UN/DPI/C. Sattleburger).

In the aftermath of the massacre at the anti-pass demonstration in Sharpeville she wrote that:

The child is not dead
the child lifts his fists against his mother
who shouts Africa!. . .
The child is not dead
Not at Langa nor at Nyanga
nor at Orlando nor at Sharpeville
nor at the police post at Philippi
where he lies with a bullet through his brain. . .
the child is present at all assemblies and law-
giving
the child peers through the windows of houses
and into the hearts of mothers
this child who only wanted to play in the sun at
Nyanga
is everywhere
the child grown to a man treks on through all
Africa

the child grown to a giant journeys
over the whole world
without a pass!

And in this glorious vision, she instructs that our endeavours must be about the liberation of the woman, the emancipation of the man and the liberty of the child.

It is these things that we must achieve to give meaning to our presence in this chamber and to give purpose to our occupancy of the seat of government.

And so we must, constrained by and yet regardless of the accumulated effect of our historical burdens, seize the time to define for ourselves what we want to make of our shared destiny.

The government I have the honour to lead and I dare say the masses who elected us to serve in this role, are inspired by the single vision of creating a people-centred society.

Accordingly, the purpose that will drive this government shall be the expansion of the frontiers of human fulfilment, the continuous extension of the frontiers of the freedom.

The acid test of the legitimacy of the programmes we elaborate, the government institutions we create, the legislation we adopt must be whether they serve these objectives.

Our single most important challenge is therefore to help establish a social order in which the freedom of the individual will truly mean the freedom of the individual.

We must construct that people-centred society of freedom in such a manner that it guarantees the political and the human rights of all our citizens.

As an affirmation of the government's commitment to an entrenched human rights culture, we shall immediately take steps to inform the Secretary General of the United Nations that we will subscribe to the Universal Declaration of Human Rights.

We shall take steps to ensure that we accede to the International Covenant on Civil and Political

Rights, the International Covenant on Social and Economic Rights and other human rights instruments of the United Nations.

Our definition of the freedom of the individual must be instructed by the fundamental objective to restore the human dignity of each and every South African.

This requires that we speak not only of political freedoms.

My government's commitment to create a people-centred society of liberty binds us to the pursuit of the goals of freedom from want, freedom from hunger, freedom from deprivation, freedom from ignorance, freedom from suppression and freedom from fear.

These freedoms are fundamental to the guarantee of human dignity. They will therefore constitute part of the centrepiece of what this government will seek to achieve, the focal point on which our attention will be continuously focused.

The things we have said constitute the true meaning, the justification and the purpose of the Reconstruction and Development Programme, without which it would lose all legitimacy.

When we elaborated this Programme we were inspired by the hope that all South Africans of goodwill could join together to provide a better life for all. We were pleased that other political organisations announced similar aims.

Today, I am happy to announce that the Cabinet of the Government of National Unity has reached consensus not only on the broad objective of the creation of the people-centred society of which I have spoken, but also on many elements of a plan broadly based on that Programme for Reconstruction and Development. . . .

My government is equally committed to ensure that we use this longer period properly fully to bring into the decision-making processes organs of civil society.

This will include the trade union movement and civic organisations, so that at no time should the government become isolated from the people. At the same time, steps will be taken to build the capacity of communities to manage their own affairs.

Precisely because we are committed to ensuring sustainable growth and development leading to a better life for all, we will continue existing programmes of fiscal rehabilitation.

We are therefore determined to make every effort to contain real general government consumption at present levels and to manage the budget deficit with a view to its continuous reduction.

Similarly, we are agreed that a permanently higher general level of taxation is to be avoided.

To achieve these important objectives will require consistent discipline on the part of both the central and the provincial governments.

Furthermore, this disciplined approach will ensure that we integrate the objectives of our Reconstruction and Development Plan within government expenditure and not treat them as incidental to the tasks of government, marginalised to the status of mere additions to the level of expenditure.

There are major areas of desperate need in our society.

As a signal of its seriousness to address these, the government will, within the next 100 days, implement various projects under the direct supervision of the President. Let me briefly mention these.

Children under the age of six and pregnant mothers will receive free medical care in every state hospital and clinic where such need exists. Similarly, a nutritional feeding scheme will be implemented in every primary school where such need is established. A concrete process of consultation between the major stakeholders in this area will be organised immediately.

A programme is already being implemented to electrify 350,000 homes during the current financial year.

A campaign will be launched at every level of government, a public works programme designed and all efforts made to involve the private sector, organised labour, the civics and other community organisations to rebuild our townships, restore services in rural and urban areas, while addressing the issue of job creation and training, especially for our unemployed youth.

Many details of the overall reconstruction and development plan remain to be discussed, agreed and put in place. But I believe that the broad outline I have given and the immediate initiatives I have mentioned, will allow you to share my joy at the progress already made by the Government of National Unity with regard to this important matter.

We shall carry out this plan within the context of a policy aimed at building a strong and growing economy which will benefit all our people. . . .

The Government is determined forcefully to confront the scourge of unemployment, not by way of handouts but by the creation of work opportunities.

The Government will also deal sensitively with the issue of population movements into the country, to protect our workers, to guard against the exploitation of vulnerable workers and to ensure friendly relations with all countries and peoples.

The Government is also taking urgent measures to deal firmly with drug trafficking some of which is carried out by foreign nationals who are resident in the country.

We must end racism in the workplace as part of our common offensive against racism in general. No more should words like Kaffirs, Hottentots, Coolies, Boy, Girl, and Baas be part of our vocabulary.

I also trust that the matter of paying the workers for the public holidays proclaimed in order to ensure their participation in the elections and the inauguration ceremonies will now be resolved as a result of recent consultations.

This would be a welcome demonstration by the private sector of its involvement in the beautiful future we are all trying to build.

We have devoted time to a discussion of economic questions because they are fundamental to the realisation of the fundamental objectives of the reconstruction and development programme.

Below I mention some of the work in which the relevant governments are already involved to translate these objectives into reality.

The Government will take steps to ensure the provision of clean water on the basis of the principle of water security for all and the introduction of proper sanitation sensitive to the protection of the environment.

We are determined to address the dire housing shortage in a vigorous manner, acting together with the private sector and the communities in need of shelter.

Health also remains a fundamental building block of the humane society we are determined to create through the implementation of the Reconstruction and Development Programme.

We must address the needs of the aged and disabled, uplift disadvantaged sectors such as the women and the youth, and improve the lives of our people in the rural communities and the informal settlements.

We must invest substantial amounts in education and training and meet our commitment to introduce free and compulsory education for a period of at least 9 years. Everywhere we must reinculcate the culture of learning and of teaching and make it possible for this culture to thrive.

We must combat such social pathologies as widespread poverty, the break down of family life, crime, alcohol and drug abuse, the abuse of children, women and the elderly, and the painful reality of street children. We are giving urgent attention to the long waiting lists for the payment of social grants which have developed in some areas, owing to lack of funds.

I am especially pleased that we have a ministry dedicated to the issue of the environment. Its work must impact on many aspects of national activity and address the question of the well-being of society as a whole and the preservation of a healthy environmental future even for generation not yet born.

As we began this address, we borrowed the words of Ingrid Jonker to focus on the plight of the children our country.

I would now like to say that the Government will, as a matter of urgency, attend to the tragic and complex question of children and juveniles in detention and prison.

The basic principle from which we will proceed from now onwards is that we must rescue the children of the nation and ensure that the system of criminal justice must be the very last resort in the case of juvenile offenders.

I have therefore issued instruction to the Departments concerned, as a matter of urgency, to work out the necessary guidelines which will enable us to empty our prisons of children and to place them in suitable alternative care. This is in addition to an amnesty for various categories serving prisoners as will be effected in terms of what I said in my Inauguration Address two weeks ago.

In this context, I also need to make the point that the Government will also not delay unduly with regard to attending to the vexed and unresolved issue of an amnesty for criminal activities carried out in furtherance of political objectives.

We will attend to this matter in a balanced and dignified way. The nation must come to terms with its past in a spirit of openness and forgiveness and proceed to build the future on the basis of repairing and healing.

The burden of the past lies heavily on all of us, including those responsible for inflicting injury and those who suffered.

Following the letter and the spirit of the Constitution, we will prepare the legislation which will seek to free the wrongdoers from fear of retribution and blackmail, while acknowledging the injury of those who have been harmed so that the individual wrongs, injuries, fears and hopes affecting individuals are identified and attended to.

In the meantime, summoning the full authority of the position represent, we call on all concerned not to take any steps that might, in any way, impede or compromise the processes of reconciliation which the impending legislation will address.

The problem of politically motivated violence is still with us. We depend on our country's security forces to deal with this problem using all resources at their disposal. In this, and in their efforts to deal especially with criminal violence, they have our personal support and confidence.

We have also directed that all relevant ministries should engage the structures set up in terms of the National Peace Accord so that these can be invigorated to pursue their noble mission in the context of the changed circumstances in our country.

The Government will otherwise not spare any effort in ensuring that our security forces enjoy the standing they deserve of being accepted by all our people the defenders of our sovereignty, our democratic system, the guarantors of a just peace within the country and the safety and security of all citizens and their property.

Let me also take this opportunity to reiterate our assurance to the rest of the public service that the Government is firmly committed to the protection of the rights of all members of this service.

We are also determined to work with the organisations of the service to ensure that we have the democratic, non-racial, non-sexist, honest, and accountable corps of public servants which members of the Public Service themselves desire.

In this context, we must also make the observation that the Government will not waver from the principle of achieving parity in remuneration and conditions of service among all workers in the public sector.

The youth of our country are the valued possession of the nation. Without them there can be no future. Their needs are immense and urgent. They are at the centre of our reconstruction and development plan.

To address them, acting with the youth

themselves, the Government will engage the representative organisations of the youth and other formations, among other things to look at the siting of a broad-based National Commission on Youth Development among the structures of Government.

Building on this base, the Government and the Commission would then work together to ensure that the nurturing of our youth stands at the centre of our reconstruction and development, without being consigned to a meaningless ghetto of public life.

Similar considerations must attach to the equally important question of the emancipation of the women of our country.

It is vitally important that all structures of Government, including the President himself, should understand this fully that freedom cannot be achieved unless the women have been emancipated from all forms of oppression.

All of us must take this on board that the objectives of the Reconstruction and Development Programme will not have been realised unless we see in visible and practical terms that the condition of the women of our country has radically changed for the better and that they have been empowered to intervene in all aspects of life as equals with any other member of society.

In addition to the establishment of the statutory Gender Commission provided for in the Constitution, the Government will, together with the representatives of the women themselves, look at the establishment of organs of Government to ensure that all levels of the public sector, from top to bottom, integrate the central issue of the emancipation of women in their programmes and daily activities.

Tomorrow, on Africa Day, the dream of Ingrid Jonker will come to fruition. The child grown to a man will trek through all Africa. The child grown to a journey will journey over the whole world—without a pass!

Tomorrow, on Africa Day, our new flag will be hoisted in an historic ceremony at the OUA Headquarters in Addis Ababa, with the OUA having already agreed to accept us as its latest member.

Tomorrow, on Africa Day, the UN Security Council will meet to lift the last remaining sanctions against South Africa and to position the world organisation to relate to our country as an honoured, responsible and peace-loving citizen.

As such, the Government is involved in discussion to determine what our contribution could be to the search for peace in Angola and Rwanda, to the reinforcement of the peace process in Mozambique, to the establishment of a new world order of mutually beneficial cooperation, justice, prosperity and peace for ourselves and for the nations of the world.

Yesterday the Cabinet also decided to apply for our country to join the Commonwealth. This important community of nations is waiting to receive us with open arms.

We have learnt the lesson that our blemishes speak of what all humanity should not do. We understand this fully that our glories point to the heights of what human genius can achieve.

In our dreams we have a vision of all our country at play in our sportsfields and enjoying deserved and enriching recreation in our theatres, galleries, beaches, mountains, plains, and game parks, in conditions of peace, security and comfort.

Our road to that glorious future lies through collective hard work to accomplish the objective of creating a people-centred society through the implementation of the vision contained in our reconstruction and development plan.

Let us all get down to work!

Study Question

1. The details of reform laid out by Nelson Mandela in 1994 were enormously ambitious. Was this blueprint attainable and, if so, under what circumstances?

PHILIP GOUREVITCH

Philip Gourevitch is a staff writer at The New Yorker *magazine. He travelled to Rwanda in 1995, one year after the genocide which killed somewhere near 800,000 people, mostly Tutsis, in a matter of a few months. After several more trips into the region Gourevitch published* We Wish to Inform You that Tomorrow We Will Be Killed with Our Families *in 1998. One of the*

book's central themes concerns the absence of western intervention during the genocide, despite the presence of a small UN *peacekeeping force, under Canadian General Roméo Dallaire, who called repeatedly for assistance in the face of the escalating massacres. Another theme, more clearly illustrated in the excerpt below, concerns the human capacity for evil.*

WE WISH TO INFORM YOU THAT TOMORROW WE WILL BE KILLED WITH OUR FAMILIES

In the province of Kibungo, in eastern Rwanda, in the swamp and pastureland near the Tanzanian border, there's a rocky hill called Nyarubuye with a church where many Tutsis were slaughtered in mid-April of 1994. A year after the killing I went to Nyurabuye with two Canadian military officers. We flew in a United Nations helicopter, traveling low over the hills in the morning mists, with the banana trees like green starbursts dense over the slopes. The uncut grass blew back as we dropped into the center of the parish schoolyard. A lone solider materialized with his Kalashnikov, and shook our hands with stiff, shy formality. The Canadians presented the paperwork for our visit, and I stepped up into the open doorway of a classroom.

At least fifty mostly decomposed cadavers covered the floor, wadded in clothing, their belongings strewn about and smashed. Macheted skulls had rolled here and there.

The dead looked like pictures of the dead. They did not smell. They did not buzz with flies. They had been killed thirteen months earlier, and they hadn't been moved. Skin stuck here and there over the bones, many of which lay scattered away from the bodies, dismembered by the killers, or by scavengers—birds, clogs, bugs. The more complete figures looked a lot

like people, which they were once. A woman in a cloth wrap printed with flowers lay near the door. Her fleshless hip bones were high and her legs slightly spread, and a child's skeleton extended between them. Her torso was hollowed out. Her ribs and spinal column poked through the rotting cloth. Her head was tipped back and her mouth was open: a strange image—half agony, half repose.

I had never been among the dead before. What to do? Look? Yes. I wanted to see them, I suppose; I had come to see them—the dead had been left unburied at Nyarubuye for memorial purposes—and there they were, so intimately exposed. I didn't need to see them. I already knew, and believed, what had happened in Rwanda. Yet looking at the buildings and the bodies, and hearing the silence of the place, with the grand Italianate basilica standing there deserted, and beds of exquisite, decadent, death-fertilized flowers blooming over the corpses, it was still strangely unimaginable. I mean one still had to imagine it.

Those dead Rwandans will be with me forever, I expect. That was why I had felt compelled to come to Nyarubuye: to be stuck with them—not with their experience, but with the experience of looking at them. They had been killed there, and

Victims of the Rwandan genocide. A number of memorial sites have been created in post-genocide Rwanda. REUTERS/ Peter Andrews (RTXHRLF).

they were dead there. What else could you really see at first? The Bible bloated with rain lying on top of one corpse or, littered about, the little woven wreaths of thatch which Rwandan women wear as crowns to balance the enormous loads they carry on their heads, and the water gourds, and the Converse tennis sneaker stuck somehow in a pelvis.

The soldier with the Kalashnikov—Sergeant Francis of the Rwandese Patriotic Army, a Tutsi whose parents had fled to Uganda with him when he was a boy, after similar but less extensive massacres in the early 1960s, and who had fought his way home in 1994 and found it like this—said that the dead in this room were mostly women who had been raped before being murdered. Sergeant Francis had high, rolling,

girlish hips, and he walked and stood with his butt stuck out behind him, an oddly purposeful posture, tipped forward, driven. He was, at once, candid and briskly official. His English had the punctilious clip of military drill, and after he told me what I was looking at I looked instead at my feet. The rusty head of a hatchet lay beside them in the dirt.

A few weeks earlier, in Bukavu, Zaire, in the giant market of a refugee camp that was home to many Rwandan Hutu militiamen, I had watched a man butchering a cow with a machete. He was quite expert at his work, taking big precise strokes that made a sharp hacking noise. The rallying cry to the killers during the genocide was 'Do your work!' And I saw that it *was* work, this butchery; hard work. It took many hacks—two, three, four, five hard hacks—to chop through the cow's leg. How many hacks to dismember a person?

Considering the enormity of the task, it is tempting to play with theories of collective madness, mob mania, a fever of hatred erupted into a mass crime of passion, and to imagine the blind orgy of the mob, with each member killing one or two people. But at Nyarubuye, and at thousands of other sites in this tiny country, on the same days of a few months in 1994, hundreds of thousands of Hutus had worked as killers in regular shifts. There was always the next victim, and the next. What sustained them, beyond the frenzy of the first attack, through the plain physical exhaustion and mess of it?

The pygmy in Gikongoro said that inhumanity is part of nature and that we must go against nature to get along and have peace. But mass violence, too, must be organized; it does not occur aimlessly. Even mobs and riots have a design, and great and sustained destruction requires great ambition. It must be conceived as the means toward achieving a new order, and although the idea behind that new order may be criminal and objectively very stupid, it must also be compellingly simple and at the same time absolute. The ideology of genocide is all of those things, and in Rwanda it went by the bald name of Hutu Power. For those who set about systematically exterminating an entire people—even a fairly small and unresisting subpopulation of perhaps a million and a quarter men, women, and children, like the Tutsis in Rwanda—blood lust surely helps. But the engineers and perpetrators of a slaughter like the one just inside the door where I stood need not enjoy killing, and they may even find it unpleasant. What is required above all is that they want their victims dead. They have to want it so badly that they consider it a necessity.

So I still had much to imagine as I entered the classroom and stepped carefully between the remains. These dead and their killers had been neighbours, schoolmates, colleagues, sometimes friends, even in-laws. The dead had seen their killers training as militias in the weeks before the end, and it was well known that they were training to kill Tutsis; it was announced on the radio, it was in the newspapers, people spoke of it openly. The week before the massacre at Nyarubuye, the killing began in Rwanda's capital, Kigali. Hutus who opposed the Hutu Power ideology were publicly denounced as 'accomplices' of the Tutsis and were among the first to be killed as the extermination got under way. In Nyarubuye, when Tutsis asked the Hutu Power mayor how they might be spared, he suggested that they seek sanctuary at the church. They did, and a few days later the mayor came to kill them. He came at the head of a pack of soldiers, policemen, militiamen, and villagers; he gave out arms and orders to complete the job well. No more was required of the mayor, but he also was said to have killed a few Tutsis himself.

The killers killed all day at Nyarubuye. At night they cut the Achilles tendons of survivors and went off to feast behind the church, roasting cattle looted from their victims in big fires, and drinking beer. (Bottled beer, banana beer—

Rwandans may not drink more beer than other Africans, but they drink prodigious quantities of it around the clock.) And, in the morning, still drunk after whatever sleep they could find beneath the cries of their prey, the killers at Nyarubuye went back and killed again. Day after day, minute to minute, Tutsi by Tutsi: all across Rwanda, they worked like that. 'It was a process,' Sergeant Francis said. I can see that it happened, I can be told how, and after nearly three years of looking around Rwanda and listening to Rwandans, I can tell you how, and I will. But the horror of it—the idiocy, the waste, the sheer wrongness—remains uncircumscribable. . . .

Rwanda is spectacular to behold. Through-out its center, a winding succession of steep, tightly terraced slopes radiates out from small roadside settlements and solitary compounds. Gashes of red clay and black loam mark fresh hoe work; eucalyptus trees flash silver against brilliant green tea plantations; banana trees are everywhere. On the theme of hills, Rwanda produces countless variations: jagged rain forests, round-shouldered buttes, undulating moors, broad swells of savannah, volcanic peaks sharp as filed teeth. During the rainy season, the clouds are huge and low and fast, mists cling in highland hollows, lightning flickers through the nights, and by day the land is lustrous. After the rains, the skies lift, the terrain takes on a ragged look beneath the flat unvarying haze of the dry season, and in the savannas of the Akagera Park wildfire blackens the hills.

One day, when I was returning to Kigali from the south, the car mounted a rise between two winding valleys, the windshield filled with purple-bellied clouds, and I asked Joseph, the man who was giving me a ride, whether Rwandans realize what a beautiful country they have. 'Beautiful?' he said. 'You think so? After the things that happened here? The people aren't good. If the people were good, the country might be OK.' Joseph told me that his brother and sister had been killed, and he made a soft hissing click with his tongue against his teeth. 'The country is empty,' he said. 'Empty!'

It was not just the dead who were missing. The genocide had been brought to a halt by the Rwandese Patriotic Front, a rebel army led by Tutsi refugees from past persecutions, and as the RPF advanced through the country in the summer of 1994, some two million Hutus had fled into exile at the behest of the same leaders who had urged them to kill. Yet except in some rural areas in the south, where the desertion of Hutus had left nothing but bush to reclaim the fields around crumbling adobe houses, I, as a newcomer, could not see the emptiness that blinded Joseph to Rwanda's beauty. Yes, there were grenade-flattened buildings, burnt homesteads, shot-up facades, and mortar-pitted roads. But these were the ravages of war, not of genocide, and by the summer of 1995, most of the dead had been buried. Fifteen months earlier, Rwanda had been the most densely populated country in Africa. Now the work of the killers looked just as they had intended: invisible.

From time to time, mass graves were discovered and excavated, and the remains would be transferred to new, properly consecrated mass graves. Yet even the occasionally exposed bones, the conspicuous number of amputees and people with deforming scars, and the superabundance of packed orphanages could not be taken as evidence that what had happened to Rwanda was an attempt to eliminate a people. There were only people's stories.

'Every survivor wonders why he is alive,' Abbé Modeste, a priest at the cathedral in Butare, Rwanda's second-largest city, told me. Abbé Modeste had hidden for weeks in his sacristy, eating communion wafers, before moving under the desk in his study, and finally into the rafters at the home of some neighboring nuns. The obvious explanation of his survival was that the RPF had come to the rescue. But the RPF didn't reach Butare till early July, and roughly seventy-five per cent of the Tutsis in Rwanda had been killed by early May. In this regard, at least, the genocide had been entirely successful: to those who were targeted, it was not death but life that seemed an accident of fate.

'I had eighteen people killed at my house,' said Etienne Niyonzima, a former businessman who had become a deputy in the National Assembly. 'Everything was totally destroyed—a place of fifty-five meters by fifty meters. In my neighborhood they killed six hundred and forty-seven people. They tortured them, too. You had to see how they killed them. They had the number of everyone's house, and they went through with red paint and marked the homes of all the Tutsis and of the Hutu moderates. My wife was at a friend's, shot with two bullets. She is still alive, only'—he fell quiet for a moment—'she has no arms. The others with her were killed. The militia left her for dead. Her whole family of sixty-five in Gitarama were killed.' Niyonzima was in hiding at the time. Only after he had been separated from his wife for three months did he learn that she and four of their children had survived. 'Well,' he said, 'one son was cut in the head with a machete. I don't know where he went.' His voice weakened, and caught. 'He disappeared.' Niyonzima clicked his tongue, and said, 'But the others are still alive. Quite honestly, I don't understand at all how I was saved.'

Laurent Nkongoli attributed his survival to 'Providence, and also good neighbors, an old woman who said, "Run away, we don't want to see your corpse."' Nkongoli, a lawyer, who had become the vice president of the National Assembly after the genocide, was a robust man, with a taste for double-breasted suit jackets and lively tics, and he moved, as he spoke, with a brisk determination. But before taking his neighbor's advice, and fleeing Kigali in late April of 1994, he said, 'I had accepted death. At a certain moment this happens. One hopes not to die cruelly, but one expects to die anyway. Not death by machete, one hopes, but with a bullet. If you were willing to pay for it, you could often ask for a bullet. Death was more or less normal, a resignation. You lose the will to fight. There were four thousand Tutsis killed here at Kacyiru'—a neighborhood of Kigali. 'The soldiers brought them here, and told them to sit down because they were going to throw grenades. And they sat.'

'Rwandan culture is a culture of fear,' Nkongoli went on. 'I remember what people said.' He adopted a pipey voice, and his face took on a look of disgust: '"Just let us pray, then kill us," or "I don't want to die in the street, I want to die at home."' He resumed his normal voice. 'When you're that resigned and oppressed you're already dead. It shows the genocide was prepared for too long. I detest this fear. These victims of genocide had been psychologically prepared to expect death just for being Tutsi. They were being killed for so long that they were already dead.'

I reminded Nkongoli that, for all his hatred of fear, he had himself accepted death before his neighbor urged him to run away. 'Yes,' he said. 'I got tired in the genocide. You struggle so long, then you get tired.'

Every Rwandan I spoke with seemed to have a favorite, unanswerable question. For Nkongoli, it was how so many Tutsis had allowed themselves to be killed. For François Xavier Nkurunziza, a Kigali lawyer, whose father was Hutu and whose mother and wife were Tutsi, the question was how so many Hutus had allowed themselves to kill. Nkurunziza had escaped death only by chance as he moved around the country from one hiding place to another, and he had lost many family members. 'Conformity is very deep, very developed here,' he told me. 'In Rwandan history, everyone obeys authority. People revere power, and there isn't enough education. You take a poor, ignorant population, and give them

arms, and say, "It's yours. Kill." They'll obey. The peasants, who were paid or forced to kill, were looking up to people of higher socio-economic standing to see how to behave. So the people of influence, or the big financiers, are often the big men in the genocide. They may think that they didn't kill because they didn't take life with their own hands, but the people were looking to them for their orders. And, in Rwanda, an order can be given very quietly.'

As I traveled around the country, collecting accounts of the killing, it almost seemed as if, with the machete, the *masu*—a club studded with nails—a few well-placed grenades, and a few bursts of automatic-rifle fire, the quiet orders of Hutu Power had made the neutron bomb obsolete.

'Everyone was called to hunt the enemy,' said Theodore Nyilinkwaya, a survivor of the massacres in his home village of Kimbogo, in the southwestern province of Cyangugu. 'But let's say someone is reluctant. Say that guy comes with a stick. They tell him, "No, get a *masu*." So, OK, he does, and he runs along with the rest, but he doesn't kill. They say, "Hey, he might denounce us later. He must kill. Everyone must help to kill at least one person." So this person who is not a killer is made to do it. And the next day it's become a game for him. You don't need to keep pushing him.'

At Nyarubuye, even the little terracotta votive statues in the sacristy had been methodically decapitated. 'They were associated with Tutsis,' Sergeant Francis explained.

Study Question

1. Under what circumstances would ordinary people participate actively in the massacre of their fellow citizens?

STEPHEN LEWIS

Stephen Lewis was the UN Secretary-General's Special Envoy for HIV/AIDS in Africa (2001–06). Prior to accepting this position Lewis had been Canada's Ambassador to the United Nations in the 1980s and, before that, leader of the NDP opposition in Ontario in the 1970s. His first encounter with Africa came in the 1950s and 1960s when he worked with the World Assembly of Youth—an outgrowth of the Socialist International—in Ghana. In 2001 Kofi Annan selected Lewis to be the special envoy, assigned the unenviable duty of focusing western attention on the plight of AIDS-stricken sub-Saharan Africa. He gave the following briefing to the United Nations on 9 January 2003.

UN BRIEFING ON HIV/AIDS IN AFRICA

Last month, I spent two weeks touring four countries in Southern Africa: Lesotho, Zimbabwe, Malawi, and Zambia. The primary purpose was to view the link between hunger and AIDS. I want to look back at that visit, because little will have changed between then and now (except, perhaps, that things will have deteriorated further), and then look forward to the prospects for addressing the pandemic in 2003.

At the outset, however, let me express, yet again, the fundamental conviction I have every time I visit Africa: there is no question that the pandemic can be defeated. No matter how terrible the scourge of AIDS, no matter how limited the capacity to respond, no matter how devastating the human toll, it is absolutely certain that the pandemic can be turned around with a joint and Herculean effort between the African countries themselves and the international community.

I am weary to the point of exasperated impatience at the endless expressions of doubt about Africa's resolve and Africa's intentions and Africa's capacities. The truth is that all over the continent, even in the most extreme of circumstances, such as those which prevail today in the four nations I visited, Africans are engaged in endless numbers of initiatives and projects and programmes and models which, if taken to scale, if generalized throughout the country, would halt the pandemic, and prolong and save millions of lives.

What is required is a combination of political will and resources. The political will is increasingly there; the money is not. A major newspaper in the United States, reflecting on the paucity of resources, used the startling phrase 'murder by complacency'. I differ in only one particular: it's mass murder by complacency.

You will forgive me for the strong language. But as we enter the year 2003, the time for polite, even agitated, entreaties is over. This pandemic cannot be allowed to continue, and those who watch it unfold with a kind of pathological equanimity must be held to account. There may yet come a day when we have peacetime tribunals to deal with this particular version of crimes against humanity.

As bad as things are in Southern Africa—and they are terrible—every country I visited exhibited particular strengths and hopes.

The little country of Lesotho has a most impressive political leadership, but is absolutely impoverished. If it had some significant additional resources, with which to build capacity, it could begin to rescue countless lives. I vividly remember the Prime Minister of Lesotho saying to me 'We're told repeatedly by donors that we don't have capacity. I know we have no capacity; give us some help and we'll build the capacity.' It's worth remembering that Lesotho has a population greater than that of Namibia and Botswana, but it has nowhere near the same pockets of wealth. It has, however, one of the highest prevalence rates for HIV[1] on the continent . . . higher than Namibia; almost as high as Botswana . . . and is fatally compromised in its response by the lack of resources.

Zimbabwe, whatever the levels of political turbulence, has created a sturdy municipal infrastructure for the purpose of dealing with AIDS. You will know that for the last couple of years, Zimbabwe has had a three per cent surtax on corporate and personal income, devoted to work on AIDS. A good part of that money has been channelled down to district and village level, through a complex array of committees and structures which actually get the money to the grassroots. It's visible in the work of youth peer educators, outreach workers, and home care through community-based and faith-based organizations. In other words, for all the convulsions to which Zimbabwe is subject, there remains an elaborate capacity to implement programmes, if only there were more programmes to implement.

In Malawi, we may be about to see the most interesting of experiments in the provision of anti-retroviral treatment in the public sector. The Government of Malawi had originally intended to treat 25,000 people based on receipt of monies from the Global Fund. They then realized that the calculation of 25,000 was based on the purchase of patent drugs, but now that it is possible to purchase generic drugs, the numbers eligible for treatment could rise to 50,000. There has been, predictably, a great deal of skepticism in the donor and other communities. However, while we were in Malawi, the country was visited by a WHO team which carefully examined the capacity and delivery issues, and came to the conclusion that treating 50,000 people, phased in of course,

Stephen Lewis in Zimbabwe during his travels as a UN Special Envoy for HIV/AIDS in Africa. WFP/Brenda Barton.

was entirely possible. This is an exciting prospect: the treatments are meant to be free of charge, and delivered through the public health sector.

Zambia, whatever the difficulties—and they are overwhelming—is emerging from the bleak and dark ages of denial into the light of recognition. The bitter truth is that in the regime of the previous President, nothing was done. He spent his time disavowing the reality of AIDS, and hurling obstacles in the way of those who were desperate to confront the pandemic. I can recall personally attending an annual OAU Summit on behalf of UNICEF, and sitting down with the then President Chiluba, and asking him what he intended to do about AIDS, and he simply wouldn't talk to me about it. Well there's a new President in Zambia. And although he's been in place for only one year, everyone agrees that there's a dramatic change in the voice of political leadership around the subject of AIDS.

The fact is that in every country, even under the most appalling of human circumstance, there are signs of determination and hope. Whether they can be harnessed in the name of social change will be known in the year 2003. God knows, there are incredible hurdles to leap.

If I am to extract from my trip those aspects that made the greatest impression on me, they are six in number.

First, there is absolutely no doubt that hunger and AIDS have come together in a Hecate's[2] brew of horror. We saw it everywhere. How could it be otherwise? In Malawi, for example, analysis of the data shows that 50 per cent of poor households are affected by chronic illness due to HIV/AIDS. You can't till the soil, grow the crops, feed the family, when disease stalks the land. Add to that the reality of erratic rainfall and drought, and WFP and the broader UN family have a hugely daunting job.

I think the nadir was reached for me in the paediatric ward of the University Teaching Hospital in Lusaka.[3] The infants were clustered, stick-thin, three and four to a bed, most so weakened by hunger and ravaged by AIDS (a prevalence rate in the nutrition section of the ward of 56 per cent . . . in the respiratory section of the ward, 72 per cent), that they really had no chance. We were there for forty-five minutes. Every fifteen minutes, another child died, awkwardly covered with a sheet, then removed by a nurse, while the ward was filled with the anguished weeping of the mothers. A scene from hell.

Second, I couldn't help but feel, on occasion, that we were witnessing the grinding down of a society. We've all imagined the catastrophe, but no one wanted to believe that it could happen. The fact that the agricultural sector is beginning to decay could simply be a harbinger of worse to come. My own sense is that education is on the brink. In all of the countries, teachers were dead, teachers were dying, teachers were ill and away from school, children, especially girls, were being taken out of school to tend to sick and dying parents, children who had lost their parents to AIDS weren't in school because they couldn't afford the school fees. It felt, in every instance, as though the education sector was under siege. In Zambia, they lost 1,967 teachers in 2001, over two thousand teachers in 2002; the Teacher's Colleges are graduating fewer than one thousand a year. In parts of Malawi, HIV-positive teachers are estimated at over 30 per cent. How can education be sustained?

Or maybe the collapse of agriculture and education are happening simultaneously, and we fasten on agriculture simply because the human damage is visible and immediate. If you don't eat for five days, the consequence is far more dramatic than being out of school for five days. In Malawi they've done an analysis of the impact of AIDS on four different Ministries, and the erosion in each, in human terms, to a lesser or greater degree, is inescapable. It's necessary to recognize that even at a prevalence rate of 15 or 20 per cent, let alone 30 or 35 per cent as in Botswana, Lesotho, Zimbabwe, and Swaziland, the incessant, irreversible, cumulative death of so many productive members of society means, ultimately, that things fall apart. When Chinua Achebe wrote his novel of that title several decades ago, little did he know that it would be the mantra of whole societies. I wouldn't discount the possibility, 10 or 15 years down the road, of failed states.

Third, one of the saddest manifestations of a society coming apart at the seams, is the growing rate of sexual abuse of children and adolescents. I was frankly jolted by what we were told. Whether it was the plight of orphans in the mountains of Lesotho, or outreach workers telling gruesome stories, sotto voce, as we traveled in Zimbabwe, or the evidence we absorbed in Zambia, there seems little doubt that sexual assaults on children have reached shocking proportions. It's so bad in Zambia that a trio of women parliamentarians are actually introducing a private member's bill to counter 'child defilement'. The Director of the YWCA in Zambia told us that cases of sexual violation of children, reported to the Lusaka YWCA clinic, numbered 23 in 1998; 77 in 1999; 88 in 2000; 110 in 2001; 152 in the first ten months of 2002. And that's just in one of eleven clinics, and only the reported cases. Towards the end of this month, Human Rights Watch will release a powerful, heartbreaking monograph on the sexual abuse of girls in Zambia, and the link with HIV. There's something deeply, deeply wrong when children are the frequent victims of adult sexual violence.

It appears to happen to orphans especially. As they are moved from place to place, more and more distant from their origins, they become increasingly vulnerable to sexual abuse. Ironically, and bitterly, they also therefore become ever more vulnerable to HIV transmission.

Fourth, I've never before felt the impact of orphans so strongly. It struck me again that we have obvious ways of dealing with most other aspects of the pandemic, but dealing with the astronomic number of orphans is a new phenomenon for which the world has no evident solution. Public health has confronted and subdued terrible contagions of communicable disease at other moments in human history. One day, the same will be true for AIDS. But we've never before confronted the selective destruction of parents that leaves such a mass of orphans behind.

And it's necessary, I think, to recognize that the extended family, and the willing community, can never fully cope with the numbers. The result is the present and escalating reality of orphan street children, of orphan gangs, of orphan delinquency, as hordes of kids, torn from their familial roots, wander the continent, bewildered, lonely, disenfranchised from reality, angry, acting out, unable to relate to normal life. Some have already reached adulthood; they've had no love, no nurturing . . . how do they bring up their own children? And in the meantime, they can be

a high-risk group, posing a collective threat to social stability.

Fifth, if women are at the center of the pandemic, as they are, acutely vulnerable to infection on the one hand, doing all the care-giving for the sick and the orphans on the other, we saw precious little evidence of efforts at women's empowerment, sexual autonomy or gender equality. And there was certainly no effort whatsoever to relieve their unfair share of the burden. In fact, male hegemony was ubiquitous. On my return trip later this month, I intend to focus on what is being done to imbed the human rights of women in each country, such that they can save their lives.

Finally, the issue of antiretroviral treatment came up constantly and everywhere. Every single group of People Living With HIV/AIDS pounded the demand home in unrelenting fashion. There is a crescendo of rage and desperation which governments will ignore at their peril. In Malawi, the prospect of 50,000 people eligible for treatment in the foreseeable future brings a strong quotient of hope. But in Zambia, the amorphous prospect of perhaps ten thousand people entering into treatment, over time, the eligibility criteria not yet known, prompts nothing but anger. And in Zimbabwe and Lesotho, where treatment is at the earliest stage of discussion, there is a festering despair among those who need it now.

What has changed is the maturity, vehemence, and confidence of the organizations of People Living With HIV/AIDS. Time and again we met activists who know everything there is to know about CD4 counts and viral loads; they know the cost of generic drugs; they know about the treatment regimens; they know that WHO[+] has undertaken to have three million people in treatment by 2005; they know that the rich members of society vault down to South Africa for treatment, while the poor remain helplessly behind; they know about Doha and intellectual property rights and the WTO; they know, from bitter experience, about all the false political promises. Increasingly, we're dealing with sophistication and determination in equal measure.

When I met with the group of People Living With HIV/AIDS in Lusaka, they presented me with a powerful and encyclopedic brief, a small part of which read as follows: '. . . for each day that passes without people accessing treatment we attend funerals. People die. We hear a hundred reasons for not providing people with treatment. For each reason given, lives are lost. The government must realize that it has a responsibility to provide health care for its people. Any government that fails to put in place measures to ensure the health of its citizens is not a government worth its name. Such governments should resign. If it does not do so, then people are justified to remove it by any means necessary. The right to life and dignity should not be a preserve of the rich and powerful.'

'What we are seeing in Zambia is a microcosm of what is happening globally. The HIV/AIDS crisis is not a crisis of lack of resources. It is a crisis of lack of conscience. It is the obscene gap between the haves and the have-nots that is driving this holocaust. . . .'

That issue of the obscene gap brings me to the end of these notes, and to the beginning of 2003.

The crucial new component that emerged from the trip to Southern Africa was the role of the Global Fund. It is impossible to overstate how strongly people feel—from Cabinet Ministers to People Living With HIV/AIDS—that the Global Fund is the best vehicle we have to finance the struggle against the pandemic. Every country yielded the same questions: When will the money come? Does the Global Fund have enough money? Why don't governments contribute to it? What happens if it goes bankrupt?

The questions are germane. As I understand it, the Global Fund has enough resources to get through the next round of proposals at the end of this month, but then it faces the moment of truth.

The Global Fund, after January, can be said to be in crisis.

It's legitimate to ask: what's wrong with this world? What's wrong with the rich countries? Why are they willing to jeopardize the integrity of the most hopeful financial instrument we have to combat the cruelest disease the world has ever seen?

But it gets worse. I want to say what we're all saying privately to each other. If, as some suggest, there is a war in Iraq come February, then the war will eclipse every other international human priority, HIV/AIDS included. In other words, if the United States, and the other members of the G7 don't augment their contributions to the Global Fund in the immediate future, we will be in desperate trouble. Wars divert attention, wars consume resources, wars ride roughshod over external calamities.

People living with HIV/AIDS are in a race against time. What they never imagined was that over and above the virus itself, there would be a new adversary, and that adversary would be a war.

Notes

1. In 2004 Lesotho's HIV infection rate was 28.9 per cent.
2. Hecate (Hecuba) was regarded in Greece as a goddess of magic. Over the years she became associated with the dark side of magic and eventually her name became synonymous with 'witch'.
3. The capital of Zambia.
4. The World Health Organization.

Study Question

1. 'The HIV/AIDS crisis is not a crisis of lack of resources. It is a crisis of lack of conscience. It is the obscene gap between the haves and the have-nots that is driving this holocaust.' Is this an accurate assessment?

ROBERT KAPLAN

'The Coming Anarchy' was originally published in The Atlantic Monthly in February 1994. When Kaplan republished the article in 2000, he observed that "'The Coming Anarchy" opens with a dire description of Africa, where at the moment nearly a dozen wars are in progress as the boundaries fixed by colonialist powers unravel, and the criminalization of regimes . . . proceeds apace. . . . But Africa is not a bellwether for politics in the rest of the world, as I indicated six years ago when I wrote the article. I still believe, though, that so-called democratic success stories like Nigeria are epiphenomena in a larger pattern of demographic and environmental upheaval.'[1]

THE COMING ANARCHY

West Africa is becoming *the* symbol of worldwide demographic, environmental, and societal stress, in which criminal anarchy emerges as the real 'strategic' danger. Disease, over-population, unprovoked crime, scarcity of resources, refugee migrations, the increasing erosion of nation-states and international borders, and the empowerment of private armies, security firms, and international drug cartels are now most tellingly demonstrated through a West African prism. West Africa provides an appropriate introduction to the issues, often extremely unpleasant to discuss, that will soon confront our civilization. To remap the political earth the way it will be a few decades hence—as I intend to do in this article—I find I must begin with West Africa.

There is no other place on the planet where political maps are so deceptive—where, in fact, they tell such lies—as in West Africa. Start with Sierra Leone. According to the map, it is a nation-state of defined borders, with a government in control of its territory. In truth the Sierra Leonian government, run by a twenty-seven-year-old army captain, Valentine Strasser,[2] controls Freetown by day and by day also controls part of the rural interior. In the government's territory the national army is an unruly rabble threatening drivers and passengers at most checkpoints. In the other part of the country units of two separate armies from the war in Liberia have taken up residence, as has an army of Sierra Leonian rebels. The government force fighting the rebels is full of renegade commanders who have aligned themselves with disaffected village chiefs. A pre-modern formlessness governs the battlefield, evoking the wars in medieval Europe prior to the 1648 Peace of Westphalia, which ushered in the era of organized nation-states.

As a consequence, roughly 400,000 Sierra Leonians are internally displaced, 280,000 more have fled to neighboring Guinea, and another 100,000 have fled to Liberia, even as 400,000 Liberians have fled to Sierra Leone. The third largest city in Sierra Leone, Gondama, is a displaced-persons camp. With an additional 600,000 Liberians in Guinea and 250,000 in the Ivory Coast, the borders dividing these four countries have become largely meaningless. Even in quiet zones none of the governments except the Ivory Coast's maintains the schools, bridges, roads, and police forces in a manner necessary for functional sovereignty. The Koranko ethnic group in northeastern Sierra Leone does all its trading in Guinea. Sierra Leonian diamonds are more likely to be sold in Liberia than in Freetown. In the eastern provinces of Sierra Leone you can buy Liberian beer but not the local brand.

In Sierra Leone, as in Guinea, as in the Ivory Coast, as in Ghana, most of the primary rain forest and the secondary bush is being destroyed at an alarming rate. I saw convoys of trucks bearing majestic hardwood trunks to coastal ports. When Sierra Leone achieved its independence, in 1961, as much as 60 per cent of the country was primary rain forest. Now 6 per cent is. In the Ivory Coast the proportion has fallen from 38 per cent to 8 per cent. The deforestation has led to soil erosion, which has led to more flooding and more mosquitoes. Virtually everyone in the West African interior has some form of malaria.

Sierra Leone is a microcosm of what is occurring, albeit in a more tempered and gradual manner, throughout West Africa and much of the underdeveloped world: the withering away of central governments, the rise of tribal and regional domains, the unchecked spread of disease, and the growing pervasiveness of war. West Africa is reverting to the Africa of the Victorian atlas. It consists now of a series of coastal trading posts, such as Freetown and Conakry, and an interior that, owing to violence, volatility, and disease, is again becoming, as Graham Greene once observed, 'blank—' and 'unexplored'. However, whereas Greene's vision implies a certain romance, as in the somnolent and charmingly seedy

Freetown of his celebrated novel *The Heart of the Matter*, it is Thomas Malthus, the philosopher of demographic doomsday, who is now the prophet of West Africa's future. And West Africa's future, eventually, will also be that of most of the rest of the world.

Notes

1. Robert D. Kaplan, *The Coming Anarchy* (New York: Random House, 2000), xiii–xiv.

2. Strasser was deposed in 1996 but the civil war continued until a 2002 peace settlement. A UN peacekeeping force maintains this peace, but the 2005 CIA World Factbook notes that 'domestic fighting among disparate rebel groups, warlords, and youth gangs in . . . Sierra Leone perpetuate insurgencies, street violence, looting, arms trafficking, ethnic conflicts, and refugees in border areas.

Study Question

1. Kaplan resurrects the arguments of Thomas Malthus—that global population will soon outstrip available resources, with dire consequences. Is this a valid argument?

TIPS FOR ANALYSIS

Transmission of the Document

Consider how the document reached its present state. Has it been translated? Has it passed through the hands of an editor—or several editors—and, if so, how has the document been altered? Has the document been substantially shortened? If so, consider the ways in which this might affect your perception of the material.

Web Resources

Development Cooperation Directorate (OECD)
http://www.oecd.org/department/0,3355,en_2649_33721_1_1_1_1_1,00.html
Women and Development Resources
http://www.gdrc.org/gender/link-resources.html
UNESCO
http://portal.unesco.org
Library of Congress: Global Gateway
http://international.loc.gov/intldl/intldlhome.html

Recommended Reading

Gil Courtemanche, *A Sunday at the Pool in Kigali* (New York: Knopf, 2003). Courtemanche's violent novel is set in the period leading up to the Rwandan genocide. The story, part fiction and part first-hand experience, weaves AIDS, genocide, tribalism, and ethnicity into an account involving western journalists, aid workers, the UN, the IMF, and the global economy.

Zakes Mda, *Heart of Redness* (New York: Picador, 2003). Mda's *Heart of Redness* is set in post-apartheid South Africa, where the problems of the present, particularly economic development, are tied to events in the past. The story is centred on the Xhosa people who, in the era of the Zulu Wars, had followed a messianic prophet. This divided the region between followers and non-believers, a division that continues to influence the present problems.

Michael Onjdaate, *Anil's Ghost* (New York: Vintage, 2001). Onjdaate's novel, set in Sri Lanka in the 1980s and 1990s during the bloody civil war, illustrates that atrocities were committed by all sides of the conflict: government, opposition, and separatist guerrillas. *Anil's Ghost* raises issues of ethnicity, religion, identity, terror, and control.

Orhan Pamuk, *Snow* (New York: Knopf, 2004). Orhan Pamuk, an Istanbul-based author, creates a story of tension in present-day Turkey: between religion and secularism, East and West. The novel also examines issues of poverty, politics, competing cultures (Russian and Ottoman), radical Islam, Western secularism, socialism, and Kurdish separatism.

Natasha Radojcic-Kane, *Homecoming* (New York: Simon Pulse, 2002). *Homecoming* is told through the eyes of a Muslim soldier who returns home from the Bosnian War to a scene of poverty, crime, corruption, and revenge. Radojcic-Kane examines old hatreds and new grievances, as well as the ongoing clash of cultures in the Balkans.

Recommended Viewing

Before the Rain (Macedonia/France/UK, 1994). Director: Milcho Manchevski. *Before the Rain* examines the ethnic and religious violence dividing the nation of Macedonia as it gained its independence from the former Yugoslavia, as well as the political conflict that resulted and the complex relationships existing between the many peoples of the region.

God Fights Back (UK/USA, 1999). Director: Ben Loeterman/WGBH Boston/BBC (Documentary). This documentary examines religious fundamentalism in both the west and the east, focusing on the extremes of the Iranian revolution and the rise of Jerry Falwell and his 'moral majority'. Loeterman also looks at televangelists and religious fundamentalists in Egypt and Algeria.

Kandahar (Iran/France, 2001). Director: Mohsen Makhmalbaf. Part fiction and part documentary, in *Kandahar* a reporter returns to Taliban-ruled Afghanistan to find her sister. Major themes include the Taliban's impact on women and families, on education, on the traditional culture of Afghanistan, as well as the results of the land-mines that have been planted across the country.

No Man's Land (Slovenia/France, 2001). Director: Danis Tanovic. Set during the 1993 conflict between Bosnia and Serbia, *No Man's Land* reveals historical hatreds and the misunderstandings between soldiers of the two nations. It also examines the involvement of UN in the conflict, the inability of the UN to take any real action, and the role of media in war.

Hotel Rwanda (South Africa/UK/Italy, 2004). Director: Terry George. *Hotel Rwanda* recounts the real-life story of Paul Rusesabagina, manager of the Hotel des Milles Collines, which became a makeshift shelter for over 1,200 Tutsi and moderate Hutu refugees from genocide. George's film captures the savagery of the genocide and the international community's betrayal of its victims.

Khomeini's Children (Iran, 2004). Director: Yorgos Avgeropoulos (Documentary). Focusing on the children born after the Iranian Revolution, this 58-minute documentary looks at their rebellion and quest for freedom from the restrictions of the religious authorities. The film also looks at the ideologies of more radical opposition groups.

CHAPTER NINETEEN

HISTORY IN THE MAKING: INTO THE TWENTY-FIRST CENTURY

Cartoonist Anita Kunz satirizes the increasing US tendency to flex its economic and political muscle (1997). © Anita Kunz. All rights reserved.

In the concluding chapter of *Conflict and Co-operation*, the documents introduce a number of the key issues that seem poised to shape the early decades of the twenty-first century. Several of the documents focus on the trend towards globalism[1] and its consequences. S.P. Udayakumar and john a. powell evaluate the destructive relationship among race, poverty, and economic globalization.

The excerpt from Naomi Klein's *No Logo* looks at the phenomenon of 'branding' and its global implications, while Robert Kaplan points out the power held by some of the world's major corporations and its consequences. The problems and potential inherent in the spread of democracy are the focus of articles by Mangosuthu Buthelezi and Mohamed Elhachmi Hamdi. Buthelezi sees in democracy a potential solution to the problems plaguing sub-Saharan Africa. Hamdi, however, speaks of the hypocrisy inherent in the export of democracy and secularism.

There can be no doubt that the first decade of the twenty-first century has been profoundly influenced by the 11 September 2001 terrorist attack on the World Trade Center in New York, the subsequent American intervention in Iraq, and the removal of Saddam Hussein from power. The article excerpted from *The Guardian* brings together leading historians to debate the justification for the war, while Noam Chomsky assesses the state of the early antiwar movement. One of the consequences of American intervention—namely, the further radicalization of America's enemies—is made clear in a 2004 speech by Osama bin Laden.

The early twenty-first century has also seen a renewed shift to the left in South America and the reemergence of Russian power in Europe. A speech by Hugo Chávez reflects on the possibility of a brighter future for Latin America, inspired by the vision of its liberator, Simon Bolivar. Finally, Vladimir Putin discusses the end of American dominance and future global security in a multipolar world.

Note

1. 'Globalism' is used here rather than 'globalization' since the latter tends to have a more exclusively economic connotation.

S.P. UDAYAKUMAR AND john a. powell

S.P. Udayakumar was a Research Associate and Co-Director of Programs at the Institute on Race and Poverty, University of Minnesota, Minneapolis. He currently runs the South Asian Community Center for Education and Research (SACCER) at Nagercoil, Tamil Nadu, India. john a. powell is director of the Institute for the Study of Race and Ethnicity in the Americas at Ohio State University and the Gregory H. Williams Chair in Civil Rights and Civil Liberties in the Moritz College of Law. The following article, written in 2000, examines many of the worst effects of globalism, especially on people of colour.

RACE, POVERTY, AND GLOBALIZATION

The world economy is in a state of what is commonly viewed as unprecedented growth. But with this growth has come dangerous and destructive economic disparity. On the one hand, we see the 'impressive' economy in the Northern Hemisphere, particularly in the United States, where Silicon Valley, a region of 2.3 million people, has produced tens of thousands of millionaires, with 64 new ones every day. There are regular US reports of historically low unemployment rates, labor shortages, and booming economy.

On the other hand, many people of color, particularly those in the Southern Hemisphere, do not have enough food to eat, resulting in malnutrition and disease. They face growing inflation while their governments, which used to subsidize some aspects of their marginal living, are urged to stop subsidies for food and adopt a more market-oriented economics. Many workers in these economies are trapped in poor working conditions with low pay. Women are often expected to do back-breaking farm and domestic work, with few rights or benefits. Yet many of the fiscal policies pushed onto developing countries and adopted in northern countries exacerbate the problem of the most marginal while celebrating the wealth of the rich.

In the North as well, people of color often find themselves being left farther and farther behind. Even as states in the US and the nation as a whole report budget surpluses, we seem unable or unwilling to provide adequate housing for the growing number of working-class and homeless families, to repair the physical structure of schools that house low-income students of color, or to provide social services or medical attention for those most in need.

Sweatshops that employ people of color working as virtual slave laborers are tolerated—even encouraged—as part of the new world trade. The public space people of color and marginal groups are most dependent on—whether it is public hospitals, schools, parks, or a social welfare system—is constantly attacked as inconsistent with the needs of capital and the market. Indeed, we are encouraged to remake public space to mimic private space with a market, anti-democratic orientation where we are consumers, not citizens.

How are these disparate conditions related to globalism, and why are people of color under the most severe threat from this process? Certainly, other people are also under a threat from this globalization process, and some would assert that democracy and capitalism itself may be undone by this process if it is not checked. To answer the above question and to understand why minorities and other marginal populations are most at risk, it is first necessary to better understand what globalism is, particularly the type of globalism that dominates today's markets.

What Is Globalism?

In the most general sense, globalism refers to the process in which goods and services, including capital, move more freely within and among nations. As globalism advances, national boundaries become more and more porous, and to some extent, less and less relevant.

Since many of our early industries, such as steel, were location-sensitive, there was a natural limitation to globalization. To be sure, some things remain location-sensitive, but mobility is the trend. It is assumed that liberalizing laws and structures, so that goods and services can become more globally focused, will produce more wealth, and indeed this seems to be true. Using this general understanding of globalism and globalization, it would be accurate to say this process has been developing and growing for well over a hundred years.

But there have been many changes in the globalization process in the last two decades that makes it distinct from earlier incarnations. The major thing being traded in today's global market is information and capital itself, rather than commodities or other products. Technological change allows capital to move almost instantaneously. Changes in monetary policies, as well as in what is being traded and the importance of capital, have created a global market distinctively different from previous eras. Earlier products and capital were more rooted to a place. Today, many of the things traded and produced in the global market, such as knowledge and computer technology, are extremely mobile or rootless.

The United States has emerged as the only world superpower. This has allowed the US tremendous influence in setting the terms for global trade. The style of globalism pushed by the United States has favored the free movement and protection of capital, while being at best indifferent and at worst hostile to the more place-dependent labor. It is the dual relationship of mobile capital and fixed, unorganized, and unprotected labor that has created the conditions for capital to dominate. This has been greatly enhanced by the US position toward organized labor and capital. While the US has been aggressive in protecting capital both at home and abroad, it has encouraged both the weakening of organized labor and removing protections for workers.

While both Japan and Europe have aggressively pushed for globalism, each has been more willing to protect labor, the environment, and certain markets—at least within their own borders. It is the United States that has consistently been the most radical on liberalizing capital and protecting it as it moves across boundaries, and the most hostile to protecting labor and fragile markets. Protecting labor expresses itself not only in strong unions and workers' benefits but also in a strong social welfare system. The United States has purposefully moved toward weaker labor unions, as well as an anemic social welfare system. It has used the globalism it advocates as justification for keeping workers' jobs insecure, pay and benefits relatively low. Workers are told that pushing hard for benefits will cause capital to leave to another location in the country or the world where workers are willing to work for less with fewer benefits.

The United States and the international organizations over which it has substantial influence, such as the International Monetary Fund, have demanded protection of capital and encouraged or tolerated the suppression of labor and the environment in the weaker southern countries. Capital is actively being directed to markets with low wages, where workers are sometimes abused, and labor organizations suppressed. The wealth this globalism is creating is being forcefully subsidized by vulnerable workers and the environment, especially in the Southern Hemisphere. This logic is then used to weaken the position of labor in the North, as we are required to compete with unorganized, suppressed labor in the South.

While sweatshops and slave labor may attract capital investments, what about the futures of black welfare mothers in Detroit or the Aborigines in Australia, who need government assistance to take advantage of, say, the educational system? How or why does US-style globalism affect their needs? US-style globalism not only attempts to suppress labor, but also seeks to suppress social welfare systems and support for public expenditures that do not directly benefit the expansion of capital. The social welfare system and other public services, such as schools, social services in the North, and food subsidies in the South, are supported through taxes, and taxes reduce short-term benefits to capital.

In the North, it is women and minorities who are most dependent on the public sector. These racial and gender correlations make it all the easier to attack the legitimacy of taxation for this purpose. Taxes are seen as undesirable because they reduce profits and interfere with the market. But the public space, including the welfare system, can only be supported by the public in the form of taxes. Whether we are talking about education or other public services, we are encouraged to believe that they should be as limited as possible and made to mimic the market. Those who cannot thrive in the market environment without help, especially if they are people of color, are seen as free-loaders and illegitimate. In many ways, much of the public space in the United States becomes associated with people of color.

Goodbye, Democratic Vision?

Public purposes and civic goods—to the extent they are even recognized—are no longer to be achieved through public institutions but are to be privatized. The democratic vision associated with public functions is to be abandoned or seriously curtailed in favor of the ideal of efficiency. There is an abiding belief that democracy must be limited because it interferes with the private decisions of market experts, thereby reducing wealth and capital. And anything that is perceived as interfering with the growth of capitalism—be it the social welfare system, labor unions, civil rights, or government programs—is being curtailed, while government policies and structures that protect capital, including the military, are enhanced.

Although proponents of this style of globalism purport to support democracy, it is only in a role subservient to capital. In the United States, we are softly encouraged to vote, while being constantly reminded that in these global matters that shape our everyday life, we have no say. We are told that no city, state, or nation can or should try to influence this powerful but uncontrollable process. We are reminded that one can regulate capital, and any attempt to do so will hurt the economy.

The deregulation of capital is made to appear both good and natural. Our attention is drawn away from the fact that there are powerful organizations supported by the US government's leadership that protect and facilitate the flow of capital. These institutions include the World Bank, International Development Association, International Finance Corporation, International Monetary Fund, World Trade Organization, etc.

Unfortunately, there are no organizations of equal stature to protect the interests of workers, racial minorities, the environment, or women and children. There are, of course, several treaties and international instruments dealing with some of these issues, such as the Convention on International Trade in Endangered Species, Convention on the Elimination of All Forms of Discrimination Against Women, Declaration on the Rights of Persons Belonging to National or Ethnic, Religious or Linguistic Minorities, and so forth.

However, they are nearly impotent, compared with the institutions with far-reaching and substantial goals of protecting capital. When citizens try to raise such issues, it is simply asserted that making working conditions or the environment part of trade agreements would unduly interfere with free trade. American-style globalism has not just transformed the flow of capital, it has transformed the role of government and the meaning of citizenship.

People are now brought together as consumers but kept apart as citizens. The transformed role of government is not to protect citizens or the precious safety net of public space but to protect and facilitate the flow of capital. So today we speak of free markets but not of free labor. We speak of an expanding global market, but a diminishing public space, and we hardly speak at all of citizen participation and justice. This is an authoritarian vision where armies police people and nations, so capital might be free.

It is very doubtful that capital, despite advances in technology, would be nearly as mobile as it is without the nationally brokered agreements that have the force of law and the coercive power of the state behind them. But while capital relies on the government to do its bidding, we enjoy freedom as individuals without the power that only comes from the collective action of informed citizens. While it might be true that cities and states, and certainly private individuals, can do little to influence globalism, it is clearly false that nations, especially the United States, are powerless in the face of globalism.

Undermining Social Movements

During the last part of the 20th century, the Civil Rights Movement, the women's movement, and the environmental movement advanced their claims for inclusion and justice. An attack on the public role of the state is a powerful strategy to limit the aspirations of these groups. They are made impotent in a forum where wealth, not votes, dictates policies. These groups are marginalized in an economic arena that transforms the market, with decisions made behind closed doors, and not in public and civic spaces.

Destruction of the public space also results in a decline of the public voice. In the United States, this decline in the role and scope of democracy in the relationship to the market occurred just when the Civil Rights Movement began to make significant gains in securing for blacks and other minorities real access to the political process.

This article, then, is not an attack on globalism per se but on the excess and undemocratic nature of the US-style globalism popular now, which is particularly hostile to people of color and other marginal groups. This style of globalism disempowers average Americans in every way, except as consumers. Globalization has been happening for over a century and will continue.

It must be re-envisioned to appropriately protect capital, but also to protect labor, the environment, and people of color. These concerns must be seen as interrelated, not as separate. Furthermore, we must create the necessary international structures with transparency and accountability in order to make this vision a reality and to develop suitable remedies for the plight of marginalized peoples. These steps should not be seen as hostile to business, but as an appropriate cost of doing business in a justice-oriented and sustainable global economy.

Despite the rhetoric about the unmitigated good that can come from US-style globalism, there is an increasing call to look more closely at the process as it relates to people and the environment throughout the world. Some assert that US-style globalism threatens democracy. Others argue that this style of globalism threatens capitalism itself. We think that both claims may be right.

We believe it is critical to look more closely at what globalism means for people in general and people of color in particular. Given its more recent history of developing a social compact that includes all people, the United States should not be championing a style of globalism that is blind to the needs of some sectors. If this process continues, we are likely to permanently re-inscribe a subordinated, life-threatening status for people of color all over the globe and rationalize it with an invisible hand. We can change this by working to make the invisible visible.

Study Question

1. The authors argue that while people may be powerless in the face of globalism nations are not. Is this accurate?

NAOMI KLEIN

Naomi Klein was born in Montreal in 1970. Prior to authoring the best-selling No Logo *she was an award-winning journalist for* The Globe and Mail *and* The Guardian. *Klein was profoundly influenced by the December 1989 murder of fourteen women at Montreal's École Polytechnique, an event that occurred while she was a student at the University of* Toronto. *Soon after, Klein became a political activist, defending the rights of women, minorities, and the gay community. At the same time, she also began to focus on the degree to which corporations were moving onto university campuses and imposing their 'brands' on the institutions.* No Logo *begins with a look at the issue of branding and its origins.*

NO LOGO

It's helpful to go back briefly and look at where the idea of branding first began. Though the words are often used interchangeably, branding and advertising are not the same process. Advertising any given product is only one part of branding's grand plan, as are sponsorship and logo licensing. Think of the brand as the core meaning of the modern corporation, and of the advertisement as one vehicle used to convey that meaning to the world.

The first mass-marketing campaigns, starting in the second half of the nineteenth century, had more to do with advertising than with branding as we understand it today. Faced with a range of recently invented products—the radio, phonograph, car, light bulb and so on—advertisers had more pressing tasks than creating a brand identity for any given corporation; first, they had to change the way people lived their lives. Ads had to inform consumers about the existence of some new invention, then convince them that their lives would be better if they used, for example, cars instead of wagons, telephones instead of mail and electric light instead of oil lamps. Many of these new products bore brand names—some of which are still around today—but these were almost incidental. These products were themselves news; that was almost advertisement enough.

The first brand-based products appeared at around the same time as the invention-based ads, largely because of another relatively recent innovation: the factory. When goods began to be produced in factories, not only were entirely new products being introduced but old products—even basic staples—were appearing in strikingly new forms. What made early branding efforts different from more straightforward salesmanship was that the market was now being flooded with uniform mass-produced products that were virtually indistinguishable from one another. Competitive branding became a necessity of the machine age—within a context of manufactured sameness, image-based difference had to be manufactured along with the product.

So the role of advertising changed from delivering product news bulletins to building an image around a particular brand-name version of a product. The first task of branding was to bestow proper names on generic goods such as sugar, flour, soap and cereal, which had previously been scooped out of barrels by local shopkeepers. In the 1880s, corporate logos were introduced to mass-produced products like Campbell's Soup, H.J. Heinz pickles and Quaker Oats cereal. As design historians and theorists Ellen Lupton and J. Abbott Miller note, logos were tailored to evoke familiarity and folksiness. . . , in an effort to counteract the new and unsettling anonymity of packaged goods. 'Familiar personalities such as Dr Brown, Uncle Ben, Aunt Jemima, and Old Grand-Dad came to replace the shop-keeper, who was traditionally responsible for measuring bulk foods for customers and acting as an advocate for products . . . a nationwide vocabulary of brand names replaced the small local shopkeeper as the interface between consumer and product.' After the product names and characters had been established, advertising gave them a venue to speak directly to would-be consumers. The corporate 'personality', uniquely named, packaged and advertised, had arrived.

For the most part, the ad campaigns at the end of the nineteenth century and the start of the twentieth used a set of rigid, pseudoscientific formulas: rivals were never mentioned, ad copy used declarative statements only and headlines had to be large, with lots of white space—according to one turn-of-the-century adman, 'an advertisement should be big enough to make an impression but not any bigger than the thing advertised.'

But there were those in the industry who understood that advertising wasn't just scientific; it was also spiritual. Brands could conjure a feeling—think of Aunt Jemima's comforting presence—but not only that, entire corporations could themselves embody a meaning of their own. In the early twenties, legendary adman Bruce Barton turned General Motors into a metaphor for the American family, 'something personal, warm, and human,' while GE was not so much the name of the faceless General Electric Company as, in Barton's words, 'the initials of a friend'. In 1923 Barton said that the role of advertising was to help corporations find their soul. The son of a preacher, he drew on his religious upbringing for uplifting messages: 'I like to think of advertising as something big, something splendid, something which goes deep down into an institution and gets hold of the soul of it. . . . Institutions have souls, just as men and nations have souls,' he told GM president Pierre du Pont. General Motors

ads began to tell stories about the people who drove its cars—the preacher, the pharmacist, or the country doctor who, thanks to his trusty GM, arrived 'at the bedside of a dying child' just in time 'to bring it back to life'.

By the end of the 1940s, there was a burgeoning awareness that a brand wasn't just a mascot or a catchphrase or a picture printed on the label of a company's product; the company as a whole could have a brand identity or a 'corporate consciousness', as this ephemeral quality was termed at the time. As this idea evolved, the adman ceased to see himself as a pitchman and instead saw himself as 'the philosopher-king of commercial culture,' in the words of ad critic Randall Rothberg. The search for the true meaning of brands—or the 'brand essence', as it is often called—gradually took the agencies away from individual products and their attributes and toward a psychological/anthropological examination of what brands mean to the culture and to people's lives. This was seen to be of crucial importance, since corporations may manufacture products, but what consumers buy are brands.

It took several decades for the manufacturing world to adjust to this shift. It clung to the idea that its core business was still production and that branding was an important add-on. Then came the brand equity mania of the eighties, the defining moment of which arrived in 1988 when Philip Morris purchased Kraft for $12.6 billion—six times what the company was worth on paper. The price difference, apparently, was the cost of the word 'Kraft'. Of course Wall Street was aware that decades of marketing and brand bolstering added value to a company over and above its assets and total annual sales. But with the Kraft purchase, a huge dollar value had been assigned to something that had previously been abstract and unquantifiable—a brand name. This was spectacular news for the ad world, which was now able to make the claim that advertising spending was more than just a sales strategy: it was an investment in cold hard equity. The more you spend, the more your company is worth. Not surprisingly, this led to a considerable increase in spending on advertising. More important, it sparked a renewed interest in puffing up brand identities, a project that involved far more than a few billboards and TV spots. It was about pushing the envelope in sponsorship deals, dreaming up new areas in which to 'extend' the brand, as well as perpetually probing the zeitgeist to ensure that the 'essence' selected for one's brand would resonate karmically with its target market. For reasons that will be explored in the rest of this chapter, this radical shift in corporate philosophy has sent manufacturers on a cultural feeding frenzy as they seize upon every corner of unmarketed landscape in search of the oxygen needed to inflate their brands. In the process, virtually nothing has been left un-branded. That's quite an impressive feat, considering that as recently as 1993 Wall Street had pronounced the brand dead, or as good as dead. . . .

The Brands Bounce Back

There were some brands that were watching from the sidelines as Wall Street declared the death of the brand. Funny, they must have thought, we don't feel dead.

Just as the admen had predicted at the beginning of the recession, the companies that exited the downturn [of the late 1980s and early 1990s] running were the ones who opted for marketing over value every time: Nike, Apple, the Body Shop, Calvin Klein, Disney, Levi's and Starbucks. Not only were these brands doing just fine, thank you very much, but the act of branding was becoming a larger and larger focus of their businesses. For these companies, the ostensible product was mere filler for the real production: the brand. They integrated the idea of branding into the very fabric of their companies. Their corporate cultures were so tight and cloistered that to outsiders they appeared to be a cross between fraternity house,

religious cult and sanitarium. Everything was an ad for the brand: bizarre lexicons for describing employees (partners, baristas, team players, crew members), company chants, superstar CEOs, fanatical attention to design consistency, a propensity for monument-building, and New Age mission statements. Unlike classic household brand names, such as Tide and Marlboro, these logos weren't losing their currency, they were in the midst of breaking every barrier in the marketing world—becoming cultural accessories and lifestyle philosophers. These companies didn't wear their image like a cheap shirt—their image was so integrated with their business that other people wore it as *their* shirt. And when the brands crashed, these companies didn't even notice—they were branded to the bone.

So the real legacy of Marlboro Friday is that it simultaneously brought the two most significant developments in nineties marketing and consumerism into sharp focus: the deeply unhip big-box bargain stores that provide the essentials of life and monopolize a disproportionate share of the market (Wal-Mart *et al.*) and the extra-premium 'attitude' brands that provide the essentials of lifestyle and monopolize ever-expanding stretches of cultural space (Nike *et al.*). The way these two tiers of consumerism developed would have a profound impact on the economy in the years to come. When overall ad expenditures took a nosedive in 1991, Nike and Reebok were busy playing advertising chicken, with each company increasing its budget to outspend the other. . . . In 1991 alone, Reebok upped its ad spending by 71.9 per cent, while Nike pumped an extra 24.6 per cent into its already soaring ad budget, bringing the company's total spending on marketing to a staggering $250 million annually. Far from worrying about competing on price, the sneaker pimps were designing ever more intricate and pseudoscientific air pockets, and driving up prices by signing star athletes to colossal sponsorship deals. The fetish strategy seemed to be working fine: in the six years prior to 1993, Nike had gone from a $750 million company to a $4 billion one and Phil Knight's Beaverton, Oregon, company emerged from the recession with profits 900 per cent higher than when it began.

Benetton and Calvin Klein, meanwhile, were also upping their spending on lifestyle marketing, using ads to associate their lines with risqué art and progressive politics. Clothes barely appeared in these high-concept advertisements, let alone prices. Even more abstract was Absolut Vodka, which for some years now had been developing a marketing strategy in which its product disappeared and its brand was nothing but a blank bottle-shaped space that could be filled with whatever content a particular audience most wanted from its brands: intellectual in *Harper's*, futuristic in *Wired*, alternative in *Spin*, loud and proud in *Out* and 'Absolut Centerfold' in *Playboy*. The brand reinvented itself as a cultural sponge, soaking up and morphing to its surroundings. . . .

Saturn, too, came out of nowhere in October 1990 when GM launched a car built not out of steel and rubber but out of New Age spirituality and seventies feminism. After the car had been on the market a few years, the company held a 'homecoming' weekend for Saturn owners, during which they could visit the auto plant and have a cookout with the people who made their cars. As the Saturn ads boasted at the time, '44,000 people spent their vacations with us, at a car plant.' It was as if Aunt Jemima had come to life and invited you over to her house for dinner.

In 1993, the year the Marlboro Man was temporarily hobbled by 'brand-blind' consumers, Microsoft made its striking debut on *Advertising Age's* list of the top 200 ad spenders—the very same year that Apple computer increased its marketing budget by 30 per cent after already making branding history with its Orwellian takeoff ad launch during the 1984 Super Bowl. . . . Like Saturn, both companies were selling a hip new

relationship to the machine that left Big Blue IBM looking as clunky and menacing as the now-dead Cold War.

And then there were the companies that had always understood that they were selling brands before product. Coke, Pepsi, McDonald's, Burger King, and Disney weren't fazed by the brand crisis, opting instead to escalate the brand war, especially since they had their eyes firmly fixed on global expansion. . . . They were joined in this project by a wave of sophisticated producer/retailers who hit full stride in the late eighties and early nineties. The Gap, IKEA, and the Body Shop were spreading like wildfire during this period, masterfully transforming the generic into the brand-specific, largely through bold, carefully branded packaging and the promotion of an 'experiential' shopping environment. The Body Shop had been a presence in Britain since the seventies, but it wasn't until 1988 that it began sprouting like a green weed on every street corner in the US. Even during the darkest years of the recession, the company opened between forty and fifty American stores a year. Most baffling of all to Wall Street, it pulled off the expansion without spending a dime on advertising. Who needed billboards and magazine ads when retail outlets were three-dimensional advertisements for an ethical and ecological approach to cosmetics? The Body Shop was all brand.

The Starbucks coffee chain, meanwhile, was also expanding during this period without laying out much in advertising; instead, it was spinning off its name into a wide range of branded projects: Starbucks airline coffee, office coffee, coffee ice cream, coffee beer. Starbucks seemed to understand brand names at a level even deeper than Madison Avenue, incorporating marketing into every fiber of its corporate concept—from the chain's strategic association with books, blues and jazz to its Euro-latte lingo. What the success of both the Body Shop and Starbucks showed was how far the branding project had come in moving beyond splashing one's logo on a billboard. Here were two companies that had fostered powerful identities by making their brand concept into a virus and sending it out into the culture via a variety of channels: cultural sponsorship, political controversy, the consumer experience, and brand extensions. Direct advertising, in this context, was viewed as a rather clumsy intrusion into a much more organic approach to image building.

Scott Bedbury, Starbucks's vice president of marketing, openly recognized that 'consumers don't truly believe there's a huge difference between products', which is why brands must 'establish emotional ties' with their customers through 'the Starbucks Experience'. The people who line up for Starbucks, writes CEO Howard Shultz, aren't just there for the coffee. 'It's the romance of the coffee experience, the feeling of warmth, and community people get in Starbucks stores'.

Interestingly, before moving to Starbucks, Bedbury was head of marketing at Nike, where he oversaw the launch of the 'Just Do It!' slogan, among other watershed branding moments. In the following passage, he explains the common techniques used to infuse the two very different brands with meaning:

> Nike, for example, is leveraging the deep emotional connection that people have with sports and fitness. With Starbucks, we see how coffee has woven itself into the fabric of people's lives, and that's our opportunity for emotional leverage. . . . A great brand raises the bar—it adds a greater sense of purpose to the experience, whether it's the challenge to do your best in sports and fitness or the affirmation that the cup of coffee you're drinking really matters.

Study Question

1. Branding is not a new phenomenon. Why do authors such as Klein believe that it is presently such a destructive force in the world?

ROBERT KAPLAN

Robert Kaplan is a senior correspondent for The Atlantic Monthly *and the author of several insightful books based upon his travels to the some of the world's most embattled regions. In* 'World Government' *Kaplan considers the issue of globalization and the impact of a 'world driven . . . by financial markets that know no borders'.*

WORLD GOVERNMENT

Authoritarian or hybrid regimes, no matter how illiberal, will still be treated as legitimate if they can provide security for their subjects and spark economic growth. And they will easily find acceptance in a world driven increasingly by financial markets that know no borders.

For years idealists have dreamed of a 'world government'. Well, a world government has been emerging—quietly and organically, the way vast developments in history take place. I do not refer to the United Nations, the power of which, almost by definition, affects only the

The corporation has been likened to a psychopathic individual due to its lack of moral restraint and empathy for its 'victims'. Logo from the film *The Corporation*. Copyright 2003 Big Picture Media Corporation.

poorest countries. After its peace-keeping failures in Bosnia and Somalia—and its $2 billion failure to make Cambodia democratic—the UN is on its way to becoming a supranational relief agency. Rather, I refer to the increasingly dense ganglia of international corporations and markets that are becoming the unseen arbiters of power in many countries. It is much more important nowadays for the leader of a developing country to get a hearing before corporate investors at the World Economic Forum than to speak before the UN General Assembly. Amnesty International now briefs corporations, just as it has always briefed national governments. Interpol officials have spoken about sharing certain kinds of intelligence with corporations. The Prime Minister of Malaysia,

Mahathir Mohamad, is recognizing the real new world order (at least in this case) by building a low-tax district he calls a 'multimedia super-corridor', with two new cities and a new airport designed specifically for international corporations. The world's most efficient peacemaking force belongs not to the UN or even to the great powers but to a South African corporate mercenary force called Executive Outcomes,[1] which restored relative stability to Sierra Leone in late 1995. (This is reminiscent of the British East India Company, which raised armies transparently for economic interests.) Not long after Executive Outcomes left Sierra Leone, where only 20.7 per cent of adults can read, that country's so-called model democracy crumbled into military anarchy, as Sudan's model democracy had done in the late 1980s.

Of the world's hundred largest economies, fifty-one are not countries but corporations. While the two hundred largest corporations employ less than three-fourths of one per cent of the world's work force, they account for 28 per cent of world economic activity. The five hundred largest corporations account for 70 per cent of world trade. Corporations are like the feudal domains that evolved into nation-states; they are nothing less than the vanguard of a new Darwinian organization of politics. Because they are in the forefront of real globalization while the overwhelming majority of the world's inhabitants are still rooted in local terrain, corporations will be free for a few decades to leave behind the social and environmental wreckage they create— abruptly closing a factory here in order to open an unsafe facility with a cheaper work force there. Ultimately, as technological innovations continue to accelerate and the world's middle classes come closer together, corporations may well become more responsible to the cohering global community and less amoral in the course of their evolution toward new political and cultural forms.

For instance, ABB Asea Brown Boveri Ltd. is a $36 billion-a-year multinational corporation divided into 1,300 companies in 140 countries; no one national group accounts for more than 20 per cent of its employees. ABB's chief executive officer, Percy Barnevik, recently told an interviewer that this diversity is so that ABB can develop its own 'global ABB culture—you might say an umbrella culture'. Barnevik explains that his best managers are moved around periodically so that they and their families can develop 'global personalities' by living and growing up in different countries. ABB management teams, moreover, are never composed of employees from any one country. Barnevik says that this encourages a 'cross-cultural glue'. Unlike the multiculturalism of the left, which masks individual deficiencies through collective—that is, ethnic or racial—self-esteem, a multinational corporation like ABB has created a diverse multicultural environment in which individuals rise or fall completely on their own merits. Like the hybrid regimes of the present and future, such an evolving corporate community can bear an eerie resemblance to the oligarchies of the ancient world. 'Decentralization goes hand in hand with central monitoring,' Barnevik says.

The level of social development required by democracy as it is known in the West has existed in only a minority of places—and even there only during certain periods of history. We are entering a troubled transition, and the irony is that while we preach our version of democracy abroad, it slips away from us at home.

Note

1. Executive Outcomes was disbanded in 1999 when South Africa passed a new anti-mercenary law. However, it is reported that some of EO's members continue to operate in new organizations.

Study Question

1. Do international corporations make up a new 'world government'?

MANGOSUTHU BUTHELEZI

Mangosuthu Buthelezi (b. 1928) founded the Inkatha National Cultural Liberation Movement (Inkatha ye Nkuleleko ye Sizwe) in 1975; before that he had headed the African National Congress's Youth League from 1948–50. In the past, Inkatha supported Zulu nationalist causes but in the 1990s the movement began to take a more conciliatory approach towards other ethnic groups. Elected to the National Assembly of the South African *government in 1994, Buthelezi served as Minister of Home Affairs from 1994 until 2004. Despite the party's conciliatory language, the movement's support base tends to be heavily concentrated in the KwaZulu-Natal Province. In June 2001, Buthelezi was invited to participate in the 'Southern Africa Economic Summit'. The following speech was given at a working dinner on the topic of 'Democracy at Work in Africa'.*

DEMOCRACY AT WORK IN AFRICA

Durban: June 6, 2001

It is an honour for me to participate in such valuable discussions around the theme of *Democracy in Africa*. Having considered the rubric of this working dinner, I was inspired to express my own perspective of the democratic miracle, a perspective which has been built throughout almost half a century in politics and the leadership of my people. For much of my life I have struggled alongside my people to see democracy born in South Africa. Democratic miracles are possible and yet we need to confront the reality of their having often not delivered the expected results in terms of development and progress. I believe that our own democratic miracle is still in the making and far from having succeeded. In fact, since 1994, we have engaged in a new phase of our struggle to achieve the genuine liberation of our people in all spheres of our cultural, social, and economic life. In spite of democracy, our people are suffering under the burden of poverty, unemployment, ignorance, and lack of basic services and development.

Our economy is fighting to reach the critical point of growth which may turn these conditions around. We are doing well, but not well enough to make the difference which really matters. Because we need to make such a great difference, the miracle of democracy in Africa is expected to achieve more than in any other part of the world. We cannot avoid this expectation and must, therefore, out-perform many established or other new democracies which may to a greater extent rely on what they have, rather than focusing on what they are still to achieve. For this reason, I believe that the miracle of democracy requires courageous leadership which ensures that its initial impetus does not merely stabilise, but also grows to accommodate the vast unfulfilled needs and expectations.

I feel that Ghana and South Africa share the historical responsibility of proving that democracy can work on our continent and can indeed deliver what our people expect. On an occasion such as this, we need to express the courage of analysing what has not worked, or what has not worked well enough in many African democracies. An African Renaissance is based on our capability to turn around the conditions of our continent and having the unwavering political will to do so. This requires our willingness to move steadfastly from the old into the new, from the known into the unknown, and from the comfortable into the uncomfortable. We must talk not only about the evils of colonialism and racial oppression, but also of the evils of the ages which preceded them. Most of all, we need to find the courage to talk about the evils which have bedevilled our continent after the age of liberation. We need to have the courage to identify our own flaws and shortcomings. Without this sense of self-criticism, it will be difficult to make progress. Our capacity to criticise ourselves is indeed the beginning of improvement and the guarantee that the impetus of forward movement keeps its required pace and brings the development of our country out of the interminable age of infancy.

Too often we remain complacent before evils springing out of our land. We are often too ready to justify ourselves for the shortcomings of our government. If we wish to turn our continent around, we need to become hard on ourselves. We can no longer accept and excuse corruption, inefficiency, delays, and shortcomings as some chronic evils of our continent, part and parcel of our land. They may have been with us for a long time but they need not be here to stay. We must also accept that there is a fundamental connection between these evils and the poor social and economic conditions of many of our countries, and the inadequate functioning of our respective democracies. For me, making democracy work means identifying, exposing, and redressing things which do not work at their best or impair progress.

In order to do so, we need once and for all to bury the culture which justifies and accepts shortcomings and deficiencies. We must dedicate our respective countries to a national endeavour towards greater efficiency, progress, development, and technological improvements. I believe that this need to grow should rise from the bottom up, from our schools, families, work-places, and communities. The greatest challenge is for me that of shaping new generations who recognise that new is better than old, and who gain the power to improve on their social and economic conditions through their own efforts and dedication. We need to promote a new culture of self-help and self-reliance which breaks the shackles of the mind-set of impotence, complacency, and indolence. We need to free our people from a pervasive sense of paternalism and authoritarianism which often inhibits personal and intellectual growth. We need to promote critical thinking and personal ingenuity as the engines of an intellectual revolution to come.

In fact, to me, the most important aspect of the economic revolution which our continent must undertake lies in the need to improve the value of our most precious and least utilised resource, which is our people. The most important economic factor of our success remains the contribution that our people can make towards our growth. Therefore, I believe that our governments must focus their priority attention on training and education, and must promote across the land a new culture of intellectual stimulation and individual protagonism in social and economic activities. We must stimulate individuals to become protagonists and better citizens and role-players in what is becoming an increasingly more complex world, in which our countries must participate on an equal level. South Africa is

championing this concept by devolving as much as one per cent per year of our national payroll towards training, to include adult basic education which is essential to real human upliftment. This action by government is extremely important, but not sufficient unless it is met halfway with a concomitant effort by all the building blocks of our society to promote individual growth and upliftment.

Looking at the past and then at the present stage of our struggle for liberation, I recognise that Ghana and South Africa have much in common. Before I speak about the successful election campaign of President John Agyekum Kufuor, it is my great pleasure to congratulate His Excellency on this recent victory. I esteem it a privilege to share this table with a man who has openly agreed that politics is for long-distance runners, and not for sprinters. As leaders, we must have a long-term vision for our countries. Operating with a perspective which looks into future generations, rather than exclusively into the time of our own lives, we must bring to our countries a leadership which is not merely for today, but which will reverberate far into the future, establishing success, prosperity, and development in the years to come.

There is great affinity between South Africa and Ghana. Our soils have produced giants among men on the African continent. President Kwame Nkrumah who led his country to independence in March of 1957 with the slogan 'Self-Government Now' was serving a prison sentence for his fiery liberation passion when his party, the Convention People's Party, won the general elections. This son of Africa stepped from prison into the highest leadership of his country, the first African country to win independence from European colonisers. One cannot but draw a similarity with South Africa's own political giant, former President Nelson Mandela, whose release from twenty-seven years in prison ushered in a new era which would soon herald democracy for South Africa.

My own role in the liberation negotiations played itself out against a background of misperceptions and obfuscation of truth. I thank God that today the truth has emerged and has been embraced by all those involved in our country's transition from *apartheid* to democracy. When the grand scheme of *apartheid* would no longer hold, the then Nationalist Government of South Africa approached me, as Chief Minister of the erstwhile KwaZulu Government, seeking bilateral negotiations. I knew that we could not proceed while some political organisations remained banned and many political prisoners, particularly Nelson Mandela, remained incarcerated. Based on what I knew to be the only route to South Africa's victory, I rejected the offer of bilateral negotiations, calling as I had so many times in the past, for the release of my comrades. In so doing, I again looked to my country's future and not my own.

I mention these matters to stress that the time for foresight and selfless actions is not over. Foresight and selfless action are more easily prompted in a time of war and struggle and are often impaired during peace. As we are still at war against poverty and under-development as our enemies, now more than ever we need heroics in our leadership and the willingness to endure sacrifices and the discipline of the struggle in our people.

Former President Mandela, President Kufuor, and myself are of the same generation. We belong to the same generation of the age of democracy in Africa. I have often mentioned to my comrade, Nelson Mandela, that we are of the same age,

only ten years apart. Today, I may express the same sentiments to President Kufuor. President Kufuor campaigned on the need for change during a time in which the economy of Ghana has experienced severe difficulties. In Africa we share a dilemma, which is that the needs are so great and so extensive, demanding a rapidly growing economy. Speaking at the Annual Meeting of the World Economic Forum earlier this year, President Thabo Mbeki spoke of the global structural fault of poverty, which I believe exists in its cruellest and most visible form on this continent.

There are undoubtedly profound world imbalances and social injustices amongst nations which require to be redressed through concerted international efforts. However, as we bring about this realisation both domestically and internationally, we must also promote the notion that Africa wishes to level the playing field to be capable of standing on its own feet, and is committed to achieving the will, capacity and maturity to do so. There is a long path ahead, most of which remains uncertain and uphill. I believe that countries such as South Africa and Ghana share the responsibility to lead the way on this path and prove that through our efforts, sacrifices, and will to succeed, the miracle of democracy may indeed finally work on the African continent.

Study Question

1. What is the greatest obstacle to democracy on the African continent?

MOHAMED ELHACHMI HAMDI

Mohamed Elhachmi Hamdi was born in Tunisia and completed his doctoral work at the University of London. He was a member of al-Nahda, a Tunisian Islamic organization, for a number of years. As a

journalist he has supported cross-cultural dialogue between Islam and the west and is currently chairman of the London-based television network, Al Mustakillah. The following excerpt was written in 1996.

ISLAM AND LIBERAL DEMOCRACY

. . . Western intellectuals should take more seriously than they do the possibility that there are limitations to their brand of democracy. Consider the ever-increasing role that money plays in determining who can run for public office in the United States, let alone who can win. Money is so important in US politics that it may in fact have more influence than the people themselves in choosing those who govern. Or consider in how many countries Western democracy has failed to prevent racism toward blacks, or anti-Semitism. Anti-Semitism, in fact, is a European product that could never have come about in the Islamic world, which is built on belief in the three main messengers of divine revelation—Moses, Jesus, and Mohammed, peace be upon them.

Although most Western writers speak of democracy as a universal set of values, Western deeds tell a very different story. The French, for instance, behave democratically in France itself, but not in Algeria, where they have committed some of this blood-drenched century's most horrific atrocities. This has also been the case with the US government's policies in parts of Central America and the Muslim world.

Nor are Western inconsistencies all that dampen the Western democratic model's appeal. Not all societies stand to benefit from a multiparty system, for in some circumstances such pluralism might only serve to deepen existing tribal or sectarian divisions (Rwanda, the Sudan, Liberia, and even Lebanon come to mind). It is also questionable whether the rule of 51 per cent is a workable solution for many African and Asian societies, which need the efforts of all political groups, not only the one that gains victory in an election.

On certain moral questions, moreover, Western democracy appears—not just to outside critics but to many Westerners—to be running amok. It is hard to see why lax Western mores that weaken or destroy the family—that most crucial of all social institutions—should be exported to the rest of the world under the banner of democracy. Indeed, I cannot foresee any Islamic country under any circumstances accepting certain social practices that until recently were not generally accepted in the West either, but have now become common there.

There is no chance for a constructive dialogue among cultures and civilizations as long as those who dominate public discourse in the West continue to see themselves as the upholders of political and moral standards for the entire world. Unfortunately, a bit of this self-satisfaction is discernible in the way in which Wright and Lewis insist on comparing tendencies of thought in the Islamic world today to the Reformation in Christian Europe five centuries ago. This fails to account for the huge differences in concepts and movements, and drives home the point that only by seeing the limitations of their own standards can Westerners look more positively and objectively at the histories and cultures of other peoples. . . .

Why on earth should all the world convert to Western norms? Would it not be better to preserve a fruitful pluralism in the world, by which nations can express themselves in different ways, while respecting the basic values that are essential for all human beings?

The only way that secularism can be kept alive in the Islamic world is by local Muslim dictatorships, supported by Western power. Lewis is wrong to claim that most Islamic countries have gained independence from Western forces, and that their misfortunes on the road to democracy have been the result of their own mistakes. Every objective observer would admit that the West is still very much involved in the day-to-day affairs of most Muslim countries, especially those in the Arab world. This involvement takes the sad form of an unholy alliance with corrupt, isolated elites who do not respect democracy in any form, Western or otherwise. What keeps all too many regimes in power in the Arab world is not their own legitimacy, but rather control over the armed forces and support from the Western nations whose interests they serve.

Here we see the true face of secularism in most of the Islamic world: a new form of submission to the same old colonial powers. These powers may have democratic polities, but it is democracy meant for Westerners only, and does not imply any moral duties toward other nations. Useful antidemocrats in the Muslim, and especially the Arab, world easily gain Western help. Ordinary Arabs know this, which is why they stand ready to support whoever raises the flag of true independence, including the Islamists of Turkey, Algeria, Egypt, the Sudan, and Iran.

Of course, secularism is not the only obstacle confronting the cause of political liberty in the Islamic world. We had our own problems even before being dominated by the West. Islam may have been misused and may continue to be misused by corrupt and tyrannical rulers intent on legitimizing their policies by giving them what appears to be religious sanction. Here, indeed, lies one of the most formidable challenges facing contemporary Islamic thought as it strives to outline a regime that is Islamic but also representative and accountable. There is no doubt that we can benefit from the rich experience of Western democracy. I will go further: we Muslims not only can, but must learn from the West if we are to overcome the many problems prevalent in the Islamic world. But for this to be possible we need a dialogue between peoples in which the respective identities and interests of each are accorded equal respect. Muslims know this well, and are ready to extend the hand of respect to their Western counterparts. The question is: Are those in the West ready to do the same for Muslims?

> **Study Question**
>
> 1. Will negative actions committed by democratic countries in the Islamic world prove to be a perpetual barrier to the spread of democratic ideals?

THE GUARDIAN

In February 2003 the British newspaper The Guardian *invited a number of leading historians to comment on the increasingly strident claims of pro-war activists that to ignore the threat of Iraq would be to repeat the mistakes of appeasement in the 1930s. Several of the commentators also refer to parallels between intervention in Iraq and Britain's disastrous intervention in the Suez in 1956.*

BLAST FROM THE PAST

By Ian Kershaw[1]

The foreign secretary, Jack Straw, is among those who have looked to the mistakes of the past to justify the present policy against Iraq. It would be repeating the disastrous appeasement policy of the 1930s, it is said, if we were not now to act against Saddam Hussain. But this is no more than a spin on history. The parallels are as good as non-existent.

Donald Rumsfeld meets Saddam Hussein in Baghdad, 20 December 1983. Getty images.

The US was then isolationist, largely uninterested in Europe. Stalinist Russia was isolated for other reasons. Britain had to take the concerns of a world empire into account. France was petrified about the growing danger on the other side of the Rhine. The threat was indeed in the very heart of Europe, and unmistakably real. Britain's very existence was at stake. No weapons inspectors were needed to see whether Hitler was building 'weapons of mass destruction'. Everybody knew he was doing this illegally even before he openly announced it. He then used military might and bullying tactics to force changes to state borders within Europe. The annexation of what was left of Czechoslovakia in 1939, without any pretext of uniting ethnic Germans, finally convinced the government to take a stand, at the risk of a war they did not want.

Today, there is no self-evident threat from Iraq. There is no invasion of a sovereign territory (as in 1991) to repulse. We have to take it on trust that Saddam is building weapons of mass destruction. Even if he has them, he is unlikely to use them against Britain or America—seemingly bent on war and towing Britain in its slipstream. The tanks at Heathrow are not there to fend off an attack from Saddam. But we can't destroy the invisible source of that menace, which is likely to grow, not diminish—fostered by a war for which the reason is far from plain. In 1939, the reason was all too obvious.

By Simon Schama[2]

I don't think it's a case either of 1939 or of 1956. I'm allergic to lazy historical analogies. History never repeats itself, ever. That's its murderous charm. The poet Joseph Brodsky, in his great essay 'A Profile of Clio', wrote that when history comes, it always takes you by surprise, and that's what I believe, too.

It is not 1939 because Saddam Hussein is not a rolling juggernaut of confident invasion and annexation (although he would probably like to be). Nor is it 1956 because the US is at the clumsy beginning of an imperial career, not the pathetic end of one.

There are two complicated modern problems that make this present situation extremely dangerous but unique. The first is in the shape of Islamic fundamentalist terrorism, where you have a movement that hates modernity but is equipped with hi-tech modern weapons. In the past, where you have had a culture that resists modernity, they have had primitive weapons. This is a rich man's terrorism with rich man's toys. Osama bin Laden is a capitalist of death.

The second issue is that, even though it is a struggle to prove a direct link between Bin Laden and Saddam, there is a kind of pond of availability of very nasty chemical and biological weapons. In 1939, you had the spectacle of the German army marching into Austria and Poland with tanks. Then, in a sense, all you had to do to oppose Hitler was meet his tanks with yours. With these weapons, the threat is less familiar, less visible, less clear—but you still need to drain the pond.

Finally, the 1939/1956 controversy does not move the argument on: there has been extraordinarily little debate about what the postwar settlement would be. Anyone could fight this war; it will be easy to win. But no one in the US or UK seems really to have any idea of what to do afterwards: what kind of regime there will be, who to protect and who to do the protecting, what legitimacy a new government will have, and so on.

As a consequence, if you were Bin Laden, you would be thrilled about the prospect of war: either there will be a great fat target of a western presence in Iraq for several years or there will be a broken and chaotic state: either way it will be a teddy bears' picnic for terrorism.

By Linda Colley[3]

For connected reasons, neither 1939 nor 1956 offer appropriate parallels to a projected second Gulf war. Saddam may in essence be as evil and megalomaniac a man as Adolf Hitler (how would one judge?). He is certainly a dictator who has killed large numbers of people. But, as a determinedly secular ruler, he lacks the international ideological underpinning fascism gave Hitler. And, crucially, he lacks comparable hardware. In 1939, Germany had the strongest, most modern army, navy and air force in the world. In 2003, it is Iraq's primary enemy, the US, that unquestionably possesses the world's greatest stock of weapons of mass destruction.

Nor is Suez a useful parallel. To be sure, Colonel Nasser was seen by the French and British as an uppity Muslim leader who did not know his place. The British had demonised Tipu Sultan of Mysore in the 1790s, and the Mahdi in the Sudan in the 1890s for much the same reason. Worrying about renegade Islamic leaders is an old western imperialist tradition. But the British were bound to fail in 1956, because Washington had set its face against them. Two thousand and three will be different. If we invade Iraq, it will be on the coat-tails of the Americans. And they will not fail.

But the vital reason why history in this case offers limited help is that, since September 11, 2001, we have entered a different world in terms of both danger and paranoia. In the past, terrorists killed hundreds at most. Now we know they can kill thousands; and that they may in the future kill millions. Whether invading Iraq will make this more or less likely is the question that really divides us, and to which we possess no answer. All I know is that I look at photographs of ordinary Iraqis caught between the rock of a foul ruler, and the hard place of approaching Armageddon, and it breaks my heart.

By Eric Hobsbawm[4]

The war which is likely to break out shortly is not like the Second World War. All comparisons with appeasement and Munich are so much hot air which merely justifies starting a war. No historian will believe them for a moment.

This is not a war against an aggressor, still less against one capable of overrunning Europe. It is not in any sense a war of defence but of aggression by the greatest military power on earth against a smallish, though very nasty, dictatorship. It's a war that the US wants and nobody else in the world wants, except the government of Sharon and the UK cabinet. If the US did not insist upon it, nobody would have proposed it or thought about it. Even today, the neighbours of Iraq are extremely reluctant to take part in it.

It is not like Suez either. Suez in 1956 was the last throw of two declining imperial powers, plus Israel, which, then as today, has its own agenda. It ended in humiliation for Britain, not for military reasons but because the US pulled the plug on us.

The US will win the new Iraq war. There is no real doubt about that. They won it quickly in 1991 and there's no reason to suppose it will not be won quickly again—even though the US remains extremely reluctant to get any one of its citizens killed. Whether this will work in a few days, nobody can tell.

And then? Will the US stay? Unless they are prepared to stay as long as they did in Japan, Germany, and Korea, they cannot guarantee stability. Have they any clear idea of what they want to happen with Iraq and the Middle East after the war? I can detect no serious plans but only a lot of editorialising about the benefits of multi-party democracy. There is not much evidence in the Balkans that this alone will be sufficient.

Finally, in short, the US, it seems to me, has used 9/11 to proclaim its global hegemony and its capacity to make other countries go along with it. I think they underestimate the complexities of the world; hi-tech means of mass destruction are not enough.

By Richard Evans[5]

History never repeats itself, so anyone looking for parallels between the present situation and past events is likely to be disappointed. Not that there has been any shortage of such parallels drawn in the past few weeks by politicians seeking to encourage their supporters or discredit their opponents. But all of them are specious in one way or another.

NATO's disarray over policy towards Saddam Hussein's Iraq has been compared to the League of Nations' impotence when confronted with Mussolini's invasion of Ethiopia in 1936. But the League of Nations was trying to stop a war, while NATO is talking about starting one. Mussolini's weapons of mass destruction included poison gas, deployed against the poorly-equipped armies of the Ethiopian emperor. But the case for intervention in terms of the real political interests of the leading member-states of the League of Nations, such as France and Britain, was feeble, given that Ethiopia was a miserably poor state of no strategic importance, and wars are fought over real political interests, not for reasons of morality.

It is easy enough to brand the opponents of an invasion of Iraq as 'appeasers', but this is another specious parallel with the past. Britain and France did not declare war on Germany in 1939 because Hitler was maltreating his own people, but because Hitler invaded Poland, and because his invasion of Poland followed his invasion of Czechoslovakia earlier the same year. This was enough to convince most people who had thought he could be appeased by revising the 1919 peace settlement to include more Germans within the Reich that this would not appease him at all, since he was now taking over non-German parts of Europe at a rapidly increasing pace. Even so, the allies did not invade Germany in 1939. Instead, it was Hitler who ended the 'phony war' in 1940 by invading France, Belgium, Holland, Denmark, and Norway.

Saddam is not Hitler. He has not invaded anywhere since the Gulf War and has shown no signs of wanting to do so. Possessing weapons of mass destruction is one thing, intending to use them quite another. There is no credible evidence to link him with international terrorism. He is not threatening to take over the world. His country does, however, possess economic and strategic importance. And given the fact that the Iraqi regime is a murderous tyranny that once, some time ago, invaded a neighbouring country, it offers a morally convenient and geographically tangible outlet for the frustrations of combating the real threat of global terrorism.

The Franco–British invasion of Suez in 1956 owed something to similar psychological factors, particularly in the case of the British prime minister Anthony Eden, who saw a Hitler in every little dictator and wanted to compensate retrospectively for his failure as foreign secretary before the war. But principally the French and British invaded Egypt because the Egyptian government had taken over the Suez Canal, which they had previously controlled, and which still seemed to them to be of vital strategic importance as an artery of seaborne communication with their remaining colonial possessions in Africa and Asia. The invasion was intended to recover the canal, not to occupy Egypt, and so was a very limited operation.

It failed because it was not supported by the world's leading superpower, then as now the US. The US is the driving force in the imminent invasion of Iraq and so the project is likely to succeed, at least in its immediate aims. Its wider consequences, however, are wholly incalculable.

By Avi Shlaim[6]

The failure to stand up to Adolf Hitler is increasingly being invoked as a reason for standing up to Saddam Hussein. In a clear allusion to the appeasement of the 1930s, Tony Blair insisted that 'all our history—especially British history—points to the lesson that if international demands are not backed up with force, the result is greater insecurity.' But to compare Saddam with Hitler is to greatly inflate his importance and the danger he poses to international order. A much closer parallel is the Suez crisis of 1956. Anthony Nutting [foreign office minister in Anthony Eden's government], who resigned over Suez, called his book *No End of a Lesson*. Tony Blair would be well advised to ponder some of these lessons before embarking on another imperial adventure in the Middle East.

Eden thought that he was applying the lessons of the 1930s in dealing with Gamal Abdel Nasser and the result was a fiasco that brought his own career crashing down. Eden demonised Nasser, personalised the issues, and went to the length of colluding with France and Israel with the aim of knocking Nasser off his perch. The chiefs of staff had deep misgivings about the war. One senior officer exclaimed: 'The prime minister has gone bananas. He has ordered us to attack Egypt!' Britain attacked Egypt without the authority of the UN and it was roundly condemned for its aggression. There is, however, one important difference between 1956 and the current crisis. Over Suez, the US upheld the authority of the UN and led the pack against the law-breakers. Today, the Bush administration is hell-bent on the use of force to topple Saddam, with or without UN sanction.

Blair would be taking a huge gamble if he ignores public opinion and joins George Bush in an imperialist war to oust the Iraqi dictator. The Suez war brought to an end Britain's moment in the Middle East. Eighteen months after the attack on Egypt, Britain witnessed the defenestration of her royal friends in Baghdad. A war on Iraq today could go badly wrong, result in heavy casualties, fuel terrorism and end up by destabilising the entire region. As the moment of truth approaches, Blair would do well to reflect on the lessons of Suez. Politicians, like everyone else, are free to repeat the mistakes of the past, but it is not mandatory to do so.

By Paul Kennedy[7]

Nineteen thirty-nine it is not. There a country which had already unilaterally moved its armed forces across international borders three times (the Rhineland in 1936, Austria in 1938, and Prague in 1939) committed a further breach against Poland in September 1939, causing the British empire and France to fulfil their clear international obligations under the League Charter and their military alliances with Poland. War was formally declared. No one has said that the British and French actions were wrong; the criticism has always been that they should have taken place earlier. When Neville Chamberlain reluctantly declared war, even his strongest critics conceded that he had striven, for years, to avoid military action.

None of the above elements will be in place if the US and UK go to war without a further UN resolution. Having taken the matter to the security council last autumn—in clear recognition that the world community gave it extraordinary powers in matters of war and peace in 1945—they cannot thumb their noses at the council now. There is no transnational aggression by Saddam Hussein this time around. There is no military alliance to fulfil. And the White House hawks give the impression that they are eager for war.

This would change markedly, of course, if the security council backs the US/UK position by a further resolution next month, declaring Iraq to be in breach and authorising all necessary measures to cease that. But if such a resolution

is not forthcoming, then military action would indeed look like a Suez adventure, *a folie de grandeur* with strong possibilities of backfiring. President Bush models himself a great deal on Churchill; but the model in question might turn out to be Mussolini.

It is also worth noting that, when Gladstone's government intervened in Egypt in 1882—to uphold 'order' against Muslim, anti-western radicals—it claimed it would leave that country soon. As it turned out, Britain didn't leave for another 73 years.

By Richard Overy[8]

It doesn't look like 1939 or 1956. The effort to grab historical examples off the shelf and use them to legitimise what you're doing at the moment seems to me to be treating history irresponsibly. You cannot compare this with the past; this is a unique set of circumstances.

If you must have a historical analogy, my choice would be the Boer war, where you had a large, heavily armed imperial power trying to eradicate the threat from an awkward regional state which happened to control an important raw material. Attempts to cast the present as a re-run of the past do not work because Germany was a military superpower in the 30s. This time around, all the superpowers are on the western side. Likewise 1956, because the US and UK are not fading imperial powers about to be disgraced, but very powerful states seeking a military success—which they will almost certainly achieve.

But I think a postwar settlement will be extremely difficult to broker. Again, if we need historical analogies, we need only remind ourselves of Britain's interventions in Iraq in the early 1920s and during the Second World War that ended in humiliation.

To me, this is not about the moral high ground Tony Blair has been speaking of. This is about the US retaliating for September 11, and the coming confrontation is really to do with American concerns rather than those of the international community.

Notes

1. Ian Kershaw is a British historian who has written throughout his career on Hitler and the Third Reich.
2. Simon Schama is a professor at Columbia University. His most recent work, *The American Future: A History,* seeks to explain the sources of past American actions.
3. Linda Colley is a British historian who currently teaches at Princeton University.
4. Eric Hobsbawm is an emeritus professor of history at Birkbeck, University of London.
5. Richard J. Evans is Regius Professor of Modern History at Cambridge University and the author of *The Third Reich at War.*
6. Avi Shlaim is a Fellow of the British Academy.
7. Paul Kennedy is a professor of British History and director of International Security Studies at Yale University.
8. Richard Overy is a professor of Modern History at the University of Exeter.

> **Study Question**
>
> 1. Given the outcome of the American intervention in Iraq, which of these assessments seems closest to the true situation?

Noam Chomsky

Born in 1928, Noam Chomsky has become one of the best-known left-wing intellectuals in North America. His educational background is in linguistics, in particular the issue of natural language. However, he is more often recognized for his bitterly anti-American critiques and his opposition to all 'unjustified hierarchy'.

Chomsky has also been unfailingly critical of Israel's treatment of Palestinians and has worked actively to improve Arab–Jewish relations. This interview on the impending war with Iraq was conducted on 4 February 2003 with Matthew Tempest, a journalist from The Guardian.

On the Antiwar Movement

Noam Chomsky: The [peace] demonstrations were another indication of a quite remarkable phenomenon. There is around the world and in the United States opposition to the coming war that is at a level that is completely unprecedented in US or European history both in scope and the parts of the population it draws on.

There's never been a time that I can think of when there's been such massive opposition to a war before it was even started. And the closer you get to the region, the higher the opposition appears to be. In Turkey, polls indicated close to 90 per cent opposition, in Europe it's quite substantial, and in the United States the figures

US troops pull down a statue of Saddam Hussein following the occupation of Baghdad in April 2003. © Patrick Robert/ Corbis.

you see in polls, however, are quite misleading because there's another factor that isn't considered that differentiates the United States from the rest of the world. This is the only country where Saddam Hussein is not only reviled and despised but also feared, so since September polls have shown that something like 60–70 per cent of the population literally think that Saddam Hussein is an imminent threat to their survival.

Now there's no objective reason why the US should be more frightened of Saddam than say the Kuwaitis, but there is a reason—namely that since September there's been a drumbeat of propaganda trying to bludgeon people into the belief that not only is Saddam a terrible person but in fact he's going to come after us tomorrow unless we stop him today. And that reaches people. So if you want to understand the actual opposition to the war in

the US you have to extract that factor. The factor of completely irrational fear created by massive propaganda, and if you did I think you'd find it's much like everywhere else.

What is not pointed out in the press coverage is that there is simply no precedent, or anything like a precedent, for this kind of public opposition to a war. And it extends itself far more broadly, it's not just opposition to war it's a lack of faith in the leaderships. You may have seen a study released by the world economic forum a couple of days ago which estimated trust in leaders, and the lowest was in leaders of the United States. Trusted by little over quarter of the population, and I think that reflects concerns over the adventurism and violence and the threats that are perceived in the actions and plans of the current administration.

These are things that ought to be central. Even in the United States there is overwhelming opposition to the war and that corresponding decline in trust in the leadership that is driving the war. This has been developing for some time but it is now reaching an unusual state, and, just to get back to the demonstrations over the weekend, that's never happened before. If you compare it with the Vietnam war, the current stage of the war with Iraq is approximately like that of 1961—that is, before the war actually was launched, as it was in 1962 with the US bombing of South Vietnam and driving millions of people into concentration camps and chemical warfare and so on, but there was no protest. In fact, so little protest that few people even remember.

The protests didn't begin to develop until several years later when large parts of South Vietnam were being subjected to saturation bombing by B-52s, hundreds of thousands of troops where there, hundreds of thousands had been killed, and then even after that, when the protests finally did develop in the US and Europe it was mostly focused on a side-issue—the bombing of North Vietnam which was undoubtedly a crime, it was far more intense in the south which was always the US target, and that's continued.

It's also, incidentally, recognised by the government. So when any administration comes into office the first thing it does is have a worldwide intelligence assessment—'What's the state of the world?'—provided by the intelligence services. These are secret and you learn about them 30 or 40 years later when they're declassified. When the first Bush administration came in 1989 parts of their intelligence assessment were leaked, and they're very revealing about what happened in the subsequent 10 years about precisely these questions.

The parts that were leaked said that it was about military confrontations with much weaker enemies, recognising they were the only kind we were going to be willing to face, or even exist. So in confrontations with much weaker enemies the United States must win 'decisively and rapidly' because otherwise popular support will erode, because it's understood to be very thin. Not like the 1960s when the government could fight a long, brutal war for years and years practically destroying a country without any protest. Not now. Now they have to win. They have to terrify the population to feel there's some enormous threat to their existence and carry out a miraculous, decisive and rapid victory over this enormous foe and march on to the next one.

Remember the people now running the show in Washington are mostly recycled Reaganites, essentially reliving the script of the 1980s—that's an apt analogy. And in the 1980s they were imposing domestic programmes which were quite harmful to the general population and which were unpopular. People opposed most of their domestic programmes. And the way they succeeded in ramming it through was by repeatedly keeping the population in a state of panic.

So one year it was an airbase in Grenada which the Russians were going to use to bomb the United States. It sounds ludicrous but that was the propaganda lie and it worked.

Nicaragua was 'two days marching time from Texas'—a dagger pointed at the heart of Texas, to borrow Hitler's phrase. Again, you'd think the people would collapse with laughter. But they didn't. That was continually brought up to frighten us—Nicaragua might conquer us on its way to conquer the hemisphere. A national emergency was called because of the threat posed to national security by Nicaragua. Libyan hitmen were wandering the streets of Washington to assassinate our leader—hispanic narco-terrorists. One thing after another was conjured up to keep the population in a state of constant fear while they carried out their major terrorist wars.

Remember, the same people declared a war on terror in 1981 that was going to be the centrepiece of US foreign policy focused primarily on Central America, and they carried out a war on terror in central America where they ended up killing about 200,000 people, leaving four countries devastated. Since 1990, when the US took them over again, they've declined still further into deep poverty. Now they're doing the same thing for the same purposes—they are carrying out domestic programmes to which the population is strongly opposed because they're being harmed by them.

But the international adventurism, the conjuring up of enemies that are about to destroy us, that's second nature, very familiar. They didn't invent it, others have done the same thing, others have done it in history but they became masters of this art and are now doing it again.

I don't want to suggest that they have no reasons for wanting to take over Iraq. Of course they do—long-standing reasons that everyone knows. Controlling Iraq will put the US in a very powerful position to extend its domination of the major energy resources of the world. That's not a small point.

But look at the specific timing. It's rather striking that the propaganda drumbeat began in September—what happened in September? Well, it's when the Congressional campaign began and it was certain that the Republicans were not going to win it by allowing social and economic issues to dominate. They would have been smashed. They had to do exactly what they did in the 80s. Replace them by security issues and in the case of a threat to security people tend to rally around the president—a strong figure who'll protect us from horrible dangers.

The more likely direction this will take [after a war with Iraq] will be Iran, and possibly Syria. North Korea is a different case. What they are demonstrating to the world with great clarity is that if you want to deter US aggression you better have weapons of mass destruction [WMD], or else a credible threat of terror. There's nothing else that will deter them—they can't be deterred by

conventional forces. That's a terrible lesson to teach, but it's exactly what's being taught.

For years, experts in the mainstream have been pointing out that the US is causing weapons proliferation by its adventures since others cannot protect themselves except by WMD or the threat of terror. Kenneth Waltz is one who recently pointed this out. But years ago, even before the Bush administration, leading commentators like Samuel Huntington in *Foreign Affairs*, the main establishment journal, were pointing out that the United States is following a dangerous course. He was talking about the Clinton administration but he pointed out that, for much of the world, the US is now regarded as a rogue state and the leading threat to their existence. In fact one of the striking things about the opposition to the war now, again unprecedented, is how broadly it extends across the political spectrum, so the two major foreign policy journals, *Foreign Affairs* and *Foreign Policy*, have just in their recent issues run very critical articles by distinguished mainstream figures opposing the resort to war in this case.

The American Academy of Arts and Sciences rarely takes a position on controversial current issues but has just published a long monograph on this issue by its committee on international security giving as sympathetic as possible an account of the Bush administration position then simply dismantling it line by line on very narrow grounds—much narrower than I would prefer—but nevertheless successfully.

[There is] just a lot of fear and concern about this adventurism, what one analyst called 'sillier armchair fantasies'. My concern is more 'What's it going to do to the people of Iraq' and 'What's it going to do to the region?' but these concerns are 'What's it going to do to us?'

Matthew Tempest: Will the propaganda rebound if democracy is not established in Iraq after 'liberation'?

NC: You're right to call it propaganda. If this is a war aim, why don't they say so? Why are they lying to the rest of the world? What is the point of having the UN inspectors? According to this propaganda, everything we are saying in public is pure farce—we don't care about the weapons of mass destruction, we don't care about disarmament, we have another goal in mind, which we're not telling you, and that is, all of a sudden, we're going to bring democracy by war. Well, if that's the goal, let's stop lying about it and put an end to the whole farce of inspections and everything else and just say now we're on a crusade to bring democracies to countries that are suffering under miserable leadership. Actually that is a traditional crusade, that's what lies behind the horrors of colonial wars and their modern equivalents, and we have a very long rich record to show just how that worked out. It's not something new in history.

In this particular case you can't predict what will happen once a war starts. In the worst case it might be what the intelligence agencies and the aid agencies are predicting—namely an increase in terror as deterrence or revenge, and for the people of Iraq, who are barely on the edge of survival, it could be the humanitarian catastrophe of which the aid agencies and the UN have been warning.

On the other hand, it's possible it could be what the hawks in Washington hope—a quick victory, no fighting to speak of, impose a new regime, give it a democratic façade, make sure the US has big military bases there, and effectively controls the oil.

The chances that they will allow anything approximating real democracy are pretty slight. There's major problems in the way of that— problems that motivated Bush No. 1 to oppose the rebellions in 1991 that could have overthrown Saddam Hussein. After all, he could have been overthrown then if the US had not authorised Saddam to crush the rebellions.

One major problem is that roughly 60 per cent of the population is Shi'ite. If there's any form of democratic government, they're going to have a say, in fact a majority say, in what the government is. Well they are not pro-Iranian but the chances are that a Shi'ite majority would join the rest of the region in trying to improve relations with Iran and reduce the levels of tension generally in the region by re-integrating Iran within it. There have been moves in that direction among the Arab states and Shi'ite majority in Iraq is likely to do that. That's the last thing the US wants. Iran is its next target.

It doesn't want improved relations. Furthermore if the Shi'ite majority gets for the first time a real voice in the government, the Kurdish minority will want something similar. And they will want a realisation of their quite just demands for a degree of autonomy in the northern regions. Well Turkey is not going to tolerate that. Turkey already has thousands of troops in Northern Iraq basically to prevent any such development. If there's move towards Kirkuk, which they regard as their capital city, Turkey will move to block it, the US will surely back them, just as the United States has strongly supported Turkey in its massive atrocities against the Kurds in the 1990s in the south-eastern regions. What you're going to be left with is either a military dictatorship with some kind of democratic façade, like maybe a parliament that votes while the military runs it behind the scenes—it's not unfamiliar—or else putting power back into the hands of something like the Sunni minority which has been running it in the past.

Nobody can predict any of this. What happens when you start a war is unknown. The CIA can't predict it, Rumsfeld can't predict it, nobody can. It could be anywhere over this range. That's why sane people refrain from the use of violence unless there are overwhelming reasons to undertake it—the dangers are simply far too great. However it's striking that neither Bush nor Blair present anything like this as their war aim. Have they gone to the Security Council and said let's have a resolution for the use of force to bring democracy to Iraq? Of course not. Because they know they'd be laughed at.

Bush and his administration were telling the Security Council back in November very openly and directly that the UN will be 'relevant' if it grants us the authority to do what we want, to use force when we want, and if the UN does not grant us that authority it will be irrelevant. It couldn't be clearer.

They said we already have the authority to do anything we want, you can come along and endorse that authorisation or else you're irrelevant. There could not have been a more clear and explicit way of informing the world that we don't care what you think, we'll do what we want. That's one of the primary reasons why US . . . authority [is] collapsing in the World Economic Forum poll.

Other countries will presumably go along with the US war—but out of fear.

Study Question

1.   Is the United Nations now irrelevant in the face of US global power?

OSAMA BIN LADEN

Osama bin Laden was born in 1957 in Riyadh, Saudi Arabia. His father was a wealthy businessman, with close ties to the Saudi monarchy. Sources on his education often provide conflicting information, but it is possible that bin Laden completed a degree in either civil engineering or public administration. He travelled to Afghanistan in either the late 1970s or early 1980s and began working with US-backed mujahedeen *factions. After the Soviet withdrawal he founded al-Qaeda ('The Base') and was responsible for a number of subsequent terrorist attacks on targets identified as sympathetic to the United States. Many analysts point to the first Gulf War as the key to bin Laden's hatred of the US. The following speech explains the motives behind the 11 September 2001 attack on targets inside the US.*

Speech on American Policy, October 2004

Praise be to Allah who created the creation for his worship and commanded them to be just and permitted the wronged one to retaliate against the oppressor in kind. To proceed:

Peace be upon he who follows the guidance: People of America this talk of mine is for you and concerns the ideal way to prevent another Manhattan, and deals with the war and its causes and results.

Before I begin, I say to you that security is an indispensable pillar of human life and that free men do not forfeit their security, contrary to Bush's claim that we hate freedom.

If so, then let him explain to us why we don't strike for example—Sweden? And we know that freedom-haters don't possess defiant spirits like those of the 19—may Allah have mercy on them.[1]

No, we fight because we are free men who don't sleep under oppression. We want to restore freedom to our nation, just as you lay waste to our nation. So shall we lay waste to yours.

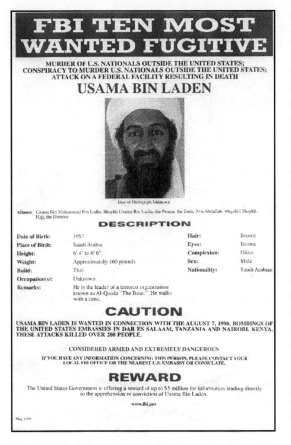

FBI TEN MOST WANTED FUGITIVE

MURDER OF U.S. NATIONALS OUTSIDE THE UNITED STATES;
CONSPIRACY TO MURDER U.S. NATIONALS OUTSIDE THE UNITED STATES;
ATTACK ON A FEDERAL FACILITY RESULTING IN DEATH

USAMA BIN LADEN

Date of Photograph Unknown

Aliases: Usama Bin Muhammad Bin Ladin, Shaykh Usama Bin Ladin, the Prince, the Emir, Abu Abdallah, Mujahid Shaykh, Hajj, the Director

DESCRIPTION

Date of Birth:	1957	Hair:	Brown
Place of Birth:	Saudi Arabia	Eyes:	Brown
Height:	6' 4" to 6' 6"	Complexion:	Olive
Weight:	Approximately 160 pounds	Sex:	Male
Build:	Thin	Nationality:	Saudi Arabian
Occupation(s):	Unknown		
Remarks:	He is the leader of a terrorist organization known as Al-Qaida "The Base." He walks with a cane.		

CAUTION

USAMA BIN LADEN IS WANTED IN CONNECTION WITH THE AUGUST 7, 1998, BOMBINGS OF THE UNITED STATES EMBASSIES IN DAR ES SALAAM, TANZANIA AND NAIROBI, KENYA. THESE ATTACKS KILLED OVER 200 PEOPLE.

CONSIDERED ARMED AND EXTREMELY DANGEROUS

IF YOU HAVE ANY INFORMATION CONCERNING THIS PERSON, PLEASE CONTACT YOUR LOCAL FBI OFFICE OR THE NEAREST U.S. EMBASSY OR CONSULATE.

REWARD

The United States Government is offering a reward of up to $5 million for information leading directly to the apprehension or conviction of Usama Bin Laden.

www.fbi.gov

May 1999

The 'Most Wanted' poster created by the FBI for Osama bin Laden in 1999. Department of Justice, Federal Bureau of Investigation. Courtesy of the Office of Public Affairs, Fugitive Publicity Office.

No one except a dumb thief plays with the security of others and then makes himself believe he will be secure. Whereas thinking people, when disaster strikes, make it their priority to look for its causes, in order to prevent it happening again.

But I am amazed at you. Even though we are in the fourth year after the events of September 11th, Bush is still engaged in distortion, deception, and hiding from you the real causes. And thus, the reasons are still there for a repeat of what occurred.

So I shall talk to you about the story behind those events and shall tell you truthfully about the moments in which the decision was taken, for you to consider.

I say to you, Allah knows that it had never occurred to us to strike the towers. But after it became unbearable and we witnessed the oppression and tyranny of the American/Israeli coalition against our people in Palestine and Lebanon, it came to my mind.

The events that affected my soul in a direct way started in 1982 when America permitted the Israelis to invade Lebanon and the American Sixth Fleet helped them in that. This bombardment began and many were killed and injured and others were terrorised and displaced.

I couldn't forget those moving scenes, blood and severed limbs, women and children sprawled everywhere. Houses destroyed along with their occupants and high rises demolished over their residents, rockets raining down on our home without mercy.

The situation was like a crocodile meeting a helpless child, powerless except for his screams. Does the crocodile understand a conversation that doesn't include a weapon? And the whole world saw and heard but it didn't respond.

In those difficult moments many hard-to-describe ideas bubbled in my soul, but in the end they produced an intense feeling of rejection of tyranny, and gave birth to a strong resolve to punish the oppressors.

And as I looked at those demolished towers in Lebanon, it entered my mind that we should punish the oppressor in kind and that we should destroy towers in America in order that they taste some of what we tasted and so that they be deterred from killing our women and children.

And that day, it was confirmed to me that oppression and the intentional killing of innocent women and children is a deliberate American policy. Destruction is freedom and democracy, while resistance is terrorism and intolerance.

This means the oppressing and embargoing to death of millions as Bush Sr did in Iraq in the greatest mass slaughter of children mankind has ever known, and it means the throwing of millions of pounds of bombs and explosives at millions of children—also in Iraq—as Bush Jr did, in order to remove an old agent and replace him with a new puppet to assist in the pilfering of Iraq's oil and other outrages.

So with these images and their like as their background, the events of September 11th came as a reply to those great wrongs, should a man be blamed for defending his sanctuary?

Is defending oneself and punishing the aggressor in kind, objectionable terrorism? If it is such, then it is unavoidable for us.

This is the message which I sought to communicate to you in word and deed, repeatedly, for years before September 11th.

And you can read this, if you wish, in my interview with Scott in *Time Magazine* in 1996, or with Peter Arnett on CNN in 1997, or my meeting with John Weiner in 1998.

You can observe it practically, if you wish, in Kenya and Tanzania and in Aden. And you can read it in my interview with Abdul Bari Atwan, as well as my interviews with Robert Fisk.

The latter is one of your compatriots and coreligionists and I consider him to be neutral. So are the pretenders of freedom at the White House and the channels controlled by them able to run an interview with him? So that he may relay to the American people what he has understood from us to be the reasons for our fight against you?

If you were to avoid these reasons, you will have taken the correct path that will lead America to the security that it was in before September 11th. This concerned the causes of the war.

As for its results, they have been, by the grace of Allah, positive and enormous, and have, by all standards, exceeded all expectations. This is due to many factors, chief among them, that we have found it difficult to deal with the Bush administration in light of the resemblance it bears to the regimes in our countries, half of which are ruled by the military and the other half which are ruled by the sons of kings and presidents.

Our experience with them is lengthy, and both types are replete with those who are characterised by pride, arrogance, greed and misappropriation of wealth. This resemblance began after the visits of Bush Sr to the region.

At a time when some of our compatriots were dazzled by America and hoping that these visits would have an effect on our countries, all of a sudden he was affected by those monarchies and military regimes, and became envious of their remaining decades in their positions, to embezzle the public wealth of the nation without supervision or accounting.

So he took dictatorship and suppression of freedoms to his son and they named it the Patriot Act, under the pretence of fighting terrorism. In addition, Bush sanctioned the installing of sons as state governors, and didn't forget to import expertise in election fraud from the region's presidents to Florida to be made use of in moments of difficulty.

All that we have mentioned has made it easy for us to provoke and bait this administration. All that we have to do is to send two mujahidin to the furthest point east to raise a piece of cloth on which is written al-Qaida, in order to make the generals race there to cause America to suffer human, economic, and political losses without their achieving for it anything of note other than some benefits for their private companies.

This is in addition to our having experience in using guerrilla warfare and the war of attrition to fight tyrannical superpowers, as we, alongside the mujahidin, bled Russia for 10 years, until it went bankrupt and was forced to withdraw in defeat.

All Praise is due to Allah.

So we are continuing this policy in bleeding America to the point of bankruptcy. Allah willing, and nothing is too great for Allah. . . .

Your security is in your own hands. And every state that doesn't play with our security has automatically guaranteed its own security.

And Allah is our Guardian and Helper, while you have no Guardian or Helper. All peace be upon he who follows the Guidance.

Note

1. Bin Laden is referring to the nineteen hijackers who were part of the September 11th attacks.

Study Question

1. To what extent have the enemies of the United States and its Allies been strengthened since 2001 and why has this occurred?

Hugo Chávez

Hugo Chávez (b. 1954) was elected president of Venezuela in 1998, and took office in 1999. He had previously attempted, unsuccessfully, to topple the repressive government of Carlos Andrés Pérez, inspired by an ideology he called Bolivarianism developed during his university days and based on the actions of Latin American liberator Simón Bolívar. Since taking office Chávez has spoken out against globalization and the economic policies supported by organizations such as the IMF and World Bank, while promoting regional economic cooperation and socialist policies at home.

Speech on the Opening of the G-15 Summit, 2004

. . . Welcome to this land washed by the waters of the Atlantic Ocean and the Caribbean Sea, crossed by the magnificent Orinoco River. A land crowned by the perpetual snow of the Andean mountains. . . !

A land overwhelmed by the never-ending magic of the Amazon forest and its millenary chants. . .!

Welcome to Venezuela, the land where a patriotic people has taken over again the banners of Simon Bolivar, its Libertador, whose name is well known beyond these frontiers!

. . . In his letter to Jamaica in 1815, Bolivar [wrote] . . .

I wish one day we would have the opportunity to install there an august congress with the representatives of the Republics, Kingdoms, and Empires to debate and discuss the highest interests of Peace and War with the countries of the other three parts of the world.

Bolivar reveals himself as an anti-imperialist leader, in the same historic perspective that 140 years after that insightful letter at Kingston materialized in the Bandung Conference in April 1955. Inspired by Nehru, Tito y [and] Nasser, a group of important leaders gathered at this conference to face great challenges and expressed their wish of not being involved in the East–West conflict and rather work together toward national development. This was the first key milestone: the first Afro-Asian conference, the immediate precedent of the Non-Aligned Countries that gathered 29 Heads of State and from which the 'Conscience of the South' was born.

Two events of great political significance occurred in the '60s: the creation of the Non-Aligned Movement in Belgrade in 1961 and the Group of the 77 in 1964[1]: Two milestones and a clear historic trend: the need of the self-awareness of the South and of acting together in a world reality characterized by imbalance and unequal exchange. . . .

All those struggles, ideas and proposals sunk in the Neo-liberal Flood and the world began to witness the so-called 'end of History' and the triumphant chant of the Neo-liberal Globalization, which today, besides an objective reality, is a weapon of manipulation intended to force us to passiveness faced to an Economic World Order that excludes our South countries and condemns them to the never-ending role of producers of wealth and recipients of leftovers.

Never before had the world such a tremendous scientific-technical potential, such a capacity to generate wealth and well-being. Authentic technological wonders that have made any place in the world to be always close with regard to distances and communications have not been capable of bringing well-being for everybody, but only for a meager 15 per cent living in the countries of the North.

Globalization has not brought the so-called interdependence, but an increase in dependency. Instead of wealth globalization, there is poverty wide spreading. Development has not become general, or been shared. To the contrary, the abysm between North and South is now so huge, that the unsustainability of the current economic order and the blindness of the people who try to justify continuing to enjoy opulence and waste, are evident.

The face of this world economic order of globalization with a neo-liberal sign is not only [the] Internet, virtual reality or the exploration of the space.

This face can also be seen, and with a greater dramatic character in the countries of the South,

in the 790 millions of people who are starving, 800 millions of illiterate adults, 654 millions of human beings who live today in the south and who will not grow older than 40 years of age. This is the harsh and hard face of the work economic order dominated by the Neoliberalism and seen every year in the south, the death of over 11 millions of boys and girls below 5 years of age caused by illnesses that are practically always preventable and curable and who die at the appalling rate of over 30 thousand every day, 21 every minute, 10 each 30 seconds. In the South, the proportion of children suffering of malnutrition reaches up to 50 per cent in quite a few countries, while according to the FAO, a child who lives in the First World will consume throughout his or her life, the equivalent to what 50 children consume in an underdeveloped country.

The great possibilities that a globalization of solidarity and true cooperation could bring to all people in the world through the scientific-technical wonders, has been reduced by the neo-liberal model to this grotesque caricature full of exploitation and social injustice. . . .

We are, dear friends, in Latin America, the favorite scenario of the neo-liberal model in the past decades. Here, neoliberalism reached the status of a dogma and was applied with greatest severity.

Its catastrophic results can be easily seen and are the explanation for the growing and uncontrollable social protest that the poor people and the excluded people of Latin America have been expressing, every day more vigorously, for some years now, claiming their right to life, to education, to health, to culture, to a decent living as human beings.

Dear friends:

I saw with my own eyes, a day like today but exactly 15 years ago, the 27th of February 1989, when an intense day of protest broke out on the streets of Caracas against the neo-liberal package of the International Monetary Fund and ended in a real massacre known as 'The Caracazo'.

The neo-liberal model promised Latin Americans greater economic growth, but during the neo-liberal years growth has not even reached half the growth achieved in the 1945–1975 period with different politics.

The model recommended the most strict financial liberalization and exchange freedom to achieve a greater influx of foreign capitals and greater stability. But in neo-liberal years the financial crises have been more intense and frequent than ever before, the external regional debts non-existent at the end of the Second World War amounts today to 750 billion dollars, the per capita highest debt in the world and in several countries is equal to more than half the GDP. Only between 1990 and the year 2002, Latin America made external debt payments amounting to 1 trillion 528 billions of dollars, which duplicates the amount of the current debt and represented an annual average payment of 118 billions. That is, we pay the debt every 6.3 years, but this evil burden continues to be there, unchanging and inextinguishable.

It is a never-ending debt!!

Obviously, this debt has exceeded the normal and reasonable payment commitments by any debtor and has turned into an instrument to undercapitalize our countries additionally to the imposition of socially adverse measures that subsequently generate powerful politically destabilizing factors for the governments that insist in their implementation.

We were asked to be ultraliberal in trade and to lift any barrier, which may obstruct the imports coming from the North, but the oral champions of free trade actually are the champions in the praxis of protectionism. The North spends 1 billion dollars a day in practicing what Latin America has been banned from doing, that is, subsidizing inefficient products. . . .

Neoliberalism promised Latin American people that if they accepted the demands of the multinational capital, investments would overflow the region. Indeed, the incoming capital increased. A portion to buy state-owned companies sometimes at bargain prices, another portion was speculative capital to seize the opportunities involved in the financial liberalization environment.

The neo-liberal model promised that after a painful adjustment period necessary to deprive the State of its regulatory power over economy and liberalize trade and finance, wealth would spread over Latin America and the long-lasting history of poverty and underdevelopment would be left behind. But the painful and temporary adjustment became permanent and appears to become everlasting. The results cannot be concealed.

Taking 1980 as the conventional year of the commencement of the neo-liberal cycle, by that time around 35 per cent of the Latin American population were poor. Two decades thereafter, 44 per cent of Latin American men and women are poor. Poverty is particularly cruel to children. It is a sad reality that in Latin America most of the poor people are children and most children are poor. In the late 90s, the Economic Commission for Latin America reported that 58 per cent of children under 5 were poor, as well as 57 per cent of children with ages ranging from 6 to 12.

Poverty among children and teenagers tends to reinforce and perpetuate inequalities of access to education, as shown by a survey conducted by the Inter-American Development Bank on 15 countries where householders in 10 per cent of the population with the highest income had an average schooling of 11 years, whereas among householders in 30 per cent of the lowest income population such average was 4 years.

Neoliberalism promised wealth. And poverty has spread, thus making of Latin America the most unequal region over the world in terms of income distribution. In the region, the wealthiest

10 percent of the population—those who are satisfied with neoliberalism and feel enthusiastic about the FTAA—receive nearly 50 per cent of the total income, where the poorest 10 per cent—those who never appear in high class society chronicles of the oligarchic mass media—barely receive 1.5 per cent of such total income.

This exploitation model has turned Latin America and the Caribbean into a social bomb ready to explode, should anti-development, unemployment and poverty keep increasing.

Even though the social struggles are growing sharp and even some governments have been overthrown by uprisings, we are told by the North that the neo-liberal reform has not yielded good results because it has not been implemented in full.

So, they now intend to recommend the formula of suicide. But we know, brothers and sisters, that countries do not commit suicide. The people of our countries awake, stand up and fight!

As a conclusion, their Excellencies, because of its injustice and inequality, the economic and social order of neo-liberal globalization appears to be a dead-end street for the South.

Therefore, the passive acceptance of the excluding rules imposed by this economic and social order cannot be the behavior to be exercised by the Heads of State and Government who have the highest responsibility before our peoples.

The history of our countries does not admit any doubt—passivity and grieving are useless, instead, the joined and firm action is the sole conduct enabling the South to rise from its sad role of exploited and humiliated rearguard.

Thanks to the heroic struggle against colonialism, the developing countries broke the economic and social order condemning them to the condition of exploited colonies. Colonialism was not defeated by the accumulations of tears of sorrow or by the repentance of colonialists, but by centuries of heroic fights for independence and sovereignty in which the resistance, tenacity and sacrifice of our peoples worked wonders.

Here, in South America, this year we are precisely commemorating 180 years of the heroic deeds of Ayacucho battle, where people joined and became a liberating army after almost 20 years of revolutionary wars under the bright leadership of José de San Martin, Bernardo O'Higgins, José Inacio Abreu e Lima, Simon Bolivar and Antonio José de Sucre, sending away the Spanish empire hitherto extended from the warm Caribbean beaches to the cold lands of Patagonia, thus ending 300 years of colonialism.

Today, vis-à-vis the obvious failure of neoliberalism and the great threat that the International Economic Order represents for our countries, it is necessary to retake the Spirit of the South. . . .

Ladies and Gentlemen, thank you very much.

Note

1. Both organizations attempted to counter the dominant bipolar cold war world and to allow developing countries to gain greater global influence.

Study Question

1. Is the era of neo-liberal economic policies the most important reason for the wealth disparity in Latin America today?

VLADIMIR PUTIN

Vladimir Putin (b. 1952) was Boris Yeltsin's hand-picked successor as president of the Russian Federation. He served two terms as president, from 2000 to 2008, enjoying exceptionally high approval ratings, and was subsequently chosen as Russia's prime minister when term limits prevented him from continuing to serve as *president. Putin's critics have pointed to an increasing loss of democratic rights in Russia, repression of the media, and rampant corruption. However, under Putin's tenure Russia's economy expanded—driven by high oil and gas prices—and its power in the world recovered substantially.*

SPEECH AT THE 43RD MUNICH CONFERENCE ON SECURITY POLICY, 2007

Thank you very much dear Madam Federal Chancellor, Mr Teltschik, ladies and gentlemen!

I am truly grateful to be invited to such a representative conference that has assembled politicians, military officials, entrepreneurs and experts from more than 40 nations.

This conference's structure allows me to avoid excessive politeness and the need to speak in roundabout, pleasant but empty diplomatic terms. This conference's format will allow me to say what I really think about international security problems. And if my comments seem unduly polemical, pointed, or inexact to our colleagues, then I would ask you not to get angry with me. After all, this is only a conference. And I hope that after the first two or three minutes of my speech Mr Teltschik will not turn on the red light over there.

Therefore, it is well known that international security comprises much more than issues relating to military and political stability. It involves the stability of the global economy, overcoming poverty, economic security, and developing a dialogue between civilisations.

This universal, indivisible character of security is expressed as the basic principle that 'security for one is security for all'. As Franklin D. Roosevelt said during the first few days that the Second World War was breaking out: 'When peace has been broken anywhere, the peace of all countries everywhere is in danger.'

These words remain topical today. Incidentally, the theme of our conference—global crises, global responsibility—exemplifies this.

Only two decades ago the world was ideologically and economically divided and it was the huge strategic potential of two superpowers that ensured global security.

This global stand-off pushed the sharpest economic and social problems to the margins of the international community's and the world's agenda. And, just like any war, the Cold War left us with live ammunition, figuratively speaking. I am referring to ideological stereotypes, double standards and other typical aspects of Cold War bloc thinking.

The unipolar world that had been proposed after the Cold War did not take place either.

The history of humanity certainly has gone through unipolar periods and seen aspirations to world supremacy. And what hasn't happened in world history?

However, what is a unipolar world? However one might embellish this term, at the end of the day it refers to one type of situation, namely one centre of authority, one centre of force, one centre of decision-making.

It is a world in which there is one master, one sovereign. And at the end of the day this is pernicious not only for all those within this system, but also for the sovereign itself because it destroys itself from within.

And this certainly has nothing in common with democracy. Because, as you know, democracy is the power of the majority in light of the interests and opinions of the minority.

Incidentally, Russia—we—are constantly being taught about democracy. But for some reason those who teach us do not want to learn themselves.

I consider that the unipolar model is not only unacceptable but also impossible in today's world. And this is not only because if there was individual leadership in today's—and precisely in today's—world, then the military, political and economic resources would not suffice. What is even more important is that the model itself is flawed because at its basis there is and can be no moral foundations for modern civilisation.

Along with this, what is happening in today's world—and we just started to discuss this—is a tentative effort to introduce precisely this concept into international affairs, the concept of a unipolar world.

And with which results?

Unilateral and frequently illegitimate actions have not resolved any problems. Moreover, they have caused new human tragedies and created new centres of tension. Judge for yourselves: wars as well as local and regional conflicts have not diminished. Mr Teltschik mentioned this very gently. And no less people perish in these conflicts—even more are dying than before. Significantly more, significantly more!

Today we are witnessing an almost uncontained hyper use of force—military force—in international relations, force that is plunging the world into an abyss of permanent conflicts. As a result we do not have sufficient strength to find a comprehensive solution to any one of these conflicts. Finding a political settlement also becomes impossible.

We are seeing a greater and greater disdain for the basic principles of international law. And independent legal norms are, as a matter of fact, coming increasingly closer to one state's legal system. One state and, of course, first and foremost the United States, has overstepped its national borders in every way. This is visible in the economic, political, cultural and educational policies it imposes on other nations. Well, who likes this? Who is happy about this?

In international relations we increasingly see the desire to resolve a given question according to so-called issues of political expediency, based on the current political climate.

And of course this is extremely dangerous. It results in the fact that no one feels safe. I want to emphasise this—no one feels safe! Because no one can feel that international law is like a stone wall that will protect them. Of course such a policy stimulates an arms race.

The force's dominance inevitably encourages a number of countries to acquire weapons of mass destruction. Moreover, significantly new threats—though they were also well-known before—have appeared, and today threats such as terrorism have taken on a global character.

I am convinced that we have reached that decisive moment when we must seriously think about the architecture of global security.

And we must proceed by searching for a reasonable balance between the interests of all participants in the international dialogue. Especially since the international landscape is so varied and changes so quickly—changes in light of the dynamic development in a whole number of countries and regions.

Madam Federal Chancellor already mentioned this. The combined GDP measured in purchasing power parity of countries such as India and China is already greater than that of the United States. And a similar calculation with the GDP of the BRIC countries—Brazil, Russia, India and China—surpasses the cumulative GDP of the EU. And according to experts this gap will only increase in the future.

There is no reason to doubt that the economic potential of the new centres of global economic growth will inevitably be converted into political influence and will strengthen multipolarity.

In connection with this the role of multilateral diplomacy is significantly increasing. The need for principles such as openness, transparency and predictability in politics is uncontested and the use of force should be a really exceptional measure, comparable to using the death penalty in the judicial systems of certain states.

However, today we are witnessing the opposite tendency, namely a situation in which countries that forbid the death penalty even for murderers and other, dangerous criminals are airily participating in military operations that are difficult to consider legitimate. And as a matter of fact, these conflicts are killing people—hundreds and thousands of civilians!

But at the same time the question arises of whether we should be indifferent and aloof to various internal conflicts inside countries, to authoritarian regimes, to tyrants, and to the proliferation of weapons of mass destruction? As a matter of fact, this was also at the centre of the question that our dear colleague Mr Lieberman asked the Federal Chancellor. If I correctly understood your question (addressing Mr Lieberman), then of course it is a serious one! Can we be indifferent observers in view of what is happening? I will try to answer your question as well: of course not.

But do we have the means to counter these threats? Certainly we do. It is sufficient to look at recent history. Did not our country have a peaceful transition to democracy? Indeed, we witnessed a peaceful transformation of the Soviet regime—a peaceful transformation! And what a regime! With what a number of weapons, including nuclear weapons! Why should we start bombing and shooting now at every available opportunity? Is it the case when without the threat of mutual destruction we do not have enough political culture, respect for democratic values and for the law?

I am convinced that the only mechanism that can make decisions about using military force as a last resort is the Charter of the United Nations. And in connection with this, either I did not understand what our colleague, the Italian Defence Minister, just said or what he said was inexact. In any case, I understood that the use of force can only be legitimate when the decision is taken by NATO, the EU, or the UN. If he really does think so, then we have different points of view. Or I didn't hear correctly. The use of force can only be considered legitimate if the decision is sanctioned by the UN. And we do not need to substitute NATO or the EU for the UN.

When the UN will truly unite the forces of the international community and can really react to events in various countries, when we will leave behind this disdain for international law, then the situation will be able to change. Otherwise the situation will simply result in a dead end, and the number of serious mistakes will be multiplied. Along with this, it is necessary to make sure that international law have a universal character both in the conception and application of its norms.

And one must not forget that democratic political actions necessarily go along with discussion and a laborious decision-making process. . . .

Dear ladies and gentlemen!

In conclusion I would like to note the following. We very often—and personally, I very often—hear appeals by our partners, including our European partners, to the effect that Russia should play an increasingly active role in world affairs.

In connection with this I would allow myself to make one small remark. It is hardly necessary to incite us to do so. Russia is a country with a history that spans more than a thousand years and has practically always used the privilege to carry out an independent foreign policy.

We are not going to change this tradition today. At the same time, we are well aware of how the world has changed and we have a realistic sense of our own opportunities and potential. And of course we would like to interact with responsible and independent partners with whom we could work together in constructing a fair and democratic world order that would ensure security and prosperity not only for a select few, but for all.

Thank you for your attention.

<table>
<tr><td>

Study Question

1. Based upon events to date, what seems more likely: a unipolar world dominated by American power, or a multipolar world dominated by several major centres of power?

</td></tr>
</table>

TIPS FOR ANALYSIS

From Document to Documentary

Many of the films recommended in the preceding chapters are documentaries. All of the same analytical tools can be used in evaluating historical documentaries: consider the film-maker, his or her biases, and the time period in which the film was created. In the case of documentaries it is sometimes useful to consider the sources of funding for the film too.

WEB RESOURCES

Resources on Globalization
http://hawaii.edu/emailref/internet_resources/Globalization.html
Global Gateway: World Culture and Resources
http://international.loc.gov/intldl/intldlhome.html
Resources on the events of September 11, 2001
http://www.nyu.edu/fas/projects/vcb/case_911/resources/web.html
Teaching with the News: A Guide to Current Issues in the Classroom
http://www.choices.edu/resources/current.php

RECOMMENDED READING

Dan Brown, *The Da Vinci Code* (New York: Doubleday, 2003). This best-selling novel explores the Christian Church's campaign to enforce a masculine-dominated version of the faith, contrary to the intentions of its founders. The idea of a deliberate campaign to eliminate the sacred feminine elements from the faith provoked outraged debunkers, despite the fictional nature of the story.

Khaled Hosseini, *The Kite Runner* (New York: Riverhead Books, 2003). *The Kite Runner* is set in Afghanistan as the monarchy collapses and Soviet troops invade the country. The novel's greatest strength, however, is in its recounting of the power of tribal loyalties and their resulting, often disastrous, implications.

Kurt Vonnegut, *Timequake* (Berkley, Ca: Berkley Publishing Group, 1998). Part unfinished novel and part Vonnegut memoir, *Timequake* sees the universe move back ten years, forcing the world to relive the 1990s in exactly the same way. En route, Vonnegut reflects on numerous issues including war, the state of humanity, spirituality, and evolution.

Ruth Linnea Whitney, *Slim* (Dallas, TX: Southern Methodist University Press, 2003). Set in Africa at the onset of the AIDS epidemic, the novel examines the problems of dictatorship, patriarchal society, and indifference amidst a gradually rising awareness of the potential social, political, and economic devastation of the unchecked epidemic.

RECOMMENDED VIEWING

Lilya 4-Ever (Sweden, 2002). Director: Lukas Moodysson. *Lilya 4-Ever* documents the poverty of life in the former Soviet Union and its impact on children, especially those who find themselves drawn to alcohol, drugs, and prostitution across Europe. The film is fictional, but it was filmed in documentary style.

The Corporation (Canada, 2003). Directors: Mark Achbar/Jennifer Abbott (Documentary). This Canadian-made documentary gained critical acclaim for its exploration of the 'personality' of the corporation. The three-hour film examines the history of the corporation beginning in the nineteenth century, and the basis of its power under the law. The film also discusses the current global power of corporations, their environmental impact, and the nature of global capitalism.

Fahrenheit 9/11 (USA, 2004). Director: Michael Moore (Documentary). Winner of the Palme d'Or at Cannes, Moore's controversial documentary focuses on the events of 11 September 2001, the Bush presidency, its questionable legitimacy, and the second Iraq War. The film examines political manipulation, the role of corporations in politics, US foreign policy, and the causes and impact of terrorism.

United 93 (USA, 2006). Director: Paul Greengrass. *United 93* follows the events surrounding the hijacking of the fourth airplane on 11 September 2001, on the plane and on the ground. Greengrass received praise for the film because he refused to revel in the heroism of the passengers who are believed to have ultimately overwhelmed the terrorists (forcing them to crash the plane in rural Pennsylvania). Instead, Greengrass provides insights into the decisions of all of the parties involved.

World Trade Center (USA, 2006). Director: Oliver Stone. Based on actual events, the film follows the activities of two Port Authority police officers—John McLoughlin and William Jimeno—as they react to the chaos of the terrorist attacks on the World Trade Center. After entering the South Tower, the two men are trapped as the concourse collapses. The rest of the film follows their struggle to survive, the effect on their families, and the efforts of rescuers. The film avoids Stone's usual focus on conspiracy theories.

Charlie Wilson's War (USA, 2007). Director: Mike Nichols. Nichols's film examines the role of US Congressman Charlie Wilson in setting up American funding to the Afghan Mujahedeen during the era of Soviet involvement in Afghanistan. The film provides the background to the rise of the Taliban and subsequent developments as the Soviets withdrew in 1988 and 1989.

Battle in Seattle (France, 2008). Director: Stuart Townsend. *Battle in Seattle* effectively combines actual event footage with fictional portrayals of key characters involved in the November 1999 protests at the World Trade Organization meetings in Seattle. The film examines the impact on the city, as well as world opinion on globalization and public protest.

Suggestions for Further Reading

Chapter One: The World and the West

Best, Antony, ed. 2004. *International History of the Twentieth Century*. London/New York: Routledge.

Conquest, Robert. 2001. *Reflections on a Ravaged Century*. New York: W.W. Norton.

Goto, Kenichi. 2003. *Tensions of Empire: Japan and Southeast Asia in the Colonial and Postcolonial World*. Athens, OH: Ohio University Press.

Gran, Peter. 1996. *Beyond Eurocentrism: A New View of Modern World History*. New York: Syracuse University Press.

Hobsbawm, E.J. 1996. *The Age of Extremes: A History of the World, 1914–1991*. London: Vintage.

Howard, Michael, and Wm. Roger Louis, eds. 1998. *The Oxford History of the Twentieth Century*. Oxford: Oxford University Press.

Ponting, Clive. 1998. *Progress and Barbarism: The World in the Twentieth Century*. London: Chatto & Windus.

Teich, Mikuláš, and Roy Porter, eds. 1990. *Fin-De-Siècle and its Legacy*. Cambridge: Cambridge University Press.

Tuchman, Barbara. 1966. *The Proud Tower: A Portrait of the World before the War, 1890–1914*. New York: Macmillan.

Von Laue, Theodore H. 1987. *The World Revolution of Westernization: The Twentieth Century in Global Perspective*. New York: Macmillan.

Watson, Peter. 2000. *A Terrible Beauty: A History of the People and Ideas that Shaped the Modern Mind*. London: Weidenfeld & Nicolson.

Chapter Two: Global Capitalism and Imperialism

Blue, Gregory, Martin Bunton, and Ralph Croizier, eds. 2002. *Colonialism and the Modern World: Selected Studies*. Armonk, NY: M.E. Sharpe.

Cooper, Frederick, and Ann Laura Stoler, eds. 1997. *Tensions of Empire: Colonial Cultures in a Bourgeois World*. Berkeley: University of California Press.

Ferro, Marc. 1997. *Colonization: A Global History*. London: Routledge.

Fieldhouse, D.K. 1999. *The West and the Third World: Trade, Colonialism, Dependence and Development*. Oxford: Blackwell.

Hobsbawm, E.J. 1987. *The Age of Empire, 1875–1914*. London: Vintage.

Johnson, Robert. 2003. *British Imperialism: Histories and Controversies*. New York: Palgrave Macmillan.

Porter, Andrew. 1994. *European Imperialism*. New York: St. Martin's Press.

Wolf, Eric. 1982. *Europe and the People Without History*. Berkeley, CA: University of California Press.

Young, Crawford. 1994. *The African Colonial State in Comparative Perspective*. New Haven: Yale University Press.

Chapter Three: War and Peace

First World War

Dadrian, Vahakn N. 2003. *The History of the Armenian Genocide: Ethnic Conflict from the Balkans to Anatolia to the Caucasus*. Oxford: Berghahn Books.

Eksteins, Modris. 1989. *Rites of Spring: The Great War and the Birth of the Modern Age*. Toronto: Mariner Books.

Ferguson, Niall. 1999. *The Pity of War: Explaining World War I*. New York: Basic Books.

Herwig, Holger. 1996. *The First World War: Germany and Austria Hungary*. London: Arnold Publishers.

Joll, James. 2000. *The Origins of the First World War*. London: Longman.

Mackaman, Douglas, and Michael Mays, eds. 2000. *World War I and the Cultures of Modernity*. Jackson, MS: University Press of Mississippi.

Winter, Jay, Geoffrey Parker, and Mary R. Habeck, eds. 2000. *The Great War and the Twentieth Century*. New Haven, CT: Yale University Press.

Postwar Settlement

Ferrell, Robert H. 1985. *Woodrow Wilson and World War I*. New York: HarperCollins.

Macmillan, Margaret. 2002. *Paris 1919: Six Months that Changed the World*. New York: Random House.

Marks, Sally. 2002. *The Ebbing of European Ascendancy: An International History of the World, 1914–1945*. London: Arnold Publishers.

Northedge, F.S. 1986. *The League of Nations: Its Life and Times, 1920–1946*. Leicester: Leicester University Press.

Overy, R.J. 1994. *The Inter-War Crisis 1919–1939*. London/New York: Longman Publishing Group.

Chapter Four: The Appeal of Revolutionary Change

Beasley, W.G. 1987. *Rise of Modern Japan: Political, Economic and Social Change since 1850*. London: Palgrave Macmillan.

Bergere, Marie-Claire. 1989. *The Golden Age of the Chinese Bourgeoisie, 1911–1937*. Stanford: Cambridge University Press.

Bix, Herbert P. 2000. *Hirohito and the Making of Modern Japan*. New York: Perennial.

Brovkin, Vladimir N., ed. 1997. *The Bolsheviks in Russian Society: The Revolution and the Civil Wars*. New Haven, CT: Yale University Press.

Brown, Judith M. 1994. *India: The Origins of an Asian Democracy*. Oxford: Oxford University Press.

Eastman, Lloyd E. 1974. *The Abortive Revolution: China under Nationalist Rule, 1927–1937*. Cambridge, MA: Harvard University Press.

Eley, Geoff. 2002. *Forging Democracy: The History of the Left in Europe, 1850–2000*. Oxford: Oxford University Press.

Figes, Orlando. 1996. *People's Tragedy: The Russian Revolution, 1891–1924*. New York: Penguin.

Freeze, Gregory L., ed. 2002. *Russia: A History*. Oxford: Oxford University Press.

Goldman, Merle, and Leo Ou-Fan Lee, eds. 2002. *An Intellectual History of Modern China*. Cambridge/New York: Cambridge University Press.

Harding, Neil, 1996. *Leninism*. Basingstoke, UK: Palgrave Macmillan.

Inkster, Ian. 2001. *Japanese Industrialisation: Historical and Cultural Perspectives*. London/New York: Routledge.

Mamdani, Mahmoud. 1996. *Citizen and Subject: Contemporary Africa and the Legacy of Late Colonialism*. London: James Currey.

Narangoa, Li. 2003. *Imperial Japan and National Identities in Asia, 1895–1945*. London/New York: Routledge.

Nove, Alec. 1992. *Economic History of the USSR*. London: Penguin.

Perry, Elizabeth J. 2002. *Challenging the Mandate of Heaven: Social Protest and State Power in China*. Armonk, NY: M.E. Sharpe.

Schoppa, R. Keith. 2001. *Revolution and its Past: Identities and Change in Modern Chinese History*. Englewood Cliffs, NJ: Prentice Hall.

Service, Robert. 1999. *The Russian Revolution, 1900–1927*. New York: Palgrave Macmillan.

Spence, Jonathan D. 1999. *The Search for Modern China*. New York: W.W. Norton.

Stern, R.W. 1993. *Changing India: Bourgeois Revolution on the Subcontinent*. Cambridge: Cambridge University Press.

Wade, Rex A. 2001. *The Bolshevik Revolution and Russian Civil War*. Westport, CT: Greenwood Press.

Wheatcroft, Stephen G., ed. 2002. *Challenging Traditional Views of Russian History*. New York: Palgrave Macmillan.

Wolpert, Stanley A. 1984. *Jinnah of Pakistan*. New York: Oxford University Press.

Wong, R. Bin. 1998. *China Transformed: Historical Change and the Limits of European Experience*. Ithaca, NY: Cornell University Press.

Chapter Five: The Authoritarian Alternative

Beasley, W.G. 1987. *Japanese Imperialism, 1894–1945*. Oxford: Oxford University Press.

Bessel, Richard. 2004. *Nazism and War*. London: Modern Library.

Conquest, Robert. 1990. *The Great Terror: A Reassessment*. New York: Oxford University Press.

Gellately, Robert. 2001. *Backing Hitler: Consent and Coercion in Nazi Germany*. Oxford: Oxford University Press.

Laqueur, Walter. 1996. *Fascism: Past, Present, Future*. New York: Oxford University Press.

Larsen, Stein Ugelvik. 2001. *Fascism Outside Europe: The European Impulse against Domestic Conditions in the Diffusion of Global Fascism*. New York: Columbia University Press.

McCauley, Martin. 2003. *Stalin and Stalinism*. Harlow: Longman.

Paxton, Robert O. 2004. *The Anatomy of Fascism*. New York: Vintage.

Payne, Stanley G. 1995. *A History of Fascism, 1914–1945*. Madison, WI: University of Wisconsin Press.

Todd, Allan. 2002. *The European Dictatorships: Hitler, Stalin, Mussolini*. Cambridge: Cambridge University Press.

Tucker, Robert. 1990. *Stalin in Power: The Revolution from Above*. New York: W.W. Norton.

Wiarda, Howard, and Harvey Kline, eds. 1990. *Latin American Politics and Development*, 3rd Edition. Boulder, CO: Westview Press.

Chapter Six: Global Depression

Balderston, Theo, ed. 2003. *The World Economy and National Economies in the Interwar Slump*. New York: Palgrave Macmillan.

Bernanke, Ben. 2000. *Essays on the Great Depression*. Princeton, NJ: Princeton University Press.

Clavin, Patricia. 2000. *The Great Depression in Europe, 1929–1939*. London: Palgrave Macmillan.

Heale, M.J. 1999. *Franklin D. Roosevelt—The New Deal and War*. London: Routledge.

Himmelberg, Robert F. 2001. *The Great Depression and the New Deal*. Westport, CT: Greenwood Press.

Kindleberger, Charles P. 1973. *The World in Depression 1929–1939*. London: University of California Press.

Klein, Maury. 2001. *Rainbow's End: The Crash of 1929*. New York: Oxford University Press.

Latham, A.J.H. 1981. *The Depression and the Developing World, 1914–1939*. London: Barnes and Noble Books.

Rothermund, Dietmar. 1996. *The Global Impact of the Great Depression, 1929–1939*. London: Routledge.

———. 1992. *India in the Great Depression, 1929–1939*. Columbia, MO: South Asia Publications.

Chapter Seven: Global War and Genocide

Second World War

Calvocoressi, Peter, and Guy Wint. 1988. *Total War: The Story of World War II*. London: Penguin.

Chickering, Roger, and Stig Förster, eds. 2003. *The Shadows of Total War: Europe, East Asia, and the United States, 1919–1939*. Cambridge: Cambridge University Press.

Irye, Akira. 1987. *The Origins of the Second World War in Asia and the Pacific*. London: Longman.

Keegan, John. 1990. *The Second World War*. New York: Penguin.

Overy, R.J. 1999. *The Road to War*. London/New York: Penguin.

Weinberg, Gerhard. 1994. *A World at Arms: A Global History of World War II*. Cambridge: Cambridge University Press.

Genocide

Bartov, Omer. 2000. *Mirrors of Destruction: War, Genocide, and Modern Identity*. New York: Oxford University Press.

Burleigh, Michael. 1997. *Ethics and Extermination: Reflections on Nazi Genocide*. Cambridge/New York: Cambridge University Press.

Gellately, Robert, and Ben Kiernan, eds. 2003. *The Specter of Genocide: Mass Murder in Historical Perspective*. Cambridge/New York: Cambridge University Press.

Hilberg, Raul. 1992. *Perpetrators Victims Bystanders: The Jewish Catastrophe, 1933–1945*. New York: Perennial.

Jones, Adam, ed. 2004. *Genocide, War Crimes and the West: History and Complicity*. London/New York: Zed Books.

Valentino, Benjamin A. 2004. *Final Solutions: Mass Killing and Genocide in the Twentieth Century*. Ithaca, NY: Cornell University Press.

Chapter Eight: A New World Order?

Aoi, Chiyuki, et al, eds. 2007. *Unintended Consequences of Peacekeeping Operations*. Tokyo/New York: United Nations University Press.

Hamburg, David A. 2002. *No More Killing Fields: Preventing Deadly Conflict*. Lanham, MD: Rowman and Littlefield Publishers.

Hunnicutt, Susan. 2007. *The United Nations*. Detroit: Greenhaven Press.

James, Stephen. 2007. *Universal Human Rights: Origins and Development*. New York: LFB Scholarly Publishers.

Meyer, Howard N. 2002. *The World Court in Action: Judging among the Nations*. Lanham, MD: Rowman and Littlefield Publishers.

Mingst, Karen A. 2006. *The United Nations in the Twenty-first Century*. Boulder, CO: Westview.

Newman, Edward, and Roland Rich, eds. 2004. *The UN Role in Promoting Democracy: Between Ideals and Reality*. Tokyo/New York: United Nations University Press.

Parsons, Anthony. 1995. *From Cold War to Hot Peace: UN Interventions 1947–1994*. New York: Penguin.

Weiss, Thomas. 2007. *The Oxford Handbook on the United Nations*. New York: OUP.

Chapter Nine: Origins and Implications of the Cold War

Alperovitz, Gar. 1997. *Decision to Use the Atomic Bomb*. New York: Vintage.

Ash, Timothy Garton. 1993. *In Europe's Name: Germany and the Divided Continent*. London: Vintage.

Brands, H.W. 1993. *The Devil We Knew: Americans and the Cold War*. Oxford: Oxford University Press.

DePorte, Anton. 1987. *Europe between the Superpowers*. New Haven: Yale University Press.

Fried, Albert. 1997. *McCarthyism: The Great American Red Scare*. Oxford: Oxford University Press.

Fursenko, Aleksandr, and Timothy Naftali. 1998. *One Hell of a Gamble: Khrushchev, Castro and Kennedy, 1958–1964*. New York: W.W. Norton.

Gaddis, John. 1997. *We Now Know: Rethinking Cold War History*. Oxford: Oxford University Press.

Knight, Amy. 2006. *How the Cold War Began: The Igor Gouzenko Affair and the Hunt for Soviet Spies*. New York: Carroll & Graf.

Paterson, James. 1996. *Grand Expectations: The United States, 1945–74*. Oxford: Oxford University Press.

Rhodes, Richard. 1988. *The Making of the Atomic Bomb*. London: Simon & Schuster.

Smyser, W.R. 1999. *From Yalta to Berlin: The Cold War Struggle Over Germany*. New York: St Martin's Press.

Takaki, Ronald. 1995. *Hiroshima: Why America Dropped the Atomic Bomb*. New York: Bay Back Books.

Zubok, Vladislav, and Constantine Pleshakov. 1996. *Inside the Kremlin's Cold War: From Stalin to Khrushchev*. Cambridge, MA: Harvard University Press.

Chapter Ten: China and Japan: The Re-Emergence of Asian Power

Borthwick, Mark. 1998. *Pacific Century: The Emergence of Modern Pacific Asia*. Boulder, CO: Westview Press.

Dickson, Bruce J. 2003. *Red Capitalists in China: The Party, Private Entrepreneurs, and Prospects for Political Change*. Cambridge: Cambridge University Press.

Gibney, Frank. 1992. *The Pacific Century*. New York: Scribner.

Goldman, Merle, and Roderick MacFarquhar, eds. 1999. *The Paradox of China's Post-Mao Reforms*. Cambridge: Harvard University Press.

Gries, Peter Hays. 2004. *China's New Nationalism: Pride, Politics and Diplomacy*. Berkeley: University of California Press.

Hane, Mikiso. 2003. *Peasants, Rebels, and Outcastes: The Underside of Modern Japan*. Lanham, MD: Rowan and Littlefield Publishers.

Iriye, Akira, and Robert A. Wampler, eds. 2001. *Partnership: The United States and Japan, 1951–2001*. Tokyo: Kodansha International.

Kingston, Jeffrey. 2001. *Japan in Transformation, 1952–2000*. New York: Longman.

Meisner, Maurice. 1999. *Mao's China and After: A History of the People's Republic*, 3rd edition. New York: Free Press.

Moore, Thomas Geoffrey. 2002. *China in the World Market: Chinese Industry and International Sources of Reform in the Post-Mao Era*. New York: Cambridge University Press.

Nolan, Peter. 2003. *Transforming China: Globalization, Transition and Development*. London: Anthem Press.

Perry, Elizabeth J., and Mark Selden, eds. 2000. *Chinese Society: Change, Conflict and Resistance.* New York: Routledge.

Schlesinger, Jacob M. 1999. *Shadow Shoguns: The Rise and Fall of Japan's Postwar Political Machine.* Stanford, CA: Stanford University Press.

Schwartz, Frank J., and Susan J. Pharr, eds. 2003. *The State of Civil Society in Japan.* Cambridge: Cambridge University Press.

Stockwin, J.A.A. 1988. *Governing Japan: Divided Politics in a Major Economy.* London: Blackwell Publishers.

Vogel, Erza. 1991. *The Four Little Dragons.* Cambridge, Mass: Harvard University Press.

Chapter Eleven: Anti-Colonial Movements and Independence

Anderson, David M. 1992. *Policing and Decolonization: Politics, Nationalism and the Police, 1917–65.* Manchester: Manchester University Press.

Berger, Mark T. 2004. *The Battle for Asia: From Decolonization to Globalization.* London/New York: Routledge.

Betts, Raymond F. 2004. *Decolonization: Making of the Contemporary World.* New York: Routledge.

Brown, Judith M. 1989. *Gandhi: Prisoner of Hope.* New Haven, CT: Yale University Press.

Chafer, Tony. 2002. *The End of Empire in French West Africa: France's Successful Decolonization?* Oxford/New York: Berg Publishers.

Elkins, Caroline. 2004. *Imperial Reckoning: The Untold Story of Britain's Gulag in Kenya.* New York: Henry Holt and Company.

Grimal, Henri. 1979. *Decolonization: The British, French, Dutch, and Belgian Empires, 1919–1963.* Boulder, CO: Westview Press.

Hahn, Peter L., and Mary Ann Heiss, eds. 2001. *Empire and Revolution: The United States and the Third World since 1945.* Columbus, OH: Ohio State University Press.

Le Sueur, James D., ed. 2003. *The Decolonization Reader.* New York: Routledge.

Springhall, John. 2001. *Decolonization since 1945: The Collapse of European Overseas Empires.* New York: Palgrave Macmillan.

Wolpert, Stanley A. 2003. *A New History of India*, 7th Edition. New York: Oxford University Press.

Chapter Twelve: Technology and the Environment

Adas, Michael. 1996. *Machines as the Measure of Men.* Ithaca, NY: Cornell University Press.

Bramwell, Anna. 1989. *Ecology in the Twentieth Century: A History.* New Haven, CT: Yale University Press.

Diamond, Jared. 2005. *Collapse: How Societies Choose to Fail or Succeed.* New York: Viking.

Ehrlich, Paul. 2008. *The Dominant Animal: Human Evolution and the Environment.* Washington DC: Island Press.

Flannery, Tim. 2006. *The Weather Makers: How We Are Changing the Climate and What It Means for Life on Earth.* Toronto: HarperCollins Canada.

Hård, Mikel. 2005. *Hubris and Hybrids. A Cultural History of Technology and Science.* New York: Routledge.

Horowitz, Roger and Arwen Mohun. 1998. *His and Hers: Gender, Consumption, and Technology.* Charlottesville, VA: University Press of Virginia.

McNeill, J.R. 2000. *Something New Under the Sun: An Environmental History of the Twentieth-Century World.* New York: W.W. Norton & Co.

Radkau, Joachim. 2008. *Nature and Power: A Global History of the Environment.* Washington, DC: German Historical Institute.

Strate, Lance. 2005. *The Legacy of McLuhan.* Cresskill, NJ: Hampton Press.

Chapter Thirteen: The Challenge of Neo-Colonialism

Amin, Samir. 1973. *Neo-colonialism in West Africa.* New York: Monthly Review Press.

Dirks, Nicholas B. 2001. *Castes of Mind: Colonialism and the Making of Modern India.* Englewood Cliffs, NJ: Princeton University Press.

Donghi, Tulio Halperin. 1993. *The Contemporary History of Latin America.* Durham, NC: Duke University Press.

Esedebe, P. Olisanwuche. 1982. *Pan-Africanism: The Idea and the Movement, 1776–1963.* Washington, DC: Howard University Press.

Iweriebor, Ehiedu. 1997. *The Age of Neo-Colonialism in Africa: Essays on Domination and Resistance after Independence.* Ibadan: African Book Builders.

Perez, Louis A. 1995. *Cuba: Between Reform and Revolution.* Oxford: Oxford University Press.

Smith, Peter H. 1999. *Talons of the Eagle: Dynamics of US–Latin American Relations*, 2nd Edition. Oxford: Oxford University Press.

Wiarda, Howard, and Harvey Kline, eds. 1990. *Latin American Politics and Development*, 3rd Edition. Boulder, CO: Westview Press.

Chapter Fourteen: Paths to Modernization

Bayart, Francois. 1993. *The State in Africa: The Politics of the Belly.* London: Longman Group UK.

Clark, Nancy L., and William H. Worger. 2004. *South Africa: The Rise and Fall of Apartheid.* New York: Longman.

Cooper, Frederick. 2002. *Africa since 1940: The Past of the Present.* Cambridge: Cambridge University Press.

Dirks, Nicholas B. 2001. *Castes of Mind: Colonialism and the Making of Modern India.* Englewood Cliffs, NJ: Princeton University Press.

Goodman, David. 1999. *Fault Lines: Journeys into the New South Africa.* Berkeley: University of California Press.

Hoogvelt, Ankie. 2001. *Globalization and the Postcolonial World:*

The New Political Economy of Development. Baltimore, MD: Johns Hopkins University Press.

Werbner, Richard, and Terence Ranger, eds. 1996. *Postcolonial Identities in Africa*. London: ZED Books.

Chapter Fifteen: The Postwar Era in the Middle East

Bhutto, Benazir. 2008. *Reconciliation: Islam, Democracy, and the West*. New York: Harper.

Horowitz, Dan, and Moshe Lissak. 1989. *Trouble in Utopia: The Overburdened Polity of Israel*. Albany, NY: State University of New York Press.

Keddie, Nikki. 2007. *Women in the Middle East: Past and Present*. Princeton, NJ: Princeton University Press.

Lapidus, Ira M. 2002. *A History of Islamic Societies*. Cambridge/New York: Cambridge University Press.

Mottahedeh, Roy. 1985. *The Mantle of the Prophet: Religion and Politics in Iran*. New York: Simon & Schuster.

Nasr, Seyyed Vali Reza. 2006. *The Shia Revival: How Conflicts within Islam will Shape the Future*. New York: W.W. Norton.

Said, Edward. 1994. *The Politics of Dispossession: The Struggle for Palestinian Self-Determination, 1969–1994*. New York: Vintage.

Saikal, Amin. 2003. *Islam and the West: Conflict or Cooperation?* New York: Palgrave Macmillan.

Yapp, Malcolm. 1991. *The Near East since the First World War*. London: Longman Group UK.

Zahan, Rosemary Said. 1989. *The Making of the Modern Gulf States*. London: Ithaca Press.

Chapter Sixteen: Ideological Change

Dierenfield, Bruce J. 2004. *The Civil Rights Movement*. New York: Longman.

Gitlin, Todd. 1993. *The Sixties: Years of Hope, Days of Rage*. New York: Bantam.

Hagan, John. 2001. *Northern Passage: American Vietnam War Resistors in Canada*. Cambridge, MA: Harvard University Press.

Isserman, Maurice, and Michael Kazin. 1999. *America Divided: The Civil War of the 1960s*. Oxford: Oxford University Press.

Klatch, Rebecca E. 1999. *A Generation Divided: The New Left, the New Right, and the 1960s*. Berkeley: University of California Press.

Kurlansky, Mark. 2003. *1968: The Year that Rocked the World*. New York: Ballantine Books.

Middlemas, Keith. 1995. *Orchestrating Europe: The Informal Politics of European Union 1973–1995*. London: Fontana Press.

Polenberg, Richard. 1993. *One Nation Divisible: Class, Race and Ethnicity in the United States since 1938*. New York: Peter Smith Publisher Inc.

Rosen, Ruth. 2000. *The World Split Open: How the Modern Women's Movement Changed America*. New York: Penguin.

Chapter Seventeen: The End of the Cold War and Its Aftermath

Antohi, Sorin, and Vladimir Tismaneanu, eds. 2000. *Between Past and Future: The Revolutions of 1989 and their Aftermath*. Budapest: Central European University Press.

Brown, Archie. 1996. *The Gorbachev Factor*. Oxford: Oxford University Press.

Fitzgerald, Frances. 2000. *Way Out there in the Blue: Reagan, Star Wars, and the End of the Cold War*. New York: Simon & Schuster.

Garthoff, Raymond. 1994. *The Great Transition: American Soviet Relations and the End of the Cold War*. Washington: Brookings Institution Press.

Holm, Hans-Henrick, and Georg Sorensen. 1995. *Whose World Order: Uneven Globalization and the End of the Cold War*. Boulder, CO: Westview Press.

Howard, Marc Morjé. 2003. *The Weakness of Civil Society in Post-Communist Europe*. Cambridge: Cambridge University Press.

Remnick, David. 1993. *Lenin's Tomb: The Last Days of the Soviet Empire*. London, UK: Vintage.

Suny, Ronald Gregor. 1993. *The Revenge of the Past: Nationalism, Revolution, and the Collapse of the Soviet Union*. Stanford: Stanford University Press.

Tsyganov, Andrei P. 2004. *Whose World Order? Russia's Perception of American Ideas after the Cold War*. Notre Dame, IN: University of Notre Dame Press.

Chapter Eighteen: State Building and Its Discontents

Bakan, Joel. 2004. *The Corporation: The Pathological Pursuit of Profit and Power*. Toronto: Penguin Books Canada.

Barber, Benjamin. 1995. *Jihad vs. McWorld: How Globalism and Tribalism are Reshaping the World*. New York: Ballantine Books.

Berkeley, Bill. 2001. *The Graves are Not Yet Full: Race, Tribe, and Power in the Heart of Africa*. New York: Basic Books.

Landes, David S. 1998. *The Wealth and Poverty of Nations: Why Some Are So Rich and Some So Poor*. New York/London: W.W. Norton & Company.

Mazama, Ama. 2007. *Africa in the 21st Century: Toward a New Future*. London: Routledge.

Melvern, Linda. 2004. *Conspiracy to Murder: The Rwanda Genocide*. London/New York: Verso.

Morton, Jeffrey S., ed. 2004. *Reflections on the Balkan Wars: Ten Years after the Break-Up of Yugoslavia*. New York: Palgrave Macmillan.

Veltmeyer, Henry, ed. 2004. *Globalization and Antiglobalization: Dynamics of Change in the New World Order*. Aldershot, Hants, UK: Ashgate Publishing.

Weitz, Eric D. 2003. *A Century of Genocide: Utopias of Race and Nation*. Princeton, NJ: Princeton University Press.

Chapter Nineteen: History in the Making: Into the Twenty-first Century

Black, Jeremy. 2004. *War and the New Disorder in the 21st Century*, rev. edition. New York/London: Continuum International Publishing Group.

Chomsky, Noam. 2003. *Hegemony or Survival: America's Quest for Global Dominance*. New York: Metropolitan Books.

Dyer, Gwynne. 2004. *Future: Tense: The Coming World Order?* Toronto: McClelland & Stewart.

Fernandez-Armesto, Felipe. 1995. *Millennium*. London: Free Press.

Frank, Andre Gunder. 1998. *Reorient: Global Economics in the Asian Age*. Berkeley: University of California Press.

Fukuyama, Francis. 2004. *State-Building: Governance and World Order in the 21st Century*. Ithaca, NY: Cornell University Press.

Kennedy, Paul. 1993. *Preparing for the Twenty-First Century*. New York: Vintage.

Lukacs, John. 1993. *The End of the Twentieth Century and the End of the Modern Age*. New York: Ticknor and Fields.

Orbinski, James. 2008. *An Imperfect Offering: Humanitarian Action in the Twenty-first Century*. Toronto: Doubleday Canada.

ACKNOWLEDGEMENTS

Amur Society, 'Anniversary Statement', Wm. Theodore de Bary, *Sources of Japanese Tradition*, Vol. Two (New York: Columbia University Press, 1958), pp. 254–59. Reprinted by permission of the publisher.

Anglo-American Committee of Inquiry, 'Testimony by Chaim Weizmann'. From Chaim Weizmann, United Nations General Assembly, Working Documentation Prepared by the Secretariat, Volume I, *Reference Library on Palestine* (A/296, 28 April 1947). The United Nations is the author of the original material. Reprinted by permission.

Kwame Anthony Appiah, excerpt from *MULTICULTURALISM AND THE POLITICS OF RECOGNITION* by Charles Taylor © 1992 Princeton University Press, 1994 expanded paperback edition (*Multiculturalism: Examining the Politics of Recognition*). Reprinted by permission of Princeton University Press.

Armenian National Institute, 'Press Reports on the Armenian Genocide'. Courtesy of the Armenian National Institute (www.armenian-genocide.org).

David Buffum, 'On Kristallnacht', *Nazism 1919–1945: A Documentary Reader, Volume 2: State, Economy and Society*. Edited by J. Noakes and G. Pridham, new edition, 2000 pp. 186–7, pp. 255–6 and pp. 360–2. Reprinted by permission of the University of Exeter Press.

Fox Butterfield, excerpt from *China: Alive in a Bitter Sea*, copyright © 1982 by Fox Butterfield. Used by permission of Times Books, a division of Random House, Inc.; Reproduced by permission of Hodder and Stoughton Limited.

Rachel Carson, excerpt from 'A Fable for Tomorrow' from *Silent Spring*. Copyright © 1962 by Rachel L. Carson, renewed 1990 by Roger Christie. Reprinted by permission of Houghton Mifflin Harcourt Publishing Company. All rights reserved. Reproduced by permission of Pollinger Limited and the Estate of Rachel Carson.

Rami Chhabra, excerpt from 'Population Policy in India: Two Comments', *Population and Development Review* Volume 1, No. 1 (March 1981): 168–171. Reprinted with permission.

Antonio Cippico, from Count Antonio Cippico, *Italy: The Central Problem of the Mediterranean* (New Haven: Yale University Press, 1926). Reprinted by permission of Yale University Press.

Milovan Djilas, excerpts from *The New Class*, copyright © 1957 by Harcourt, Inc. and renewed 1985 by Milovan Djilas, reprinted by permission of Houghton Mifflin Harcourt Publishing Company.

Sinisa Djuric, 'Police Report on the Cleansing of Serbs'. Reprinted by permission of Sinisa Djuric, translator.

W.E.B. DuBois, 'Liberia, the League, and the United States, 1933'. Reprinted by permission of FOREIGN AFFAIRS, (Vol. 11, No. 4, July 1933). Copyright 1933 by the Council on Foreign Relations, Inc. www.ForeignAffairs.com

Frantz Fanon, excerpt from *The Wretched of the Earth*, copyright © 1963 by *Présence Africaine*. Used by permission of Grove/Atlantic, Inc.

Paul Comly French, 'Children on Strike'. Reprinted with permission from the May 31, 1933 issue of *The Nation*. For subscription information, call 1-800-333-8536. Portions of each week's *Nation* magazine can be accessed at http://www.thenation.com.

Fortune Magazine, excerpt from 'South America VI: Brazil', *Fortune Magazine*, Volume 19, No. 6 (June 1939), pp. 140–42. © 1939 Time Inc. All rights reserved.

Evgeniia Ginzburg, Excerpt from *JOURNEY INTO THE WHIRLWIND*, copyright © 1967 by Arnoldo Mondadori Editore-Milano, English translation by Paul Stevenson and Max Hayward copyright © 1967 by Harcourt, Inc. reprinted by permission of Houghton Mifflin Harcourt Publishing Company.

Joseph Goebbels, 'The Reich Ministry of Popular Enlightenment and Propaganda', from *Nazism 1919–1945: A Documentary Reader, Volume 2: State, Economy and Society*. Edited by J. Noakes and G. Pridham, new edition, 2000 pp. 186–7, pp. 255–6 and pp. 360–2. Reprinted by permission of the University of Exeter Press.

Albert Gore, 'Nobel Lecture', Oslo, Norway, 10 December 2007. © The Nobel Foundation 2007.

Philip Gourevitch, excerpts from Chapter 1 from *We Wish To Inform You That Tomorrow We Will Be Killed With Our Families: Stories from Rwanda*. Copyright © 1998 by Philip Gourevitch. Reprinted by permission of Farrar, Straus & Giroux.

Mohamed Elhachmi Hamdi. 'Islam and Liberal Democracy: The Limits of the Western Model', *Journal of Democracy* 7:2 (1996), 81–85. © 1996 National Endowment for Democracy and the Johns Hopkins University Press. Reprinted with permission of The Johns Hopkins University Press.

Ito Hirobumi, 'On the Constitution of 1889', Wm. Theodore de Bary, *Sources of Japanese Tradition*, Vol. Two (New York: Columbia University Press, 1958), pp. 161–64. Reprinted by permission of the publisher.

Adolf Hitler, 'To the National Socialist Frauenbund', *Nazism 1919–1945: A Documentary Reader, Volume 2: State, Economy and Society*. Edited by J. Noakes and G. Pridham, new edition, 2000 pp. 186–7, pp. 255–6 and pp. 360–2. Reprinted by permission of the University of Exeter Press.

Adam Hochschild (excerpt), *King Leopold's Ghost*. Excerpt from *KING LEOPOLD'S GHOST* by Adam Hochschild. Copyright © 1998 by Adam Hochschild. Reprinted by permission of Houghton Mifflin Harcourt Publishing Company. All Rights Reserved.

Robert Kaplan, excerpts from *Balkan Ghosts: A Journey through History*, copyright © 1993 by the author and reprinted by permission of St. Martin's Press, LLC.

Robert Kaplan, excerpts from *The Coming Anarchy: Shattering the Dreams of the Post Cold War*. Published by Random House. Copyright © 2000 by Robert D. Kaplan. Reprinted by permission of Brandt & Hochman Literary Agents, Inc.

Kamei Katsuichiro, 'Return to the East', Wm. Theodore de Bary, *Sources of Japanese Tradition*, Vol. Two (New York: Columbia University Press, 1958), pp. 393–99. Reprinted by permission of the publisher.

Nikita Khrushchev, excerpt, 'Khrushchev Remembers', in *Khrushchev Remembers*, trans. Strobe Talbott (Boston, MA: Little, Brown and Company, 1971). Reprinted by permission of Andrew Nurnberg Associates.

Nikita Khrushchev, excerpt, 'Secret Speech', in *Khrushchev Remembers* trans. Strobe Talbott (Boston, MA: Little, Brown and Company, 1971). Reprinted by permission of Andrew Nurnberg Associates.

Martin Luther King, Jr., 'I Have a Dream'. Reprinted by arrangement with The Heirs to the Estate of Martin Luther King Jr., c/o Writers House as agent for the proprietor, New York, NY. Copyright 1963 Dr. Martin Luther King Jr.; copyright renewed 1991 Coretta Scott King

Muriel Kitagawa, *This Is My Own: Letters to Wes and Other Writings on Japanese Canadians, 1941–1948*, Roy Miki, ed. © 1985 Muriel Kitigawa, Roy Miki, Talon Books Ltd., Vancouver, BC. Reprinted by permission of the publisher.

Naomi Klein, excerpt from *No Logo: Taking Aim at the Brand Bullies*. Copyright © 2000 by Naomi Klein. Reprinted by permission of Alfred A. Knopf Canada.

Victor Klemperer, excerpt from *I WILL BEAR WITNESS* Vols. 1 & 2 by Victor Klemperer, translated by Martin Chalmers, translation copyright © 1998 by Martin chambers. Used by permission of Random House, Inc.

Kido K in, 'Observations on Returning from the West, 1873', Wm. Theodore de Bary, *Sources of Japanese Tradition*, Vol. Two (New York: Columbia University Press, 1958), pp. 143–45. Reprinted by permission of the publisher.

Alexandra Kollontai, *Alexandra Kollontai: Selected Articles and Speeches* (New York: International Publishers, 1984). Reprinted by permission of International Publishers Co., NY.

Stephen Lewis, 'UN Briefing on HIV/AIDS in Africa'. From Stephen Lewis, 'Text of UN Briefing by Stephen Lewis on HIV/AIDS in Africa'. Available online: http://www.worldrevolution.org/article/279. Reprinted courtesy of the United Nations Publications, Department of Public Information.

Syed Abul A'ala Maududi, 'Replacing Western Forms with Islamic Law,' Wm. Theodore de Bary et al., *Sources of Indian Tradition*, Vol. Two, Second Edition (New York: Columbia University Press, 1988), pp. 406–09. Reprinted by permission of the publisher.

Marshall McLuhan, From the *Playboy* Interview: Marshall McLuhan, *Playboy* magazine (March 1969). Copyright © 1969 by Playboy. Reprinted with permission. All rights reserved.

Dadabhai Naoroji, 'The Blessings of British Rule', Wm. Theodore de Bary et al., *Sources of Indian Tradition*, Vol. Two, Second Edition (New York: Columbia UP, 1988), pp. 93–94. Reprinted by permission of the publisher.

Jawaharlal Nehru, 'The Socialist Creed (1936)', Wm. Theodore de Bary et al., *Sources of Indian Tradition*, Volume Two, Second Edition (New York: Columbia University Press, 1988), pp. 317–19. Reprinted by permission of the publisher.

P.J. O'Rourke, 'Inside Tanzania'. From *Rolling Stone* (10 July 1997), 100, 102–3, 106, 108, 113–14. Reprinted by permission of the author. P.J. O'Rourke, Journalist.

Lester Pearson, selected text of speech entitled 'On Peacekeeping', 2 April 1965. Library and Archives Canada / Lester B. Pearson fonds / MG26 N9, Volume 33, File April 1965. © Government of Canada. Reproduced with the permission of the Minister of Public Works and Government Services Canada (2009).

D. Zizwe Poe, excerpt from *Kwame Nkrumah's Contribution to Pan-Africanism: An Afrocentric Analysis* (New York: Taylor & Francis/Routledge, 2003), pp. 161–63. Reprinted by permission.

john a. powell and S.P. Udayakumar, 'Race, Poverty and Globalization', *Global Exchange*, http://www.globalexchange.org/economy/econ101/globalization072000.html. Reprinted by permission of john a. powell.

William Ratliff, 'A New Old Che Guevara Interview', in *Hispanic American Historical Review*, Volume 46, no. 3, pp. 288–300. Copyright 1966, Duke University Press. All Rights Reserved. Used by permission of the publisher.

Erich Maria Remarque, excerpt from *All Quiet on the Western Front*. Reproduced by permission of the Estate of the Late Paulette Goddard Remarque.

Edward Said, 'Truth and Reconciliation', originally published in *al-Ahram Weekly On-line*. Copyright © 1999 by Edward Said, reprinted with permission of The Wylie Agency LLC.

Jean-Paul Sartre, excerpt from *Existentialism*. Copyright © 1957, 1985 Philosophical Library, Inc. All rights reserved. Reprinted by arrangement with Kensington Publishing Corp. www.kensingtonbooks.com.

Miriam Schneir, ed., *Feminism in Our Time: The Essential Writings, World War II to the Present* (New York/Toronto: Vintage Books, 1994), pp. 127–29. Reprinted by permission of the author.

Leopold Senghor, 'Some Thoughts on Africa', *International Affairs* Vol. 38, No. 2 (April 1962): 189–95. Reprinted by permission.

Aleksandr Solzhenitsyn, excerpts from 'At the End of Our Endurance' and 'Urgent Measures for the Russian Union' from *Rebuilding Russia*, translated by Alexis Klimoff. Translation copyright © 1991 by Farrar, Straus & Giroux, Inc.

Li Ta-chao, 'The Victory of Bolshevism', November 15, 1918, reprinted by permission of the publisher from *China's Response to the West: A Documentary Survey, 1839–1923*, by Ssu-yü Têng and John King Fairbank, pp. 246–249, Cambridge, Mass.: Harvard University Press, Copyright © 1954, 1979 by the President and Fellows of Harvard College, Copyright renewed 1982 by Ssu-yü Têng and John King Fairbank.

Matthew Tempest, 'Chomsky on the Antiwar Movement: An Interview in *The Guardian*', 4 February 2003. Copyright Guardian News & Media Ltd., 2003.

Bal Gangadhar Tilak, 'Tenets of the New Party', Wm. Theodore de Bary et al., *Sources of Indian Tradition*, Vol. Two, Second Edition (New York: Columbia UP, 1988), pp. 143–47. Reprinted by permission of the publisher.

Total War Research Institute, 'The Greater East Asia co-Prosperity Sphere', Wm. Theodore de Bary, *Sources of Japanese Tradition*, Vol. Two (New York: Columbia University Press, 1958), pp. 294–98. Reprinted by permission of the publisher.

Desmond Tutu, excerpt from *The Voice of Crying in the Wilderness*, ed. John Webster (London: Mowbray, 1982). Reproduced by kind permission of Continuum International Publishing Group.

United Nations, 'UN Declaration on Colonial Independence'. The United Nations is the author of the original material. Available online: http://www.un.org/documents/ga/res/15/ares15.htm. The United Nations is the author of the original material. Reprinted by permission.

United Nations, 'The Universal Declaration of Human Rights'. From The United Nations, 'The Universal Declaration of Human Rights, Adopted and Proclaimed by General Assembly Resolution in December 1948'. The United Nations is the author of the original material. Reprinted by permission.

United Nations, UN Resolution 242: United Nations Security Council, 'Resolution 242, 22 November 1967'. Available online: http://www.un.org/documents/sc/res/1967/scres67.htm. The United Nations is the author of the original material. Reprinted by permission.

Rex Weyler, author, *Greenpeace: The Inside Story* (Raincoast 2004). Reprinted by permission of the author.

Stella Wieseltier, 'Rejoining the Human Race', *Hasidic Tales of the Holocaust*, Yaffa Eliach, ed. By permission of Oxford University Press, Inc.

Chitoshi Yanaga, *Big Business in Japanese Politics* (New Haven: Yale University Press, 1968). Reprinted by permission of Yale University Press.

Kang Youwie, 'Comprehensive Consideration of the Whole Situation', Wm. Theodore de Bary, et al. eds, *Sources of Chinese Tradition: From 1600 through the Twentieth Century* (New York: Columbia University Press, 2001), pp. 269–70. Reprinted with permission of the publisher.

INDEX

11 September 2001 attacks, 467, 494, 495–6

advertising, 472, 473
Africa, 2, 276, 283–5, 340–1, 462–3, 479–81; colonialism in, 20,
    40–1, 65; HIV/AIDS in, 439, 457–61; neo-colonialism in, 317–19
Albanian peoples; conflict with Serbians peoples, 430–2
Algeria: Front de Libération Nationale (FLN), 268, 273
Amritsar Massacre, 16, 201; accounts of, 30–4
Amur Society, 110; 'Anniversary Statement', 110–12
Anglo-American Committee of Inquiry, 205; 'Testimony on the
    Creation of the State of Israel', 206–9
anti-colonialism, 29; see also independence movements
apartheid, 268, 285–7, 481
Appiah, Kwame Anthony, 407; 'Identity, Authenticity, Survival', 407–9
Arab-Israeli War, 360
Arab peoples: control of Middle East, 56–7; in Palestine, 206–7,
    363–4, 367
Armenian National Institute: 'Press Reports on the Armenian
    Genocide', 57–61
Atatürk, Mustapha Kemel, 94; 'October 1927 Speech', 95–6
Atlantic Charter, 192–4
Atlantic Monthly, 352; 'Rwanda 1964', 353–6
atomic bomb, 185, 292
Attlee, Clement, 278; 'Debates of the House of Commons, 15 March
    1946', 278–80
authoritarian governments, 99–101

Balfour, Arthur James, 55
Balfour Declaration, 55, 57, 206, 362, 369
Barber, Benjamin, 425; 'Jihad versus McWorld', 426–30
Baring, Evelyn, Earl of Cromer, 25; 'British Rule in Egypt', 26–7
Behrendt, Richard F., 329; 'The Uprooted: A Guatemala Sketch',
    329–32
Belgian Congo, 19, 21–2, 41, 354
Belgium, 41, 268
bin Laden, Osama, 494; 'Speech on American Policy, October 2004',
    494–7
black peoples, 19, 40–2, 404–7: identity and, 408–9; nationalism
    and, 64
Blair, Eric Arthur. See Orwell, George.
Blakeslee, G.H., 235; 'Draft Memorandum, Far Eastern Division,
    Department of State, April 1945', 235–7
Body Shop, 475
Bolívar, Simón, 497
Bolshevism, 91–3, 108, 112–13
branding, 472–6
Brazil, 101, 125–7; coffee cycle in, 37–9
Brezhnev, Leonid, 373, 412, 414
British Empire, 19, 43, 191–2; in Egypt, 26–7; in India, 28–30
Bruce, Hamish, 305–6
Buffum, David, 122; 'On Kristallnacht', 122–4
Buthelezi, Mangosuthu, 478; 'Democracy at Work in Africa', 479–81
Butterfield, Fox, 247; 'Lihua', 247–9

Canada: effects of Depression on, 153; peacekeeping role of, 212
Cárdenas, Lázaro, 146; 'Speech to the Nation', 146–8
Carson, Rachel, 302; 'A Fable for Tomorrow', 302–3; Silent Spring,
    292, 302
Castro, Fidel, 324; 'On the Exploitation of the Cuban Nation',
    324–8
Chai Ling, 249; 'June Four: A Chronicle of the Chinese Democratic
    Uprising', 249–52
Chamberlain, Neville, 152; 'Speech to the House of Commons,
    3 October 1938', 153–4
Cha Ruizhen, 166
Chávez, Hugo, 497; 'Speech on the Opening of the G-15 Summit,
    2004', 497–500
Chhabra, Rami, 439–40; 'An Interview with Indira Gandhi', 440–1
Chiang Kai-Shek, 194; 'The Potsdam Proclamation', 194–5
Chicago Seven Trial Transcript, 398–403
child labour, 143–5
China, 252–4; Great Proletarian Cultural Revolution, 242, 247–9;
    Opium Wars in, 2; post-Second World War, 242–3; reform in, 2,
    3, 11–12, 13–15; revolution in, 76, 85–8, 89–91
Chinese Communist Party (CCP), 89–90, 91, 242, 244, 246
Chitoshi Yanaga, 259–60; 'Big Business in Japanese Politics', 260–2
Chomsky, Noam, 489; 'On the Antiwar Movement', 489–94
Churchill, Winston S.', 191, 192, 194, 217, 218; 'Iron Curtain
    Speech', 217–21; 'On India', 35–6; Stalin's response to, 221–5;
    'The Atlantic Charter', 192–4; 'The Potsdam Proclamation',
    194–5
Cippico, Antonio, 101–2; 'Italy: The Central Problem of the
    Mediterranean', 102–4
civil rights movement, 386, 471
climate change, 293, 307–9, 311
cold war, 216–17
Colley, Linda: on threat of Iraq, 485
colonialism, 19, 340; defence of, 23–5, 191–2; legacy of, 315–36,
    338–9; resistance to, 19, 28–30
Commonwealth of Independent States, 413
communism, 220, 225–8, 228–31; in Eastern Europe, 224, 231, 412;
    in Germany, 100
Communist Party of the Soviet Union (CPSU), 221, 216, 231–4,
    418–22
Congo: independence movement in, 338, 342–4; see also Belgian
    Congo
Congolese National Movement (MNC), 338
corporations: as governments, 477–8; in Japanese politics, 260–2
Croatia: conflict with Serbia, 181–4
Cuba, 324–8, 332–5
Czechoslovakia, 412, 414–16, 416–18

Darnell, Bill, 306
democracy, 106, 219, 471: in Africa, 479–81; in China, 86–7
Deng Xiaoping, 243, 247, 249
Devi, Rattan: statements before Congress Enquiry Committee, 33
Djilas, Milovan, 228; 'The New Class', 228–31

Djuric, Sinisa (translator), 181; 'Police Report on the Cleansing of the Serbs', 182–4

Dresden, firebombing of, 158; Freyer's account of, 159–61

Du Bois, W.E.B., 19, 149; 'Liberia, the League, and the United States', 149–52; 'The Negro', 40–2

Dyer, R.E.H., 30, 34; report on Amritsar Massacre, 31; statements before Hunter Committee, 31–2

Egypt: British rule in, 26–7

environmental issues, 292–3, 304–7, 307–9; pesticides and, 302–3

environmental movement, 471

Equal Rights Amendment, 386

ethnic cleansing, 158, 182–4; *see also* genocide

Europe, 47, 48, 66–8; post-Second World War, 191, 215; revolutionary thought in, 76; Soviet Union in Eastern, 411–13

Evans, Richard: on threat of Iraq, 486–7

existentialism, 396–8

Fanon, Frantz, 320; 'The Collaborating Class in Neo-Colonialism', 320–2

fascism, 99, 191; in Italy, 102, 105–7, 108–9

feminism, 394–5

Ferry, Jules, 23; 'Speech Before the French Chamber of Deputies', 24–5

First World War, 48; Remarque's account, 49–52; Russian women in combat, 52–5; treaties, 48

Fortune Magazine, 125; 'Getúlio Vargas and the "*Estado Novo*"', 125–7

France, 24–5, 27, 41, 268, 271; in Algeria, 273–5; in Indochina, 235–7; in Vietnam, 204

French, Paul Comly, 143; 'Children on Strike', 143–5

Freyer, Margaret, 159; 'Eyewitness Account of Firestorm in Dresden', 159–61

Front de Libération Nationale (FLN), 268, 273; 'Proclamation, 1 November 1954', 274–5

Gandhi, Indira: Chhabra's interview with, 440–1

Gandhi, Mohandas K., 30, 36, 201; non-violent resistance and, 35, 201; '"Quit India" Draft Resolution', 201–3

Gao Xingzu, 166

Garvey, Marcus: 'Advice of the Negro to the Peace Conference', 64–6

genocide, 48, 158; Armenian, 57–61; Jewish, 158, 180; in Rwanda, 355, 452–6

Germany, 67–8, 99–101, 132–5: in Brazil, 39; First World War and, 49–52; propaganda in, 119–20

Geyer, A.L. (Albertus Lourens), 285; 'The Case for Apartheid', 285–7

Ghana, 283–5, 317–19

Ginzburg, Evgeniia, 115; 'Journey Into the Whirlwind', 115–18

globalism: vs. globalization, 467, 468–70, 501

globalization, 428, 476–8, 498; race and poverty and, 468–71

global warming. *See* climate change.

Goebbels, Joseph, 118; 'The Reich Ministry of Popular Enlightenment and Propaganda', 119–20

Gorbachev, Mikhail, 412, 418; 'On the Closing of the 27th Congress of the CPSU', 418–22

Gore, Albert, 307; 'Nobel Lecture', 307–9

Gourevitch, Philip, 452; 'We Wish to Inform You That Tomorrow We Will Be Killed With Our Families', 452–6

Great Britain: Great Depression and, 135–9; pro-independence policy of, 267; relationship with US, 219

Great Britain, Government of, 361; 'The White Paper of 1939', 209, 360, 361–5

Great Depression, 130–2, 135–9, 139–42

'Greater East Asia Co-Prosperity Sphere', 161–3

Great Proletarian Cultural Revolution, 247–9

Greenpeace, 293, 306

Guardian: on threat of Iraq, 483–9

Guatemala: movement of labour in, 329–32

Guevara, Ernesto 'Ché', 332–5; 'A New Old Interview', 332–5

Guinea, 276–8

Hamas, 374; 'Covenant of the Islamic Resistance Movement', 374–8

Hamdi, Mohamed Elhachmi, 481; 'Islam and Liberal Democracy', 482–3

Hauser, Heinrich, 132; 'With Germany's Unemployed', 132–5

Havel, Václav, 416; 'Disturbing the Peace', 416–18

Hawking, Stephen, 310; 'Why We Should Go Into Space', 310–12

Heath, Graham, with Patrice Lumumba, 'Congo: My Country', 342–4

Hiroshima, 158, 191

Hitler, Adolf, 120; genocide of Jews, 158; 'Speech to National Socialist *Frauenbund*', 120–2

HIV/AIDS, in Africa, 457–61

Hobsbawm, Eric: on threat of Iraq, 486

Ho Chi Minh, 203, 235; 'Declaration of Independence of the Democratic Republic of Viet Nam', 203–5

Hochschild, Adam, 21; 'King Leopold's Ghost', 21–2

Hoffman, Abbie: Chicago Seven Trial Transcript, 398–403

Holocaust, 158, 179, 434

Hu Jintao, 252; 'China's Development is an Opportunity for Asia', 252–4

Hu Yungong, 166

hydrogen bomb, 292

identity, 408–9

imperialism, 42–4; *see also* colonialism

independence movements, 48, 192, 267–8, 338

India, 3–4, 28–30, 35–6, 316; anti-colonialism in, 3, 28–30; British rule in, 28–30; independence of, 201–3, 268–9, 278–80, 280–2; population growth, 316, 440–1; socialist thought in, 93–4

Indian National Congress, 19, 28–30, 35, 93

Indochina: France in, 235–7

Iraq: *Guardian* writers on, 483–9

Irving, Miles: 'Amritsar Deputy Commissioner's Letter to the Commissioner of Lahore Division', 30–1

Islam, 482–3

Islamic law, 442–3

Islamic Resistance Movement (Hamas), 374–8

Islamic socialism, 444

Israel, 360, 361, 370–2; creation of, 206–9, 369

Italy: fascism in, 99, 102–4, 108–9

Ito Hirobumi, 7; 'On the Constitution of 1889', 7–9

Jallianwala Bagh Massacre. *See* Amritsar Massacre.

Jamal al-Din al-Afghani, Sayyid, 9; 'Lecture on Teaching and Learning', 9–10

Japan, 5–6, 255–9; 1990s economic collapse, 263–4; Amur Society in, 110–12; big business in, 260–2; Great Depression and, 132; Meiji period, 2–3, 11; post-Second World War, 242, 243–4

Jews: in Germany, 122–4, 158, 175–8; in Palestine, 57, 205, 206–7, 207–9, 363–4, 364–5, 379; in Romania, 434

Jihad: Barber's concept of, 426, 429–30

'Joint US/Soviet Statement on Peace in the Middle East, September 1977', 373–4

Kakuchi, Suvendrini, 262; 'Amid Recession the Poor Demand Safety Nets', 263–4

Kamei Katsuichirō, 254; 'Return to the East', 255–9

Kang Youwei, 11; 'Comprehensive Consideration of the Whole Situation', 11–12

Kaplan, Robert, 430, 462, 476; 'Moldova: "Conditioned to Hate"', 432–5; 'Old Serbia and Albania: Balkan "West Bank"', 430–2; 'The Coming Anarchy', 462–3; 'World Government', 476–8

Kennedy, John F., 294, 301; 'On the Space Race', 294–6

Kennedy, Paul: on threat of Iraq, 488

Kershaw, Ian: on threat of Iraq, 483–4

Keynes, J.M., 66; 'The Economic Consequences of the Peace', 66–8

Khrushchev, Nikita, 83, 216, 231; 'Khrushchev Remembers', 83–4; 'Secret Speech', 231–4

Kido Kōin, 5; 'Observations on Returning from the West, 1873', 5–6

King, Martin Luther, Jr, 386, 403–4; 'I Have a Dream', 404–7

King, William L. Mackenzie, 152; 'Telegram from Prime Minister William L. Mackenzie King to British Prime Minister Neville Chamberlain', 155

Kitagawa, Muriel, 169–70; 'Letters to Wes', 170–4

Klein, Naomi, 472; 'No Logo', 472–6

Klemperer, Victor, 175; 'I Will Bear Witness", 175–8

Kollontai, Alexandra, 392; 'The Soviet Woman—A Full and Equal Citizen of Her Country', 392–3

Kristallnacht, 122–4

League of Nations, 68–70, 70–2, 149–52, 191, 206; Mandates, 360

Lenin, Vladimir Ilyich (V.I.), 19, 42, 80, 101, 231–3; 'Imperialism, the Highest Stage of Capitalism', 42–4; 'The Beginning of the Revolution in Russia', 80–2

Lewis, Stephen, 457; 'UN Briefing on HIV/AIDS in Africa', 457–61

Liberia, 149–52

Li Dazhao, 91; 'The Victory of Bolshevism', 91–3

Lodge, Henry Cabot, 70; 'On the League of Nations', 70–2

Lumumba, Patrice, 341–2; 'Congo: My Country', 342–4

Luxemburg, Rosa, 77; 'The Junius Pamphlet', 77–80

MacMahon, A. Henry, 55

Malcom X, 386

Mandela, Nelson, 446, 480; 'State of the Nation Address, 1994', 446–51

Mao Zedong, 242, 243, 244–5, 247; 'The Foolish Old Man Who Removed the Mountains', 245–6

Maududi, Syed Abul A'ala, 442; 'Replacing Western Forms with Islamic Law', 442–3

McCarthy, Joseph, 225; 'On Communists in Government', 225–8

McLuhan, Marshall, 299; 'The Playboy Interview, March 1969', 299–302

McMahon Letter, 55, 56–7

McNamara, Robert, 237; 'Memorandum for the President, 8 November 1961', 238–9

McWorld: Barber's concept of, 426–30

media: McLuhan on, 299–302

Meir, Golda, 370; 'Remarks to President Sadat', 370–2

Mexico, 146–8

Middle East: after First World War, 56–7; joint US/Soviet statement on peace in, 373–4; map of, 365; after Second World War, 360–83

moon landing, 292, 295

Mozambique, 357–8

Mussolini, Benito, 102, 103, 104, 104–5; 'Fascist Doctrines', 105–7

Nagasaki, 158, 191

Nanjing massacre, 164–5, 166–9

Naoroji, Dadabhai, 3; 'The Blessings of British Rule', 3–4

Nehru, Jawaharlal, 93, 201, 280; 'The Socialist Creed', 93–4; 'Tryst with Destiny, 14 August 1947', 281–2

neo-colonialism, 19, 20, 317–19, 320–2

neo-liberalism, 498–500

Newton, Huey P., 357; 'Uniting Against a Common Enemy', 357–8

Nicholas II (tsar of Russia), 75

Nike: branding and, 474–5

Nitti, Francecso, 108; 'Probabilities of War in Europe', 108–9

Nkrumah, Kwame, 283, 317, 323–4, 480; 'I Speak of Freedom', 283–5; 'Neo-Colonialism: The Last Stage of Imperialism', 317–19

non-alignment, 318, 338, 341

Novoe Vremya, 52–5; 'Russian Women in Combat', 53–5

nuclear bomb, 185–8, 305

Nyerere, Julius, 345; 'The Arusha Declaration', 345–7

O'Rourke, P.J., 347; 'Inside Tanzania', 348–51

Orwell, George, 135; 'The Road to Wigan Pier', 135–9

Ottoman Empire, 2, 94

Overy, Richard: on threat of Iraq, 488–9

Palestine, 378–83; Arab peoples in, 206–7, 362, 372; Hamas in, 374–8; Jews in, 57, 205, 206–7, 207–9, 363–4, 364–5, 379; liberation war, 368–9; Mandate of, 360, 361–5, 369

Palestine National Council: 'The Palestinian National Charter', 367–9

Palestinian Liberation Organization, 377–8

Pan-African movement, 41–2, 323–4

Pearson, Lester B., 210; 'On Peacekeeping', 210–13

Poe, D. Zizwe, 322; 'Afrocentric Summary of Nkrumah's Major Contributions', 323–4

Potsdam Proclamation, 194–5

poverty, 499; globalization and race and, 468–71

powell, john a., 467; 'Race, Poverty, and Globalization', 468–71

Prado, Caio, Júnior, 37; 'The Coffee Cycle in Brazil', 37–9

Prague Spring, 414, 416

propaganda, 119–20

protest movements, 386; environmental, 306–7

Putin, Vladimir, 413, 501; 'Speech at the 43rd Munich Conference on Security Policy, 2007', 501–4

al-Qadhafi, Mu'ammar, 444; 'The Green Book', 444–6

race: globalization and poverty and, 468–71

Ram, Lala Nathu: account of Amritsar Massacre, 32–3

Ramadier, Paul, 270–1; 'Speech to the National Assembly, 18 March 1947', 271–3

Redstockings, 394; 'A Feminist Manifesto', 394–5

Remarque, Erich Maria, 49; 'All Quiet on the Western Front', 49–52

revolution, 76, 92, 327

Romania, 433–5

Roosevelt, Eleanor, 197, 387; 'Women Must Learn to Play the Game as Men Do', 387–91

Roosevelt, Franklin D., 132, 139, 192; 'Inaugural Address of the President, 4 March 1933', 139–42; 'The Atlantic Charter', 192–4

Russia, 422–5, 503–4: First World War and, 48, 52–5; revolution in, 76

Russian Revolution, 80–2

Rwanda: *Atlantic Monthly* report on, 353–6; genocide in, 452–6; map of, 352

Said, Edward, 378; 'Truth and Reconciliation', 378–83
Sartre, Jean-Paul, 396; 'Existentialism', 396–8
Saturn (car company), 475
Schama, Simon: on threat of Iraq, 484–5
Schlemmer, Eva, 175
Second World War, 157–8, 220–1; technology in, 292
Senegal, 340–1
Senghor, Leopold, 339–40; 'Some Thoughts on Africa', 340–1
Serbian peoples, 430–2
Shlaim, Avi: on threat of Iraq, 487
Sierra Leone, 462–3, 477
Sino-Japanese War, 11, 85, 158, 244
Six-Day War, 1967, 361, 366
socialism, 76, 93–4, 113–14; fascism and, 106; Islamic, 444–6
Solzhenitsyn, Aleksandr, 422; 'Rebuilding Russia', 422–5
Soong Ching-Ling, 88–9; 'The Struggle for New China', 89–91
South Africa, 268, 287–9, 438, 446–51
Soviet Union, 418–22; dissolution of, 413; in Eastern Europe,
    411–13; fascism in, 101; German invasion of, 223; under
    Gorbachev, 412–13; nationalism in, 215, 216; space programme,
    297–8; women in, 392–3
space exploration, 292, 294–6, 310–12; Soviet, 297–8; United States,
    294–6
Spong, Paul, 304–5
Stalin, Joseph, 99, 101, 112, 218, 221, 231–3; 'On Opposition, 1927',
    112–13; purges of, 115; 'Response to Churchill, 14 March 1946',
    221–5; 'The Socialist Fatherland, 1931', 113–14
Starbucks, 475–6
Steinem, Gloria, 385
stock market, crash of 1928, 130–1
Suez Canal, 25
Sun Yet-Sen, 85; 'Fundamentals of National Reconstruction', 85–8, 89
sweatshops, 143–4, 468, 469

Tagore, Rabindranath, 16; 'East and West', 16–17
Tanzania, 345–7, 348–51
technology, 294–5, 428: advancements, 1–2; in China, 13; in Second
    World War, 292
Tereshkova, Valentina, 296; 'On the Soviet Space Programme', 297–8
Tiananmen Square, 249–52
Tilak, Bal Gangadhar (B.G.), 28; 'The Tenets of the New Party', 28–30
Timperly, Harold, 164; 'An Eyewitness Account at Nanjing', 164–5
Total War Research Institute, 161; 'Greater East Asia Co-Prosperity
    Sphere', 161–3
Touré, Sekou, 275; 'The Republic of Guinea', 276–8

Trinity Project, 185, 194
Truman, Harry S., 194, 218; 'The Potsdam Proclamation', 194–5
Turkey, 27, 94, 95–6
Tutu, Desmond, 287; 'My Vision for South Africa', 287–9

Udayakumar, S.P., 467; 'Race, Poverty, and Globalization', 468–71
United Nations, 191, 196, 210, 211, 269, 476–7; Charter of, 191;
    Declaration on Colonial Independence, 268, 269–70; Middle
    East and, 360; military personnel, 211–12; Resolution 242, 361;
    in Rwanda, 356; 'The Universal Declaration of Human Rights',
    196–200
United Nations Security Council, 191; 'Resolution 242, 2 November
    1967', 366
United States: anti-communism in, 216; in Cuba, 328; in First World
    War, 61; on French Empire in Indochina, 235–7; globalism and,
    469, 470, 471; Great Depression and, 130, 132; Japan and,
    243–4; nationalism in, 215–16; neo-colonialism and, 19; space
    exploration and, 294–6; war on terror, 491–2, 493–4, 496
United States War Department, 185; 'Release on the New Mexico Test,
    16 July 1945', 185–8

Vaculík, Ludvík, 414; 'Two Thousand Words to Workers, Farmers,
    Scientists, Artists, and Everyone', 414–16
Vargas, Getúlio, 125–7
Venezuela, 497
Vietnam: colonialism in, 203–4; France in, 272; independence of,
    203–5, 235; United States in, 237, 238–9
Vietnam War, 212, 491

Weizmann, Chaim, 207–9
Wells, H.G., et al., 68; 'The Idea of the League of Nations', 68–70
Weyler, Rex, 304; 'Waves of Compassion', 304–7
Wieseltier, Stella, 179; 'Rejoining the Human Race', 179–81
Wilson, Woodrow, 61; 'Fourteen Points Speech', 62–4
women, 120–2, 387–91, 392–3, 441; HIV/AIDS in Africa and, 460;
    oppression of, 394–5
women's movement, 386–7, 471
Wu Shimin, 166
Wu Tingfang, 12; 'The Awakening of China', 13–15

Yeltsin, Boris, 413
Yippie movement, 401–3
Yugoslavia (former), 412, 438: ethnic cleansing in, 158

Zionism, 369, 378–83